THE TRINITARIAN THEO
SAINT THOMAS AQU

The Trinitarian Theology of Saint Thomas Aquinas

GILLES EMERY OP

Translated by

FRANCESCA ARAN MURPHY

OXFORD

UNIVERSITY PRESS

OXFORD

UNIVERSITY PRESS

Great Clarendon Street, Oxford OX2 6DP

Oxford University Press is a department of the University of Oxford.
It furthers the University's objective of excellence in research, scholarship,
and education by publishing worldwide in

Oxford New York

Auckland Cape Town Dar es Salaam Hong Kong Karachi
Kuala Lumpur Madrid Melbourne Mexico City Nairobi
New Delhi Shanghai Taipei Toronto

With offices in

Argentina Austria Brazil Chile Czech Republic France Greece
Guatemala Hungary Italy Japan Poland Portugal Singapore
South Korea Switzerland Thailand Turkey Ukraine Vietnam

Oxford is a registered trade mark of Oxford University Press
in the UK and in certain other countries

Published in the United States
by Oxford University Press Inc., New York

© Oxford University Press 2007
French edition © Éditions du Cerf 2004

The moral rights of the authors have been asserted
Database right Oxford University Press (maker)

First published 2007
First published in Paperback 2010

British Library Cataloguing in Publication Data

Data available

Library of Congress Cataloging in Publication Data

Emery, Gilles. The trinitarian theology of Saint Thomas Aquinas
Gilles Emery; translated by Francesca Aran Murphy.
Includes bibliographical references and index.
1. Thomas, Aquinas, Saint, 1225?–1274. 2. Trinity-History of
doctrines–Middle Ages, 600–1500. I. Title.
BT111.3. E4413 2007
231'.044092—dc22   2006032595

Typeset by SPI Publisher Services, Pondicherry, India
Digitally printed and bound in Great Britain by CPI Antony Rowe,
Chippenham and Eastbourne

ISBN   978-0-19-920682-7 (Hbk.)
ISBN   978-0-19-958221-1 (Pbk.)

1 3 5 7 9 10 8 6 4 2

Acknowledgements

Many people have helped me to prepare this book. In attracting my attention to what is interesting and difficult in many of the questions of Trinitarian theology, the students of the Faculty of Theology of the University of Fribourg have encouraged me to project this introductory work. My confrères at the Dominican House of Studies in Washington DC gave me the fraternal and intellectual hospitality which enabled me to redraft it. Father Jean-Pierre Torrell's critical reading of the book gave me the benefit of his valuable observations and suggestions: my cordial thanks go to him.

I must finally give a particular acknowledgement to Francesca Murphy, who took the initiative in making this English translation and who has made many ameliorations to the original French text in the course of completing it. My gratitude is all the more active because the making of the translation has created the opportunity for stimulating and fraternal dialogue with a spirited theologian and a sister in the Order of St Dominic. In her patient and determined withstanding of my suggestions, Francesca Murphy has reminded me of the meaning of St Thomas' remark that, 'while safeguarding the meaning of the truths which he translates, a good translator must adapt his style to the spirit of the language in which he expresses it'. If this work holds the attention of English-speaking readers, the credit belongs to Francesca Murphy. Both the author and translator are grateful for the work of David Sanders.

Contents

Abbreviations

ACO	*Acta Conciliorum Œcumenicorum*, Berlin and Leipzig.
AFP	*Archivum fratrum praedicatorum*, Rome.
AHDLMA	*Archives d'histoire doctrinale et littéraire du moyen âge*, Paris.
BA	Bibliothèque augustinienne (Œuvres de saint Augustin), Paris.
BT	*Bulletin thomiste*, Kain / Etiolles.
CCCM	Corpus christianorum - continuatio mediaevalis, Turnhout.
CCSL	Corpus christianorum - series latina, Turnhout.
CSEL	Corpus scriptorum ecclesiasticorum latinorum, Vienna.
EThL	*Ephemerides theologicae lovanienses*, Louvain.
FZPT	*Freiburger Zeitschrift für Philosophie und Theologie*, Fribourg.
MM	*Miscellanea mediaevalia*, Berlin.
NRT	*Nouvelle Revue théologique*, Louvain.
PG	Patrologia graeca (ed. J.-P. Migne), Paris.
PL	Patrologia latina (ed. J.-P. Migne), Paris.
RSPT	*Revue des sciences philosophiques et théologiques*, Paris.
RT	*Revue thomiste*, Toulouse.
RTAM	*Recherches de théologie ancienne et médiévale*, Louvain.
SC	Sources chrétiennes, Paris.
SE	*Sciences ecclésiastiques / Science et Esprit*, Montreal.
CEG	Thomas Aquinas, *Contra errores Graecorum*.
CT	Thomas Aquinas, *Compendium of Theology*.
SCG	Thomas Aquinas, *Summa contra Gentiles*.
ST	Thomas Aquinas, *Summa Theologiae*.
Sent.	Thomas Aquinas / Albert the Great / Bonaventure: *Scriptum super libros Sententiarum* (commentary on the *Sentences*).
a.	article
arg.	argument (objection)
ch.	chapter

d.	distinction
div. text	divisio textus
exp. text.	expositio textus
lect.	lectio
lib.	liber
prol.	prologue
q.	question
qla	quaestiuncula

Introduction

> There is no subject where a mistake is more dangerous, or the search
> more laborious, or discovery more advantageous than the unity of the
> Trinity: of the Father, the Son and the Holy Spirit.

Augustine's remark, which Peter Lombard put on the first page of his study of
the Trinity in the *Sentences*,[1] gives us the flavour of Trinitarian reflection in the
golden age of scholasticism. As St Thomas' Master, Albert the Great saw the
matter, precisely because it belongs to this field, to show the goal of human
existence—making mistakes here will divest faith and theology of their
purpose: 'The whole of human knowledge comes to fruition in knowledge
of the Trinity. For every science and every thing to which the mind applies
itself is looking for that which gives us happiness. Speaking about other things
is only worthwhile when it derives from and guides us to this search.'[2]
St Thomas would follow that up by saying that, 'The whole of our life bears
fruit (*fructus*) and comes to achievement (*finis*) in the knowledge of the Trinity.'[3]

This 'knowledge of the Trinity' is supplied by Christian faith, and so paves
the way for the vision of the Trinity. It is the way to happiness: 'The Lord taught
that the knowledge that makes us happy consists in knowing two things: the
divinity of the Trinity and the humanity of Christ.'[4] Faith in the mystery of
Christ enshrines and implies faith in the Trinity.[5] Within the pilgrimage of
faith made in the hope of happiness, the theologian's vocation consists in giving
an account of the mystery which he has received, after the pattern of 1 Peter 3.15,
a verse which St Thomas loved to quote in order to describe the task to which
he dedicated his life within the Order of St Dominic: 'Always be prepared to
satisfy everyone that asketh a reason for the hope and faith which are in you.'[6]

---

[1] Augustine, *De Trinitate* I.III.5; Peter Lombard, I *Sent.* dist. 2, ch. 1 (vol. I/2, ed. PP. Collegii
S. Bonaventurae ad Claras Aquas, Grottaferrata, 1971, p. 62).

[2] Albert, I *Sent.* d. 2, a. 6–7.

[3] Thomas, I *Sent.* d. 2, exp. text.

[4] *CT* I, ch. 2. See *De rationibus fidei*, ch. 1; *De articulis fidei* I.

[5] *ST* II–II, q. 2, a. 8.

[6] St Thomas usually cites a version of this verse which refers to faith (hope and faith); see *De
rationibus fidei*, ch. 1; *ST* II–II, q. 2, a. 10, sed contra; q. 10, a. 7, ad 3; etc. On the history of this
theological emblem, see J. De Ghellinck, *Le Mouvement théologique du XIIe siècle*, Brussels and
Paris, 1948, pp. 279–284.

Reflecting on the Trinitarian faith is thus the theologian's primary task and this is
where the heart of St Thomas' teaching rests.[7]

A fresco in the Dominican monastery of St Anne in Nocera Inferiore in
Campania bears witness to the central role which Trinitarian faith played in
Thomas' life. St Thomas is pictured in this icon as one who has received the
gift which the Trinity makes of itself to the saints. Images like this are not
common within the iconography of the Dominican saint, which usually
displays different motifs, like his triumph, his meditation on the Blessed
Sacrament, his prayer before the crucifix, his composing the office of the
Blessed Sacrament, and so on, along with various insignia, like the chair, the
dove, and the lily. In a collection of frescos dating from the fourteenth and
fifteenth centuries, in the monastery of St Anne, Thomas is set between
St Paul and St Lucy, and pictured with a pen and a book, two recurrent
figures in his iconography.[8] The book pictured here is not the *Summa
Theologiae*, but the 'Writing on the *Sentences*', and we can see its first lines,
taken from Ecclesiasticus, *I, Wisdom have poured out rivers* (Eccli. 24.40, in the
Vulgate). St Thomas' prologue to the 'Writing' explains that Wisdom refers to
the person of the Son: Wisdom who reveals the Trinity in its intimate mystery
and in its works, Wisdom who creates, Wisdom who saves the world through
his incarnation, and leads humankind to the Father's glory.[9] When the
believer looks at the Son–Wisdom, he is engaged in contemplation of the
creative and saving Trinity. And the artist at Nocera has depicted the Trinity as
dwelling in the heart of the Dominican master. This icon represents a Trinity
as 'two heads with the dove between them', an iconographic type which is
fairly infrequent and of which one finds almost no trace after the fifteenth
century.[10] Here it suggests the Pauline and Johannine idea of the indwelling of
the divine persons: 'We will make our abode in him' (Jn 14.23).[11] It was also

[7] See the magisterial discussion by J.-P. Torrell, *Thomas Aquinas: Spiritual Master*, trans.
Robert Royal, Washington DC, 2003, pp. 23–224.
[8] On these frescos, see G. Ruggiero, 'Il monastero di Sant' Anna di Nocera. Dalla fondazione
al concilio di Trento', *Memorie Domenicane* n.s. 20 (1989), 5–166, esp. pp. 114–131 (including 24
plates alongside the text). This essay was also published in book form in the same year and with
the same title, by the Centro Riviste della Provincia Romana in Pistoia.
[9] This text is translated in our book, *La Trinité créatrice*, Paris, 1995, pp. 531–535.
[10] See F. Boespflug, *Dieu dans l'art, Sollicitudini nostrae de Benoît XV (1745) et l'affaire
Crescence de Kaufbeuren*, Paris, 1984, p. 285. In the wake of theologians like Bellarmine, who
jumped into linking this figure with the 'Three-headed Trinity' and so criticized this way of
representing the Trinity, Benedict XV prohibited it (ibid., p. 41). This kind of iconogaphy does
not bear the hallmarks of the 'monstrosity' which Bellarmine ascribed to it: it hints at the
communion of Father and Son who, as distinct persons, are united in their common nature and
in the Holy Spirit, their mutual bond.
[11] Perhaps because they are dubious about this kind of iconography of the Trinity, some
people have wanted to see the Nocera Fresco as picturing the humanity and the divinity of

in his 'Writing on the *Sentences*' that St Thomas created his most expansive treatise on the missions of the divine persons; this was the work which medieval commentators pored over most minutely. The artist's message is transparent: what St Thomas taught in his theology, he had received and channelled into his own life experience through living faith and charity, remaining constantly open to the gift of Father, Son, and Holy Spirit: 'The whole of our life bears fruit (*fructus*) and comes to achievement (*finis*) in the knowledge of the Trinity.'

St Thomas was happy to speak of the topic of his enquiry as 'the mystery of the Trinity' (*mysterium Trinitatis*). Those who follow his steps often encounter this turn of phrase, used to signify the three distinct persons in the unity of their identical divinity.[12] We can take it as read that for Thomas, 'mystery' means God in his revelation, seen from the outlines of creation and salvation, moving through its different scenes down to the summative restoration of the creation at the end of time, and with the advent of the Son in the flesh and the gift of the Holy Spirit at its centre. For St Thomas, 'Mystery is the secret of Wisdom, the Word of God insofar as He manifests God, and reveals the cosmic dimensions of salvation.'[13] 'The mystery of the Trinity' is a two-sided expression: it refers to God himself, as he reveals himself in the economy of the Son and Holy Spirit,[14] making a free gift of himself that surpasses anything at which human reason could arrive by its own devices.[15] What was veiled under the Old Covenant is exhibited to the eyes of faith under the New: the mystery of Christ.[16]

When he reflects on the lines of Augustine cited at the beginning, St Thomas comments that 'disordered' explanations, or ones which 'make light of the matter', lead straight to the recreation of the ancient errors, especially Arianism and Sabellianism. Since it transcends our reason, reflection on the Trinitarian mystery can only be achieved along the 'modest and prudent' path of the minute analysis of our own thinking and language. A singular kind of care has to be taken in the patient weighing and evaluation of the import of all the sources: Scripture first of all, then the tradition of the Fathers, and also metaphysics, anthropology, logic, and the other human disciplines.

Christ as two heads. We have taken the Trinitarian interpretation from the well-documented study of Santo Pagnotta, *La figura di San Tommaso d'Aquino nell'arte: Tentativo di analisi storico-teologica dell'iconografia tommasiana*, Fribourg, 1995, pp. 55–57.

[12] See for instance *ST* I, q. 46, a. 2.

[13] M.-J. Le Guillou, *Christ and Church: A Theology of the Mystery*, preface by M. D. Chenu, trans. Charles E. Schaldenbrand, New York, 1966 p. 214.

[14] See *ST* II–II, q. 174, a. 6.

[15] *ST* II–II, q. 180, a. 4, arg. 3.

[16] III *Sent.* d. 25, q. 2, a. 2, qla 4, ad 3.

'Modesty' and 'prudence' keep us going on an investigative journey whose complexity discourages even the most ardent applicants. Thomistic studies of the Trinitarian mystery often contain the steepest ascents. Most of these are simply specialist research. Bear it in mind that St Thomas' Trinitarian theology is demanding. This has put some readers in such a hurry to get through it that they want to shrug it off as a logical or metaphysical disquisition detached from revelation and the history of salvation or as an abstract exercise which only the most highfalutin intellects should attempt to scale. But the *Summa Theologiae* was not written for professors: it was addressed to students, in order to help them take the first steps in understanding revelation.

To help people to understand the wealth of Thomas Aquinas' Trinitarian doctrine, without making a secret of the complexity of some questions, this book hopes to offer an introduction to the reading of the Trinitarian treatise in the *Summa*. It is written for students and for those who want to take an overview of the main questions and the issues they raise, and to get an idea of the lie of the land before they commence their study of the articles of the treatise.

So this book does not comment on the Trinitarian treatise as a whole, and nor does it analyse every single question in this part of the *Summa*. Even though Trinitarian research has made much progress since the 1960s, Father Hyacinthe Dondaine's wonderful set of comments have yet to be replaced.[17] Even though we will not refer to Father Dondaine's notes, the reader could learn a great deal from them.

But the *Summa*'s treatise lends itself to being read as an organic whole and this book seeks to show this way into it. Finding our way to this opening must begin by getting a feel for the foundations of Trinitarian thought, and thus of the driving aim or intention behind the theologian's quest for an understanding of the mystery of the Trinity. Reading the treatise also calls for a sense of the way that St Thomas structured his meditation. Our first three chapters attempt to set out these preliminary elements. They can stand as a general introduction to the *Summa*'s Trinitarian treatise.

The twelve following chapters travel the roads which Trinitarian theology takes. The first and foremost of these are the three basic routes of the doctrine of the processions, that of relations, and that of the persons (Chapters 4, 5, and 6). No one could call these easy questions. They take up all the resources and the capacity for complexity which theology has to offer. But it is through

---

[17] H.-F. Dondaine, 'Notes explicatives' and 'Renseignements techniques', in Thomas Aquinas, *Somme théologique, La Trinité*, vol. 1: *1a, Questions 27–32*, Paris, Tournai and Rome, 1943, 1950; vol. 2: *1a, Questions 33–43*, Paris, Tournai and Rome, 1946, 1950. The two volumes were reissued by Cerf in 1997.

these questions that the issue of whether one can lay out an authentically Trinitarian monotheism is decided (Chapter 7). These questions pave the way for the enquiry into Father, Son, and Holy Spirit as grasped in each of their unique, distinguishing properties (Chapters 8–11) and within the reciprocal interiority of their communion (Chapter 12). We attempt to disclose the properties of the persons within the eternal Trinity, but also to show how these properties shed light on the persons' action in the economy of creation and of grace. The last three chapters (13–15) will indicate, finally, St Thomas' teaching on the creative and salvific action of the Trinity, since this is the overall theme and end of the revelation of the Trinity: to give us a fair idea of the creation and salvation which the divine persons bring about.

Our reading of St Thomas' Trinitarian doctrine often remarks upon the deepening scope or progress which one can find amongst his synthetic works, showing also how his biblical commentaries illuminate the doctrine; and it does not neglect to note the sources which enable one better to see where it is innovative, and where traditional. This historical moment is not at the forefront of this work, but it is not without importance. Without leading the reader into the thickets of historical research, we have sought to indicate the key issues, pointing out the works which take these matters further. The historical development of St Thomas' own Trinitarian thought and where it fits into the thirteenth-century Trinitarian debates must not be neglected, because we cannot fully understand Thomas' speculative thought without knowing something of them. The fact that we think it necessary to attend to the history of doctrines does not mean that St Thomas can be tucked away into the past, but it does enable us to disengage the circumstances and the motivations which helped to concentrate his attention during his speculative journey. It is our profound conviction that a truly speculative understanding of Thomas' thought can benefit from grasping the historical state of play at the time of his writing. We cannot show St Thomas' relevance for today without paying the price of historical research.

To pin down what the *Summa* means, or to illustrate particular aspects of its Trinitarian treatise, we refer to other works by St Thomas, but we have no intention of mentioning every text that is related to the questions with which we deal. The bibliographical references are likewise restricted. Referring to a greater diversity of works would have led us into refinements and critical discussions that are way beyond the purview of this book. Although we do not make detailed references to them we have tried to take on board up-to-date research and the contemporary debates over the interpretation of St Thomas' thought. The notes will indicate some reference works for further study. The reader can also consult the bibliography at the back of this book.

1

The Revelation of the Trinity

Trinitarian faith rests on receiving God's revelation within salvation history. This means that we have to consider what the revelatory action of the Trinity is, before we can begin a theological reflection on the Trinitarian mystery. In making this first step with St Thomas, we will have already entered upon an important theological reflection about our knowledge of the Trinity.

1. REVELATION, CREATION, AND SALVATION

St Thomas explains in the first article of the *Summa Theologiae* that the philosophical sciences, which provide knowledge of God through human reason, are not sufficient for human salvation. Salvation requires a sacred doctrine (*sacra doctrina*), in which God is known through revelation. The necessity (*necessarium*) of this doctrine is founded on the end of human life:

> man is directed to God, as to an end that surpasses the grasp of his reason: *The eye hath not seen, O God, besides Thee, what things Thou hast prepared for them that love* (Isa. 56.4). But the end must first be known by men who are to direct their thoughts and actions to the end. Hence it was necessary for the salvation of man that certain truths which exceed human reason should be made known to him by divine revelation.[1]

The 'necessity' which is in question here is not conceived as an absolute necessity which imposes itself on God himself, as if God had to reveal himself—God is free and his self-revelation is gratuitous—but as a necessity relative to the end which is sought.[2] Since God freely wishes that humanity be saved, God also wills the means required to that end: the revelation which makes known to man his transcendent end, from beyond our natural

---

[1] *ST* I, q. 1, a. 1.
[2] Cf. *ST* III, q. 46, a. 1; on the distinction between absolute and relative necessity (*necessitas ex suppositione finis*), see J.-P. Torrell, *Le Christ en ses mystères: La vie et l'oeuvre de Jésus selon St Thomas d'Aquin*, vol. 2, Paris, 1999, pp. 310–322.

resources. St Thomas puts this same reason first when he explains the 'necessity' of the revelation of the Trinity:

There are two reasons why the knowledge of the divine persons was necessary for us. It was necessary for the right idea of creation. The fact of saying that God made all things by His Word excludes the error of those who say that God produced things by necessity. When we say that in Him there is a procession of love, we show that God produced things not because He needed them, but on account of the love of His own goodness. . . . In another way, and chiefly, the knowledge of the divine persons was necessary so that we may think rightly concerning the salvation of the human race, accomplished by the Incarnate Son, and by the gift of the Holy Spirit.[3]

Trinitarian faith is required for a firm grasp on God's creative activity, and, by extension, on the whole of God's activity in the world (in other words, the exercise of divine providence). Knowledge of the Son and of the Holy Spirit, that is, of the Word and of Love, give the best perspective on the gratuity and freedom of creation: so we cannot understand creation well without receiving knowledge of the Trinitarian mystery. Philosophical reflection on creation can appreciate that God's creative activity is free, since it can work out that God does not act without wisdom or volition; but it is Trinitarian faith which gives us God's deep personhood. Moreover, the Trinitarian character of creation lays the foundation of that Trinitarian reality which is salvation. The Trinitarian mode of divine action is not restricted to salvation: one and the same God creates and saves us through his Trinitarian action.

St Thomas effectively makes the soteriological dimension of Trinitarian doctrine its primary dimension (*principalius*). This soteriological dimension concerns the action of the persons, and, more precisely, our *knowledge* of the divine persons, given by revelation. That faith in Christ which brings about salvation is inseparable from faith in the Trinity:

It is not possible to believe explicitly in the mystery of Christ, without faith in the Trinity, since the mystery of Christ includes that the Son of God took flesh; that he renewed the world through the grace of the Holy Spirit; and again, that he was conceived by the Holy Spirit.[4]

To grasp the salvation which is accomplished through the mysteries of the incarnate Son, one also has to know by faith the mystery of the Trinity. This soteriological dimension does not imply either that Trinitarian doctrine should be reduced to its 'practical' aspects, or that St Thomas limited his investigations to what today is called the 'economic Trinity'. In effect, to know who the 'Word', or the 'Son', is, and to know who 'Love', or the 'Holy Spirit', is, it is necessary to consider the persons in their relations and subsistence at the

---

[3] *ST* I, q. 32, a. 1, ad 3.   [4] *ST* II-II, q. 2, a. 8.

heart of the eternal Trinity. It is on this basis that Christian theology is able to illuminate the economy of salvation: understanding creation and salvation requires knowledge of the divine persons, and it is this knowledge which revelation offers.[5] And it is this knowledge that Trinitarian theology endeavours to disclose.

2. THE REVELATION OF THE TRINITY THROUGH ITS WORKS

We must distinguish the pathway by which we discover the Trinity (the Trinity's self-revelation by acting in the world) from the way in which theological understanding lays out the revealed mystery (the processions and the eternal properties of the persons), illuminating their action in the world. On the path giving us access to the Trinitarian mystery, the manifestation of the Trinity through the action of the Son and the Holy Spirit takes precedence. According to the Apostolic witness, the Trinity reveals itself in the words and actions of Jesus and also in the gift of the Spirit. More precisely, the recognition of a Trinity of persons in God unfolds from that of the divinity of the Son and Holy Spirit, and of their distinction.[6] St Thomas follows this path in the *Summa Contra Gentiles*: wanting to explain the biblical passages in relation to their interpretation by the ancient Christian heretics, he examines here the biblical testimonies to the divinity of the Son and the Holy Spirit.[7] Thomas' New Testament commentaries (on Matthew, John, and the Pauline Epistles) pay attention to the same question.

For St Thomas, the divinity of Christ is manifested in many ways. First one finds the revelation which is Christ's very person. Christ manifested his own divinity in two ways: through his *teaching* and by his *actions*.[8] As Thomas explains it, these are bound together. The Father's presence in Christ accounts for the unique revelatory value of Christ's words and deeds.[9] Such is what one

---

[5] Creation and salvation nonetheless imply this central difference: salvation itself (and not only the theologians' understanding of it!) requires that men and women know the Trinity; cf. *ST* II-II, q. 2, a. 8. *CT* I, ch. 1: love, through which we turn toward our ultimate end, requires hope in this end, 'and this cannot exist if one does not have knowledge of the truth [that is to say, faith]'.

[6] See B. Rey, *A la découverte de Dieu: Les origines de la foi trinitaire*, Paris, 1982; A. W. Wainwright, *The Trinity in the New Testament*, London, 1962.

[7] *SCG* IV, chs. 2–9; chs. 15–18. See our study, 'Le traité de St Thomas sur la Trinité dans la *Somme contre les Gentils*', *Revue Thomiste* 96 (1996), 11–21; ET 'The Treatise of St. Thomas on the Trinity in the *Summa Contra Gentiles*', in *Trinity in Aquinas*, Michigan, 2003, pp. 33–70.

[8] Cf. *In Ioan.* 14.10 (no. 1893).   [9] Ibid.

may call the sacramental structure of revelation, composed of words and of acts. St Thomas next finds the expression of the divinity of Christ in the Apostles' teaching (the titles which they attributed to Christ, the expressions concerning the unity of Christ with his Father, and so forth), and then in the activity of the Church (especially in the worship rendered to Christ). The passages are so numerous that we will limit ourselves to a few examples.

Thomas begins by reflecting on the words of Christ, because his 'words... show the power of the divinity in Christ'.[10] For example, when, in the Gospel of John, Jesus explains to Philip: *Who sees me, sees the Father...I am in the Father and the Father is in me* (14.9–10), St Thomas regards this as the expression of the consubstantial divinity of the Father and the Son; this interpretation is based on many patristic authors.[11] When Christ declares: *The Father and I are one* (Jn 10.30), Thomas explains that this unity is not limited to the union which their mutual affection creates, nor to a vague similarity in power, but, rather, invites us to acknowledge the unity of essence of the Father and the Son.[12] The same divinity of Christ appears in the sayings of Jesus which express his intimacy of knowledge and love with the Father, an intimacy and unity in which St Thomas finds the sign of the eternal procession of the Son within the one God.[13] One could multiply similar examples; they are very numerous because St Thomas pays minute attention to these expressions whenever he meets them in his reading of the Gospels.

St Thomas observes that Christ gives himself the most significant divine name: *I am* (Jn 8.24, 28, 58; 13.19). In applying this name to himself, Christ 'recalls that which was said to Moses in Exodus 3.14: *I am who am*, for being itself [*ipsum esse*] is the property of God';[14] this name expresses Jesus' eternity and divinity: '*that I am*, that is, that I have in me the nature of God, and that it is I who spoke to Moses, saying [Exodus 3.14): *I am who I am.*'[15] Christ does not 'become,' as do worldly realities (Jn 1.3); in giving the divine name to himself, he shows 'that he was not made as a creature is, but was eternally

---

[10] *In Ioan.* 14.12 (no. 1898). Thomas' exegesis, which, like the Fathers and the medieval writers takes the Gospels literally, attributes to Christ himself sayings which modern exegetes interpret as an expression of the Easter faith of the evangelists and of their community.

[11] *In Ioan.* 14.9–10 (nos. 1885–1891).

[12] *In Ioan.* 10.30 (nos. 1450–1451).

[13] *In Ioan.* 17.24 (no. 2262).

[14] *In Ioan.* 8.24 (no. 1179).

[15] *In Ioan.* 8.28 (no. 1192); cf. 8.58 (no. 1290). Thomas here takes up a very ancient tradition which, at the least since Justin Martyr, recognized the person of the Son in the angel which spoke to Moses from the burning bush; cf. Justin, *Apology* I.63, (ed. Ch. Munier, Fribourg, 1995, pp. 116–119). The words 'I am that I am', as pronounced by the Son, manifest that the Son is God, that he possesses the fullness of being and eternity belonging to God alone (Basil of Caesaria, *Against Eunomius* II.18; SC 305, pp. 70–75).

begotten from the essence of the Father.'[16] Trinitarian faith is born out of the recognition of the divine unity of Jesus and his Father, with which the Holy Spirit is immediately associated.

Alongside the sayings of Jesus, St Thomas pays a great deal of attention to the revelatory value of those of Jesus' actions which disclose his divine unity with the Father. Commenting on St John, Thomas particularly considers judgement, the giving of life, and forgiveness: these properly divine works can only be exercised by God, and Christ effectively carries them out. Thomas notes the relation which the action observes with the nature in which it is founded and which it manifests. Because of the human mode of knowledge, 'it is natural to man to know the power and the nature of things from their actions; and therefore our Lord fittingly says that the sort of person he is can be learned from the work he does. So since he performs divine works by his own power, we should believe that he has divine power within him.'[17] One can see from this last passage that, if St Thomas often associates operation and nature, he also connects them to a consideration of power.[18] This is why, since *everything was made by him* (Jn 1.3), believers acknowledge that the Word has the totality of divine power. St Thomas conceives power as the principle of action, and he explains it as follows: 'To be the principle of all things that have been made is the property of the great all powerful God: *All that the Lord wills, he has done, on heaven and on earth*' (Ps. 134.6 (135.6)). Thus, the Word through whom all things have been made is the great God and co-equal with the Father.[19]

Concerning the life-giving power of the Son, St Thomas observes: 'Here we should point out that in the Old Testament the divine power is particularly emphasized by the fact that God is the author of life.'[20] In related passages, Thomas notes that 'the clearest indication of the nature of a being is taken from its works'.[21] If one applies this to Christ, 'the fact that he does the works of God' entails that 'it can be clearly known and believed that Christ is God'.[22] Conversely, in the realities in which one observes different actions, one must

---

[16] *In Ioan.* 8.58 (no. 1290). Thomas rests his position here on Augustine's interpretation. For an evaluation of these interpretations, see A. Feuillet, 'Les *ego eimi* christologiques du quatrième évangile', *Recherches de Science Religieuse* 54 (1966), 5–22 and 213–40; M.-E. Boismard, *Moïse ou Jésus: Essai de christologie johannique*, Leuven, 1988, pp. 127–130.

[17] *In Ioan.* 5.36 (no. 817).

[18] On the patristic argument from power (and on operation), see M. R. Barnes, *The Power of God: Dunamis in Gregory of Nyssa's Trinitarian Theology*, Washington DC, 2001.

[19] *In Ioan.* 1.3 (no. 69).

[20] *In Ioan.* 5.21 (no. 761).

[21] *In Ioan.* 10.38 (no. 1466).

[22] Ibid.

recognize a diversity of substance because 'different actions indicate different natures'.[23] St Thomas explains:

when we want to know if a certain thing is true, we can determine it from two things: its nature and its power. For true gold is that which has the species of true gold; and we determine this if it acts like true gold. Therefore, if we maintain that the Son has the true nature of God, because the Son exercises the true activities of divinity, it is clear that the Son is authentically God. Now the Son does perform true works of divinity, for we read, '*Whatever he* [the Father] *does, that the Son does likewise* (5.19); and again he said, '*For as the Father has life in himself,*' which is not a participated life, '*so he has granted the Son also to have life in himself*' (Jn 5.26); '*That we may be in his true Son, Jesus Christ. This is the true God and eternal life*' (1 Jn 5.20).[24]

These actions are not restricted to the miracles which Christ once performed, but extend to the whole of his activity; he continues to act on believers' behalf today, as Scripture attests. For this reason, the experience of salvation which we receive from Christ leads us to recognize his divinity and his eternal unity with the Father:

a person participating in the word of God becomes god by participation. But a thing does not becomes this or that by participation unless it participates in what is this or that by its essence . . . Therefore, one does not become god by participation unless he participates in what is God by essence. Therefore, the Word of God, that is the Son, by participation in whom we become gods, is God by essence.[25]

One recognizes here the soteriological argument that Athanasius liked, as did many other Fathers of the Church.[26] Thomas takes it over not only from St Hilary, but also from St John Chrysostom and palpably from St Augustine (as the *Catena aurea* on the passages which we have indicated here shows): if Christ is not God, he could not save, for he could not renew the faithful in the grace of the new creation, which is adoptive Sonship (meaning divinization). The reality of salvation rests on the divinity of Christ who, because he is God, enables us to participate in what he really is.

Alongside Christ's own words and actions, Thomas examines the titles and the names given to Christ by others (such as Son of God, Son, the Son, Word): they express the divine intimacy of the Son with His Father, the divine relationship which the Son has with the Father.[27] St Thomas also considers the New

---

[23] *In Ioan.* 14.16 (no. 1912). Taken to its logical conclusion, this would mean that, if the works of the divine persons are different, the persons would not be of the same nature. But, according to Thomas, the action of persons is identical: only the mode of this common action is distinct (see below, in Chapter 14, 'The Persons' Distinct Modes of Action and their Unity in Action').

[24] *In Ioan.* 17.3 (no. 2187).

[25] *In Ioan.* 10.35 (no. 1460). On this theme, see L.-B. Geiger, *La participation dans la philosophie de St Thomas d'Aquin*, Paris, 1953, pp. 238–258.

[26] Cf. for example Athanasius, *De synodis* 51 (PG 26.784).   [27] Cf. *SCG* IV, chs. 2–3.

Testament passages which explicitly attribute the name *God* to the person of Christ: Jn 1.1 (*And the Word was God*); Jn 20.28 (*My Lord and my God*); Rom. 9.5 (*Christ... who is over all, God blessed for ever*), or Titus 2.13 (*the glorious appearing of our great God and saviour, Jesus Christ*), etc.[28] In applying the name God to Christ, Christian revelation enriches the meaning of this word: as signifying 'that which has the divine nature', the name *God* can designate each and all of the persons who commune in one and the same divine nature.[29]

In his reading of Scripture, St Thomas also meditates on the way in which Jesus is addressed in the liturgy: Jesus is glorified in the same way as the Father is. For example, commenting on Romans 16.27, he explains that glory and honour are rendered to Christ 'by every creature's worship of his full divinity'.[30] In honouring the Son alongside the Father, the faithful offer a worship of 'latria' which expresses faith in the Father and the Son in their common divinity and their distinct persons.[31] Thus, the adoration of Christ is a practical recognition of his personal divinity.[32]

These considerations, for which one could easily multiply examples, affect how we should enter into Thomas' Trinitarian theology. His practice in the *Summa Theologiae* is to explain the secondary reality (our salvation) from the primary reality (the divinity of the Son and the Spirit): the Son deifies and the Spirit gives life, because the Son and the Spirit are God; such is the order of doctrinal exposition which one habitually encounters in Thomas' synthesizing texts. But his biblical commentaries, in close contact with his patristic sources, also follow the opposite order: Thomas establishes the primary reality (the divinity of the persons) *on the basis of* the secondary reality (our salvation). He starts off from the faith-experience of salvation, that is, the authentic re-creation (divinization) of believers, to show the divinity of the persons: only the true God can divinize and re-create. Here he follows the order in which we discover the mystery: the action of the persons in the economy leads to the discovery and disclosure of a truth concerning the Trinity itself. This shows that, behind the *ordo disciplinae* of the *Summa*, Thomas was seriously concerned to recapture the patristic roots of Trinitarian doctrines and their foundation in the economy of salvation.

He takes the same approach when he reflects on the Holy Spirit. St Thomas focuses on the biblical passages witnessing to the divinity of the Holy Spirit

---

[28] *SCG* IV, ch. 3; *In Ioan.* 1.1 (no. 59). For an introduction to the exegetical discussion of these passages, see especially Raymond Brown, *Jésus dans les quatre évangiles*, Paris, 1996, pp. 237–273; M. J. Harris, *Jesus as God: The New Testament Use of Theos in Relation to God*, Grand Rapids, 1992.

[29] *ST* I, q. 39, a. 5; *In Ioan.* 1.1 (no. 44). See below, in Chapter 7, 'The Word *God*'.

[30] *In Rom.* 16.27 (no. 1228).   [31] *In Ioan.* 5.23 (nos. 768–769).

[32] *ST* III, q. 25, a. 1–2.

and to the Spirit's subsisting as a person. Even though Scripture does not directly ascribe the name *God* to the Holy Spirit—as it does to the Son— Thomas' biblical reading here is like his practice of exegesis in relation to the Son. Once again we find the soteriological argument which Thomas developed in relation to the Son, this time for the Holy Spirit. The divinity of the Holy Spirit sets the scene for one of Thomas' best formulations of the soteriological argument:

It is clear that the Holy Spirit is God, since he says, *unless one is born again of water and the Holy Spirit, he cannot enter the kingdom of God....* From this we can form the following argument: He from whom men are spiritually reborn is God; but men are spiritually reborn through the Holy Spirit ... therefore, the Holy Spirit is God.[33]

St Thomas presents this reflection as an argument (*ratio*) which believers, working from scriptural teaching, can use their reason to formulate. The divine action of the Holy Spirit manifests the Spirit's divinity. In the same way, the unity of action of the Holy Spirit and of Christ discloses their consubstantiality: although his action has a different modality, the Spirit does not accomplish something different from what Christ does; thus, his nature, the principle of his action, is not different from that of the Son of God.[34] When Thomas approaches the subject in this way, he is drawing out the legacy of the fourth-century Church Fathers.[35] On this issue, one can look at many chapters in the *Summa Contra Gentiles* which focus on the patristic exegesis springing from the anti-pneumatological controversy (the *Pneumatomachai*, or 'fighters against the Spirit').[36] Thomas presents the works of the Holy Spirit in detail. This is a matter of works which God alone can perform, so the witness of Scripture induces one to acknowledge the divinity of the Spirit: the Holy Spirit creates, gives life to the dead, observes, instructs and inhabits human hearts, brings about justice, receives divine glory, speaks through the prophets, reveals the mysteries of God, and is the source of sanctification (one can hear the echoes of the Creed of Constantinople). This is one example of Thomas' soteriological reflection, chosen from amongst many:

[33] *In Ioan.* 3.5 (no. 444).

[34] *In Ioan.* 14.15 (no. 1912). On the strict parallelism of the actions of the Spirit and of Christ in St John and St Paul, see especially Yves Congar, *I Believe in the Holy Spirit, vol. 1: The Holy Spirit in the 'Economy'*, trans. David Smith, London, 1983, pp. 55–59 and 84–86; cf. Congar, *The Word and the Spirit*, trans. David Smith, San Francisco, 1986. On Thomas' idea of the mutual work of the Son and Spirit, see the beautiful collection of texts, brought together, translated and annotated by L. Somme: *Thomas d'Aquin: La divinisation dans le Christ*, Geneva, 1988.

[35] For instance, Athanasius of Alexandria explains: 'If [the Holy Spirit] divinizes, there is no doubt that his nature is that of God' (*Letter to Serapion* I.24; SC 15, p. 126); cf. *Letter to Serapion* I.23; I.27; I.29 (SC 15, pp. 124, 132, 135). Basil of Caesarea mines the same vein (see especially Basil, Letter 159, in *Lettres*, ed. and trans. Y. Courtonne, in SC 17, 2nd edn, pp. 132–133).

[36] *SCG* IV, chs. 15–17.

to sanctify men is the proper work of God, for Leviticus (22.32) says: *I am the Lord who sanctify you.* It is of course the Holy Spirit who sanctifies, as the Apostle says: *You are washed, you are sanctified through the name of Jesus Christ and in the Spirit of our God* (1 Cor. 6.11). And in 2 Thessalonians (2.13) one reads: *God has chosen you from the beginning to be saved by the Spirit which sanctifies and by faith in the truth.* It is thus necessary that the Holy Spirit be God.[37]

The discussion thus far has been about the manifestation of the *divinity* of the Son and of the Holy Spirit. But Thomas pays as much attention to the *distinction* of the persons: One with the Father, the Son is nonetheless distinct from Him; and for all that the Holy Spirit is of the same nature as the Father and the Son, the Spirit is yet distinct from them. St Thomas shows this when he presents the standard set of biblical quotations, drawn together because of the Sabellian controversy, and which he knew through its patristic documentation.[38] He also uses it to show that the New Testament does not present the Holy Spirit as just a 'force', like an attribute of God, but really as a *person.* He brings the biblical witness to the action of the Spirit: into focus the Spirit proceeds, he teaches, he witnesses, he intercedes, he reveals, he knows, he inhabits the faithful. Thomas concludes: 'One could not say that if the Holy Spirit were not a subsistent person'; 'Scripture speaks to us of the Spirit as a divine person which subsists.'[39] Faith in the divinity of the Father, the Son, and the Holy Spirit, in their personal subsistence and in their distinction, rests on the historical manifestation of the divine persons, and above all on recognizing their action, following the witness of Scripture received in the Church.

Special witnesses to the unity and the distinction of the persons include the disclosure of the Trinity in Christ's conception and nativity,[40] his baptism ('the Son is present in his flesh, the Father in the voice which speaks, and the Holy Spirit under the appearance of a dove'[41]), and his transfiguration ('the whole Trinity appears: the Father in the voice, the Son in the humanity, the Holy Spirit in the luminous cloud'[42]). According to Thomas, the sending of the Son and Holy Spirit into our world discloses their personal properties.[43] The passion of Christ also discloses the Trinity: far from seeing in the passion the separation of the three divine persons— how could one do that?—St Thomas finds in it the expression of their unity and their relations: 'by infusing him with charity, the Father inspires Christ with the will to die for us',[44] charity in which we recognize the Holy Spirit, with which Christ's humanity is filled. He looks at the resurrection from the

---

[37] *SCG* IV, ch. 17 (no. 3528).
[38] *SCG* IV, chs. 5 and 9.
[39] *SCG* IV, ch. 18 (no. 3553).
[40] *In Matt.* 1.18 (no. 112).
[41] *In Matt.* 3.16–17 (no. 305).
[42] *ST* III, q. 45, a. 4, ad 2.
[43] On this see below, Chapter 15.
[44] *ST* III, q. 47, a. 3.

same perspective: living with the Father, the Son is exalted 'according to the Spirit of sanctification', in that he pours forth the Holy Spirit.[45]

Finally, of all the New Testament sayings, the locus to which we particularly return is the Trinitarian baptismal formula in the last chapter of Matthew's Gospel: *Go and baptize in the name of the Father, the Son and the Holy Spirit* (Mt. 28.19). This baptismal formula, which was the source of the 'rule of faith', played a central role in the development of the patristic doctrine of the Trinity in the fourth-century Trinitarian controversies; St Basil especially used it to show the order and the equal divinity of the Father, the Son and the Holy Spirit. It is just the same in St Thomas' writings. In the Matthean formula and in the Creed, the Holy Spirit is placed on the same level as the Father and the Son (the name of the Holy Spirit is 'numbered together' with that of the Father and the Son, the Spirit is 'counted with' the Father and the Son), following an order which discloses his personality at the heart of the Triune God:

Since the Father and the Son are subsistent persons and divine in nature, the Holy Spirit would not be 'counted with' them if he were not also a divine, subsistent person. And this is very well shown when the Lord says to his disciples (Mt. 28.19): *Go and teach all nations, baptizing in the name of the Father, the Son and the Holy Spirit.*[46]

Thomas explains that,

The reason [for this formula] is as follows. Regeneration [which baptism brings about] involves three things: that *in view of which* it is done, that *through which* it is done, and that *whereby* it is achieved. In view of what [is one baptized]? In view of God the Father, as the Apostle says in Romans 8.29: *For whom he did foreknow, he also did predestine to be conformed to the image of his Son....Through what* [are we baptized]? *Through* the Son: *God has sent his Son...so that we may receive adoption as sons of God* (Gal. 4.4–5), for it is by adoption to the image of the one who is Son by nature that we are made sons. *Whereby* [are we baptized]? In the gift of the Holy Spirit, which we receive: *You have not received the spirit of bondage again to fear; but ye have received the Spirit of adoption, whereby we cry Abba, Father* (Rom. 8.15). So it is suitable to mention the Father, the Son and the Holy Spirit.[47]

Thomas concludes his exegesis of the Trinitarian baptismal formula by observing that it discloses the Trinity and excludes heresies, such as Sabellianism, which conflates the persons, and Arianism, which separates them.[48] The baptismal formula thus bears witness to the *order* of the persons, and to their *consubstantiality*. This is precisely what speculative theology will attempt to account for.

---

45 *In Rom.* 1.4 (no. 58).   46 *SCG* IV, ch. 18 (no. 3554).
47 *In Matt.* 28.19 (no. 2465).   48 *In Matt.* 28.19 (no. 2466).

So, in the same way that, as St Thomas explains them, the mission of the Son and the gift of the Holy Spirit reveal to us their *divine unity* with the Father, these missions reveal the mutual relations which the divine persons engender. 'Everything that the Son does is directed to the glory of the Father':[49] the Son 'relates everything to the Father because he derives everything he has from the Father'.[50] Similarly, the Holy Spirit glorifies the Son and brings human beings together with the Son, because of his relation with the Son: 'Just as the effect of the mission of the Son was to lead us to the Father, so the effect of the mission of the Holy Spirit is to lead the faithful to the Son.'[51] The missions of the Son and Holy Spirit in the economy of salvation provide believers with knowledge of the eternal origin of the persons: 'a mission . . . indicates an origin'.[52] The expression of the Father through the Son, and the manifestation of the Son through the Holy Spirit thus enables us to recognise the eternal processions of the persons: this is the pathway of our discovery of the Triune mystery, within faith. But, conversely, knowing the eternal processions gives us a better perspective on the foundation (the 'reason') of the action of the Son and the Holy Spirit in the world.[53] And this will be the precise task of speculative Trinitarian theology.

In sum, Thomas finds in the action of the Trinity, as brought into focus by Scripture and received by faith, the revelation of the *divinity* of the three persons, their *personal existence*, and their relations. This rapid survey shows us the path on which Thomas will lead us through Trinitarian theology. The spring of Trinitarian theology is the reception of the revelation of the Trinity in the economic actions of the Father, the Son, and the Holy Spirit. The Trinitarian teaching in the *Summa Theologiae* will seek to present this same reality which the action of the persons discloses: their unity and their distinction. And, in studying the eternal mystery of the three persons who are one God, speculative theology will equally seek to show the depth of the creative and salvific action of the Father, the Son, and the Holy Spirit.

---

[49] *In Ioan.* 14.14 (no. 1906).

[50] *SCG* IV, ch. 24 (no. 3622).

[51] *In Ioan.* 14.26 (no. 1958).

[52] *In Ioan.* 5.23 (no. 769); 15.26 (nos. 2061–2062). See below, in Chapter 15, 'The "Visible" Missions of the Son and Holy Spirit'.

[53] *In Ioan.* 16.14 (no. 2107): 'For everything which is from another manifests that from which it is. Thus the Son manifests the Father because he is from the Father. And so because the Holy Spirit is from the Son, it is appropriate (*proprium*) that the Spirit glorify the Son'; cf. *In Ioan.* 14.17 (no. 1916); *In Ioan.* 17.2 (no. 2185): 'whatever the Son has he has from the Father; and thus it is necessary that what the Son does manifests the Father'. On this theme, see A. Cirillo, *Cristo Rivelatore del Padre nel Vangelo di S. Giovanni secondo il commento di S. Tommaso d'Aquino*, Rome, 1988.

2

Thomas' Exposition of Speculative
Trinitarian Theology

In order correctly to understand Thomas' treatise on Trinitarian theology in the *Summa Theologiae*, one has to begin by paying attention to the broad underlying intention in his presentation of the treatise. Thomas does not launch his treatise with epistemological and methodological prologues, describing his intention. He refines it in the course of his research, when particular questions come up, following the procedure which one can see in other parts of the *Summa*: the epistemological elements appear in the main body of the theological investigation.[1] In practice, our knowledge of a reality does not just depend on our own faculties, but on the reality itself: so one needs to clarify what the object of study is before one can adequately assess the knowledge we can have of it.

One cannot get a true idea of the Trinitarian teaching in Thomas' synthesizing texts without perceiving their animating intention. Some popular misconceptions can set the interpretation of the treatise off on the wrong track. This is why, without proposing to reverse the order of the questions which Thomas adopted, we will take the opportunity to tackle some of these topics at the beginning. To read the treatise on the Trinity in the *Summa Theologiae* correctly, it is not enough to raise the question of the method and content of Trinitarian theology; one also has to answer the question: What does speculative study of the Trinity intend to achieve? This question will make us reflect on how theology draws on revelation when, with the help of human intelligence, it seeks to present our faith.

1. BIBLICAL EXEGESIS AND TRINITARIAN THEOLOGY

The previous chapter brought to our attention some fundamental features of Thomas' reading of Scripture: Written in the faith of the Church, Scripture

---

[1] Thus, for instance, the question of our knowledge of God ('How can we know God?') and that of our language for God (the 'divine names') are not placed at the beginning of the treatise on God, but in the middle of it (*ST* I, qq. 12–13), after the discussions of the existence of God and of the attributes of God's being.

directs us to the divinity of the three Persons, their personal existence, their distinction. But what is the difference, for Thomas, between scriptural exegesis and biblical theology? We have elsewhere compared St Thomas' Trinitarian theology in his biblical exegesis with that in his *Summa Theologiae*.[2] Without labouring the details of the comparison here, one can mention some of its consequences, which tell us a lot. One can see that Thomas' Commentary on John contains the essential core of the Trinitarian doctrine taught by the *Summa Theologiae*: the notion of procession, the immanent modes of procession of the Son and the Holy Spirit (the intellectual mode and the mode of volition or love), the theory of relations and of relative opposition, personal subsistence, the conception of the Word, the eternal origin of the Spirit, the eternal property of the Father, the unity of the Father and the Son as the principle of the Holy Spirit, the personal properties, the connections between the persons and the divine essence and the relations, the 'order of nature' in God, the connections of the divine persons with creatures, the persons' missions, not forgetting the many problems of Trinitarian language. The biblical commentary exhibits these points of doctrine with a striking luxury of detail and refinement. On some points, especially on the speculative doctrine of the Word (set out in the Commentary on John 1.1–3), the *Lectura* on St John is more complete than the *Summa Theologiae*.

Within the main features of Thomas' doctrine of the Trinity, we found two which are deficient in the John Commentary, in comparison with the *Summa*: the investigation of the word 'person', which makes use of Boethius, and the deepened reflection on the 'imprint of love' which permits one to grasp the personal property of the Holy Spirit.[3] The other differences relate to academic issues whose absence is not surprising in a biblical commentary.[4] As regards essentials, the John Commentary is a striking demonstration that St Thomas does not separate biblical Trinitarian theology from speculative Trinitarian theology: it is the same theology. Both the biblical commentary and the synthesizing text have the same purpose, the reflective explanation of Scripture. The doctrinal resources are similar. Nonetheless, the biblical commentary develops some themes more fully which, without being

[2] G. Emery, 'Biblical Exegesis and the Speculative Doctrine of the Trinity in St. Thomas Aquinas' Commentary on St. John', in id., *Trinity in Aquinas*, Ypsilanti, MI, 2003, pp. 271–319.

[3] See below, in Chapter 6, 'What is a Person?' and in Chapter 10, 'The Holy Spirit is Love in Person'.

[4] The John Commentary does not stretch either to questions which touch on the 'reasons' for the number of processions, of persons, and of real relations in God, or to some problems about the notional acts and notional power in God. In the same way, the Commentary on John does not discuss some linguistic questions, like the meaning of the word 'Trinitas', the attribution of essential names to the persons, or the attribution of personal names to the essential terms (questions which are dealt with in the *Summa Theologiae*).

completely absent from the treatise on the Trinity in the *Summa*, are touched on briefly there: the unity of knowledge and will of the Father and the Son, the action of the divine persons in the world, and the soteriological dimension of Trinitarian reflection.

How does St Thomas bring speculative reflection into effect in his reading of the Fourth Gospel? His way of reading the Bible uses the three levels of literal exposition described by Hugh of St Victor: the *littera* in the strict sense (textual analysis with reference to grammar and linguistics, an overview of the words' meaning in their immediate context), the *sensus* (the analysis of the signification of each member), and the *sententia* (a genuine understanding of the text, which draws out its theological and philosophical meaning).[5] This *sententia*, that is, the development of the theological themes constituting the teaching in the finished exposition, exhibits two modalities which are at work in the John Commentary. It engages either in commentary following upon the biblical pericope (this is what it does most often), or in questions, objections or digressions raised by the reading of the text (this occurs more rarely).[6] In every case, speculative theology is not superimposed on or juxtaposed with the biblical text, but is part and parcel of the biblical reading: it aims at disclosing the doctrinal meaning of the 'letter', the literal sense, of the Gospel.

As to the theological resources, one must observe that the John Commentary (like the *Summa Contra Gentiles*) pays much attention to Trinitarian heresies; this flows from Thomas' exegesis being rooted in the theology of the Church Fathers. One example of this is the equality in power of the Father and the Son. In the *Summa Theologiae*, the article on this (Ia, q. 42, a. 6) mentions many Johannine texts in the objections (Jn 5.19; 5.20; 5.30; 14.31) and in the *sed contra* (Jn 5.19). Thomas' professorial reply does not indicate any patristic authority, even though one can see a reference to Saint Hilary's *De Trinitate* (Bk. IX) in the reply to the first objection.

The John Commentary tells us much more about Thomas' patristic sources for the equality in power of the Father and the Son. The patristic sources themselves also illuminate our perception of his doctrinal exegesis. On John 5.19 (*The Son can do nothing of himself, only that which he sees the Father doing*), the Commentary presents in near-entirety the anti-Arian reading

---

[5] See G. Dahan, *L'exégèse chrétienne de la Bible en Occident médiéval XIIᵉ–XIVᵉ siècle*, Paris, 1999, pp. 239–297; M.-D. Chenu, *Toward Understanding St Thomas*, trans. A.-M. Landry and D. Hughes, Chicago, 1963, pp. 83–86 and 221–222. Cf. Hugh of St Victor, *Didascalicon* VI. 8: 'Expositio tria continet: Litteram, sensum, sententiam' (ed. Ch. H. Buttimer, Washington, 1939, p. 125).

[6] One can see the detail of these types of exegesis, including many examples, in the article mentioned above ('Biblical Exegesis and the Speculative Doctrine of the Trinity').

given by Hilary's *De Trinitate* (Bk. VII); by relating power to nature, this text shows that the Son receives power from the Father as he receives nature, being and operation, without incurring inequality by so doing.[7] The Commentary also cites Augustine's interpretation, which synthesizes Hilary and John Chrysostom's differing approaches to the text.[8] The Commentary on John enables one to see that, in the *Summa*, Thomas' reply to the objections drawn from John 5.20 and 5.30 largely come from St Augustine (mainly, his *Homilies on John*); when it is said that the Son has received a command from the Father or that the Son listens to the Father and so receives knowledge of Him, this refers to Christ's human nature, or to the eternal generation through which the Father communicates divine knowledge and will to the Son.[9] As to the incommunicable relations or personal properties (the Son receives his essence from the Father but not the property of paternity), the John Commentary (like the *Catena aurea*) shows that the reply in the *Summa* is taken from Didymus' *Treatise on the Holy Spirit*.[10] In this way, one can see that the *Summa* organizes and summarizes the patristic teachings which the John Commentary presents in greater detail. One could multiply similar instances: the exegesis in the Commentary is guided by the legacy of the Fathers (and by their concern to avoid heresy), so it helps us to rediscover the way in which the *Summa*'s Trinitarian doctrine is rooted in patristic theology.

Ultimately, the main difference between the biblical Commentary and the *Summa Theologiae* concerns the order of exposition, the organization of the material: whilst the *Summa Theologiae* follows the teaching order (*ordo disciplinae*) which guides us through Trinitarian doctrine as laid out according to the coherence and internal organization of its elements, the biblical Commentary puts its development of doctrinal points into the hands of the text, although the speculative perspective becomes apparent in some specific explanations.

Comparison of the Commentary on St John and the *Summa Theologiae* enables us to see the unity which *Sacra doctrina* has for Thomas. The aim which he pursues in explaining Scripture is identical to the goal of Scripture itself and to that of Christian theology: to teach revealed truth, to distance it from error, in order to perceive that which we hope one day to contemplate in broad daylight. In the John Commentary and in the *Summa*, speculative reflection is engaged in disclosing the truth taught by revelation (that is to

---

[7] *In Ioan.* 5.19 (no. 749); cf. *Catena in Ioan.* 5.19 (ed. A. Guarienti, Turin, 1953, vol. 2, pp. 401–403). This throws light on the reply in *ST* I, q. 42, a. 6, ad 1.

[8] *In Ioan.* 5.19 (nos. 747 and 751).

[9] *In Ioan.* 5.20 (no. 754) and 5.30 (nos. 795–797): cf. *Catena in Ioan.* 5.20 and 5.30 (ed. Guarienti, pp. 402–403 and 407–408). This illuminates the reply in *ST* I, q. 42, a. 6, ad 2.

[10] *In Ioan.* 16.15 (no. 2111, cf. no. 2114); cf. *Catena in Ioan.* 16.15 (ed. Guarienti, p. 541).

say: in *making it more articulate* for us). The most speculative reflection on the properties and Trinitarian relations is inscribed in his biblical teaching, for its purpose is to disengage the deep meaning of the scriptural text, using reason within faith. In the light of these observations, it is doubtless necessary to advise people not to read the *Summa Theologiae* without Thomas' biblical commentaries.

2. THE AIM OF SPECULATIVE TRINITARIAN THEOLOGY

The John commentary shows the intention of Trinitarian theology: to disclose revealed truth and distance it from errors in order to account for the faith. This requires some fine-tunings.

(a) The Prerogatives of the Faith

Only faith, the reception of revelation, gives us access to knowledge of the Trinity. St Thomas rules out the idea that natural human reason working on its own resources could realize that there are three divine persons. The exclusive role given to faith, as opposed to natural reason, was a common feature of Trinitarian theology from its origins, but in the Middle Ages, discussion of it was reopened by Peter Abelard. Abelard effectively attempted to identify the properties of the three divine persons with the attributes of, respectively, power (the Father), wisdom (the Son), and goodness (the Holy Spirit): 'God is thus three Persons, Father, Son, Holy Spirit—which comes down to saying that the divine substance is powerful, wise, good.'[11] As a result, Abelard claimed, philosophers and all men of good will who could know the power, wisdom, and goodness of God, had borne witness to the Trinity— above all, Plato, 'the greatest of the philosophers'; according to Abelard, Plato had 'taught a summary of the whole Trinity'.[12]

Like all his contemporaries, St Thomas taught that the existence of the divine persons cannot be known by natural reason: faith alone can know the Trinity. But when he explains why philosophers could not achieve

---

[11] Abelard, *Theologia Summi Boni* I.II (CCCM 13, pp. 86–88).

[12] Abelard, 'Theology of the Supreme Good', I.V (CCCM 13, pp. 98–99). For a more complete discussion, with the references to Abelard's works and bibliographical notes, see our article, 'Trinité et Unité de Dieu dans la scolastique, XIIe–XIVe siècles', in *Le christianisme est-il un monothéisme?*, ed. P. Gisel and G. Emery, Geneva, 2001, pp. 196–201. See also below, Chapter 13, 'The Origin of the Doctrine of Appropriations'.

knowledge of the Trinity by natural reason, Thomas relates it neither to original sin, as Alexander of Hales did,[13] nor to the 'opposition' between Trinitarian faith and the principles of natural reason, as with Albert the Great.[14] Thomas' response is based on two principles: the proper mode of human knowledge, and the nature of divine causality:

Using natural reason, man can know God only from creatures. Now, creatures lead us to the knowledge of God as effects do to their cause. Accordingly, by natural reason we can know of God that only which of necessity belongs to Him as the principle of all things, and we have cited this fundamental principle in treating of God as above (q. 12, a. 12). Now, the creative power of God is common to the whole Trinity; and hence it belongs to the unity of the essence, and not to the distinction of the persons. Therefore, by natural reason we can know what belongs to the unity of the essence, but not what belongs to the distinction of the persons.[15]

A 'nature' is an inner principle of action. God acts by virtue of his nature, which is common to the three persons (otherwise one undermines the divine unity: one person does not create 'more' than another, or to the exclusion of the others), and this is why creatures can enable us to demonstrate what their creative cause is, its nature, but not the distinct properties of the persons. St Thomas works out a remarkable Trinitarian doctrine of creation in the light of the faith which makes us know the Trinity, but this Trinitarian dimension cannot be achieved by natural human reason. He is very firm about this: knowledge of the Trinity rests exclusively on the faithful reception of revelation in the history of salvation. Philosophical reason can know the essential attributes of God, but no more than that.

(b) The Rejection of Rationalism

St Thomas also sets aside the 'necessary reasons' through which some theologians tried to show that reason is compelled to acknowledge the Trinity. This idea of 'necessary reasons' was brought into play in the eleventh century by Anselm's *Monologium*. St Anselm chose a method which drew on 'necessary reasons' over one which made direct use of sacred Scripture, and which proposed rational arguments leading to 'quasi-necessary conclusions';[16] this

---

[13] *Summa fratris Alexandri*, Book I, no. 10, (ed. Collegii S. Bonaventure, vol. 1, Quaracchi, 1924, p. 19).

[14] Albert, I *Sent.* d. 3, a. 18, sol. (*Opera omnia*, vol. 25, ed. Auguste Borgnet, Paris, 1893, p. 113).

[15] Thomas, *ST I*, q. 32, a. 1; cf. *De veritate*, q. 10, a. 13. On the originality of this response, see G. Emery, *La Trinité créatrice*, Paris, 1995, pp. 345–351.

[16] For the references to St Anselm and Richard of St Victor, see our study, 'Trinité et Unité de Dieu dans la scolastique XIIe–XIVe siècles', pp. 207–213.

enabled him to see in God both Word (the Son) and Love (the Holy Spirit).
The track which Anselm had opened up was explored in an original way by
Richard of St-Victor, in his *De Trinitate* (*c*.1170). At the heart of knowledge
by faith, Richard wanted to present 'necessary reasons' supporting the Trinity,
that is to say, 'to understand through reason that which we believe'; since the
Trinity is not a contingent, but a necessary reality, one can establish it through
'arguments which are not only plausible or probable, but necessary'. Richard
wants to show that the plenitude of the goodness of God, God's plenitude of
happiness, and of glory, like the plenitude of divine charity, all require that
there is in God a plurality of persons amongst whom goodness, happiness,
and charity are communicated. This project of demonstrating the Trinity, by
an exercise which is simultaneously logical, metaphysical, contemplative, and
aesthetic, will exert a lasting fascination in the history of theology.

St Bonaventure (+1274) brought together the legacy of Anselm and
Richard of St-Victor with that of Pseudo-Dionysius. Prior to his work, the
first Franciscan masters put forward the notion of the Good to account for the
plurality of the divine persons: it belongs to goodness to communicate itself
(*bonum diffusivum sui*). Since the divine goodness is perfect, its communication must be perfect, and that requires an alterity of persons within God: the
perfect goodness of God implies the communication of the divine substance
in God himself by the generation of the Son and the spiration of the Holy
Spirit.[17] Bonaventure develops this teaching when he elaborates the 'necessary
reasons' with the following motifs:

- It is natural for the good to diffuse itself; so if God did not communicate
  himself through a perfect diffusion of the entirety of the divine substance,
  he would not be sovereign and perfect Good;
- the beatitude, charity, liberality, and joy of God require that one posit a
  plurality of persons in God, since their perfection cannot exist in solitary
  confinement;
- the primacy (*primitas*) in God entails a plurality of persons, since when one
  reality is first, it is the principle of another; in virtue of his primacy, one
  must recognize that God has a sovereign fecundity and 'Sourceness' (*fontalitas*), according to the two modes which pertain to God: an emanation of
  nature (generation of the Son) and an emanation of will (the procession of
  the Holy Spirit);
- the perfect actuality of God demands that this communication be not only
  possible but necessary, for in God no state of potentiality exists: God's

---

[17] Alexander of Hales, *Summa theologica*, Book I, no. 317 (ed. Collegii S. Bonaventurae, vol. 1,
Quaracchi, 1924, pp. 465–466).

entire existence is in a state of perfect actuality. 'It is thus necessary to affirm a plurality of persons.'[18]

Thus, according to Bonaventure, affirmation of the Trinity necessarily follows from balanced consideration of the unity of God: the recognition of the Trinity is 'included' in the affirmation of divine unity, and the reasons he gives enable one to explain this inclusion in a way that imposes itself with the force of necessity. So, for Bonaventure, the believing mind can rise to the contemplation of the Trinity on the basis of the perfection which reason must necessarily recognize in God.

Many other writers embarked on the quest for necessary reasons. So, for instance, Henry of Ghent (+1293) acknowledged that we can only know the Trinity by faith; but at the same time, after faith has given us access to the Trinity, we can 'prove its necessity' by rational argument. Henry held that the perfection of intellectual activity in God necessarily requires the fruitful production of a personal Word; likewise, God's perfect voluntative and loving activity demands the spiration of the Holy Spirit. Reason can prove this. Henry of Ghent concluded that, if God were not Triune, he could not have created the world with wisdom and freedom. The person of the Word (wisdom) and the person of the Spirit (love, freedom), are thus necessarily required to think through the act of creation.[19]

St Thomas was vigorously opposed to this apologetic project in Trinitarian theology. Neither the goodness nor the happiness of God, nor his intelligence, are arguments capable of proving that the existence of a plurality of divine persons imposes itself by rational necessity.[20] Only the 'truth of faith', to the exclusion of any other reason, leads us to acknowledge God's tripersonality.[21] This thesis is a fundamental and characteristic feature of his Trinitarian theology. For Thomas, Bonaventure's reasons could be probable arguments, but they do not have the force of necessity. And, in Thomas' judgement, the attempt to give necessary reasons in Trinitarian theology jeopardizes the faith: 'this undermines the faith'.[22] Such a project ignores the dignity of faith— because faith deals with realities that are beyond reason—and it makes the faith liable to ridicule by non-believers, by indicating to them that Christians profess the Trinity on very shaky grounds.[23] St Thomas' stance implies

---

[18] Bonaventure, I *Sent.* d. 2, a. un., q. 2; I *Sent.* d. 27, p. 1, a. un., q. 2, ad 3; *Quaestiones disputatae de Mysterio Trinitatis*, qq. 1–8; *Hexaemeron* XI. 11; *Itinerarium mentis in Deum*, ch. 6.

[19] Henri of Ghent, *Quodlibet* VI, q. 2 (*Opera omnia*, vol. 10, Leuven and Leiden, 1987, pp. 33–40); cf. q. 1 (pp. 2–31). In a completely different spirit to the medievals, modern philosophers have discussed the Trinity in a more rigorously rationalist vein (see on this, in particular, S. M. Powell, *The Trinity in German Thought*, Cambridge, 2001).

[20] *ST* I, q. 32, a. 1, ad 2.   [21] I *Sent.* d. 2, q. un., a. 4; cf. *ST* I, q. 32, a. 1.

[22] *ST* I, q. 32, a. 1.   [23] Ibid.

a clear-cut divide between the domain of faith and that of natural reason: this straightforward distinction is one of Thomas' most outstanding features, particularly by comparison with Bonaventure. This means that the reasons which theology uses to exhibit the Trinitarian mystery will never be demonstrative proofs. Rather they will be one of two things: either 'approximations' or 'probable arguments'[24] that is, arguments which show that what the faith proposes is not impossible, or arguments drawn only from faith.[25]

In his approach to the Trinity, Thomas' epistemic method is thus characterized by two constant features: First, the strict exclusion of the idea that Trinitarian faith can be established by necessary reasons,[26] and second, taking it to be impossible either to conceive the Trinity by deducing it from the divine unity or to think of the plurality of persons as deriving from the essential attributes.[27] This second thesis, which is too often neglected, is one of the fundamental features of Thomas' Trinitarian theology. Thomas was a more rigorous thinker than most of his contemporaries, and he wields that rigour in his barring any confusion between our knowledge of the divine essence and our knowledge of personal plurality in God; he strictly refuses to consider God's personal plurality as the fruit of an essential fecundity of the divine being. Hence it is necessary to pin down what we mean by the role of human reason in Trinitarian theology.

(c) Understanding the Faith

We are now in a position to understand the problem which presents itself to Trinitarian theology: if, on the one hand, natural human intelligence has no access to the existence of a Trinity of persons in God (since only faith gives knowledge of it), and if, on the other hand, the speculative reasons advanced by Christian theology are not demonstrations, what could be the value of a speculative discussion which makes use of 'reason', and what is the discussion for?

The treatise on the Trinity develops many themes which are applied to God by the use of analogy (person, relation, order, origin, procession, etc.); the properties of the persons are also set out by means of analogies derived from

---

[24] I *Sent.* d. 3, q. 1, a. 4, ad 3 (*adaptationes quaedam*); *SCG* I, chs. 8–9.

[25] *ST* II–II, q. 1, a. 5, ad 2.

[26] See R. L. Richard, *The Problem of an Apologetic Perspective in the Trinitarian Theology of St. Thomas Aquinas*, Rome, 1963.

[27] See our study: 'Essentialisme ou personnalisme dans le traité de Dieu chez St Thomas d'Aquin?' *RT* 98 (1998), 5–38; cf. H. C. Schmidbaur, *Personarum Trinitas: Die trinitarische Gotteslehre des heiligen Thomas von Aquin*, St Ottilien, 1995.

anthropology (word, love). The use of these analogies enables St Thomas to say precisely what the purpose of his Trinitarian theology is. Thus, in reference to the notion of *person* in the Trinity, he explains:

The plurality of persons in God belongs to those realities which are held by faith and which human reason can neither explore nor sufficiently understand; but we hope to know them when we reach our Mother Country, when the essence of God will be seen, when faith will give way to sight. Nonetheless, when they were pressed by those who denied the faith, the holy Fathers were compelled to discuss this and other matters of faith, yet they did so humbly and reverently, avoiding any pretence to comprehension. Nor is such a discussion useless, since it gives the mind enough of a glimpse of the truth to steer clear of error.[28]

This observation in the *Quaestiones Disputatae de Potentia Dei*, which is echoed in the *Summa Theologiae*,[29] summarizes the purpose of speculative understanding of the mystery of the Trinity. We will come upon other remarks akin to these in the course of the discussion. This is the project which St Thomas puts to work in all of his writings: driven by the ultimate purpose of contemplation, Trinitarian theology supplies believers with ways to defend the faith.[30] The expression of truth and the critique of error are the two facets of a single theological project. To eliminate error, it is not enough to produce Bible quotes; one has also to show the conformity of Catholic faith with Scripture, and to reply to arguments opposing the Church's faith. The truth is not fully disclosed until it has been distinguished from the errors set against it. To disclose the truth and to separate out errors: such is the twofold task of the Sage as Thomas formulates and works it out in the *Summa Contra Gentiles*.[31]

The purpose of defending the faith is more tacit in the *Summa Theologiae*, but it is in fact present. Thomas evokes the double task of the Sage when, in the first question of the *Summa*, he explains that sacred doctrine is an argumentative science: sacred doctrine 'does not argue to prove its principles' because it receives them (i.e. the articles of faith), but 'it disputes with those who deny its principles'.[32] The treatise on the Trinity confirms this project: it begins precisely by showing the misjudgements which give rise to Arianism and Sabellianism, signposting the route away from the quicksand of such heresies.[33] This has two sides to it, historical and speculative.

---

[28] *De potentia*, q. 9, a. 5.   [29] *ST* I, q. 29, a. 3, ad 1.

[30] Trinitarian theology is thus woven into an extension of the ancient *Credos* which developed and refined the ecclesial expression of faith in Father, Son, and Holy Spirit, against heresies (*ST* II-II, q. 1, a. 8, ad 3).

[31] Cf. *SCG* I, ch. 1: one can find a very clear description of this topic in R.-A. Gauthier, *St Thomas d'Aquin, Somme contre les Gentils, Introduction*, Paris, 1993, pp. 143–163 ('le métier de sage').

[32] *ST* I, q. 1, a. 8.

[33] *ST* I, q. 27, a. 1; see below, in Chapter 4, 'The Problems of Arianism and of Sabellianism'.

On the historical side, as Thomas says, heresies gave the Fathers the opportunity to deepen their understanding of revelation and hence to refine the deposit which they passed on to others.[34] The main topics in question were adoptionism, Arianism, Sabellianism, and the heresy concerning the Holy Spirit attributed to Macedonius.[35] Taking this on board, Thomas connects up with an important feature of patristic theology, and finds it a stimulus to his own presentation of Trinitarian faith, which will occupy an eirenic genre. He also pays attention to the Islamic rejection of the Trinity, but, on this occasion his efforts at documentation were rather more limited.[36] The 'errors' which Thomas discussed were mainly Christian heresies of patristic times, those which occasioned the Fathers' elaborations of Trinitarian doctrine. The reasons for this preference should probably be sought in the interesting metaphysical themes found in Trinitarian errors: 'The only errors which interest the Christian sage are those which have contributed to the deepening of Christian truth.'[37] The manifestation of the faith is tied to the refutation of errors which are opposed to it. As Fr R.-A. Gauthier has very well shown, Thomas is interested in an error, not only because of the number of adherents it has or will attract, but rather, an error 'is more interesting in the degree that it is opposed to a deeper truth'.[38] St Thomas tries to discover these heresies' internal logic and their roots, so that, ultimately, by contrast, he can find a way to disclose the Catholic faith.

The construction of a speculative reflection on the Trinity, using analogies and philosophical resources, is thus guided by a double-sided theme: the contemplation of revealed truth, which makes it possible, secondly, to defend the faith against error. The goal of Trinitarian theology is to show the intelligibility of the faith, and thus that arguments against it are not compelling. Since the principles of human reason come from God, they cannot contradict the faith given by God. St Thomas firmly maintains that the principles of human reason 'cannot be contrary to the truth of Christian faith.'[39] For this reason, the arguments against Trinitarian faith 'do not have demonstrative force, but are either probable reasons or sophisms'.[40] In some

[34] *De potentia*, q. 9, a. 5; *ST* I, q. 29, a. 3, ad 1; cf. *CEG*, prol.

[35] For documentation on St Thomas and the Trinitarian heresies, see our articles, 'Le photinisme et ses précurseurs chez St Thomas', *RT* 95 (1995), 371–398; 'Le Traité de St Thomas sur la Trinité dans la *Somme contre les Gentils*', *RT* 96 (1996), pp. 14–18, in *Trinity in Aquinas*, pp. 71–120.

[36] See our note in *Thomas d'Aquin, Traités: Les raisons de la foi, les articles de la foi et les sacrements de l'Église*, trans. Gilles Emery, Paris, 1999, pp. 30–35. This is a translation of Thomas' *De rationibus fidei*.

[37] Gauthier, *St Thomas d'Aquin*, p. 127.

[38] Ibid., p. 142.   [39] *SCG* I, ch. 7; cf. *Super Boetium de Trinitate*, q. 2, a. 3; *ST* I, q. 1, a. 8.

[40] *SCG* I, ch. 7 (no. 47).

cases, one can refute the arguments against Trinitarian faith by establishing that they are erroneous (sophisms); but at other times, one cannot directly show that the argument is inherently false: 'The realities belonging to faith cannot be proven in a demonstrative way; for this reason, the falsity of certain [statements] contrary to the faith eludes the possibility of demonstration, but one can show that they are not necessary proofs.'[41] In the latter case, one can only prove that the arguments against the faith are just 'probable reasons', which do not necessarily bind our thinking. And, to show that, one must establish an alternative, by making use of different 'probable reasons'.

In effect, when St Thomas discloses the intelligibility of the faith through 'likely arguments', he shows—without *demonstrating* the faith—that the arguments of the heretics (Arianism, Sabellianism), and the arguments of those who reject the Trinity, do not have the force of necessity: he does this by indicating a different approach which establishes a *cogent* alternative. It is not a matter of showing the complete convergence of faith and reason, but rather their non-divergence or, still better: the fittingness of truth. If there is an apologetic dimension in Thomas' Trinitarian theology, it will be a somewhat indirect one.[42] Thomas explains this in broad strokes in the first question of the *Summa Theologiae*:

Since it has no science above itself, Holy Scripture can dispute with one who denies its principles only if the opponent admits at least some of the truths obtained through divine revelation; thus we can argue with heretics from texts in Holy Writ, and against those who deny one article of faith we can argue from another. If our opponent believes nothing of divine revelation, there is no longer any means of proving the article of faith by reasoning, but only of answering his objections—if he has any— against faith. Since faith rests upon infallible truth, and since the contrary of a truth can never be demonstrated, it is clear that the arguments brought against faith are not demonstrations, but are arguments that can be solved.[43]

On the one hand, the theologian puts forward scriptural arguments, reasoning which is compelling for believers, and, on the other, he makes use of 'similitudes', that is, the analogies which allow one to give an account of faith in three divine persons, in the main, the Augustinian analogy of word and love.[44] These 'similitudes' constitute arguments from congruity or fitting-ness,[45] 'persuasive arguments which show that what the faith proposes *is not*

---

[41] *Super Boetium de Trinitate*, q. 2, a. 3.

[42] On the apologetic put forward by St Thomas, see our *Thomas d'Aquin. Traités*, pp. 24–30.

[43] *ST* I, q. 1, a. 8.

[44] *Super Boetium de Trinitate*, q. 2, a. 3: 'It is thus that Augustine, in his book on the Trinity, inserts numerous comparisons drawn from philosophical doctrines to manifest the Trinity'; cf. *SCG* I, chs. 7–9.

[45] *ST* I, q. 32, a. 1, ad 2.

impossible.[46] They do not aim either to give a rational demonstration of the faith or to convince those who do not share the Christian faith in the Trinity.[47] If one refuses to use speculative reason like this, one can *assert* that God is a Trinity, but one cannot *disclose* the truth of Trinitarian faith, or make its truth more visible to human eyes. The task of speculative theology is very well expressed in a celebrated *Quodlibet* in which Thomas explains that, if the master or professor is content to rest his case on 'authorities' (the texts which are authoritative within theology), his audience will doubtless know what is true and what is false, but they will not have any idea of what the truth proposed to them means:

So it is necessary to rest one's case on reasons which seek out the roots of the truth and which enable people to see how what one proposes is true. Unless one does this, if the master's response is based purely on authorities, the listener will know that things are so, but he will have achieved neither knowledge nor understanding and will go away with an empty head.[48]

This is what speculative theology aims to do: to seek out the root of truth, with the ultimate purpose of discovering how one can know the truth of the revealed texts and the teaching of the Church. The doctrine of Trinitarian processions, relations, persons, and so on, are very precisely engraved into this intention. In offering us understanding of the truth, Trinitarian theology provides believers with a foretaste of that which they hope to contemplate in the beatific vision of God: this is Trinitarian theology's essential contemplative dimension. This goal, which Thomas takes over from Augustine, is thus simultaneously modest and high-reaching: 'To disclose this kind of truth [truth which belongs to faith alone], it is necessary to propose likely arguments, for the *exercise and support of the faithful*.'[49]

As Thomas sees it, the seat of his vocation as a theologian is to perform a 'contemplative' exercise, the purpose of which is to take a 'small sip'[50] of the divine knowledge which is communicated in revelation. In presenting 'likely reasons', the Christian theologian enters into the understanding of a mystery which loses none of its transcendence and which, for that reason, is a profound source of spiritual joy. Thomas states that,

---

[46] *ST* II–II, q. 1, a. 5, ad 2.   [47] *SCG* I, ch. 9; cf. *De rationibus fidei*, ch. 2.

[48] *Quodlibet* IV, q. 9, a. 3. See J.-P. Torrell, 'Le savoir théologique chez S. Thomas', *RT* 96 (1996), 355–396.

[49] *SCG* I, ch. 9 (no. 54): *ad fidelium quidem exercitium et solatium*. On Trinitarian theology as a 'spiritual exercise' for Christians, see Augustine, *De Trinitate* XIII. XX. 26; XV. I. 1; XV. VI. 10. St Thomas himself sets the study and teaching of Wisdom amongst the spiritual exercises [*spiritualia exercitia*]: see *SCG* III, ch. 132 (no. 3047); *ST* II–II, q. 122, a. 4, ad 3.

[50] *SCG* IV, ch. 1.

it is useful for the human reason to exercise itself in such arguments, however weak they may be, provided only that there is no presumption to comprehend or to demonstrate. For to be able to see something of the loftiest realities, however thin and weak the sight may be, is . . . a cause of the greatest joy. The testimony of Hilary agrees with this. Speaking of this same truth, he writes as follows in his *De Trinitate*: 'Enter these truths by believing, press forward, persevere. And though I may know that you will not arrive at an end, yet I will congratulate you on your progress. For, though he who pursues the infinite with reverence will never finally reach the end, yet he will always progress by pressing forward. But do not intrude yourself into the divine secret, do not, presuming to comprehend the sum total of intelligence, plunge yourself into the mystery of the unending nativity [the begetting of the only begotten God by the only unbegotten God]; rather, understand that these things are incomprehensible.'[51]

For this reason, an accurate interpretation of the treatise on the Trinity in the *Summa* must distance itself from every sort of rationalism. It is by a serious misreading that some writers have believed they have found an attempt at a rational demonstration of the Trinity in St Thomas' works. Those who can never stop contrasting the spiritual aims of the Fathers with Thomas' scholastic theology make the same mistake. Thomas undertakes a speculative or contemplative[52] exercise which, addressing itself to believers, enables them to touch lightly upon 'something of the truth' (*aliquid veritatis*),[53] in developing 'approximations' and analogies which suffice to exclude errors, because they show that the Trinity fulfils our minds without violating them.

(d) Why Investigate Notions, Relations, and Properties?

In his treatise on the Trinity, Thomas seeks to clarify the *relations* of the persons, that is, the *properties* which, by distinguishing the persons in a way which accounts for their plurality, enables us to perceive the features proper to each person. Why did the Schoolmen and Thomas devote such painstaking attention to relations, properties, and notions? Was it necessary or wise? At first glance, it is tempting to see it as a brilliant logical exercise, a sort of theological Glass-Bead Game.

---

[51] *SCG* I, ch. 8 (nos. 49–50). Cf. Hilary, *De Trinitate* II. 10–11 (SC 443, pp. 294–297); as we noted, he is speaking about the eternal begetting of the Son.

[52] When they come from Thomas' hand, the terms 'contemplative' and 'speculative' mean practically the same thing and designate the same reality (*speculativus* is more often used in the treatises that are inspired by Aristotelianism, whereas the word *contemplativus* appears more frequently in the treatises drawing on Christian sources; cf. S. Pinckaers, 'Recherche de la signification véritable du terme spéculatif', *NRT* 81 (1959), 673–695).

[53] *De potentia*, q. 9, a. 5.

This is not a new problem. St Thomas met and reflected on it, under a different guise. The opinions of Praepositinus of Cremona gave him his opportunity. Chancellor of the University of Paris at the outset of the thirteenth century, Praepositinus sparked off a great debate about the 'notions' (*notiones*) in God. This technical term in Trinitarian theology means the proper characteristics of the persons, enabling us to distinguish the persons. Since the three divine persons are distinct, it is necessary to recognize something which is proper to each of them, by which they distinguish themselves and through which we can know them. For Peter Lombard, whom most Masters had followed since William of Auxerre,[54] there are five *notions*: the Father's *unbegottenness* and *paternity*, the *filiation* of the Son, the *procession* of the Spirit, and his *spiration* (the latter is common to Father and Son, who breathe or 'spirate' the Holy Spirit).[55] We will return to this much later in the investigation of the relations and persons.[56] In the twelfth century and even into the thirteenth century, there was an animated debate about this: some theologians computed that these 'notions' are infinite in number; others considered that there are six, others three, and still others refused to accept that there are any at all.[57]

Praepositinus of Cremona positioned himself with the latter solution: he found no place for such notions. He claimed that when we say that the Father characterizes himself through *paternity*, or that 'The Father distinguishes himself from the Son through paternity,' these propositions just mean 'the Father is the Father.' The persons' relative properties (fatherhood, filiation, procession) are only 'manners of speaking.' Our concepts and our analogical language, in as much as they signify the truth of God himself, are therefore reduced to the common *essence* of the three persons and to the three *persons* themselves: all that we can properly say is that the three persons are distinct and that they are one God. All the rest of it can be eliminated: God has no 'properties,' and it is not for us to recognize 'notions' in God.[58]

Faced with this question, St Thomas began by recalling God's *simplicity*. God is not composed of this and that element: in God, the person is really

---

[54] William of Auxerre, *Summa aurea* I, tr. 7, ch. 2 (ed. J. Ribaillier, Paris and Grottaferrata, 1980, pp. 116–118). Cf. J. Schneider, *Die Lehre vom dreieinigen Gott in der Schule des Petrus Lombardus*, Munich, 1961, pp. 172–180.

[55] This was what the Masters commonly taught in Thomas' time. See *ST* I, q. 32, a. 3.

[56] See below, in Chapter 5, 'Relative Opposition: Paternity, Filiation, Spiration, Procession', and in Chapter 8, 'Unbegottenness: the Unengendered Father'.

[57] Praepositinus of Cremona, *Summa 'Qui producit ventos'*, Book I, ch. 12.2 (ed. G. Angelini, *L'ortodossia e la grammatica: Analisi di struttura e deduzione storica della Teologia Trinitaria di Prepositino*, Rome, 1972, p. 277). Praepositinus stood on the shoulders of earlier writers; cf. J. Schneider, *Die Lehre vom dreieinigen Gott*, pp. 172–180.

[58] Praepositinus of Cremona, *Summa* I, ch. 12 (ed. Angelini, pp. 275–280); see G. Angelini's exposition, which discerns a certain 'nominalist orientation' in Praepositinus' thought (pp. 154 ff., especially pp. 181–185).

identical to the divine essence and is not composed of a property. 'But our natural reason cannot know the divine simplicity as it is in itself: this is why our mind apprehends and names God according to its own mode, that is, from the milieu of sensible objects, whence its knowledge is derived.'[59] In our world, we employ concrete words to designate concrete realities (such as a flower or a bird), and abstract words to signify the principles or 'forms' of these realities (like the whiteness of the flower, or the animality of the bird): language parallels our knowledge of things, and this knowledge itself is based in the composition or the complexity of the bodily realities which we can observe. We cannot do otherwise when we speak of God, since we speak about God in our own human language: we speak of the *wisdom* or the *goodness* of God (abstract names) and even of *God* himself ('concrete' name), and in the same way we speak of the *Father* (concrete name) and of his *paternity* (abstract name). In so doing, we are not claiming that the *property* or the *relation* of paternity is really something different from the *person of the Father himself*, but our grasp of the mystery is affected by the double mode of our knowledge and our language. Why must one take this into account in reflecting on the mystery of the Trinity? Thomas' answer is that,

We are obliged to do so for two reasons. The first is at the insistence of heretics. For since we confess the Father, the Son, and the Holy Spirit to be one God, they demand to know: *How can they be one God, and how can they be three Persons?* And to the first question, we answer that: they are one through their essence or deity; so there must also be some abstract terms whereby we may show that the persons are distinguished: these are the 'properties' or 'notions', that is, abstract terms like 'paternity' or 'filiation'. Therefore, the divine essence is signified as *What* (quid), the person as *Who* (quis); and the property as *Whereby* (quo).[60]

These explanations are very instructive. They take us back to the questions which the Cappadocian Fathers met when they were dealing with Arianism and Sabellianism. The faith professes three hypostases or three persons in God: Father, Son, and Holy Spirit. But how can one show that the Three, whilst being the same God, are not mixed up with each other? That is, how does one show that the Father is not the Son or the Holy Spirit? To disclose the true divinity of the three persons, it is necessary to draw on the concept of essence (*ousia*), through which each of the three persons is truly God; and in the same way, to show the genuine plurality and distinction of the persons, one must pick out the characteristic through which the Father is Father, the Son is Son, and the Spirit is Spirit. The theory of the properties, such as one finds in Gregory Nazianzus, for instance, comes from this question: in seeking out the

---

[59] *ST* I, q. 32, a. 2.   [60] Ibid.

characteristics of the persons, one can show their distinction in unity, in the teeth of Arianism, which denies the true divinity, and Sabellianism, which denies the real plurality of the persons.[61] Thomas' investigation of persons and properties has the same goal. The theologian who rejects this undertaking will have no means of contesting Arianism or Sabellianism, and will not be able to account for Trinitarian faith. We see once again that, being aware of theories that distance themselves from doing so, Thomas took care of the requirement to give an account of the faith in relation to Trinitarian theology.

So, in attempting to refine our understanding of relations and properties, Trinitarian theology will examine 'that through which' the persons distinguish themselves, through which they are constituted as such (for instance, that through which the Son is Son, that through which he is distinguished from the Father). This question about properties as signified by abstract names is less a matter of the divine reality in itself than of *our human knowledge of the mystery*.[62] The person of the Father is simple: there is not, within the Father, a difference between *what* he is (God), *who* he is (Father), and *that through which* he is Father (paternity). But our grasp of the mystery requires that we perceive *that through which* he is Father, in order to be able to know and disclose his personal distinction, that is to say, to be able to account for the mystery of three persons being one God.

St Thomas puts this in another way as well: to be able to show how the Father distinguishes himself from the Son and the Holy Spirit, one must show that the Father has one relation with the Son and another, different relation with the Holy Spirit; so it is necessary to distinguish the relation of paternity (the relation of the Father to the Son), and the relation of spiration (His relation to the Holy Spirit), without which one could offer a very fine affirmation of the Trinity of persons, but could not explicate the distinction of persons. But, in the Father, paternity is not a different reality from spiration; the two 'notions' of paternity and spiration do not divide the person of the Father: the Father is one. To account for Trinitarian faith, one has to use the 'abstract' language of notions and properties, with the ultimate purpose of showing 'that through which' the Father distinguishes himself from the Son and the Holy Spirit, they themselves being distinct from one another.[63]

---

[61] See, for example, Gregory of Nazianzus, *Oration* 31. 8–9 (SC 250, pp. 290–293).

[62] This has been rightly stressed by Cajetan, who observes, in relation to 'notions': 'This question does not concern the reality [the divine reality: the three persons] considered absolutely in itself, but the reality *in so far as it is described and apprehended by us*' (*In I^{am}* q. 32, a. 2; Leon. ed., vol. 4, p. 352).

[63] *ST* I, q. 32, a. 2; this is the second reason which compels us to recognize notions or properties. For a more prolonged discussion, see H. Dondaine, *La Trinité*, vol. 1, pp. 211–214.

We will return to this in the course of our exploration of relation and person; for the meantime, our discussion suffices to indicate the purpose of investigating processions, relations and properties. The goal is far-reaching: to show that Trinitarian faith can be thought out in a reasonable way. But it is also modest: in presenting the persuasive reasons through which to reply to objections raised against the faith, the theologian carries out a contemplative exercise in order to grasp a droplet of the divine knowledge communicated by revelation, without losing sight of the limits of our knowledge. For St Thomas Trinitarian theology is a spiritual exercise for believers.

3

The Structure of Thomas' Treatise on the Triune God

The meaning of the Trinitarian doctrine of the *Summa Theologiae* is closely related to its structure. The structure is important because it contains a miniature depiction of the basic ideas guiding Thomas' unfolding of the doctrine. It has also been the occasion of some misunderstandings.[1] So it is worthwhile to look at how the principle aspects of Trinitarian faith are integrated within Thomas' treatise.

1. ST THOMAS: VARIOUS ACCOUNTS OF THE MYSTERY OF THE TRINITY

Several of Thomas' works examine Trinitarian faith synthetically. The first thing which strikes one, and which is perhaps surprising, is that on each occasion Thomas gave his treatise a different structure, in relation to the circumstances and particular aim of the book. In his first synthesis, the Commentary on the *Sentences* (1252–1256), Peter Lombard's text provides the structure of the treatise on God. So the general organization of the treatise does not reveal St Thomas' personal intention, even though this is apparent in the prologues (and in the internal arrangement of the questions within each distinction): one cannot fail to notice the key position of the notion of 'procession' and of the exitus–reditus structure. Thomas' Commentary on the *Sentences* is guided by this central thesis: The procession of the divine persons in their unity of essence is the cause and the reason for the procession of creatures.[2]

---

[1] The debate mainly concerns the relation of the divine essence and the persons, as well as the distinction between the immanent being of God and the economic Trinity; see our article, 'Essentialisme ou personnalisme dans le traité de Dieu chez St Thomas d'Aquin?' *RT* 98 (1998), 5–38, cf. pp. 5–9; English translation in *Trinity in Aquinas*, pp. 165–208.

[2] See our book, *La Trinité créatrice*, Paris, 1995, pp. 251–341. For the chronology of Thomas' works, see J.-P. Torrell, *St Thomas Aquinas*, vol. 1: *The Person and His Work*, trans. Robert Royal, Washington DC, 1996. He discusses the date of the redaction on the *Sentences* on pp. 45–47.

In the *Summa Contra Gentiles* (1259–1264/1265), the investigation of the divine mystery falls into two parts: what natural reason can know of the mystery of God (Book I), and that which faith alone can make known to us (Book IV, which also discusses Christology and eschatology). The way of structuring the study of God corresponds to the specific aim of the *Summa Contra Gentiles*. If St Thomas distinguishes the investigation of the essential attributes of God from that of the Trinitarian mystery, this is primarily connected to the two ways in which we know: the first deals with what is accessible to philosophical reason, the second deals with that which surpasses reason.[3] The Trinitarian treatise of the *Summa Contra Gentiles* is structured in a particular way, into two main parts: the generation of the Son (Book IV, chs. 2–14) and then the procession of the Holy Spirit (chs. 15–25); a concluding chapter (ch. 26) shows that there are no other processions in God. Each of the two main parts involves three levels, as follows: (1) the fundamental givens of Scripture; (2) Scripture as interpreted by Catholic faith by contrast with heresies (Thomas' references to the Fathers play an important part in this); (3) discussion and refutation of objections to Catholic faith in the Son and the Holy Spirit. It is in this third stage that St Thomas makes use of the conceptions of the Word and Love, and also the other major speculative themes (notably the theory of relation)[4] which are given primacy in the *Summa Theologiae*.

The plan of the treatise on the Trinity in the *Compendium of Theology* (1265–1267) is like and unlike this. The doctrine of God is set out in three parts: '(1) the unity of the divine essence; (2) the Trinity of persons; (3) the divinity's effects.'[5] As in the *Summa Contra Gentiles*, the distinction between the study of the divine essence and the Trinity of persons is justified by the pathways our knowledge takes.[6] In the matter of the divine persons, the *Compendium* first presents the doctrine of the Word (I, chs. 37–44), then the doctrine of Love (I, chs. 45–49); then it shows how the theory of relation, founded on that of the Word and Love, enables one to conceive the plurality of persons in the unity of essence (I, chs. 50–67, including properties and notional acts). So this treatise is comprised of three parts: the first illuminates faith in the Son (the Word); the second throws light on faith in the Holy Spirit

---

[3] The *Summa Contra Gentiles* is thus built on a threefold distinction: (1) the study of God in himself; (2) the study of the procession of the creatures made by God; (3) the investigation of the relation of creatures to God as final end. Each of the three sections is divided into two parts: that which is accessible to reason, and that which only revelation can make known (cf. *SCG* I, ch. 9; III, ch. 1; IV, ch. 1).

[4] See our article, 'Le traité de St Thomas sur la Trinité dans la *Somme contre les Gentils*', *RT* 96 (1996), pp. 7–14; *Trinity in Aquinas*, pp. 73–84.

[5] *CT* I, ch. 2.   [6] *CT* I, ch. 36.

(Love), and the third shows how one can know that the three divine persons are not three gods but one single God.[7] The treatise called *De rationibus fidei* (written shortly after 1265) has a very analogous structure (chs. III–IV).[8]

In the same period (1265–1276), the Disputed Questions *De potentia*, which were composed a little while before the *Summa Theologiae*, are especially instructive. Among the ten questions, the last four deal with the mystery of the Trinity and unfold like this: Question 7 is about the simplicity of the divine essence, Question 8 deals with the Trinitarian relations, Question 9 treats the persons, whilst Question 10 is devoted to the processions. On the one hand, the connection between divine simplicity and Trinitarian doctrine is very telling, since it highlights the possibility of thinking about the Trinitarian plurality in a way which takes the requirements of God's simplicity into full account. The primary position of the divine simplicity will be recaptured in the *Summa Theologiae*, since it is the first divine attribute which Thomas examines.[9] With its extensive development of the idea of relation, in the context of God's relations with the world, Question 7 is also setting the ground rules for Trinitarian doctrine. On the other hand, the set of the three last questions reveals a serious interest in relations, persons, and processions. None of Thomas' earlier works provides such a profound study of these three notions, brought together into a single collection.

In these questions *De potentia*, St Thomas does not present the scriptural testimonies, as he had done in the *Summa Contra Gentiles*, but rather organizes and refines the theological notions which enable one to know the Trinity in unity. For the theologian who has received faith in the Trinity, the plurality of persons in God requires the positing of a real *distinction* of the persons; this distinction can only be situated within the *relations* which enable one to know the *persons*; and, in their turn, these relations are founded on the actions which give place to the *processions*.[10] In sum, the *De potentia* questions supply a highly developed reflection on the relations, processions, and persons, and do the same in their accounts and arrangements of these three notions in the theological understanding of the mystery of the Trinity. It is obvious that the elaboration of the Trinitarian treatise in the *Summa*

---

[7] Cf. *CT* I, ch. 36.

[8] See our brief survey in Thomas d'Aquin, *Traités: Les raisons de la foi, les articles de la foi et les sacrements de l'Église*, pp. 19–24 and 35–40.

[9] *ST* I, q. 3. On the foundational value of the study of the divine simplicity, see S.-Th. Bonino, 'La simplicité de Dieu', in *Istituto S. Tommaso, Studi 1996*, ed. D. Lorenz, Rome, 1997, pp. 117–151.

[10] Cf. *De potentia*, q. 8, a. 1.

Theologiae owes much to the clarifications which the *De potentia* brings to bear on relation, person, and procession.[11]

2. THE PLAN OF THE TRINITARIAN TREATISE IN THE *SUMMA THEOLOGIAE*

St Thomas assembles the whole of Christian reflection around the mystery of God considered as he is in himself, and considered as the source and goal of creatures: this is what theology is about, its 'subject'.[12] Evidently, the concern is to bring out the theocentricity of Christian doctrine, while maintaining the transcendence of God. The treatise on God in the *Summa Theologiae* is a well-organized unity. The structure appears in the Prologues, enabling one to grasp the purpose of the treatise. Contrary to one widespread opinion (division of the treatise on God into a 'De Deo Uno' and a 'De Deo Trino'), this comprises not two but *three* parts:

The treatment of God will fall into three parts: first we will consider that which pertains to the divine essence, secondly, that pertaining to the distinction of the persons; and thirdly that concerning the procession of creatures from God.[13]

This structure is not out of the ordinary, for Thomas. As we recall, we found it in the *Compendium of Theology*,[14] and Thomas also uses it in some of the Catechetical works where he explains the Creed.[15] It is not alien to the *Summa Contra Gentiles*, even though Thomas connects the tripartite scheme to the general bipartite structure (that which reason can attain, and that which only faith can make known to us).[16] The first thing we must observe is that Thomas does not announce a treatise *De Deo Uno* followed by a treatise

[11] Cf. J. A. Weisheipl OP, 'In fact, *De potentia* is chronologically and speculatively the immediate predecessor of the first part of the theological *Summa*.' *Friar Thomas D'Aquino: His Life, Thought and Work*, New York, 1974, p. 200.

[12] *ST* I, q. 1, a. 7.

[13] *ST* I, q. 2, prologue; cf. q. 27, prologue; q. 44, prologue.

[14] *CT* I, ch. 2.

[15] *De Articulis Fidei*, prologue: 'On the subject of the Trinity, it is necessary to consider three things: the unity of the divine essence, the Trinity of persons and the effects of divine power.'

[16] See n. 3 above, in this chapter. The consequence of this complex plan is that the *Summa Contra Gentiles* deals with the works of God in two sections: St Thomas discusses 'the procession of creatures' [which come] 'from God' in Book II, whilst he considers 'that which is made by God beyond reason' in Book IV (*SCG* I, ch. 9; *SCG* IV, ch. 1). Thus, the Trinitarian dimension of creation does not appear in the treatise on creation in Book II, but in the Trinitarian treatise (bk. IV, chs. 11–13, 20 and 26). The same is true of the investigation of the goal of human beings (bk. III and bk. IV).

De Deo Trino, but a single *consideratio de Deo* which begins by examining 'that which concerns the divine essence', followed by 'that which concerns the distinction of persons'. The way he formulates it clearly suggests that this is a matter of two aspects of one and the same reality.

Further, the economy is not separated from the investigation of God but is made part of it, as a chapter of this treatise on God is dedicated to it. St Thomas describes God's works here as 'the procession of creatures *from God*'. This 'procession of creatures' is not limited to creation in the restricted sense (the original institution of creatures in their natural being), but is rather a general matter of the divine action in the world; it extends to divine 'government' (the realization of providence),[17] which also involves some aspects of the return of creatures to God. In addition, the language of 'procession' enables one to attach the economy, that is, the 'procession of creatures', to its origin in the inner-Trinitarian-ness of the divine persons.[18] God's works are not exclusively attached to the divine essence, but to the mystery of the triune God, considered under all of its aspects (the essence *and* the distinction of persons). Within one single investigation *De Deo,* the structure of the treatise thus rests on a double distinction: (1) between God in his immanent life and in his creative and salvific action; (2) between that which relates to the divine essence and that which relates to the distinction of persons. This double distinction, which produces a three-part structure, requires some explanation.

(a) Immanent and Economic Trinity

The first distinction is between God in his immanent being (*ST* I, qq. 2–43), and God in his creative and saving action (qq. 44 ff.). This distinction takes us back to the origins of speculative Trinitarian theology. It is founded on the Christian doctrinal requirement, as formulated in the fourth century: the existence of the divine persons and their personal properties is dependent neither on creation nor on the divine action in the world. To avoid considering the Son and the Holy Spirit as creatures (as Arianism did), one's conception of the divine persons and their mutual relations must work on the level of eternal divinity, clearly distinguishing the created and the uncreated.

[17] Cf. *ST* I, q. 44, prologue. The 'return to God' is already present in the *Prima pars,* as can particularly be seen in the Treatise on Angels (cf. q. 62) and that on the image of God (q. 93).
[18] In his treatise on creation, St Thomas explains that: 'the processions of the divine persons are the reasons behind the production of creatures' (*ST* I, q. 45, a. 6). See below, in Chapter 14, 'The "Efficacy" of the Trinitarian Processions'.

The distinction between the immanent life of the Trinity and its action in the world comes out in a theme which especially belongs to Trinitarian theology. As Thomas explains them, Arianism and Sabellianism had committed the error of conceiving the processions of the Son and Spirit like an action of God in the world, that is, in the way that an effect proceeds from its cause; this kind of action does not allow one to account for the authentic divinity of the persons and their real distinction. Arianism effectively conceives the Son and the Holy Spirit like creatures, that is, like God's created effects. On the other hand, Sabellianism conceived the generation of the Son as the mode of a divine action in the world: God took the form of the Son when he became incarnate. Far from being marginal, this observation is the point of departure of the Trinitarian treatise of the *Summa Theologiae* (q. 27, a. 1). For this reason, the Trinitarian treatise begins precisely by showing that one ought not to conceive the procession of the divine persons like a divine action in the world, but like an immanent action brought about within God.

This distinction also rests on the philosophical analysis of action, which Aquinas took from Aristotle:

There are two sorts of operations, as Aristotle teaches in *Metaphysics* IX: The first has its place in the operating agent, remaining in it and constituting the perfection of that agent; for example, the act of sensing, knowing, and willing. The second passes over into an external thing, and is a perfection of the thing made as a result of that operation, as for instance, the acts of heating, cutting, and building.

Both kinds of operation belong to God: the former, in that He knows, wills, rejoices, and loves; the latter in that He brings things into being, preserves them, and governs them. But, since the former operation is a perfection of the operator, the latter a perfection of the thing made, and since the agent is naturally prior to the thing made and is the cause of it, it must be that the first of these types of operation is the ground (*ratio*) of the second, and naturally precedes it, as a cause precedes its effect. We can see this very well in human experience: for the architect's plan and his will are the principle and the reason for the construction.[19]

St Thomas distinguishes 'immanent' action, which remains in the acting subject, and 'transitive' action, which is transmitted to a reality outside the acting subject. This explanation, which is not the only one,[20] contains the fundamental principles of Thomas' reflection on what we today call the 'immanent Trinity' and the 'economic Trinity'. They allow one to take account of the plenitude of the Triune God which enjoys complete happiness in its own immanent life, without anything 'lacking' to it.[21] This ensures the

[19] *SCG* II, ch. 1 (nos. 853–854).
[20] See particularly *ST* I, q. 27, a. 1; *De potentia*, q. 9, a. 9; q. 10, a. 1.
[21] *ST* I, q. 26, a. 1; cf. q. 18, a. 3. These features are recalled, in an entirely different context, by the Vatican I constitution *Dei Filius* (cf. Denzinger, nos. 3001–3002).

freedom and gratuity of the creation: whereas immanent action is 'necessary' within God (this action and the fruit or term which proceeds from it are strictly identical to the divine being), God's work in the world springs from a free decision: God creates that which he conceives in his wisdom, following the design of his will.[22] This manifests the first motif of the revelation of the Trinity which we recalled above: in teaching us that God creates through his Word and his Love, Trinitarian faith shows us that God creates the world as a free gift, and not because he is under a necessary compulsion to do so.[23]

As Thomas further refines the point, the immanent action of God (knowledge and will, the processions of the Word and the Holy Spirit) undergird his action in the world: the immanent action is the ground of the latter. Since it is in knowing himself that God knows the creatures of which he is the exemplar and Creator, and since it is in loving himself that God wills and loves his creatures,[24] we cannot study creation until we have considered God's immanent actions. For the same reason, the investigation of the Trinity's action in the world must be preceded by the study of the processions of Word and Love in God's eternity: the generation of the Word and the procession of Love are the source of God's works in the world.[25] So investigation of God's immanent activity, which is essential and personal, must take first place before the consideration of creation and salvation. With St Thomas, the strong perception of God's transcendent unity does not separate thinking about God from thinking about the world or human beings. Rather, it shows and ensures the gratuity of divine action in the world, by showing the depth at which the world's bond to God is rooted within God.

This approach has great benefits. By respecting the absolute transcendence of God's being, knowledge and love, Thomas founds the participation of creatures in the divine life, and ensures the total liberty of the action which God exercises in the world on behalf of creatures. Still more, the fruits of God's activity in the world (creation, exercise of providence, salvation) have their source and rationale in the eternal, immanent activity of God: it is by the same wisdom that God knows himself and knows us; it is by the same love that God loves himself and loves each of his creatures.[26] Here, what may look superficially like an approach which is detached from the economy of creation and salvation, turns out in reality to be a teaching which contains a deep-seated window into the divine foundations of the economy. For St Thomas,

---

[22] *ST* I, q. 14, a. 8; q. 19, a. 4; q. 20, a. 2; cf. q. 44. Using a doctrine which he took from the Fathers, St Thomas explains that the Father engenders the Son and breathes the Holy Spirit *by nature*, whereas he creates the world *by volition* (see below, in Chapter 4, '"Notional" Action').

[23] *ST* I, q. 32, a. 1, ad 3.   [24] *ST* I, q. 14, a. 8; q. 19, a. 4; q. 20, a. 2.

[25] Cf. *ST* I, q. 37, a. 2, ad 3; q. 45, a. 6.

[26] *SCG* I, chs. 48–49 and 74–76; cf. *ST* I, q. 14, a. 5; q. 19, a. 2.

creation and salvation are illuminated from within the doctrine of God himself. One does not take God's action seriously by allowing his relations to the world to condition him, but, rather, one discovers the source of the economy by contemplating the immanent and transcendent being of God. As a result, Thomas refuses to subordinate Trinitarian theology to other theological or anthropological interests. The 'instrumentalization' of Trinitarian discourse, which one sometimes encounters today, is alien to St Thomas. As the Thomist tradition emphasizes, the subject of theology is 'God qua God'.[27]

This is how the 'procession of creatures' is made a part of the study of the Triune God, as the prologue of the second question of the *Summa Theologiae* indicates. This thesis is connected to Thomas' conception of theology. Just as the specifying difference of the philosophical sciences issues from human reason, so *sacra doctrina* has divine revelation as its principle.[28] Philosophical theology (i.e. metaphysics) achieves its goal by considering God as the principle of being; but the subject of the 'theology transmitted by sacred Scripture' is God considered in himself. If one looks at it like this, theology and philosophy take inverse routes. Philosophy derives from the consideration of creatures and knows God as the principle of these creatures; whereas Christian doctrine issues from revelation and takes its departure from the study of God, using this to illuminate our knowledge of creatures.[29] In other words, whereas the human sciences study creatures 'in the nature proper to them', Christian theology studies them in so far as they come from God, disclose God and are related to God. If one follows Thomas, this epistemology implies an *ordo* appropriate to Christian doctrine, where what is at stake is nothing less than the status of revelation within theology:

in the teaching of philosophy, which considers creatures in themselves and leads us from them to the knowledge of God, the first consideration is about creatures; the last, of God. But in the teaching of faith, which considers creatures only in their relation to God, the consideration of God comes first, that of creatures afterwards.[30]

It is this conception of sacred doctrine which the *Summa*'s teaching on the subject of theology expresses: 'In sacred doctrine, everything is treated of under the aspect of God (*sub ratione Dei*): either because it concerns God himself, or because it is a question of realities in so far as they relate to God as

---

[27] One of the episodes in this debate is presented in our article, 'Dieu, la foi et la théologie chez Durand de Saint-Pourçain', *RT* 99 (1999), 679–687.

[28] *ST* I, q. 1, a. 1.

[29] *Super Boetium de Trinitate*, q. 5, a. 4; see J.-P. Torrell, 'Philosophie et théologie d'après le Prologue de Thomas d'Aquin au *Super Boetium de Trinitate*. Essai d'une lecture théologique', *Documenti et Studi sulla tradizione filosofica medievale* 10 (1999), 299–353.

[30] *SCG* II, ch. 4 (no. 876); cf. *ST* I, q. 1, ad 2: the natural ('philosophical') sciences study realities as known 'in the light of natural reason', whereas theology studies them in the degree that they are known 'in the light of revelation'.

their principle and end.'[31] The investigation of creatures need not only disclose their relation to God, but also helps us to have a better grasp of God himself: theology invites us to meditate on the works of God so as to deepen our knowledge of God.[32] The analogies deployed by Trinitarian doctrine are a case in point: a good understanding of the mystery of God requires an accurate assessment of the creatures who make an analogical disclosure of our faith in God possible. This is the theocentrism animating Thomas' theology: theology derives from the revelation of the Triune God, and it goes on to illuminate the 'procession of creatures' within a ground-plan which never loses sight of the mystery of the Trinity.

The treatise on the Trinity must show that the three persons are one God, in virtue of a single essence, and that they are really distinct, by dint of the processions immanent to the heart of the Trinity. When it clarifies the relations that creatures have with the Triune God, it must also show that the creative and salvific action of the Trinity is founded on the common essence and in the properties of the Father, the Son, and the Holy Spirit; all with the aim of helping us to know God better. Even though it comes after the investigation of the immanent life of God, considering the works of God is also part of the study of the Triune God.

(b) The Essence and the Distinction of Persons: the Common and the 'Proper'

The second distinction structuring the treatise on God in the *Summa Theologiae* touches specifically on Trinitarian doctrine. It is about 'that which concerns the divine essence' and 'that which concerns the distinction of persons'. It is not, as some have said, about dividing the treatise into *De Deo Uno* and *De Deo Trino* in the style of certain neo-scholastic theology manuals.[33] Still less is it a matter of a division between a philosophical approach to God and a theological one, as if the first part of the treatise had a philosophical nature and the second was properly theological. In effect, the whole treatise on God is about the Triune God seen in the light of revelation.[34] The distinction between 'that which concerns the divine essence' and 'that which concerns the distinction of persons' rests principally on a theological exigency, deriving, once again, from the Arian controversy. The question at

---

[31] *ST* I, q. 1, a. 7.   [32] *SCG* II, chs. 2–3.

[33] We do not intend to disparage neo-scholasticism. If one reads a number of these treatises, one can easily see that they contain significant divergences on this point.

[34] *ST* I, q. 1, a. 1. On this integral aim of theology, see J.-P. Torrell, 'Le savoir théologique chez St Thomas', *RT* 96 (1996), 355–396.

issue is the distinction between that which is *common* to the three persons, and that which is *proper* to each of them, their own property.

This distinction was developed in the fourth century by St Basil of Caesarea, in the course of his response to the radical Arianism of Eunomius of Cyzicus. Eunomius conceived the 'Unbegotten' (God) in a way which excluded, *a priori*, the recognition of three persons of the same substance. To avoid this dead end, Basil found it necessary to distinguish the divine substance and what properly belongs to the unbegotten Father, so as to show that the Son is of the same substance as the Father (the Son is 'begotten of the substance of the Father', according to the Nicene Creed), even though the Son is not the Father. Consequently, Christian theology will have to distinguish, within our knowledge of God's mystery, that which pertains to the substance and that pertaining to each of the persons' own properties:

The divinity is common, but the paternity and the filiation are properties (*idiomata*); and combining the two elements, the common (*koinon*) and the proper (*idion*), brings about in us the comprehension of the truth. Thus, when we want to speak of an *unbegotten light*, we think of the Father, and when we want to speak of a *begotten light*, we conceive the notion of the Son. As light and light, there is no opposition between them, but as begotten and unbegotten, one considers them under the aspect of their opposition (*antithesis*). The properties (*idiomata*) effectively have the character of showing the alterity within the identity of substance (*ousia*). The properties are distinguished from one another by opposing themselves, [...] but they do not divide the unity of the substance.[35]

Basil also used the *common/proper* contrast to establish the formula 'one substance, three hypostases', which became one expression of Trinitarian orthodoxy.[36] The challenge of radical Arianism ('Anomoeanism') played a decisive part in this. The Arian controversy, and especially the need to answer Eunomius of Cyzicus, led orthodox theology to posit the distinction between 'common' and 'proper' in order to account for the undivided and unconfused unity of the Trinity: 'The Three are One from the perspective of their divinity, and the One is Three from the perspective of the properties.'[37]

[35] Basil, *Against Eunomius* II. 28 (SC 305, pp. 120–121). On this key passage, see B. Sesboüé, *Saint Basile et la Trinité. Un acte théologique au IVᵉ siècle: Le rôle de Basile de Césarée dans l'élaboration de la doctrine et du langage trinitaires*, Paris, 1998, pp. 122–127.

[36] 'The substance (*ousia*) relates to the hypostasis (*hypostasis*) as the common (*koinon*) relates to the proper (*idion*)' (Basil, *Letter* 214.4, ed. Y. Courtonne, *Saint Basile: Lettres*, vol. 2, Paris, 1961, p. 205). Gregory of Nazianzus: 'We speak in harmony with the orthodox doctrine of the unique substance (*ousia*) and of the three hypostases: the former expresses the nature (*phusis*) of divinity, the second expresses the properties belonging to each of the three' (*Orations* 21.35; SC 270, pp. 184–187).

[37] Gregory of Nazianzus, *Orations* 31.9 (SC 250, pp. 292–293). It is this reduplication (One–Three) which is expressed in the structure of Thomas' treatise on God (that which concerns the unity of the divine essence and that which concerns the distinction of the three persons).

From here onwards, Trinitarian theology effects a sort of 'reduplication'.[38] To express the Triune mystery, one must use two words, two formulas, in a reflection that joins the aspect of the unity of the divine substance to that of the distinction of persons. Basil expressed this with the example of light: the 'unbegotten light' designates the Father and the 'begotten light' designates the Son; there is no distinction as far as light, or the divine substance, is concerned, but there is one in relation to the properties (the unbegotten and the begotten). The other Cappadocians adopted this teaching: 'If I say *God,* you would be struck by the lightning bolt of one single light and of three lights: three in what touches upon the properties, or, again, the hypostases, (...) but this light is one if one speaks of the substance, of the Godhead.'[39]

Because of this, an adequate understanding of Trinitarian faith can only be achieved through the 'redoubling' which we have indicated. If we are to avoid the quicksand of Arianism, we must make a conceptual distinction between the divine substance and the proper characteristics of the persons (paternity and filiation), without separating them; as Basil of Caesaria puts it, it is necessary to create a 'combination of the common and the proper'. It is this distinction, which Thomas took from the tradition, especially from Augustine and John Damascene,[40] which structures his treatise on God. The *common* is very precisely signified by the phrase 'that which concerns the divine essence'; on the other hand, the *proper* (the properties) is designated by the phrase, 'that which concerns the distinction of persons'.[41] So the treatise on God is structured by the 'combination' of the investigation of the divine essence *common* to the three persons (qq. 2–26) and the *properties* which distinguish the persons (qq. 27–43).

St Thomas further refines this point when he notes that, *in our conceptual order, common* precedes *proper.* We grasp the divine essence before we grasp the personal properties:

Common terms taken absolutely, in the order of our intelligence, come before proper terms; because they are included in the understanding of proper terms; but not conversely: in effect, when we grasp the person of the Father, the notion of God is included in that, but not conversely.[42]

---

[38] Cf. G. Lafont, *Peut-on connaître Dieu en Jésus-Christ?* Paris, 1969, p. 130.

[39] Gregory of Nazianzus, *Orations* 39.11 (SC 358, pp. 170–173).

[40] See especially John Damascene, *The Orthodox Faith* I, ch. 8.

[41] The 'proper' (*proprium*) is that which belongs to a single person, constituting its distinctive or characteristic property (cf. *ST* I, q. 33, a. 4, arg. 4; q. 34. a. 2, arg. 3; q. 40, a. 2). On the other hand, the 'common' (*commune*) is nothing other than the divine essence (cf. for example q. 30, a. 4, arg. 1); thus, that which is 'common to the whole Trinity concerns the unity of essence and not the distinction of persons' (q. 32, a. 1).

[42] *ST* I, q. 33, a. 3, ad 1; cf. I *Sent.* d. 7, q. 1, a. 3, arg. 4, and ad 4; I *Sent.* d. 29, q. 1, a. 2, qla 2, arg. 1 and sol. If the word 'God' included the notion of paternity (that is, if the divinity boils down to that which is Father), then the Son could not be acknowledged to be God, since he is not the Father.

When we conceive a divine person, we think it precisely as a *divine* person. We cannot grasp the person of the Father just by conceiving his typical characteristic or property: we think of the Father as a person who subsists in the divine being; that is, as a person who is God. It follows that when we grasp the property of paternity as it exists in the Father's person, we include the thought of deity. Our knowledge of the property of the person presupposes and includes the knowledge of the divinity of that person. But, conversely, when we think 'God', we do not think that the Father alone is God (otherwise, we fall into the linguistic and conceptual trap of Arianism, for then we cannot conceive of the Son as God): in this sense, we do not necessarily include the property of Father in the name 'God'. This rule of our knowledge of the persons, which deepens our meditation on the meaning of the word 'God',[43] is required by the patristic distinction of the common and the proper, as St Thomas understood it.

For this reason, which derives from the internal requirements of Trinitarian doctrine, the study of God begins from that of the essence common to the three persons (qq. 2–26), and this is then *integrated* into the study of the properties which distinguish the persons and the understanding of which presupposes our grasp of the divine essence (qq. 27–43). This approach was not invented by St Thomas, or by the 'Augustinian' West. It is effectively present in Cappadocian theology, particularly in Gregory of Nyssa. Gregory's reflections on the Trinity also take their departure from the nature of God, going on to the distinct persons, after a clear conceptual support has been set up for grasping the nature common to the three persons. Trinitarian theology has this starting-point so that it can avoid being caught up in radical Arianism, like that of Eunomius of Cyzicus, which, precisely, premises its thinking on the identity between the divinity and the Unbegotten: a reply to this which works exclusively from the distinct persons would find it difficult to resist the doctrinal manoeuvres of the Arians.[44]

One can add to the arguments a discussion of the paths which our knowledge of God can take, and the place for philosophy within it. The distinction of 'common' and 'proper' enables the theologian to put philosophy to many purposes. He or she uses it in two ways: in relation to that which human rationality can establish through necessary arguments, and secondly, in conjunction with 'likenesses', or 'arguments from congruity', which permit an elaborated presentation of that which faith alone enables one to know.[45] The first instance applies to God's essential attributes, which are attainable by

---

[43] *ST* I, q. 39, a. 4. See below, in Chapter 7, 'The Word *God*'.

[44] See M. R. Barnes, *The Power of God: Dunamis in Gregory of Nyssa's Trinitarian Theology*, Washington DC, 2001, pp. 263–264.

[45] Cf. *ST* I, q. 32, a. 1, ad 2; *Super Boetium de Trinitate*, q. 2, a. 3.

natural reason (qq. 2–26), and where conclusive philosophical arguments are integrated into theology, although not uncritically.[46] St Thomas explains that creatures lead us to the recognition that God exists, and they are also conducive to 'know[ing] of God what must necessarily belong to him, as the first cause of all things, exceeding all things caused by him'.[47] Created things cannot make us know the divine essence as being the essence of Father, Son, and Holy Spirit, but it induces us to grasp the features which one must acknowledge as belonging to the divine essence in its capacity as the principle of creatures; and these essential features are common to the three persons which are known by their revelation in the history of salvation. The second instance applies to the distinction of the persons within the Trinity: as we have recalled earlier, Thomas draws on analogies which, without having demonstrative force outside of faith, enable one to present the Trinity to believers' thinking.

(c) The Game Plan of the Treatise on the Trinity

Using the elements which we have just brought to mind (the *common* and the *proper*), and in line with the project of thinking about faith which we sketched in the previous chapter, Thomas' thesis aims at giving an account of the divine persons who are the one God (the common essence), each of whom is characterized by a personal property (the distinction of persons). The notion of person as 'subsistent relation'—which we will look at in detail later on[48]— is thus the synthesizing principle of Thomas' treatise about God. Since the divine person is to be conceived as a subsistent relation, the study of *person* must be preceded by a study of *relation*: and since our minds perceive procession as the foundation of relation, the theory of relation requires a preliminary study of *procession*. As we try to think about the mystery of the Trinity, the order in which we conceptualize things will thus be as follows: (1) the processions; (2) the relations; (3) the persons. Here again one finds the fundamental elements of this meditation, as St Thomas developed them in his

---

[46] Theology does not restrict itself simply to repeating the thinking of philosophers, for human reason easily commits 'numerous errors' about God (*ST* I, q. 1, a. 1). At the conclusion of his study of the essential attributes of God, in the *Compendium Theologiae*, St Thomas observes: 'That which we have taught about God has been treated with finesse by many pagan philosophers, even though some have commited errors on this topic' (*CT* I, ch. 36). St Thomas was not satisfied with borrowing and using other people's philosophy: he created a philosophy.

[47] *ST* I, q. 12, a. 12. This does not refer to everything which could be said about the divine essence: the treatise on the Trinity will show this by making further refinements about the relation of the essence with the divine persons.

[48] See below, Chapters 6 and 7.

Disputed Questions *De potentia*. Following the explanations given in the prologue of the treatise on the Trinity in the *Summa*, the study of 'that which concerns the distinction of the persons' is presented like this:

I. THE ORIGIN OR THE PROCESSIONS (q. 27)
II. THE RELATIONS OF ORIGIN (q. 28)
III. THE PERSONS (qq. 29–43).
    (a) The persons, considered absolutely (qq. 29–38)
        1. The persons in their common properties (qq. 29–32)
          - The meaning of the name 'person' (q. 29)
          - The plurality or 'number' of the persons (q. 30)
          - Consequences of the plurality of the persons (q. 31)
          - Our knowledge of persons (q. 32)
        2. The persons in the features which are proper to each of them (qq. 33–38)
          - The Father (q. 33)
          - The Son (qq. 34–35)
          - The Holy Spirit (qq. 36–38)
    (b) The persons, considered in comparison (qq. 39–43)
        1. The persons compared to the essence (q. 39)
        2. The persons compared to the properties (q. 40)
        3. The persons compared to notional acts (q. 41)
        4. The persons in their mutual relations (qq. 42–43)
          - The persons' relations of equality and of similarity (q. 42)
          - The missions of the persons (q. 43).

This structure does not reflect the order of our discovery of the Trinitarian mystery, as one would find it in the *Summa Contra Gentiles* or the biblical commentaries.[49] And it does not offer an historical approach which reflects the centuries-long genesis of the Church's confessions of the Trinity. The *Summa Theologiae* proposes a speculative understanding of the faith (*intellectus fidei*) which exhibits the notions, so to speak, in the inverse order to that in which we would find them out.[50] This method of exposition consists in treating procession, relation, and person in their conceptual sequence, so that

[49] A comparison of the two *Summas* shows that, in the *Summa Theologiae*, the exposition is mainly dedicated to notions which, in the *Summa contra Gentiles*, are aimed at giving an account of the faith in the face of arguments against Trinitarian faith.

[50] In faith, we know God through his action in the world and we confess the three divine persons; then theology refines that the persons, in virtue of the processions (generation of the Son, procession of the Spirit), are distinguished by relations. The *Summa Theologiae* in a sense follows the reverse order: processions, relations, persons (including the foundations of creation and grace which are studied in a detailed way in the rest of the *Summa*).

the reader can benefit at each stage from the elements conditioning our understanding of each of the notions. We reminded ourselves in the previous chapter that the only purpose of this speculative doctrine is to take us back to the profound teaching of revelation, conveyed by Scripture. To read the treatise on the Trinity in the *Summa* requires knowledge of biblical revelation, of the liturgy, and, to an extent, knowledge of Christian tradition.

The investigation of the three persons is structured in a similar way: each point of doctrine is situated in such a way that it draws on the preceding expositions and illuminates the subsequent scene. The study of the persons is the centre of the treatise on the Trinity. If one leaves out the two first questions dedicated to processions and to relation, the whole Trinitarian treatise comes under the heading: 'the divine persons' (qq. 29–43). St Thomas' teaching about the Trinity mainly concentrates on the reality of the Trinity itself, that is, on Father, Son, and Holy Spirit. So, Thomas first of all explains the notion of 'person', the meaning of this word and our knowledge of divine persons (qq. 29–32), then he studies each of the divine persons one at a time (qq. 33–38), in order finally to compare the persons (qq. 39–43). These comparisons are diverse. The study of some of them is mainly aimed at organizing the different aspects of our knowledge of the Triune mystery and of our language: it is a matter of comparing the person with the essence, with the properties, and with the notional acts of generation and spiration (qq. 39–41). The others concern the mutual relations of person to person, either at the heart of the immanent life of the Trinity (equality, relation of principle, order of origin, perichoresis: q. 42), or in the Trinity in its gracious action, when the Son and the Holy Spirit are sent to the saints (mission: q. 43).

The placement of the last question about the divine missions means, on the one hand, that, in studying the sending of the Son and the Holy Spirit, the theologian never takes his attention off the intra-Trinitarian mystery. On the other hand, it means that the divine persons are sent and given in their personal distinction, that is in their distinctive properties. Trinitarian doctrine, in illuminating our knowledge of the divine persons in the bosom of the eternal Trinity, furnishes the elements required to appreciate creation and to grasp the salvation effected by the sending of the Son and the gift of the Spirit. In this light, the treatise on the Trinity provides the foundation of the whole teaching which the rest of the *Summa Theologiae* offers. The Trinitarian treatise is thus constructed in a way that will disclose the three divine persons in their subsistence, in their properties, in their relations, and in their actions on our behalf. The fundamental structure of this theological exposition expresses Thomas' determined option for the central place of the *person* and for the role of *relation* in grasping the meaning of person.

4

The Processions

In the *Summa Theologiae*, the very first question in the treatise on the Trinity is about the processions. To see why he begins by asking about this, one must look at where the question is leading: St Thomas wants to show that, because it secures a roundly Trinitarian monotheism, relation enables one to grasp the divine person.

In the previous chapter, we noted the contribution of the systematic reflection in the Disputed Questions *De potentia*; the truth is that the role of the processions in understanding the relations is already apparent in the *Commentary on the Sentences*.[1] The *Summa Contra Gentiles* also elucidates the matter, in the context of the procession of the Holy Spirit: faith in three *persons* implies that these persons are really distinct; and since it concerns consubstantial persons whose essence is indivisible, their distinctness can only be through the pure opposition of relation; relation itself must be founded on the *origin* of the persons, that is in an action giving rise to a procession.[2] We see this in our own world: real relations do not spring from nowhere, but rather come from something which ensures its being real. Our mind perceives the foundation of personal relations in God precisely as procession. So, if one wants to use a relational conception of the person as a means of illuminating our faith in the Trinity, one must be able to give a presentation, in analogies, of the processions which allow us to account for the real relations in God.

It follows that the role which the investigation of the processions plays is propaedeutic: it prepares the way for the study of relations, which in its turn prepares the way for us to think about the persons. That means that the analysis of the processions and relations will be seen to have been worth it when we reach the study of the persons.[3] What is at stake in the question of the processions is assuring the bases of the theories of relation and person. But what kind of procession are we talking about? The tonality of the entire

---

[1] See particularly, I *Sent.* d. 26, q. 2, a. 1; a. 2, ad 4; cf. d. 11, q. 1, a. 1.

[2] *SCG* IV, ch. 24 (no. 3612).

[3] Cf. *ST* I, q. 29, prol: 'Now that we have dealt with what were seen as the necessary preliminaries about processions and relations (*quae de processionibus et relationibus praecognoscenda videbantur*), it is necessary to grapple with the persons.'

Trinitarian treatise comes from this question. St Thomas regards it as necessary for the disclosure of the properties and consubstantiality of the divine
persons. So it calls for our close scrutiny.

1. THE WORD 'PROCESSION'

St Thomas considers the existence of 'processions' in God as a given, scriptural teaching: 'In relation to God, sacred Scripture uses words which indicate
procession.'[4] Theology attempts no rational proof of the personal processions:
it simply offers itself as a disclosure of the sense of Scripture.[5] But, so that the
affirmation of 'processions' in God can make some sense to us, it is necessary
for us to grasp what a procession is; and we can only do that by moving on by
analogy from what is better known to us, processions in our own world.
Unless one does this, one can assert the existence of the divine processions,
but one will not have enlightened anyone's mind as to the meaning of such an
assertion.

St Thomas also accepts as a scriptural fact (he was reading the Bible in
Latin), that the word *procession* applies to the origin of the Son and of the
Holy Spirit.[6] But he also gathered from the Eastern terminology used by the
Greek Fathers that *procession* designates, more precisely, the origin of the Holy
Spirit. In the teaching on the properties, the word *procession* will actually be
applied by Thomas to what belongs to the person of the Spirit, and not to the
Son.[7] The word *procession* thus exposes two meanings: in its common usage it
refers as much to the origin of the Son as the Holy Spirit, and it also has a
restricted sense which exclusively relates to the Holy Spirit. Here is the reason:
'In the created world, one finds a subsistent reality which proceeds by way of
nature: this enables us to give the procession of the Son a proper name:
generation. But we do not find, in the created world, a subsistent reality which
proceeds by way of love, as the Holy Spirit proceeds; and this is why we are not
able to give this procession a proper name, but only a common name.'[8]

---

[4] *ST* I, q. 27, a. 1. St Thomas notes the language concerning the origin of the Son (ibid., sed
contra) and the origin of the Holy Spirit (q. 27, a. 3, sed contra): 'Ego ex Deo processi' (Jn 8.42
Vulgate); 'The Spirit of truth which proceeds from the Father' (Jn 15.26). See also *De potentia*,
q. 10, a. 1, sed contra 1–2; *SCG* IV, chs. 2 and 15.

[5] Cf. *ST* I, q. 32, a. 1, ad 2.

[6] See above, n. 4.

[7] See for instance *ST* I, q. 28, a. 4; q. 32, a. 3. See below, Chapter 5: 'Paternity, Filiation,
Spiration, Procession'. In this context, the term *processio* corresponds to the Greek word *ekporeusis*
which was used by Gregory Nazianzus to designate the personal property of the Holy Spirit; see for
instance, St Gregory, *Orations* 31.8–9; 39.12 (SC 250, pp. 290–293; 358, pp. 172–177).

[8] I *Sent.* d. 13, q. 1, a. 3, ad 2.

Thomas adds, 'But this procession can be called *spiration*, since it is the procession of the *Spirit*.'[9]

St Thomas is quite well aware that the Holy Spirit has its own proper and distinct procession—he will show its characteristics later on—but the *word* which refers to it does not have as much precision as the word 'generation', which we use to designate the origin of the Son. One need not leap to the conclusion that this drawback in our way of talking about it automatically undermines our ability to think about it. Thomas knows that, in Greek theology, procession (*ekporeusis*) designates the relation of the Holy Spirit to the Father as the sole 'primary source' ('principle without principle').[10] We will come back to this in relation to the *Filioque*.[11] For the moment, what we need to notice is that in speaking of the 'procession' of the Holy Spirit, the drawback is a matter of the language, and not of the reality which it is intended to designate.

Lastly, like every theologian, St Thomas immediately separates the conception of divine 'procession' from the sense of local movement (which only has a metaphorical sense when applied to God).[12] In the case of God, procession must be grasped as 'the drawing out of a reality that has issued from a principle', that is, as a pure 'relation of emanation'.[13]

2. ACTION, THE SOURCE OF RELATION

The genuine alterity of the divine persons requires the acceptance that there are such things as real relations. To show that there are, Thomas must establish that there is a difference between real relations and conceptual relations. So, what is the foundation for real relations? Answering this question involves us in a general reflection about the source of relations. Taking over and interpreting Aristotle's thought on this, Thomas accepts only two foundations for real relations. Within this analysis, the word 'foundation'[14] does not designate the substrate of the relation (the thing which carries the relation) but the cause or the source which entails the existence of a relation, that which brings the relation about. Thomas writes,

---

[9] *ST* I, q. 27, a. 4, ad 3.   [10] I *Sent.* d. 12, q. 1, a. 2, ad 3; *In Ioan.* 15.26 (no. 2065).

[11] See below, Chapter 11, 'The Terminology: the Spirit "Proceeds" from the Father and the Son'.

[12] I *Sent.* d. 13, q. 1, a. 1; *De potentia*, q. 10, a. 1; *ST* I, q. 27, a. 1, sol. and ad 1.

[13] I *Sent.* d. 13, q. 1, a. 1; cf. ad 1; *De potentia*, q. 10, a. 1, ad 2.

[14] Real relation is 'founded' (*fundatur*) on a reality giving rise to the existence of this relation. Cf. *ST* I, q. 28, a. 4; *SCG* IV, ch. 24 (no. 3612); etc.

According to the Philosopher, in *Metaphysics* V, every relation is founded either on quantity (for example, double and half); or on action and passion (for example, that which does something and the thing which it produces, or father and son, or master and servant). And there is no quantity in God: he is 'great without quantity', as Augustine says. It follows that a real relation in God can only be founded on action.[15]

This analysis takes place in the context of the Aristotelian theory of the categories (the ten modes of being), amongst which Thomas is looking for the foundation for real relations. He considers all the possibilities, one by one. Amongst the accidents, he first excludes those which do not entail a relation but are, rather, consequent upon a relation.[16] He follows Avicenna's lead in ruling out the idea that a relation could really refer to something through another relation, or that this real relation could be founded on another relation.[17] As to quality and substance, it is only 'accidentally' that they exercise a foundational role towards a relation, that is, in so far as they are reduced to action and passion (active and passive power) or so far as one considers them under the aspect of quantity (this is why unity of substance entails the relation of 'sameness', whereas unity of quality entails the relation of similitude).[18] These explanations leave nothing to chance. St Thomas makes a precise examination of the nature of relations in our world, and concludes to the existence of two possible foundations for the existence of a real relation: action/passion, and quantity. 'Hence the Philosopher, in giving the species of relations in *Metaphysics* Book V, says that some are founded on quantity and some on action and passion.'[19]

The reader may be surprised to find this Aristotelian analysis in the middle of a treatise on the Trinity. We will see later on that, in this field, the use of Aristotle goes back to the Patristics. For Thomas, the analysis is rooted in the following consideration. If there are real relations in God (and faith leads one to accept that there are), then these relations must be able to stand the test of comparison with the constitutive elements of any real relation; otherwise attributing such relations to God would add nothing to our understanding of our faith in the Trinity. To put it another way: if, when we speak of 'real relations' in God, the word *relation* means something to us, by analogy with

---

[15] *ST* I, q. 28, a. 4; Cf. I *Sent.* d. 26, q. 2, a. 2, ad 4; *SCG* IV, ch. 24 (no. 3612); *De potentia*, q. 7, a. 9; q. 8, a. 1; *In Metaph.* V, lect. 17 (nos. 1001–1004); *In Physic.* III, lect. 1 (no. 280). Aristotle, *Metaphysics*, Δ. 15 (1020^{b}26–29). See M.-J. Dubois, *Aristote, livre des acceptions multiples. Commentaire philosophique*, Saint-Maur, 1998, pp. 123–130, 'Le relatif'.

[16] Cf. *In Metaph.* V, lect. 17 (no. 1005); amongst the predicaments, this is the case for 'when', 'where', 'position', and 'habitus'.

[17] *De potentia*, q. 3, a. 3, ad 2; q. 7, a. 9, ad 2. The 'relations of relations' are conceptual, not real (I *Sent.* d. 26, q. 2, a. 1; II *Sent.* d. 1, q. 1, a. 2, ad 5).

[18] Cf. *De potentia*, q. 7, a. 9; cf. *SCG* IV, ch. 24 (no. 3612).

[19] *De potentia*, q. 7, a. 9.

relations in our world, it must be possible to pick out one of the two foundations of real relations from within the world. Unless one can do this, one will not be able to show how real relations exist.

St Thomas goes on to say that 'quantity' must be excluded from God. Augustine's explanation ('God is great without quantity') is enough to indicate this. A relation founded on quantity would imply a difference in the relative terms (such as 'greater', 'smaller') which is incompatible with the consubstantiality of the divine persons; or it would not entail a distinction but rather presuppose distinction without causing it.[20]

The upshot of performing this philosophical analysis and integrating it into theology is that the only foundation which can account for real relation in God is action. More precisely, Thomas speaks of 'action and passion'. Action effectively involves a subject acting plus a terminus for the action, its recipient. In other words: action implies both an acting subject and some reality which issues from this agent, that is to say, something which *proceeds* from it. From this fact it follows that such action entails a double relation: the relation of the agent to the terminus of his action, and the relation of the terminus to the agent from which it issues. It is this analysis which serves as the analogy which helps one to pin down how to grasp the processions in God.

3. THE PROBLEMS OF ARIANISM AND OF SABELLIANISM

Trinitarian theology is looking for an analogy which gives due respect to its subject, and which enables it to bring an authentic procession within God to light. Refining on what the analogy must do, St Thomas adds that it must enable one to grasp an 'immanent procession'. The starting-point of the Trinitarian treatise is the idea of 'immanent procession'. Thomas' reflection is based on an interpretation of the problems of Arianism and Sabellianism: because they conceive procession like a transitive action, these heterodox theories cannot work out how a Son could genuinely exist within God. As we mentioned in relation to the structure of the treatise,[21] Thomas appropriated Aristotle's distinction between two kinds of actions: 'immanent' action, which remains within the acting subject (such as knowing, willing, and feeling), and 'transitive' action which passes over (*transit*) to a reality external to itself (such as heating, constructing, and making).[22] In both cases, the action gives rise to a procession:

---

[20] *SCG* IV, ch. 24 (no. 3612).
[21] See above, in Chapter 3, 'Immanent and Economic Trinity'.
[22] See especially *ST* I, q. 27, a. 1; *SCG* II, ch. 1; *De potentia*, q. 9, a. 9; q. 10, a. 1.

procession of an interior reality, for the immanent action, and procession of an external reality, for the transitive action. One must recognize two analogous kinds of actions in God: the Trinitarian processions, in the one case, and the actions of creation and government in the other.[23]

The example constantly used by St Thomas is that of the architect: the immanent action takes place when the architect mentally conceives the plan of the building which he is going to construct, and he wills its construction; then, in the transitive action, the architect concretely realizes his plan by getting the building constructed. The next step is that the transitive action, or 'procession *ad extra*', implies a difference between the agent and the reality which proceeds from his action.[24] If one applies this to the processions of the divine persons, then 'the persons who proceed from it will be external to the divine nature', just as the house is of a different nature from the mind of the architect who conceives and wills it.[25] For Thomas, this is the trap into which both Arianism and Sabellianism fall, in their own different ways:

Some have understood this procession in the sense of an effect proceeding from its cause; so Arius took it, saying that the Son proceeds from the Father as the first amongst his creatures, and that the Holy Spirit proceeds from the Father and the Son as the creature of both. But then, neither the Son nor the Holy Spirit would be true God ... Others take the procession to mean the cause proceeding to the effect, as moving it, or impressing its own likeness on it; in which sense it was understood by Sabellius, who said that God the Father is called Son in assuming flesh from the Virgin Mary, and that the Father also is called Holy Spirit in sanctifying the rational creature and moving it to life.[26]

By conceiving the generation of the Son as if it were a transitive action, Arianism sets up an *a priori* interdiction against understanding the authentic divinity of the Son and the Holy Spirit. Sabellianism does something analogous from the opposite end of the spectrum: it allows one to maintain the divinity of the Son and Holy Spirit but only by conflating them with the Father, treating them as the modes through which the Father acts in the world. It is no surprise that Arianism and Sabellianism both make the same misjudgement. It is true that, in trying to avoid Sabellianism, Arius went for the opposite mistake,[27] but nevertheless the contraries meet on one point: both connect the generation of the Son to an 'external nature',[28] Arius relating it to the production of a creature, and Sabellius to incarnation. Thus: 'Careful

---

[23] *De potentia*, q. 10, a. 1; *SCG* II, ch. 1 (no. 854).
[24] *ST* I, q. 27, a. 1, ad 2.   [25] *De potentia*, q. 9, a. 9.   [26] *ST* I, q. 27, a. 1.
[27] *SCG* IV, ch. 6 (no. 3387); *De rationibus fidei*, ch. 9: 'Arius, trying to avoid Sabellius' error, which conflated the persons of the holy Trinity, fell into the opposite error, dividing the essence of the deity.'
[28] *SCG* IV, ch. 7 (no. 3425).

examination shows that Arius and Sabellius understood the procession as something brought about within an external reality.'[29]

These thoughts are very useful for understanding what Thomas is aiming at here. His consideration of the processions is undergirded by the necessity of creating an alternative to the two outstanding Trinitarian heresies. As he explains in the *De potentia*:

The ancient doctors of the faith were compelled to discuss matters of faith because the heretics drove them to it. Thus Arius thought 'holding one's existence from another' is incompatible with the divine nature. Since Scripture teaches that the Son and the Holy Spirit hold their existence from another, Arius maintained that the Son and the Holy Spirit are creatures. In order to refute this error the holy Fathers had to show that it is not impossible for someone to proceed from God the Father and yet be consubstantial with him, inasmuch as he receives from him the same nature as the Father has himself.[30]

The exigence of defending the faith supplies the opportunity to unfold a Catholic doctrine of the Trinitarian processions. As we saw above, Thomas had already formulated the same intention regarding the plurality of the divine 'persons'. He conceived his own meditation as an extension of the Fathers', both manifesting the true faith as against the mire of heresy. The heresies are linked to a philosophical misjudgement: St Thomas explains elsewhere that the Arians did not want to believe in the divinity of the Son and that *they could not understand it*: so their position was motivated by deliberate rejection, but also by an intellectual difficulty.[31] He does not present the diverse aspects of Arianism and Sabellianism in detail in q. 27 of the *Summa*,[32] but he does propose a doctrinal interpretation of their common error, with the aim of finding a speculative route which, by enabling us to avoid their dead-end, permits us to contemplate the truth. This is why Thomas chose to build his Trinitarian treatise on the immanent processions of the word and of love.

4. A PROCESSION WHICH IS THE GENERATION OF THE WORD

Catholic faith 'advances on a middle ground'[33] between the errors, but also radically overturns their perspective. It does this by considering procession not as an action *ad extra*, but as an *immanent* action:

[29] *ST* I, q. 27, a. 1. [30] *De potentia*, q. 10, a. 2.
[31] *SCG* IV, ch. 6 (no. 3387). This idea is drawn from Augustine, *De Trinitate* XV.XX.38.
[32] See especially *SCG* IV, chs. 5–6. On Thomas' knowledge of Arianism, see P. Worrall, 'St. Thomas and Arianism', *RTAM* 23 (1956), 208–259; 24 (1957), 45–100.
[33] *SCG* IV, ch. 7 (no. 3426).

In the case of an action which remains within the agent himself, one observes a procession which comes about *ad intra*. One observes this above all (*maxime patet*) in the intellect, whose action, that is, intellection, remains in the knowing subject. For whenever we understand, by the very fact of understanding there proceeds something within us, which is a conception of the object understood, a conception issuing from the intellectual power and proceeding from our knowledge of the object. It is this conception which the spoken word signifies; and it is called the word of the heart signified by the word of the voice.[34]

From the *Summa Contra Gentiles* onward, this doctrine of the word, based on the analysis of language and of the process of meaning, is the means by which St Thomas accounts for the procession of the Son.[35] When he applies this within his meditation on God, Thomas invites us to consider God's spiritual nature: 'God has a spiritual or intellectual nature, or rather, he overarches every mind: so generation in God must be understood in a way that suits an intellectual nature.'[36] He knows, from Hilary and Augustine, that the doctrine of the 'prolation' or 'emanation' of the Word was sometimes suspect amongst the ancient writers, because of Gnostic philosophizing about the emission of aeons in the pleroma. Irenaeus encountered this problem; it need not remain an issue with Aquinas because analysis of the mode of the procession of the Word in God shows that this doctrine has nothing in common with Gnostic philosophizing.[37]

The most original exposition of the doctrine of the word is found in St John (Jn 1.1; 1.14; 1 Jn 1.1; Rev. 19.13). To articulate it, Thomas works with a modification of Aristotle's anthropology which repays observation. For Aristotle, properly speaking, the immanent operation of the mind and will effectively 'produces' nothing.[38] In order to be able to acknowledge that the acts of knowing and loving produce an immanent issue, St Thomas reinterprets Aristotle in the light of the Augustinian tradition: this relates to the word, and, as we will see later, to love's affection. For the moment, Thomas concentrates his attention on the *procession* of this word. Intellectual knowledge is a fertile act within which something 'proceeds': this is the 'word of the heart' (the expression comes from Augustine), which Thomas identifies as the concept of the thing known. This word *proceeds* from the knowing mind,

---

[34] *ST* I, q. 27, a. 1.

[35] See our article, 'Le traité de St Thomas sur la Trinité dans la *Somme contre les Gentils*', *RT* 96 (1996), 21–31. On the development of Thomas' doctrine of the Word, see below, in Chapter 9, 'Studies in the Analogy of the Word: Anthropology and Trinitarian Theology'.

[36] *De rationibus fidei*, ch. 3.

[37] *ST* I, q. 34, a. 2, arg. 2 and ad 2. Thomas refers here to St Hilary (*De Trinitate* VI.9; SC 488, pp. 182–185), and to St Augustine (*De haeresibus* 11; CCSL 46, pp. 295–296). Cf. St Irenaeus, *Adversus Haereses* II.28.6.

[38] Aristotle, *Metaphysics* θ. 8 (1050^a23–$^b2$).

whilst remaining within the mind. This gives us an analogous conception of the substantial unity of the Father and his Word, that is to say the divinity of the Word, and its distinction:

whatever proceeds within (*ad intra*) by an intellectual process is not necessarily diverse [from its principle]; to the contrary, the more perfect the procession is, the more closely it is one with that from which it proceeds. For it is clear that the more a thing is known, the greater the intimacy of its intellectual conception with the one who knows it; and the more it is one with him; because the intellect by the very act of knowing, becomes one with the known. Thus, since the divine intellect is the summit of all perfection, as we said above [q. 14, a. 1], it is necessary that the divine Word be perfectly one with Him from whom he proceeds, without the least diversity.[39]

The act of thought consists in a union, an assimilation: the knowing subject somehow makes the perfections which belong to other beings exist within himself. When the mind knows, 'that which is known is in a certain way in the knower', because 'the form of the known is in the knower'.[40] When it knows, the mind intentionally 'becomes' the thing known.[41] This union with the known thing abides in the intimacy of the word within the intellect itself. The intellect unites itself to the known thing through the word which abides within itself. It is this intimacy between the word and the intellect (the immanence of the word within the mind) to which St Thomas refers here. On such a basis, he can assess the prerogatives of the divine intellect. The divine Word is not an accident, since there are no accidents in God: everything 'there is' within God, is God himself.[42] The Word is not something that 'happens' to God, but rather has the nature of God, from all eternity.[43] In addition, the 'object' of the divine understanding is God himself. In the act through which God knows himself, the unity of the divine intellect and the Word is thus 'the most intimate'.[44] So, when one considers how it takes place within God, the act of intellectual understanding enables one to disclose a procession occurring within a substantial unity ('without the least diversity').

In this way, St Thomas can show the principle aspects of divine generation by means of the analogy of intellectual procession: the distinction of the Word and its principle (the Father), the Word's relation of origin with this principle, the intimacy and immanence of the Word and his principle (Jn 1.1–2: 'The

---

[39] *ST* I, q. 27, a. 1, ad 2.   [40] *De veritate*, q. 2, a. 2; *ST* I, q. 14, a. 1.
[41] 'This is what makes the Philosopher say, in Book III of *De Anima*, that "the soul is in a certain way all things"' (*ST* I, q. 14, a. 1).
[42] *ST* I, q. 3, a. 6; cf. q. 34, a. 2, ad 1; q. 14, a. 4.   [43] *ST* I, q. 27, a. 2, ad 2.
[44] This intimacy is the starting-point for the meditation in the *Summa Contra Gentiles* (IV, ch. 11, no. 3461).

Word was with God and the Word was God. It was at the beginning with
God'; Jn 14.10: 'I am in the Father and the Father is in me'), the unity of the
Word and his principle (Jn 10.30: 'The Father and I are one'). In the *Summa
Contra Gentiles*, at the end of an explanation comparable to the one given
back in the John Commentary, Thomas concludes that this is the teaching
contained in the Prologue to the Fourth Gospel.[45] In his treatise, *De rationibus
fidei*, he concludes his exposition by showing that this doctrine allows one to
show that the divine Word is 'of the same nature as the Father and co-eternal
with the Father, unique and perfect', that is to say, it enables one to give an
account of the Creed.[46]

In the first article of the Trinitarian treatise in the *Summa Theologiae*,
Thomas does not mention 'generation': the reader could well be put out by
this, since that is what he is dealing with! St Thomas wants to avoid the
misdirected conception, found in Arianism and Sabellianism, of the generation of the Son as being like one of the acts which God performs within this
world. So Thomas does not place the notion of 'generation' (as the communication of nature to the engendered) at the beginning of his exposition, but
starts with the intellectual procession of the Word instead, because this
enables one clearly to grasp an *immanent* action whose issue is *consubstantial*
with its principle, both being a *unity*. The analogy of intellectual procession
does not work to the exclusion of all others, but Thomas considers it the most
enlightening. He observes that our world does not provide us with any
examples of procession which could perfectly represent the divine generation,
because the Son is born in identity of substance and eternity with the Father.
'Hence we need to gather an analogical representation from many of these
modes [which one can observe in creatures], so that what is lacking in one
may be partially supplied by another . . . Yet, within all these likenesses, it is the
procession of the word which represents [divine generation] in the most
adequate way.'[47] It is here that one effectively finds the deepest intimacy. So
here the theologian deploys an analogy which, primarily, suits the spiritual
perfection of God; and which, secondly, enables one to grasp clearly what
procession is like *in God*; and, thirdly, roots it apart from where Arius and
Sabellius had so unproductively planted it.

In the second moment of his exposition, St Thomas shows that the procession of the Word allows one to know that which in God is the *generation* of
the Son. In our world, generation comes about in diverse ways. It is an
observable fact for every being which undergoes genesis: it is 'the passage

---

[45] *SCG* IV, ch. 11 (no. 3473).
[46] *De rationibus fidei*, ch. 3.   [47] *ST* I, q. 42, a. 2, ad 1.

from non-being to being'. Amongst living things, generation has its own way of coming about, at a higher level: then it means 'the origin of a living being from a living principle conjoined to it', entailing the communication of a similar nature (the likeness of the specifying nature: we say that a human being is 'born' from another human being). This is the precise meaning of the word 'generation'. Thomas explains that, when it takes place in God, generation is disassociated from the passage of non-being to being, but retains the analogical rationale which it has amongst living beings. Having set out these elements, St Thomas concludes:

So in this manner the procession of the Word is generation. The Word effectively proceeds by way of an intellectual activity, and it is a living operation.[48] It also proceeds from a conjoined principle, as we have said (a. 1). And it proceeds by the rationale of similitude, since what the intellect conceives is the likeness of the thing known. And it exists in the same nature, since in God knowing is identical to being, as we have shown above (q. 14, a. 4). This is why the procession of the Word in God is called *generation*, and the Word itself proceeding is called 'Son'.[49]

The identification of generation with the Word's procession rests on the constitutive features of both conceptions, and also on what belongs to divinity (such as substantial identity).[50] Without going any further into Thomas' view of generation, one should notice what he is aiming at: the procession of the Word passes the test of the constitutive features of generation, insofar as they are applicable to God.[51] The procession of the word is thus apt for *disclosing what generation is in God*, without getting bogged down in Arianism and Sabellianism, and it serves as an analogy characterizing the first divine procession as well as distinguishing it from the second. The study of the person of the Son is approached in the same way: it is on the basis of the doctrine of the Word that Thomas shows how one must understand filiation and the name 'Son' itself.[52]

[48] On the activity of the intellect as a living operation, see *ST* I, q. 18; cf. *De potentia*, q. 10, a. 1.
[49] *ST* I, q. 27, a. 2; cf. *ST* III, q. 32, a. 3. Thomas' words 'ratio' and 'rationes' have no direct English equivalent. In the course of this book, 'ratio' and 'rationes' are translated variously as *rationale, idea, eidetic pattern, pattern*, and *model*.
[50] *ST* I, q. 27, a. 2, ad 2. Unlike our human word (which is not really 'engendered'), the divine Word 'proceeds as subsisting in the same nature'; so one can properly recognize, in the speaking of the Word, a genuine *generation*. Cf. *SCG* IV, ch. 11; *De rationibus fidei*, ch. 3.
[51] Procession 'by the mode of nature' (the notion of generation) is thus identical to 'procession in an intellectual mode' (the emanation of the Word); the second enables one to understand the first; *ST* I, q. 30, a. 2, ad 2.
[52] See below, in Chapter 9, 'The Son, Word of God'.

5. A DIFFERENT PROCESSION, WHICH IS THAT OF LOVE

The method of studying the second procession is analogous to the first. In the *Summa Theologiae*, Thomas first of all shows the existence of the procession of Love, then he shows that this procession is not a generation and that it is distinct from the first (q. 27, aa. 3–4). Here again, Thomas wants to avoid the Arian (or semi-Arian) conception of the Spirit as a creature, which came about by imagining the procession of the Spirit as being like one of God's actions within the world:

Since the Son receives the Father's nature, he is said to be *begotten* or *engendered* of the Father. But the Holy Spirit is not said to be either *begotten* or engendered in the Scriptures, although it is said that the Holy Spirit derives his existence from God (*est a Deo*). This is why Macedonius thought that the Holy Spirit is not consubstantial with the Father but is one of his creatures. For Macedonius did not believe it possible for anyone to receive from another that other's very nature, unless one was born of him and was his son. Hence he considered that if the Holy Spirit receives the Father's very nature and essence from the Father, it must necessarily follow that the Holy Spirit is begotten and is a Son.[53] So, to refute this error it was necessary for our doctors to show that the divine nature can be communicated by a twofold procession, the one being a begetting or nativity, and the other not: and this is the same as to look for the distinction between the divine processions.[54]

The attribution of this argument to Macedonius himself is dubious,[55] but it does appear in the patristic debate about the procession of the Holy Spirit, from the time of Athanasius' *Letters to Serapion*,[56] and perhaps earlier. Gregory of Nazianzus also gave his undivided attention to it, proposing the notion of *ekporeusis* to distinguish the origination of the Spirit and the generation of the Son.[57] As with the investigation of the procession of the Son,

---

[53] In the *Summa Contra Gentiles*, where he uses the same argument, St Thomas adds: 'And a healthy faith will find this revolting' (*SCG* IV, ch. 16, no. 3523).

[54] *De potentia*, q. 10, a. 2.

[55] Following the usage which he took over from his patristic texts, Thomas tends to identify the Macedonians with the 'semi-Arians' in general (cf. *SCG* IV, ch. 16, no. 3525). In other words, he did not make the precise distinction between the 'Macedonians' and the 'Tropikoi' who Athanasius targeted in his *Letters to Serapion*. Through Nicolas of Cotrona's *Libellus de fide Trinitatis* which Pope Urban IV had submitted to his expert scrutiny (nos. 10–21; Leon. edn., vol. 40, p. A 113–126), St Thomas was aware of large extracts from the first *Letter to Serapion*, although, unfortunately, in a text which had been enlarged and glossed. For a sketch of the pneumatological question in St Thomas, see J. A. Riestra, 'El error de Macedonio y la doctrina de Santo Tomás', in *Credo in Spiritum Sanctum*, ed. J. Saraiva Martins, vol. 1 Vatican City, 1983, pp. 461–471.

[56] Athanasius, *Letter to Serapion* I.15–16 (SC 15, pp. 108–112).

[57] Gregory of Nazianzus, *Orations* 31.8–9 (SC 250, pp. 290–293).

we find here that the intention to defend the faith furnished the opportu..., for the Fathers' speculative meditation (*our doctors*). St Thomas conceives his enquiry as an extension of patristic reflection.[58] *To disclose the divinity of the Spirit and the kind of existence which belongs to him, it is necessary to show that his procession is of a different kind from that of the Son.* And one cannot show this on the basis of the concept of 'generation', simply because the procession of the Spirit is not a generation. As he did with the Son, Thomas concentrates his meditation on the notion of 'immanent procession'. The explanations in the *Summa Theologiae* are extremely concise:

Procession exists in God only according to an action which does not tend to anything external, but remains in the agent himself. And, in an intellectual nature, such action is that of the intellect, and of the will. The procession of the Word belongs to an act of the intelligence. As to the operation of the will, for us it gives rise to a different procession which is that of love, whereby the object loved is in the lover (in the same way that, by the procession of the word, the thing spoken or known is in the knower). Hence, in addition to the procession of the Word, there exists in God another procession which is the procession of Love.[59]

St Thomas is looking for an analogy which enables one to grasp the procession of the Holy Spirit (without which one can assert it, but one cannot disclose it!). To this end, he uses the analogy of spiritual life, which had already worked well in conceiving the generation of the Son, this time referring it to affective action: volition belongs to intelligent beings.[60] To understand how he draws out the theme in Trinitarian theology, we must consider Thomas' original idea of love.

Thomas sets his presentation of affective life within a metaphysics of action that is governed by one fundamental principle: 'every form gives rise to a certain inclination which corresponds to it'.[61] One can understand it like this. A being is what it is through a 'form' which gives it being in this or that way, for instance as a hazel tree, a piano, or a bat. This form is a principle of being and it is also the principle of an *inclination* towards something, that is, the principle of an action. For example, a case of a substantial form, a dog barks, eats bones, engenders other dogs, and so forth by virtue of its dog-form: the form which specifies its dog-being entails inclinations corresponding to that form, inclining the dog to certain acts which fit what it is. Thomas distinguishes on this basis three types of form, which are the source of three sorts of 'appetites' (*appetitus*) or inclinations of a being towards that which conforms

---

[58] The question about the Holy Spirit's proceeding without being begotten is central to Augustine's thinking: see *De Trinitate* I.V.8; II.III.5; IX.XII.17–18; XV.XXV.45; XV.XXVI.47; XV.XXVII.48; XV.XXVII.50.

[59] *ST* I, q. 27, a. 3.   [60] *SCG* IV, ch. 19 (no. 3558).   [61] *ST* I, q. 80, a. 1.

to its nature. (1) *Natural appetite*: this is the tendency every being has by virtue of its natural form (fire heats; it is inclined to heat what it touches); (2) *animal appetite*: this is the tendency of beings which know through their senses towards the things which they have understood through their senses (dogs are inclined to the bones which they munch); (3) *intellectual appetite*: this is the inclination of beings that know intellectually towards that which they grasp through their intellectual understanding (human beings are inclined to the truth as their good). This latter inclination or intellectual appetite is volition, or *will*.[62] Volition is the inclination towards the good apprehended by intelligence, the capacity to convey oneself towards an end grasped by one's mind:

Through the form which constitutes their species, natural beings have an inclination to their fitting operations and to the end which fits their operations—as one is, so one acts—and they tend to what belongs to them. Thus, the intelligible form in an intelligent being unfolds towards the operations and end proper to it. In an intelligent nature, this inclination is volition: it is the principle of the operations in us and through which an intelligent being acts towards its end, for ends and goods are the object of the will. So one must recognize that intelligent beings have volition.[63]

All beings act to attain a good to which they are inclined, either by nature or through sensible knowledge, or through intellectual knowledge. We learn what love is from this inclination, that bowling for the good which orients every being to what fits and satisfies it. Love is the aboriginal affection, reaching for the good, the principle of movement towards the beloved good:

In each of these appetites [natural, sensitive, and intellectual], the name *love* is given to the principle of movement toward the beloved end. In the natural appetite the principle of this movement is the connaturality of the subject with that towards which it tends, and may be called 'natural love'; thus, the connaturality of the heavy body with the place which, because of its weight, suits it, can be called 'natural love'. Likewise the adaptation (*coaptatio*) of the sensitive appetite and that of the will to a good, that is to say its very complacency (*complacentia*) in good is called sensible love [in the case of sensitive appetite], and intellectual or rational appetite [in the case of the will].[64]

Love is the gravitation of one being toward another which is its good, by dint of connaturality, or a relationship of conformity between oneself and the

---

[62] *ST* I-II, q. 26 a. 1; cf. *ST* I, q. 80, a. 1. *De veritate*, q. 23, a. 1: 'This free inclination (*libera inclinatio*) constitutes the essence of the will.' See S. Pinckaers, *Les sources de la morale chrétienne: Sa méthode, son contenu, son histoire*, Fribourg and Paris, 1990, pp. 384–460.

[63] *SCG* IV, ch. 19 (no. 3558); cf. *ST* I, q. 19, a. 1.

[64] *ST* I-II, q. 26, a. 1; *SCG* IV, ch. 19 (no. 3559): St Thomas' teaching here shows the homogeneity between his anthropology and his Trinitarian theology, which are mutually illuminating.

other. It is the inclination of things to come into line with the good congruent to them. This conception of creaturely love stands under the ensign of finality: what makes things act is the good which fits them, doing so either by nature or because they can perceive their own good. The arc they trace out has their good as its end or goal. Love is something which is teleological, belonging to the order of finality, and also analogical, authenticating its presence on the diverse rungs of being. Without love, nothing would act, nothing would become, nothing would change, because nothing would seek its good. Love is thus the root of action. With the helping hands of Stoicism and Nemesius of Emesa behind him, Thomas recognizes love as the source of our central affections:

Every inclination of the will derives from the fact that, through it, something is apprehended as 'congruent' or as 'arousing the affections': to experience affection for something is to love it. Thus, every inclination of the will, and even of the sensible appetite, originates from love. It is because we love something that we desire it in its absence, that we are joyous in its presence, that we are sad when we cannot attain it, and that we experience hate and anger towards whatever separates us from it.[65]

So love is the principle of the affective life, the absolutely primary affection of the appetite in contact with the desirable, and native complacency in the good, which the will has as its object. This is why love motivates action: it is the 'primitive root' of all appetitive movements.[66] Whenever we act, it is because we are moved by a good which we want to attain, and it is always because of a love. This is why, analogously, God's creative activity will be attributed to his Love, as the principle of his works. Understanding the creative action of the Holy Spirit will benefit a great deal from knowing about this.

On this basis, St Thomas proposes one more step, which is of central importance for the application of the analogy of love to the procession of the Holy Spirit. In the spiritual order, our union with another is achieved by the *presence of the other to ourselves*. Earlier, we brought to mind that, in the case of knowledge, this presence is secured by a similitude to the thing known in the knowing subject, and particularly by the *word* which renders the item present, and known. Love is not achieved by the presence of a similitude of the 'object': the presence of another through a likeness is the mode which fits understanding.[67] When we love, this love is not a likeness or resemblance in us

---

[65] *SCG* IV, ch. 19 (no. 3559). Joy, sadness, hope, and fear are the four 'principal passions': *ST* I-II, q. 25, a. 4. Cf. E. Dobler, *Zwei syrische Quellen der theologischen Summa des Thomas von Aquin, Nemesios von Emesa und Johannes von Damaskus*, Fribourg, 2000, pp. 330–335.

[66] *ST* I-II, q. 28, a. 6: 'Whatever it is, every agent carries out all its actions because of a love'; cf. q. 27, a. 4; *ST* I, q. 20, a. 1.

[67] *ST* I, q. 30, a. 2, ad 2.

of the beloved being. In other words, the process of knowledge comes about in the mind of the knowing subject, and truth or falsity are located within this mind; whereas love is brought about outside of ourselves, in the realities which we love and in which good and evil are found.[68] So how can one account for the *presence* of the beloved being *in* the one who loves? This is a crucial issue, if we remember that Thomas is attempting to disclose an *immanent* procession in God. The same question will also play a central role in grasping the divine missions, especially the Holy Spirit's dwelling within the just: how can God make himself present in those who love him?[69] Thomas writes,

There is a certain difference between the intellect and the will. The intellect is made to be in act by the thing known, which is in the intellect through its likeness; whereas the will is actualized, not because a likeness of the willed thing is in the will, but because the will has an inclination towards the thing which is willed. Thus the procession of the intellect is by the mode of similitude, and it is under this aspect that it authenticates the notion of generation, for anything that engenders, engenders its own likeness. But the procession which comes about through the mode of will, does not present itself by way of similitude: rather, it is achieved under the aspect of what impels and moves toward something (*secundum rationem impellentis et moventis in aliquid*). So what proceeds in God by way of love does not proceed as engendered, but rather as a 'Spirit'. This word effectively designates a sort of vital movement (*vitalis motio*) or impulsion (*impulsio*) in the sense that one says that love pushes us or entrains us to doing something.[70]

This is the nub of St Thomas' meditations: the beloved being is present in the loving will in a different way from that in which the known being is in the mind. The beloved being is present in a *dynamic* mode, like a vital momentum, a weight of love entraining the will toward the beloved being. This follows from the 'ecstatic' character of love: the understanding of a reality is achieved within the interiority of the knowing subject (knowledge makes things 'exist' in our minds, in an intelligible mode), whereas love carries the will outside of itself toward the beloved good. The presence of the beloved being in the lover thus displays the modality of an interior weight of love ('what impels and moves') which arises in the will when it loves something (when it is activated). It is thus that Thomas can show, analogously, that the love-procession of the Holy Spirit is different from generation: that which proceeds by the way of love is not 'begotten'.[71] The way he explains it in the *Summa Contra Gentiles* is akin to this.

[68] *De veritate*, q. 4, a. 2, ad 7.
[69] *ST* I, q. 43, a. 3; cf. q. 8, a. 3. See below, in Chapter 15, 'God's Presence as Known and Loved'. The conjunction of these two issues (the procession of the Holy Spirit in the Trinity and the presence of God in the saints) is thus a matter of trying to conceive how love brings human beings to the image of the Trinity.
[70] *ST* I, q. 27, a. 4.   [71] See also *SCG* IV, ch. 19 (no. 3565).

what is loved is not only in the intellect of the lover, but in his will as well, but in one way and another. It is in the intellect by reason of the likeness of its species; it is in the will of the lover, however, as the term of a movement is in its proportioned motive principle by reason of the congruence and proportion which the principle has for that term. Just so, in a certain way, there is in fire the upper place by reason of that lightness which gives it proportion and congruity to such a place, but the fire which is generated [the engendered flame] is in the fire which generates [the generator flame] by reason of the likeness of its form.[72]

Thomas puts in the example of fire so as to distinguish two aspects which suggest the difference between generation and the procession of love. When one lights one flame with the help of another flame, there is in fact a procession which one can call 'generation', in the broad and colloquial sense of the term: the flame is 'engendered' by the flame which sets it alight. There is here a relation of species likeness in virtue of which one can recognize the presence of fire in an illuminated flame (the relation is that of likeness, which Thomas explained when he was talking about generation).[73] But this is not what happens in the case of love. To suggest the mode of presence which belongs to love, St Thomas takes the example of fire, and considers the momentum of a rising flame. It rises because that is 'congruent' with the natural properties of flame: the flame of fire—this is the aspect which the example is trying to illustrate—rises to a higher place because it has an inclination to or 'congruence' with the higher region to which it is attracted. Thus, 'the higher place' is 'in a certain sort of way' present in the flame itself, in so far as the flame is carried to rise itself toward it by its own inclination.

Whatever the limitations of this example, it does indicate a dynamic mode of presence, under the form of an 'impression' (*impressio*) of the beloved, which moves or inclines the will towards the beloved being (affection, attraction, impulsion).[74] Thus, St Thomas notices that there is a dynamic presence of the beloved being in the will which actually loves: the one whom I love is present to my will as inclining me towards him, like the attraction to the goal of movement which one can observe in the moving principle, to which it has proportion and 'congruence'.

It is not difficult to see that this explanation rests on the precise notion of love which we briefly recalled above: inclination, congruence, affection, impulsion, motion. This conception of love is original and St Thomas himself did not always put it forward as clearly as this. As with the doctrine of the Word, one can see that he has made progress here. In his Commentary on the

---

[72] *SCG* IV, ch. 19 (no. 3560).

[73] Looked at from this angle, the example of fire is close to the patristic image of light: the Son is the 'light' [born] of 'light', as the Constantinopolitan *Creed* confesses.

[74] *SCG* IV, ch. 19; *CT* I, ch. 46 (*attractio*); *ST* I, q. 37, a. 1 (*affectio*).

Sentences, he posed the topic of the procession of the Holy Spirit by means of the theme of creative Love.[75] He conceives love as an 'in-formation' (*formatio, informatio, transformatio*) of the will by the loved good, explaining that love consists in the reception of a *form*, a form which is analogous to that received by the intellect in the act of knowledge; love would thus be a 'transformation' of the appetite by the beloved thing.[76] Thomas' first attempt is characterized by an excessively narrow parallel between intelligence and will, built around the notion of 'form'. The Disputed Questions *De veritate* evince a similar conception,[77] and even though love is more finely distinguished from intelligence here, the basic problem remains intact: St Thomas still acknowledges that 'the will has nothing which, proceeding from it, remains in it, except by mode of operation'.[78] This absence of a fertility immanent to the will prevents one from finding the procession of a term in it, and this leads Thomas, as in his Commentary on the *Sentences*, to think along the lines of a 'subsistent operation' or an 'action which proceeds' when one conceives the Holy Spirit.[79]

St Thomas' mature solution appears in the *Summa Contra Gentiles*, from which we have already cited several pages, and also in the Commentary on Pseudo-Denys' *Divine Names*. After these various blind-shots and focusings, the light of Thomas' mature anthropology and Trinitarian theology dawns in the *Summa Theologiae*.[80] Using the model of an imprint of love, Thomas no longer just discerns an *action* in the loving will, but sees in it a 'fruit' which proceeds from volition and remains in the will.[81] We will come back later to why the Holy Spirit is named 'Love'.[82] What we have said so far is enough to show how beneficial the investigation of love is. Through it, Thomas can disclose: (1) the emanation of a reality which proceeds from the will and remains immanent within it (this is what gives one an analogue for understanding the Holy Spirit's relation of origin); (2) the existence of a spiritual

---

[75] I *Sent.* d. 10, q. 1, a. 1.   [76] III *Sent.* d. 27, q. 1, a. 1.

[77] *De veritate*, q. 27, a. 4: 'The passion of love is nothing other than the formation of the appetite by the "appetizing" good.' The *De veritate* nonetheless shows a clearer understanding of the will as an 'inclination' toward the good (q. 22, a. 12).

[78] *De veritate*, q. 4, a. 2, ad 7. At one time, this passage gave rise to a heated debate, because it shows the incompleteness of Thomas' thought at the time when he wrote the *De veritate*; cf. the discussion by H. Dondaine in the *Bulletin thomiste* 5 (1937–1939), 547–549.

[79] I *Sent.* d. 32, q. 1, a. 1; cf. Emery, *La Trinité créatrice*, pp. 368–383 and 430–434.

[80] For St Thomas' development, with the main texts and the interpretation of the Thomist school, see H.-D. Simonin, 'Autour de la solution thomiste du problème de l'amour', *AHDLMA* 6 (1931), 174–276.

[81] Cf. *SCG* IV, ch. 26: 'when the mind (*mens*) loves itself, it produces its own self as loved in the will (*seipsam producit in voluntate ut amatum*)'.

[82] See below, in Chapter 10, 'The Holy Spirit is Love in Person'.

procession distinct from that of the word (the procession of the Holy Spirit is not the generation of the Son); (3) the procession of a term which is consubstantial to its principle (since the will of God is identical to the being of God, the Spirit which proceeds by the mode of love has the very nature of God, whilst being personally distinct from the Father and the Son).[83]

Such is the path which enables one to grasp the procession of the Holy Spirit and which by doing so, sidesteps arguments against the truth of Faith. The theologian is not content with asserting this truth, but can actually show that there is a procession which is distinct from that of the Word, thus indicating that the criticisms of Trinitarian faith are not compelling.

6. THE ORDER OF THE TRINITARIAN PROCESSIONS

Reflecting on the procession of the Holy Spirit creates another refinement. It relates to the *order* of the processions.[84] In using the analogies of mind and will, does Thomas grasp the procession of the divine persons on the basis of God's mind and will, taken as essential attributes? In that case, would he not be conceiving the Son and the Spirit as somehow deriving from the divine essence? But then, the project of understanding the faith would be empty, since as Thomas himself has explained, the distinction of the persons is not drawn from the divine essence, since that essence is common to the Three. The intellect and will of God are really identical to the one single being and substance of God.[85] So in God, intellect and will are a single, identical reality. But then how can one think the procession of two *really distinct* persons, when one uses the mode of two attributes (intellect and will or love) which are, in God, *really identical*? Would such an enterprise not be doomed to failure from the start?

The first point to clarify is that Thomas does not reserve the activity of thought to the procession of the Son, nor the activity of love to the procession of the Spirit: there is no more 'intellect' in the begetting of the Son, nor is there 'more love' in the procession of the Holy Spirit. The begetting of the Son is also, and eminently, an act of love; and the procession of the Holy Spirit is not without wisdom. Thomas explains that, in each of the processions, all of the divine attributes are brought into play 'concomitantly'.[86] All of the divine

---

[83] *ST* I, q. 27, a. 4, ad 1; cf. *SCG* IV, ch. 19 (no. 3563); *De rationibus fidei*, ch. 4.
[84] This is the premier aspect in the Disputed Questions *De potentia*, q. 10, a. 2.
[85] Cf. *ST* I, q. 14, a. 4; q. 19, a. 1.
[86] I *Sent.* d. 6, q. 1, a. 2 and 3; cf. *ST* I, q. 41, a. 2; *De potentia*, q. 2, a. 3.

attributes concur in the begetting of the Son, and all concur in the breathing-forth of the Spirit. In begetting as in spiration, one must recognize the fullness of God, by the mode of the speaking of the Word and the procession of Love.

Thomas' next step is to explain that intellect and will, or love, taken as such, are incapable of distinguishing two persons in God.[87] Intellect and Love are essential attributes which are in reality identical and which are only logically distinct. A distinction amongst such essential attributes would not suffice to disclose the real plurality of the divine persons. Otherwise put, the distinction of the persons is neither that of mind and will, nor, properly speaking, of wisdom and love since they too are essential attributes. Rather, it concerns the immanent terms or fruits which *proceed* by dint of an action of knowledge and love: the Word, distinct from the Father who speaks him, and Love (affection, amorous 'impression'), distinct from the Father and the Son from which he proceeds. Further, at the heart of the processions of the Son through intellect and the Spirit through love, St Thomas distinguishes an 'order', a relation which excludes their being conflated. It is this *order*, and not intellect or will as such which enables one to disclose Trinitarian faith: 'It is only the order of the processions, which arises from their origin, that multiplies processions in God.'[88] Thomas writes that,

To distinguish the Holy Spirit and the Son, it is not enough to say that the Son proceeds by the mode of the intellect and the Holy Spirit by the mode of volition, unless one adds that the Holy Spirit proceeds from the Son . . . From the very fact that the Holy Spirit proceeds by way of volition and the Son by way of intellect, it follows that the Holy Spirit exists from the Son. For love proceeds from the word: we cannot love anything if we have not conceived it by the word in our heart.[89]

So one cannot give a reason for the processions just by talking about their modes, of intellect and love; one also needs to speak of *the order which these modes make manifest*:

All that exists in God is one with the divine nature. Hence it is not from this unity that one can grasp the rationale which belongs to this or that procession, that is, that which distinguishes the one from the other. The rationale of each of the processions must be taken from the order which they have amongst themselves. *And this order is derived from the very nature of volition and intellect.*[90] [. . .] It is necessary that Love proceeds from the Word; this is why we cannot love something unless we have first conceived of it in our mind.[91]

---

87 *De potentia*, q. 10, a. 2; *SCG* IV, ch. 24 (no. 3616); cf. *ST* I, q. 40, a. 2.
88 *De potentia*, q. 10, a. 2.   89 *SCG* IV, ch. 24 (nos. 3616–3617).
90 *ST* I, q. 27, a. 4, ad 1.   91 *ST* I, q. 36, a. 2.

So the distinction of the processions is rooted in the 'order of origin', that is to say the relation which the procession of the Spirit has to the generation of the Son, or, to put it in full, in the Son's relation of origin to the Father, and in the Spirit's relation of origin to the Father and the begotten Son. This is the order which the notions of intellect and will permit one to present, because of the character of these two modes of action. St Thomas also explains this when he formulates the processions in terms of *nature* (generation) and *will* (spiration):

In God, procession by way of nature is one that presupposes no other. But that which takes place by the mode of will takes its origin from a procession which it presupposes. So it is necessary that there is procession from procession, and that one of the [Persons] proceeds from another; and this is what makes for a real distinction in God.[92]

This theme of *order*, which is integrated here into a Trinitarian theological structure which is obviously Latin and Catholic, comes from the Trinitarian doctrine of the Cappadocian Fathers.[93] This *order*, which makes it impossible to conflate the persons, is expressed in the baptismal formula and in the Creed: Father, and Son, and Holy Spirit. Thomas explains that the 'order' in God, refers only to the *relations of origin* that the persons maintain in the processions: the Father does not proceed from anyone, but is rather the source of the Son and the Holy Spirit; the Son receives the substance of divinity from the Father who eternally begets him; and the Holy Spirit receives the substance of divinity from the Father and the Son from whom he eternally proceeds.[94] This order excludes not only temporal intervals in between the existence of the persons, but also any kind of 'priority' of a person or procession in relation to another. St Thomas puts this very strongly: 'The Father has no priority in relation to the Son: neither in duration, nor in nature, nor conceptually, nor in dignity... There is no priority whatsoever of one person over another in God.'[95]

One has to interpret Thomas' intention in saying that the generation of the Son is 'presupposed' in the procession of the Holy Spirit by the same lights: 'in the divine reality, begetting has no priority at all over procession [of the Holy Spirit].[96] The order solely consists in the relations of origin. In the simultaneity of divine eternity, the three persons are absolutely equal and inseparable. There is for this reason no priority of the generation of the Son over the procession of the Spirit, even if, for the purposes of describing it in

---

[92] *De potentia*, q. 10, a. 2, ad 7.
[93] See for instance Basil of Caesarea, *Against Eunomius* III.1–2 (SC 305, pp. 145–153).
[94] Cf. *ST* I, q. 42, a. 3.
[95] I *Sent.* d. 9, q. 2, a. 1; d. 12, q. 1, a. 1.
[96] I *Sent.* d. 12, q. 1, a. 1. This 'priority' only exists in the flawed 'likenesses' which creatures present.

terms taken from our knowledge of this-worldly things, we have to consider one procession at a time. This point will be important for getting a good grasp on the reciprocity of the divine persons.

7. THE CYCLE OF THE TRINITARIAN PROCESSIONS

In the *Summa Theologiae*, after having set out the procession of the Word and Love, St Thomas concludes his investigation of the processions by showing that no other procession takes place in God (q. 27, a. 5). This last stage could seem odd. Since, effectively, it is solely by faith that we hold the generation of the Son and the procession of the Spirit, one could ask why anything should be added to this. The final article actually supplies a synthesis, which success-fully authenticates the value of the earlier explanations of the processions:

One can only conceive a procession in God that derives from actions which remain in the agent. In a nature that is intellectual and divine, there are only two actions of this type: understanding and volition. The act of sensation, which also seems to be an operation that remains immanent to the sensing subject, does not belong to an intellectual nature; nor is it entirely alien to the sphere of *ad extra* actions, since the act of sensation is brought about by the action of a sensible object on the senses. It follows that no other procession is possible in God except that of Word and Love.[97]

This takes us back to the foundation of the study of the processions: the immanent actions of understanding and volition, the only actions enabling one to disclose the origin of the persons. And, since God knows in a pure and simple act, we are led to perceive that the procession of the Word is unique, just as the procession of Love is unique.[98] St Thomas is very rigorous about this: the other divine attributes cannot account for the immanent processions.

The apparent subtlety of this question should not hide what is at stake in it. Faith teaches us that the processions of the Son and the Holy Spirit do in fact take place within the Trinity. Neither Arianism nor Sabellianism can succeed in showing this: 'Only the Catholic faith, which affirms the unity of the divine nature in really distinct persons can assign a reason why there are three [persons] in God.'[99] This 'reason for the tripling' (*ternarii numeri ratio*) is the generation of the Son and the procession of the Spirit, these two being

---

[97] *ST* I, q. 27, a. 5.

[98] *ST* I, q. 27, a. 5, ad 3; cf. *SCG* IV, ch. 13; *De rationibus fidei*, ch. 3; *De potentia*, q. 9, a. 9. This is also how Thomas conveys the notion of the 'only begotten' (Jn 1.14–18); cf. *In Ioan.* 1.1 (no. 27); *SCG* IV, ch. 13 (no. 3485).

[99] *De potentia*, q. 9, a. 9.

really distinct persons who are yet consubstantial with the Father. Theology receives this as a gift of faith; it cannot prove it. But the only way to disclose such processions, according to Thomas, is the origin which one can observe in the immanent actions of intellect and volition, because this is the only way we can perceive, in a way that fits God's spiritual nature, the intimate personal fertility in the Trinity. Thomas' expressions are very clear: one can not grasp them in any other way (*accipi non possunt*), one can not think another procession (*nulla possit*), without being caught in the trap of heresy or abandoning trying to illuminate the faith.[100] Otherwise put: this is all we have at our disposal for giving a reasonable account of the faith, but it is still to be highly valued, since it permits us to succeed here, 'in some way', or 'in as much as we can'.[101] St Thomas is so profoundly convinced of this that he explains, in the *De potentia*:

In God there cannot be any origination but what is immaterial and consistent with spiritual nature: such is the origin of Word and Love. This is why if the procession of Word and Love is not enough to insert a personal distinction (*ad distinctionem personalem insinuandam*), no distinction of persons will be possible in God. Thus St John both in the beginning of his Gospel and in his first canonical epistle employs the term *Word* to designate the Son.[102]

If there is another procession, it will be of a different order, of a different kind: this is the 'procession' of creatures, the divine economy. When he considers the 'cycle' of processions, Thomas says that,

There is in God, as there is in us, a sort of 'circulation' (*circulatio*) in the operations of mind and will: for the will returns to that which understanding initiated. But with us the 'circle' (*circulus*) closes in that which is outside of us: the external good moving our intellect, our intellect moving the will, and the will returning through its appetite and love to the external good. But in God, the 'circle' is completed within himself: for when God understands himself, he conceives his Word which is the 'rationale' of everything known by him, since he understands all things by understanding himself; and through this Word, he 'proceeds' to the love of all things and of himself... And the circle being completed, nothing more can be added to it: so that a third procession within the divine nature is impossible, although there follows a procession toward external nature.[103]

In this passage, St Thomas shows that since God's actions in the world ('procession toward external nature')[104] add nothing to the processions which

---

[100] *ST* I, q. 27, a. 5.   [101] *SCG* IV, ch. 13 (no. 3496); *CT* I, ch. 36.

[102] *De potentia*, q. 9, a. 9, ad 7.

[103] *De potentia*, q. 9, a. 9. Cf. *SCG* IV, ch. 26 (no. 3632): 'There is no other procession in the divine nature, only a procession toward external effects.'

[104] The terminology of *procession* (like that of *distinction*) enables one to make an analogous connection between the immanent life of the Trinity and its action in the world: 'There is a

constitute a perfect 'circle', they are not to be numbered amongst the intra-Trinitarian processions. God's actions in the world are of a different order, even though they are attached to the intra-Trinitarian processions. On the one hand, the intra-Trinitarian processions somehow include God's principles of creative and salvific action: God knows all things through the begotten Word; God loves all beings through the Love which proceeds. St Thomas explains this in more detail in his study of the persons, and in that of the divine missions and creation.[105] On the other hand, the creative and salvific action is somehow especially connected to the procession of the Holy Spirit. Love is responsible for our own external acts: 'there is a procession toward external effects, when our spirit proceeds to do something, by means of its love'.[106] In the same way, it is by his Love (the Holy Spirit) that God 'proceeds' toward external effects. This is why the procession of the Holy Spirit is responsible for the creative impulse initiating the cycle of the procession of creatures: 'the cause of creation is the Love through which God loves his own goodness.'[107] The investigation of the Trinitarian processions, whose principal object remains the distinction of the persons in God, also opens another chapter in theology: the study of creation and grace.

8. 'NOTIONAL' ACTION

We must pinpoint one further element of the 'action' which we have been discussing. Thomas has explained that the relations are based on an action giving rise to a procession. So we conceive procession, or the divine nature communicated, as the basis of relation.[108] This basis is important, enabling Thomas to account for the real relations in God.

These three words, *action, procession, relation*, do not designate different entities within the God who is simple. The plurality of terms derives from the use of our intelligence in tackling the mystery of the Trinity under many different aspects, because our way of thinking is tied to the worldly realities

double procession: one is that in which one person proceeds from another, and this is how the divine persons are mutually distinguished [...]; the other procession is that through which creatures proceed from God: and this is how the multiplicity of things appears, and the distinction of creatures from God' (*Super Dion. de div. nom.* II, lect. 2; no. 153).

[105] *ST* I, q. 34, a. 3; q. 37, a. 2, ad 3; q. 45, a. 6. See below, Chapter 14.

[106] *SCG* IV, ch. 26 (no. 3631).

[107] *SCG* IV, ch. 20 (no. 3570). We will come back to this in the investigation of the Holy Spirit in Chapter 10.

[108] *De potentia*, q. 10, a. 3; I *Sent.* d. 26, q. 2, a. 1.

amongst which we belong (how could we do otherwise?). So one single reality is envisaged from many different angles. First of all, it can be considered under the aspect of the *action* in which one person communicates the divine substance to another. This is a matter of generation and spiration. This *action* is signified in a dynamic way, 'like the surging of one person toward another'. To designate the personal action of the generation of the Son and the breathing of the Holy Spirit (the Father 'begets', the Father and the Son 'breathe'), Thomas speaks of a 'notional' act or action.[109] This same reality can also be considered under the aspect of the process of the 'outcoming' person: this is then the *procession*, signified as the 'pathway' leading to the constitution of that person; the Son 'is begotten', the Holy Spirit 'proceeds'. The very same reality can be further considered in the light of the property or characteristic which the persons possess in virtue of the processions: this is then a matter of the *relation* which distinctly characterizes each person. Thomas explains it like this:

generation signifies the relation to the manner of an operation [...] And it is through one and the same action that the Father begets and the Son is born, but this action finds out two distinct relations in the Father and the Son.[110]

Finally, the same reality can be considered under the aspect of that which possesses this relation, based on procession: this is the *person*, signified in the manner of the reality which exists or subsists.[111]

In the *Summa Theologiae*, St Thomas devotes an entire question (q. 41) to the 'notional acts' (the act of begetting and the act of spiration) which correspond to processions. One must acknowledge that such acts exist, since 'these acts are the only fitting way to designate the origination [of the Son and the Holy Spirit]'.[112] Without going into every aspect of this topic, we must at least mention its patristic roots, which are especially apparent when St Thomas explains that notional acts are actions which come about 'through nature'. Arius maintained that the Son was engendered 'through volition': the

---

[109] *ST* I, q. 41, a. 1. 'Origin can only be designated by actions. So, to signify the order of origin in the divine persons, we must attribute notional acts to the persons.' This way of speaking (*notional*) indicates the idea of 'notions', which have been an issue earlier, in Chapter 2. It enables one to distinguish, on the one hand, generation and spiration, and, on the other hand, the acts that are common to the three persons (essential acts) which are also acts exercised by the persons, but which do not entail a real procession within God.

[110] I *Sent.* d. 20, q. 1, a. 1, ad 1. This is difficult to think through, and yet it is compelling: the fact of being begotten does not imply any 'passivity' in the Son. To be begotten is an action— that is, to be born. For the Son to receive the divine nature is to be born of the Father. And when one says that the Son 'receives the divine nature from the Father' this 'reception' refers to a pure relation of the Son to the Father: this is the relation of origin.

[111] *ST* I, q. 40, a. 2; q. 41, a. 1, ad 2; *De potentia*, q. 8, a. 3.

[112] *ST* I, q. 41, a. 1.

Father did not beget the Son out of his own substance, but rather produced him as he does creatures, through his 'will', or 'as a gift'. Because of this, Arius claims that the Son is not of the same nature as the Father, but is created 'out of nothing' (*ex ouk ontôn, ex nihilo*).[113] Thus, for Arius, the Son is a work issuing from God's will: to say that the Son is engendered *volitionally* is to say he is not Son *naturally* but as a free creation of God, something which he has cheerfully volunteered to do. Before Arius, many Catholic authors (such as St Justin, for instance[114]) had affirmed that the Son was begotten 'by will'. Because of Arianism, this was ruled out, for saying that the Son is begotten by a free choice boils down to designating him as a creature. In reply to Arius, Athanasius and many other of the Fathers explained that begetting the Son is not an act of God's will but rather an act of God's *nature*. This is what the council of Nicaea professed: The Son is begotten 'from the substance of the Father'. St Thomas knew the historical aspects of the discussion, particularly the discussions of Hilary and Augustine, which had been set out by Peter Lombard.[115]

When he employs his patristic armoury, St Thomas extends the question to the two processions: those of the Son and the Spirit. He puts this forward as a response to Arianism. The generation of the Son and the procession of the Holy Spirit do not depend on the creative will of God (divine will being the principle of creation), but are a matter of the divine nature: the Son and the Holy Spirit proceed 'by nature'.[116] Divine will is concomitant with the Son's generation, but its principle is the divine nature.[117] Thomas also reminds us of the difference between immanent and transitive acts. With his idea of immanent processions, it is not difficult to show that the Son and the Holy Spirit are 'of the substance of the Father', since they do not proceed 'outside' of God, but 'within' God himself.[118] The power through which the Father begets the Son must be designated as the divine nature itself in the person of the Father.[119]

---

[113] Arius, *Thalia* and *Letter to Eusebius*; cf. Athanasius, *Werke*, vol. III/1, ed. Hans-Georg Opitz, Berlin and Leipzig, 1935, p. 3.
[114] Justin, *Dialogue with Trypho* 61.
[115] See Peter Lombard's *Sentences*, Book I, dist. 5 and 6.
[116] *ST* I, q. 41, a. 2.
[117] *De potentia*, q. 2, a. 3; *ST* I, q. 41, a. 2.
[118] *ST* I, q. 41, a. 3.
[119] *ST* I, q. 41, aa. 4 and 5. On this question of the 'power of begetting' (a notional power), one can look at our exposition in *La Trinité créatrice*, Paris, 1995, pp. 455–562. Compared to the *Commentary on the Sentences*, the *Summa Theologiae* puts more emphasis on the divine nature or essence. This question had held Thomas' attention at length in the Questions *De potentia* (q. 2, aa. 1–6).

Thomas also uses his theory of *immanent* processions and his idea that 'notional acts' come about 'by nature' to show the 'co-eternity' of the divine persons. He realizes that one of Arius' basic theses is the negation of the eternity of the Son: the rejection of the co-eternity of the Son with the Father results in the denial of his consubstantiality.[120] He replies to this by explaining that,

the Father does not beget the Son by will but by nature.... the Father's nature is perfect from eternity. And again, the action through which the Father produces the Son is without successiveness, because if it were so the Son would be generated sucessively, and this generation would be material, and accompanied with movement; which is impossible. Therefore, the Son existed whensoever the Father existed. He is thus co-eternal with the Father, and likewise the Holy Spirit is co-eternal with both.[121]

The idea of immanent processions and notional acts enables one to sharpen the critique of Arianism by means of a more precise conception of the generation of Son and the procession of Holy Spirit.[122] The goal of giving reasons for faith as against heresies is thus found at the beginning as well as the end of Thomas' teaching on the processions in God, in a manner that is not unlike what took place in the patristic debates. For Thomas, its greatest fruit is that it enables him to give a basis for the theory of relations of origin.

---

[120] *SCG* IV, ch. 6 (no. 3387).

[121] *ST* I, q. 42, a. 2. This formulation is a reply to Arius' slogan: 'There was a time when God was alone and was not yet Father... There was a time when the Word was not.'

[122] See G. Reichberg, 'La communication de la nature divine en Dieu selon Thomas d'Aquin', *RT* 93 (1993), 50–65.

5

Relations

For St Thomas, the relations which distinguish the divine persons constitute these persons. Relation thus becomes the basis of a theological understanding of the divine persons. In working this out, Thomas is following the path opened up by his teacher, St Albert the Great, which diverges from that of the Franciscan school. The theme of relation does not occupy a comparable position in the theology of St Bonaventure, for example. But for Thomas, even more than for Albert the Great, the notion of relation is of utmost significance. The treatise on the Trinity begins with a consideration of the processions precisely in order to show that this is its foundation.

Hence, the theory of relations will be found throughout the *Summa*'s Trinitarian treatise: it is not confined to question 28, but influences the whole of the subsequent meditation. When we trace out the main stages of question 28, we will see that Thomas is laying the groundwork out of which the treatise develops. He shows the existence of real relations in God, the identity of these relations with the single divine essence, the mutual distinction of the relations, and he provisionally completes his reflection by pinning down what sort of relations we are talking about. Once he has completed this part of the construction, the elements which give us the ability to conceive a divine person have been put on view.

The first time St Thomas tackled the question of relation, he observed that, 'for all Catholics, it is certain that there are relations in God'.[1] 'The truth of the faith (*veritas fidei*) implies that the only distinction that can be in God is taken from opposed relations.'[2] And when he explains that these relations are absolutely real ones, he begins his exposition with a similar observation, zeroing in on the fact that, like the preceding one, this question arises because of issues raised by the heresies of the patristic era:

Those who follow the teaching of the Catholic faith must hold that there are real relations in God. The Catholic faith acknowledges that there are in God three persons of one single Essence. And, any number results from a distinction. So there must be in God a distinction [not only] in comparison to creatures, which essentially differ from

---

[1] I *Sent.* d. 26, q. 2, a. 1.   [2] *Quodlibet* XII, q. 1, a. 1.

God, but also a distinction in respect of that which subsists in the divine essence. And this distinction cannot issue out of a reality that is absolute, for anything that is attributed to God as an absolute reality signifies the divine essence, so it would follow from that that the divine persons are distinguished through their essence: this is the heresy of Arius. But this distinction cannot be purely conceptual either, for... it would follow that the Father is the Son, and that the Son is the Father,... and thus the divine persons are only verbally distinct from one another: this is the heresy of Sabellianism. It remains thus to be said that the relations in God are real. So, in following the teaching of the saints [the Fathers], one must try to work out how this can be, although of course our reason cannot fully grasp it.[3]

This takes us back to the themes which we indicated earlier, in studying processions. Theological investigation of the relations comes from the encounter between Catholic faith and Arianism or Sabellianism. St Thomas understands his own work as the extension of that of the Fathers of the Church who prized relation as a way of expressing an authentic Trinitarian monotheism, as against the heresies. This project is not an attempt to 'comprehend' the Trinity, because our reason cannot fully grasp the mystery of relations in God. When the theologian tries to perceive the divine relations, he wants to show believers that there is a rational basis from which to resist objections to faith in the Trinity. By enabling them not to be confused by erroneous reasoning, theological research opens believers to contemplation of the mystery.

St Thomas is not very forthcoming about the patristic sources of his theory of relation. He makes his debt to Augustine and Boethius explicit, but his references to the Greek fathers are less numerous, even though he was at least indirectly aware of them.[4] To get a perspective on what the idea of relation means within his Trinitarian theology, and to grasp its roots, we must briefly retrace our steps to the Fathers.

1. ELEMENTS OF THE PATRISTIC TEACHING ON RELATION

Relation was brought into Trinitarian theology right at the start of the Arian crisis. Before the Council of Nicaea, in his Profession of Faith to Alexander of

[3] *De potentia*, q. 8, a. 1.

[4] For instance, the *Libellus de fide Trinitatis* (a compilation of Eastern patristic commentaries, that St Thomas examined at the request of Pope Urban IV) presented the thought of Gregory Nazianzus like this: 'The Father is called "unbegotten" and Father not because of his essence, but in a relative way because of his property of paternity; and the Son, likewise, since he takes his origin from the Principle, is not so called because of his nature but because of his relation to another' (no. 23; Leon. edn., vol. 40A, p. 127); cf. Gregory of Nazianzus, *Orations* 29.16 (SC 250, pp. 210–211); *Orations* 31.7 and 31.9 (SC 250, pp. 286–289 and 290–293); *Orations* 42.15 (SC 384, pp. 80–83).

Alexandria, Arius maintained that the Son is not co-eternal with the Father, explaining that: 'He did not exist at the same time as the Father, as some have said in speaking of "relatives" (*ta pros ti*).'[5] Arius' remark is a good indication that, already at the beginning of the fourth century, some Alexandrian Catholics (whose identity remains a tricky question[6]) were using the Aristotelian category of relation to show the co-eternity of the Father and the Son: relative beings are simultaneous;[7] if 'Father' and 'Son' are indeed mutually related names, then whenever there was a Father, there must have been a Son. But it was left to the Cappadocians to exploit the theory of relation more systematically; the first of them to do so was Basil of Caesarea. In his *Contra Eunomius*, St Basil made relation a central feature of his argument against radical Arianism. We have already mentioned this, when we were talking about 'common' and 'proper'.

Remember why this problem matters. As a radical Arian (Anomoeanist), Eunomius identified the 'Unengendered' with the very substance of God: to be God is to be unengendered substance (*ousia agennêtos*).[8] As a result, God-the-Unengendered could not beget an equal, for by doing so he would divide or introduce composition into himself, and cease to be the Unengendered. Nothing can coexist with the Unengendered.[9] The name 'Father' does not designate the substance of the Unengendered, but rather an action (*energeia*) of the Unengendered, different from his substance. As for the 'Son', his name designates the filial substance, which is created.[10] This complex thesis, hinting at the idea of an hierarchical emanation of beings out of the One, involves a recondite theory of language and a subtle metaphysics.[11] It excludes *a priori* any possibility of generation within God.

The challenge of Eunomius of Cyzicus' 'technology' led Basil to develop the first speculative theory of relation within Trinitarian theology. The first tool which Basil took to hand was linguistic analysis. He showed that our knowledge of God is analogical and that it derives from God's actions within the world; this means that we must use many names to express the mystery of God, in so far as we can grasp it at all. Some of these names are positive, expressing the substance of things, and others are negative and

---

[5] *Athanasius Werke*, vol. III/1, ed. H.-G. Opitz, Berlin and Leipzig, 1935, p. 13. This is Aristotle's language (*ta pros ti*), which one finds from the beginning of the history of the use of the idea of 'relation' in Trinitarian theology.

[6] M.-O. Boulnois, *Le paradoxe trinitaire chez Cyrille d'Alexandrie*, Paris, 1994, pp. 391–393.

[7] Aristotle, *Categories* 7 (7^{b}15).

[8] Eunomius of Cyzicus, *Apology* 8 (SC 305, pp. 250–251).

[9] Eunomius, *Apology* 9–10 (SC 305, pp. 250–255).

[10] Eunomius, *Apology* 12–18 and 22–23 (SC 305, pp. 256–271 and 278–281).

[11] See B. Sesboüé, *Saint Basile et la Trinité: Un acte théologique au IVe siècle*, Paris, 1998, pp. 19–53.

designate that which the thing is not. The name 'Unengendered' belongs to the latter category: without implying any imperfection, it signifies that God is 'not-engendered'.[12] By showing that 'Unengendered' is not a positive description of the divine substance, which in fact cannot be defined, Basil withdraws this appellation from the commanding heights upon which Euno-mius had set it. In the context of this analysis of language and concepts, St Basil introduces the category of relation:

Amongst the names, some are connected to the thing itself, as an absolute, and when they are pronounced they signify the substrate of the realities in question; others are said in connection with beings other than themselves, and are only made known through their relation (*schesis*) with the others in connection with which they are spoken. For example, man, horse, cow, express each of the named entities; but *son, slave*, or *friend* just indicate a connection with the term to which it is joined. This is why what is expressed by the word 'offspring' (*gennêma*) does not lead one to think of a substance (*ousia*), but it conceives the entity in question as connected to another. For 'offspring' is called 'offspring' as springing *from someone*. In fact, since what it puts before us is not the notion of a subject but an indication of relation (*schesis*) to another thing, isn't it the height of insanity to decide that it means the substance?[13]

It is clear from the examination of these names, that is, *father and son*, that they are not of such a kind as primarily to evoke the idea of corporeal passion; but spoken through themselves, they just express the relation (*schesis*) of the one to the other. A *father* is one who supplies for another the principle of his being in a nature like his own, a *son* is one who receives from another through generation the principle of his being . . . [14]

There are thus two kinds of appellations: names which refer to substance, and names which refer to relations. In the same way, there are two levels in our approach to God, and our language for God: that of substance and that of the properties of the hypostases. So, as we mentioned before, language about God must be effected by the 'combination' of the two levels.[15] The main point of the use of relation is to show that, even though he is neither Father nor 'Unengendered', the Son is nonetheless fully God: 'not to be Father' does not strip the Son of his divinity, because the names *Father* and *Son* do not express the substance of divinity, but the mutual *relation* of Father and Son. The

---

[12] Basil of Caesarea, *Contra Eunomius* I.5–14 (SC 299, pp. 168–225). See Sesboüé's exposition in the work mentioned in the previous footnote. We can note that most of the elements set out here by St Basil will reappear in Thomas' treatise on God: analogical knowledge, plurality of divine names, affirmative and negative names, the incomprehensibility of God, and so on (*ST* I, qq. 12–13).

[13] Basil, *Contra Eunomius* II.9 (SC 305, pp. 36–37).

[14] Basil, *Contra Eunomius* II.22 (SC 305, pp. 92–93).

[15] Basil, *Contra Eunomius* II.28 (SC 305, pp. 118–121).

category of relation also enables one to put across the eternal coexistence of the Son: 'As soon as the Father is, the Son is, and the Son immediately enters into the notion of the Father.'[16] So relation allows one to disclose the consubstantiality of the divine persons and to show that, within God, generation does not imply any of the imperfection tied to corporeality or mutability: it is not a 'passion', but a 'relation from one to another'. St Basil can thus dispose of the objections prompted by the suggestion of becoming or change in God.

From now onwards, the notion of relation becomes a prerequisite for giving an account of Trinitarian monotheism. So, for instance, one finds it in Gregory Nazianzus when he goes about synthesizing the properties of the divine persons.[17] St Augustine takes over this theory and hands it on to the West. Gregory of Nazianzus and Basil's reflections on the name 'Unengendered' reappear in a strikingly similar form in the writings of the bishop of Hippo.[18] As it was for the Cappadocians, likewise for Augustine, *Father* and *Son* are relational terms. Everything that we say about God, we say either substantially or relationally. Saint Augustine employs many elements of the Aristotelian theory of predicaments here, in Trinitarian theology:

With God, nothing is said under the heading of accident, because he is unchangeable. And yet, not everything that is said of him is said substance-wise. Some things are posited as relations (*ad aliquid*): for instance, the Father is relative to the Son and the Son is relative to the Father, which is not an accident. The one is always Father, the other is always Son ... This is why, if being the Father and being the Son is not the same, the substance is nonetheless not different. These appellations do not belong to the order of substance but to that of relation (*relativum*), relation which is not an accident because change is foreign to it.[19]

Thus, Augustine's view that the persons are formally characterized by their mutual relations is an extension of the Cappadocians' theory. It is through their relations that we grasp what belongs to them as persons.[20] 'In the case of the Trinity, expressing the proper and distinct characteristics of each of the persons, comes back to expressing their mutual relations (*quae relative dicuntur ad*

---

[16] Basil, *Contra Eunomius* II.12 (SC 305, p. 47).
[17] Gregory Nazianzus, *Orations* 31.9 (SC 250, pp. 290–293).
[18] Augustine, *De Trinitate* V.VI.7–VII.8 (BA 15, pp. 434–443).
[19] Augustine, *De Trinitate* V.V.6 (BA 15, pp. 432–435). The decrees of the 11th Council of Toledo, in the high Middle Ages, echo this Augustinian doctrine: if one speaks of three persons in God, this is in as much as 'the three persons are said relationally to one another'; 'it is in relation that the number of persons appears' (*Denzinger*, nos. 528 and 530).
[20] See in particular I. Chevalier, *Saint Augustin et la pensée grecque: Les relations trinitaires*, Fribourg, 1940; id., *La théorie augustinienne des relations trinitaires*, Fribourg, 1940.

invicem): it is in this way that we speak of the Father and of the Son, and of the Gift of them both, the Holy Spirit.'[21]

In the wake of the Cappadocians and Augustine, Boethius pushed the boat out a little further, at the beginning of the sixth century. Boethius is an important link in the chain which transmitted this patristic teaching to the medievals and to St Thomas in particular.[22] Like the Fathers, Boethius uses relation to keep Arianism and Sabellianism at bay. He made a systematic examination of Aristotle's ten categories, so as to determine the value and status of our affirmations about God. He pinpointed the fact that, when we acknowledge substance and relations in God, these attributions are linguistically distinct from those which we apply to creatures, for everything in God is the divine substance. So relation is not attributed to God in the same way as it is to creatures. It adds nothing to the divine substance; it cannot be counted up alongside it. Boethius explains that relation adds no perfection whatsoever to the divine essence: it does not modify the substance, nor does it perfect the divine essence, since it is simply an interconnection. This permits one to account for divine immutability and for the perfection of the persons. Boethius also explains that the correlatives are inseparable. For these reasons, relation entails no inequality of the persons and allows one to grasp that there is real plurality in God and yet no diversity within God's nature:

It cannot be affirmed that a category of relation increases, decreases, or alters in any way the substance of the thing to which it is applied. The category of relation, then, has nothing to do with the essence of the substance; it simply denotes a condition of relativity, and that not necessarily to something else, but sometimes to the subject itself.... Accordingly those predicates which do not denote the essential nature of a thing cannot alter, change, or disturb its nature in any way. Wherefore if Father and Son are predicates of relation, and, as we have said, have no other difference but that of relation ... it will effect no real difference in its subject ... the plurality of the Trinity is secured through the category of relation, and the unity is maintained through the fact that there is no difference of substance, nor of activity...[23]

Boethius summarizes his perspective in a formula which was later very influential with the medievals, and to which St Thomas often refers:

---

[21] Augustine, *De Trinitate* VIII, prol. (BA 16, pp. 24–25).

[22] See *ST* I, q. 28, a. 1, arg. 1 and ad 2; q. 28, a. 3, sed contra; q. 30, a. 1, arg. 3 and ad 3; q. 36, a. 1, arg. 2; q. 39, a. 1; q. 40, a. 2, sed contra; q. 41, a. 1, arg. 1 and sol. (this one is about relation and not the Boethian definition of the person which we will discuss later).

[23] Boethius, *The Trinity is One God not Three Gods*, chs. 5–6 (English–Latin in the Loeb edition: Boethius, *The Theological Tractates and The Consolation of Philosophy*, trans. H. F. Stewart and E. K. Rand, London, 1918, 1968).

So then, the category of substance preserves the Unity, that of relation brings about the Trinity (*substantia continet unitatem, relatio muliplicat trinitatem*). Hence only terms belonging to relation may be applied singly to each.[24]

Later on, we will mention other echoes of the Patristics in St Thomas' writings; this must be enough for the time being. Thomas was able to draw on an enormously rich vein of tradition for his use of the category of relation. Relation enables us to articulate the names of the divine persons, and, more generally, to spell out how language about the Trinity works (through substance-relation). It also permits us to get hold of the properties of the persons, the immutability of the Trinity, the co-eternity of the persons and their consubstantiality. Thomas' original contribution consisted in systematically deepening the patristic legacy. His innovation was to extend this theological tradition in two directions: toward the theory of real relation, as presented in his conception of the word and the 'impression' of love (Thomas' own doctrine of the Word and Love), and, following from this, the constitution of the divine persons through relation, that is, the conception of subsistent relation.

2. REAL RELATIONS IN GOD

Thomas explains that Catholic faith in the Trinity requires the acknowledgement of real relations. To show this, he does not just argue from authority, on the basis of the tradition we have described, but looks for the *reasons* for the truth which has been handed on to him. These reasons depend on a detailed analysis of relation, or, more precisely, 'relatives'. A 'relative'[25] is the *thing* itself which is referred to another thing, or the *word* by which our language signifies one thing which is referred to another. Conversely, 'relation' (*relatio*) refers to the accident in a relative thing which consists in its connection to another thing: it is through this relation that one thing is referred to another. Thomas' meditation starts from Aristotle's teaching on this subject. We can recall the definitions Aristotle gives in the *Categories*:

Those things are called relative which, being either said to be *of* something else or *related to* something else, are explained by reference to that other thing. For instance, the word 'superior' is explained by reference to something else, for it is superiority *over something else* that is meant. Similarly the expression *double* has this external reference, for it is the double *of something else* that is meant.... These terms, then, are

---

[24] Boethius, *The Trinity is One God not Three Gods*, ch. 6.
[25] In Thomas' Latin: *relativum, id quod ad aliquid dicitur, id quod est ad aliquid.*

called relative, the nature of which is explained by reference to something else, the preposition 'of' or some other preposition being used to indicate the relation.[26]

even if our definition of that which is relative was complete, it is very difficult, if not impossible, to prove that no substance is relative. If, however, our definition was not complete, if those things only are properly called relative in the case of which relation to an external object is a necessary condition of existence, perhaps some explanation of the dilemma can be found. The former definition does indeed apply to all relatives, but the fact that a thing is explained with reference to something else does not make it essentially relative.[27]

Like Aristotle (and Augustine, Boethius, etc.), Thomas envisages relation in our world as an accident, that is, as one of the categories of being. Following Aristotle, he gives this definition of it:

Relative terms by their very meaning indicate only a reference to something (*ad aliud*).... To be relative means having a relationship to another thing.[28]

This definition expresses the essence of the relative as such, the notion or *ratio* of the relative. So a word will be relative when it formally signifies a relation to another thing. Likewise, a reality will be relative when it formally implies this relation to another thing.

Among relative things and names, there are those whose entire being formally consists in relation to another thing, for example, 'larger', 'smaller', 'double', 'half', 'father', and 'son'. The entire content of these words and the reality formally signified by them consists in a relation to something else; these words and realities are the ones which properly belong to the category of relation. When he wants to indicate them, Thomas speaks of 'relatives according to being' (*relativa secundum esse*). But there are also relative names which designate realities from which relations derive. Thomas calls them 'relatives as to speech' (*relativa secundum dici*).[29] This distinction, which goes back to Aristotle, is expressed in Boethian terminology. But different authors give the terms different meanings. For Albert the Great or Alexander of Hales, for instance, the relatives which are just 'as to speech' indicate a logical or conceptual relation.[30] One must handle the terminology carefully, because Thomas uses these same words with a totally different meaning. Within his usage, 'relatives according to being' are relative terms which signify the relation itself (these are the relatives which primarily or solely present a relation),

---

[26] Aristotle, *Categories* 7 (6ª36–6ᵇ8); in *The Basic Works of Aristotle*, ed. Richard McKeon, New York, 1941.

[27] Ibid., 7 (8ª31).

[28] *ST* I, q. 28, a. 1; a. 2, arg. 3.

[29] *ST* I, q. 13, a. 7, ad 1.

[30] Cf. A. Krempel, *La doctrine de la relation chez St Thomas d'Aquin*, Paris, 1952, pp. 398–402.

whereas 'relatives as to speech' refer to things which are accompanied by a relation: 'This distinction between relatives "as to being" and "as to speech" has nothing to do with the reality of the relation.'[31] The relatives studied by Trinitarian theology (*Father, Son* and *Word, Love* and *Gift*) are relatives 'according to being': they properly or formally refer to the connection itself, that is, the relation to another. Therefore, even when we have fine-tuned the topic thus far, we have yet to show that relation can be real.

St Thomas recognizes two main types of relation: (1) *real* relations; (2) logical relations. He designates as a 'real relation' (*relatio realis*) a relation which has a concrete existence in things, independent of whether we are thinking about it, when the connection to another thing exists 'in the very nature of the things themselves'.[32] In these cases, the relation does not just exist 'between' things, but '*in* the things': given its ontological texture, the relation concretely qualifies the substance which carries it, in the same way that an accident does. This radically distinguishes Thomas' teaching from the later nominalism which reduces relation to a mental comparison and thereby makes its function in Trinitarian theology rather rarefied.[33] For William of Ockham, in the fourteenth century, relations will be exclusively predicated of names, that is, of relative *words*, and not of things outside of our minds (for him, only the singular thing exists, in its irreducibility). Ockham firmly distances himself from the existence of relations in the reality of things, and only upholds the existence of the extra-mental real relations 'where faith obliges one to do so', that is, in Trinitarian doctrine;[34] thus, the recognition of real relations in God is no longer replenished by an analogy within our world and ceases to throw much light on it. So, to understand Thomas' intention, it is necessary to observe this concrete reality of relations which exists in the very reality of things, outside of our minds: this is the decisive point. Already, before Thomas, this was the thesis which Albert the Great maintained.[35]

Thomas called the relation which does not exist in the concrete reality of things, which is not ontologically inherent in things, 'logical' (*rationis, secundum rationem*, etc.), for its fabric is conceptual. There will only be a

---

[31] *De potentia*, q. 7, a. 10, ad 11.

[32] *ST* I, q. 28, a. 1.

[33] R. Schönberger, *Relation als Vergleich: Die Relationstheories des Johannes Buridan im Kontext seines Denkens und der Scholastik*, Leiden, 1994.

[34] On this idea of relation, see B. Beretta, *Ad Aliquid: La relation chez Guillaume d'Occam*, Fribourg, 1999.

[35] For St Albert, see my article, 'La relation dans la théologie de saint Albert le Grand', in *Albertus Magnus: Zum Gedenken nach 800 Jahren, Neue Zugänge, Aspekte und Perspektiven*, ed. W. Senner, Berlin, 2001, pp. 457–458.

conceptual distinction between this relation and the thing to which one attributes it. For instance, this is the case for a thing's relation of identity with itself, or of a relation to things which do not really exist, or of the relation which does not exist concretely in a relative even though it really exists in its correlative, or of the relation between relations,[36] and the same goes for all relations which derive purely from a mental conception.[37] Relation is the only predicament which can have purely 'logical' existence: all the other 'modes of being', St Thomas says, properly signify something which concretely exists, that is, the substance or the accidents which inhere in a substance (quantity, quality, etc.). The very nature of relation makes it an exception to this rule, as we will see again later on. So far as its formal notion is concerned, relation properly consists in a connection to another thing, not in a determination of the subject bearing the relation.[38] This unique characteristic of relation will play an important role in showing that, in God, relation adds nothing to the divine essence and does not perfect this essence: 'When one considers a relative, its proper reason as a relative is not taken from a comparison with its subject but by comparison to another.'[39] This is the reason why relation can exist either 'in the nature of things' (real relations) or 'only in the apprehension of our reason which attributes this or that to a thing' (logical relation).[40]

Since every relation involves two correlative terms, it follows that there are three classes of relation: (1) those which are real in both one and the other, that is to say, which really exist in both of the relatives; (2) those which are 'logical' relations in both the one and the other; (3) those which are real in one relative, and merely 'logical' in the other.[41]

The third class of relations is especially important in theology, since one can see it in the relationship between God and the world. St Thomas customarily compares it to the relation of knowledge: in the mind of the knowing subject, the relation is 'real'; but in the thing known, the relation to the knowing subject is simply a 'logical' one.[42] This example can make this easy to understand. When we say that a collection of paintings is admired by the visitors to an art gallery, the fact of 'being admired' is not positively inscribed within the paintings themselves; 'being admired' adds nothing to the works of art in themselves: so far as the ontology of the artwork is concerned, the fact of being admired is a 'logical' relation. But when the visitor admires the artwork, it is very much an objective event in the person vis-à-vis the work of art, that

---

[36] Thomas, I *Sent.* d. 26, q. 2, a. 1 (Thomas indicates his sources here: Aristotle and Avicenna).
[37] *ST* I, q. 13, a. 7; *De potentia*, q. 7, a. 11.   [38] *De potentia*, q. 8, a. 2.
[39] *ST* I, q. 28, a. 1, ad 1.   [40] *ST* I, q. 28, a. 1.
[41] *ST* I, q. 13, a. 7; cf. I *Sent.* d. 26, a. 2, q. 1; *De potentia*, q. 7, a. 10.
[42] *ST* I, q. 13, a. 7.

is, a gaze, a knowledge, an emotion, a pleasure which positively qualifies the admirer: so far as the visitor is concerned, the relation to the artwork is very much 'real'. This is how St Thomas explains that the relations which we have with God are real, whereas, for God, the relation to creatures is 'logical'. This language must be understood properly: it absolutely does not mean either that God is 'indifferent' to his creatures, or that God's relationship to the world is illusory. Rather, it means that God is not enriched or modified by this relation to the world because God is of another order from the world. The relation to the world adds nothing to God, it does not make God more perfect; it is the creature who is enriched by the divine action.[43] God's action in the world is very much real. It is real to the point that it is the substance and very being of God, but it makes no addition to God, and this is why it does not introduce any difference into God himself. God surpasses the relation which we have with him, because he is its transcendent cause.[44]

Nonetheless, it is the first class of relations which mainly concerns Trinitarian theology: a real relation in each of the two relatives. As we've seen, the existence of such a real relation requires that it be founded on quantity, action, or passion.[45] This has already been secured through the study of the processions (action). The bilateral reality of relation takes us even further into the implications of the fact that the relatives *must be of the same order*. 'A relation exists in the very nature of the thing...when things are naturally pointed at each other and have an inclination toward one another.'[46] Since a real relation consists in the interconnection with, or the order (*ordo*) of, one thing towards another, one only finds a mutually real relation between two things which communicate from within one and the same 'order' of connections.[47] This is the further reason why, unlike the mutual relations of the divine persons, God's bonds to creatures are not 'real': 'God is outside the order of creatures.'[48] God does not belong to any genus;[49] nothing can bracket God and creatures together as the possessors of the same perfection. It is otherwise

---

[43] Cf. *De potentia*, q. 7, a. 10.
[44] *ST* I, q. 13, a. 7; cf. *De potentia*, q. 7, a. 11. This teaching clearly derives from that of St Albert: see our article, *La relation dans la théologie de saint Albert le Grand*, pp. 457 and 462–464.
[45] *ST* I, q. 28, a. 4; cf. q. 13, a. 7.
[46] *ST* I, q. 28, a. 1; cf. q. 13, a. 7.
[47] *De potentia*, q. 7, a. 10.
[48] *ST* I, q. 13, a. 7; q. 28, a. 1, ad 3. The relation that God maintains with creatures is not of the same nature as the relation of creatures to God. God transcends the relation which creatures have toward him. This point had already been established in Christian theology well before St Thomas, in the East as well as in the West. For instance, in Denys' wake, St Maximus the Confessor explains that, in his creative causality, God remains immutable and 'without relation' (*aschetos*); cf. Maximus the Confessor, *Ambigua* 23 (PG 91.1260); Denys, *The Divine Names* IV.16 (PG 3.713). It is this teaching which Thomas is taking over, when he distinguishes the 'real' relation of creatures to God and the 'logical' relation of God to creatures.
[49] *ST* I, q. 3, a. 5: this is a requirement of divine simplicity.

with the divine persons who share in the same divine nature communicated through generation and spiration:

> When a being proceeds from a principle which has the same nature, then both that which causes the procession and that which proceeds from it necessarily belong to the same order; and so they must have real relations with one another. Since processions in God exist within an identity of nature, as we have shown, it is necessary to consider the relations made by the divine processions as real relations.[50]

Within this argument, the fact that the relation of origin is a real one rests on two factors: (1) divine consubstantiality, which ensures the unity of the inter-connections of the persons who share the same divinity; (2) the communication of the divine nature, that is, the generation of the Son and the procession of the Holy Spirit, which tests out as an action capable of founding real relations. In his Commentary on the *Sentences*, St Thomas insists on this second factor. A relation needs two legs to be real: a connection to another thing, but also a 'foundation' in reality, that is, a 'cause' giving rise to the relation. Without these two factors, the reality of the relation disappears.[51] And relations of origin prove to contain the two elements: they involve a connection to someone else within the same order, and they are founded on the 'communication of the divine nature' (generation and spiration).[52] With the second factor, Thomas takes further care to emphasize that it is not about a relationship of knowledge and love with a known and loved being (and which it is necessary to acknow-ledge analogously in God, as a logical relation), but concerns, rather, the procession of the *Word* engendered by its Principle, and the procession of the *impression* or *affection of Love*, in which one can see a real distinction, as was indicated in the earlier discussion of the processions.[53]

3. THE BEING OF DIVINE RELATIONS

The existence of real relations having been laid out, it remains to be shown that the relations do not divide the divine essence. The theory of relations seeks to account for the fact that Trinitarian faith is monotheist. Along

---

[50] *ST* I, q. 28, a. 1. In his questions *De potentia*, Thomas mentions the three factors which are required for two things to have a mutual 'order': these things must really exist (*ens*), they have to be distinct from each other (*distinctum*), and they must be 'orderable' (*ordinabile*).

[51] I *Sent.* d. 26, q. 2, a. 1, ad 3.

[52] I *Sent.* d. 26, q. 2, a. 2, ad 4; q. 2, a. 1, sol. If his use of the category of relation is not innovatory, the systematic and synthetic character of his analysis shows a typical feature of Thomas' thought, from his very first teaching.

[53] *ST* I, q. 28, a. 1, ad 4; cf. above, Chapter 4.

with the conception of person as a subsistent relation for which it is the preparation, this stage of the argument supplies the key to St Thomas' Trinitarian theology.

At an historical level, Thomas formulates this question in reference to Gilbert de la Porrée (+1154). The Chancellor of Chartres, professor in Paris and then bishop of Poitiers, Gilbert had been an outstanding figure within twelfth-century theology. When commenting on Boethius, he had taken care to show that the Trinity is compatible with the unity of God. So as to hold on to the unity of the divine essence, which is absolutely identical in each divine person, he had explained that the divine persons are not contrasted on the level of their essence, which is identical, but distinguish themselves from one another by a relation which Gilbert defines as 'extrinsic' or as 'extraneously labelled' (*extrinsecus affixa*).[54] Gilbert uses the word 'external' to indicate that the relation does not belong to the order of essence, that is, the divine unity, but to the order of the distinction of the persons, which does not touch their essential unity. He also takes over from Boethius the distinction between abstract forms (that *by which* a thing is such) and the concrete subject (the concretely existing subsistent individual). He makes an analogous distinction in God: there will be a difference between the divine person and his relative property, for instance, between the Father and his paternity. This idea elicited heated reactions, especially from Bernard of Clairvaux, who counter-attacked in the name of God's *simplicity*. The theory would be rejected at the synod of Reims (1148), whose doctrinal decision was accepted by Gilbert. Whatever its accuracy with respect to Gilbert's actual thinking, the criticism which it addressed to him constituted the scholastic form of 'Porretanism', as the kind of Trinitarian theology which Peter Lombard's *Sentences* characterized as 'heretical'.[55] It is found throughout the whole of theological Trinitarian writing, from the middle of the twelfth century right down to the fourteenth century and beyond.

At a theoretical level, St Thomas draws out the thinking of his teacher Albert the Great.[56] Albert had stressed that relation simultaneously secures the plurality of divine persons and the simplicity and immutability of God.

[54] Gilbert of Poitiers, *Expositio in Boecii de Trinitate* I. 5, nn. 42–43 (ed. N. M. Häring, *The Commentaries on Boethius by Gilbert of Poitiers*, Toronto, 1966, p. 148); cf. II.1, n. 37 (pp. 170–171). For an overview and bibliographic references, see our article, 'Trinité et Unité de Dieu dans la scolastique, XIIe–XIVe siècles', in *Le christianisme est-il un monothéisme?*, ed. P. Gisel and G. Emery, Geneva, 2001, pp. 201–204.

[55] Peter Lombard, *Sentences*, Book I, dist. 33, ch. 1 (vol. I/2, Grottaferrata, 1971, pp. 240–243).

[56] For more details and reference to Albert's texts, see our article, *La relation dans la théologie de saint Albert le Grand*, pp. 457–461.

Following Aristotle and Averroes,[57] Albert went back to the idea that relation has a 'minimal degree of being' and is thus workable for giving an account of a 'minimal distinction' at the heart of the sovereignly simple divinity, that is, a distinction which makes for no difference in essence. This enabled him to sort out two different aspects or components in a real relation: (1) the being which the relation derives from the subject in which it exists or 'inheres', as all accidents do; (2) the connection to another. Under the first aspect, the relation does not remain in God; since God's simplicity excludes him from having any accidents, the accidentality of a relation disappears when one attributes it to God, in whom the relation has the being of the divine substance itself. Trinitarian relations take this prerogative from their divine status, from the fact that it is a divine relation. But, under the second aspect, (connection to another), relation does not need to be reconstructed in order to be attributed to God. Because of its purity, the connection to another constituting the essence of the relation can properly be acknowledged in God.

St Albert's Commentary on Pseudo-Deny's *Divine Names*, which Thomas knew at first hand, supplies a brilliant synthesis.[58] Albert explains that, so far as their second aspect, connection to someone, is concerned, there is no modification to what relation is like within God; whereas, from the perspective of its *being* (the first aspect), relation in God loses its accidentality and is purely and simply identified with the divine substance. St Albert can thus show the existence of real relations, distinguishing the divine persons (through connection to someone else), but also the substantial unity of these three persons (the being of the relation). St Thomas' meditation is engrafted within the framework St Albert opened up.

In the *Summa Theologiae*, Thomas' discussion requires three stages: first, he takes over Albert's analysis of the twin aspects of relation, then he uses this analysis to rectify what Gilbert de la Porrée had said about relation, and finally he exhibits the way in which we can understand the existence of relations in God. The twin aspects of relation are presented in the general setting of the Aristotelian theory of accidents:

[57] Cf. Aristotle, *Metaphysics* N.1 (1088ᵃ22–24). St Thomas takes over this theme: I *Sent.* d. 26, q. 2, a. 2, contra; *De potentia*, q. 8, a. 1, arg. 4 and ad 4.

[58] See F. Ruello, 'Une source probable de la théologie trinitaire de St Thomas', *Recherches de science religieuse* 43 (1955), 104–128; F. Ruello, 'Le commentaire inédit de saint Albert le Grand sur les *Noms divins*. Présentation et aperçus de théologie trinitaire', *Traditio* 12 (1956), 231–314; see also my article, 'La relation dans la théologie de saint Albert le Grand', pp. 458–461. We have a copy of this commentary which is handwritten by St Thomas himself, in his famous *littera illegibilis*; cf. J.-P. Torrell, *St Thomas Aquinas*, vol. 1: *The Person and His Work*, trans. Robert Royal, Washington, 1996, pp. 21–22 and 25.

two aspects can be considered in each of the nine categories of accidental being. The first is being (*esse*) which belongs to each of them as accidents. For everything, commonly, this is existence in (*inesse*) a subject; for an accident to be is to be in another. The second aspect that can be considered in each category is the specific character (*proprio ratio*) of each of these genres. In categories other than relation, for example, quantity and quality, the specific character of the genre is defined by its connection to the subject; so one says that quantity is the measure of the substance and quality its disposition. But in relation the specific character is thought of with regard to something other (*ad aliquid extra*), not to the subject in which it is.[59]

As we have seen earlier, the second aspect (*ratio*) constitutes the essence of relation: it is 'only the connection to another thing' which states the definition of the relation.[60] Relation occupies a unique place here, and it is just this which Trinitarian theology is going to put to use. The specific character of the relation, its essence, is not taken from its connection to the subject in which the relation is inlaid, but concerns rather a connection to something or someone other.[61] Relation is an ec-stasis, a pure 'outside referring': this is its own special feature, its perfection, and allows it to be attributed directly to God. In his 'Writing on the *Sentences*', Thomas explains that,

If one considers the proper notion (*propria ratio*) of all the genres [of accidents], with the exception of relation each of these genres involves an imperfection. For instance, the proper notion of quantity derives from its connection to its subject: quantity is a measure of the substance, quality is a disposition of this substance; and it works the same for the other genres. This is why, under the aspect of their generic notion, one must exclude them from things which we attribute to God, just as one must exclude them under the aspect of their accidentality [...] But, conversely, even if one looks at the relation from the perspective of its generic notion, relation does not imply a dependency-connection to a subject: it refers itself rather to something external (*aliquid extra*). And this is why, under the aspect of its generic notion, it can also be found in God.[62]

As Augustine and Boethius had already seen, it follows from this that our language about God can only accurately attribute two modes to him: *substance* and *relation*.[63] The other kinds of attributes, such as action for instance,

---

[59] *ST* I, q. 28, a. 2. Thomas had already worked out this doctrine in his first teaching: see I *Sent.* d. 8, q. 4, a. 3; d. 26, q. 2, a. 1; d. 33, q. 1, a. 1.

[60] *ST* I, q. 28, a. 1; *De potentia*, q. 8, a. 2.

[61] Cf. I *Sent.* d. 8, q. 4, a. 3; *ST* I, q. 28, a. 1, ad 1.

[62] I *Sent.* d. 8, q. 4, a. 3.

[63] Ibid.; *ST* I, q. 28, a. 2, ad 1: 'There are thus only two predicaments in God. For the other predications imply a connection to the subject of attribution from the point of view both of existence and the proper characteristics of the genus. Nothing can be attributed to God in any other way than as identical to him, since he is absolutely simple.' This takes us back to the foundational structure of the treatise on God: substantial unity of essence and relational

cannot be attributed to God in an unmodified way, because of the divine simplicity: God acts, but without changing, without passing from potentiality to act; he is good but without disposition or 'habitus'; he is great, but without dimensions, and so forth. Unlike the other genres of being, relation has no need to be reconstituted for us to acknowledge it within God; it fits the divine simplicity in and of itself.[64] It can be applied immediately to God on the basis that its specific characteristic is pure connectivity. When one recognizes 'relations' in God, the relation preserves its formality of relation.[65]

The last point is central for Trinitarian theology. The relation as such (its essence, its proper notion) adds nothing positive, it does not modify its subject, it is purely outward-bound; it does not perfect the subject. 'Relation adds nothing real to essence.'[66] The 'outgoing/ec-static' mode, which can also be called a 'mode of exteriority' of predicamental relation, reveals its special intelligibility. 'Its formal content free of the bondage and limitation of the material subject, this notion can be immediately transposed into the spiritual world' because 'what it says about its subject is this order, this pure looking outwards toward its aim, leaving the rich positivity of the subject untouched.'[67]

This pure connectivity to something other only indicates one aspect of relations in our world. Real relations are part of the texture of things, they exist *in* and *through* an other: that is the definition of an accident. If one looks at it like this, a real relation derives its being from the subject in which it inheres, as all accidents do, and it creates a compound with its subject (a subject is not a relation to another, but it has a relation to another, it is qualified by this relation). In short: a real relation only concretely exists because it is the relation *of* something or *of* someone. A real relation 'cannot exist without something absolute', that is to say, without a reality which itself does not belong to the order of relativity.[68] In Thomas' terms, Gilbert de la Porrée's error was in only looking at relation from the perspective of its connection to another (its *ratio*): from this viewpoint, relations can indeed be considered as 'positioned from outside', since they formally consist in the connection 'to the outside'. But this is only one aspect of relation. So far as its being is concerned, relation inheres 'from within', it has its being in the subject in which it exists.[69] This other aspect is an absolute requirement—as Thomas

---

distinction of persons; see above, in Chapter 3, 'The Essence and the Distinction of Persons: the Common and the "Proper" '.

[64] Cf. *De potentia*, q. 8, a. 2.   [65] Cf. I *Sent.* d. 33, q. 1, a. 1.

[66] *De potentia*, q. 8, a. 2, ad 3.   [67] H. Dondaine, *La Trinité*, vol. 1, pp. 234–235.

[68] *SCG* IV, ch. 10 (no. 3455); ch. 14 (no. 3506). In God relation will be identified with this absolute.

[69] *ST* I, q. 28, a. 2; q. 39, a. 1; I *Sent.* d. 33, q. 1, a. 1. Albert had already said this (I *Sent.* d. 33, a. 5). For this reason, the only relations which can properly be called 'positioned from outside'

has already said—for the relation to be real; without it, one cannot show the real distinction of the persons, and the use of relations would just turn us around into dedicated Sabellians. So it is necessary to state very precisely how this twin aspect can be transposed into God. The key to the theory of Trinitarian relation lies in this explanation:

Whatever has accidental existence within creatures has substantial existence when transferred into God; for nothing is in God as an accident in its subject, but whatever is in God is his essence. Consequently from this point of view, while relation in created things exists as an accident in a subject, in God a really existing relation has the being of the divine essence and is wholly identical with it. But in so far as it is a pure reference (*ad aliquid*), relation does not bear upon essence, but on its opposed term. It is thus manifest that a real relation in God is really identical to God's essence, and only differs in our way of thinking, in so far as the relation implies a reference to its opposed term which is not implied by the term 'essence'. Therefore it is clear that in God there is no distinction of being-as-relation and essential-being: this is one and the same being.[70]

(1) From the perspective of its being, like all the other accidental predicates which we attribute to God (such as good, wise, great, and so on), relation does not retain the mode of an existential accident when it is ascribed to God, but exhibits the substantial mode of existence of divinity itself. In God, relation is not something which *inheres*: it *is* what God is. Its existence is that of the incomprehensible being which God is: from this angle, relation is identified with an 'absolute' in God. This identification is hard for us to deal with intellectually, because, in our experience, a relation is not an 'absolute': 'a substance is never a relation'.[71] St Thomas appeals to the transcendence of God, for God cannot belong to any genus: 'No substance that is in a genus can be a relation, because it is limited to one genus and is therefore excluded from another. But the divine essence is not in the genus of substance, but is, rather, above every genus, embracing in itself the perfections of all genera. This is why nothing prevents one from finding that which pertains to relation within it.'[72] In the final analysis, the real identity of the divine substance and the divine relation hangs on the supereminent mode of the divine being.

---

are 'logical' relations, which have no ontological reality in the subject itself (*De potentia*, q. 8, a. 2).

[70] *ST* I, q. 28, a. 2; cf. q. 39, a. 1.

[71] *De potentia*, q. 8, a. 2, arg. 1. The word 'absolute' literally means 'that which is not bound, the boundless', and thus that which is not relative to something else.

[72] *De potentia*, q. 8, a. 2, ad 1: 'God is not in the genus of substance like a species of this genus, but he belongs to the genus of substance in that he is the principle of the genus' (*De potentia*, q. 9, a. 3, ad 3). Cf. *ST* I, q. 3, a. 5, ad 1; *SCG* IV, ch. 14 (no. 3506).

(2) But from the perspective of its formal character (reference to another), relation can be transposed to God without any qualification, since it does not entail any imperfection. It is here that the metaphysical purity of the relation comes into the picture, its formal character in comparison to other accidents, for this character does not pertain to the divine essence but to the correlative term ('relation does not bear upon essence, but on its opposed term'). The connection between the existence and the *ratio* of the relation are thus different in God than in creatures. Whereas, in creatures, a real relation adds to the subject who has it, and is really different from this subject, in God the absolute and the relation 'are one and the same reality'.[73] Albert the Great had already explained this, in very similar terms. One can thus grasp the divine relation in its authentic formality of relation (reference to another) and in the identity of the divine substance.

The application of this teaching to Trinitarian relations will go like this. Christian faith recognizes *paternity* in God. Under the aspect of its formal characteristic (*ratio*), the relation of paternity does not condition the divine essence, but consists in the reference of the Father to the Son. And paternity, under the aspect of its being, is identical to the essence or substance of God; paternity is God himself, not something other than God: the Father is God. One can thus account for the divinity of the Father *and* the real relation which he maintains with the Son and which distinguishes him from his Son.

The investigation of relation gives rise to a twin distinction, and one has to observe what is happening here very carefully. On the one hand, each personal relation is distinguished from its opposite correlate, and this distinction is entirely real (paternity is not filiation). But, on the other hand, from within the divine essence, relation is just a logical distinction. Effectively, when we speak of 'paternity' in God, we *signify* the reference of the Father to the Son but we do not pinpoint 'anything other' than God himself. In our language and in our thinking, relation remains a mode of attribution which is distinct from substance,[74] but without naming anything which could be distinct from the divine substance. Thomas explains: 'Even though they signify the divine essence, the divine relations do not signify it by way of essence, since they do not convey the idea of existence in something, but of reference towards something else.'[75]

[73] *ST* I, q. 28, a. 2, ad 2. In the created world, real relation produces a composition with its subject. Such composition has no place in God, in whom relation is really identical to the essence and the person; cf. I *Sent.* d. 33, q. 1, a. 1.

[74] *ST* I, q. 28, a. 2, ad 1; cf. ad 2; *De potentia*, q. 8, a. 2. This discussion is important. It shows that relation is the divine essence, without making the divine essence into a relative reality (cf. I *Sent.* d. 33, q. 1, a. 1, ad 1).

[75] *De potentia*, q. 8, a. 2, ad 4.

One can see that there is for Thomas no question of creating clear blue water between the divine essence or substance and the relations. And likewise, as we will see in the next chapter, there is no intention of making a gulf between the divine essence and the divine persons. Those of Thomas' interpreters who read his Trinitarian theology as investing in a sort of concurrence between essence and relation, or as opposing essence to person, make a serious mistake touching on the heart of his teaching. The divine relations integrate or draw together everything that exists in God, in their two aspects: the common essence and the mutual connections of the persons. Thus the divine unity and the distinction of persons are brought together. This is also why the theologian tackles the Trinitarian mystery by following the law of 'redoubling' which we mentioned earlier: to grasp the mystery, we must join these two aspects together. This conclusion is central to understanding St Thomas' thought. *The doctrine of relation integrates all of the aspects of our knowledge of the mystery of God*, and this is why relation permits us to conceive the divine person.

4. RELATIVE OPPOSITION: PATERNITY, FILIATION, SPIRATION, AND PROCESSION

Down to this stage, Thomas has exhibited the existence of real relations in God and these relations' identity in being with the divine essence. After having seen how these factors can direct one to understanding the divine person, two further frontiers must still be crossed. One must fine-tune the way in which the relations entail a real distinction, and determine precisely what relations are at issue. The first question is filled out in the idea of relative opposition, whilst the second comes back to showing the four relations of origin which Trinitarian doctrine traditionally acknowledges in God.

(a) Relative Opposition

The recognition of real distinctness amongst the divine relations results from the analysis of the structure of relation, as Thomas has earlier described it:

To attribute a predicate to a subject necessarily involves attributing to it everything that belongs to the definition of this predicate. For instance, calling anyone 'man' involves conceiving him as endowed with reason. Now by definition relation implies reference to another, according to which the two things stand in relative opposition to one another. Therefore since there is in God a real relation, as we said earlier, there must also be real opposition. And by its very meaning such opposition implies distinction. Therefore there must be real distinction in God, not indeed when we consider the absolute reality of his nature, where there is sheer unity and simplicity, but when we thing of him in terms of relation.[76]

This consideration is founded on the two aspects of relation which were discussed earlier. On the side of its *ratio*, relation involves a reference to another, and this reference formally distinguishes the two relatives which are mutually referred to one another: paternity is not filiation. Amongst all the divine attributes, only relation entails formal distinction; it is unique in involving an 'opposition'[77] in its formal character. And, from the side of its *being*, the relation of origin is entirely real, as St Thomas has already shown. Thus, the opposition of relations of origin includes a real distinction. As Thomas has already shown, this real distinction is not a matter of the reference of the relations to the essence, but the mutual connection of the relatives: it is a distinction from relative to relative, and not of relative to essence. The real distinction of the relations thus maintains the simplicity and unity of the divine essence, without partitioning it out: it does not divide the single essence of God. The distinction must be seen as the 'smallest possible distinction' in so far as the difference it entails is concerned, that is a distinction which is 'closest to unity'[78] (the three persons are one single God), even though it has the status of the sovereign distinction, since it is a distinction within God.[79]

The idea of 'opposition' was not a new one. Well before Thomas, Anselm of Canterbury had foregrounded it:

It follows from God's unity, which has no parts, that whatever we say about the one God, who in his entirety is whatever he is, we say about the entire God, the Father, and the Son and the Holy Spirit, since each is the sole and whole and complete God. And the relational opposition, which results from the fact that God is from God through the two aforementioned ways [the generation of the Son and the procession of the Spirit], prevents us from predicating Father and Son and Holy Spirit of one another, and from attributing the properties of each to the others. Therefore, the consequences of this unity and this set of relations are so harmoniously mixed that neither the plurality resulting from the relations is transferable to the things in which the simplicity of the aforementioned unity resounds, nor does the unity suppress the plurality whereby we signify the same relations. The unity should never lose its consequences, except when a relational opposition stands in the way, nor

---

[76] *ST* I, q. 28, a. 3.

[77] *ST* I, q. 28, a. 3, ad 2. Goodness or power, for instance, do not have this element of distinction.

[78] *ST* I, q. 40, a. 2, ad 3.   [79] I *Sent.* d. 26, q. 2, a. 2, ad 2.

should the relations lose what belongs to them except when the indivisible unity stands in the way.[80]

The idea of 'opposition' was not discovered in the Middle Ages; it does not even come from the Latin West. As early as Basil of Caesarea, one finds the comment that, under the aspect of the divine substance, there is no opposition between the Father and the Son, but 'in so far as one engenders and the other is engendered, one must consider them under the aspect of their opposition (*antithesis*)'.[81] This way of talking about relations becomes commonplace with the Scholastics. The characteristic feature of Thomas' investigation is the way he put his mind to fine-tuning the concept of *opposition* in order to determine the nature of the *distinction* in God. The word 'opposition' obviously does not indicate competition, but must be taken in its formal meaning: opposition is the *principle of a distinction*.[82] This opposition is required because the distinction of the divine persons is not 'material'. No opposition, no distinction: to reject such 'opposition' comes down to an acceptance of Sabellianism.

Assisted by his reading of Aristotle, Thomas allows for the existence of four kinds of opposition: (1) opposition of affirmation and negation; (2) opposition of privation and possession; (3) opposition of contrariety; (4) opposition of relation. The first kind of opposition implies a difference in being, the second necessarily involves inequality, and the third entails an essential difference (a 'difference of form') between the opposed terms: none of these can be applied to the three consubstantial divine persons. Rigorous analysis shows, then, that the only remaining possibility is 'opposition of relation'[83] or 'relative opposition',[84] whose 'very definition includes opposition'. A relative opposition can rest on many foundations, as we indicated in the study of processions: quantity, action, and passion. The only relation which can be attributed to the Trinity is that founded on immanent action, the relation of origin. Here we have the

[80] Anselm of Canterbury, *The Procession of the Holy Spirit* (ET by Richard Regan, in *Anselm of Canterbury: The Major Works*, ed. Brian Davies and G. R. Evans, Oxford, 1998, pp. 390–434 (p. 393). The first section of this formula is repeated by the Council of Florence, in 1442: in God 'Hae tres personae sunt unus Deus, et non tres dii: quia trium est una substantia, una essentia, una natura, una divinitas, una immensitas, una aeternitas, omniaque sunt unum, ubi non obviat relationis oppositio' (Denzinger, no. 1330). One might perhaps expect to find a citation from this passage of Anselm's in the Trinitarian treatise of Thomas' *Summa Theologiae*, but it is not there. But Thomas integrates this doctrine into his own theology (see especially *ST* I, q. 28, a. 3). He refers explicitly to Anselm, on this point, in the *De potentia*, q. 10, a. 5, sed contra 2.
[81] Basil of Caesarea, *Contra Eunomius* II.28 (SC 305, pp. 120–121). Cf *Contra Eunomius* II. 26 (*SC* 305, pp. 108–109): 'opposition (*antithesis*) between the unengendered and the engendered'. The Latin word *oppositio* is the literal equivalent of the Greek term *antithesis*.
[82] *SCG* IV, ch. 24 (no. 3612).
[83] *SCG* IV, ch. 24 (no. 3612); I *Sent.* d. 27, q. 1, a. 1.
[84] *Quodlibet* IV, q. 4, a. 2.

principle of the intra-Trinitarian distinction: 'relative opposition as to origin'.[85] His scriptural *lectura* gives rise to reflections which accord with this and which lead Thomas to the same conclusion.[86]

Relative opposition consequent on origin does not just put the real distinction of the divine persons on show. It also exhibits the inseparability of the persons, because a relative, as such, cannot exist without its correlate. It cannot even be thought without its correlate. This is why, 'as to the distinction of the Persons, which is by relations of origin, knowledge of the Father does indeed include knowledge of the Son, for He would not be Father, had he not a Son; and the Holy Spirit is their mutual bond'.[87] In this way, relative opposition shows that the persons are distinct *and* inseparable. One can easily see why the theory of relative opposition plays such a central role in accounting for the distinction and unity of the three persons.

Finally, with respect to the terminology, one should note that Thomas generally uses the expressions 'relative opposition' and 'opposition of relation'. He also speaks of 'opposed relations',[88] of 'mutually opposed relations',[89] or of 'relations which have a mutual opposition'.[90] In all of their uses, the formulas refer to the kind of opposition which takes place through relation, or they home in, precisely, on a pair of relations. In contemporary theology textbooks, one often comes across the phrase 'relation of opposition', but this formula—which St Thomas never uses—is inapt. For Thomas, the relations of origin, which by definition include opposition, specify a kind of opposition. These relations involve a special mode of distinction, the kind which the doctrine of the Trinity recognizes in God. So it is preferable to speak of 'relative opposition', and, when one wants to refer to a pair of relations (such as paternity and filiation), of 'opposed relations'.

(b) Paternity, filiation, spiration, procession

At the completion of his study of relations, St Thomas pares down and gives names to these real relations that are made 'oppositional' by the processions.[91] Such a list of relations presents no novelty: it draws together common doctrines. It gives us *paternity* (the relation of the Father to the Son), *filiation* (the relation of the Son to the Father), the *spiration* of the Holy Spirit (the

85 *SCG* IV, ch. 24 (no. 3612).
86 *In Ioan.* 15.26 (no. 2063); *In Ioan.* 16.14–15 (nos. 2112–2115).
87 *ST* II–II, q. 1, a. 8 ad 3.
88 See for example *ST* I, q. 30, a. 2; q. 36, a. 2, sol. and ad 1; q. 39, a. 1.
89 See for instance *ST* I, q. 36, a. 2.
90 See for example *ST* I, q. 39, a. 1, ad 1.   91 *ST* I, q. 28, a. 3, ad 3.

relation of the Father and the Son in respect to the Holy Spirit), and the
procession of the Holy Spirit (the relation of the Holy Spirit in respect to
the Father and the Son).[92] This enumeration summarizes the traditional
triad of personal properties established by the Capaddocians,[93] inscribes
in it the Catholic teaching about the procession of the Holy Spirit, and refines
the point that the generation of the Son involves a pair of opposed relations
(paternity–filiation), just as much as the procession of the Spirit does
(spiration–procession). One nonetheless finds Thomas' original orientation
in the manner in which he exhibits these four relations. By linking his
explanation of them to *relative opposition*, Thomas exhibits the *relations* by
way of the *immanent processions* of the Word and of Love:

In each of the processions, one must consider two opposed relations: the relation of
what proceeds from its principle or source, and the relation of the principle itself. The
procession of the Word is called 'generation' in the proper sense of the term which
belongs to living beings; and, in the perfection of the living, the relation of being the
principle of generation is called *paternity*; and the relation of the one who proceeds
from this principle is called *filiation*. For the procession of Love, however, there is no
proper name, as we have said above (q. 27, a. 4), neither is there for the relations
which it founds. All the same the relation of being the principle of this procession may
be called *spiration* and the relation of what proceeds *procession*, although these two
words have to do with the processions or origins themselves, not with relations.[94]

Here, where Thomas makes a unified presentation of ideas whose main
features he has already established, the first striking move is the use of relative
opposition. Generation founds the relation of Father to Son, and, correlatively, of Son to Father: these are 'opposed relations'. Not all of the connections of the four relations touch on opposition, just the mutual connection
of paternity and filiation, on the one hand, and the mutual connection of
spiration and procession, on the other. We are on familiar terms with the
analogy of Word and Love, since Thomas used it in his discussion of the
processions. It is this which, by enabling one to grasp the immanent processions, gives rise to the conception of opposed relations. St Thomas explains
the relation of the Father and the Son by applying his analysis of the

---

[92] See for instance Saint Bonaventure, *Breviloquium* I, ch. 3 (*Opera omnia*, vol. 5, pp. 211–
212). Bonaventure puts forward here a portfolio of academic refinements, the like of which is
not found in St Thomas (!): two processions, three hypostases, four relations, five notions.

[93] See Saint Gregory of Nazianzus, *Orations*, 31.9 (*SC* 250, 292–293); *Orations*, 39.12 (*SC* 358,
174–177): the unengendered Father engenders the Son; the Son is engendered, the Holy Spirit
proceeds. Peter Lombard offers a synthesis of these ideas on the basis of Augustine's theology:
paternity, filiation, procession (*Sentences*, Book I, dist. 27).

[94] *ST* I, q. 28, a. 4; one finds a comparable discussion in *SCG* IV, ch. 24 (no. 3613).

procession of the Word to it.[95] One should observe that, as in the study of the processions,[96] it is the mode of emanation of the Word which allows for the elucidation of paternity and filiation: the relation of filiation is the relation of the Word to his principle or source, and paternity is simply the correlative relation. The relation in question is not that which the divine intellect enjoys with the realities which it knows—St Thomas underlines this once again—but the mutual relation which the Word, in proceeding by an intellectual action, enjoys with his Principle.[97] The same goes for Love.

Finally, Thomas comes back to the linguistic problem which we have in talking about the procession of the Holy Spirit: we must use a common name ('procession') to designate both the origin proper to the Holy Spirit and the relations springing from this origin.[98] Whereas, when we are speaking about the mutual reference of the Father and the Son, we can make a linguistic distinction between the *procession* ('generation') and the *relations* which it founds, ('paternity' and 'filiation'), linguistic constraints compel us to designate the relations by the procession and the action themselves ('procession' and 'spiration').

Opposition is strictly a matter of what the processions can tell us about the two pairs of opposed relations. There is, on the one hand, a mutual 'opposition' of paternity and filiation, and, on the other, an 'opposition' of spiration and procession. There is, for instance, no opposition of paternity and spiration, or of filiation and spiration. St Thomas explains this in more detail a little further on. Since they are opposed, paternity and filiation belong to two distinct persons: the Father and the Son. But there is no opposition between 'being Father' and 'breathing the Holy Spirit'; because there is no opposition here, these two relations do not cut across the Father (they do not really distinguish the Father from himself).[99] In the same way, there is no opposition between 'being Son' and 'breathing the Holy Spirit together with the Father': the Son is not really distinguished in himself by these two relations.[100] The only relative opposition is the opposition which the one who 'breathes'

[95] The Commentary on the *Sentences* counts up the relations in the same way (I *Sent.* d. 27, q. 1, a. 1), but without making use of a doctrine of the Word and of Love that Thomas would only propose, in an exact form, starting with the *Summa Contra Gentiles*.

[96] *ST* I, q. 27, a. 2.

[97] *ST* I, q. 28, a. 4, ad 1; cf. q. 27.

[98] See above, in Chapter 4, 'The Word "Procession" ' and 'A Different Procession, Which is That of Love'.

[99] Otherwise put: since they are not opposed, paternity and spiration do not make the Father two persons.

[100] *ST* I, q. 30, a. 2. Likewise, the 'procession' does not enter into relative opposition with paternity or filiation as such. So Thomas appeals here to the 'order' of the processions of Word and Love to complete his explanations: this order entails that procession cannot belong to the one who has paternity or to the one who has filiation.

(the spiration of the Spirit) enjoys with 'being breathed' (the procession of the Holy Spirit); because of their 'opposition', these two relations cannot belong to the same person; they thus entail a person-to-person distinction. In this way, the spiration belongs to the Father and the Son, whilst the procession properly comes back to the Holy Spirit, and thus distinguishes the Spirit from the Father and the Son.[101]

The theory of relative opposition shows that the Father is distinguished and known by the relations of *paternity* and of spiration, the Son by the relations of filiation and spiration, and the Holy Spirit by the relation of *procession*. Since paternity, filiation, and procession properly and exclusively belong to only one person, they are called 'personal properties' (*proprietates personales*).[102] According to Catholic doctrine, spiration is not proper to the Father alone, but belongs to Father and Son; it is very much a real relation, but it is not named a 'property'. As for 'Unbegottenness', which so heavily preoccupied fourth-century theologians (the Father is *unengendered*), it is a property of the Father's person, which does not precisely consist in a relation but rather in the negation of a relation (the Father is not-engendered).[103] This gives us our tally of five 'notions', as mentioned above.[104] The meditation on relation sometimes overwhelms one with its logical formulations, and it is important to pick out what is going on here. When St Thomas teaches on the four real relations and three personal properties in God, he does not restrict himself to invoking the authority of the Fathers, like a Catechism or a textbook of the history of doctrines. He intends to show that the tradition conveys the truth about the three divine persons,[105] and he is trying to exhibit the rationale of this truth to believers.

There is still more to be said about relations beyond this discussion. The outstanding task is to show how the relations belong to the persons, and, in particular, what role is played by the relations in constituting the divine persons. This requires a preliminary fine-tuning of how 'person' must be understood, within God. Such will be the object of the next question.

---

[101] *ST* I, q. 30, a. 2; cf. ad 1; *CT* I, ch. 60; *SCG* IV, ch. 24 (no. 3613).

[102] *ST* I, q. 30, a. 2, ad 1; cf. q. 32, a. 3.

[103] We will come back to this in the investigation of the Father in Chapter 8, 'Unbegottenness: the Unengendered Father'.

[104] See above, in Chapter 2, 'Why Investigate Notions, Relations, and Properties?'

[105] As we observed at the beginning of the chapter: it is 'in following what the saints said', that is the Fathers and the doctors of the Church, that St Thomas proposes his doctrine of divine relation (*De potentia*, q. 8, a. 1).

6

The Person

St Thomas conceives the divine person as a subsisting relation. Relation distinguishes and identifies the person which it 'constitutes'. His notion of person has been much studied, in connection with Trinitarian theology, Christology and anthropology.[1] Instead of going into all of the aspects of his notion of 'person', we mainly plan to throw light on this conception of the person as relational. In the context of Trinitarian doctrine, the first thing we should note is that Thomas ties his own investigation to the Fathers of the Church, who developed the notion of *person* in response to various heresies:

> The Scriptures of the Old and New Testaments do not apply the name 'person' to God, although they often attribute to God what is meant by this name, namely that God exists sovereignly through himself and is perfect in knowledge. If, in speaking of God we could only employ the words which Scripture literally ascribes to God, it would follow that one could never speak of him in any other language than that in which the Old and New Testaments were delivered. We have to look for new words to express the ancient faith in God because of the necessity of arguing with heretics. And there is no need to avoid such innovation ... —the apostle teaches us to 'avoid profane verbal innovations' (1 Tim. 6.20)—since it is not profane but is in harmony with the meaning of Scripture.[2]

This way of thinking goes hand in hand with the purpose of speculative theology. It also reminds us of the observations which have already been formulated in connection with the notions of procession and relation. St Thomas tests the use of the word 'person' in theology against the patristic criterion which came down to him through Pseudo-Denys: one must not think or speak of God 'outside of that which has been divinely revealed by the sacred Scriptures'.[3] The sole aim of our reflections on the person is to help us understand what revelation says about God. The meditation comes about because of the need to address heresies. In connection with the 'number' of

---

[1] Amongst the many available works, we would like to note: E. Bailleux, 'Le personnalisme de St Thomas en théologie trinitaire', *RT* 61 (1961), 25–42; A. Malet, *Personne et amour dans la théologie trinitaire de St Thomas d'Aquin*, Paris, 1956.

[2] *ST* I, q. 29, a. 3, ad 1.

[3] Ibid., arg. 1; cf. *SCG* IV, ch. 24 (no. 3621); *De potentia*, q. 10, a. 4, arg. 12.

persons in God, St Thomas explained in his Questions *De potentia* that, without any pretension to 'comprehend' God, the theologian can grasp something of the truth, in a contemplative exercise which, clearing mistakes out of the path, gives believers a pre-glimpse of what they hope to contemplate in the beatific vision.[4]

1. WHAT IS A PERSON?

St Thomas does not tell us much about the history of the word 'person'. In the context of Christology, he does present solid background information on the historical context, connecting the discussion of *hypostasis* and *person* to the Councils of Ephesus and Chalcedon, particularly focusing on how these words emerge from the Nestorian controversy.[5] The well-known definition by Boethius, whose Thomist interpretation we will be examining, itself arose within a Christological context. In Trinitarian theology, he alludes to the fourth-century patristic controversies,[6] but without giving very much detail. Like all his peers, he discusses three main definitions of the 'person' in Trinitarian theology: those of Boethius and of Richard of Saint-Victor, and the 'definition of the masters', to which the early Franciscan school was much attached. He makes his preference for Boethius' definition very clear; for him, it eclipses the others. At least in the exclusive form it presents in Thomas' writing, this choice was not obvious. In the twelfth century, and likewise at the beginning of the thirteenth century, many authors criticized Boethius' definition for being 'more philosophical than theological', and thus inadmissible in Trinitarian theology.[7] It was not unusual for theologians to rework the meaning of Boethius' definition in the light of other conceptions of the person.

St Thomas is much more decisive. His investigation of the person is clearly based on Boethius' definition, set within a Christological context which requires that one steers clear of Nestorianism and Monophysitism: 'The person is an individual substance of a rational nature' (*persona est rationalis [rationabilis]*

---

[4] *De potentia*, q. 9, a. 5; see above, in Chapter 2, 'Understanding the Faith'.

[5] Cf. *ST* III, q. 2, aa. 2 and 3; *De unione Verbi incarnati*, aa. 1 and 2. On the nature of Thomas' information of the Councils, see G. Geenen, 'En marge du Concile de Chalcédoine. Les textes du Quatrième Concile dans les oeuvres de St Thomas', *Angelicum* 29 (1952), 43–59; M. Morard, 'Une source de St Thomas d'Aquin: le deuxième concile de Constantinople (553)', *RSPT* 81 (1997), 21–56.

[6] Cf. *De potentia*, q. 9, aa. 4 and 5.

[7] See for instance Peter of Poitiers, I *Sent.* 4 and I *Sent.* 32 (PL 211. 801 and 923).

naturae individua substantia).[8] His explanation of this definition starts off from the conception of the *individual*: 'the individual belongs in a special way to the genus of substance. For a substance is individuated through itself'.[9] The first thing which one sees about the person is its character as an irreducibly real singular, a determinate entity, singular and distinct from everything else. St Thomas immediately goes on to say that the 'individual' in question belongs to the genus of substance, in the sense of Aristotle's 'primary substance' (the concrete substance, subject, or hypostasis). An individual substance is characterized by its own 'mode of existence': it does not exist in and through another, but in and through itself. This fact of existing through itself is the fundamental characteristic of substance, and thus of the person. A *person* is the individual substance which possesses its own being in and through itself, having complete purchase on the exercise of its own act of existence. To specify what he means by individual substance, Thomas makes an analysis of action:

particularity and individuality are found in a still more special and perfect way in rational substances, which have control over their actions, and are not just acted upon as other beings are, but act of their own initiative; and actions are carried out by singular beings. It follows from this that, amongst all the substances, individual beings with rational nature have a special name: that of 'person'.[10]

The theme at the heart of this way of approaching the person is *freedom of action*: persons act through themselves. The presence of this theme shows that, when he talks about 'rational nature', Thomas is picturing all of the spiritual faculties of the person. Intellectuality implies volition and freedom: it characterizes a way of acting that is in step with beings who recognize and conceive goals in their minds and freely direct themselves towards them. Free will only belongs to those beings which have mind: they are not just 'driven' toward an attainable end, but have the capacity freely to take themselves off toward a goal upon which they have intelligently decided. This free inclination, or 'intellectual appetite', is free will.[11] A mode of action exhibits a mode of being: as one is, so one acts. The mode of acting freely through oneself is based on the mode of being through oneself.[12] The experience of

[8] *ST* I, q. 29, a. 1; cf. I *Sent.* d. 25, q. 1, a. 1; *De potentia*, q. 9, a. 2. Boethius, *Contra Eutyches and Nestorius*, ch. 3 (PL 64. 1343). Cf. C. Schlapkohl, *Persona est naturae rationabilis individua substantia, Boethius und die Debatte über den Personbegriff*, Marburg, 1999, pp. 199–217.

[9] *ST* I, q. 29, a. 1; cf. *De potentia*, q. 9, a. 2. On this topic see L. Dewan, 'The Individual as a Mode of Being according to Thomas Aquinas', *The Thomist* 63 (1999), 403–424.

[10] *ST* I, q. 29, a. 1.

[11] *ST* I, q. 80, a. 1; q. 82, a. 1; cf. *SCG* IV, ch. 19 (no. 3558); *De veritate*, q. 23, a. 1.

[12] *De potentia*, q. 9, a. 1, ad 3.

acting enables one to apprehend the existence of the reality which founds this action. At the root of action is a 'self' which engages with and knows itself as such because it is so constituted through its ontological principles: free action manifests the genuine nature of persons. So we need not contrast Thomas' metaphysical attitude to the topic with one which stresses the 'psychological' elements of the person (such as the life of the mind: knowledge, freedom, action, and openness to another), because these elements are integrated into his own approach.

Thus, 'individual substance' is the genus nearest to the definition of a person, whilst its specific difference is tied to its being a 'rational nature'. The word 'rational' does not only indicate mental activity, but the power, capacity, or faculty of intellectual knowledge and spiritual life. Elsewhere, St Thomas clarifies that the adjective 'reasonable' should not just be taken in the strict sense of reason as a discursive faculty proper to human beings (unless one says this, one could not apply this definition of the person to God, since God knows without reasoning[13]); instead, it should be taken to embrace all the branches of intellectual nature, whatever its modalities (for instance, intuitive or discursive). It thus has an analogical fit with God, with angels, and with human beings. In addition, 'nature' is not only taken here in its original meaning of 'principle of action' (the principle of movement or rest),[14] but denotes the specific essence.[15] Boethius used these features in order to draw up a complete definition which is targeted not only at a mental conception but at the whole concrete reality of the person.[16]

In conclusion, the person is defined by its existing through itself (subsistence), in an irreducible and entirely singular way (individuality), with a freedom of action which is drawn from its essence (intellectual nature). All of these character traits ground the dignity of the person. The theological use of this definition secures the divinity of the three persons (the divine intellectual nature), as against Arianism, it preserves the real distinction of the persons and the subsistence which fits them (the individual substance) against Sabellianism, and it founds their action (as an individual substance which is intelligent and free).

---

[13] *ST* I, q. 29, a. 3, ad 4; cf. q. 14, a. 7; q. 79, a. 8; I *Sent.* d. 25, q. 1, a. 1, ad 4; *De potentia* q. 9, a. 2, ad 10: 'Boethius takes the word "rational" broadly here, in the sense of "intellectual".'

[14] Aristotle, *Physics* II.1 (192^b21–23); *Metaphysics* Δ 4 (1014^b18–20); cf. *ST* III, q. 2, a. 1.

[15] *ST* I, q. 29, a. 1, ad 4; *De potentia*, q. 9, a. 2, ad 11. It is a plausible assessment that, on this point, St Thomas distinguishes himself from 'most of the interpreters of his times' by interpreting Boethius' definition correctly (Schlapkohl, *Persona*, p. 209).

[16] I *Sent.* d. 25, q. 1, a. 1, ad 8; *De unione Verbi incarnati*, a. 2.

2. PERSON AND ANALOGY

According to Boethius' precise definition of its features, the person signifies 'that which is most perfect (*perfectissimum*) in all of nature': and thus the name *person* is eminently applicable to God.[17] Like most other theologians,[18] Thomas recognizes that the name *person* is a term which is applied analogously, in diverse modalities, to human beings, to angels, and to God. As with all analogous attribution, one has to be aware of the fact that one is in the presence of a perfection which God possesses in a way unique to him.[19] This rule for analogous usage is important. It can be applied on the same basis to other suitable words by which we name God: Father, Son, Spirit, Goodness, Wisdom, Love, Life, and so on. We should take a little time to remind ourselves what is going on here.

The analogous attribution of a name to God implies that one distinguishes the perfection under consideration (wisdom, for example), from its mode of existence (the way of being wise). On a linguistic level, therefore, one will find this distinction: (1) the perfection signified by a word; (2) the mode of signification, that is, the manner of signifying this perfection.[20] Thomas explains that in our language the mode of signification is connected to the mode by which we understand the perfections in so far as they exist in creatures. Under this second aspect, our words are always tied to the way in which we know creatures, since it was primarily to express our knowledge of created realities that these words were forged. Thus, for instance, there will be two aspects of the name 'wise', which we attribute to human beings and which we also attribute pre-eminently to God. We can look at these two aspects.

(1) The first aspect relates to the *perfection signified* by this name (the perfection signified by the name 'wisdom'). Under this first aspect, our words can properly be applied to God. When it comes to proper analogies, these words apply to God better than to creatures, in terms of the thing they signify.[21] What they signify fits God more genuinely than creatures, because these perfections flow from God to creatures. This is how Thomas explains, for instance, Jesus' remark that 'Only one is good' (Mt. 19.17).[22] God is good

---

[17] *ST* I, q. 29, a. 3. This superlative echoes in the Disputed Questions *De potentia*, q. 9, a. 3, where Thomas qualifies the person as 'dignissima' three times in a row: the nature of the person is 'the most dignified of all natures', and 'the mode of existence of the person is the most dignified'.

[18] See Albert, I *Sent.* d. 25, a. 2; Bonaventure, I *Sent.* d. 25, a. 2, q. 2.

[19] *ST* I, q. 29, a. 3; cf. I *Sent.* d. 25, q. 1, a. 2; *De potentia*, q. 9, a. 3.

[20] *ST* I, q. 13, a. 3.   [21] *ST* I, q. 13, a. 6.

[22] *ST* I, q. 6, a. 2, ad 2; cf. *In Matt.* 19.17 (no. 1582).

through his essence, whereas creatures receive this quality through their participation in God.

(2) The second aspect touches on the reality's *mode* of signification, the way in which our words signify the perfection which we can see in God. We conceive and signify wisdom like a quality, the habit which a subject *has*, and which is not identical to the subject itself, which is acquired or received and can be lost (and so on). Under this second aspect, of the mode of signification, our words are not at all fitting for God. God is wise and good in an entirely different way from the wisdom and goodness of creatures, for he is identical with his own wisdom and goodness, is good through himself; his goodness is simply his substance.[23]

When we recognize that 'God is wise' we do not intend to denote something which would be different from his essence, his power, or his being. The attribution of 'wisdom' to God infinitely overflows the mode of signification of this term: 'what it signifies in God goes beyond the meaning of the name, leaving the signified reality uncomprehended'.[24] In this way, analogy obtains an authentic knowledge of God, but one which profoundly respects the incomprehensibility of the divine essence which, in the mode of existence belonging to itself alone, its intimate reality, remains unknown to us. This is the way it is for all the words which we put to service for naming God (the condition of use being that the property belongs to God), even in the most appropriate language that we have at our disposal. This criterion must thus apply also to the word *person*,[25] as also to the names *Father, Son,* and so on. We touch on the truth when we apply the name *person* to God, and doing so makes something about God known, even though the divine person's mode of being remains incomprehensible to us, infinitely surpassing what a created person is like.[26] Despite what a commonplace prejudice puts abroad, these features of the theory of analogy are not idiosyncratic to Thomas Aquinas or to Catholicism; one also finds them in Reformed writers like Karl Barth whom one would suspect would only mention analogy to take a pot-shot at it.[27]

---

[23] *ST* I, q. 13, a. 3.

[24] *ST* I, q. 13, a. 5: *relinquit rem significatam ut incomprehensam.*

[25] I *Sent.* d. 25, q. 1, a. 1; *De potentia,* q. 9, a. 3, ad 1.

[26] To apply the definition of person to God should not tempt one to define God (*De potentia,* q. 9, a. 3, ad 2): God cannot be defined, any more than he can be comprehended (*ST* I, q. 3, a. 5). God is not defined by names like this; but the notion of *person,* what the definition of this name means, belongs to God.

[27] Karl Barth, *Church Dogmatics* II/1, pp. 221–227. Barth rejects what he calls *analogia entis,* but he explains clearly that talking about faith in God is subjected to the rule of analogy: 'If in this fellowship there can be no question of either parity or disparity, there remains only what is generally meant by analogy: similarity, partial correspondence and agreement.... the object itself—God's truth in His revelation as the basis of the veracity of our knowledge of God—does not leave us any option but to resort to this concept' (ibid., p. 225).

Thus, one attributes the name *person* to God because of the eminent perfection which this name signifies, 'not in the same way that one says of a creature that it is a person, but in a supremely excellent way'.[28] If one wants to use Boethius' definition correctly, one must bring these refinements of the notion to bear on it:

We can say that God has a *reasonable nature* if reason is taken to imply, not the process of discursive thought, but an intelligent nature in a general sense. God cannot be called an 'individual' in the sense that this implies matter which is the principle of individuation, but only in the sense of incommunicability. Finally, 'substance' can be applied to God inasmuch as it refers to self-grounded existence.[29]

Thomas can thus conclude: 'Both the word *person* and the definition of person given above are applicable to God.'[30] For these reasons, the interesting etymologies of the word *person* are of little use in Trinitarian theology. Like other people in his time, Thomas mentions the theatrical mask which seems to have historical connections with the word *person*.[31] But if a name can be attributed to God, it is not because of the way the word was originally used: it is on account of the perfection which the word indicates.[32] We could perhaps register the value of the idea of 'representation' (the face, that which presents itself, the role: the social and moral dimension of the person).[33] St Thomas remarks that a name often comes from a property, action, or effect of the thing which it wants to name. Even so, when it comes to the proper names for God, one has to give priority to the deep perfection to which the name points.[34]

The second definition of the person came from the 'Masters'. This definition embeds itself in etymology, precisely by evoking the *dignity* of the person (in the sense in which one calls an important personage a 'dignitary'): 'the person is an hypostasis distinguished by a property pertaining to dignity'.[35]

---

[28] *ST* I, q. 29, a. 3.   [29] *ST* I, q. 29, a. 3, ad 4.   [30] *De potentia*, q. 9, a. 3, ad 2.

[31] *ST* I, q. 29, a. 3, arg. 2 and ad 2; *De potentia*, q. 9, a. 3, arg. 1 and ad 1; etc. Thomas took this theme over from Boethius: see *Contra Eutyches and Nestorius*, ch. 3.

[32] *ST* I, q. 29, a. 3, ad 2: 'The word *person* is not suitable for God when its meaning is drawn from its original reference.'

[33] As early as Aristotle, the word *prosopon* designates the part of the human body between the cranium and the neck, that is, the face, the countenance, that which appears in front (Aristotle, *Parts of Animals* III.1); this meaning of *prosopon* also appears in the Septuagint. By the end of a striking development, particularly in Cicero, the word *persona* has acquired a cluster of meanings: the social, moral, legal, active roles which are given to individual humans, acting in a social context: the human being as such. See M. Nédoncelle, '*Prosopon* et *persona* dans l'Antiquité classique', *Revue des Sciences Religieuses* 22 (1948), 277–299; A. Milano, *Persona in teologia: Alle origini del significato di persona nel cristianesimo antico*, Rome, 1966, pp. 53–66.

[34] *ST* I, q. 29, a. 3, ad 2; *De potentia*, q. 9, a. 3, ad 1.

[35] *ST* I, q. 29, a. 3, ad 2: 'Hypostasis proprietate distincta ad dignitatem pertinente.' St Thomas also mentions this definition under a variant which foregrounds the nobility of the person: 'Alia [definitio] datur a magistris sic: persona est hypostasis distincta proprietate ad

The early Franciscan school often used this definition, and it is still the primary one for St Bonaventure.[36] St Thomas was quite well aware that God is eminent in dignity or, rather, 'surpasses every dignity'. He does not oppose the Master's definition, but it is only interesting to him as an evocative allusion; it does not have the wealth or precision of that of Boethius.

The third traditional definition comes from Richard of Saint-Victor: a person is 'an incommunicable existence of divine nature'.[37] Richard substituted this definition for Boethius', because, in his opinion, Boethius' definition leads one to conceive the divine substance as a person and thus creates a confusion between the common substance and the distinct Three in God. This is why Richard's definition indicates what distinguishes the persons (the principle of 'individuation'), that is, the *ex-sistere* (indicating directly the origin from another; holding his existence from someone) which is *incommunicable* (the distinct singularity and irreducible singularity of the person). In addition, Richard replaced the adjective 'reason' with a conditioning quality, 'divine'. The accuracy of Richard's criticisms is debatable, since for Boethius divine substance is not an 'individual substance' in the meaning which his definition of person gives it,[38] and the note of incommunicability is expressed by the notion of 'individual'. However that may be, very many theologians united around Richard's objections. In every quarter, even amongst those who retained Boethius' definition, the criticisms attracted great attention. One still finds traces of them in Albert, who judges that 'as Boethius defines it, the person does not fit into God, unless one explains substance in the sense of existence, as Richard puts it'.[39] Bonaventure, who was likewise receptive to Boethius' definition, explains that it applies as much to creatures as to God, whereas Richard's applies exclusively to God: the Franciscan master concludes that one can say that Richard's definition uses language 'more appropriately'.[40]

nobilitatem pertinens' (I *Sent.* d. 25, q. 1, a. 1, ad 8). St Albert the Great observed that 'The masters got their definition by way of a comparison with social values or civil functions' (Albert, I *Sent.* d. 25, a. 1 *in fine*).

[36] See Bonaventure, I *Sent.* d. 23, a. 1, q. 1; d. 25, a. 1, q. 1.

[37] Richard of Saint-Victor, *De Trinitate*, Book IV, ch. 22 (SC 63, pp. 280–283): 'naturae divinae incommunicabilis exsistentia'. This definition has lately given rise to several anachronistic interpretations of Richard's idea. For the Victorine, the definition is based on the concept of *nature* and also implies the notion of *substance*, for 'the word *existence* signifies substantial being' (Book IV, ch. 23; SC 63, pp. 282–283); cf. N. Den Bok, *Communicating the Most High: A Systematic Study of Person and Trinity in the theology of Richard of St. Victor (+ 1173)*, Paris and Turnhout, 1996.

[38] Cf. Schlapkohl, *Persona*, pp. 150–151, 155.   [39] Albert, I *Sent.* d. 25, a. 1.

[40] Bonaventure, I *Sent.* d. 25, a. 1, q. 2, ad 4. Although the Scotist definition of person is not identical to Richard's, Duns Scotus takes over Richard of Saint Victor's definition and his critique of Boethius (see Schlapkohl, *Persona*, pp. 155–169; F. Wetter, *Die Trinitätslehre des Johannes Duns Scotus*, Münster, 1967, pp. 272–273).

St Thomas shows himself to have been unimpressed by Richard's objections to Boethius. He notes that Richard wanted to 'correct' Boethius' definition, and that 'some people say Boethius' definition does not define "person" in the sense we use when speaking of person in God',[41] but he does not accept the points of criticism. He maintains that, 'if one interprets it correctly', Boethius' definition 'is fitting for God'.[42] In Boethius' definition, '*individual*' designates a singularity which we do not attribute to several subjects; this expresses precisely the incommunicability which Richard so much values.[43] It does not follow from this that individual substance is conflated with divine essence: 'in our way of speaking about it, the divine essence is not an individual substance since we attribute it to many persons'.[44] Nonetheless, Thomas does not reject Richard's definition. He recognizes that it is a good expression of what it means to be a 'person' in God; but it has only marginal interest for him.[45] The reason for this is clear from Bonaventure's observation that Boethius' definition fits both God and creatures, whereas Richard's only applies to God. If one takes Richard's definition as the basis of one's reflection, one will deprive oneself of the power of the analogy: the word 'person' no longer indicates the knot between human and angelic persons and the divine persons, and so one's grasp of the persons in God is very much loosened. Boethius' definition has to its credit that it does not specify what the principle of distinction in a person is. Since it supplies an 'analogical concept', it leaves the word open to the diverse attributions from which Trinitarian theology, angelology, and anthropology can all benefit in their diverse ways.[46]

3. CORRELATIONS IN THE GREEK AND LATIN TERMINOLOGY

Boethius' contribution does not end with his well-known definition of the person. He also nailed down for posterity a series of correlations between Greek and Latin Trinitarian terminology, 'not without some artificiality and a certain inflexibility which does not facilitate the interpretation of Conciliar texts'.[47] The discussion of these correlations has an extraordinary position in

---

[41] *ST* I, q. 29, a. 3, ad 4.   [42] *De potentia*, q. 9, a. 3, ad 2.
[43] Cf. *ST* I, q. 29, a. 3, ad 4.   [44] *De potentia*, q. 9, a. 2, ad 12.
[45] Thomas does not discuss Richard's definition within the main body of his arguments, but it does appear in the responses to objections, following upon expositions which have centred on the Boethian definition: I *Sent.* d. 25, q. 1, a. 1, ad 8; *De potentia*, q. 9, a. 2, ad 12; *ST* I, q. 29, a. 3, ad 4.
[46] I *Sent.* d. 25, q. 1, a. 2, ad 5.   [47] H. Dondaine, *La Trinité*, vol. 1, p. 180.

thirteenth-century Trinitarian texts.[48] This is a witness to the remarkable way in which Thomas and his contemporaries applied themselves to remaining in direct contact with the language of the ancient Councils and with the Trinitarian doctrine of the Greek Fathers. In his Commentary on the *Sentences*, Thomas devotes a strikingly complex discussion to these correlations.[49] He tries to give a little order to the catalogue of information; some of the facts came from logic, some from metaphysics, and when these issues were blurred, that often led to equivocation.

We can briefly bring to mind that the scholastic theologians knew and maintained one of the main formulas of Trinitarian orthodoxy: there are in God 'three *hypostases* and one *ousia*'.[50] Investigation of this formula brought about an examination of the language for talking about the Trinity which Boethius had passed on to them (substance, essence, subsistence, hypostasis, ousia, and so on), and of its connections with the word 'person'. The writers usually accept the following correlations: the Greek work *ousia* corresponds to the Latin term *essentia* (essence); *hypostasis* corresponds to *subsistentia* (subsistence); and *prosopon* corresponds to the Latin word *persona* (person).[51]

Thomas explains that these terms are not synonymous, and he sets himself to accounting for the correlations in a way that protects their pliability, so as to avoid rigid parallelisms. In the *Summa*, his exposition is organized around the notion of *substance*. If one considers substance in so far as it exists through itself and not in another, one speaks of *subsistence*; if one considers substance in so far as it is the subject or substrate which underlies accidents, one speaks of *hypostasis*. Since, as we have seen, the person is defined as a 'substance' (an 'individual substance of a rational nature'), it can be called both *substance* and *hypostasis*.[52]

We should point out that the word 'subsistence' does not have here the abstract meaning which it sometimes accrued in the later Thomistic tradition. The word refers to the reality itself: 'Subsistence is the same thing as the subsisting reality.'[53] Thomas preserves the usage of the Fathers and the Councils which came to him in the Latin language: the hypostasis is the subsistence (*subsistentia*).[54] So he customarily talks about 'three subsistences'

[48] See for instance the *Summa fratris Alexandri*, Book I, pars 2, inq. 2, tract. 2, sect. 1, q. 1, mm. 2–3 (ed. Quaracchi, vol. 1, nos. 395–404); Albert, I *Sent.* d. 23, aa. 4 and 7; Bonaventure, I *Sent.* d. 23, a. 1, q. 3.

[49] Thomas, I *Sent.* d. 23, q. 1, a. 1.

[50] This is the title of one of Albert's articles: I *Sent.* d. 23, a. 7.

[51] Albert, I *Sent.* d. 23, a. 4; Bonaventure, I *Sent.* d. 23, a. 1, q. 3; Thomas, I *Sent.* d. 23, q. 1, a. 1.

[52] *ST* I, q. 29, a. 2; *De potentia*, q. 9, a. 1, ad 2. Cf. I *Sent.* d. 26, q. 1, a. 1; Albert, I *Sent.* d. 23, a. 4.

[53] *ST* III, q. 2, a. 3.

[54] Thomas is using the Latin text of the Acts of Ephesus, Chalcedon, and Constantinople II, which usually translates the word 'hypostasis' by the Latin term 'subsistentia': see for instance *ST* III, q. 2, a. 1, ad 1; *ST* III, q. 2, a. 3; *ST* III, q. 2, a. 6; etc.

in God when he speaks of the three hypostases or the three persons. Without rejecting this expression, he also explains that Richard of Saint Victor's terminology posits three 'existences' (*existentiae*) in the Triune God,[55] since, properly speaking, there is nothing that could stand underneath within God; but this is not his own habitual way of speaking.[56]

The correlation of *hypostasis* and *person* does not create any problem: 'In the same way that we [the Latins] say three *persons*, the Greeks say three *hypostases*.'[57] There is nonetheless a fine shade of difference between them. For Thomas, the term *hypostasis* properly means the whole individual in the genus of the substance, and not just the persons: hypostasis identifies the primary substance. For instance, a horse or a dog is just as much an hypostasis as a human being. He considers that it is this usage, rather than the strict meaning of the word, which led the Greek theological terminology to reserve the word *hypostasis* for substances of a rational nature, that is, for persons.[58]

The main hazard for the Latin terminology is its close etymological connection between the two words *substance* and *hypostasis*, for both suggest 'something which stands underneath'. And, within the healthiest tradition, Christians recognize one single 'substance' but three 'hypostases' in God; clearly, the two words cannot have the same meaning in Trinitarian theology. Thomas writes that:

Just as we [Latins] speak in the plural of three 'persons' and three 'subsistences', so the Greeks speak of three 'hypostases'. But the word substance [*substantia*] which properly speaking corresponds in meaning to 'hypostasis' is equivocal in Latin, since it refers sometimes to 'essence' and sometimes to 'hypostasis'. It was to avoid this opportunity for error that they preferred to translate 'hypostasis' by 'subsistence' rather than by 'substance'.[59]

This analysis is reminiscent of the fourth-century Trinitarian controversy. Because the Arians liked it, it took a long and laborious debate before the expression *three hypostases* was imposed. Since the recognition of the three hypostases must not imply a diminution of the consubstantiality of Father, Son, and Holy Spirit, professing three hypostases required Neo-Nicene orthodoxy to make a clear distinction between *hypostasis* and *ousia*. And, in Latin, *ousia* was often translated by the term *substantia* (or *essentia*). Thus, despite the literal correspondence of the words *substantia* and *hypostasis*, Latin Trinitarian theology had to find another word with which to translate

---

[55] *ST* I, q. 29, a. 2, ad 2; *De potentia*, q. 9, a. 2, ad 8.
[56] I *Sent*. d. 23, q. 1, a. 2, ad 3; I *Sent*. d. 34, q. 1, a. 1. The word 'subsistentia' literally means a reality which 'stands beneath'.
[57] *ST* I, q. 30, a. 1, ad 1.   [58] *ST* I, q. 29, a. 2, ad 1.
[59] *ST* I, q. 29, a. 2, ad 2; cf. q. 30, a. 1, ad 1.

hypostasis: they chose *subsistentia*. St Thomas was aware of this patristic debate, and of the related translation problems, particularly through the discussions of the subject in Augustine and Jerome.[60]

4. SUBSISTENT RELATIONS

St Thomas has shown what a *person* is, and, when he explained the parallels in the Greek theological terminology, he established that the name is sovereignly fitting to God. When he drew on the rules of analogy, he pin-pointed the fact that the person exists in God in a different way from in creatures. Faith recognizes three 'distinct subsistents' in the unity of the divine substance: it was precisely in order to articulate this that the Church called on the words *person* and *hypostasis*. What becomes of our notion of *person*, and what is the meaning of the term when it is applied to God? Here one is touching on the mystery of the irreducible features of the person at the heart of the Trinity (the *individual* of Boethius' definition), or the incommunicable properties (Richard of Saint-Victor's *incommunicable existence*).

This question gives rise to the theory of the 'subsistent relation'. Using his preliminary analysis of relation, Thomas makes 'subsistent relations' the synthesizing agents in his speculative Trinitarian theology. In the *Summa Theologiae*, the heart of the synthesis emerges in question 29, the investigation of the meaning of the word *person*. The discussion is pursued later on in the treatise, with the comparison of person, essence, and relations (qq. 39–40).

The question is tackled from the perspective of language: What does the word 'person' signify when it is applied to God? This is not just a verbal matter, because in trying to see where our doctrinal language points us, the theologian is actually considering the divine reality. What does it mean for Father, Son, Spirit to be the distinct and incommunicable reality which we call '*person*'? The scholastics have a common formula for putting this question: Does the word 'person' indicate the substance or the relation, the essence or the distinctive character of each of the Three? Every time he examines this question, Thomas begins by discussing the different current opinions about it: 'One finds multiple responses in the masters.'[61] The opinions are almost more numerous than the theologians pronouncing them. For instance, St Albert described no fewer than seven different verdicts in the masters,

[60] One can see the file on this material put together by Peter Lombard in his *Sentences*, bk. I, dist. 23–26. St Thomas connects his own thinking on the translation of *hypostasis* to Jerome (I *Sent.* d. 26, q. 1, a. 1, ad 1; *ST* I, q. 29, a. 2, ad 3).
[61] Thomas, I *Sent.* d. 23, q. 1, a. 3.

before giving the eighth, which he adopts![62] For Thomas the discussion of the sources is restricted to the listing of the three most important opinions. We will briefly look at them, in the same order as we find them in the *Summa*.[63]

Thomas begins by marking his distance from an essentialist conception of *person* for which, properly understood, it purely and simply signifies the divine substance, just as the word *God* does. In that case, the use of the term 'persons', in the plural, to indicate the distinct Three would be merely an accommodation to our way of speaking, a verbal convention based on the Church using it in the ancient Councils. If we examine this opinion, we can see the problem arises for those who take Augustine too literally (Peter Lombard is no exception to this).[64] For St Augustine, the term *person* is effectively, in and of itself, an absolute name: 'in this Trinity, when we speak of the person of the Father, ... we mean nothing other than the substance of the Father. ... Person is an absolute term [*ad se dicitur*] and not a term which is relative to the Son or the Holy Spirit, like absolute terms such as: God, great, good, just, and other qualitatives of that kind.'[65] It is clear that Augustine's analysis ultimately fails, for he has to say that *person* means the substance, and cannot genuinely refer to the distinct Three: 'If one asks oneself, three whats? Human language is too bare so say. But one can reply: three persons, less in order to say what is there than in order not to be reduced to silence.'[66] Thomas considers that this solution is completely unsatisfactory. If one accepts that it is only by linguistic convention or because of historical accident that the word *person* is used to refer to the distinct Three (the 'relatives'), then, when it introduced this word to articulate the Trinitarian faith, the Church exposed itself to even more serious error than the heresies it was dealing with at the time.[67]

Other theologians had maintained that the word *person* directly refers to the divine essence, and only indirectly indicates the relation: it would thus be a substantial name with the connotation of, or 'co-signifying' a relation. This opinion, advanced by Simon of Tournai,[68] leaves the problem exactly where it

---

[62] Albert, I *Sent.* d. 23, q. 1, a. 2. St Thomas evidently utilized the research assembled by Albert, and Bonaventure: one often finds the listed opinions in his writings, couched in very similar phraseology.

[63] *ST* I, q. 29, a. 4. These discussions are nearly all paralleled in the Commentary on the *Sentences* (I *Sent.* d. 23, q. 1, a. 3) and in the Disputed Questions *De potentia* (q. 9, a. 4). For a historical analysis, see M. Bergeron, 'La structure du concept latin de personne', *Études d'histoire littéraire et doctrinale du XIIIᵉ siècle*, Second series, Paris and Ottawa, 1932, pp. 121–161.

[64] Thomas (*De potentia*, q. 9, a. 4) explicitly attributed this opinion to Peter Lombard (*Sentences*, Book I, dist. 25).

[65] Augustine, *De Trinitate* VII.VI.11.

[66] Augustine, *De Trinitate* V.IX.10; cf. *De Trinitate* VII.VI.11.

[67] *ST* I, q. 29, a. 4; *De potentia*, q. 9, a. 4.

[68] Simon of Tournai, *Disputatio* 83, q. 1 (ed. J. Warichez, *Les Disputationes de Simon de Tournai*, Namur, 1932, p. 241). Cf. M. Schmaus, 'Die Texte der Trinitätslehre in den Sententiae des Simon von Tournai', *RTAM* 4 (1932), 62–63.

was, because it puts the main stress on the divine substance or essence which is common to the Three. It is hard to see how one can justify the use of 'persons' in the plural on this basis. Conversely, a third opinion holds that *person* refers primarily to the relation, and only in the second place to the divine essence. Albert reports that this was the approach suggested by William of Auxerre.[69] But William of Auxerre's solution is shaky. It doubtless disengages *person* from the essentialist meaning it took on in the Augustinian tradition, but only by an argument which has a utilitarian flavour: if that is what *persona* means, it cannot be used without making mistakes.[70] And if, Thomas adds, person primarily means a relation, an individual person can hardly be described as being an 'in itself' or a 'for itself'.

On this question, Albert and Bonaventure took the middle ground, holding that person simultaneously means substance and relative property. Bonaventure explains that the name *person* is aiming at the essence, plus the relation: this is how our minds can grasp the hypostasis which is distinct through a property.[71] Albert's solution is similar to Bonaventure's: he prudently explains that, in God, the word *person* refers to the essence or substance and additionally to the singular property, in such a way that once we add the relative property to the substance, 'person' includes both.[72]

Thomas is more resolute in seizing on the direction pointed out by William: those who go this way 'are closer to the truth'.[73] He thought the middle way tried out by Albert and Bonaventure was unsatisfactory because it divided the meaning of person or conceived it as a kind of specification or addition. And, by definition, 'person' means that which is distinct in an individual nature, including its individuating principles. 'Hence "person" in human nature refers to *this* flesh, *these* bones and *this* soul which are the sources of a human being's individuality.'[74] Consequently, when we attribute the name *person* to God it must also express, in the fullest sense of the term, that which entails distinction amongst the divine persons. This is where the preparatory study of relation enters the question. 'Relation does not exist in God like an accident inheres in a subject: it is the divine essence itself, it is thus subsistent just as the divine essence is.' On this basis, Thomas explains that,

The 'divine Person' means relation as something subsisting (*relatio ut subsistens*). Otherwise put, it means the relation by way of that substance which is the subsistent hypostasis in the divine nature (*relatio per modum substantiae quae est hypostasis*

---

[69] Albert, I *Sent.* d. 23, a. 2 (this is the sixth opinion Albert lists).

[70] William of Auxerre, *Summa aurea* I, tr. 6, ch. 3 (ed. J. Ribaillier, Paris and Grottaferrata, 1980, vol. 1, pp. 84–90).

[71] Bonaventure, I *Sent.* d. 25, a. 1, q. 1. One notices that Bonaventure is guided by the Masters' definition of the person, not that of Boethius.

[72] Albert, I *Sent.* d. 23, a. 2.   [73] *ST* I, q. 29, a. 4.   [74] *ST* I, q. 29, a. 4.

subsistens in natura divina); though that which subsists in the divine nature is nothing other than the divine nature.[75]

One can very easily see the originality of Thomas' thought on this, and the advance which it marks by comparison to Bonaventure or Albert. His doctrine of the person rests on his analysis of relation. We have already seen that, as far as its proper notion or *ratio* is concerned, relation consists in a pure reference to another (a connection of origin) but in its own being it is purely and simply identical with the existence of the divine essence.[76] This is worked out in such a way that, in God, the principle of distinction (the relation) is no different from the reality thus distinguished (the person).[77] It is no longer seen as an 'addition', as in the previous explanations, but rather as an 'integration', so to speak, since what is involved is a divine relation under the aspects of its personal distinction and essence: this is, therefore, what we mean by the word *person* in God. To clarify this, and ensure that there is no ambiguity here, this is not a matter of a relation considered simply according to its *ratio* (the pure connection) to the exclusion of its being; as has been discussed earlier, it is very much relation taken in its integral status in God. In this way, the divine person *is* the relation in so far as it is a *subsisting* relation; it is the relation of origin in God, enjoying the prerogatives of the absolute in the mode of the hypostatic incommunicability, and it is this subsisting relation which is signified by the word *person*. It is thus in an entirely fitting way, and not just by linguistic convention, that we confess Father, Son, and Holy Spirit as distinct persons in God.

Yet person does not simply mean relation as relationality, but relation as *subsistence*. The words *relation* and *person* continue to signify in their own distinct modes. Throughout his discussion, Thomas ceaselessly pays attention to our *language*, since this language expresses the notions and concepts through which we grasp the realities in question. When we say that the Father is a person, we do not signify the Father as one would a relation, but in the style due to a subsistent. In the same way that the notion of relation is conceptually distinct from that of person, their mode of referring also differs: if you pay attention to how our language works, what *relation* naturally signifies is a form, a reference to another; whereas what *person* naturally signifies is a concrete subject, a subsistent.[78] The word *person* 'thus does not signify relation after the manner of relation, but after the manner of the substance which is the hypostasis'.[79] Relation derives this capacity to be referred to hypostatically

[75] *ST* I, q. 29, a. 4. This response is already clear in the Commentary on the *Sentences*: 'I thus affirm that "person" in God means a relation in the mode of substance . . . , not the substance which is the essence but the substance qua the supposit possessing the essence' (I *Sent.* d. 23, q. 1, a. 3).
[76] *ST* I, q. 28, a. 2; see above, Chapter 5.   [77] *De potentia*, q. 9, a. 4, ad 16.
[78] *ST* I, q. 40, a. 2.   [79] *ST* I, q. 29, a. 4, ad 1; cf. I *Sent.* d. 26, q. 1, a. 1, ad 5.

from its being situated in God: it perfectly preserves its formality of 'relation to another' (relation of origin) and simultaneously really identifies itself *existentially* with the divine subsistent essence.[80]

Having set out the heart of his own position, Thomas can draw out the truth in the other responses to the question. The first opinion is right to say that it belongs to Christianity to have disengaged the profound significance of the *person*, as happened during its confrontation with Arianism and Sabellianism, for the authentic meaning of this word 'was not grasped before the heretics abused it'. The defence of the faith was therefore the occasion for the discovery of the Trinitarian meaning of the word 'person'. This explanation involves a particular understanding of the theologian's vocation. Without reducing it to the historical circumstances which produced it, he has communicated the truth of the dogmatic expression put forward by the Spirit-led Church to express its faith. If the name *person* is applied to the Father, the Son, and the Holy Spirit, it is not just a matter of convention, however venerable, but because of what this term means.

Likewise, the second opinion is correct to say that in a certain way 'person' signifies essence plus relation, so long as one sees that the essence is really identical to the hypostasis and that the axes of distinction amongst the hypostases are their relations. It is also true that, as the third solution had it, the name *person* signifies the relation directly and the essence indirectly, on condition that one grasps that this is a matter of signifying 'in the mode of an hypostasis', as Thomas put it in his own explanation.[81] One can then see what makes Thomas' explanation different from this third opinion. Properly speaking, *person* does not mean relation *first* and essence *afterwards* but rather, relation as subsisting. It is not an addition to or juxtaposition of relation with essence, but their integration or identity, thanks to a precise idea of what relation is. It is this integrative approach which enables Thomas to draw together all the other patristic and medieval contributions to the subject.

Thomas restricts his discovery of 'person-relation' to the divine persons. He observes that 'it is one thing to research the meaning of person in general, and another to study the meaning of the *divine person*'.[82] Human beings are very much persons but they are not subsistent relations! Because of the analogical character of the name *person*, it is necessary to recognize, in the first place, a *common* notion of person which applies analogically to God, human beings and angels, and, in the second place, a *formal* notion of person which comes

[80] *ST* I, q. 28, a. 2.   [81] *ST* I, q. 29, a. 4.
[82] Ibid., cf. *De potentia*, q. 9, a. 4. The advantage of Boethius' definition is precisely that of offering a 'common' meaning for person, whereas Richard of Saint-Victor's definition, although it is valuable in other respects, is restricted to the divine person.

back to God alone, along with another notion of persons which is exclusively attached to creatures. The common notion had been expressed in Boethius' definition, and Thomas summarizes it like this: in all these cases, a person is 'a distinct subsistent in an intellectual nature'.[83] To be able then to carve out a more precise notion of person as it belongs to God and as it does to human beings, it is necessary to determine the mode of individuation appropriate to it. That is, it is necessary to bring into the discussion the individuating principles which account for the person's incommunicability, whether it is human or divine. If one considers the human person by itself, its 'formal meaning' is specified by the human principle of individuation, that is, the union of this soul and that body, according to the Aristotelian conception of individuation through matter. If one considers the Triune God, the 'formal meaning' of the word *person* is the 'distinct subsistent in the divine nature', that is, a 'relation by way of subsistence' or in other words, 'the relation by way of substance... qua hypostasis'.[84]

So one must not conflate Boethius' common and analogical definition with the 'formal' signification of person in God (the person as subsisting relation). St Thomas does not bring relation either into the common definition of the person or into the particular signification of the human person: 'Even though relation is contained in the meaning of the divine person, it is not like this for the meaning of person in angels or the meaning of the human person.'[85] This means in practice that 'in creatures the distinction of *supposits* does not come back to relations, but to essential principles; because in creatures, relations are not subsistent'.[86] The relational understanding of person is set aside for the Trinity, because of the status which relation has in God, that is, because only in God are there 'subsistent relations'.[87]

This theory of subsistent relation provides the key to Thomas' theological understanding of the mystery of the divine tri-personhood. This is his means of disclosing the plurality of persons, their genuine alterity, the mystery of 'number' in God, the identity of relation and person with the divine essence, and the distinction and the actual constitution of the persons through their relations. Without going into every shade of meaning or exhibiting a complete portrait of the different aspects of this teaching, one must at least indicate them, so that we can estimate the extent of the implications of this discovery.

---

[83] St Thomas had already taken on this definition when he wrote the Commentary on the *Sentences*; see for instance I *Sent.* d. 23, q. 1, a. 4: 'persona dicit aliquid distinctum subsistens in natura intellectuali'.

[84] *De potentia*, q. 9, a. 4.   [85] *ST* I, q. 29, a. 4, ad 4.

[86] *ST* I, q. 39, a. 1, ad 1.   [87] Ibid.

5. RELATION THE HEART OF TRINITARIAN THEOLOGY

Once we have got hold of the divine person as a 'subsistent relation' Thomas follows up his meditation by systematically comparing persons and relations. This thorough analysis is carried out in question 40 of the *Summa*, in the section devoted to comparing the persons with what we conceive as the other aspects of the Trinitarian mystery, so far as we can grasp it. This question deals with 'The most arduous problems in Latin Trinitarian theology'.[88] Here the points of divergence between the schools are especially noticeable. After the end of the thirteenth century, the scholastics abandoned themselves to 'interminable disputes' on these topics.[89] St Thomas is more restrained but, despite this self-denying ordinance, expresses ideas which can doubtless count amongst the most difficult in the whole of his theology. Their degree of subtlety discourages readers from working them out. It is certainly not through question 40 that one should commence one's study of the Trinitarian treatise in the *Summa*. But, for all its complexity, we would not want to give up on saying something about this question, however briefly, because it shows the unique approach of Thomas' Trinitarian theology.

Set out in four stages, it shows that the personal relations are identical to the persons themselves, that they distinguish the persons, and, what goes deeper, that they constitute these persons in such a way that if we mentally abstract from the relations, we cease to be able to grasp the divine persons: the person cannot be known independently of the relative property which constitutes it as such. To understand this thesis properly, one most observe that the investigation does not touch only on the reality of the three persons in themselves in their divine transcendence, but also bears on the persons *in so far as these persons are apprehended by our minds*, and designated by us in the language of faith.[90] In the precise meaning of the term, this is a theological exercise.

St Thomas begins by showing that, in God, the relation *is* the person. When he explained that a person is a subsisting relation, he was envisaging the question from the aspect of the persons. Now he is looking at it from the aspect of the relations, so as to bring out the same conclusion. To this end, he reconfigures Gilbert de la Porrée's view of relation as 'positioned from outside' and also corrects Praepositinus of Cremona, who had reduced relative properties to 'ways of speaking'.[91] He reminds us that 'in so far as it is a divine

---

[88] H. Dondaine, *La Trinité*, vol. 2, p. 349.

[89] Ibid.   [90] See above, ch. 2, n. 62, on 'notions'.

[91] On Praepositinus, see above, Chapter 2, in our discussion of notions; on Gilbert of Poitiers, see above, in Chapter 5, 'The Being of Divine Relations'.

reality, relation is the essence itself'. This is what the discussions of the being of relations showed; relation formally consists in a connection to another, and its being is identical to that of the divine essence.[92] The person is likewise not 'something other' than the essence (each person *is* God). For these reasons, 'the relation is identical to the person'.[93] This is a direct consequence of the theory of subsistent relations.

Because of this theory of subsistent relations, Thomas can stake two claims on behalf of the divine simplicity. The first is that all the divine attributes are really identical to the very essence of God. Since there does not exist within God a collocation of this, that and the other, there is no genuine difference between God's *goodness*, his *power*, and his *essence*. The second is that what we mean by the concrete names is not really different from what we signify by the abstract names: *God* is his *deity*. Thus, the relative properties are really identical to the divine person, not only because everything we recognize in God is the divine essence itself,[94] but also because what we concretely signify, the 'person', in God is really identical to what we speak of abstractly ('properties', 'relation'). Another way of putting it is that *relative property* and *person* designate the *same* reality, even though their mode of signifying it differs. In the final analysis, this identity of relative property and person rests on the nature of a divine relation, and, as the study of relation in question 28 showed, divine relations formally possess the being of the divine essence. This applies in full to the three personal relations, that is, to the three relative properties which constitute the persons: paternity, filiation, and procession. These relations or relative properties 'are the subsisting persons themselves': paternity is the Father himself, filiation is the Son, and 'procession' is the Holy Spirit.[95]

In the second stage, which gives us one of the governing ideas of his Trinitarian theory, Thomas explains that the distinction and constitution of the persons *comes down to relation*. We are here in the order of the Trinitarian mystery, such as we can grapple with it. In God, the relations are persons: there is no other reality than that of the three persons, the Father, the Son, and the Holy Spirit. But how to grasp the distinction of these persons, so far as it

---

[92] *ST* I, q. 28, a. 2; see above, Chapter 5, 'The Being of Divine Relations'.

[93] *ST* I, q. 40, a. 1; cf. I *Sent.* d. 33, q. 1, a. 2.

[94] *ST* I, q. 40, a. 1, ad 1. It is by means of this rule of the real identity of the divine attributes and essence that Thomas shows that the other relations, which are not 'personal subsistent relations' are identical to the divine essence and to the persons. This is applied first to the real relation of 'spiration' which the Father and Son have with the Holy Spirit; the relation of spiration is really identical to the persons of the Father and the Son. This can then be applied to the other relations (for instance, the mutual knowledge of the three persons), which are not the sources of personal distinction in God.

[95] *ST* I, q. 40, a. 1, ad 1.

can be achieved at all? This point is so important in Thomas' eyes that he deals with it in all of his great synthesizing works and even in his biblical commentaries.[96] What is at stake for him is nothing less than the possibility of giving an account of the real plurality of persons which are one single God, according to the teaching of Scripture as received within the Church.

We touched on this a long way back, when we were speaking of the processions: the essential attributes are incapable of giving an account of personal distinction in God. Because they are essential attributes, understanding and will cannot create such a distinction.[97] St Thomas rigorously forbids us to conceive the personal plurality as if it were a derivative of the divine essence: this leads to Sabellianism. Neither can the distinction result from the divine attributes which the Son receives in his begetting and those the Holy Spirit receives through his procession, for each receives divinity in its fullness. The Three have each the same divine nature in all its plenitude.

This is where the theological schools reach their crossways. For one large theological current, it is the *origin* of the persons which accounts for their distinctness, that is, the *generation* of the Son and the *procession* of the Holy Spirit: the Son is *begotten*, the Holy Spirit *proceeds* (from Father and Son)—so that is what constitutes the principle of personal distinction in God: the Father is distinguished from the Son as his *begetter*, the Son is distinguished from the Father because he *is begotten* by the Father, and the Holy Spirit is distinct from Father and Son in that he *proceeds* from them. In that case, relation will not be presented as the principle of the distinctness, but rather as a *result* of the origin which it expresses. From Thomas' perspective, this opinion considers relation in the light of its being founded in action and thus as resulting from this action. This thesis could invoke the authority of Richard of Saint-Victor, who had insisted that, 'in God, it is solely in origin that one should seek the distinction of the persons or existents'.[98] To a great extent, Bonaventure sets the stamp of his approval upon this theory. For the Franciscan master, the property which distinguishes the persons implies origin *and* relation, but the priority must be given to origin (generation and procession).[99] If one enquires into the source of the personal distinctions, one would then have to reconsider the origins, looking to the generation of the Son and the procession of the Holy Spirit.

---

[96] See *In Ioan.* 15.26 (nos. 2063–2064); 16.14–15 (nos. 2110–2115).

[97] See above, in Chapter 4, 'The Order of the Trinitarian Processions'.

[98] Richard of Saint-Victor, *De Trinitate* IV.XV (SC 63, pp. 260–261). According to St Thomas, Richard's thesis leads to holding that the persons are distinguished by origin, not by relations (cf. *De potentia*, q. 8, a. 3, arg. 13).

[99] Bonaventure, I *Sent.* d. 26, a. un., q. 3. See A. Stohr, *Die Trinitätslehre des heiligen Bonaventura*, Münster, 1923, pp. 114–120.

St Thomas finds this response unsatisfactory or that it goes too fast: 'it cannot be held'.[100] In the world as we know it, when two realities are distinct, they are distinguished not only by the respective processes of their coming into being, but by their own, idiosyncratic properties.[101] What makes for the differences between a cow and a horse is the nature or 'specific form' of a cow or a horse; what makes two colts out of the same mare different is the 'matter' into which the horse's nature is concretely diversified, and this is how the two colts are distinct individuals.[102] Whatever the stretch between these examples and the divine transcendence, they show that plurality is grounded in a property which is internal to the distinct individuals. And, with God, the plurality consists neither in matter, since the divine persons are non-material, nor in the specific nature, since the three persons are the same God, nor in a difference between the nature and the concrete subject in possession of this nature, since each person is the divine nature.

Thomas goes on from here to take a look at what the words 'origin' and 'relation' reflect about their objects. Origin signifies the kind of act that is a process moving from a principle to an end-result. And so generation means an action which comes out of the Father and comes to completion in the Son: within the exact inflection of its meaning, generation picks out the operation which, so to say, 'lands up' in the distinct existence of the Son; it does not indicate what characterizes the Son as such, it intends the operation that 'results' in him. Even if one conceives it as entailing a relation, origin is not enough formally to distinguish and to constitute the Father and the Son.[103] One still needs to show what precisely in the Father distinguishes him from the Son, and what it is about the Son that makes him distinct from the Father. And relation does this because it really means an intrinsic character of a subject, like a form: filiation is a property, one exclusively belonging to the Son. So it is filiation, rather than generation, which can distinguish and constitute the Son's personality.[104] Thomas' analysis plumbs everything there is to relation: relation then distinguishes and constitutes the person in that relation is the person himself. One can see elsewhere how Thomas gives a lot of thought to the relations signified in the divine persons' names, like Father, Word, Love, so as to show that these relation-names intend the subsisting person.

Thus, so as we can grasp the Triune mystery, and if we pay attention to our own language, 'origin' means a process: generation means the 'way' (*via*) of an action which goes from the Father to the Son; 'birth' signifies the way into

---

[100] *ST* I, q. 40, a. 2.   [101] Ibid.
[102] Cf. *SCG* IV, ch. 24 (no. 3615).   [103] *De potentia*, q. 8, a. 3.
[104] *ST* I, q. 40. a. 2; see also I *Sent.* d. 26, q. 2; *De potentia*, q. 8, a. 3; *Quodlibet* IV, q. 4, a. 2.

the constitution of the Son as person, but it does not signify that which
distinguishes and constitutes the Son in himself. 'The hypostasis of the Son
must be formally constituted and distinguished by Filiation and not by its
origin [birth, begetting] ... since the origin signifies something not as yet
subsistent in the nature but as tending toward it.'[105] Properly speaking, the
distinction and the 'constitution' of the divine persons comes down to
relations, that is, to the three relative properties: paternity, filiation, procession. 'It is thus better to say that the persons or hypostases are distinguished
by relations rather than by origin. For, although they are distinguished in both
ways, nevertheless in our mode of understanding they are distinguished
mainly and primarily by relations.'[106]

To understand why relation is given this role, we have to go back once again
to the preliminary investigation of relation. When he takes the two aspects of
relation into account (reference to another and being of the divine essence),
St Thomas shows that relation distinguishes the persons: paternity is not
filiation, for these two real relations are mutually opposed. And if one takes a
good look at relations within the divinity, one finds that relation exists here as
the divine essence, it subsists, thus constituting the persons: paternity is the
subsisting of the Father, filiation is the Son, the property of procession is
the Holy Spirit himself.[107] Thomas turns to relation, as that which *distinguishes* the persons and *constitutes* them as such. If relation 'constitutes' the
persons, it is because it is endowed with the divine being. And it has this
divine being not only because it is necessary to recognize that everything
which is in God is identical with the divine being itself, but also because this
belongs to relation in virtue of its formality as a divine relation. It is thus
relation which enables one to understand personhood in God. In reference to
the Son, Thomas explains that: 'it is through his relation that the Son is a
subsisting person, for his relation is his characteristic personhood'.[108]

Cajetan has accurately remarked in this context that, it is one thing to say
that relation has this prerogative to the extent that it is otherwise identical to
the divine essence; and another thing to say that relation has this prerogative
because it is formally identical to the divine essence. In the debates amongst
the schools,[109] in which the Thomists themselves were divided, Cajetan seems

[105] *De potentia*, q. 8, a. 3. Cf. *ST* I, q. 40, a. 2.
[106] *ST* I, q. 40, a. 2.   [107] Cf. *De potentia*, q. 10, a. 3.
[108] I *Sent.* d. 19, q. 3, a. 2, ad 1: *sua enim relatio est sua personalitas.*
[109] There were heated controversies about this in the fourteenth century, particularly
between Thomists and Scotists. Using Bonaventure as his authority, Duns Scotus was in fact
tempted to conceive the constitution of a divine person, not as a relation but rather as an
absolute reality; see especially Scotus' *Lectura* on I *Sent.* d. 26, q. 1 (*Opera omnia*, vol. 17, Vatican
City, 1966, pp. 328–337); cf. F. Wetter, *Die Trinitätslehre des Johannes Duns Scotus*, Münster,
1967, pp. 283–315.

to us to have grasped Thomas' thesis which he clarifies by interpreting it in this way: 'Relation constitutes the person through its own condition as relation'[110]; and again, 'relation constitutes the person in this way alone: by positing itself, since it is the person as such'.[111]

St Thomas presents his famous formula for this by way of an extension to this discussion: 'It is because he is the Father that the Father engenders' (*quia Pater est, generat*).[112] Bonaventure, because he thinks that it is origin which makes for the constitution of the divine person, affirms that the Father is Father *because he engenders*.[113] The Dominican master adamantly asserts the reverse: if one considers the property of the Father not just in terms of relation to another, but on the basis that his property constitutes his personality (by being identical to the divine substance paternity is subsistent being itself), then one has to acknowledge that the Father is Father through his paternity. It is thus *as* constituted by his relative property that the Father exercises his own particular actions, the chief of which is generation. It is because he is God the Father, in virtue of his relative property of paternity, that the Father engenders the Son. In this sense, the relative property of the Father is 'presupposed' in all that he does as person.

This question may seem over subtle, but its outcome is not trivial. What Thomas is rejecting is the idea that the person who exercises an action can be conceived extra-relationally, independently of his constitution as person through his relative property. Otherwise put, the role of relations is not restricted to putting the persons on show. The relative properties are not adventitiously added on to persons who have already been constituted in some other way. We can express it as St Albert does: one cannot think a distinct person other than by grasping his relative property.[114] Since the actions are not performed by the divine essence but rather by the persons as such (it is the *person* of the Father which engenders), the Father cannot be grasped as an acting subject outside his relative property of paternity. This is why, in the order of our understanding of the mystery, getting hold of

[110] Cajetan, In I^{am}, q. 40, a. 4 (Leon. ed., vol. 4, p. 419, nos. 6 and 8). The debate largely bore on the issue of how to interpret the *Summa Theologiae* and the *De potentia* (q. 8, a. 3, ad 7) in relation to one another. See P. Vanier, *Théologie trinitaire chez Thomas d'Aquin*, Montreal and Paris, 1953, pp. 77–80; id., 'La relation trinitaire dans la Somme théologique de St Thomas d'Aquin', *Sciences ecclésiastiques* 1 (1948), 143–159, cf. 156–159.

[111] Cajetan, ibid. (no. 10); see our article, 'Essentialisme ou personnalisme dans le traité de Dieu chez St Thomas d'Aquin?', *RT* 98 (1998), p. 36; *Trinity in Aquinas*, pp. 205–206.

[112] *ST* I, q. 40, a. 4; cf. I *Sent.* d. 27, q. 1, a. 2; *De potentia*, q. 10, a. 3. This is also the teaching of Albert the Great, who Thomas follows in this. Cf. Albert, I *Sent.* d. 27, a. 2; *Super Dion. de div. nom.*, ch. 2, no. 26 (ed. Colon., vol. 37/1, p. 60).

[113] Bonaventure, I *Sent.*, d. 27, p. 1, a. un., q. 2.

[114] Albert, *Super Dion. de div. nom.*, ch. 2, no. 25 (ed. Colon., vol. 37/1, p. 60).

paternity, the property of the Father, comes before grasping the personal action performed by the Father. Otherwise, one would have conceive the Father independently of his relative property or anteriorly to this relative property. Attached to his doctrine of relation, St Thomas shows that this is not possible, because it boils down to conceiving the Father in some way as a pre-relational divine being. He does not conceive the Father as the 'absolute person of God'[115] but rather conceives the one who is the Father *through his paternity*.

For the same reason, if we prescind from the relations which are the three personal properties (paternity, filiation, procession), then the divine persons evaporate from our thought.[116] Without an understanding of the relations, one can still conceive the divine essence; this is why believing Jews or non-Christians who recognize the existence of God understand God as a being who exists or subsists, and also perceive his essential attributes (wisdom, power, etc.). If we abstract from the relations, then within our minds at least, the tri-personhood of God vanishes. Without the relative properties of paternity, filiation, and procession, it becomes impossible to conceive the divine persons, since it is these relative properties which distinguish and constitute the persons. The reason which Thomas gives for this goes back to one of Albert's formulae. There is not, on the one hand, person, and on the other hand, relation, but 'the relations bear their supposits within themselves'.[117]

The meaning of this reasoning must be understood properly. It is not a matter of putting the Trinitarian faith, so to speak, into parentheses, but rather of authenticating the depth at which the person in God is attached to relation. Thomas' reflection manifests the fact that our grasp of the divine persons is totally bound up with the relations. And when one considers relation in a divine condition properly, such as Christian theology recognizes it to be (according to its two aspects: relation to another and the being of the divine essence), then if we mentally suppress the relations, the whole divine reality vanishes within our minds. There will remain neither the persons, since they are constituted by the relations, nor the essence, since relation is formally identical to the divine essence; nor will hypostasis remain, nor even

---

[115] The expression is used by W. Kasper, whose position borders on the one Thomas is challenging: see Walter Kasper, *The God of Jesus Christ*, trans. Matthew J. O'Connell, London, 1983, p. 298.

[116] *ST* I, q. 40, a. 3; cf. I *Sent.* d. 26, q. 1, a. 2; *De potentia*, q. 8, a. 4.

[117] Thomas, *ST* I, q. 40, a. 3; Albert, *Super Dion. de div. nom.*, ch. 2, nos. 25–26 (ed. Colon., vol. 37/1, p. 60); Albert, I *Sent.* d. 28, a. 4, ad 5 ('I am obdurate!', Albert explains in the main body of his reply: without the relational property, we cannot conceive the divine person as Trinitarian faith understands it).

the divine absolute, since that absolute is itself also identical to the subsistent relation: 'nothing remains'.[118]

One could scarcely formulate more forcibly and profoundly the central role of relations in the theological disclosure of Trinitarian faith. The doctrine of subsistent relation, which exhibits the persons and their plurality, is the soul of Thomas Aquinas' speculative Trinitarian theology.

---

[118] Thomas, I *Sent.*, d. 26, q. 1, a. 2: 'Unde, abstracta relatione proprie loquendo nihil manet, neque absolutum, neque relatum, neque hypostasis, neque essentia.' Thomas shows himself here a true disciple of his master, Albert the Great. See Albert, *Super Dion. de div. nom.*, ch. 2, no. 25 (ed. Colon., vol. 37/1, p. 60): 'et ita nihil manet'; cf. I *Sent.* d. 26, a. 5. From this viewpoint, even the divine nature or essence will disappear from our minds, because the divine essence is not determined by relations as a substance is determined by an accident.

7

Trinitarian Monotheism

When it is explained in terms of relation, the idea of personhood enables one to put forward an authentic Trinitarian monotheism. The expression 'Trinitarian monotheism' is not part of Thomas' own way of speaking,[1] but it represents what he is working toward: a plurality of persons who are one same and single God. That is why the first article of the Trinitarian treatise, studying the 'immanent' processions in order to side-step Arianism and Sabellianism, is written with this aim already in view, as are the studies of relation and person which follow it. The *Summa Theologiae* pictures this characteric feature of Christian faith from many complementary angles: as the 'plurality of persons' (q. 30), as the 'upshot' of unity and plurality in God (q. 31), and in terms of the 'comparison' of the persons with the common essence (q. 39).[2]

1. PERSONAL PLURALITY IN THE TRIUNE GOD

The first harvest yielded by the theory of subsistent relations is the disclosure of an authentic plurality and alterity within the Triune God. St Thomas begins by exhibiting the *plurality* of persons professed by Christian faith. The theme of plurality within unity has nothing to do with any kind of mathematical hypothesizing or hermetic speculation on the meaning of numbers. Thomas explains it with the utmost clarity in his Questions *De potentia*:

the plurality of persons in God is an article of faith, and natural human reason is unable to investigate and adequately understand it . . . The holy Fathers, however, were compelled to discuss this and other matters of faith by the objections raised by those who denied the faith. . . . Nor is such a discussion useless, since it enables the mind to get enough of a glimpse of the truth to steer clear of error.[3]

---

[1] The term 'monotheism' was unknown to the medievals. It only emerged in the seventeenth century (cf. R. Hülsewiesche, 'Monotheismus', in *Historiches Wörterbuch der Philosophie*, vol. 6, ed. J. Ritter and K. Gründer, Basel and Stuttgart, 1984, cols. 142–146).

[2] See the prologues to questions 29, 30, 31, and 39.

[3] *De potentia*, q. 9, a. 5; this observation echoes an analogous comment by St Albert on the same question (Albert, I *Sent.* d. 23, a. 3). See above, in Chapter 2, 'Understanding the Faith'.

Faith acknowledges that God is Father, Son, and Holy Spirit. Theology seeks to disclose the truth of this credal confession, by showing how and why we can truly say that the Father, Son, and Holy Spirit are 'three persons'. It is faith, and not a rationalization deriving simply from human reasoning, which leads to this affirmation.[4] Theological investigation envisages its task as avoiding the dead-ends of Arianism and Sabellianism, in a exercise in contemplation whose fruits are passed on to believers. Standing on this ground, the exposition puts the study of relation and person to work, with precision:

From what we have said it follows that there are several persons in God. For it was shown above that 'person' used of God means relation as a reality which subsists in the divine nature. It was also established that in God there are several real relations. Hence it follows that there are several subsisting realities in the divine nature. And this is to say that there are several persons in God.[5]

One can easily see that this response is the upshot of question 29 ('relation as a reality which subsists') and also of the ideas which Thomas drew out of the study of relation in question 28 (it gave him 'several real relations'). What interests Thomas in these discusses is *plurality*. The recognition of a plurality of real subsistent relations enables one to show how we can understand the plurality of persons in God. And, by giving us a plurality of persons, it gives thinking believers the chance of seeing why the language of faith can accurately use the word 'persons' in the plural. This plurality is not a matter of three 'absolute' entities within God (which would undermine the simplicity and unity of God, by colluding with tritheism). The issue is one of a 'plurality of relations' in God, leaving the unity of the divine nature intact, since the being of the relation is the being of the nature.[6]

As he formulates it in his synthesizing works, this response is less banal than one might be led to suspect. Albert, for instance, had been content with fine-tuning the Patristics' discourse on Trinitarian plurality, and exhibiting specimens of it,[7] reminding people that the distinction of the persons derives from the relative properties.[8] Following the lead of Alexander of Hales, whose *Summa* likewise calls on the relations,[9] and refining the traditional terminology, St Bonaventure looked to the fruitfulness in the Trinity (the fact that goodness, charity, primacy, and perfection require a plurality of persons) to bring about plurality amongst the persons.[10] But none of these authors

[4] See above, in Chapter 2, 'The Rejection of Rationalism'.
[5] *ST* I, q. 30, a. 1; cf. *De potentia*, q. 9, a. 5.   [6] *ST* I, q. 30, a. 1, ad 3.
[7] Albert, I *Sent.* d. 23, aa. 3–7.   [8] Albert, I *Sent.* d. 23, a. 8; cf. d. 2, a. 9.
[9] *Summa fratris Alexandri*, Book I (ed. Quaracchi, vol. 1, nos. 314–316).
[10] Bonaventure, I *Sent.* d. 2, art. 1, q. 2 and q. 4.

presents a response comparable to Thomas'.[11] The comparison of their
responses with the one Thomas gave in his Commentary on the *Sentences*
also shows the development of his thinking on the topic. In his 'Writing on
the *Sentences*', he explained perfectly well that the name *person* signifies
relation as subsisting, but he does not turn to the notion of relation when
he needs to account for the use of the word *persons* in the plural.[12] The notion
of subsistent relation appears in a more developed form in the *De potentia*,
where Thomas' main concern is to validate his theory of the Word.[13] The
Summa's response to this question is a benchmark.

From this same position,[14] Thomas can show why there are neither more
nor less but *three* persons in God. It can be surprising that he raises this as a
problem, since the confession of *three* persons rests on the Church's received
revelation alone. So one can ask if speculative reason is applicable here. When
he poses this question, Thomas is pursuing the same goal as in the preceding
question. It is not a matter of proving the Trinitarian faith by an intellectual
contrivance. Rather, the theologian seeks to disclose the clarity of the mystery
to the minds of believers, that is, to give an account of the Church's profession
of faith in three persons, not limiting himself to arguments from authority
found in the Councils or the Fathers, but taking the light of faith into those
avenues which reason offers us for grasping a little piece of the truth of this
profession. This question also creates the opportunity for testing the mettle of
the idea of processions, relations, and persons, letting it prove itself. We can
briefly look at these features.

(1) So far as the *persons* are concerned, it has been shown that to say 'many
persons' is the same as saying 'many subsistent relations', each of which is
really distinct. Here one takes up the bearings which q. 29 has on the person,
and also the results of q. 28, where Thomas showed that relations of origin
which are 'opposed' are really distinct from one another.

(2) On the topic of the *relations*, the real distinction is derived from
relative opposition, as q. 28 established. And there are four opposed relations;
this has also been established earlier. These relations constitute relatively
opposed pairs: paternity and filiation, and spiration and procession. As
opposed, paternity and filiation are linked to two really distinct persons;
and as subsisting, they *are* these persons: 'subsisting Fatherhood is the person
of the Father, and subsisting Sonship is the person of the Son'.[15] As we have

---

[11] Bonaventure, I *Sent.* d. 23, a. 2, qq. 1–3. There are three persons in God, but not three
substances (unless we take 'substance' to mean 'hypostasis'), nor three essences, nor three gods.
[12] Thomas, I *Sent.* d. 23, q. 1, a. 4.   [13] *De potentia*, q. 9, a. 5.
[14] *ST* I, q. 30, a. 2.   [15] Ibid.

already indicated on the topic of relative opposition, spiration is not opposed either to Fatherhood or to filiation; the fact of being Father and the fact of breathing the Spirit do not set up a differentiation of two persons within the Father! So it remains the case that, because of the relative opposition between spiration and procession, and because of the 'origin order' of Word and Love, procession is due to a third person who is really distinct from the Father and the Son: procession 'must belong to another person who is called the "Holy Spirit"'.[16] The personhood of the Father, Son, and Holy Spirit must not be sought either beyond or prior to these relations of paternity, filiation, and procession. These three relations enable one to disclose three persons, neither more nor less. In combination with the theory of subsistent relations, in a meditation which makes use of its rigorous internal coherence, relative opposition also shows the divine tri-personhood, as taught by Scripture. It is not enough to say the persons 'have' these relations. One must also acknowledge that they 'are' the relations. One can see very clearly the consequences of the theory of subsistent relations.

(3) Finally, in relation to the *processions*, Thomas comes back to the distinction between the generation of the Son and the spiration of the Holy Spirit in the terms posited by q. 27. The one is the procession of the Word as through the intellect, and the other has the mode of Love. As we have seen, these two are the only immanent processions that can be reasonably grasped in God, by means of an action that founds a real relation. This prohibits the conflation of procession with Fatherhood or filiation.[17]

As one considers them, each of the building-blocks of this meditation, such as subsistent relation and especially the idea of the Word and of Love, puts Thomas' own way of presenting Trinitarian faith to work. Even though the other Masters posed exactly the same question, it is not astonishing that their thought should follow different paths.[18] One can also notice the progress Thomas achieved after his 'Writing on the *Sentences*'. On the same question, of why *three* persons in one God, our author was still thinking in terms of 'natural-mode' or 'voluntative-mode' processions, without also clearly making use of the theory of subsistent relations.[19] The issue of the number of the persons is perhaps not a central question in the treatise, but it does highlight the theological resources which Thomas is now able to put at the heart of his theological doctrine.

---

[16] Ibid.

[17] *ST* I, q. 30, a. 2, sol., ad 3 and ad 4; cf. q. 27, aa. 3 and 5. See above, in Chapter 4, 'The Cycle of the Trinitarian Processions'.

[18] The most proximate exposition is doubtless Albert's: I *Sent.* d. 10, a. 12.

[19] Thomas, I *Sent.* d. 10, q. 1, a. 5.

2. THE THEOLOGICAL TERMINOLOGY OF PLURALITY

Following upon these elucidations, St Thomas examines the name which Christians give to God: *Trinity.* The discussion of this term sometimes takes up a very large place in the scholastic Trinitarian treatises.[20] The mid-thirteenth-century authors generally recognize that this is a relative name.[21] Thomas confines himself to a rapid exposition, emphasizing both the plurality of the persons (numerically *three*) and their essential unity. The word *Trinity* refers to 'the determinate number of persons'. Otherwise put: what the word *plurality* states vaguely, the name *Trinity* puts into a determinate form. Applied to God, the name *Trinity* refers in a precise way to 'the number of persons having one single essence'. It does not precisely signify the relations, but rather the number of persons who are mutually referred to one another through the relations.[22] We will lay out the question of 'number' in more detail further on.

The plurality of persons, to which the word *Trinity* refers, implies a genuine *alterity* amongst the persons. St Thomas pays serious attention to the connection between plurality and alterity. The occasion is furnished by a conventional scholastic debating-point: 'is the Son "other" (*alius*) than the Father?'[23] The *Summa Theologiae* brings together two problems which the *Sentences* consider separately: what is the *alterity* of the persons, and can one speak of a *diversity* of persons?[24]

Philosophically, according to Aristotle, the 'plural' is that which is 'divisible' or 'divided'.[25] To account for the multiplicity, one must turn to the cause or explanation of the division. And this is not identically the same in things which are secondary and composed, and in those which are primary and simple. The cause of the division of secondary and composed things is the diversity of that which is simple and primary. This latter presupposes a plurality amongst primary and simple things. So the first 'division' comes from affirmation and negation (being and non-being). If there is alterity in things, it is because the negation of the one is in some way included in the other.[26] The explanation of the alterity of creatures is connected to a reflection on being and non-being, on 'division' and diversity.

---

[20] For instance, the *Summa* of Alexander of Hales dedicates seven chapters or questions to it (Book I, ed. Quaracchi, vol. 1, nos. 441–447).

[21] Albert, I *Sent.* d. 5, a. 6, ad 1; *Summa fratris Alexandri,* Book I (ed. Quaracchi, vol. 1, no. 443).

[22] *ST* I, q. 31, a. 1, sol. and ad 1; cf. I *Sent.* d. 24, q. 2, a. 2.

[23] *ST* I, q. 31, a. 2. cf. Augustine, *De Civitate Dei* XI, X, 1.

[24] I *Sent.* d. 9, q. 1, a. 1; d. 24, q. 2, a. 1.

[25] *Super Boetium de Trinitate,* q. 4, a. 1; cf. Aristotle, *Metaphysics* X, ch. 3 (1054ᵃ22).

[26] *Super Boetium de Trinitate,* q. 4, a. 1; St Thomas is discussing here how best to understand Boethius' statement that: 'the principle of plurality is alterity' (Boethius, *De Trinitate* 1, Leonine edn., vol. 50, p. 69).

When one turns to Trinitarian theology as such, the study of the plurality of persons will require a special kind of analysis, and fresh conceptual instruments. It also requires that one fine-tunes the terminology: not 'division' but 'distinction through relations'; not 'diversity' but 'distinction'.[27] As to relation itself, it doesn't follow from distinction; relation is what entails distinction and personal alterity.[28]

By the end of the chapter, we should be able to see how to get hold of the Trinitarian plurality. But making our start with a consideration of the theological vocabulary used for plurality will enable us to stake out the question much better. Following his constant method, with which we are by now familiar, Thomas begins from the Trinitarian heresies which he wants to avoid, and concludes by indicating the path which gives an accurate view of things:

Now in speaking of the Trinity we must beware of two opposite errors, proceeding along a crest lined up between Arius' error in allocating three substances to the three persons, and the error of Sabellius, in attaching one single person to the single divine essence.[29]

The genuine distinction of the persons and their plurality requires that one recognize a genuine personal *alterity* in God. The Son is 'an other' (*alius*) from the Father, but he is not 'something else' and the Holy Spirit is 'an other' from the Father and the Son without being 'something else' than the Father and the Son are. We find here once again a double-mapping in our path to the mystery of the Trinity, or the double aspect which was brought out in our study of what relation is in God. The alterity of the Father, the Son, and the Holy Spirit is an alterity of 'supposits', an alterity of persons based on a relation-distinction, but not an alterity of essence, nature, or substance.[30] Not acknowledging the personal or hypostatic alterity would backfire on us as Sabellianism; conceding an alterity of essence leads to Arianism.

Thus, the pitfalls of the heresies require us to take care about the words we use, so easily do they conceal ambiguous fault-lines. Paying attention to terminology is not a second-rate pastime. It expresses a very vivid sense of the rigour which it takes, whether in theology or catechesis and preaching, to express the faith authentically. The words we use have an enormous impact, since we refer to faith through them. Thomas recalls this in his appropriation of an ancient warning, made by Jerome at the time of the sensitive Trinitarian

---

[27] *De potentia*, q. 9, a. 8, ad 2 and ad 4.

[28] *De potentia*, q. 8, a. 3, ad 12; see above, in Chapter 6, 'Relation the Heart of Trinitarian Theology'.

[29] *ST* I, q. 31, a. 2. Cf. what Thomas already says in the *Sentences*, Book I, d. 24, q. 2, a. 1.

[30] *ST* I, q. 31, a. 2; I *Sent.* d. 9, q. 1, a. 1, sol. and ad 2; *De potentia*, q. 9, a. 8; cf. *In Ioan.* 14.16 (no. 1912).

controversies of the fourth century: 'careless words are a slippery slope to heresy'. Here more than anywhere else, it is necessary to take care to speak prudently or with circumspection (*cautela*).[31] Reflection on the two main heresies calls for the elimination of certain words from our Trinitarian language.

To avoid the error of Arius, one avoids speaking of *diversity* (*diversitas*) or *difference* (*differentia*) in God; that would destroy the unity of essence. But we can use the word 'distinction', on account of relative opposition. So if we come across a reference to diversity or difference of persons in any authoritative text, we take it to mean 'distinction'. Then, to safeguard the simplicity of the divine nature, it is necessary to avoid the words *separation* (*separatio*) and *division* (*divisio*) which are a matter of a whole divided into parts. To safeguard equality we avoid the word *disparity* (*disparitas*). To safeguard the likeness [of the persons] one avoids the words *alien* (*alienus*) and *divergent* (*discrepans*), following Saint Ambrose . . . and Saint Hilary . . . .

On the other hand, to avoid the error of Sabellius, one avoids the words *singularity* (*singularitas*) so as not to negate the communicability of the divine essence; this is why Hilary says *it is sacrilege to call the Father or the Son a single God*. We must also avoid the term *unique* (*unicus*) so as not to negate the plurality of persons: Hilary also says that *the idea of someone singular and unique* is inapplicable to God. If we speak of 'the only Son' that is because there are not several sons in God. But we do not call him 'the only God' since the deity is common to several [persons]. We also avoid the term *conflated* [*confusus*] lest we endanger the order of nature amongst the persons. Ambrose thus writes: *What is one is not 'conflated', and what is undifferentiated cannot be manifold*. We must also avoid 'solitary' (*solitarius*) in order to respect the fellowship of the three persons; for Hilary says, *We should profess belief in neither a solitary nor a diversified God*.[32]

This discussion goes back over the rules for terminology which he gave in the Commentary on the *Sentences* and in the Questions *De potentia*.[33] This list of proscribed words is not peculiar to him. It is an expression of the attention paid to the quality of words, within the context of respect for language which typifies scholastic theology. Such a glossary is significant to us because of the way it is organized. Using a well-known method, St Thomas has pulled his language together with the object of side-stepping Arianism and Sabellianism.[34] One can also observe the references to the Fathers of the

---

[31] *ST* I, q. 31, a. 2; cf. I *Sent.* d. 24, q. 2, a. 1; *De potentia*, q. 9, a. 8: 'it is necessary to speak of God in such a way that one never creates an occasion for error'.

[32] *ST* I, q. 31, a. 2.

[33] I *Sent.* d. 24, q. 2, a. 1; *De potentia*, q. 9, a. 8.

[34] This includes a study of antithetical parallelisms: there are thus *four* groups of words to avoid in relation to Arianism, and also *four* for Sabellianism, as Thomas explains in his Commentary on the *Sentences* (I *Sent.* d. 24, q. 2, a. 1) and in his Disputed Questions *De potentia* (q. 9, a. 8).

Church (Western, as it happens, because the issue is Latin terminology) together with whom Thomas draws out the rules of Trinitarian language.

It is especially notable that 'difference' is excluded from this language. Today, it has become a common practice to indicate the Trinitarian plurality in terms of 'difference', or 'unity within difference'. Thomas does not invite us to speak like this. Although he does use the notion of 'difference' in some explanations requiring a philosophical vocabulary (speaking of 'difference' is often introduced by an objection), he does not recognize 'difference' amongst the divine persons. The reason is simple: the word *difference* implies a 'distinction of form',[35] which is to suggest a distinction within the nature or essence of the divine persons. In fact, according to a classic patristic exegesis of Philippians 2.6–7 ('Christ Jesus, though he was in the form [*morphe; forma*] of God... *poured himself out*, taking the *form* of a slave')[36] if we often use the language of accommodation to speak of 'form' within God, this is to designate the divine essence. The word *diversity* is even more serious, because diversity derives from substantial forms and so implies a difference in essence.[37] But Thomas would have come across the word *differentia* in his reading of the Fathers, for instance in the Latin translation of John of Damascus' *De fide orthodoxa*.[38] He invites us to explain such formulae as 'difference of persons' as an expression of Trinitarian *distinction* (*distinctio*): one must take *different* to mean *distinct*. This is a recognizable example of the method of *expositio reverentialis*, from which, at opportune moments, Thomas did not refrain.[39]

Within the work as a whole, and both in its practice and in its theory, the investigation into Trinitarian plurality gives a central place to the language of *distinction*. The reason for selecting this word is obvious: in itself, distinction

[35] *De potentia*, q. 9, a. 8, ad 2; *ST* I, q. 31, a. 2, ad 2.
[36] Cf. Thomas, *In Phil.* 2.6 (no. 54): 'one calls the nature of a thing its "form"'. The meaning of *morphe* (which St Paul only uses in this one passage) is discussed; although it is also necessary to hold on to its sense of a 'manifestation of being' and of 'image', the anti-Arian controversy usually led patristic exegesis to find its meaning in nature or substance. See for instance Hilary of Poitiers, *De Trinitate* VIII. 45–47 (SC 488, pp. 450–455); Basil of Caesarea, *Contra Eunomius* I.18 (SC 299, pp. 236–237). Cf. P. Grelot, 'La traduction et l'interprétation de Ph 2.6–7. Quelques éléments d'enquête patristique', *NRT* 93 (1971), 897–922 and 1009–1026.
[37] *De potentia*, q. 9, a. 8, ad 2; *ST* I, q. 31, a. 2, ad 1. It is commonplace to proscribe attribution of 'diversity' to God: see for instance Bonaventure, I *Sent.* d. 19, p. 1, a. un., q. 1, ad 4; d. 23, dubium 4.
[38] See the passage cited in *ST* I, q. 32, a. 2, sed contra, and also *De potentia*, q. 9, a. 8, arg. 2. Cf. John of Damascus, *De fide orthodoxa*, versions of Burgundio and Cerbanus, ed. E. M. Buytaert, New York, 1955, p. 183.
[39] *De potentia*, q. 9, a. 8, ad 2; cf *ST* I, q. 31, a. 2, ad 2. On this topic, see Y. Congar, 'Valeur et portée oecuméniques de quelques principes herméneutiques de St Thomas', *RSPT* 57 (1973), 611–626; J.-P. Torrell, 'Autorités théologiques et liberté du théologien. L'exemple de St Thomas d'Aquin', *Les Échos de Saint-Maurice* NS 18 (1988), 7–24.

does not designate a difference of essence or substance, and it is thus perfectly suitable to express the alterity of persons sharing a single essence. Thomas uses *distinction* as much as he does *relation* to pinpoint the way in which the plurality of this world is a causal reflection of the plurality of the divine persons, which in turn confers an eminently positive character on the manyness of creatures.[40]

St Thomas very seldom either refers to the Father as 'first person', or uses the phrase 'second person' to name the Son; he designates the Holy Spirit as 'third person' a little less rarely, but it is not a repeated formula within his Trinitarian vocabulary. This is despite the fact that, at least from Tertullian onwards,[41] such language is common in the Latin tradition. So, for instance, the Trinitarian treatise in the *Summa* does not use the 'first' or 'second person.' The phrase 'third person' appears in one argument, and in the response to it, where the terminology is determined by the sources of the discussion,[42] and in the response to one other argument, where Thomas shows that the Holy Spirit is not an 'intermediary' or 'mediate' person within the Trinity, but that he is the 'third person'.[43] One can see that this way of speaking is rather peripheral. To our knowledge, St Thomas' complete works only contain one single text which uses the three formulae all at once, as in 'the first, second, and third person'; this passage, which comes from an argument in a disputed question, clearly presents the manner of speaking which was current in the school rather than the language habitually chosen by St Thomas himself.[44]

The accurate meaning of the expressions, 'first, second, third person' excludes any kind of priority of one person over another. One must be yet more precise than that, if one wants to render the consubstantiality of the Trinity. Taken in an absolute sense, 'where there is unity, there is no relationship (*ordo*) of first or of third'. So one cannot say that the Son is 'the second God', or that the Holy Spirit is 'the third God'. One can only say that the Son is the 'second person' or that the Holy Spirit is the 'third person'; this usage is recognized 'because of the plurality of persons'.[45] Such expressions, which Thomas seldom employs, designate the order of origin or 'order of nature' in God, conforming to the baptismal and credal formulae. Otherwise put, the

[40] I *Sent.* d. 26, q. 2, a. 2, ad 2; see below, in Chapter 14, 'Trinity and Creation: the Meaning of the Plural'.
[41] See Tertullian, *Contra Praxeas* 6.1; 11.7; 12.3; 18.2 (CCSL 2, pp. 1165, 1172, 1173, 1183), etc.
[42] *ST* I, q. 32, a. 1, arg. 1 and ad 1; cf. Bonaventure, I *Sent.* d. 3, p. 1, a. un., q. 4, arg. 2.
[43] *ST* I, q. 37, a. 1, ad 3.
[44] *De potentia*, q. 10, a. 4, sed contra 2 (one can see a related expression in q. 9, a. 9, sed contra 3).
[45] *CEG* I, ch. 3.

meaning of these formulae is just the 'number' we signify when we refer to many persons in their standing order: one, two, three, persons. So we need to examine more closely the idea of 'number' within the Trinity.

3. A TRANSCENDENTAL MULTIPLICITY

The study of the plurality of persons has made us touch on the question of 'number' in God. We have already hinted at this in relation to the word *Trinity*. Trinitarian faith compels us to acknowledge 'multiplicity': no 'multiple', no real Trinity.

But what is this plurality to do with? The problem arose very early, and with an acerbic punch, in the very first Trinitarian debates within scholastic theology. One of Abelard's first masters, Roscelin de Compiègne, aroused a heated debate by refusing to accept that the three divine persons could be one single reality (*una res*). For Roscelin, the affirmation that the three divine persons are a single reality cannot enable one to safeguard the givens of faith, since, amongst these persons, only the Son became incarnate. Consequently, Roscelin held that the three persons are three realities (*tres res*), which nonetheless have power and will in the way in which three angels or three human souls do so.[46] This is the origin of the scholastics' question, which is still there in St Thomas' writings: 'Can the three persons be called "three realities" (*tres res*)?'[47]

Anselm of Canterbury hit back at Roscelin's thesis in his *Letter on the Incarnation of the Word*. Conceiving Roscelin as a nominalist dialectician, Anselm accuses anyone who holds his view of tritheism: 'Surely either they intend to profess three gods, or they do not understand what they are saying.'[48] In Anselm's analysis, the cause of this error is a misunderstanding of how individual and universal are connected: 'For in what way can those who do not yet understand how several specifically human beings are one human being understand in the most hidden and highest nature how several persons, each of whom is complete God, are one God?'[49] According to Anselm, Roscelin's thesis introduces a fissure into God's unitary nature.

---

[46] According to Anselm, *Epistola de incarnatione Verbi*. See also Roscelin's letter to Abelard (PL 178. 357–372). For an exposition of Roscelin's thought about the Trinity, see J. Hofmeier, *Die Trinitätslehre des Hugo von St. Viktor*, Munich, 1963, pp. 9–26.

[47] Thomas, I *Sent.* d. 25, q. 1, a. 4; cf. Bonaventure, I *Sent.* d. 25, dubium 3. The question was carried into the twelfth century by Peter Lombard, who notes the Augustinian sources of the idea (I *Sent.* dist. 25, ch. 2, nos. 4–5; vol. I/2, pp. 193–194).

[48] Anselm, *Epistola de incarnatione Verbi* (2nd version), in *Anselm of Canterbury: The Major Works*, ed. Brian Davies and G. R. Evans, Oxford, 1998, pp. 233–259, p. 238.

[49] Ibid, p. 237.

Thus Anselm faults 'Those contemporary dialecticians (rather, those heretical dialecticians) who consider universal substances to be merely vocal emanations'.[50] On a theological level, the abbot of Bec replies to Roscelin by making a distinction between that which is common within God (the divine essence) and that which is distinct (the persons and their properties). The three persons are one single *res* (substance or essence); if one chooses to speak of three *res*, one can only be making the word 'res' stand for the relations, not the substance.[51] Anselm retraced the main steps of his reply in a letter addressed to Foulques, bishop of Beauvais, to be read before the assembled Council of Soissons (1092); the council would condemn Roscelin's erroneous conception of the Trinity.

Abelard also reacted against Roscelin's thesis. In a letter sent to the bishop of Paris around 1120, the Master of Pallet explained that the principal aim of his writings on the Trinity was to refute Roscelin's tritheism, condemned by the Council of Soissons.[52] The *Theologia Summi Boni* (and its later elaborations, the *Theologia Christiana* and the *Theologia Scholarium*) aim to furnish a defence of traditional Trinitarian doctrine in response to the new 'dialecticians'. In his own thesis, Abelard developed an understanding of the Father, Son, and Holy Spirit by means of the attributes of power, wisdom, and goodness: we will return to it in connection with the theory of appropriations.[53] Abelard avoids the perils of tritheism by excluding numerical plurality from God. So, he does not accept that one can speak of God as being 'three' or 'many' (*multa*) in an unqualified way: God is 'many persons', but he is not 'many', and there is, 'in an absolute sense', no 'three' (*tria per se*) in God. For Abelard, prefixing 'three' to 'persons', in the phrase 'three persons' is accidental (*accidentaliter*). Properly speaking, the number is not applicable to God. Because he was quite clearly taking into account only the numerical terms which derive from quantity, Abelard rejects numerical plurality in God and excludes the idea that there is in God a 'three in an absolute sense'. There is a multiplicity of properties or of 'definitions' but there is neither numerical plurality nor diversity in God.[54] Thus, it was Abelard who opened the question of 'numerical terms' within scholastic Trinitarian theology.

---

[50] Anselm, *Epistola de incarnatione Verbi* (2nd version), in *Anselm of Canterbury: The Major Works*, ed. Brian Davies and G. R. Evans, Oxford, 1998, p. 237; Evans and Davies have 'logicians', not 'dialecticians'. Roscelin's nominalism or 'vocalism' (which claims that only words or vocal sounds and singular things exist) is considered to have been the starting-point for the debate about universals; cf. A. de Libera, *La querelle des universaux de Platon à la fin du Moyen Age*, Paris, 1996, pp. 142–146.

[51] Anselm, *Epistola de incarnatione Verbi*, ch. 2.

[52] C. J. Mews, 'Introduction', in *Petri Abaelardi Theologia 'Summi Boni'*, CCCM 13, Turnhout, 1987, p. 39; cf. PL 178. 355–358.

[53] See below, in Chapter 13, 'The origins of the Idea of Appropriations'.

[54] Abelard, *Theologia Summi Boni*, Book III, ch. I, nos. 5–7 (CCCM 13, pp. 159–161).

In the *Sentences*, Peter Lombard still thinks of the terms for number and quantity as being closely connected. 'When we say three persons, the number *three* does not affirm either numerical quantity nor any diversity within God.' For this reason, the Lombard ascribes a purely negative meaning to the 'numbers' we use in speaking of God, as in *one, two, three* persons. The phrase, '*one Father*' is used to exclude the idea that there are many Fathers. The expression 'one God' rules out a plurality of gods. The phrase 'many persons' or 'three persons' excludes the idea of God as one single, solitary person (that is, Sabellianism). When we say 'the Father and the Son are two persons', we mean that the Father is not the only person within God, that neither is the Son the only person, and that the Father is not the Son—and so on.[55] How can one make positive affirmations about there being 'number' in God without fragmenting the divine unity?

Much nearer to Thomas, the *Summa* of Alexander of Hales explains that, 'in the divine persons, there is no number in an absolute (*simpliciter*) sense, and nor can one properly speak of there being so', for that would entail a diversity of substances: there is no 'number' in the quantitative sense, but there is just a 'certain number' of persons at least to the extent that one person is distinguished from another as to origin.[56] Albert the Great provides a more detailed consideration, one which distinguishes several kinds of 'numbers'. The important step is his acknowledgement that, 'in a certain way' one can positively affirm that there is a number in God, in relation to the personal distinctions which come about through the properties of origin.[57] On the matter of divine *unity*, Albert has also thought through why one should notice the difference between 'one' as a numerical principle, (relating to number as quantity) and the 'one which is convertible with being' (relating to the oneness which every being has).[58] Benefiting from Albert's analysis, Thomas excludes quantitative, numerical manyness from God but recognizes that there is in God a transcendental 'multiplicity'. He takes up this approach in his Commentary on the *Sentences* (and thus in his tenth *Quodlibet*), and then, in a more developed way, in the Questions *De potentia* and in the *Summa theologiae*.[59]

Like St Albert, Thomas sets aside the reply to the question made by the Master of the *Sentences*. In attributing a merely negative function to the numerical terms in our language for God, Peter Lombard only took into account the connection

---

[55] Peter Lombard, *Sentences*, Book I, dist. 24 (vol. I/2, pp. 187–189).

[56] *Summa Fratris Alexandri*, Book I (ed. Quaracchi, vol. 1, nos. 313–316).

[57] Albert, I *Sent.* d. 24, a. 1.

[58] Albert, I *Sent.* d. 24, a. 3.

[59] *De potentia*, q. 9, a. 7; *ST* I, q. 30, a. 3; cf. I *Sent.* d. 24, q. 1, a. 4; *Quodlibet* X, q. 1, a. 1.

between plurality and *quantity*. But the numerical terms in our Trinitarian speech do not just play a negative role: they say something true about the Triune God. It is here that the transcendentals enter the picture. In the same way that one must distinguish between *one* as the 'numerical principle' and *one* as 'convertible with being', so one must distinguish the multiplicity which results from quantity and the multiplicity which embraces every genus (like the *one*), that is, the multiplicity pertaining to the 'transcendentals'.[60] *One* as transcendental ('convertible with being') stands for being in its undividedness: being is one in the degree that it is not divided. This had already been thought through in the study of the unity of God: 'one does not add anything to being, but is just the negation of division; *one* effectively just means undivided being'.[61] Like the affirmation of the unity of each person, affirming the unity of the Triune God thus consists in the affirmation of the reality to which one attributes unity, and in the denial of division.

The one which is convertible with being adds to being only the denial of division; for 'one' means 'undivided being'. Therefore, whenever we call anything 'one' we mean that it is an undivided reality; for instance, to speak of 'one man' is to signify an undivided human substance.... when we say 'the [divine] essence is one', the term 'one' refers to the undivided essence; when we say 'person is one' we mean that the person is undivided.[62]

The originality of Thomas' thought is expressed by the application of this idea to plurality or 'multiplicity' in the Trinity:[63]

In so far as they enter into statements about God, numerical terms, ... are taken from the 'multiplicity' which is transcendental (*multitudo secundum quod est transcendens*). This multiplicity has the same relationship to the many things of which it is predicated which 'one' has to the 'being' with which it is convertible .... when we speak of a 'multiplicity of things', 'multiple' here refers to the things in question with the implication that none of them is divided.... and when we say 'there are many persons', we signify those persons, each in its own indivision. For, by definition, a 'multiple' is something made up of unities.[64]

    [60] *ST* I, q. 30, a. 3; *De potentia*, q. 9, a. 7.

    [61] *ST* I, q. 11, a. 1. Being (*ens*) is one in so far as it is 'non-divided', 'undivided'.

    [62] *ST* I, q. 30, a. 3; *De potentia*, q. 9, a. 7: 'The one which is convertible with being affirmatively posits being itself and adds nothing to it but the denial of a division.'

    [63] On this topic, see G. Ventimiglia's excellent book, *Differenza e contraddizione*, Milan, 1997, pp. 191–245.

    [64] *ST* I, q. 30, a. 3. In his response to the first objection (ibid., ad 1), Thomas repeats: 'Since "one" is a transcendental, it has a wider range of meaning than "substance" or "relation"; so, too, has "many". Hence when used of God both terms can stand for both substance and relation according to the context.'

The numerical terms in our Trinitarian language affirmatively posit each reality which they qualify, without adding anything positive to it—for if it did, one would fall straight back into the composition which Abelard and Peter Lombard rightly tried to avoid—except the affirmation of the unity of each person. The transcendental multiplicity of the persons thus consists in the affirmation of each one person, and in the affirmation of the distinction of each person from another. Otherwise put: it affirms each person by adding two negations: the person is undivided, and that person is not someone else.[65] In the same way, the theologian can show that multiplicity genuinely belongs to the reality of the Triune God: 'the unity and the multiplicity intended by the numerical terms which we attribute to God does not only exist in our minds, but really exists in God'.[66]

These remarks show the seriousness with which Thomas addresses himself to the real plurality of the divine persons, without attenuating his concern for the unity and simplicity of the three persons: the upshot is that he can articulate a Trinitarian monotheism. Unity does not exclude plurality, and plurality does not obstruct unity. ' "One" does not exclude the "many", but rather division .... And "many" does not exclude unity, but rather division between the realities out of which the manyness comes together.'[67] One thus has a theoretical explanation of why it should matter that faith affirms a real plurality of persons. The original concept of *transcendental multiplicity* expresses the new step which Christianity takes in its understanding of the relation between the one and the many; it is placed at the heart of Trinitarian theology. The introduction of multiplicity (*multitudo*) into the transcendentals is an expression of the key status of plurality in Thomas' own thought. The intelligibility of the profession of faith in a plurality of persons is thus theoretically ensured.

4. THE CONSUBSTANTIALITY OF THE PERSONS

The recognition of the plurality of the persons is the counterpart of the unswerving affirmation of the identity of person and essence. This identity was emphasized earlier in the scrutiny of the notion of 'person' (q. 29). Thomas comes back to this examination when he deals systematically with the relationships of persons and essence, much later in the *Summa Theologiae*

---

[65] *De potentia*, q. 9, a. 7. The transcendental multiplicity thus consists in one affirmation and two negations.

[66] *De potentia*, q. 9, a. 7, ad 4.   [67] *ST* I, q. 30, a. 3, ad 3.

(q. 39). The point of this question is to show that the divine persons each have their own prerogatives and simultaneously to bring to light and consider every possible aspect of the authenticity of Trinitarian monotheism. This thesis entails making numerous refinements to the way we speak about faith and to our grasp of the Trinitarian mystery. It will bring out once again the benefits of the theory of subsistent relations.

Recalling the historical origins of this question takes us back first of all to the twelfth century, and Gilbert de la Porrée. In order to safeguard the unity of the divine nature of the three persons, Gilbert declared that the relations are 'positioned from outside' or 'externally imposed'. St Thomas replied by distinguishing two aspects within relation, and he showed that relation in God is really identical to the divine nature.[68] A further question has now to be asked, not in regard to relation, but to person. Is the person different from the essence? Gilbert de la Porrée had taken over from Boethius the distinction between abstract forms (that *through which* a thing is what it is) and concrete subjects (the concretely existing individual), and he posited an analogous distinction within God. So people criticized him for introducing a difference between *God* (to which we refer in the concrete) and the divine essence (to which we refer in the abstract: that *through which* God is God) and of creating an apparent difference between the divine person, the Father for instance, and the relation or property, for example, paternity, as that through which the Father is Father. Pope Eugene III gave his doctrinal sanction to this latter foreboding. Theologians must not cast a division between God's essence and the persons. The divine essence is not just 'that through which' God is God, it is God himself.[69] Gilbert's stalwart opponent, Peter Lombard, gave a lot of space to the debate in his *Sentences*.[70]

Thomas' doctrine of subsistent relation enables him to tackle the problem in an eirenic way. As regards person and essence, he begins by referring to the historical aspect of the question:

Because, as Boethius says, it is relation which multiplies the persons of the Trinity, some have affirmed that in God the person differs from the essence. This difference derived from the fact that, as they thought, the relations are 'added on' (*assistentes*) to the essence; effectively seeing in the relations nothing but the idea of reference to another, forgetting that they themselves are realities.[71]

---

[68] *ST* I, q. 28, a. 2. See above, in Chapter 5, 'The Being of Divine Relations'.

[69] For more detail and bibliographical material, see our own brief exposition: 'Trinité et Unité de Dieu dans la scolastique, XIIᵉ–XIVᵉ siècles', pp. 201–204; *Trinity in Aquinas*, pp. 9–12.

[70] Peter Lombard, *Sentences*, Book I, dist. 33 and 34.

[71] *ST* I, q. 39, a. 1; cf. I *Sent.* d. 33, q. 1, a. 1; d. 34, q. 1, a. 1.

One can see in this the criticisms which he had earlier directed at the school of Gilbert de la Porrée in his investigation of relations.[72] On this basis, he can easily show the identity of person and essence in God, in a discussion which provides a remarkable synthesis of his theory of the person. In order to create this synthesis, all of the by now well-known features of the problem are drawn up: the exclusion of accidentality from God, the twin aspects of relation, relative opposition, and subsistent relation. Thomas remarks:

> But as it was shown above (q. 28, a. 2) just as relations in created things inhere [in a subject] in an accidental way, so relations in God are the divine essence itself. It follows from this that in God the essence is not really distinct from the person even though the persons are really distinguished from one another. In effect, as we also showed above (q. 29, a. 4), person signifies relation in so far as this relation subsists in the divine nature. But, considered in comparison to essence, relation only differs from it conceptually; and, in comparison to the opposed relation, it is really distinguished by virtue of this relative opposition. Thus there is one essence and three persons.[73]

So the theory of relation enables one to respect God's simplicity in the very act of disclosing God's authentic plurality. Simplicity lays itself down as a fundamental rule of Trinitarian doctrine: God is his own essence or nature,[74] and the persons themselves are this nature.

This meditation began as a criticism of Gilbert de la Porrée, but that is not the whole of what it is aiming to achieve. On a deeper level, it is about the faith professed against Arianism at the Council of Nicaea: the Son is begotten 'of the substance of the Father' and he is 'coessential' or 'consubstantial' with the Father.[75] Once he has completed his appraisal of Gilbert de la Porrée, Thomas immediately raises the question of the unitary essence of the three persons: 'Must it be said that the three persons are of a single selfsame essence?'[76] In short, 'the word homoousion, which the council of Nicaea adopted against the Arians, means that the three persons are of one essence'.[77]

Following the lead of Athanasius, Hilary of Poitiers, and Augustine, St Thomas strongly applies the 'numerical unity' of the essence to the three persons. The essence of the three persons should be 'one in number' (*una numero*).[78] This phrase means that the three divine persons are not just of one

---

[72] *ST* I, q. 28, a. 2.

[73] *ST* I, q. 39, a. 1; cf. I *Sent.* d. 34, q. 1, a. 1.

[74] *ST* I, q. 3, a. 3; q. 39. a. 1.

[75] 'Consubstantial' and 'coessential' are the two translations of Nicaea's *homoousios* which Thomas uses (*Super II Decret.*; Leon. edn., vol. 40, p. E 41).

[76] *ST* I, q. 39, a. 2.

[77] Ibid., sed contra. Like Athanasius of Alexandria in his own time, St Thomas extends what Nicaea says about the Father and the Son to the Holy Spirit.

[78] *Super II Decret.*; cf. *ST* I, q. 33, a. 2, ad 4; q. 39, a. 5, ad 2.

specific nature, like the human persons in whom one recognizes 'the same nature' because they have the same humanity. In the Triune God, the essence is not 'multiplied' by the three persons, but the three persons are one and the same identical essence. St Thomas came upon this claim in his reading of Scripture.[79] This numerical unity is an absolute prerequisite for maintaining the confession of the unity of God and crediting Son and Holy Spirit with their authentic divinity.[80] St Thomas sees it as a strict exigency of the Niceno-Constantinopolitan Creed; the theory of the immanent processions of the Word and of Love enable one to disclose this precise numerical unity.[81] Thomas states that,

Since the Father, the Son, and the Holy Spirit are not distinguished through their divine nature but solely by their relations, it is therefore appropriate that we do not call the three persons 'three gods', but confess one single, true and perfect God. And if, among human beings, three persons are called three men and not one single man, that is because the human nature common to the three is theirs in a different way, divided up materially amongst them, which could not take place in God. This is because, since three men have three numerically different humanities, only the essence of humanity is common to them. But it must be the case that in the three divine persons, there are not three numerically different divinities but one single and simple deity,[82] since the essence of the Word and of Love in God is nothing but the essence of God. So, we do not confess three Gods but one sole God, because of the single, simple deity in the three persons.[83]

St Thomas is looking at the fact of distinction by means of relation alone, making it play a role analogous to that of a 'principle of individuation'. In physical beings, the principle of individuation is the material which renders an *individual*, in relation to the species whose nature the individual has.[84] All of them have, of course, the nature appropriate to the human species, but this humanity is, as it were, 'multiplied' in each one of them.[85] It works out differently in the Triune God. The divine essence is *numerically* one: the essence is absolutely one and the same identical reality in the three persons.

[79] See for instance *In Ioan.* 14.10 (nos. 1887–1888, 1891); 15.9 (no. 1999); 16.28 (no. 2161), etc.
[80] *SCG* IV, ch. 7 (no. 3421); ch. 14 (no. 3502); ch. 8 (no. 3427).
[81] Cf. *ST* I, q. 27, a. 1, ad 2; q. 34, a. 2, ad 4.
[82] 'Deity': *deitas*. As so often with Thomas, the word is used here with a meaning equivalent to 'divinity' (*divinitas*), so as to designate the divine nature, despite the subtle difference between these two terms: 'divinity' can refer to participated divine being, whereas 'deity' refers exclusively to the divinity possessed through essence (I *Sent.* d. 15, *exp. text*: dist. 29, *exp. text*).
[83] *De rationibus fidei*, ch. 4.
[84] Cf. for instance *SCG* III, ch. 65 (no. 2400): 'There is such a thing as *this* man (*hic homo*) from the fact that human nature is in this material (*in hac materia*), which is the principle of individuation.'
[85] Cf. *ST* I, q. 39, a. 3.

What makes the persons of the Trinity plural is not the common essence but relation as a personal property, a 'quasi principle of individuation'. One of the outstanding benefits of the doctrine of the immanent processions is that its perception of the origin of the Word and Love in the Trinity shows this: the Word and Love proceed within the unity of the divine nature. Relative opposition as to origin makes the relations really distinct from one another, but each of them is really identical to the single divine essence or substance.[86] In sum, this body of ideas (the person, relative opposition, Word and Love, and subsistent relation), coheres around the depiction of the Trinitarian unity of God.

5. PERSON AND ESSENCE: A PROBLEM RAISED BY JOACHIM OF FIORE

Once the controversy created by Gilbert de la Porrée was over, a different misapprehension led to a more precise articulation of the relation between the Trinity and Unity of God. It came about in Joachim of Fiore's polemics against Peter Lombard. Peter Lombard's *Sentences* take up a radically different position on this from what we described earlier as being Roscelin's stance. Doubtless with Gilbert de la Porrée in mind, the Lombard affirmed the absolute prerogatives of the unity of God: the Triune God is 'a single, once-off supreme reality'.[87] Since the divine essence is an 'unitary, sovereign reality', Peter Lombard refuses to accept formulae like 'the Father engenders the divine essence', or 'the divine essence engenders the Son'. Since the essence or divine substance is the unitary reality of the Triune God, Peter Lombard figured that one cannot say the essence engenders, or is engendered, or proceeds: this would mean that the essence engenders itself, that is, that the Trinity engenders itself. It does not belong to the essence or to the substance but to the person to be the subject of generation and procession.[88]

This understanding of the three persons aroused both deep incomprehension and steely opposition in Joachim of Fiore (+1202). Joachim was attached to different formulae from these, which did use the words 'substance' or 'essence' to mean the person or hypostasis (and patristic precedents for these are not uncommon). So he rejected the terminology which Peter Lombard had imposed. Failing to grasp the way the Lombard's analysis

---

[86] *ST* I, q. 29, a. 4; cf. q. 28, a. 2.
[87] Peter Lombard, *Sentences*, book I, dist. 25, ch. 2, n. 5 (vol. I/2, p. 194).
[88] Peter Lombard, *Sentences* I, book I, dist. 5, ch. 1 (vol. I/2, pp. 80–87).

distinguishes the reality from the ways our language works (like Thomas after him, Peter Lombard does not attribute generation to the substance but to the person who has this substance), Joachim could not accept a 'supreme reality which does not engender, which is not engendered, and does not proceed'. In his eyes, such a 'supreme reality' would be a fourth reality, alongside the 'reality which engenders', the 'reality which is engendered', and the 'reality which proceeds' (Father, Son, and Spirit). So he thought Peter Lombard's doctrine put forward a 'quaternity' in God, creating a synthesis which allies Arianism to Sabellianism.[89]

In 1215, the Fourth Lateran Council sharply rejected Joachim of Fiore's interpretation of Peter Lombard. The Council condemned the treatise in which Joachim formulated his accusation of heresy against the Lombard; and, not without generating yet another misunderstanding, it criticized Joachim for conceiving the divine unity like a collective union, that is, in the way that many men are one single people.[90] As a result, the Council propounded a profession of faith in the unique divine reality which does not engender, is not engendered, and does not proceed, since each of the persons *is* this divine reality.

St Thomas commented on the Lateran IV decree *Damnamus*. He also mentions Joachim's difficulties in the *Summa Theologiae*.[91] Joachim 'has not properly understood the formulae of Master Peter Lombard',[92] 'he is mistaken'.[93] On this basis, Thomas repeats that 'the divine essence is not something other than the three persons; so there is no quaternity in God'. Likewise, 'there is no distinction of the divine essence in the three persons'.[94] The distinction is purely a matter of the divine persons in their mutual relations. This is a strict requirement of the Nicene Creed.[95]

As far as our language is concerned, Thomas recalls this fundamental rule: we speak of God not after the mode of God himself, but in a creaturely modality, and it is from this that we structure the words which we use to name God. This is why, in our language about God, we signify the essence as if we were referring to a form: we *signify* 'that through which' God is God, even though, in the divine reality itself, the divine essence is nothing other than the person (there is in God none of that composition of form and supposit which

---

[89] For the references to Joachim's works and for the bibliographical references, see our exposition, 'Trinité et Unité de Dieu dans la scolastique XIIᵉ–XIVᵉ siècles', pp. 204–205; *Trinity in Aquinas*, pp. 12–14.

[90] *Decress of the Ecumenical Councils*, 2 vols., ed. Norman P. Tanner, Washington DC, 1990, vol. 1, pp. 231–233; Denzinger, nos. 803–807.

[91] *ST* I, q. 39, a. 5.   [92] *Super II Decret.* (Leon edn., vol. 40, p. E 41).

[93] *ST* I, q. 39, a. 5.   [94] *Super II Decret.* (Leon edn., vol. 40, p. E 43).

[95] Ibid. (pp. E 41 and 43).

characterizes corporeal creatures[96]). And we *signify* the person as the concretely existing subject or subsistent, even though the person has no other
reality than the divine essence itself. Our words cannot do any better than
this. The different ways of signifying the essence and the person follow from
this. For this reason, because of the mode in which it is signified in our speech,
the essence cannot take the place of the person: that which properly belongs
to the person is thus not attributed to the essence. Since the divine acts are
performed by the supposits, that is, the persons, one does not say that the
'essence engenders', even though the Father who engenders is nothing other
than the divine essence. The entire discussion is governed by what it means to
be a divine *person*.[97]

But Thomas' reading of the Fathers had put him in contact with the
'essentialist' figures of speech, which attributed divine generation to the divine
essence or substance (speaking of 'the engendering essence', 'the engendered
essence', and so on). In the texts he had at his disposal, he found this especially
in Athanasius of Alexandria, from whom Hilary passed it on to the West, and
even in Basil of Caesarea.[98] It is notable that when he focuses on Cyril,[99] he has
to explain that 'the Fathers sometimes impelled their language beyond the
borders of terminological precision'. Because of the real identity of the essence
and the person in God, Cyril sometimes overlooks the terminological propri-
eties, swapping one of them for another. When we read in the Fathers that the
'essence engenders' or that 'the essence is engendered', Thomas suggests that we
take it as meaning that, through generation, the Father has given his own
essence to the Son. Thomas concludes that these figures of speech have to be
interpreted before one makes any generalizations on their basis.[100]

The same hermeneutic rules are applied to more important figures of
speech. We have already remarked upon the outstanding case in point, the
formula 'three persons of a single selfsame essence'. This formula is a direct
consequence of the terms 'consubstantial' and 'coessential', put forward by the
Council of Nicaea. In this phrase, we mean the essence as 'that through which'
the three persons are the same God, whereas we refer to the persons as
supposits or subjects possessing this essence. Such a distinction does not
exist within God's own reality, but in our way of understanding and talking
about the mystery of God. Since in God the essence is single and the persons

[96] *ST* I, q. 3, a. 3.
[97] *ST* I, q. 39, a. 5; cf. I *Sent.* d. 5, q. 1, aa. 1 and 2; *De unione Verbi incarnati*, a. 1, ad 12.
[98] For the texts which Thomas had from the Greek Fathers, see *CEG* I, ch. 4. Peter Lombard
was doubtless unaware of the extent of the linguistic tradition by which Joachim was so
captivated. Hilary's position was more well known in the West, and Peter Lombard had brought
it into the discussion of this question (see the *Sentences*, book I, dist. 5).
[99] *CEG* I, ch. 4.
[100] *ST* I, q. 39, a. 5, ad 1; *CEG* I, ch. 4. On the method of reverential exposition, see above, n. 39.

plural, our dogmatic formulae profess the consubstantiality of the three persons like this. It works in the same way when we say that 'the Father and the Son are of the same nature'.[101]

The person and the essence are identical in reality, even though our respective notions for them are not precisely the same. We meet again the two sides to our language for God, which is not neutral or interchangeable. Observing this enables us to explain why one attributes certain properties to the person which one does not ascribe to the divine essence: even though the essence is not distinct, the person is distinct; the essence does no engendering, but the person of the Father engenders the Son. On this basis, it is the theory of subsistent relation which supplies an understanding of the conceptual distinction between the person and the essence and likewise of their identity in the reality of God.[102] The essence is not something additional on top of the three persons, and is thus in no way a 'fourth' thing alongside the three persons. When it is added to the linguistic analysis which Thomas never lets out of sight, the theory of subsistent relations enables one to present a genuinely Trinitarian monotheism.

6. THE WORD *GOD*

Having already entered the frame in connection with person and essence, Gilbert of Porrée's name comes up yet again in connection with a linguistic problem which is proximate to the foregoing issue. Gilbert had pinpointed the fact that in our way of speaking about the Trinity, the name *God* is attributed ('predicated') substantially, that is, as to the essence (*ousia*), whereas the name *Trinity* is not substantially attributed to God.[103] On the one hand, the masters criticized Gilbert for having denied that 'God is Trinity'.[104] On the other hand, the debate had a bearing on the meaning of the word *God*: is this an 'essential name', properly signifying the divine essence and thus not designating the person except when a personal name is connected to it (for instance, 'God the Father')?[105]

---

[101] *ST* I, q. 39, a. 2.   [102] *ST* I, q. 39, a. 1, ad 2.

[103] Gilbert de la Porrée, *In Boet. de Trin.* II.2 (ed. N. M. Häring, *The Commentaries on Boethius by Gilbert of Poitiers* Toronto, 1966, pp. 175–180).

[104] See the comments in Alexander of Hales' *Summa* (Book I, ed. Quaracchi, vol. 1, no. 365). Such a judgement is not, however, fair to Gilbert.

[105] *Summa Fratris Alexandri*, Book I, Prologue of no. 358 (ed. Quaracchi, vol. 1, p. 535 and n. 1). Thomas' conception of the problem in the *Summa* and the way he solves it is close to that of the 'Hales' *Summa*. See also William of Auxerre, *Summa aurea*, Book I, tract. 4, chs. 3–7 (ed. Ribaillier, vol. 1, pp. 43–61).

Thomas rejected the notion of reducing the word *God* to an essentialist meaning. *God* is a 'thick' name. Properly speaking, according to Thomas, the word means 'the divine essence in he who has it', or 'the divine essence in as much as it is in that which possesses it', not in an abstract way but in the style of substantive concrete names: it is thus that the word *man*, for example, refers to a human nature in a concrete individual; that is to say, a human-natured individual. Using an analytic process which was commonplace in his time, St Thomas distinguishes, on the one hand, what a word means, and, on the other hand, the 'supposition' (*suppositio, supponere*) of this word. This procedure is too important to Thomas for us to run over it lightly.

On the one hand, a word conveys a conceptual content: this is what it formally signifies. On the other hand, in our speaking, a word is often used as a 'place holder' for a reality or to 'represent' it. When we say for instance, 'these men have their freedom taken from them', the word *men* in this proposition, 'substitutes for', 'represents', 'stands in for', or 'refers to' the persons who are taken captive. The 'supposition' is linked to the signification, since it is because of what it signifies that a word can have such a reference within our speech.[106] And, not just through an accommodation to our language use but through its own proper weight, the name *God* has a good fit for standing in for a distinct divine person (the Father is '*God* who begets the Son'), or for designating many divine persons ('God born of God', 'God who breathes the Holy Spirit') or even for representing the divine essence.[107] Commenting on the first verse of John's Gospel (*the Word was with God*), Thomas explains that,

The name *God* signifies the divinity, but in a supposit and in a concrete way, whereas the name *deity* signifies divinity in an absolute and abstract way. From this it follows that, through its natural capacity and mode of signifying, the word *deity* cannot stand in for person; it can only be a place holder for the nature. But, from its own mode of signifying, the word *God* can naturally stand in for the person, just like the word *man* takes the place of a human natured supposit... Thus, when it is said here that the *Word was with God*, the word *God* must necessarily be standing in for the person of the Father, since the preposition *with* signifies a distinction from the Word which is said to be *with God*.[108]

When, in the same verse of the Prologue to the Fourth Gospel, St Thomas reads *the Word was God* (or: *God was the Word*), he explains that in this instance the word *God* refers to the person of the Word, not the person of the

---

[106] See E. Sweeney, 'Supposition, Signification and Universals: Metaphysical and Linguistic Complexity in Aquinas', *FZPT* 42 (1995), 267–290. The theories of supposition are complex; for an introductory survey and the bibliographical details, see A. de Libera, 'Suppositio', in *Dictionnaire du Moyen Âge*, ed. C. Gauvard, A. de Libera and M. Zink, Paris, 2002, pp. 1358–1360.

[107] *ST* I, q. 39; I *Sent.* d. 4, q. 1, a. 2.   [108] *In Ioan.* 1.1 (no. 44).

Father, because the word *God* can stand in for the three persons together, or for one of them.[109] It is also by means of the 'supposition' of the word *God* that he presents the confession of faith that the Son is 'God born of God',[110] and other New Testament passages which apply the name *God* to the person of Christ: John 20.28 (*My Lord and my God*), Romans 9.5 (*the Christ… who is over all, God blessed for ever*), or Titus 2.13 (*the glory of our great God and saviour, Jesus Christ*), and so on.[111] For the same reason, and in its own proper sense, the name *God* can designate many persons: 'God is three persons', 'God is Trinity'.[112] This pliable and yet precise analysis of the word *God* expresses the novel character of the Christian faith put forward by the Council of Nicaea. In this connection, restricting the word *God* within the language of faith to the person of the Father alone is indubitably a retrograde step and a diminishment, not an improvement.[113]

Some other questions deserve a mention at this point. This is especially the case for the Trinitarian 'appropriations', because of the difficulties which they raise today; when we are much further down the line, we can give a whole chapter to it.[114] In the *Summa*, Thomas exhibits the appropriations in the context of the problems which we have just discussed. Appropriation effectively presents a similar linguistic fact: it comes about when an essential attribute is connected to a person with which this attribute has a special affinity; an attribute such as power which is common to the divine essence of the three persons is 'appropriated' to the person of the Father who is Principle without Principle. The process of appropriation belongs to the rules which devolve from faith in three consubstantial divine persons.

In all of these instances, the synthesis which renders the plurality of the persons rests on the two aspects of the mystery of God (unity of essence and personal distinction) which the theologian constantly brings together, without conflating the divine reality with the language through which we refer to it. These two aspects are neither superimposed one on top of the other nor juxtaposed alongside each other, but are united and integrated in the theory of the person as subsistent relation. It is by means of this theory that St Thomas discloses the unseparated plurality and unconfused unity of the Trinity.

---

[109] *In Ioan.* 1.1 (nos. 53–59), cf. *In Ioan.* 14.1 (no. 1851).

[110] I *Sent.* d. 4, q. 1, a. 2: 'God has begot God'; cf. sed contra, 'God begotten by God' (this is the formula of the Niceno–Constantinopolitan Creed).

[111] *In Ioan.* 1.1 (no. 59).

[112] *ST* I, q. 39, a. 6; I *Sent.* d. 4, q. 2, a. 2, ad 5.

[113] This formula is put forward today by various authors: see for instance B. Studer, 'Credo in unum Deum Patrem omnipotentem', *Connaissance des Pères de l'Eglise* 73 (1999), 2–17. Karl Rahner's fundamental investigation played a decisive part in this development: '*Theos* in the New Testament', in *Theological Investigations*, vol. 1, trans. C. Ernst, New York, 1982, pp. 79–148.

[114] See below, Chapter 13.

8

The Person of the Father

Once he has given his exposition of the divine persons in their *plurality*, which was based on the notion of *person*, and which in its turn was built on the analysis of procession and relation, Thomas considers the distinctive character of each divine person. This methodology is unique to the *Summa Theologiae*. Since it tracks Peter Lombard's text, the *Commentary on the Sentences* mixes these questions together with other problems. Both in the *Summa Contra Gentiles* and in the *Compendium of Theology*, the exposition is structured with a view to the generation of the Son and the procession of the Holy Spirit. The *Summa Theologiae* creates a special section for 'each of the divine persons in particular' (qq. 33 to 38).[1] But this does not entail losing sight of the general plan of the Trinitarian treatise. It is not, for instance, just in the question devoted to the person of the Father (q. 33) that one finds Thomas' teaching about the Father, for this is present throughout the treatise: from the study of generation and the procession of the Spirit (q. 27) to that of the relations and persons (qq. 28–32), and likewise also in the comparison of the persons (qq. 39–43). Someone who wants to understand what Thomas has to say about the person of the Father cannot confine themselves to q. 33, but will have to read the whole treatise, and treat it as a unity. In the section given over to 'each of the divine persons in particular', Thomas especially examines the *unique properties* of each person. To narrow it down still further, these properties are envisaged from the perspective of the names through which we can truly designate the divine persons.

Thus, what Thomas is proposing to do when he considers each person distinctly in itself is to create an exposé of the 'divine personal names': *Father, Unbegotten, Son* and *Word, Image, Holy Spirit, Love* and *Gift*. This doesn't mean that his approach is exclusively concerned with language. It is the reality of the property of each person which is intended by means of the language, so it is at bottom an investigation of the persons themselves. But putting a terminological slant on the enquiry reminds theologians of the nature of their project. It is revelation, received in the Church, which makes knowledge

---

[1] *ST* I, q. 33, prol.; cf. q. 29, prol.

of the divine persons accessible to us. So it is by tracing the words of the confession of faith that one can pick out the characteristics of the divine persons.

The names of the divine persons indicate both the properties which are unique to them at the heart of the Trinity and also these persons' relations with creatures, in creation and in the economy of grace. Taking the divine persons in turn, St Thomas looks at each of them under two lights: first of all, in terms of the properties which are personal to them within the eternal Trinity, and then in respect of their relations to creatures. In these questions, 'theology' and 'economy' will be closely connected. This investigation builds up like a crescendo: one question about the Father, then two questions about the Son, and finally three for the Holy Spirit.

The name 'Father' has to go through a process of purification before it can be applied properly to God. By the fourth century, the patristic debates about Arianism had already showcased many of the reasons for this. As Christians ascribe it to God, the name 'Father' is removed from corporeal generation, sexual difference, temporal succession, ageing, and change. The study of the processions has shown this already: like the word *generation,* the name *Father* must be understood in terms congruous with God's spiritual nature (this is why the idea of the uttering of the word is set in the foreground), and in step with the elements which are unique to God, like simplicity, eternity, and so forth. This process is worked through carefully in the *Summa Contra Gentiles.*[2] The *Summa Theologiae* takes it up again, more briefly.[3]

As one clears away the features incompatible with God's perfection and with the Nicene confession of faith, what must one hold on to in the name *Father?* Two major features must be acknowledged, the two characteristics of the first person of the Trinity: (1) the Father is Father of the Son whom he begets and with whom he breathes the Holy Spirit; (2) the Father has no origin. The first of the features is expressed in the personal property of *paternity,* and the second by the notion of unbegottenness (the Father is unbegotten). According to Thomas, these two properties indicate the essence of the meaning which Trinitarian doctrine ascribes to the name 'Father'. The theologian can arrange the many facets of Christian faith in the Father around them, and this is how the treatise in the *Summa Theologiae* organizes its study of the Father (q. 33).

[2] See *SCG* IV, chs. 7–14.
[3] On generation see, *ST* I, q. 27, aa. 1–2; q. 42, aa. 2 and 4.

1. THE NAME WHICH FITS BEST: FATHER

The most fitting way of referring to the first person of the Trinity is to call him *Father*. This is one of the claims made by the council of Nicaea. Whereas, for Arius, to be God is to be *unengendered*, Nicaea, followed by Athanasius and Basil, sets the name *Father* in the foreground. God is *Father of a Son*.[4] Reappropriating what he learned in his study of divine persons, St Thomas takes account of this as follows:

A name proper to any person indicates that by which the person is distinct from all others.... Now, that which distinguishes the person of the Father from all others is Fatherhood. Thus the name *Father*, signifying his fatherhood, is the name proper to the person of the Father.[5]

One might imagine that it would have been simpler just to call on the New Testament evidence, and show the centrality which the name 'Father' has in it. We need to understand what Thomas is aiming at here. His purpose is precisely to address the language of Scripture. He is trying to show why we are required to use this specific, scriptural way of speaking. To achieve this, he does not just wrap himself up in the authority of the biblical language (he mentions it briefly[6]), but attempts to show the deeper reason for the language of faith, that is, to give the speculative key which enables one to unfold the priority given to the name *Father* by Scripture.

On the one hand, as a name, *Father* is neither an image nor a metaphor but a name which *properly* applies to the divine person. It signifies a 'perfection' in God: the relation according to which the Father is the source of the Son; in an act by which, in the identity of substance, he vitally communicates to him the fullness of divinity. Here St Thomas has the study of generation in q. 27 to draw on.[7] Whilst explaining that the divine Word is a reality which subsists, or exists, in God, he had shown how the procession of the Word allows one to understand what generation means in God. Whereas one only speaks metaphorically of a 'generation of the word' in relation to human thinking, all of the authentic features of generation can be shown to occur in the procession of the divine Word. So when one names God as *Son* and *Father* one is using language in an entirely appropriate way, not speaking metaphorically or using a verbal accommodation.[8]

---

[4] Cf. J. Wolinski, 'Le monothéisme chrétien classique', in *Le christianisme est-il un mono-théisme?*, pp. 158–160.

[5] *ST* I, q. 33, a. 2.   [6] *ST* I, q. 33, a. 2, sed contra.

[7] *ST* I, q. 27, a. 2; see above, in Chapter 4, 'A Procession which is the Generation of the Word'.

[8] *ST* I, q. 33, a. 2, ad 3; cf. a. 3.

As with all the names which make up our right-fitting language for God, *Father* must be considered in relation to the rules of analogy. The perfection indicated by this word is found primarily in God himself; this perfection is communicated to creatures through participation, and it is by this participation that some are genuinely 'fathers'; but, for the latter, the reality of paternity is merely derivative, for in God alone does there come about a perfect unity of Father with Son, that is, 'a perfection notion of paternity and filiation'.[9] We will come back to this later on.

On the other hand, the name *Father* properly designates the distinct person who is the Father. It is not a matter of an accommodation, as with the other names by which we indicate one person, by appropriating it to them (as with the 'Eternal', the 'All-Powerful', and so on), nor is it an 'activity' of the deity, as Eunomius of Cyzicus argued. The reason has already been stated: the name *Father* signifies that relation which is paternity. Since the persons are distinguished by their relations, the Father's relative property of paternity means the Father *in his distinct personhood*. Building on what has been shown by his theory of subsistent relations, St Thomas can explain that the name *Father* does not merely refer to a relation which the first person has, nor just to an activity of that person, but really signifies the person as such. The name *Father* refers to the relation of paternity as it exists in God, that is, to the divine person himself.[10] St Thomas says that,

the name *Father* signifies not just a property, but the person itself ... the reason: the name *Father* signifies the relation that is distinctive and constitutive of the hypostasis.[11] ... the relation to which the name *Father* points is a subsisting person.[12]

Thus, both in his speculation on personhood and in his linguistic analysis, Thomas very clearly aims at showing the primacy of the name *Father*. He accepts some other names which were current in patristic theology, like 'Begettor' or 'Progenitor', but he explains that these ones do not convey the same precision: they refer to the Father as source of generation, taken as a process, whereas the name *Father* means 'fulfilled generation', that is, the person himself, as a relative property.[13] He also refuses to foreground the name 'Unengendered' in the way that Eunomius of Cyzicus did. The negative meaning of 'Unengendered' must rest on a prior affirmation, expressing the Father's positive property: the positive property which

---

[9] *ST* I, q. 33, a. 3; cf. a. 2, ad 4.
[10] *ST* I, q. 33, a. 2, sol. and ad 1; cf. q. 29, a. 4. In respect of human beings, the name 'father' designates a relationship, that is, one of the person's relationships. In God, the person is no different from the relation itself: it is this relation which subsists; thus, the name *Father* properly refers to the person himself in his distinct subsistence.
[11] *ST* I, q. 40, a. 2.   [12] *ST* I, q. 33, a. 2, ad 1.   [13] *ST* I, q. 33, a. 2, ad 2.

constitutes the Father and is the source of the other words which we use to name the Father is paternity.[14] We will come back to it later, but the unswerving direction of Thomas' argument is already clearly in view: the name Father must take priority over every other aspect.

The Father's paternity is filled with his manifold relationships with his Son. It is surely in the relation which Jesus expressed in his humanity that we discover his divine relation towards the one he called *Abba*, his Father. The relationship which he experienced in his humanity is the personal relation of the Word to his Father: sonship is a relation which one person has with another, and it is by a Sonship unique to himself that Christ is the Son of the Father.[15] Many notions are involved in paternity. Without trying to give a complete overview, we can bring forward the moments which St Thomas accentuates.

(1) Paternity involves a moment of the Father's *affectivity and love* towards his Son: eternal generation is marked by love. Where the resemblance is perfect, St Thomas explains, love also is perfect. The Father has absolute delight in his Son *because he is his Father*:[16] 'the only Son is called "Son of charity" [of the Father] (cf. Col. 1.13), because the depths of the Father's charity falls upon him'.[17] Paternity also implies the Father and the Son's communion in the same volition, since the Father has by his eternal generating communicated the fullness of his will to the Son.[18]

(2) Paternity also brings with it a moment of *knowledge, understanding*. The Father and the Son know each other in a mutual 'comprehension'.[19] The Father communicates his knowledge to the Word by eternal generation;[20] it is his own knowledge which he expresses in his Word, in such a way that the Word is 'the doctrine of the Father' in person.[21] The Father and the Son communicate in the same divine *life*.

---

[14] *ST* I, q. 33, a. 4, ad 1.   [15] *ST* III, q. 23, a. 4; q. 32, a. 3; q. 35, a. 5.

[16] Cf. *In Ioan.* 3.35 (no. 545); 5.20 (no. 753); *In Matt.* 3.17 (no. 302); 17.5 (nos. 1436–1437).

[17] I *Sent.* d. 5, exp. text.

[18] Cf. *In Ioan.* 11.41 (no. 1553); 1.2 (no. 60: 'concordia voluntatis'); 5.30 (no. 798); etc.

[19] Cf. *In Ioan.* 10.15 (no. 1414): 'to know the Father as he is known by him is proper to the Son alone, because only the Son knows the Father comprehensively'.

[20] *ST* I, q. 42, a. 6, ad 2. Like Augustine, Thomas describes generation in terms of *vision*: 'the procession of the Son is nothing other than the procession of the divine Wisdom. And since "vision" refers to the derivation of the knowledge and wisdom coming from someone, generation of the Son coming from the Father has the right to be called "vision": to say the Son sees the Father acting, is the same as to say that he proceeds, through an intelligible procession, from the Father acting' (*In Ioan.* 5.18; no. 750).

[21] *In Ioan.* 7.16 (no. 1037). The Son sees and knows the Father because he is personally 'the Word of the intellect of the Father' (*In Ioan.* 3.32; no. 534).

(3) Paternity implies also the moment of a *common action* by Father and Son, because the Father eternally communicates his power of action to the Son: the Father achieves all that he does through the Son.[22] The persons have their distinctness within a unity of operation which the Father gives to the Son.[23]

(4) All these moments, plus more which could be added linked to the other divine attributes, have as their fundamental basis the eternally generated *communication of the whole divine being* by the Father to the Son, which the relative property of *paternity* expresses.

Divine paternity includes the features which belong to mothers, in creatures: conception, childbirth, caring for the child. In accordance with Scripture, maternal traits are ascribed to the Father: the Word is born 'from his womb' (*ex utero*), and he remains 'in the heart of the Father' (*in sinu Patris*). And it is 'for a mother to conceive and give birth'. In line with Scripture, St Thomas accepts maternal expressions like this, but, nevertheless, keeps the name *Father* for God. The 'things which belong distinctly to the father or to the mother in fleshly generation, in the generation of the Word are all attributed to the Father by sacred Scripture; for the Father is said not only "to give life to the Son", but also "to conceive" and to "bring forth"'.[24] Likewise, he uses the maternal image of childbirth to describe creation. And he also uses the image of the wise-woman to describe the providential activity of God, who does not just create the world, but cares for his creatures by leading them where they will flourish.[25] These maternal features are integrated into the description of the name *Father*.

The Father *as Father* thus communicates to his Son the whole treasure of divinity, except for the fact of being Father which, precisely, indicates his relation to the Son.[26] In the *Summa Theologiae*, Thomas sums up all the elements of his biblical exegesis in the more formal statement that paternity signifies the Father's 'relation of principle' towards the Son, that is, that the Father is the Son's 'principle'.

2. THE FATHER: PRINCIPLE AND SOURCE

The Father's two properties are exhibited by means of the notion of 'principle', which is present throughout the question devoted to the Father and which governs the whole theological discussion of the Father. To be able to grasp

---

[22] *In Ioan.* 5.17 (no. 740); 5.18 (nos. 750–751); 5.21–22 (nos. 761–763); etc.
[23] *In Ioan.* 17.22 (no. 2246).   [24] *SCG* IV, ch. 11 (no. 3479).
[25] See especially II *Sent.*, prol.   [26] *In Ioan.* 16.15 (nos. 2111–2112).

paternity and unbegottenness, one must first clarify what one means by *principle*. This theme takes us back to the origins of Trinitarian theology, and is commonplace in the Augustinian medieval tradition. But in Thomas the typical feature is the way he puts this notion at the heart of his investigation of the Father, because of its conceptual precision. Effectively, when we speak of one reality being the 'principle' of another, this does not intrinsically imply that the reality deriving from the principle is posterior or inferior to it. There are certain principles which do imply such an inequality or posteriority, because principle is an analogical notion; there are many ways of being a principle. One speaks of a principle to indicate a local position (a 'point of departure'), or to designate the foundation of a reasoning, or to refer to an end which one proposes to obtain, or again, to mention an efficient cause, and so on.[27] But, in its general usage, inequality of this kind is not included in the term's formal meaning.

This conception is not arbitrary, but rests on observation of our language and concepts. 'We also use the term *principle* to refer to things amongst which there is no difference [in perfection or of substance or distance], but which simply have a relation of origin: for instance, it is thus that we say that a point or even the first segment of a line is its principle.'[28] We can see once again how carefully St Thomas works on weighing the soundness of our language. It is not just by linguistic convention that we can name the Father as 'principle'— it belongs to the meaning of the term: 'without specifying how the origination happens, the name principle means an order of origin'.[29] It simply designates the reality from which something else proceeds. This name is thus apt for being used in reference to God, to signify a divine person in the relation which he has with another person who proceeds from him.[30] In this context, Thomas comments on a general rule in relation to our language for God:

Of all the terms relating to origin, the word *principle* is most appropriate to God. For since we are unable to comprehend the things of God it is better for us to indicate them by means of general terms which have an indefinite meaning, than to employ special words that have a definite signification. Wherefore the name *He who is* (Exod. 3.13–14) is said to be the most appropriate, seeing that according to Damascene it signifies *the boundless sea of substance*.[31]

This discussion shows the advantage of the name *principle* over that of *cause*. The term *cause* is more determinate than *principle*. 'Cause says more

[27] Cf. *ST* I, q. 42, a. 3.   [28] *ST* I, q. 33, a. 1.
[29] I *Sent.* d. 29, q. 1, a. 1; cf. *ST* I, q. 33, a. 1, sol. and ad 3.
[30] *ST* I, q. 33, a. 1; cf. q. 42, a. 3.
[31] *De potentia*, q. 10, a. 1, ad 9; cf. *ST* I, q. 33, a. 1; I *Sent.* d. 29, q. 1, a. 1; see also *ST* I, q. 13, a. 11.

than principle'[32] because it expresses a certain way of being a principle. And in our world, this way implies an externality and inequality of the effect in relation to the cause. The 'word cause seems to denote a diversity of substances and the dependence of the one on the other; "principle" does not suggest this. For in the genus of causality, there is always a certain distance in perfection or power between a cause and its effect. But, conversely, we use the word "principle" even with regard to matters in which there is no difference of this kind, but merely one based on some sort of order (*ordo*)'.[33]

If this linguistic analysis actually makes sense of the Latin and Greek traditions, that cannot be a matter of restricted interest: 'The Greeks use the names *cause* and *principle* interchangeably; but the Latin doctors do not employ the word *cause*: they only use the word *principle*.'[34] Behind the term *cause* can be found the Greek word *aitia* which, along with *arche*, Eastern Trinitarian tradition frequently uses with reference to the Father. In his very first teaching on this topic, Thomas calculated that, since it essentially implies dependence plus externality, 'the name *cause* is not suitable for designating the order of origin [of the divine persons]'.[35] So he regarded using it to refer to the Father as 'unfitting'.[36] Much later, St Thomas perceived rather better the traditional significance of this term, finding it in Latin translations of Athanasius of Alexandria, Basil of Caesarea, Gregory of Nyssa, and many others.[37] He fine-tuned his assessment, explaining that, 'by using this word, [the Greek Fathers] just wanted to show the origin of the persons, as we do by the word *principle*'.[38]

The study of this information gave him the opportunity to observe: 'There are many words which resonate well in the Greek language, but which do not sound right in Latin, and this is why the Greeks and the Latins profess the same faith in different words.'[39] In his *De potentia*, he specifies that the Latin Fathers 'only rarely or even never' apply the name *cause* to the Father, because of the meaning evinced by this term 'in our language' (*apud nos*). From the Greek side we find the use of 'the word *cause* to speak of God in a more absolute way, taking it to mean the sole origin'. Moreover, 'a term can be unsuitable in Latin, but, because of the character of the languages, could work in the Greek language'.[40] These findings are drawn into the *Summa Theologiae*.[41]

The Father's character is equally well designated by *auctor* as by principle, and by the cognate term *auctoritas* (principle, source), proximate to the Greek term *aitia* (cause). Difficult to translate into French or English, especially because of its moral sense and the hierarchical connotations exhibited by the

---

[32] *CEG* I, ch. 1.
[33] *ST* I, q. 33, a. 1; cf. *De potentia*, q. 10, a. 1, ad 9.   [34] *ST* I, q. 33, a. 1.
[35] I *Sent.* d. 29, q. 1, a. 1.   [36] Ibid., ad 2; cf. I *Sent.* d. 12, q. 1, a. 2, ad 1.
[37] See for instance the texts compiled in *CEG* I, ch. 1.   [38] *CEG* I, ch. 1.
[39] *CEG* I, prol.   [40] *De potentia*, q. 10, a. 1, ad 8.   [41] *ST* I, q. 33, a. 1.

word *authority*, these terms occupy quite a large position in the scholastic Trinitarian vocabulary deriving from the Latin Fathers.[42] 'With the Latins, it is not common to say that the Father is *cause* of the Son or of the Holy Spirit; one would say rather that he is their *principle* or their *auctor*.'[43] St Thomas explains that the name *auctor* denotes the principle which does not derive its being from another: 'This is why, even though the Son can be called *principle* [of the Holy Spirit], only the Father is named *auctor*.'[44] The name *auctor* thus denotes the relation of principle found in the person of the Father.[45] It just indicates the relation through which the Father is the source of the Son, without implying any inferiority in him.[46]

The language by which we refer to the Father as principle can be further enriched by other names. Later on, our investigation of unbegottenness will bring out the Augustinian terms 'principle without principle', 'principle of the divinity', and other expressions coming from the Greek Fathers. For the moment, we will mention the word 'source' (*fons*), which St Thomas took mainly from Pseudo-Denys, but also from Athanasius and Cyril of Alexandria.[47] The language of 'originary plenitude' (*fontalitas*) is more common in the Commentary on the *Sentences*,[48] but one also finds it in the *Summa Theologiae*.[49] St Thomas can easily take it on board by connecting the name to the foregoing analysis: the Father is named *source* under his aspect of 'principle without principle',[50] *auctoritas*.

Finally, in relation to the notion of *principle*, it is necessary to observe that St Thomas distances himself from the idea of a 'hierarchy' within the Trinity. The hierarchy theme, linked to the reception of the works of Pseudo-Denys

[42] St Hilary of Poitiers, in particular, uses this language very amply: the Father is *auctor* of the Son and of his generation (cf. e.g. *De Trinitate* IV.6; IX.54; XII.21; XII.25; SC 448, pp. 20–21; SC 462, pp. 128–129, 414–415 and 418–419). See L. F. Ladaria, 'Dios Padre en Hilario de Poitiers', in *Dios es Padre*, Semanas de estudios trinitarios, Salamanca, 1991, pp. 141–177, cf. pp. 149–150. This vocabulary is passed on by Peter Lombard (see particularly Peter Lombard, *Sentences*, Book I, dist. 29, ch. 3).

[43] *CEG* I, ch. 1.

[44] I *Sent.* d. 29, q. 1, a. 1. In other passages, Thomas takes the term *auctor* in a wider sense which equates to that of *principle* (see for instance *CEG* II, ch. 23). This usage can claim to be founded on his patristic sources, cf. for instance Hilary of Poitiers, *De Trinitate* II.29 (SC 443, pp. 322–323; the Father and the Son are *auctores* of the Holy Spirit).

[45] *De potentia*, q. 10, a. 1, arg. 17 and ad 17; cf. *ST* I, q. 33, a. 1, ad 2.

[46] Distancing himself from a common scholastic way of talking, St Thomas advises against using the word *subauctoritas* to denote the corresponding relation of the Son (or the Holy Spirit) to the Father, since it can suggest a certain subordination (*De potentia*, q. 10, a. 1, ad 9).

[47] Cf. *CEG* I, ch. 1; II, chs. 25 and 27.

[48] See for instance I *Sent.* d. 11, q. 1, a. 1, arg. 1; d. 12, q. 1, a. 2, ad 3; d. 28, q. 1, a. 1, sol. and ad 4; etc.

[49] Cf. *ST* I, q. 33, a. 4, ad 1.

[50] *In Dion. de div. nom.*, ch. 2, lect. 2 (no. 155); lect. 4 (no. 181).

the Areopagite, won through in some quarters. For instance, St Bonaventure connects the universe of 'created hierarchies' to the divine hierarchy. For the Franciscan master, this divine hierarchy consists in the perfect Unity and Trinity in God, which implies an order within the communication of the Good.[51] The Dominican theologian is more reticent about it, because the word 'hierarchy' connotes an inequality of degrees or levels, so it is incongruous to speak of a 'hierarchy' within the Triune God.[52] He is very firm about this: between the divine persons, there is *no priority whatsoever*, neither in rank, nor in dignity, nor in any other way.[53] The notion of *principle* enables one to avoid these ambiguities,[54] and St Thomas remains strictly attached to it. It is by means of this notion (plus the related theme of *order*[55]) that he describes paternity as a personal property, and the Father's unbegottenness: ' "to be principle" is proper to the Father in so far as the Father is the principle of the Son through generation'.[56]

3. THE PATERNITY OF THE FATHER: FATHER OF THE SON AND FATHER OF HIS CREATURES

(a) The Analogous Network of the Name 'Father'

When we call God *Father*, we can do so in many ways. As we have seen, the word *father* means a relation of paternity. And it is necessary to acknowledge many relations in virtue of which God is called Father: Father of his only Son, Father of all creatures, Father of humanity, Father of the saints. What is put into the word 'Father' in each of these cases is not identical. Or in other words, the relation intended by the word *Father*, or the corresponding relation of sonship, does not cover one single reality in an univocal way. This network of meanings is also connected to the progressive revelation of the paternity of

---

[51] See especially Bonaventure, II *Sent.* d. 9, *Praenotata*; cf. J. G. Bougerol, 'Saint Bonaventure et la Hiérarchie dionysienne', *AHDLMA* 36 (1969), 131–167.

[52] Thomas, II *Sent.* d. 9, q. un., a. 1, ad 6.

[53] I *Sent.* d. 9, q. 2, a. 1; d. 12, q. 1, a. 1. See above, in Chapter 4, 'The Order of the Trinitarian Processions'.

[54] *De potentia*, q. 10, a. 1, ad 10; *ST* I, q. 33, a. 1, ad 3.

[55] *Order* properly denotes the relation between the principle and what issues from the principle, without there being priority or inequality in God (*ST* I, q. 42, a. 3); cf. above, in Chapter 4, 'The Order of the Trinitarian Processions'.

[56] *In Ioan.* 8.25 (no. 1183). It belongs to the Father to be principle in three ways: as principle of the Son, principle of the Holy Spirit, and, in another way, principle of creatures. All the divine modes of being 'principle' coalesce in the Father.

God in the history of salvation. In the Old Covenant, the Father was revealed as the 'All-powerful God' (creation and election: providence), but not in the full sense that the Christian God would be. It is only in his relation to the one Son, Jesus Christ, that the Father reveals himself fully as Father, Father of his consubstantial Son.[57]

In the most proper, and the primary, sense of the term, the name *Father* refers to the Father's eternal relation to his only Son. The reason for this has already been given: 'It is in the Father and in the Son that the perfection of paternity and sonship is found, because the Father and the Son have the same nature and glory.'[58] Genuine fatherhood is a relation implying neither difference nor superiority in the Father, but only that the Father is related to the Son as 'principle': 'the very fact that in God the distinction of begetter and begotten is based on relation alone is part of the truth of the divine begetting and fatherhood'.[59] It is within the Triune God that paternity exists in its perfect modality, and this mode touches on the personal relation of the Father with his Son. To say 'Father' is not primarily to refer to God's relationship with his creatures, but to the eternal relation of the Father with his only Son, communicating to him from within their unity the fullness of divine life. The reason for these elaborations is to avoid the difficulties raised by Arianism. The upshot is that the Father's paternity toward his consubstantial Son is given primacy.

God's relationship of fatherhood toward his creatures is not eschewed, but it is understood to have a secondary position, derived from the first: 'fatherhood in God applies to God first as connoting the relation of the one [divine] person to another, before it applies as connoting the relation of God to creatures'.[60] The reason is as follows: 'the notion of being God's son is not present in creatures in its fullest sense, since God and creatures do not have the same nature: the sonship one sees here is based in a limited likeness'.[61] In other words: the Father is not our Father in the same way that he is the Father of the only Son, because he is Father of the Son by nature whereas he is our Father through creation and by grace, that is, by means of a similarity to the sonship of the only Son.[62] This 'similarity' is the creatures' participation in the sonship of the Son: just as the Son receives the fullness of divine being from all eternity, which is why he must be understood as 'Son by nature', so 'derivatively', creatures receive from God a participation in the divine being and goodness, aligned to the resemblance or similarity of the Son.[63] Thomas

---

[57] *In Ioan.* 8.19 (no. 1161).   [58] *ST* I, q. 33, a. 3.

[59] *ST* I, q. 33, a. 2, ad 4.   [60] *ST* I, q. 33, a. 3.   [61] Ibid.

[62] *In Ioan.* 20.17 (no. 2520). It is evident that St Thomas is particularly careful to avoid the Arian confusion between Christ's sonship and the sonship of creatures.

[63] *ST* I, q. 33, a. 3, ad 2; cf. *In Eph.* 3.15 (no. 169).

follows on from Albert the Great in adding an explanation of this by reference to the term *principle*: 'the procession of creatures has as its exemplar the procession of the divine persons. This is why *principle* is referred in absolute terms to the person and subsequently to the creature'.[64] The Son's eternal generation by the Father is in this respect 'the exemplar and the rationale' of the participation of creatures in being.[65]

From one perspective, human fatherhood is a participation in the paternity of the Father. And although St Thomas does not put it in these words (he is in this respect a child of his times, and depends on antiquated ideas which are now outdated), the same participation primarily effects human maternity, since 'Scripture attributes to the Father, in the generation of the Son, all of that which, in the physical generation of children, belongs to the father and the mother.'[66] This applies to parental paternity and maternity, and also extends, by analogy, to spiritual paternity and maternity: 'someone who leads someone else to an act of life, such as acting well, knowledge, willing, loving, deserves to be called "father" '.[67] In all of the areas of what we today describe as the progress of human dignity, or concern for life, St Thomas invites us to find a participation in the Father's paternity.

From another perspective, God's paternity with respect to creatures carries many different modes of realization. Even here, analogy remains. When we call God Father of creatures, we do not always take the name 'Father' in the same way, because we are speaking of diverse relations which creatures have with God. Thomas shows this when he discusses the degrees of participation. He states,

the more perfect the likeness to sonship is, the closer one approaches to a true notion of sonship. (1) God is called *Father* of some creatures by reason of a mere vestigial likeness: this is the case for sub-rational creatures; as we see in Job: *Who is the Father of the rain? or who begot the drops of dew?* (Job 38.28). (2) There are other creatures of whom God is the *Father* through an image-likeness; as Deuteronomy 36.6 puts it, *Is he not thy Father, who possessed, and made, and created thee?* These are rational creatures. Amongst these he is for some *Father* because of the likeness of grace; they are called his adoptive sons in that their receiving the gift of grace empowers them to come into eternal glory, as Saint Paul said; *The Spirit himself gives testimony to our spirit that we are the sons of God; and if sons, heirs also* (Romans 5.2, Vulgate): *We glory in the hope of the glory of the sons of God.*[68]

[64] I *Sent.* d. 29, q. 1, a. 2, qla 2. Most of what Thomas' Commentary on the *Sentences* says in relation to *principle* is connected to the discussion of *paternity*, in the *Summa Theologiae*. See Albert, I Sent. d. 29, a. 2, sed contra 2.

[65] I *Sent.* d. 10, q. 1, a. 1.

[66] *SCG* IV, ch. 11 (no. 3479).

[67] *In Eph.* 3.15 (no. 168). St Thomas explains that such spiritual paternity also touches the angels.

[68] *ST* I, q. 33, a. 3.

The theological model of 'nature–grace–glory' can be recognized in this discussion, and its connection to the distinction between sub-rational creatures and those which are to the image of God. The themes of vestige[69] and image are couched within God's paternity. The same model will be used in the study of the divine image, in the treatise on creation.[70] So the idea of participation and analogy discourages us from limiting the appelation 'sons of God' to the life of grace alone, and invites us to appreciate that it is realized in a diversified way in the thorough-going participation of creatures in God's being. Creation and the exercise of providence already give us a universal notion of paternity.[71] On the deeper level brought to light by Trinitarian faith, God's fathering of the saints comes about increasingly as the stage-posts of the economy of salvation are achieved: paternity of grace amidst the pilgrimage of faith, paternity of glory within the beatific vision. We will come back to the theme of sonship later on, in the study of the personhood of the Son, but we can already observe its fundamental structure.

(b) The Name 'Father': the Person of the Father and the Trinity

For these reasons, Thomas follows St Augustine[72] in recognizing that the name *Father* can also refer to the Trinity, that is to the three persons taken together under the aspect of sole Creator and unitary Providence. One has to get hold of what this extended sense of the name *Father* means. St Thomas looks closely at the *relation* to which we refer when we call God 'Father'. All three persons create us, take care of us, and save us, so if the relation in question is a matter of our relationship to the Creator and Saviour God, then it affects what the three persons have in common; so, in this connection, the name *Father* refers to the Trinity as one single God, 'our Father'.[73] God is called 'our Father' under the aspect of creation, through which he establishes us in his image, but also because of the providence through which he leads his children as free beings, not slaves, and finally under the aspect of adoption as sons through grace.[74] According to St Thomas, our relation to God in these

---

[69] *ST* I, q. 45, a. 7. Thomas also recalls here that 'the processions of the persons are in a certain way the cause of creation' (ad 3).

[70] *ST* I, q. 93, aa. 1–4.

[71] Hence, persons of very different beliefs can be grouped together in acknowledging the *Father* God, without it following that they use the word to mean the same reality or the same relation (analogy).

[72] Augustine, *De Trinitate* V.XI.12 (*BA* 15, pp. 450–451).

[73] See especially *In 1 Cor.* 1.3 (no. 10); *In Col.* 1.3 (no. 7), etc.; cf. also *In Ioan.* 14.18 (no. 1922).

[74] *Expositio in orationem dominicam*, prol. (no. 1028). Commenting on the 'Our Father' in Matthew's Gospel, Thomas particularly draws out these features of the Father: providence (God

aspects is not restricted to the person of the Father alone, but touches on the whole Trinity.[75]

To understand this elucidation, first recall what the name *Father* properly means. When we confess the Father, signifying by this word the first person of the Trinity, we profess him as a distinct person: we conceive him according to his relation to the Son, since it is through his relation to the Son, with whom he breathes the Holy Spirit, that the Father exists as a distinct person. To name God *Father* in its complete Christian meaning is always to name him *under the aspect in which he is the Father of his only Son*. St Thomas sees this as a requirement of the dogma professed at Nicaea and at Constantinople. It is not a divine action within this world which renders God *Father*, but rather God is Father because of his relation to the Son, at the heart of the Trinity. God does not happen to have the attribute of paternity, but is Father from before the foundation of the world through his relation to the Son whom he begets of himself. So the primary thing is the Father's paternity in respect of the Son, and it is to this eternal person-to-person relation that the name *Father* properly refers. When it draws human beings into its ambience, God's paternity takes place in a different order of relations: not on the plane of the relations immanent within the Trinity, but on that of the relations which God sustains with the world. And it is not these relations with the world which make the Father a distinct person: relations with the world do not introduce a real distinction into the Triune God. In his relations with the world, God is engaged simply as God, so to speak. We can use the name Father to indicate his relation with the world, but strictly taken in itself the term means the divine reality of the three persons. When we use the name 'Father' to signify God's relation to the world, this word actually connotes the whole Trinity.

Consequently, when he comes on the name *Father* in his scriptural exegesis, St Thomas first of all seeks to pin down from the context and word meanings what kind of paternity it affects. If the name *Father* is actually conditioned by the Father–Son relation, then the word *Father* denotes the divine person in its proper distinctness. If the name *Father* touches on the creature–relation, then it will refer to the whole Trinity.[76] St Thomas often recalls the following rule covering divine personal names like Son, Word, Love, or Gift: in these names,

takes active care for human beings), love which invites a response of love, imitation (mercy), and humility (acknowledgement of our condition as the Father's children); cf. *In Matt.* 6.9 (no. 584). Affection will thus be a special sign of sonship in relation to the Father (*In Ioan.* 8.42; no. 1234).

[75] In the statement, 'God is our Father', we refer to an action of God's (creation, providence, care for human beings, etc.), which in and of itself brings out the whole Trinity, since the three persons are God and inseparably exercise this action.

[76] See *In 1 Thess.* 1.1 (no. 5); *In Gal.* 1.1 (no. 7); 1.4–5 (nos. 14–15); *In Rom.* 1.7 (no. 72), etc.

the personal distinction is lodged in the intra-Trinitarian relation, divine person to divine person, and not in the relationship with creatures. This relationship with creatures attaches to the person in virtue of the nature common to the entire Trinity.[77] In the case at hand, Thomas draws two senses out of the name *Father*, the second being linked to the first: one sense in which the name *Father* indicates the intra-divine relation of the Father to his Son, and one sense in which *Father* designates the action or relation of God towards creatures in creation, in providence, and in the gift of grace. In this second sense, on the ontological level, the name *Father* applies to the whole Trinity.

St Thomas explains this in detail in his investigation of our adoption as sons. To adopt is an *action*, and this action engages the three divine persons. The Father, Son, and Holy Spirit achieve the work of adoption inseparably, because they bring it about in virtue of their divinity, and in this divinity each person is reciprocally in the other. And since the action is achieved by the three persons, the effect which results from it must also be attributed to the three persons, in such a way that the relationship of adoptive sonship onto-logically refers us to the Trinity in its entirety. Since it is not to be exclusively reserved for any one divine person, filial adoption will thus be appropriated to the three persons: 'filial sonship is appropriated to the Father as to its author, to the Son as to its exemplar, and to the Holy Spirit as to the one who imprints in us the resemblance to that model [the Son]'.[78] The appropriation is not founded in a Trinity-to-human relation, for the three persons act through a common action (it is this, precisely, which is appropriated), but on the properties of the three persons, that is, on a divine person-to-person relation.

The Father is the personal source of the action in which adoption consists, for it is he who sends the Son and the Holy Spirit through whom he achieves filial adoption. The Son is the exemplar or model of our enfiliation, in virtue of the fact that he is Son to the Father, for 'adoptive sonship is a similitude of eternal sonship'.[79] And, through the gift of his grace, the Holy Spirit inscribes this sonship in our hearts, by dint of the property personal to him: 'the Holy Spirit makes us sons of God because he is the Spirit of the Son'.[80] The Father effects adoption in that he is the *author* or *principle of the Son and of the Holy Spirit*. The Son effects adoption in that he is the *Son of the Father*.

---

[77] Cf. *ST* I, q. 34, a. 3, ad 1. When he is considering the procession or communication of the divine nature within God, St Thomas also formulates this rule like this: since the procession of persons is the cause of the procession of creatures, a divine personal name can signify not only the intratrinitarian relation but also, and as a consequence, the relation of the divine persons towards creatures (I *Sent.* d. 27, q. 2, a. 3, ad 6).

[78] *ST* III, q. 23, a. 2, ad 3.   [79] Ibid.; q. 45, a. 4; *In Eph.* 1.5 (no. 9); etc.

[80] *SCG* IV, ch. 24 (no. 3606).

The Holy Spirit effects adoption in that he is the *Spirit of the Son*. These are the features upon which appropriation is based. These features are taken from the personal properties, that is from the relations of the divine persons to one another. They ground the appropriation of an *action* (adoption) which, as such, is exercised by the three persons, and this action results in a *relation* (adoptive sonship) which refers us ontologically or objectively to the whole Trinity.

This teaching is common doctrine. St Albert is very straightforward about it: when one speaks of God as 'our Father', the word *Father* means the Trinity as a whole.[81] Bonaventure is equally explicit: adoptive sonship makes us children of the Trinity: 'there can be no doubt about this'. In language which is very close to Thomas' own, the Franciscan Master explains that: 'If the name *Father* is said in respect of one person, it bears a personal sense; and if it is said in respect of the rational creature, it bears an essential sense. This is why, in the same way that, by producing its nature, the Father, Son, and Holy Spirit are one single principle of the creature, in the same way they are one single Father in the gift of grace.'[82] Bonaventure concludes that, 'We are sons of Christ's Father... but not of the Father alone, because Christ is the Son in a different manner from that in which we are sons: Christ is the Son through begetting, which is a personal action, whereas we are sons through creation and the gift of grace, which is an essential action that the Father communicates to the whole Trinity.'[83]

St Bonaventure's comments involve two important distinctions which one also finds in Thomas.[84] Firstly, the name *Father* has two meanings because the natures of the eternal Son and of human beings are different. This is why we are not children of God in the same way that the only Son is. St Thomas explains that, 'through adoption, we become brothers of Christ in having the same Father, but the Father is Father of Christ in one way and of us in another... He is Father of Christ by begetting him of his own nature, and this is his own character; whereas he is our Father by volition, and this belongs to him together with the Son and the Holy Spirit'.[85] In this context, Thomas emphasizes that filiation sets up a 'community' between Christ and believers ('we have the same Father as him'), but indicates the exclusive prerogatives of

---

[81] Albert, *Super Matt.* 6.9 (ed. Colon., vol. 21/1, p. 178); the name Father 'stands in for' the whole Trinity.

[82] Bonaventure, III *Sent.* d. 10, a. 2, q. 3.

[83] Ibid., ad 2.

[84] Thomas, *In Ioan.* 20.17 (no. 2520). It follows from Thomas' view that the error of Arianism consists in thinking that the only Son is son in the same way as we are, through an act of creation.

[85] *ST* III, q. 23, a. 2, ad 2.

the only Son. The only Son is 'begotten not created', whereas human beings are children of God through creation and re-creation. For Thomas, this is required by the Nicene creed. The essential dividing line is not between the Father and everything else, including the Son, but between the Trinity and those other realities which creatures are. The distinction of Uncreated and created thus leads one to recognize that the Father, Son, and Holy Spirit are on the one side of it, and creatures on the other. For this reason, on an ontological and objective level, our relationship with God is a relationship with the Triune God, that is, Father, Son, and Holy Spirit in their inseparable divinity. We are children of the Father of Christ, 'but not of the Father alone', because the Son and the Holy Spirit bring about our filiation in unity with him.

This teaching does not obviate the distinct character of the person of the Father (this has already been suggested by the appropriation). This is the second piece of fine-tuning: in an action on the part of the Trinity, performed by the divine persons, the property personal to the Father is engaged from within the mutual intra-Trinitarian relationships. It is from the Father that the Son and the Holy Spirit take their divine being, and it is from the Father that the Son and the Holy Spirit receive their action. The modes of action of the Son and Holy Spirit take their distinct stamp from their relationship to the Father. Adoption is an 'essential action communicated by the Father through the whole Trinity'.[86] This is why one expresses the Father's action as proper to him (and not through appropriation), when one acknowledges that: 'the Son is the one through whom the Father acts' or in confessing that 'the Father achieves his works through his Son in the Spirit': the Father alone acts through his Son in the Spirit. One thus points not only to the Father's relationship with creatures, but primarily to the Father's personal relation with the Son and the Holy Spirit, in which he co-engages when he acts on behalf of creatures. The personal distinction is not effected from the side of the divine action, since he acts from his essence, nor from the side of its results, for the same effects flow from the Father, the Son, and the Holy Spirit, but from that of the mutual relations of the divine persons which characterize their mode of being and of action.

To sum it up, this analysis can be restructured around three basic themes. First, the Father's paternity consists primarily in his relation to his only Son: the perfection of paternity and of sonship rests here, and it is this relation to which the name *Father* refers in the full and proper sense given to it by Trinitarian faith. Second, the relationships of creatures towards God the Father are not situated on the same plane as the Son's inner-Trinitarian

---

[86] See below, in Chapter 14, 'The Persons' Distinct Modes of Action and their Unity in Action'.

relation with the Father; they are not 'of the same order' or 'of the same nature'. So the person of the Father can only be understood as distinct on the basis of the first plane, the intra-Trinitarian relationship of paternity. Third, it is through participation (by 'derivation') in the eternal filiation of the Son by the Father that creatures have a filial relationship with God the Father. Hence, God is called Father of creatures by analogy with the eternal paternity of the Father (the Father's inner-Trinitarian relation to the Son), by a different avenue whose highest realization is found in the gracious adoption of the saints.

St Thomas thus develops an understanding of the economy centred in the person of the Father as the origin and ultimate goal of the universe and of human life. But, before one can tackle this 'paternal' theology of creation and the economy of grace, one has to pin down what one means when one designates the Father as 'Unengendered' and 'principle not from a principle'.

4. UNBEGOTTENNESS: THE UNENGENDERED FATHER

Thomas' exposition of the Father's paternity is based on the notion of *principle*. He also uses this notion to explain the Father's characteristic property of unbegottenness. Seen in the perspective of his action on the world, the Father is the principle of creation and of the economy in conjunction with the Son and the Holy Spirit: the three persons are thus recognized as 'one single principle' of creatures.[87] Seen in the perspective of the intra-Trinitarian life, in a completely different order of relations, ' "to be principle" belongs to the Father, in that the Father is the principle of the Son through generation'. And, according to Catholic doctrine, the Father is also the 'principle' of the Holy Spirit, with the Son.[88] And since the Son takes his being the principle of the Holy Spirit from the Father, Thomas falls in behind St Augustine in teaching that the Holy Spirit proceeds 'principally' (*principaliter*) from the Father: the word *principaliter* means the Father is the 'principle' of the Son with whom he breathes the Holy Spirit.[89] He adds to this that the Father himself is *without principle*, something which cannot be said of the Son or the Holy Spirit since they

---

[87] Creation does not make creatures enjoy three different relations with God (one with the Father, one with the Son, and yet another with the Holy Spirit), but rather one single relation with the creating Trinity.

[88] *In Ioan.* 8.25 (no. 1183).

[89] I *Sent.* d. 12, q. 1, a. 2, ad 3; cf. *ST* I, q. 36, a. 3, ad 2.

proceed from the Father. The Latin tradition uses the term *innascibility* (*innas-cibilitas*) to express this latter feature of the Father: the Father is *unengendered*.

One must immediately clarify this: Thomas eliminates the confusion between the two meanings of 'unbegotten' which had created the problematic behind the Arian crisis. Arianism was the vehicle of a conception which had yet to make a distinction between 'to be engendered' and 'to become'. The problem could be even more subtle when, in Greek, the formulation of the difficulty hung on one single alphabetical letter, *nu*. According to a common standpoint within Hellenistic culture, the word 'unbegotten' can refer to an essential property of God: God is not the product of any becoming, he is not subject to genesis, he is not begotten (*agenêtos*). But this word can also refer to the Father's unengenderedness, for what distinguishes the Son from him is that he is engendered by the Father: it properly belongs to the Father to be unbegotten (*agennêtos*). For a time, the terminology wavered. In many ancient texts, the meaning of the words is only apparent from the context. The Arian crisis compelled Christian theology clearly to distinguish the two concepts and the language which expresses them: the Son is *begotten*, but he does not *become*. Thomas is put in mind of this by John of Damascus: the word *unengendered* can refer to 'that which is uncreated' (which does not become), and in this sense it applies to each of the three divine persons; but it can also designate 'that which is not engendered or which does not proceed from another', and here it indicates, not the common divine substance of the three persons, but the property of the Father. It is in this latter sense that one speaks of the Father as unengendered or unbegotten.[90]

The exposition in the *Summa* presents the unbegottenness of the Father in combination with the Augustinian idea of the Father's being 'principle not from a principle'.[91] The Commentary on the *Sentences* adjoins this to an Eastern theme coming from Pseudo-Denys: the Father is the 'fountain of divinity'.[92] In his reconsideration of the 'notions' through which we grasp his person, Thomas uses these bases for his examination of how we know the Father.[93] This point of departure tells us a great deal. Since he goes on to explain

[90] *ST* I, q. 33, a. 4, ad 3. Cf. St John of Damascus, *De fide orthodoxa* VIII.8, in the translation made by Burgundio of Pisa (ed. E. M. Buytaert, New York, 1955, p. 35): 'oportet scire quod ageniton per unum n scriptum, increatum, scilicet quod non factum, significat; agenniton per duo n scriptum, ostendet quod non genitum est'.

[91] *ST* I, q. 33, a. 4.

[92] I *Sent.* d. 28, q. 1, a. 1. For an initiation into this theme both in Eastern theology and in the Western tradition, see Y. Congar, 'The Father, the Absolute Source of Divinity', in *I Believe in the Holy Spirit*, vol. 3: *The River of the Water of Life (Rev 22.1) Flows in the East and in the West*, pp. 133–143.

[93] On these 'notions,' see above in Chapter 2, 'Why Investigate Notions, Relations, and Properties?'

that unbegottenness consists in a negation (the Father is not-engendered), St Thomas is clearly looking at this from the perspective of *our knowledge* of the mystery. Amongst created beings, two traits make something known as a 'first principle' as such: on the one hand, the fact that this first principle is the source out of which something derives; and, on the other hand, the fact that this principle does not issue from something else: it is, precisely, first. There is properly speaking no 'first principle' in God, because there is no priority amongst the divine persons, but, in one respect, the two traits can still be found within our knowledge of the Father's person:

The Father is known to us in one respect through his paternity and spiration, that is to say, through his relation to the persons who proceed from him. But, in a different respect, in so far as he is "principle not from a principle", the Father is known to us under the aspect in which he himself does not come from the person of another: That is what constitutes the property of not being begotten, to which the term "unengendered" refers.[94]

Thomas explains next that the name *Unengendered* and the property of *unbegottenness* refer to a negative. Basil of Caesarea had already expounded this in response to Eunomius of Cyzicus, and St Augustine had brought it into the West.[95] Thomas explicitly refers to the latter: 'According to Augustine, it must be acknowledged that the name *Unengendered* indicates the negation of being engendered: "Saying he is unbegotten means the same as that he is not the Son." '[96] This is not a matter of a privation which would undercut the divine perfection of the Father, since the fact of not being engendered does not deprive the Father of any divine good. It speaks of a negation, more precisely, a negation of a relation of origin.[97] 'The term *Unengendered* means that which is not born; and then it is a relational term . . . since then, in the Godhead to be begotten implies relation, to be unbegotten likewise involves relation. What follows, then, is that the unbegotten Father is distinct from the Son begotten not in substance but solely by a distinction of relation, from the fact that the relation of sonship is denied of the Father.'[98] Unbegottenness is not for all that any less of a genuine property of the Father and a notion which enables us to know Him, since it is a good expression of one aspect of

---

[94] *ST* I, q. 33, a. 4; cf. I *Sent.* d. 28, q. 1, a. 1.

[95] St Basil: 'The unengendered (*to agennêton*) indicates that which is not present [. . .] If you want to call this a privative or an exclusive or a negative or something else of that kind, we will not argue with you. But I think that we have sufficiently shown that unengendered does not indicate that which exists within God' (*Contra Eunomius* I.10; SC 299, pp. 206–207); cf. Augustine, *De Trinitate* V. VI–VII.

[96] *ST* I, q. 33, a. 4, ad 1. Cf. Augustine, *De Trinitate* V.VII.8.

[97] *ST* I, q. 33, a. 4, ad 2.   [98] *ST* I, q. 33, a. 4, ad 3.

the Father's person: the Father does not derive his being from another. Albert the Great had already explained this in much detail, before St Thomas did so.[99]

The question of unbegottenness exposes a split between Bonaventure's Franciscan Trinitarian theology and the Dominican school to which Albert and Thomas belonged. For St Bonaventure, unbegottenness does have a negative face (the Father has no principle), but there is also a positive face on it. Not to receive his existence from another, as Bonaventure explains it, that is, to be first, constitutes a position of nobility: and his primacy implies fecundity. 'It is *because he is first* that the Father begets [the Son] and breathes [the Spirit].' With the Franciscan Master, Unbegottenness designates precisely the fecundity of primacy. So it does not just consist in a negation, but also in the affirmation of a positive feature of the Father, in other words, his primordial fecundity which 'produces' the other divine persons: 'the unbegottenness of the Father signifies his originary plenitude (*plenitudo fontalis*)'. According to Bonaventure, this is the meaning of the Augustinian theme of the Father as 'principle not from a principle' or 'principle of the whole deity'. As a result, the Father's proper distinction is initially posited in terms of unbegottenness ('we can conceive of the hypostasis of the Father himself without conceiving another person, and it is thus conceived without paternity'), and is drawn out to its fullness by paternity. To be even more precise, the Franciscan Master has it that, 'it is *because he is unbegotten* that the hypostasis of the Father engenders [the Son]'.[100]

On first glance, the divergence could look abstruse or trivial, but in fact it reflects a fundamental characteristic of the thought of these theologians. St Bonaventure foregrounds the theme of primacy: originary plenitude is taken to be the root or source of the Father's paternity. Despite some nuances typical of Latin theology, this conception probably could stake an affinity with Byzantine theology. On the other hand, with St Thomas, unbegottenness refers to a negation which, as such, rests on the recognition of the Father as principle within the order of relation: the Father engenders his Son and breathes the Holy Spirit, but no one has the relation of principle to the Father.[101] As St Thomas sees it, the Bonaventurian thesis implies that the Father would somehow be constituted in his personal subsistence in advance of his paternity-relation. He takes this to be an extra-relational conception of the Father. Against Bonaventure, he argues that: 'If we take paternity out of

[99] In his Commentary on the *Sentences*, St Albert dedicates no fewer than six articles to the unbegottenness of the Father (I *Sent.* d. 28, aa. 1–6).

[100] Bonaventure, I *Sent.* d. 27, p. 1, a. un., q. 2, sol. and ad 3; d. 28, a. un., q. 2; d. 28, dubium 1. There is an English translation containing some extracts from this in Y. Congar, *I Believe in the Holy Spirit*, vol. 3, pp. 108–114.

[101] Thomas, I *Sent.* d. 28, q. 1, a. 2.

consideration, then we can no longer conceive the Father's hypostasis.'[102] So he distances himself from the Bonaventurian view that the unbegottenness signifies the Father's originary plenitude: 'This cannot be true, because then unbegottenness would not be a property distinct from paternity and spiration ...: in the Godhead to be source... means exactly the same as to be principle of origin.'[103] It is clear what is at stake in this debate about the unbegottenness of the Father: it is about the relational idea of the person, that is the role of the relative properties (paternity, filiation, procession) in the distinction and the constitution of the hypostases or divine persons.

Hence, the patristic expressions are explained by means of the doctrine of person and of relation. The Father, as Augustine puts it, is 'principle without principle', 'principle of the whole divinity', or 'principle of the deity'. This means that, without receiving his being from another, the Father is the principle both of the Son whom he engenders and of the Holy Spirit who proceeds from him; he is the principle from whom the other persons come forth.[104] It is to this relation of the Father to Son and Spirit that one refers when one says that the Father is 'source'; and this is what is designated by the 'originary plenitude' of the Father.[105] When he reads in Pseudo-Denys that the Father is the 'source of the deity' (*fons deitatis*) or that the 'originary deity' (*fontana deitas*) is in the Father, Thomas explains that these expressions designate the Father as 'principle without principle' or as 'author', in the way that Augustine speaks of it.[106] This takes us back to the two main features of the investigation of the Father: being himself without principle, the Father is the principle of the Son and the Holy Spirit.

5. FROM FATHER TO FATHER

Understanding the Father as *Source* within the Trinity, or 'principle without principle', is also a good way of illuminating the economy. Taken from the perspective of appropriation, because the Father manifests himself as Source, this characteristic of the Father carries over into the attribution of power, of eternity, of creation, and of other similar features, to the person of the Father.

---

[102] I *Sent.* d. 28, q. 1, a. 2, ad 3. This had already been the teaching of St Albert the Great (I *Sent.* d. 28, a. 4). See above, in Chapter 6, 'Relation the Heart of Trinitarian theology.'

[103] *ST* I, q. 33, a. 4, ad 1; cf. I *Sent.* d. 28, q. 1, a. 1 and a. 2.

[104] I *Sent.* d. 15, exp. text.; I *Sent.* d. 29, exp. text.; cf. for example Augustine, *De Trinitate* IV.XX.29.

[105] *ST* I, q. 33, a. 4, ad 1.

[106] *In Dion. de div. nom.*, ch. 2, lect. 2 (no. 155); ch. 2, lect. 4 (no. 181); I *Sent.* d. 28, q. 1, a. 1.

St Thomas has explained earlier that the identity of the natures of the three persons accounts for their unity. But this very unity can be envisaged under the aspect of the person of the Father himself, or rather *in* the Father's person:

When we consider the properties of the persons, we find the notion of, as it were, 'first principle' in the Father. And it is in virtue of the unity of a principle without principle that, the same nature is communicated to all, within each nature. This is why *it is through the Father that all is one.*[107]

The divine unity would therefore be appropriated to the Father,[108] because the Father is the principle of unity in the Trinity. Just as 'unity of form unfolds from unity of principle', so the consubstantial unity of the Trinity comes from the person of the Father.[109] The unity of the three persons is not taken solely from the level of the common divinity, but also issues from the relations which Son and Holy Spirit have with the Father. The Son and the Holy Spirit are drawn from the Father, who bestows his unity on the Trinity.

This analysis also illuminates the Father's action within the perspective of the economy of salvation.[110] The Father's mode of action is that of the principle or source within the Trinity: his Son and Spirit issue from him, and he acts through them. In his Commentary on the *Sentences*, St Thomas explains this by describing creation and the operation of grace in terms of the going out and return to God. Coming forth from God in creation, creatures move toward the good under the hand of divine providence. With reasonable creatures, angels and human beings, this assimilation to the divine Good is refined to participation in the divine happiness, through the knowledge and love of God. One can thus see a sort of 'circulation' amongst creatures: divinely created, they return to the Creator.[111] God is the *alpha* and *omega*, the principle and the end. This creaturely movement towards, or relationship with, the God who is their principle and their end is rested in the action of the Son and the Holy Spirit, the source of which is the Father:

In the coming out of creatures from the first principle, one observes a certain circulation or 're-gyration', in the fact that all things take as their end point of return that which produced them as their principle. And therefore it is necessary that the

[107] I *Sent.* d. 31, q. 3, a. 2.

[108] This is an oft-repeated theme in Thomas, which he takes especially from Hilary and from Augustine: *ST* I, q. 39, a. 8; q. 47, a. 2, ad 2; *ST* III, q. 58, a. 2, ad 3; I *Sent.* d. 31, q. 3, aa. 1 and 2 (the second article is entirely given over to this issue); etc.

[109] I *Sent.* d. 31, q. 3, a. 2, ad 1.

[110] See our article, 'Le Père et l'oeuvre trinitaire de création selon le Commentaire des *Sentences* de S. Thomas d'Aquin', in *Ordo Sapientiae et amoris: Image et message de St Thomas d'Aquin. Hommage au Prof. J.-P. Torrell OP*, ed. C.-J. Pinto de Oliveira, Fribourg, 1993, pp. 85–117.

[111] IV *Sent.* d. 49, q. 1, a. 3, qla 1.

return to the end come about through the same realities through which the 'exit' from the principle was achieved. Thus, in the same way that the procession of the persons is the rationale for the production of creatures by the first principle, so likewise the procession of the persons is the rationale of this return to the end; since, in the same way that we have been created through the Son and the Holy Spirit, so likewise it is through them that we are united to the ultimate end, as Augustine makes clearly apparent when he writes, 'the principle to which we return', that is, the Father, 'and the form which we imitate', that is, the Son, 'and the grace through which we are reconciled' [that is to say, the Holy Spirit].[112] And Saint Hilary says:[113] to one alone without-principle and the principle of all things we refer all things by way of the Son.[114]

In this discussion, the Father appears as the *source* and *end* of the whole divine economy. On the one side, the Father is the origin of all things: he is the principle of the Son and of the Holy Spirit through whom he acts on the world. It is through the generation of the Son and by the procession of the Holy Spirit that the Father exercises his paternal action. He is in this sense the source of creation, because he is the source of the persons through whom he creates the world. The Father also acts as the *conclusion* of the missions of Son and Spirit. The work of Son and Holy Spirit consists in leading us to the Father. The Father is thus, in an Augustinian phrase which Thomas echoes, 'the principle to which we return'. The Father is the personal conclusion of our journey, because he is the source of the Son and the Holy Spirit through whom he is re-joined to us and we are led to him.

This is the reason why Christians offer praise to all three persons, but especially to the Father. Human beings are introduced to the Father by the Son and Holy Spirit: they are linked into the relation which the Holy Spirit and the Son have with the Father.[115] It is in this sign that Christian prayer is offered to the Father. Union with God is brought about, in the Holy Spirit, in our joining to the Son who leads us to the Father, principle without principle and source of all good. This is why Christ taught us to address our prayer to the Father.[116]

St Thomas underlines the close correspondence between the outlay of the immanent mystery of God and that of the Trinitarian economy. One is touching here upon the mysterious aspect of the Father's action. Source of the communication of the divine fullness at the heart of the Trinity, the Father

[112] Augustine, *De vera religione*, ch. 55, no. 113.
[113] Hilary, *De Synodis* 59. XXVI (PL 10.521).
[114] Thomas, I *Sent.* d. 14, q. 2, a. 2. For a more complete exposition of this passage, and other related texts in Thomas, see our book, *La Trinité créatrice*, pp. 390–402.
[115] Cf. I *Sent.* d. 15, q. 4, a. 1.
[116] IV *Sent.* d. 15, q. 4, a. 5, qla 3, ad 1.

appears at the end of our journey into Trinitarian life; we only have access to the Father in the Son and through the Spirit. The Father is thus the 'principle without principle' within the Trinity and the source within Trinitarian action; and, in the same way that he is source, he is also that towards which, under the operation of the Son and the Holy Spirit, human beings are lifted by grace and advance within it. Everything comes from the Father and returns to the Father.

9

The Person of the Son

In the *Summa Theologiae*, the next step after study of the person of the Father is to give two questions to the person of the Son. The remarks with which we began the last chapter about the Father apply in the same way here. On the one hand, one must not lose sight of the broader strategy of the treatise. The teaching about the Son's personhood is not pigeon-holed into questions 34–35, but is present throughout. Thomas effectively begins his Trinitarian treatise with the procession of the Son (q. 27), so as to lead the reader into the doctrine of relations and of the divine persons (qq. 28–32) where the personal alterity between the Father and the Son stands out, even as he shows their consubstantiality. Moreover, question 33, which is given over to the Father, has the Son at its heart: it is because he is the Father *of the Son* that the Father is Father. The Son will be found once again, at the centre of the enquiry into the person of the Holy Spirit (qq. 33–38), and again in the comparative study of the persons (qq. 39–43), and, especially, in the investigation of the persons' missions (q. 43). One has to read the whole treatise to understand what it has to say about the Son.

1. STUDYING THE PERSONAL PROPERTY OF THE SON

In the section which is explicitly given over to the Son's personhood (qq. 34–35), St Thomas restricts himself to examining the *personal property* of the Son, and spotlighting what makes this property distinct. One could add that the Trinitarian approach to the Son's person also involves reflection on the persons of Father and Spirit. Within the methodological and pedagogical requirements of the treatise, the theologian envisages each of the three persons in turn, but without forgetting their indissoluble unity and inseparable relations. He will give a more precise analysis of this at the end of the investigation of the persons, using the idea of perichoresis.

As with the study of the Father, the personal property of the Son is viewed through the filter of the *names* through which we specifically signify the Son's personality. The approach is not purely linguistic, but it does take the language of revelation as its starting-point. These names give rise to a twofold reflection: the Son within the immanence of the Trinity, and in the Trinitarian economy. And, as in the whole of Trinitarian theology, reflection on the person of the Son is very intimately bound to Christology.[1] One side of it aims at bringing the Son's personal existence and eternal property within the eternal Trinity to light, and its other side is economic, seeking to illuminate creation and salvation within the Son, creating the bases for Christology. Such a reflection can be organized around the many names which the Bible gives to Christ: Son, Life, Truth, Word, Image, First-Born, Wisdom, Power, Saviour, and so on. Amongst these names, some are attributed to the whole Trinity in common, and are appropriated to the Son (for instance, Wisdom, Truth, or Power); so they are not adequate means for knowing what the Son's personal property is. The tradition stemming from Augustine, which had been sys-tematized by Peter Lombard, drew up its reflection on the Son around three main names which indicate the Son in his personal property: Son, Word, and Image.[2] These three ways of formulating the Son's personal property are the foundation for the other names which Scripture and tradition give the Son.[3] More important, as we have said, they give us the basis for organizing and exposing the person and work of the Son of God.

St Thomas begins with a question about the name *Word* (q. 34), then he moves on to the name *Image* (q. 35). At first glance, the absence of a question about the name *Son* can seem surprising. What can explain it? On the one hand, the investigation of the name *Father* could not have been carried out without studying the name *Son*, which was given the same priority as *Father*, since paternity is utterly bound up with sonship. Bearing 'relative opposition' in mind, these relational ways of naming are mutually inclusive. Thomas has explained that the Father is Father as 'Father of the Son' by drawing out the fact that 'the perfection of paternity and of sonship are found in the Father and in the Son'. This is why *son* is a name which belongs primarily to the eternal Son, taking creatures in its tow within many degrees of participation as its beneficiaries, through assimilation to the filiation of the Son.[4]

---

[1] One must keep in mind the distinction between *our journey of discovery* (the reception of revelation and the economy of Christ and the Holy Spirit, opening up the way to knowledge of the Trinity), and the order of *reality-itself* (the eternal Trinity which freely reveals itself within the passage of history); see above, Chapter 1.

[2] See Peter Lombard, *Sentences*, Book I, dist. 27, ch. 3 (vol. I/2, pp. 206–207), where one also finds this reference to Augustine.

[3] Cf. *ST* I, q. 39, a. 8.

[4] *ST* I, q. 33, a. 3. See above, in Chapter 8, 'The Paternity of the Father: Father of the Son and Father of his Creatures'.

On the other hand, and at a deeper level, it is the exposition of 'Word' which discloses what the name *Son* really means within God. St Thomas' methodology can be illustrated from his exegesis of the prologue to St John's Gospel. He asks why the Fourth Gospel begins by mentioning the Word, not the Son (*In the beginning was the Word*). Basing himself on John Chrysostom, he explains this as follows:

The name *son* means something begotten, and when we hear talk of a 'generation of a son' someone might suppose that this generation is the kind he can comprehend, that is, a material and changeable generation. So, because the Word pertains to an intelligible procession, [the Evangelist] wrote *Word* rather than Son, so that it would not be understood as a material and changeable generation. And so in showing that the Son is born of God without becoming [literally, impassibly],[5] he eliminates a faulty conjecture by using the name *Word*. One can also respond that the Evangelist is about to consider the Word as having come to manifest the Father. But since the idea of disclosure is implied better in the name 'Word' than in the name 'Son', he preferred to use the name Word.[6]

We saw a similar procedure in the first question of the treatise. In order to avoid conceiving the Son either as one would a creature, or as a straightforward appearance of the Father himself, theology requires an analogy adequate to grasping the generation of the Son; one that steers clear of Arianism and of Sabellianism. This analogy was found in a word's 'proceeding' immanently within a mind.[7] The generation of the Son is set forward using this motif of the procession of the word (q. 27, aa. 1–2); in the same way, it is from the *Word* that one can now show how to get hold of a *Son* in God (q. 34, aa. 1–2). Otherwise put, as a name, *Word* offers a better way of showing what it means to be *Son* in God, by regarding the Son in a way that reflects the spiritual nature of God and the profession of faith in the consubstantiality of Son and Father. In addition, the name *Word* enables one to showcase the Son's economic work, since 'Word' inherently involves a note of manifestation or revelation (as we will see further on, it also contains a note relating to action). We have already seen that Thomas puts this even more neatly in his *Disputed Questions De Potentia*:

in God there cannot be any origination but what is immaterial and which fits the intellectual nature [of God]: such is the origin of Word and Love. For this reason, if

---

[5] The 'impassibility' indicates that the Son is begotten without the becoming which is characteristic of carnal generation. St Thomas finds this phrase in the Acts of the Council of Ephesus, which likewise connects it to the distinctive property of the Word (see below, in this chapter, n. 65).

[6] *In Ioan.* 1.1 (no. 31).

[7] See above, in Chapter 4, 'A Procession which is the Generation of the Word'.

the procession of Word and Love is not enough to insert a personal distinction, no distinction of persons could be possible in God. This is also why both in the beginning of his gospel and in his first epistle John uses the term *Word* instead of *Son*; and we may not speak of God otherwise than Holy Scripture does.[8]

These observations relate to two questions: (1) how can a human 'origin' word be competent to refer to a superior reality which is known only through revelation; and (2) how can one assign a precise place to the language of revelation within the operations of theology? In the first place, Thomas bears in mind that, like the procession of the Spirit, the generation of the Son must be grasped in a way that fully does justice to the immateriality of God, to the spirituality of his nature in love and knowledge. To be able rigorously to disclose this kind of divine origination, that is, to be able to use our human experience to conceive an immaterial origin, one needs an analogy which involves this spiritual element. Despite its very great depth, the analogy of human generation has unsuitable implications in this respect, because this kind of generation is neither immaterial nor of a purely spiritual order. To be able to grasp precisely what the *Son* is within God, one must rethink how to conceive an *immaterial and spiritual sonship*. This is where the analogy of the word comes into play. St Thomas thus recaptures the Johannine language which uses the *Word*-name to refer to Christ (*Logos*: Jn 1.1; 1.14; 1 Jn 1.1; Rev. 19.13). A close attention to the notion of Word will open up the inward meaning of the scriptural teaching, and enable us to exhibit the reason why we are bound by this scriptural language if we want to understand the personality of the Son in a way which fits the case.

The investigation of the person of the Son is therefore a *theology of the Word*. Thomas pays extraordinary attention to this theme in every one of his great works. This is a highly technical chapter of his Trinitarian doctrine, and we will restrict ourselves here to indicating its main features. Although it is difficult, it is of the first importance, because, as his comments in the *De potentia* clearly show, the doctrine of the Word is incontestably the heart of Thomas' Trinitarian theology. Amongst the Fathers, it was St Augustine who particularly worked on pinpointing the nature of the 'word' within a theory of relation.[9] Thomas' project can be seen as a personal development of this legacy. He puts forward his own viewpoint 'as following on from what Augustine has shown'.[10] The way in which he deepens the doctrine will bind Trinitarian anthropology and theology closely together. On the one hand, his Trinitarian research provides the opportunity for a more precise

[8] *De potentia*, q. 9, a. 9, ad 7.
[9] Cf. H. Paissac, *Théologie du Verbe: Saint Augustin et St Thomas*, Paris, 1951, pp. 9–100.
[10] *De potentia*, q. 9, a. 5.

disengagement of what the word means in human knowledge; and, on the other hand, the value of the Trinitarian doctrine of the Word rests on the bearings of anthropology, in the analogical order which governs our knowledge of God and our language for him.

2. STUDIES IN THE ANALOGY OF THE WORD: ANTHROPOLOGY AND TRINITARIAN THEOLOGY

St Thomas did not always set to work in such a decided way.[11] In his first synthetic text, his Commentary on the *Sentences,* he exhibits the procession of the divine persons by taking begetting as an act of nature and spiration as an act of volition. In other words, the notion of a 'generation of the Son' seemed enough to him, and above all the notion of the *Word* seemed imperfectly to fit the presentation of the faith at which he was aiming. There is a simple reason for this: he does not arrive at showing that the name *Word* refers to a distinct divine person, as opposed to the divine nature common to the three persons. Saint John uses the name Word very effectively to indicate the Son as person; and the Church does likewise. But the theologian does not find it enough just to call on Scripture or Church authority by themselves, because if one wants to account for what they do, one has to show *why* their practice is compelling, that is, to explain its *truth.* And St Thomas had not yet achieved an explanation of why the name Word means precisely one distinct person, not just because this can be tacked on to it, but because it is in and of the nature of the term itself to mean this.

This difficulty is lodged in the theory of knowledge. What is a word within our minds? If one just takes 'word' as meaning a likeness or representation of the reality known to our minds, through which the reality is known, this will not be sufficient to locate the properly personal meaning of the term *Word* when it is ascribed to God. For God knows himself and is disclosed to himself through his own essence, and one can see from this that, when it refers to God, the name *Word* can also reflect a meaning relating to essence, for it means nothing less than the divine nature common to the three persons. There is effectively no real distinction, within God, between the act by which he knows, that by which he knows, and the reality which he knows. Some

---

[11] For what follows, see especially F. von Gunten, '*In Principio erat Verbum.* Une évolution de St Thomas en théologie trinitaire', in *Ordo sapientiae et amoris,* pp. 119–141; H. Paissac, *Théologie du Verbe*; Y. Floucat, *L'intime fécondité de l'intelligence: Le verbe mental selon St Thomas d'Aquin,* Paris, 2001.

people could argue that all there is to it is that St John and the Church took the term *Word* in an entirely personal sense. But this assertion does not help us out in showing what makes this word intrinsically fitting to be the exclusive and proper name for one divine person. Conversely, if one considers the mental word as being something distinct from the intellect which conceives it, then, when it is applied to God, *Word* will refer to the distinct person of the Son; but it will only be by linguistic convention that one limits the term *Word* to this strictly personal meaning.

Returning to his analyses when he revised his Commentary on the *Sentences*, St Thomas tackled the same problem again. He now observes that the word is relative to the mind that conceives it. If one gauges its meaning from the natural workings of the created thing which the name 'word' was originally cut out to signify, then one would be forced to acknowledge that, when it is attributed to God, the term *Word* can designate either the divine essence or the person of the Son. And if one considers such a relation as real, then the term *Word* refers to the person of the Son who is in fact distinguished from the Father by his relation of origin. To put it another way, St Thomas' earliest writings hold on to two aspects in the word, as we find it in the human mind: (1) that through which the mind knows or the act of knowledge itself; (2) a relation which links the word to the principle which 'pronounces' it. If one takes nature, or the operation which it is originally intended to perform within created reality, as the gauge of its meaning, then one would be forced to acknowledge that, when it is attributed to God, the term *Word* can designate either the divine essence or the person of the Son. It will then be 'the usage of the saints' rather than the intrinsic properties of the word which drives us to maintain an exclusively personal meaning for the name *Word*. The same problem recurs when one considers the process of knowledge in the light of relation: 'The name *word* does not just signify a relation, as the names *father* and *son* do, but is used to refer to a reality which is absolute but which, at the same time, also has a relation, as happens with the word *science*.'[12] One can clearly observe the difficulties which Thomas is in here. Like St Albert,[13]

---

[12] I *Sent.* d. 27, qla 2, a. 2. On the two editions of the Commentary on the *Sentences*, see F. von Gunten, *In principio erat Verbum*, pp. 121–128; cf. G. Emery, *La Trinité créatrice*, pp. 414–420.

[13] Albert the Great, I *Sent.* d. 27, a. 6. Bonaventure escapes the problem by explaining that 'to speak the Word' implies the conception of this Word: for God, it touches on the generation of the Word in an exclusively personal sense (Bonaventure, I *Sent.* d. 27, p. 2, a. un., q. 1). From St Thomas' perspective, this reply leaves the difficulty standing. He explains, 'This question has a superficially easy look to it, if we take it that a word implies an origin in virtue of which the divine persons are distinguished. But, if one examines it more deeply, the question reveals great difficulties, on account of the fact that we find in God some aspects implying an origin which is solely conceptual, and not real' (*De veritate*, q. 4, a. 2).

he has not been able to explain why the precise denotation of the term *Word* makes it purely relative to the Father.

The disputed questions *De veritate* make a minor advance on this, but one still finds the two aspects of the 'word': the word as the token of what is known to us, and the word as it is expressed by the mind. Observing that what is known within our minds proceeds from our minds, St Thomas explains that a 'word' implies an 'out-going' or 'emanation' from the mind. So 'word' has a relation to the mind which conceives it. But he still does not clearly distinguish between this 'word' and the activity of knowledge itself. In other words, the intrinsic relation which is implied by the nature of a word could be real, but it could also just be a 'relation of reason': and this means it cannot create a real distinction between one person and another within God. This analysis leads one to hold that the name 'Word' has a double edge when it is applied to God. If one takes the term 'word' in its foremost aspect, as that which is known in us, *Word* is an analogous way of speaking of the divine nature; but here we are only holding on to one partial aspect of the notion of Word. Openness to the complete meaning of the name *Word* requires that we grasp the combined aspects, (including its being expressed by another); and then in its fullest and most inward meaning, *Word* will refer to the person of the Son who proceeds from the Father.[14]

It is only with the *Summa Contra Gentiles* that St Thomas' mature theory begins to appear. The theory he develops now is unique to him amongst his contemporaries. From now on, he considers the mental word (*verbum, intentio intellecta*) very precisely as that which the mind expresses or *forms* within its act of knowledge.[15] He makes a clear distinction between the word itself, on the one hand, and all the other aspects of intellectual knowledge on the other; the word is not the activity of knowledge, but that which, within this act of knowledge, really proceeds within the mind. The word is no longer seen as an intelligible *species* or the idea of the thing known, that is, as the likeness of the thing known in the mind, that through which the intellect knows and which puts the mind into an active state of knowing, the intelligibility of the thing in act. The word is the *expression* of the thing known in the mind of the knower; *formed* by the intellect, its existence is intrinsically relative. From now on, Thomas' earlier desire to keep the term 'word' at arms' length evaporates. Looking at it in the light of the fact that the 'word' is constituted by a relation of origin toward the mind which speaks it[16]

[14] Thomas, *De veritate*, q. 4, a. 2.
[15] *SCG* I, ch. 53; *SCG* IV, ch. 11. L.-B. Geiger, 'Les rédactions successives de *Contra Gentiles* I, 53 d'après l'autographe', in *St Thomas d'Aquin aujourd'hui*, 'Recherches de philosophie, 6', Paris, 1963, pp. 221–240.
[16] *SCG* IV, ch. 11 (no 3473).

effectively opens the way to recognizing something purely personal in what the name *Word* means within God. St Thomas can now make a precise connection between the notion of Word and his understanding of relation. The relative being of the 'word' is perfectly positioned for exhibiting the person of the Son of God.[17] The doctrine of the Holy Spirit as *Love* will be constructed on the same ground.

If one wants to show that the name *Word* means the person of the Son, it will no longer be necessary to sacralize a linguistic tradition or run for help to 'what the saints did'. The meaning towards which it naturally gravitates and which is conveyed by the function of the created reality which the name 'word' was originally invented to signify, enables one to show that, when one attributes it to God, *Word* properly refers to the person of the Son. Because he sets out to show that the Johannine use of language is perfectly fitted to indicating the Son in his relation to the Father,[18] Thomas only refers to St John's Gospel. The disputed questions *De potentia* and then the *Summa Theologiae* elaborate on the theory which was formulated in the *Summa Contra Gentiles*.[19] We will present this through a brief consideration of the John Commentary, which gives us the final state of the question.

In order to grasp what a 'word' is, one has to examine the structure of our language. The Aristotelian theory of language gives us a way into this: 'vocal speech is a signal of passions which are in the soul'.[20] In other words, our externally pronounced words are signs indicating the content of our conception of realities external to us.[21] The vocal speech is the *sign* of this interior conception, our mind's 'internal word' or the 'speech of the heart'. Vocal speech is a sign neither of our faculty of knowledge nor of the acts through which we know: when we call a cat a 'cat', we do not intend to refer either to our intellect or to its act of calling the cat a cat, but to the fact that it is a cat. It is no better to suggest that vocal speech indicates that 'through which' we know a cat: the 'that through which' which Thomas calls the 'intelligible *species*'[22] is the active intelligibility which informs our mind, that is, the form

---

[17] For a more detailed exposition, see our article, 'Le traité de St Thomas sur la Trinité dans la *Somme contre les Gentils*', *RT* 96 (1996), 21–27; *Trinity in Aquinas*, pp. 71–120.

[18] One can count seven citations from John 1.1 in Book IV of the *Summa Contra Gentiles*, two citations of 1 John 5.7 and six citations from John 1.14 (cf. F. von Gunten, *In principio erat Verbum*, p. 139).

[19] *De potentia*, q. 8, a. 1; q. 9, a. 5; q. 9, a. 9; q. 10, a. 1; *ST* I, q. 34, aa. 1–2.

[20] *In Ioan.* 1.1 (no. 24); cf. *ST* I, q. 34. a. 1. Aristotle, *On Interpretation* 1 (16ᵃ3). See also Augustine, *De Trinitate* XV.X.17–XV.XI.20.

[21] Words do not directly refer to the external realities which we know, but refer first to the conception which we form in our mind, the conception through which our mind unites itself to the known reality; cf. *SCG* I, ch. 35.

[22] The Latin word *species* translates the Greek *eidos*.

of the known reality, abstracted from material conditions, which presents the
known object to our mind and puts our mind into an active state of knowing.
This is obviously not what we intend to refer to in our use of words; 'this is
not the intention of the one who names something'.²³

So the remaining option is that what we are signifying through our spoken
words is the conception of the known reality which we *form* within us. The
conception we form is the *concept* or *word* of the known thing which our
intellect *expresses* within itself and which *proceeds* internally within our mind.
It can either be a matter of the word which we conceive when we grasp
something's nature, expressed in its definition, or the complex conception
through which we separate or connect concepts in order to build them into
phrases. The word is not that *through which* the mind knows (which is the
species) but is, rather, the *fruit* of an internal making or conceiving, the
expression of the reality known within our mind: the word is that 'in which'
(*in quo*) our mind knows realities. The word is thus relative through and
through. It is relative to the mind which forms it and to the known thing
which is manifested to the mind which conceives it. It is through the word
that we 'unite' ourselves to the known reality.²⁴ 'And with this we now know
the meaning of the term "word".'²⁵

In sum, the central feature which a word bears in itself is the fact of
proceeding from an active intellect. In so far as it expresses a known reality,
the word is also 'like' to this reality. And if that which knows is simultaneously that which is known, then the word will be the perfect expression and
likeness of the mind from which it proceeds. From this standpoint, Thomas
can see the analogical status which the word has for human beings, for
angels, and in God. When we consider the Word in God, the fact that we
are dealing with something divine constrains us to appreciate that there are
many differences here from our human word. It is not a matter of the
demands of a theological thesis forcing one to tone things down, but the
properties which are bound up with the very notion of 'divine Word'. This
Word does not travel from potency to act, and nor does it result from a
discursive noetic process, for the way in which God knows is perpetually
active and direct. So the Word is co-eternal with the One who utters him.
The Word is unique in that, whereas we know through a series of acts of
knowledge (and thus through a series of words), the Father knows himself
and knows all things in one single act. Finally, this Word is neither an

²³ *In Ioan.* 1.1 (no. 25). This is precisely the point which Thomas did not perceive so clearly in
his earlier teaching.
²⁴ See above, in Chapter 4, 'A Procession which is the Generation of the Word'.
²⁵ *In Ioan.* 1.1 (no. 25).

accident nor a qualification which 'happens to' God, but has the same nature as God, for reason can show that the divine mind in God is nothing other than God himself. The divine word is thus a distinct reality subsisting in the divine nature.[26]

Has one then fallen for the rational temptation to *prove* an article of the Creed and *demonstrated* the personal being of a Word in God? St Thomas' answer to this would be 'No', because 'the analogy with our minds does not constitute a sufficient proof to demonstrate something about God, because reason does not exist univocally in God and in us'.[27] It is a matter of an 'argument from congruity', a 'persuasive reason' which enables one to grasp only what has been received from revelation, that is to say the faith, made known to us. But, using an analogy which gets to grips with the content of the confession of faith, one has disclosed how we can get to grips with the generation of the Word in God. This analogy preserves a profound respect for God's spiritual nature, since it draws on the word's spiritual procession. It attempts to illuminate believers' minds by starting from what is closest to them, the word in our own human mind, to open the door a little way onto the mystery of the divine generation of the Word.

3. THE SON, WORD OF GOD

It is by means of his idea of *Word* that Thomas unveils a congruent way of understanding the *Son* of God. But before he does that he subjects the name *Word* to a linguistic critique, testing and fine-tuning its precise quality.

Having drawn up the results of his analysis of the word, it is not difficult to show, first, that 'Word' is very much a personal name for God. 'It appears, from what has gone before, that properly speaking the Word is always taken in a personal sense in God, since a word designates nothing other than that which is expressed by the one who knows.'[28] In its created realization, proportioned to what we can adequately know, that is, within our human minds, in its principal and primary attribution, the word properly refers to that which the mind conceives within itself when it takes a known reality as its subject; in the second place, the word designates the external speech which refers to this speaking with one's self; finally, since the spoken word comes from the imagination, it can signify the formative image of this speech. In his

---

[26] *In Ioan.* 1.1 (nos. 26–28); cf. *De rationibus fidei*, ch. 3. Augustine writes about the divine prerogatives of the Word in *De Trinitate* XV.XIII.22–XV.XVI.26.

[27] *ST* I, q. 32, a. 1, ad 2. See above, in Chapter 2, 'The Aim of Speculative Trinitarian Theology'.

[28] *In Ioan.* 1.1 (no. 29).

account of its privileged, divine make-up, Thomas has no difficulty in showing that, within God the name *Word* means a reality of a personal, rather than
essential, order, because it proves on reflection to contain an immanent
procession and a relation of origin. 'In God the proper meaning of the term
"Word" is one proceeding from another: this is numbered in the ranks of the
personal names, because the divine persons are distinct on the basis of origin,
as we have shown.'[29] From this point on he can integrate his idea of the Word
with everything he has said earlier about relations (q. 28), the person (q. 29),
and personal plurality within God (qq. 30–32).

In these elucidations, Thomas is particularly careful to put some space
between his own idea of the divine Word and all the assorted essentialist takes
on the Word. Seeing it as the intellectual idea of God's essence, or as the divine
knowledge common to the three persons, is not his style of understanding the
Word. 'Word is the only one amongst the terms referring to the intellect
which is predicated in a personal way of God ... for a word is what the intellect forms in its conceiving.'[30] As we have seen, the intellect and its
intelligent act are essential realities, absolutes. Thomas at this point brings
in a striking correction to the avenue laid out by Anselm of Canterbury in his
Monologion. One cannot disclose the personal character of the Word simply
by looking at knowledge or by reflecting on the 'Supreme Mind'.[31] Doing that
ultimately rebounds into a Sabellian conception of the Word, because it
cannot show a real relation within God between the Word and the One
from whom he proceeds. In other words, Thomas rules out understanding
the Word as if it were a derivate of the divine essence. One of the fundamental
features of his Trinitarian epistemology is brought out again here. Faith in the
Trinity cannot be adequately set forth by beginning from God's essential
attributes (which are the matter for appropriations). Their personal distinctions do not arise within the order of essence, but in the order of relative
properties.[32] To avoid confusing these two orders, one must distinguish
carefully between the following notions:

- To know (*intelligere*): this is an essential act, common to the whole Trinity;
  each person knows himself and knows the others. God knows himself
  through himself and, in this way, knows other things.

---

[29] *ST* I, q. 34, a. 1.   [30] *ST* I, q. 34, a. 1, ad 2.
[31] *ST* I, q. 34, a. 1, ad 2 and ad 3; cf. *De potentia*, q. 9, a. 9, ad 8. This relates to particular
terminological issues, but these points cut across the different theological routes which one finds
in St Anselm and in St Thomas.
[32] See above, in Chapter 3, 'The Essence and the Distinction of Persons: the Common and the
"Proper"'.

- To be known (*intelligi*): God is known through himself; each person is known by the others.

- To speak (*dicere*): this is the action proper to the Father who 'speaks' or 'pronounces' his Word; this 'notional action', which is identical to *generation*, is done by the Father alone: neither the Son nor the Holy Spirit 'speak the Word' any more than they 'engender the Son'.

- To be spoken (*dici*): each person in the whole Trinity and even creatures are 'spoken' by the Father in his Word: 'In knowing himself, in knowing the Son and the Holy Spirit, and in knowing everything which is contained in his science, the Father *conceives* the Word: and thus the Trinity is spoken in the Word, and creatures in addition.'[33]

So one needs to make a distinction between *knowledge* in God (which is an act of his nature, shared by the whole Trinity), and *speech* (which is a personal or 'notional' action of the Father). Thomas explains this in the course of reflecting on the connections between the two cases. In the case of *knowledge*, where a subject is related to a known reality, there is of course a relation. But in God the knowing subject is really identical to the known reality; thinking about this relation will not enable one to disclose the Trinitarian faith, because there is here no relation of origin, which could make for a real distinction amongst the persons. This discussion is closely configured to the theory of the processions. The essential attributes (nature and will, or intelligence and love) cannot distinguish the divine persons. The distinction must belong to a different schema, that of the *order* within the Trinity, that is, at the level of relations of origin.[34] In the case of *speech*, one can observe a relation which is very much a real one: it does not touch on the relation of the knowing subject to the known reality, but consists in the Word's link with the one who pronounces him; this is the relation of origin which makes Father and Son distinct.

Just as with the name *Father*, the name *Word* belongs to the genuine language of the faith. It is not just a metaphor or an image, but a *proper* name for speaking of the Son. What is at stake here, with the Word as for the Father, is the rejection of Arianism. If one holds that the Son is the Word of the Father but reduces the name *Word* to a metaphor, one has taken the first step on a path leading to the denial of the consubstantial divinity of the Word with his Father[35] (the same danger arises if one treats the name *Son* as a metaphor). It is only when one includes within the term 'word' the *works*

---

[33] *ST* I, q. 34, a. 1, ad 3.

[34] See above, in Chapter 4, 'The Order of the Trinitarian Processions'; or in Chapter 6, 'Relation at the Heart of Trinitarian Theology'.

[35] *ST* I, q. 34, a. 1, ad 1.

which the divine Word achieves that something metaphorical comes into play here. For creatures are also, in a sense, a 'word' which the Father pronounces, a 'word' in which God is manifested: 'all things proclaim, it is God who made us'.[36] One can metaphorically describe creatures as a 'word' because of their function as display-screens. This metaphorical sense presupposes a divine Word in the proper meaning of the term: the creatures who show God forth are the 'speech of the Word'.[37] We will come back to this later on when we reflect on the action of the Word within the world.

Once having accurately anchored our language, St Thomas can refine on the perspective opened up by the doctrine of the Word:

It looks clear from what has gone before that the divine Word is the *likeness* of Him from whom he proceeds. Likewise, the Word is *co-eternal* with the One from whom he proceeds, since he was not in potential to being formed before being actually formed, because he is always in act. The Word is also *equal* to the Father, since he is his perfect Word, expressing the whole being of the Father. And the Word is *co-essential* and *consubstantial* to the Father, since he is of his substance.[38]

The notion of 'divine Word' as such is the means of putting these features of the Word's personality on view: an expressive likeness of the Father who pronounces him, not tangled up in potentiality, consubstantial to the Father. In sum, the doctrine of the Word enables one to account for the touchstones of the Son which Christians profess in the Creed. As the *Summa Contra Gentiles* points out, this was already the teaching of the prologue to the Fourth Gospel: the Word is distinct from the Father ('the Word was *with God*') and he himself is God ('and the Word *was God*').[39] This idea of the Word eliminates the Sabellian conception of the generation of the Son, just as it does for the Arian heresy.

The crux of the matter is the relation of origin uncovered in the divine Word. This is what enables us to show that the divine Word is really distinct from the Father; the relation of origin is that the Word proceeds from the Father. St Thomas flourishes the significance of his discovery. The fact of proceeding, of being distinct from and having a relation of origin with, the conceiving intellect 'belongs to the notion of word as such'. And since the nature of the Word in God is not different from that reality which is paternal intellect, or that of God himself, 'there remains the distinction of relation ... in so far as the Word is related to the one who conceives as to Him from whom He is'.[40]

---

[36] I *Sent.* d. 27, q. 2, a. 2, qla 2, ad 3; *ST* I, q. 34, a. 1, sol., ad 1 and ad 4.   [37] Ibid.
[38] *In Ioan.* 1.1 (no. 29).   [39] *SCG* IV, ch. 11 (no. 3473).   [40] Ibid.

Thomas reckons that the same point also shows the constitutive features of the notion of *Son* within God:

in every nature, that which proceeds and has a likeness to that from which it issues, is called a son. And it is clear that the Word proceeds in a likeness and identity to the nature of the one from whom he proceeds. Thus, the Word is suitably and appropriately called Son, and his production is called *generation*.[41]

The Word is a person who subsists in himself, distinct from the Father from whom he proceeds; being equal to, and of the same nature as, the Father, he is the perfect expression and presentation of the Father. The notion of *Word* also enables one to grasp what it means for God to be Son, using an analogy which is adapted to the spiritual nature of God. To put it another way, it is the notion of the *Word* which, according to St Thomas, gives one an understanding of *begetting the Son* which is best fitted to God. He had not argued otherwise in his study of the processions, in q. 27 of the *Prima Pars*.[42] One can see the same approach from the *Summa contra Gentiles* onward. The doctrine of the Word is developed after an exposition of the problems of Arianism and of Sabellianism, and is brought in precisely in order to respond to the theological objections which were raised against faith in the Son.[43] In that work, Thomas explains that the notion of *Word* likewise enables one to show that the Word is in his essence the image of the one who speaks him: 'the Word has his very nature in common with the speaker'. He is thus properly the *Son* because 'that which proceeds from a living thing in the likeness of species is called son'.[44] The divine Word also proceeds *by nature*, since God the Father knows himself naturally (his understanding being really identical to his nature and to his being). Thomas writes:

since the Word of God is of the same nature as God speaking [the Father] and his likeness, it follows that this natural procession leads into a likeness of the one who is the source of the procession, and in an identical nature. And this is the genuine notion of generation in living beings: that which is generated proceeds from him who generates in being his likeness and of the same nature as he is. Therefore, the Word of God is truly *begotten* by God [the Father] who 'speaks' him: and his procession can be called *generation* or *birth*. This is why the Psalmist says, 'This day have I begotten

[41] *In Ioan.* 1.1 (no. 29).
[42] *ST* I, q. 27, aa. 1–2. See above, in Chapter 4, 'A Procession which is the Generation of the Word'.
[43] This sequence is a good indication of how the doctrine of the Word operates in allowing one to grasp the truth of the faith we profess and thus to distance oneself from falsehood (cf. above, Chapter 2): St Thomas sets out the arguments against the divine generation of the Son (*SCG* IV, ch. 10), then he presents his doctrine of the Word (chs. 11–13), and it is through this that he can reply to the objections brought against Christian faith in the Son (ch. 14).
[44] *SCG* IV, ch. 11 (no. 3476).

thee' [Ps. 2.7], that is: this generation is always actual in eternity, it has no past or future to it.[45]

This elucidation aims to cut out the Arian thesis that the Father engenders the Son, not through his nature, but by an act of volition; the upshot of this would be conceiving the Son as a creature.[46] But, on a deeper level, the analysis shows that, in its constitutive elements, the 'speaking of the Word' must be formally considered as a *generation*, since it proves to have the authentic notes of generation. St Thomas follows up the identification of speaking the Word and generation when he shows that the Word is *conceived* in an analogous way to human offspring. His conception is an authentic *childbirth*, like the idea of childbirth which we find in Old Testament Wisdom literature: the books of Proverbs and Wisdom speak of a giving birth within the divine immanence of the Father. The Word, who is the Son, remains 'in the heart of the Father' (John 1.18).[47] The treatise *De rationibus fidei* takes up the explanations which, once given in the *Summa Contra Gentiles*, are indefatigably repeated from one work to the next:

In human usage, one calls *son* someone who proceeds from another through the mode of likeness and who subsists in the same nature as he does. This is why, to the extent that the divine realities can be named in human words, we call the Word of the divine mind *Son of God*. God as the principle of the Word we call the *Father*. And we call the procession of the Word the *generation of the Son*, an immaterial generation, not to be imagined on the model of the physical generation of human flesh.[48]

In his Commentary on St John, Thomas makes a more detailed connection between the divine generation of the Son and the notes related to the Father, which we looked at earlier.[49] As with the paternity on which it is conditional, divine sonship involves a note of *affectivity and love*, between Son and Father. Sonship also brings with it a note of *understanding and of knowledge*. The Son knows the Father perfectly. He manifests the Father, in the economy of salvation, because he is his Word. As we will see in more detail further on, Sonship implies a *commonality of action* between the Son and the Father, because the Father eternally communicates his power of action to the Son: the Father achieves all things through his Son, through his Word.[50] All of these, and the notes which touch on other divine attributes like eternity and glory,

---

[45] *SCG* IV, ch. 11 (no. 3477).

[46] On this Arian thesis, see above, in Chapter 4, ' "Notional" Action'.

[47] *SCG* IV, ch. 11 (no. 3478).

[48] *De rationibus fidei*, ch. 3.

[49] For more detail, see above, in Chapter 8, 'The Name which Fits Best: Father'.

[50] *In Ioan.* 1.3 (nos. 69–88); *In Ioan.* 5.17 (no. 740); *In Ioan.* 5.19 (nos. 750–751); *In Ioan.* 5.21–22 (nos. 761–763); etc.

are fundamentally based on the Father's *communication of the whole divine being* in his eternal generation of the Son, which expresses the Son's relative property of sonship, disclosed by means of the doctrine of the Word.

The *Summa Theologiae* uses this analysis to show that Word is a proper name of the Son, just as Father is proper to the first person of the Trinity. *Word* is a personal name which exclusively refers to the person who is the Son. Thomas says,

> *Word*, said of God in its proper sense, is used personally, and is the proper name of the person of the Son. It effectively signifies an emanation of the intellect. And, the person who proceeds in God by way of emanation of the intellect is called Son; and this procession is called generation, as we have shown above. Hence it follows that the Son alone is properly called Word in God.[51]

Thomas is referring back to what he had shown in the preceding article (on the personal meaning of the name *Word*), and also to his work on the processions where he had already shown that all the notes belonging to actual generation can be authenticated in the procession of the Word: 'The procession of the Word in God is thus called *generation*, and the Word himself who proceeds from it is called the *Son*.'[52] The terms 'word' and 'son' are not synonyms, but in relation to God they solidly designate the same person. St Thomas makes a particular point of showing that, in relation to God, the name *Word* refers to the person himself. On the other hand, the name *Son* does not present this problem, since in our world, at the created end of the analogy, one spontaneously conceives a human son as a person, even though it does not work the same way for *word*. For us, a word is not a person but an 'accident', that is, a cognitive qualification which occurs to our minds, and which belongs to the realm of intentionality. As he had already done in the *Summa Contra Gentiles*, St Thomas draws on the fact that this Word is divine. The divine Word is God, of the same nature as the Father. One can grasp this by reflecting on the fact that the mind of God is his own being, and that that which is 'in God' is nothing other than God himself; the Word who proceeds from him is thus of the very same divine nature as the Father: 'This is why the Word must be something subsistent; for whatever is in the nature of God subsists.'[53]

Although it does not create the same nuances, this consideration is like the one which one can see in the study of subsisting relation, within God. Since he is relative to the Father, the Word is distinct from the Father. He is a distinct reality who, in virtue of his relation (his connection to Fatherhood and

---

[51] *ST* I, q. 34, a. 2.
[52] *ST* I, q. 27, a. 2; see above, in Chapter 4, 'A Procession which is the Generation of the Word'.
[53] *ST* I, q. 34, a. 2, ad 1; cf. *SCG* IV ch. 11 (no. 3471); *In Ioan.* 1.1 (no. 28).

his divinity) subsists within the divine nature, that is, he is an 'hypostasis' or 'person'.[54] Here we recoup the benefits of the investigation of subsistent relation. In relation to the notion of the Son, St Thomas had since his Commentary on the *Sentences* taken it as read that, 'From the very fact of his relation (*ex ipsa relatione*), the Son is a person who subsists.'[55]

The name *Son* designates the same relation as the name *Word*, to wit, that relative property which distinguishes and constitutes the person and which is identical to the person itself. 'The name *Word* and the name *Son* refer to the same property.'[56] As we will see later, the term *Image* also designates the same relation. And it is still this relation to which one is referring when one calls the Son *begotten Wisdom* or *Splendour of the Father*. Before we consider the repercussions of the theme of Word in the economy, like the manifestation of the Father, or creative and saving action, we will glance briefly at the extension of the Word theme into the names *Wisdom* and *Splendour*.

4. THE WORD, WISDOM, AND SPLENDOUR OF THE FATHER

The Wisdom theme is directly linked to that of the Word, 'because the Word is nothing else than the conception of Wisdom itself, which we can call *begotten Wisdom*'.[57] The idea of the Son as Wisdom has a central position in Thomas' writings. He makes it the epigraph to his first synthesized work, the Commentary on the *Sentences*. Here, in an astonishing theological miniature, Thomas had shown that one can present the entire Christian faith in the light of the Wisdom-Son: the Trinity, manifested by the Wisdom-Son; creation, work of Wisdom; salvation, achieved through the incarnation of Wisdom; eschatology, participation in Wisdom.[58] In the *Summa Contra Gentiles*, he dedicates a whole chapter to the name *Wisdom*, immediately following the discussion of the Word. Following Aristotle, he explains that wisdom refers to our knowledge of the highest things. Since the self-knowledge of God is sovereign, one must recognize Wisdom as an eminent name. Thomas states that,

From what has been said, this is clear: The Son of God is the Word and conception of God understanding himself. It follows, then, that the same Word of God, as wisely conceived by the divine mind, is properly said to be *conceived Wisdom* or *begotten Wisdom*. This is why the Apostle calls Christ 'the Wisdom of God' (1 Cor. 1.24).[59]

---

[54] See above, in Chapter 6, 'Subsistent Relations'.   [55] I *Sent*. d. 19, q. 3, a. 2, ad 1.
[56] *ST* I, q. 34, a. 2, ad 3.   [57] *ST* I, q. 34, a. 1, ad 2.
[58] *Sent*. prol. See our study, *La Trinité créatrice*, pp. 252–301.
[59] *SCG* IV, ch. 12 (no. 3482).

One can observe how precise this explanation is: it is *proper* to the Word to be engendered Wisdom. Wisdom as such is a divine attribute, shared in common by the three persons; under this aspect, it is appropriated to the Son, because of the affinity between wisdom and a conception of the mind: the Father's nature shines forth in the Son.[60] But when one takes wisdom *as proceeding* into consideration, 'Wisdom *begotten* or *conceived*', this expression specifically pinpoints the Son, since it signifies the Word in his relation to the Father who conceives him: 'the Son, who is the Word of God, is properly called *conceived Wisdom*'.[61] The Son is not 'that through which' the Father knows, as if the Father knew 'by means of' his Son. Just like the Son and the Spirit, the Father knows himself and knows all things through his own essence. But the Son is the *fruit* of the knowledge sown by the Father, he is the term conceived by the Father, he is the Word of the Father's wisdom, and, under this rubric, he is properly engendered Wisdom.[62] It is in this sense that the Father knows all things *in his Word, in his begotten Wisdom*.

Like that of the Word, the theme of Wisdom opens up a broad avenue for understanding the Son's *revelation* of the Father. The refulgence of the Father within the heart of the eternal Trinity, it is by way of his personal property that the Word, Wisdom of the Father, shows forth and reveals the Father to men. Thomas writes:

the word of wisdom conceived in the mind is a manifestation of the wisdom of the one who knows. One can see this amongst ourselves: all the habits [dispositions to act] are displayed by their acts. And since the divine Wisdom is called *light*, in the measure that it consists in a pure act of knowledge, and the manifestation or refulgence of light, it is the proper *splendour* of the light which proceeds from this light. This is why the Word of divine wisdom has the right to be called *Splendour of the light*, [Heb. 1.3] as it is worded by the Apostle who says of the Son: *he is the splendour of the glory [of God]*. And this is why the Son ascribes the manifestation of the Father to himself, when he says in John: *Father, I have manifested your name to men* [17.6].[63]

Each of the names we give the Son throws one profile of his person into relief. The theme of splendour accentuates the Son's non-sequential and yet natural procession in the divine eternity. 'But this likeness of the "splendour"

---

[60] Cf. *ST* I, q. 39, a. 7, ad 2; a. 8; *SCG* IV, ch. 12 (no. 3484).

[61] *SCG* IV, ch. 12 (no. 3484).

[62] I *Sent.* d. 32, q. 2, a. 1 and a. 2; cf. *ST* I, q. 39, a. 7, ad 2. It is in a similar sense that one can say that the Father and the Son love one another and love us *in* or *through* the Holy Spirit (*ST* I, q. 37, a. 2).

[63] *SCG* IV, ch. 12 (no. 3483). On this theme, see D. Bouthillier, '*Splendor gloriae Patris*: Deux collations du *Super Isaiam* de S. Thomas d'Aquin', in *Christ among the Medieval Dominicans*, ed. K. Emery and J. Wawrykow, Notre Dame, 1998, pp. 139–156.

(cf. Heb 1.3) lacks the feature of connaturality; and similarly the likeness of human sonship lacks the aspect of co-eternity. In practice, approaching knowledge of God requires a plurality of names taken from material realities: no single one of them is sufficient.'[64] In his John commentary, which restores the patristic idea of our route to knowledge of divine things, St Thomas reappropriates the passage in a sermon by Theodotus of Ancyrus, which he knew about through his reading in the Acts of the Council of Ephesus: 'The name *Splendour* manifests to you the eternal coexistence of the Father and the Son; that of *Word* reflects the impassibility of the Word's birth, and the name *Son* suggests his consubstantiality.'[65] This text recurs twice in the *Summa Theologiae*—a mark of Thomas' respect for it—once in the form of a literal quotation from the Acts of Ephesus,[66] and again in the guise of a personal reappraisal:

The Son's nativity, which belongs to him as a person, is indicated by the divers names which show his perfection in diverse ways. In practice, we call him Son, to show that he is of the same nature as the Father. We call him Splendour to show that he is co-eternal with the Father. One calls him Image to show he is like him in every way. And to show that he is begotten in a non-material way, we call him *Word*. One could not find a single name which designates all these aspects in a single blow.[67]

From the *Summa Contra Gentiles* onwards, the names *Son, Splendour,* and *Image* are always explained using the name *Word.* We have already met the reason for this many times: 'Amongst all these likenesses, it is that of the procession of the word from the intellect which represents [the begetting of the Son] in the most explicit way; and the word is only posterior to its principle in the instance where one has an intellect passing from potentiality to act: this condition is absolutely alien to God.'[68] By expressing a personal property of the Son, each of these names involves a relationship with the Son's

---

[64] *In Ioan.* 1.1 (nos. 41–42).

[65] *In Ioan.* 1.1 (no. 41). This sermon of Theodotus', *Clara praesentis festivitatis,* conserved in the Acts of Ephesus, is cited at greater length by Thomas in his *Catena* on John 1.1 (ed. Guarienti, vol. 2, 1953, p. 328), using Rusticus' *Synodicum* (*collectio casinensis*); cf. *Acta Conciliorum Oecumenicorum,* ed. E. Schwartz, vol. I/3, Berlin and Leipzig, 1929, p. 164 (French translation: A. Festugière, *Ephèse et Chalcédoine, Actes des Conciles,* Paris, 1982, pp. 274–275). Theodotus emphasized one of the features of the analogy of the word which Thomas will employ: 'Scripture shows the impassibility of the birth of the Word, because the human mind likewise produces a word in an impassible way' (ibid.).

[66] *ST* I, q. 42, a. 2, ad 1.

[67] *ST* I, q. 34, a. 2, ad 3; see also *In Ioan.* 1.1 (no. 42).

[68] *ST* I, q. 42, a. 2, ad 1; in reference to the existence of an immanent procession, cf. q. 27, a. 1: 'this appears maximally (*maxime*) in the intellect whose action, that is, the act of knowledge, remains in the one who knows'.

work within this world. St Thomas noted this with respect to Wisdom and Light, and especially elaborates on it in his investigation of the Word.

5. THE WORD, CREATION, AND THE ECONOMY: THE FATHER ACTS THROUGH HIS SON

As a name, *Word* has two sets of meanings: one referring to the Son's *action* and one indicating the task of *disclosure* or revelation which the Son achieves as the Father's *Word*. Thomas pays great attention to these two themes in very many of his works. This is the point at which he integrates many features of the biblical teaching: the Word or Speech reveals a content, but also a dynamism of action or of realization; the Word reveals and ordains, acts effectively, and creates. And likewise, the biblical theme of Wisdom involves the note of creation: Wisdom illuminates, and teaches, but she also creates the world and governs it. The *Summa Theologiae* draws this together organically, when it explains how the name *Word* contains a relationship to creatures:

The name 'Word' involves a reference to creatures. In knowing himself, God knows every creature. A word conceived mentally is the representation of all that is actually known. In us the diverse realities which we know occasion many words. But God knows himself and knows all things in one single act: his one single Word does not express the Father alone, but creatures as well. Moreover, whilst God's knowledge is simply cognitive with respect to himself, in relation to creatures it is simultaneously cognitive and productive. Thus, the Word of God is the expression of all that is in the Father, but, in relation to creatures, is both their expression and causative. This is why the Psalm says, *He spoke and they were made* (Ps. 33[32].9); because the Word includes the operative plan of God's works.[69]

This analysis is based on an antecedent investigation of divine knowledge. God's knowledge has a universal scope. God does not just know himself; the way he knows means he knows all things; he knows all creatures and thus everything that happens, right down to its singularity. God does not receive this knowledge from creatures, for it is by knowing himself that he knows all things, through his own essence which is the exemplary cause of all things.[70] The divine knowledge of creatures is not derived from the created world, but is rather the *cause* of creatures, in that God effectively wills to create that which he contemplates in his knowledge.[71] And the Word is the person whom

---

[69] *ST* I, q. 34, a. 3; cf. I *Sent.* d. 27, q. 2, a. 3; *De Veritate*, q. 4, a. 5; *SCG* IV, ch. 13.

[70] *ST* I, q. 14, a. 5; cf. q. 34, a. 3, ad 3.

[71] *ST* I, q. 14, a. 8. On this theme, see S.-Th. Bonino's magisterial study, *Thomas d'Aquin, de la vérité, Question 2* (*La science en Dieu*), Fribourg and Paris, 1996.

the Father conceives when he knows himself. By his own mode of procession, that is, the property distinctive to him, the Word not only knows all the Father knows, but he *articulates* all that is contained in the Father's knowledge—a word is, by definition, *expression*. From one side, the Word is the perfect expression of the Father. From another, the Word is the expression of creatures contained in the Father's knowledge, and, because this is creative knowledge, the Word is also the creative cause of all that the Father does. These two sides are bound closely together.[72] We will first consider the expression of creatures through the Word, then the Father's action through the Word.

The Word expresses creatures: 'Since God, in knowing himself, knows all things, it is necessary that the Word which God [the Father] conceives in knowing himself is also the *Word of all things*.'[73] This formula means that the Word's personal procession is that of the Exemplar, the Model, or rationale of creatures, that is to say, as the expression, contained in the wisdom of the Father, of what creatures are. The Father 'utters' all creatures through the Word in which he 'speaks' himself:

Through his knowledge, the Father knows himself, and in knowing himself, he knows all things. The consequence is that his Word also expresses, primarily the Father himself, and following from that all other realities which the Father knows by knowing himself. Thus, because of the fact that he is the Word who perfectly expresses the Father, the Son expresses all creatures.[74]

But the Word is not solely the expression of creatures. He is equally the creatures' 'productive' or 'operative cause'.[75] The name *Word* includes this, because divine knowledge is creative knowledge. In this sense, the procession of the Word is what causes the procession of creatures.[76] This theme had been developed in the Commentary on the *Sentences*:

Since not only the essence, but also the personal procession which is the reason of the procession of creatures, has a relationship to creatures, something of the personal can thus also be signified with a relation to the creature; ... and it works like this for the name *Word*...[77]

Thus one can see a relationship to creatures in the name *Word*, that is, in the reality formally signified by this name. *Word* means primarily a personal relation touching on the intra-Trinitarian relationship of the Father to the

---

[72] Since the divine knowledge also extends to that which God contemplates in his 'science' but does not create (possibles, which have never been and never will be), the Word is also their expression and manifestation, without being their creative cause, since there is no creation in this case (*ST* I, q. 34, a. 3, ad 5).

[73] *SCG* IV, ch. 13 (no. 3490): *Verbum omnium rerum.*   [74] *De veritate*, q. 4. a. 4.

[75] *ST* I, q. 34, a. 3.   [76] *ST* I, q. 45, a. 6.   [77] I *Sent.* d. 27, q. 2, a. 3, ad 6.

Son, and not the relationship to creatures. This fine-tuning enables one to avoid blending the Uncreated with the created: the Father and the Son are not 'constituted' as such by their relationship to creatures, but in their mutual relation, which is eternal. This is required by the Nicene creed. But, just as the divine relation formally includes the divine essence, the personal property also includes this essence, just as the divine person includes it. On the one hand, in as much as the Word receives the plenitude of the divine nature from the Father in his conception or generation, the Word has a relationship to creatures from the fact that creatures pre-exist in the divine essence which is the creative cause. On the other hand, the Word properly proceeds as the expression of the Father's knowledge; and the divine knowledge is the cause of creatures; thus, in line with the *proper mode* of his procession, the Word bears a special relation to creatures.[78]

The Son as Word is thus the Father's *creative Art.* 'Every artist acts through his art. And, as Augustine says, the Son is the *art of the Father,* full of the patterns of all living things: the Father acts through his Son.'[79] This image of the artist is less naive than one might think at first glance. All of the actions of an efficient cause (a cause which produces an effect within being) imply an exemplary cause. This is a metaphysical law of action.[80] Actions tend to communicate determinate forms, fabricating this and that. If the form has not been determined, the action itself cannot take place, for the activity's power vanishes into non-determination. Every agent acts with a determinate form in view. And the origin of the form cannot be found in the effect, because the effect did not exist before the action happened. So it exists in the subject who carries out the action, either in their natural being when it is a natural action, like a flame igniting another flame, or in the agent's mind, when we are looking at an action performed freely and knowingly: and the artist illustrates such action. This analogy means that creation, God's action in the world, is linked to God's immanent activity, the personal procession of the Word. It thus exhibits the economic repercussions of Trinitarian faith. St Thomas often uses the exemplar of how architects work to explain this:

Whoever makes anything by understanding does his work by mentally conceiving the form of the thing to be done. For example, the house constructed of matter is built by the builder by means of the plan ('rationale') for this house, as he conceives it in his mind. God produces things in being not through a necessity of his nature, but intelligently and voluntarily. Therefore, God made all things by His Word, which is the rationale of things

[78] For more detail, see our book, *La Trinité créatrice*, pp. 424–430.
[79] II *Sent.* d. 13, q. un., a. 5, contra 2; I *Sent.* d. 27, q. 2, a. 3, arg. 4, sol. and ad 4. Augustine, *De Trinitate* VI.X.11; cf. *Tractates on John* I, nos. 16–17.
[80] *ST* I, q. 44, a. 3.

made by Him. This is why St John says, *All things were made by him* [1.3]. In agreement
with this, Moses describes the origin of the world by using such a manner of speech for
the single works: *God said 'let there be light', and light was made . . . God said: Let there be a
firmament made* (Gen. 1.1–3), and so of the rest. All of which the Psalmist includes,
saying, *He spoke and they were made* (Ps. 148.5). Thus, therefore, one must understand
that God spoke and they were made because He articulated his Word, by which he
produced things in being as through their perfect rationale.[81]

This takes us back to something which we have already envisioned as a
revelation of the Trinity: 'On the one hand, knowledge of the divine persons is
necessary for a decent understanding of the creation of things. In effect, when
we affirm that God has made all things through his Word, one excludes the
error of those who hold that God produced things by a natural necessity.'[82]
Faith in the Word enables one to show the personal wisdom at work in
creation. Moreover, the Word's activity is not limited to the original creation
of the world, but extends to the whole exercise of divine providence in the
course of time, and in particular to maintaining creatures within the being
which they receive from God. Thomas says,

The cause conserving beings is the same as that which produces them. So, since all
things are made by the Word, so by the Word all things are conserved in being. Hence,
the Psalmist says, *By the Word of the Lord the heavens are established.* And the apostle
teaches: *The Son upholds the universe by the power of his word* (Heb. 1.3).[83]

Thus the Father achieves all that he does through his Word. Creation and
the exercise of providence are bound to the eternal begetting of the Word.
Thomas gives an especially detailed explanation of this when he is commenting on the prologue to the Fourth Gospel: *Through him all things are made*
(Jn 1.3). The Father achieves all things through his Word. This expression
does not mean that the Word could be the Father's 'instrument'; for the Word
is equal to the Father. Nor does it mean that the Word could be the source of
the Father's action: on the order of origin implied by the notion of Word
itself, it is the Father who communicates being and action to the Word, and
not the other way round. On this basis, Thomas makes a close examination of
the meaning of the preposition 'through', as in *through* him all things were
made. If one intends this preposition to mean the formal principle of the
Father's activity, one must acknowledge that this principle is none other than

<hr>

[81] *SCG* IV, ch. 13 (no. 3491).
[82] *ST* I, q. 32, a. 1, ad 3. See above, in Chapter 1, 'Revelation, Creation, and Salvation'.
[83] *SCG* IV, ch. 13 (no. 3492). Thomas has built up to this by explaining Hebrews 1.3 like this:
'Not only the conception of the divine mind is called *Word*, but one also calls *word* the
deployment of this divine conception in external works' (ibid., no. 3489). The plan of divine
providence will thus be appropriated to the Word (III *Sent.* d. 4, q. 1, a. 1, qla 3).

the divine essence itself; in this sense, it is through 'appropriation' that one can say that the Son is that 'through whom' God acts; because, just like wisdom and power, the divine essence is held in common by the three persons. But if, in the preposition 'through' one intends the relationship of causality to creatures (in that creatures are made by the Word), then it is not as an appropriation, but as language which fits his nature, that one understands the phrase, *through the Word*. Thomas affirms that,

if the 'through' denotes causality from the standpoint of the thing produced, then what we affirm in saying that 'The Father achieves all things through his Word,' is not appropriated to the Word but is proper to him; because the fact that he is the cause of creatures is had from another, namely, the Father, from whom he has being.[84]

Hence, by attributing the production of creatures to the Word, John is expounding the most proper way in which he is (*propriissime*):

God makes nothing except through the conception of his intellect, that is, the Word of God and the Son of God. So it is impossible that God make anything other than through his Son. And so Augustine says in *The Trinity* that the Word is the art full of the living rationale of all things. Thus it is clear that all things which the Father makes, he makes through him.[85]

Thomas comes back to this thread when he presents the incarnation of the Son of God. As he reappropriates the theme of the 'Art of the Father', the first thing he does is to recollect the creative role of the Word. 'That through which one makes something is also that through which one repairs it. In practice, if a house has fallen in, one repairs it on the model through which it was originally made.'[86] Scholastic writers regularly use this patristic argument[87] to create a co-ordinated view of creation and salvation which will indicate the fittingness of the incarnation of the Word. Created by the Word, human beings are saved or 'restored' ('repaired') by the Word, and the whole universe is restored in man.[88] This line of thought has tremendous value theologically, because of the precision given by the doctrine of the Word. Thomas writes that,

[84] *In Ioan.* 1.3 (no. 76); cf. *ST* I, q. 39, a. 8: 'In some cases the preposition "through" (*per*) applies to an intermediary cause, e.g. in the statement that an artisan works through his hammer. So "through" sometimes does not mean an appropriation, but a property of the Son, as John said, *All things were made through him* (Jn 1.3); not because the Son is an instrument, but because he is a principle from a principle.' We will come back to this teaching in chapter 14, 'The Persons' Distinct Modes of Action and their Unity in Action'.

[85] *In Ioan.* 1.3 (no. 77). See above, n. 79.

[86] *De rationibus fidei*, ch. 5.

[87] Cf. Athanasius of Alexandria: 'The recreation of the universe has been produced by the Word who originally created it . . . the Father realized salvation and creation in the One through whom he produces them' (*On the Incarnation of the Word* I.4; SC 199, p. 263).

[88] The same formula appears as early as the general prologue of the Writing on the Sentences (cf. G. Emery, *La Trinité créatrice*, pp. 287–289 and 534). See also *SCG* IV, ch. 42; *ST* III, q. 3, a. 8.

such as are similar are fittingly united. Now the person of the Son, who is the Word of God, has a shared relationship with all creatures. The artist's word, his conception, is in fact a model-likeness of his works of art. This is why the Word of God, who is his eternal concept, is also the model-likeness of all creatures. And therefore as creatures are constituted in their species by participation in this likeness, despite being mutable and corruptible, so it was fitting that the fallen creature be restored to its eternal and unchangeable perfection, not just by participation, but by the personal union of the Word. For if the artist's work has fallen into ruin, he restores it by means of the artistic form through which he conceived it and in accordance with which he originally realized his work.[89]

Thomas wants his next step to be to not just show that the Word has a rapport with the totality of creatures, but also to dovetail this affinity into a special relationship with human beings. He brings this out by underscoring the revelation achieved by the Word, the manifestation of the Father, and by considering the Word as the Father's *Image*. But for the moment it is important to observe the universal window opened by investigation of the Word:

The Word has a kinship not only with rational natures, but also universally with every creature. For the Word contains the 'patterns' of everything which God creates, analogously to how the human artist has an intellectual conception which contains the 'models' for his works of art. Thus, then, the totality of creatures are nothing but a kind of real expression and representation of that contained in the conception of the divine Word. This is why all things are said to be made by the Word (Jn 1.3). So it was fitting that the Word was united to the creature, namely, to human nature.[90]

The cosmic repercussions of the Incarnation are grounded in the Word's universal rapport with the entirety of his creation. Medieval theologians also indicated this cosmic dimension by considering the human being as a 'microcosm' in which the spiritual and material universe was somehow brought together, and through whom Christ's work flows on to creatures as a whole.[91] But the cosmic dimension of the Incarnation and its repercussions in the material universe are not just based on human relationships with the universe. More fundamentally, these dimensions spring from the universality of the Word's activity, on this 'real expression' or 'kinship' of all creatures with the person of the Word.

---

[89] *ST* III, q. 3, a. 8.
[90] *SCG* IV, ch. 42 (no. 3803).
[91] Cf. particularly *Sent.* prol. and III *Sent.* prol. See our study, *La Trinité créatrice*, pp. 287–294.

6. THE WORD DISCLOSES AND REVEALS THE FATHER

By examining the notion of *Word*, Thomas has shown this: since he proceeds from the Father's conceiving, 'the Word articulates the whole being of the Father'.[92] The theme of the Son as the *Splendour of the Father* has likewise shown that the Word is the manifestation of the Wisdom of the Father.[93] Since the Word expresses the Father from eternity, one can show that the disclosure of the Father in the economy is brought about by the same Word. In fact, the Word does not just involve a note of action (the Father accomplishing all things through his Son) but also a note of *revelation*. As we have seen, it is here that one espies one of the biblical features which is underlined in the Commentary on the Fourth Gospel: 'since the aspect of disclosure is suggested better by the name *Word* than by the name *Son*, the evangelist prefers to use it here'.[94] Thus, the disclosure of the Father rebounds on the person of the Word at every step of the economy, right up to the new covenant, when the Word discloses the Father in his own flesh. St Thomas tells us that,

Just as one who acts through his intelligence produces things in being by patterning them on his idea, so also a teacher brings about knowledge within another in the pattern of his idea. The science of the apprentice is drawn from the science of the teacher; it is like an image of it. And God by his intellect is not just the cause of all beings which naturally subsist; but all knowledge is derived from the divine intellect ... Necessarily, then, it is by the Word of God, which is the eidetic pattern of the divine intellect, that all intellectual know-how is caused. This is why it says in John 1.4: *And the life was the light of men.* For the Word who is himself the Life and the One in whom all things have life, discloses the truth to the human spirit, like a light does.[95]

Without making a detailed analysis of the numerous facets of this teaching, we can at least make a brief survey of them. The John Commentary, in particular, pays close attention to the role of the Word as illuminator. This action on the part of the Word is not restricted to revelation in this strict sense, but concerns, in the first instance, understanding in a more general way: 'he shines in everyone's understanding; because whatever light and wisdom there is amongst men has come to them from participating in the Word'.[96] As soon as human beings use their own natural reason, their knowledge flows from the Word, because 'it is from this true Light that human

[92] *In Ioan.* 1.1 (no. 29).
[93] *SCG* IV, ch. 12 (no. 3483). See above, in this chapter, 'The Word, Wisdom, and Splendour of the Father'.
[94] *In Ioan.* 1.1 (no. 31).   [95] *SCG* IV, ch. 13 (no. 3495).
[96] *In Ioan.* 1.26 (no. 246); cf. *In Ioan.* 1.9 (no. 125).

participation in the natural light of knowledge derives.'[97] 'Whatever truth is known by anyone is due to a participation in that light which shines in darkness.'[98] In the deepest sense, to participate in the Word is to have the knowledge given in revelation. In the Old Covenant, it was in the Word that inspired men and women spoke. 'At one time, the Only Son of God revealed knowledge of God through the prophets, whose proclamation was measured to the extent to which they had been made participants in the eternal Word.'[99] In the New Covenant, it is in his own flesh that the Word elicits knowledge of God. Thomas finds that,

People disclose their secrets by their word. This is why it is only by a person's words that we can know another person's secret.... No one can gain knowledge of the Father except by his Word, which is his Son. One reads in Matthew 11.27: *No one knows the Father except the Son.* And just as when a man wants to reveal himself through the word of his heart, uttering it in audible sounds, he clothes his inner word with the garments of writing or of speech. And in the same way, God, wanting to disclose himself to men, reveals himself in flesh and in time by his Word which he conceives from eternity. And so no one can arrive at a knowledge of the Father except through the Son.[100]

Going beyond the affinity between the Word and every creature, it is at this juncture that the *Summa* indicates a second angle on the fittingness of the incarnation of the Word:

The Word of God has a special affinity with human nature, because he is a concept of the eternal Wisdom, from which all human wisdom comes. And this is why a human being is perfected in wisdom—which is the perfection belonging to him as a rational being—in the measure that he participates in the Word of God; just like the disciple is instructed by receiving the word of his master. Hence it is said in Ecclesiasticus, *The Word of God on high is the fountain of wisdom* (1.5). And so to lead humanity to its perfection, it was fitting that the Word of God personally united himself to a human nature.[101]

In all of these instances, St Thomas especially accentuates *God's own self-knowledge*, which wisdom consists in. It is the knowledge peculiar to himself which the Father expresses in his Word, in such a way that the Word is personally the 'doctrine of the Father'.[102] Everything else we know about the

[97] *In Ioan.* 1.9 (no. 129).   [98] *In Ioan.* 1.5 (no. 103).
[99] *In Ioan.* 1.18 (no. 221). *In Ioan.* 5.38 (no. 820): 'Christ is by nature the Word of God. Every word inspired by God is a participated likeness of him, and since every participated likeness leads to its principle, it is clear that every word inspired by God leads to Christ.' See aso *In Ioan.* 10.8 (no. 1384).
[100] *In Ioan.* 14.6 (no. 1874).
[101] *ST* III, q. 3, a. 8. Cf. *SCG* IV, ch. 42 (no. 3802): 'The greatest affinity which the Word has is with human nature.'
[102] *In Ioan.* 7.16 (no. 1037). Cf. Augustine, *De Trinitate* I.XII.27.

faith flows from this knowledge of the mystery of God, revealed by the Word. Thomas writes that,

Christ the Word of God is the root and fountain of our knowledge of God. *The fountain of wisdom is the word of God* (Eccl 1.5). Human wisdom consists in knowing God. And this knowledge flows to us from the Word, because human beings know God in the measure that they participate in the Word . . . From this knowledge of the Word, which is the root and fountain, all the knowledge of the faithful flows, like rivulets and streams.[103]

In his work of revelation, the Son communicates to human beings a participation in his personal character, at the heart of the Trinity. Thus, to know the truth is to be united to the Word. As the Father's conception and the perfect expression of the Father, the Word is the Truth in person, the Truth articulated by the Father. 'Because no one can know the truth unless he adheres to the truth, it is necessary that anyone who desires to know the truth adhere to this Word.'[104] It is this way now, in our pilgrimage of faith, and will be like this even in glory: the saints know the Father in the vision of the Word which discloses him to them.[105] Thomas thus puts his presentation of the whole work of revelation, right up to the beatific vision, under the light of the Word. Needless to say, this draws on the joint action of the Holy Spirit:

Just as the mission of the Son was to lead to the Father, so the effect of the mission of the Holy Spirit is to lead the faithful to the Son. Now the Son, since he is begotten Wisdom, is Truth itself: *I am the way, the truth, and the life* (Jn 14.6). And so the effect of this mission is to render men participants in the divine Wisdom and knowers of the truth. Since he is the Word, the Son gives us teaching; and the Holy Spirit makes us able to grasp it.[106]

This analysis gives pole-position to the perfection of the Word himself. 'The Word articulates the whole being of the Father', 'The single divine Word is expressive of all that is in God, not only of the Persons but also of creatures.'[107] Human knowledge is thus presented within the framework of a theory of participation: 'Since all imperfect things take their origin from that which is perfect, all our knowledge comes from the Word.'[108] It devolves to the Word to disclose the Father, to disclose the Trinity, and to disclose everything whose source is God. St Thomas' speculative work on the Trinitarian mystery helps him out here: he can account for the Word's achieving this by means of the two central planks of his doctrine of the divine person. First, the *personal property* of the Word: since he is properly the Word, it comes down to the Son

---

[103] *In Ioan.* 17.25 (nos. 2267–2268).
[104] *In Ioan.* 14.6 (no. 1869).
[105] *In Ioan.* 16.25 (no. 2150).
[106] *In Ioan.* 14.26 (no. 1958).
[107] *In Ioan.* 1.1 (nos. 29 and 27).
[108] *In Ioan.* 8.55 (no. 1284).

to unveil the Father. Second, the Word's *relation towards the Father*: 'every-thing which is from another discloses that from which it comes: likewise, the Son discloses the Father because he is from the Father'.[109] And last, by unifying creation, revelation, and salvation within a single knot, the theology of the Word shows *the unity of the divine plan of creation and salvation*. In this way, it is the elaboration of a speculative theory about the person of the Son within the eternal Trinity, which, as it reflects on the economy, provides an authentic account of the economy of the Son.

7. THE SON GIVES US A SHARE IN HIS SONSHIP

St Thomas explains on many occasions that the filial relationship of creatures to God derives in its entirety from the filiation of the eternal Son. When he writes about filiation, Thomas always consciously emphasizes the prerogatives of the Son of God. He alone is Son by nature, whereas creatures have a filial relation to God through participation. The enfiliation of creatures is thus a 'likeness' or 'participated likeness' in the eternal filiation of the Son.[110] This is an authentic leitmotif: we have a resemblance, or a likeness to what the only Son has by nature.[111] This insistence comes from a Christological idea, that is, the rejection of adoptionism. Christ's filial relation to the Father is of a different order to ours: he is thus neither adopted by the Father nor 'deified', as the saints are. Thomas' thinking here is defined by fidelity to the Nicene Creed, and thus the necessity of blocking out Arianism. The Son is not Son to the Father in the same way that creatures are so, for he is 'begotten, not created'.[112] The Son's filiation is not on the same level as that of creatures. Rather, creatures take a filial relation to the Father God from the Son, by participating in his personal property.

Moreover, as we saw when we were considering the Father, it is not just the saints who can be called son; rather, the name operates in an analogical way, by degrees, in the filial relation of creatures to God. (1) All creatures have God as their Father and attain the name 'son' in respect of this; an affirmation

---

[109] *In Ioan.* 16.14 (no. 2107).   [110] *ST* I, q. 33, a. 3; *ST* III, q. 23, aa. 3–4.

[111] See L. Somme, *Fils adoptifs de Dieu par Jésus Christ*, Paris, 1997. Amongst the many patristic sources of Thomas' insistence on this point, we would note Hilary of Poitiers, *De Trinitate* VI.32 (SC 448, pp. 234–235): Jesus Christ is not just entitled son, but is son through his own nature; not just son by adoption, but son through a genuine birth. In the *Summa Theologiae*, Thomas refers this to Ambrose of Milan (*ST* III, q. 23, a. 4, sed contra).

[112] *ST* III, q. 23, a. 4. St Thomas thus eliminates any trace of the idea of an 'adoptive sonship' in Christ. See especially *In Ioan.* 20.17 (no. 2520). He is particularly careful to avoid the Arian mix-up between Christ's filiation and the enfiliation of creatures.

which Thomas finds in Scripture. In the same way that the fatherhood of God is universal, so the created world exhibits a deep-seated filial character. (2) Among creatures, those which are created in the image of God, angels and human beings, deserve the name 'son' in a special way, because of their narrower resemblance to the God whom they can know and love. (3) On a higher level, sonship consists in participation in the divine life which is given first by grace, and then in glory, through the gift of the Holy Spirit which conforms us to the Son.[113]

The theme of *participation in the Word* allows one to explain the diverse modes of creatures' enfiliation to God. We come back once more to the three degrees of sonship which we have already seen in the study of the Father, and this is mirrored in Thomas' characteristic foregrounding of the property of the Word to display the meaning of filiation:

the Son of God proceeds naturally from the Father as his intellectual Word, existing in unity with him. Assimilation to the Word can happen in three ways. First, through the form, but without intellectuality. Thus, the form of an external house is assimilated to the mental word of the architect, but not intellectually, because the material form of a house is not intelligible as it was in the mind of the architect. In this way, every creature is assimilated to the eternal Word, for every creature has been made by him. Secondly, a creature is assimilated to the Word not only in its formal aspect, but also as to its intelligibility; thus the knowledge which happens in the disciple's mind is likened to the word in the mind of the master. In this way the rational creature, even in its nature, is assimilated to the Word of God.[114]

This analysis must give us pause. The exposition of the first two modes of enfiliation to God primarily conceives the Son as Word; the text goes on to mention a third mode which we will examine a little later. He is the Son by nature in so far as he is properly the Word of God, the conception and perfect expression of the Father. The enfiliation of creatures is thus conceived as an 'assimilation to the Word'; it consists of being rendered 'like' the Son who is the Word of God. From one angle, this 'assimilation' is universal since, as we have seen, creatures are made through the Word, it is through him that they are sustained in being, and again it is through him that they are led to their end. This does not just happen 'from the outside', but 'from within', by dint of a participation in the Word. In themselves, creatures have and express something of the Word himself. This 'something' does not consist in the spiritual character ('intellectuality') of such a participation, but rather in the expression of the Word through each creature, or, the fact that each creature is what

---

[113] Cf. *ST* I, q. 33, a. 3. See above, in Chapter 8, 'The Analogous Network of the Name "Father"'.

[114] *ST* III, q. 23, a. 3.

it is by its 'form'. The Word is that from which all these things issue, because the Word is their creative source and uncreated model. So, as the expression of the Son, the world participates in his sonship: such is the 'filial' status of the whole universe.

From his Commentary on the *Sentences* onwards, Thomas noted this feature of the derived 'order' of creation:

The temporal procession of creatures comes from the eternal procession of the persons. This is why it says in Psalm 148.5: *He has spoken and they are created.* 'He has begotten the Word in whom their making was made,' according to St Augustine. According to the Philosopher, that which is first is always effectively the cause of that which follows on from it: this is why the first procession is the cause and pattern of every procession which follows it.[115]

So it finds its model in the procession of the Son, who, considered in relation to the creatures' reception of being from God, is the cause and pattern of creation.[116] The Son is begotten in the unity of the divine nature. From their side, creatures somehow 'imitate', on their own level, the eternal begetting of the Son, by participating in the reception of being of which eternal begetting is the model and source.[117] In his precise property as Son and Word, the Son is thus seen as the source of all creatures' participation in being, and as the source of creatures' manifestation of God. This teaching, which could be called a 'sonship theology', is characteristic of the way St Thomas thinks. The world exists by participating in the sonship of the Word.

This participation or 'assimilation' has a higher place amongst human beings or angels (this is the second mode), because these do not only bear a universal resemblance to the Word, as do all other creatures, but are more closely connected to the Word through their spiritual nature ('intellectuality'), that is, their ability to know and to love God. Human beings and angels do more than 'copy' their Creator: they can reach up to him, in knowledge and love. This is the theme of the *image* of God.[118] Angels, and all men, have this image as from their creation ('even in their nature'). It thus belongs to human nature as such, in so far as the human being is created through the Word. In this respect, all human beings are 'children of God' after the creative exemplarity of the Word. It is upon this created assimilation to the Word that filial adoption is grafted, the highest level of assimilation to the filial Word:

Thirdly a creature can be likened to the eternal Word as to the oneness of the Word with the Father, and such a likeness is made by grace and charity. This is why our Lord

---

[115] *Sent.* prol. Cf. Augustine, *On the Literal Interpretation of Genesis* II.VI; Aristotle, *Metaphysics* II (a) (993^{b}24–30).
[116] I *Sent.* d. 10, q. 1, a. 1.   [117] Cf. *ST* I, q. 33, a. 3, sol. and ad 2.
[118] Cf. *ST* I, q. 93.

prays, *That they may be one in us...as we also are one* (Jn 17.21). And this likeness brings the adoption to perfection, for those who are thus made like him inherit eternity.[119]

Just as grace assumes nature, so adoptive sonship assumes the filiality brought about by creation. And thus as grace elevates nature, so adoptive sonship raises participation in the filiation of the Son to its highest power. In this respect, adoptive sonship is a 're-generation', a new birth and a recreation: it reforms God's created human children, by raising their sonship to a higher degree of participation. On this point, Thomas stresses that adoptive sonship is characterized by unity. It is a matter of the oneness with God which is achieved through knowledge and love of God, the fruits of grace. It also concerns the ecclesial communion which this unity obtains for the children of God. The study of the divine missions and the image of God will show that this oneness consists in an embedding in the divine life which sets one within the Trinity itself: participation in the eternal communion, in the begetting of the Word and the procession of the Holy Spirit.[120] Adoptive sonship makes human beings kin to the Word *from within the oneness which he has with the Father.* In other words, adoptive sonship gives the members of the Church participation in the divine filiation of the Son shaped as it is by unity of nature and by the personal relationality of the Word. Brought about by assimilation to the Son, the oneness of the Church is thus seen as a participation in the oneness of the Trinity. Thomas states that,

our oneness will be the more perfect the more it participates in the divine oneness. Now there is a twofold unity in God. On the one hand, there is a unity of nature, in reference to which Christ says, *I and the Father are one.* And there is a unity of love in the Father and the Son, which is a unity of Spirit. Both of these are found in us, not in an identical way, but through something of a likeness. For the Father and the Son have numerically one and the same nature, while we are one in the same specific nature. In the same way, the Father and the Son are One by a Love which is not a participated gift but which proceeds from them, for the Father and the Son love another through the Holy Spirit; whereas we are one by participating in this higher Love.[121]

The 'participation' in which filial adoption consists is a divinization or deification, for Thomas conceives grace as precisely an 'assimilation' or 'participation in the divine nature', a new creation which God alone can

---

[119] *ST* III, q. 23, a. 3.

[120] *ST* I, q. 43, aa. 3 and 5; q. 93, aa. 6–8. See below, Chapter 15.

[121] *In Ioan.* 17.11 (no. 2214); cf. *In Ioan.* 17.21 (no. 2240): we are 'one' through a likeness or imitation of this double unity of the Father and the Son. On this theme, see Charles Morerod, 'Trinité et unité de l'Eglise', *Nova et Vetera* 77/3 (2002), 5–17.

bring about.[122] By affiliating human beings to the Son, adoptive Sonship affiliates them to his divine Sonship of the Father. Grace is thus a 'participation of the divine nature' (following 2 Peter 1.4, *The greatest and most precious promises we have been given, that by these you may become participants in the divine nature*), 'and it is in the reception of this nature that we are born again as sons of God'.[123] This rebirth is brought about by the gift of the Holy Spirit, a point to which we will return in the next chapter. From this gift, rooted in the eternal filiation of the Son of God, the whole Christian life is projected: new birth (re-creation), participation in God's nature (divinization), hope of the inheritance of eternal life (the beatific vision), an intimate kinship with God through prayer, and the imitation of God in virtuous action, in the moral life. The following passage is one of many which takes up this teaching in regard to assimilation:

There is added to human nature from above the perfection of grace through which the human being is made a *participant in the divine nature*, as it says in 2 Peter 1.4. This is how we are reborn as sons of God, according to John 1.12: *he gave them power to become sons of God*. And those who are instituted as sons can suitably hope for their inheritance, according to Romans 8.17: *if children, then heirs*. And hence, because of this spiritual rebirth, it belongs to human beings to have a greater hope of God, that is, to obtain eternal life, according to 1 Peter 1.3–4, *He has begotten us again unto a lively hope by the resurrection of Jesus Christ from the dead, to an inheritance incorruptible, and undefiled, and that fadeth not away, reserved in heaven for you.* And then through the Spirit of adoption which we have received, we cry *Abba, Father!*, as it says in Romans 8.15, the Lord showed us how to pray by beginning his prayer through an invocation of the Father which says, *Father*. And in saying *Father*, the heart of man is prepared to pray in purity and to gain what he hopes for. Children must become imitators of their parents, and this is why in confessing God as Father, one compels oneself to imitate God, by avoiding that which renders one unlike God, and by seeking out that which renders us like to God . . .[124]

A large number of texts are given over to this theme.[125] But those which we have briefly presented here are a sufficient indication that, because it provides an authentic idea of the Son's activity in the economy, Thomas' Trinitarian theology directs us toward a profound vision of the Son at work in creation and salvation. This idea is not set adjacent to the speculative reflection on the Son in the immanence of the Trinity, but is planted straight into it, so that it receives its fruits. Having concentrated on showing what the property of the Word can do, Thomas exhibits the action of the Son in its light, by

---

[122] *ST* I–II, q. 112, a. 1.

[123] *ST* I–II, q. 110, a. 3; cf. I–II, q. 62, a. 1.   [124] *CT* II, ch. 4.

[125] See in particular, Thomas d'Aquin, *La divinisation dans le Christ*, texts edited and translated by L.-Th. Somme, Geneva, 1998; J.-P. Torrell, *St Thomas Aquinas: Spiritual Master*, pp. 125–153.

foregrounding the Word's *divine relation* to the Father, a relation in which his action on behalf of creatures is given to participate.

8. THE WORD, IMAGE OF THE FATHER

After the question about the Word, the *Summa Theologiae* brings its investigation of the Son to completion by examining the name *Image*. We have already observed that, amongst the Son's names, that of *Image* especially highlights the Son's perfect resemblance to the Father.[126] The Image theme also belongs to the Bible: *He is the image (eikôn, imago) of the invisible God, the first-born of all creatures, for in him all have been created* (Col. 1.15); *Christ, who is the image of God* (2 Cor. 4.4). Thomas also draws on other biblical passages traditionally connected with the notion of image, even though the word is missing, such as Hebrews 1.3: The Son *being the brightness of his glory and the expression (charactěr, figura) of his substance, and upholding the universe through the power of his word*.[127] As a name, *Image* refers to Christ as pre-existing creation, as performing creation (as the model and author of creation), and in the Church. Like the name *Word*, *Image* has a bearing on the representation and the manifestation of the Father, and likewise on the work carried out by the Son in creation, revelation, and salvation.

The importance of the image theme had been illuminated by fourth-century Fathers, such as Athanasius, Hilary of Poitiers, Basil of Caesarea, and others. Using a conception which they had taken over from Platonism, the Arians saw the image as a reality which was intrinsically inferior to its model. Against the Arian position, Hilary of Poitiers, for example, explained that, by being the Image of the Father, the Son is the perfect expression of the Father and receives all of the Father's being, so that he is equal to the Father: the Son-Image has the 'form' of God himself, and it is because his eternal begetting gives him a power equal to the Father's that the Son-Image is the source of the universe.[128] St Thomas knew about this aspect of the debate with Arianism. 'The Arians have misunderstood this word [image], because they conceived the Image of the [invisible] God as being like the images which people of old fashioned in order to be able to look upon those dear

---

[126] See especially *ST* I, q. 34, a. 2, ad 3; *In Ioan.* 1.1 (no. 42).

[127] Cf. *In Heb.* 1.3 (no. 27): 'The word *figura* is taken here for the phrase *character* or *image*, as if to say, he is the image of his substance.'

[128] Hilary, *De Trinitate* VII. 37–38 (SC 448, pp. 360–361); cf. *De Trinitate* VIII.48–49 (SC 448, pp. 454–459). Amongst the numerous patristic authors in whom one can find this, see Basil of Caesarea, *On the Holy Spirit* XVIII.45 (SC 17, 2nd edn., p. 407).

ones who had been lifted above, like we make images of the saints in order to
see imaginatively those whom we cannot see substantially; and thus they
presumed…that the Son is of another nature than the Father.'[129] Along
with his patristic sources (particularly Hilary and Augustine), St Thomas
tries to bring the fact of the consubstantial expression of the Father out of
the name *Image*.

In order to show this, he first sifts through the constitutive elements of the
notion of image.[130] On the one hand, Trinitarian faith leads us to avoid the
idea of inequality between the Son-Image and the Father. But, on the other
hand, equality is not necessarily a constitutive feature of every image: for
otherwise, how could one explain that man bears the 'image of God' without
being equal to God? One must pick out a notion of image which fits
analogically between Trinitarian theology and anthropology. Saint Augustine
had already realized this, and Thomas assimilates his way of working it out.
One has to distinguish between the image, the likeness, and the equality:
not every image necessarily implies equality, and not every likeness is an
image.[131] St Thomas also takes over from Hilary the two features out of
which the notion of image is constructed within Trinitarian theology: *the
origin* of the image in relation to its model, and the *likeness in specifics*
between an image and its model (which, for God, comes down to a unity
of nature).[132] On this basis, Thomas extracts three elements in which the
notion of the image come together:

We see how [Christ] is called the *Image of God* (Col. 1.15) … The notion of image embraces
the constitutive elements: (1) there must be a likeness; (2) this likeness must issue or derive
from the reality of which it is a likeness; (3) it requires that it issues according to an aspect
which either comes from the specific nature or is the sign of the species.[133]

The first element does not create any problems: an image represents
another reality, presenting a resemblance or likeness to it. But the element
of resemblance by itself falls short of imaging. For there to be an image, the
image must be somehow derived from its model. As Augustine explains, a
partridge egg is like a chicken egg, but it is not its 'image'! In fact, 'for one
being to image another, it must proceed from it'; it must 'issue from the
other'; it is requisite that the image be the expression of its model: in short, an
image calls for a relation of origin.[134] This second feature is decisive for

---

[129] *In Col.* 1.15 (no. 32).
[130] Amongst the many studies of this, see R. Imbach and F.-X. Putallaz, 'Notes sur l'usage du
terme *imago* chez Thomas d'Aquin', *Micrologus* 5 (1997), 69–88.
[131] Augustine, *On 83 Questions*, q. 74. Thomas, *In Col.* 1.15 (no. 31); *ST* I, q. 35, a. 1.
[132] *I Sent.* d. 28, q. 2, a. 1.   [133] *In Col.* 1.15 (no. 31).
[134] *ST* I, q. 35, a. 1; *In Col.* 1.15 (no. 31). Cf. Augustine, *On 83 Questions*, q. 74.

Trinitarian theology: it is this which enables it to recognize that the name *Image* is a personal one in God, since its formal meaning involves a relation of origin.

Further, if an image represents the reality from which it is derived, one must nail down what sort of resemblance we are dealing with: 'resemblance is not enough to make an image: that requires a likeness in the specific nature, or at least a sign of the species'.[135] This is the third feature. In order to establish it, Thomas once more takes his example from the earthly realities which we call 'images'. For a representation of a man to be called an 'image' of that man, we must be able to recognize his specifically human features in it: the image must have the features proper to the species to which the model belongs.[136] This can take place in the 'likeness to the specific nature'. It is thus that a child, who has the same human species-nature as its parents, is the 'image' of its parents. But this can also come about in a 'sign of the species', that is, a sign which evokes a feature proper to the species to which the model belongs. Thomas finds this proper feature, the mark of the species, in the form and contour, which he indicates with the word 'figure' (*figura*). It is because it presents such a 'figure' that the picture representing a man or animal is called the 'image' of the man or the animal. This 'sign of the species' is the 'figure' which plays an important role in anthropology. It enables one to show that, even though human beings are of a different nature or species to God, they are nonetheless in his image because, unlike other corporeal creatures, human beings do in fact give a sign which evokes the genuine features of the divine nature: the spiritual life of the mind and the will.[137]

Having put forward the constitutive elements of the image (likeness in specifics or likeness as a sign of the species, and expression of the model or origination from it), Thomas observes further degrees of perfection in the image. Like paternity and sonship, image is an analogical notion. There are images which purely represent a sign of their species model: for instance, the image of the sovereign engraved on a coin; it is to this first degree that the image of God in man is linked. There are also images which present an authentic likeness to their model, at the level of nature: for instance, children, who are their parents' image. The highest degree of image is found in the only Son who does not just present a likeness in nature to the Father, but who has the same nature as the Father in the 'numerical unity' of the divine sub-stance.[138] Thomas summarizes his thought on this in his Commentary on the Second Letter to the Corinthians:

[135] *ST* I, q. 35, a. 1.
[136] I *Sent.* d. 28, q. 2, a. 1; *ST* I, q. 35, a. 1; *In Col.* 1.15 (no. 31).
[137] Cf. *ST* I, q. 93, a. 2.
[138] I *Sent.* d. 28, q. 2, a. 1, ad 3; *ST* I, q. 35, a. 2, ad 3; cf. *ST* I, q. 93, aa. 1–3.

Christ is the most perfect (*perfectissima*) image of God. Because, for an image to be perfect, three elements are needed, and these three elements are given perfectly in Christ. The first is likeness, the second is origin, and the third is perfect equality. [. . .] And all three are found in Christ, the Son of God: he is like the Father, he proceeds from the Father, and he is equal to him. It is thus at the highest point and in the most perfect way that he is called *Image of God*.[139]

This explanation rests on Christian faith in the person of Christ. Begotten by the Father, the Son of God is equal and like to him. To *disclose* this to our minds, the theologian has recourse to the analogy of the mental word which, as we have seen, provides the speculative foundation for Trinitarian reflection on the person of the Son:

There is a word in our minds when we actively articulate a form of the reality we know, and it is this word which we signify in our external speech. The word thus conceived is a likeness of the known thing which we grasp in our mind, it is like it in specifics. And this is why the Word of God is called *Image of God*.[140]

In other words, since the Son is the *Word* of God, he is likewise the *Image* of the Father. The theme of the Word gives the speculative basis for thinking about that of Image, and thus for taking Paul's teaching on board, and it does so by providing the analogy which creates a window through which our minds can see its truth.

Thus, as a name, *Image* indicates something belonging to the person of the Son alone. The *Summa Theologiae* discusses this in two steps. On the basis of the constitutive features of the image (specific likeness and being expressed by another), without mentioning the Word-theme, a first article begins by establishing that *Image* is a personal name when it is ascribed to God. The relation of origin, which the notion of *Image* implies, enables one to say unambiguously, 'That which implies a procession or origin within God is a personal reality. This is why the name *Image* is in fact a personal name.'[141] The same teaching is presented as early as the Commentary on the *Sentences*, but there Thomas can be seen to be more reliant on the notion of 'imitation', as found in Hilary of Poitiers. The analysis of imitation suggests that, alongside the personal meaning, one can also recognize a secondary meaning, relating to the divine nature (that is, the divine nature grasped as 'that in which' the three persons imitate one another and the divine nature as that which creatures imitate).[142] The reply in the *Summa* is not as two-sided as

---

139 *In 2 Cor.* 4.4 (no. 126).
140 *In Col.* 1.15 (no. 31); cf. *SCG* IV, ch. 11 (no. 3474); *ST* I, q. 35, a. 2.
141 *ST* I, q. 35, a. 1.
142 I *Sent.* d. 28, q. 2. a. 2. But Thomas is completely clear about the first meaning: 'So far as it is attributed to God in a proper sense, the name *Image* is always personal.'

this: the sense is exclusively personal, and there are no concessions to an essentially secondary meaning.

In a second article, St Thomas explains that, as he had said earlier for *Word*, so here again, the name *Image* indicates the person of the Son alone. He knew many texts from the Greek Fathers (some of which are unreliable translations, and others accurate) attributing the name *Image* to the Holy Spirit, for example this one, from St John of Damascus: 'The Son is the image of the Father, and the Spirit is the image of the Son, the Spirit through whom Christ makes men to be in his image.'[143] So should he restrict the name *Image* to the Son, or extend it to the Holy Spirit as well? Speaking for the Latins, Augustine had been very strict: only the Son is given the name *Image*.[144] A response to the question should begin from sacred Scripture. Only the Son is explicitly called *Image* in the New Testament.[145] But a more generous reading of the biblical passages does suggest a link between Holy Spirit and image, because, if the Holy Spirit inscribes the image of the Son in men (cf. Rom. 8.29; 1 Cor. 15.49; 2 Cor. 3.18), then he bears that image in himself.[146]

To clarify the issue, Thomas turns next to speculative reflection, starting by examining past solutions. Under the influence of Richard of Saint-Victor, all of these in one way or another habitually make use of the doctrine of the procession of the Holy Spirit from the Father and the Son to show that the name *Image* refers to the Son alone.[147] St Thomas sets aside these solutions, explaining that they do not tell us anything about the theme of Image, or that they neglect the unity of Father and Son, as the single principle of the Holy Spirit.[148] So he puts forward his own solution which considers the procession of the Son in his property as Word. Only the Son can really be called Image, 'because the Son proceeds as Word, and it belongs to the very notion of *word* to be the likeness of the principle from which the word proceeds'.[149] The Holy Spirit is likewise, of course, the perfect resemblance of the Father, but he does not have this likeness by virtue of his mode of procession, which is one of love (the procession of a word is formally effected through a likeness, whereas that

---

[143] John of Damascus, *The Orthodox Faith* (cf. the Latin translation by Burgundio of Pisa, ed. E. M. Buytaert, New York, 1955, p. 61). This linguistic difference is less important than Thomas suspects; see on this topic H. Dondaine, *La Trinité*, vol. 2, p. 318.

[144] Augustine, *De Trinitate* VI.II.3, cited in *ST* I, q. 35, a. 2, sed contra. See also *De Trinitate* XII.VI.6–7.

[145] *ST* I, q. 35, a. 2.

[146] *CEG* I, ch. 10.

[147] Richard of Saint-Victor, *De Trinitate* VI.11 (SC 63, pp. 400–405); Alexander of Hales, *Summa*, Book I (ed. Quaracchi, vol. 1), no. 418; Albert, I *Sent*. d. 28, a. 9; Bonaventure, I *Sent*. d. 31, p. 2, a. 1, q. 2.

[148] *ST* I, q. 35, a. 2; *CEG* I, ch. 10.

[149] *ST* I, q. 35, a. 2; *CEG* I, ch. 10; *SCG* IV, ch. 11 (no. 3474).

of love consists in an impulsion, or a drive[150]). This is why the Holy Spirit is not *begotten*, but *proceeds*: his origin is not formally achieved through that communication of nature which is the generation or articulation of the Word. The Holy Spirit is certainly perfectly like the Father, because he proceeds from the Father through the reception of the Father's nature, that is, because he is a *divine* person, and, more precisely, the Love *of God*. However, the Son is personally the Image in a way that belongs properly to him, from the fact that he is the Word of the Father, for the implication of the notion of Word is that likeness in which an image consists. One can show this by examining the mode of procession and the property which belongs to him.

The fact remains that Thomas accepts the attribution of the name *Image* to the Holy Spirit, when he takes *Image* not in the precise sense in which it applies to the Son, but with the broader meaning of 'perfect likeness'; so the Holy Spirit can be called the image of the Son.[151] The motivation for extending the meaning comes from its documentation in the Greek Fathers: 'it would be presumptuous to run against explicit texts from so many authoritative doctors'.[152] Despite his somewhat flawed interpretation of these Greek patristic texts, the question of attributing the name *Image* to the Holy Spirit is a good indicator of the *theological method* which Thomas tries to apply (and this is perhaps its main interest for us): he is stimulated by a linguistic difference between the Greek and Latin traditions, he puts these face to face with the New Testament vocabulary, then he makes a critical investigation of the commonplace speculative motifs in the scholastic theologians, and having proposed his own solution, based on his analysis of the modes of procession and the personal properties, he concludes by welcoming on board the expressions used in the Eastern documents, in the light which his analysis enables him to direct on them.

9. IMAGE OF THE FATHER, FIRST-BORN OF CREATION

Just as with the themes of the Son and the Word, an economic dimension opens out from the theme of the Image. As we have seen, each of these names primarily illuminates what belongs to the eternal person of the Son within the immanence of the Trinity, and, in the second place, enables us to grasp the Son in his creative and salvific acts. Because he is the perfect Image of the Father, the Son is the exemplar or model on which the Father conceives his creatures,

---

[150] See above, in Chapter 4, 'A Different Procession, Which is That of Love'.
[151] I *Sent.* d. 28, q. 2, a. 3, ad 1; *ST* I, q. 35, a. 2, ad 1.   [152] *CEG* I, ch. 10.

creates and recreates them. It is once again the analogy of the mental word which enables this to be shown:

> The word interiorly conceived is a kind of notion and likeness of the thing known. And the likeness of one thing in another has the character of an *exemplar*, if it is its principle, or, instead, it is an *image* if the likeness is drawn from another, who is its principle. And one can find examples of both aspects in our intellect. On the one hand, the likeness of a work of art existing in the mind of the artist is the principle of the operation by which the work of art is produced: it is thus related to the work of art as a model or exemplar is related to the thing which issues from the exemplar. On the other hand, the likeness of a natural reality conceived in our intellect is related to that reality, whose likeness it is, as to its principle, for our act of understanding takes its principle from the senses which are affected by natural things. And God knows both himself and he knows things, as we have seen, and his understanding is the principle of the things which he knows, since they are caused by his intellect and his will: these things are related to that Intelligible which is God himself, as to their principle. And this Intelligible which is God is identical to the [divine] intellect which knows, and of which the Word conceived is, as it were, an emanation. The Word of God is therefore related to the other things God knows as their exemplar, and he is related to God [the Father], whose Word he is, as Image. This is why Colossians 1.15 says that the Word is the *Image of the Invisible God*.[153]

These considerations give us a synthesis of Thomas' thought and of his method. The end in view is to give an account of the name *Image*, which Scripture gives to the Son (in this case Col. 1.15). This requires one to make use of analogy. By starting from that which is proportioned to our understanding, one can grasp that which transcends our reason. This analogy is in fact the *mental word*, which for St Thomas constitutes the best way of thinking about the mystery of the Son. Within this analogy, he examines the *relations* which the word has: the relation to the principle which forms the word, and the relations to the things conceived and made through the word. Transposed into God, and taking account of what belongs to God alone, the analogy enables one to unfold the relation of the Son to the Father: the Son is the *Image* of the Father, as a personal, intra-Trinitarian property. But it also allows one to disclose the relation of the Son in respect of creatures: being the Image of the Father, he is, therefore, the *Model* for creatures. This is why the Son is the *First-born of all creation*. Thomas writes that,

> God knows himself, and he does not know creatures through someone else: he knows all things in his essence, as being the first cause which produces them. And the Son is the Father's intellectual conception, through which God knows himself, and,

---

[153] *SCG* IV, ch. 11 (no. 3474).

consequently, all creatures as well. In so far as he is begotten, he thus appears as the Word who represents every creature, and he is himself the principle of all creation. For, if he were not begotten in this way, the Word would be the First-Born of the Father alone, but not the First-Born of all creation. [...] The form and the wisdom [through which God makes all things] is thus the Word, and this is why all things are grounded in him, as their exemplar: *He has spoken and they were made* (Cf. Gen. 1; Ps. 33[32].8) because it is in his eternal Word that God has created all things for what they will become.[154]

So, as with the names Word and Son, Thomas first notes a universal kinship of the Image with the entirety of the created world. The Son, as the Image of the Father, is the Model who contains the universe and through which the Father creates the universe. Such is the 'filial' status of the creation. But, within the cosmic reverberations of the Image, one can see a closer kinship, the particular relationship which the Son has with human beings:

There seems to be a kind of special affinity of the Word with human nature. For human beings get the nature which specifically belongs to them from being rational. And the Word is kin to this reason: this is why, with the Greeks, *logos* refers to the *word* and to *reason*. It was therefore supremely congruous that the Word unite himself to a reasonable nature. And it was by reason of this kinship that Sacred Scripture attributes the name *image* both to the Word and to human beings; the Apostle says of the Word that he is the *Image of the invisible God* (Col. 1.15), and he says the same thing of human beings: *man is the image of God* (1 Cor. 11.7).[155]

The *affinity* at issue entails that it is by participating in the Word, the Image of the Father, that human beings receive the image of God. 'As to its perfection, the Image indicates the property of the Son; it also rebounds on the creature, but in an imperfect sense: this is why the image "descends" from the Son to creatures, just as paternity "descends" from the Father (cf. Eph. 3.14–15).'[156] The Son is the perfect Image of the Father, he has the same nature as the Father and perfectly articulates the Father. Created and re-created in the image of God, a human being has a participation (hence, 'imperfect sense') in this relation of resemblance and expression: he participates in the Son-Image. According to St Thomas, it is this participation which one is referring to when one says that man is *to the image* of God, for one means by that 'a movement towards perfection', that is to say, one who tends toward the perfect Image who is the Son.[157]

Within the Augustinian tradition, human beings are not purely to the image of the Son, but to the image of the whole Trinity.[158] More precisely,

[154] *In Col.* 1.15–16 (nos. 35–37).   [155] *SCG* IV, ch. 42 (no. 3802).
[156] II *Sent.* d. 16, q. 1, a. 1, ad 2.   [157] *ST* I, q. 35, a. 2, ad 3; cf. q. 93, a. 1 and ad 2.
[158] Cf. Augustine, *De Trinitate* XII. VI.6–7; Thomas, *ST* I, q. 93, a. 5, ad 4.

humans have a similitude to the Son by nature, and they are recreated by conforming to Christ,[159] the Son of God, through whom they are to the image of the whole Trinity. Thomas takes over from the Greek Fathers the difference between the Son *Image* and human beings made *to the image*.[160] On the one hand, he maintains the idea that the image has a restricted sense for human beings (indicated in Latin by the preposition *ad* and in English by the preposition *to*). On the other hand, he notices a special kinship between humankind and the Son Image. As we have seen, the expression 'to the image of God' denotes a certain 'distance' between humankind and God (man is not image of God in a way equivalent to the only Son who is the perfect Image of the Father), but it also indicates a 'movement' of rapprochement to the perfect Image. It is by participating in the perfect Image, the Son and Word, that the human receives 'being-towards-the-image-of-the-Trinity': the image 'descends' (in participation) from the Son to human beings. St Thomas conceives the image in a dynamic way, in the movement towards God in which the human person fulfils his vocation.

In this way of looking at things, the Incarnation and the Son's mission of salvation consists in re-establishing the image in man, which had been watered down by sin (it was not that humans had lost the image of God which they carried in virtue of their human nature, but that sin destroys the higher realization of the image which comes about through grace), and raises it to participation in the life of God through conformation to the Son:

In his capacity as Image, the Son has a kinship with that which he must restore, that is to say, with man who is created to the image of God (cf. Gen. 1.27). This is why it is fitting that the Image assumes the image, that is to say, that the uncreated Image assumes the created image.[161]

The work of salvation performed by the Son and the Holy Spirit consists in re-establishing the image of God in humankind, and putting it into operation: *Those whom God had chosen before, he predestined to be conformed to the image of his Son* (Rom. 8.29). For St Thomas, this 'image of the Son' is the adoptive sonship in which the Holy Spirit gives a share by joining believers to the person of the Son, today, in the life of grace, and tomorrow in the sharing in glory, when 'we will be like him' (1 Jn 3.2).[162]

---

[159] On the theme of conformity to Christ, see J.-P. Torrell, *St Thomas Aquinas: Spiritual Master*, pp. 140–149.

[160] See for instance, Athanasius, *On the Incarnation of the Word* 12–13 (SC 199, pp. 306–315).

[161] III *Sent.* d. 1, q. 2, a. 2.

[162] *In Gal.* 4.5 (no. 209); *In Rom.* 8.29 (nos. 704–705).

The investigation of the names *Word, Son,* and *Image* has reached its goal: to show the personal property which distinguishes and constitutes the person of the Son, and by the same token to illuminate the action of the Son in the economy of creation and salvation. Once it had taken hold in the *Summa Contra Gentiles,* it is this original idea of the Word which, from beginning to end, offers the best way of understanding the person and work of the Son.

10

The Person of the Holy Spirit

The *Summa* follows up its reflection on the personal properties of Father and Son with three questions on the Holy Spirit (qq. 36–38). The way we brought things into focus in introducing the two earlier chapters also applies in reference to the Holy Spirit. In the first place, one must appreciate that the Spirit is present within the treatise from the first question to the last. Questions 36–38, dedicated to the person of the Holy Spirit, 'taken in a special way', are a narrower examination of his *personal property*. To grasp what Thomas is aiming at, one has to read the questions in the context of the Trinitarian treatise. In the second place, the central aim of this enquiry is to elucidate what belongs eternally to the Holy Spirit, in the immanence of the Trinity, but to do so in a way that provides the foundation for understanding his action in creation and salvation. Here perhaps more than elsewhere, theology is closely linked to the economy, because the Spirit is at the source of Christian life and of ecclesial unity. The study of the Holy Spirit will show that the ground of Christian existence, and the bond of believers, lives in the Charity who proceeds from the Father and the Son. Thirdly, as with the Father and the Son, the way of tackling the investigation into the Holy Spirit is to consider the orientation of the *names* which we give to him. So it comes down to disclosing the personal property of the Holy Spirit as it is expressed through the names which genuinely address him.

Such an investigation engages the numerous themes and diverse names through which Scripture and the tradition have indicated the Holy Spirit: Spirit (Spirit of holiness, Spirit of God, Spirit of Christ, Spirit of the Promise, and so forth), Paraclete, Unction, Gift, Pledge of our inheritance, and more. How should one frame these themes for one's research? Especially in the way it had been drawn together by Peter Lombard, the medieval Augustinian tradition focused on three particular aspects: *Holy Spirit, Love,* and *Gift*.[1] Thomas examines these and shows that a theologian can use them to structure his pneumatological meditations. They enable one to give an account of the property personal to the Holy Spirit, explain the Holy Spirit's other

---

[1] See Peter Lombard, *Sentences*, Book I, dist. 10–18 and 31–32.

names, and lay out his action within the economy. So he turns one question over to the Holy Spirit, a second to the name *Love* and a third to the name *Gift*.

On a theoretical level, the central question is surely that of *Love* (q. 37). It is this one which creates the window for explaining why it is in the Holy Spirit's character to be Gift, and it also sets the frame for the Holy Spirit's action in the economy. But the first question, which studies the name *Holy Spirit* (q. 36), is also highly elaborated. Three articles are set aside for the origin of the Holy Spirit: 'Does the person whom one calls Holy Spirit proceed from the Father and the Son?'[2] Because of the difficulties specific to this question, which are as much methodological as doctrinal, and because of its ecumenical implications, we will present it in the next chapter. But we should nonetheless keep in mind that, when he works through the questions about Love and Gift, Thomas has already laid out the Catholic doctrine of the origin of the Spirit (that he proceeds from the Father and from the Son).

1. THE NAME 'HOLY SPIRIT'

Amongst the New Testament names, the predominant one is Spirit or Holy Spirit.[3] St Thomas markedly follows this use of language. But this phraseology raises a two-sided problem. On the one hand, in and of itself, the word Spirit does not exclusively characterize the third person of the Trinity, but can also refer to God in his divinity as such, or in other words, it could mean the Father, or the Son, or the whole Trinity. 'The name *Spirit* can be apposite to the three persons; we see this in John 4.24: *God is Spirit*.'[4] Thomas explains this by noting that the incorporeality (cf. Lk. 24.39) and the power of life denoted by the word *spirit* must be seen in each of the divine persons.[5] The name *Holy* presents a similar problem, because it is in the essence of God to be holy, and each of the three persons shares in the same holiness: 'to be holy is

---

[2] This is the title of ST I, q. 36, a. 2 (cf. q. 36, prol.). One can see from this formulation that Thomas connects this doctrinal point to the expression 'Holy Spirit', that is, to the personal name.

[3] There are around 275 mentions of the divine Spirit in the New Testament (there are 379 occurrences of the word *pneuma*, but this figure also includes references to bad spirits or the human spirit).

[4] I *Sent.* d. 10, q. 1, a. 4, arg. 2; *ST* I, q. 36, a. 1, arg. 1.

[5] *In Ioan.* 4.24 (no. 615). The verse in 2 Cor. 3.17 (*The Lord, is the Spirit*) presents an analogous problem: Thomas comments that the word *Spirit* can refer either to the person of the Holy Spirit, or to Christ (*In 2 Cor.* 3.17; no. 111).

common [to the three persons], and not proper [to one of them]'.[6] The difficulty remains even if one considers holiness in the more exact perspective of *sanctification.* The Holy Spirit does in fact effect sanctification in a special way (the Father and the Son give him to us for our sanctification), but in and of itself the power of sanctification belongs to each divine person because of their sacred divinity.[7]

All of these indications show that, despite the affinity between holiness and the personality of the Spirit, and even though sanctification is the purpose of the mission upon which the Spirit is sent, one cannot set the word *Holy* on one side as designating that which from all eternity distinguishes him from the Father and the Son.[8] Moreover, Thomas shows the divinity of the Holy Spirit like this: the Spirit carries out actions which are properly or formally divine (as especially sanctification), and this is why, even if it does not affirm it as explicitly as it does for the Son, Scripture leads us to recognize him as God.[9]

St Thomas picks up the thread with a discussion of the connection between the words *Spirit* and *Holy*: 'Taken by themselves, the force of the two words in the term *Holy Spirit* is common to the entire Trinity.'[10] There will thus be two ways of looking at the name *Holy Spirit.* One could take it in the sense conveyed by weighing each of its terms individually; in this light, one will have to admit that, intrinsically, the name belongs to the whole Trinity. But one could also hold on to the meaning which Scripture and the Church have accommodated for this expression. In that case, one takes the expression *Holy Spirit* as one single name, the proper enunciation which the Church has drawn from Scripture for speaking of a distinct divine person.[11]

Even if, as is his wont, Thomas begins from questions about language, a deeper problem is lying in wait behind the verbal difficulties, and his intention is to lead the reader to it, to the very reality for which our language tries to find words. We have seen that, when they are attributed to God, the precise force of the very names *Father* and *Word*, or *Son* indicates a distinct divine person, and they are able to find out the personal property which they express, to wit, that relative property which is one of the divine persons himself. The

<hr/>

[6] I *Sent.* d. 10, q. 1, a. 4, arg. 1.

[7] Cf. *In Rom.* 1.4 (no. 58). Here Thomas gives a precise explanation: 'It is the property of the divine power to sanctify through the gift of the Holy Spirit.' The special role of the Holy Spirit in this action is well attested, but this is not enough to enable us to assign the divine power of sanctification exclusively to the Holy Spirit.

[8] Cf. Augustine, *De Trinitate* XV. XIX. 37: 'He is not alone in the Trinity in being holy or in being spirit, because the Father too is holy and the Son too is holy, and the Father too is spirit and the Son too is spirit, a truth about which piety can have no doubts.'

[9] Cf. especially *SCG* IV, ch. 17 (no. 3528): 'to sanctify men is God's proper work'. See above, in Chapter 1, 'The Revelation of the Trinity through its Works'.

[10] *ST* I, q. 36, a. 1, ad 1; cf. I *Sent.* d. 10, q. 1, a. 4, ad 1.   [11] Ibid.

particular difficulty of the name *Holy Spirit* is that the words by themselves do not give us an adequate or sufficient basis for pinpointing the personality of the Spirit. Sanctification—*Holy* Spirit—might give us an avenue for thinking it through, and Basil of Caesarea saw this as the rightful property of the Spirit,[12] but St Thomas is not satisfied by it, since, as he says, all three divine persons have the same power to sanctify. So this does not suffice to characterize the Holy Spirit as a distinct person. In addition, sanctification is one of God's works within this world, whereas the first thing Thomas is looking for is an intra-Trinitarian property, a typifying relation between one divine person and another. One could also hypothesize that the notion of procession or *ekporeusis*, put forward to this end by Gregory of Nazianzus, might help us out here, but, as we have seen, it creates another difficulty: according to Thomas, the word *procession* refers not only to the origin of the Spirit, but also to that of the Son.[13] When he first considers the question, Thomas draws together the results of his previous enquiry:

As we have already seen (q. 27, a. 4), there are two processions in God, and the one which is accomplished by way of love has no proper name. In consequence, as we have also noted (q. 28, a. 4), the relations which one can consider in it are nameless. For that reason, the person who proceeds by love has no proper name. However, common usage has adapted certain names to signify the relations in question: we call these names *procession* and *spiration*, terms which in their correct meaning indicate characteristic acts rather than relations; likewise, to designate the divine person who proceeds by way of love, Scriptural usage, by a kind of accommodation, sets aside the name *Holy Spirit*.[14]

Here Thomas is reverting to his own earlier study of processions and relations (qq. 27–28). He had observed there that our own created world indicates to us an analogous reality which enables us authentically to name how the Son originates: that is, *generation*. Our grasp of the distinct origin of the Holy Spirit is made possible by referring to procession in the mode of love. Even though we do not have a proper name with which to designate it, we can

---

[12] St Basil: 'The substantial principle is common, as with goodness, divinity, or any of the attributes like this, whereas the hypostasis is considered as the special property (*idioma*) of paternity, or sonship or of the power of sanctification' (Letter 214.4, St Basil, *Lettres*, ed. Y. Courtonne, vol 2, Paris, 1961, p. 205; cf. Letter 38).

[13] See above, in Chapter 4: 'The word "procession"'. We can add that, if one sets aside the word *ekporeusis* for the Holy Spirit, a problem remains, for we have hardly any analogy *within this world* which enables us to distinguish an '*ekporeusis*' from another spiritual origin. And, in order to *disclose* the faith to our minds, it is precisely such an analogy that Thomas is looking for, so that we can grasp something of the content of the profession of faith, by putting it in the light of the knowledge of something whose object is proportioned to what we can know through our own human experience.

[14] *ST* I, q. 36, a. 1.

make use of a common name (*procession*) to indicate the origin belonging to the Spirit. Within the commonplace terminology of the scholastic theologians, this origination is likewise called *Spiration*, since it is a matter of the procession of the *Spirit*. The Spirit is *breathed* in procession, the Father and the Son *breath* the Spirit, which is a notional act.[15] Once we get into this side of things, we see that the *relations* grounded in this procession present their own linguistic problems. When we speak of the mutual relation of Father and Son, we have at our disposal a vocabulary which is attuned to precisely pinpointing the action, as generation, their relations, as paternity and sonship, and their persons, as Father and Son. But when we turn to the Holy Spirit, this terminological precision deserts us. We have to use the same word to indicate the *action* of the Father and Son, and the *relation* which they have with the Holy Spirit: *spiration*. We likewise use the same word to designate both the Holy Spirit's *origin* and his *relation* to the Father and the Son: *procession*.[16] And to indicate his person, we make use of one single composite expression: *Holy Spirit*.

Although Thomas presents this way of speaking as an accommodation, he does not mean to say that it is purely arbitrary. It can give rise to several important arguments from congruity. Examining the word *spiritus*, whose nuances are richer in Latin than in English, the Commentary on the *Sentences* foregrounds the theme of *breath*: 'The attractions and repulsions of the air are called inspiration and expiration, and this is why the winds are also called *spiritus*.' The highest token of esteem is thus given to the Spirit's 'subtlety', his lightness, capacity for diffusion, movement and communication, or immateriality.[17] In his opuscule, *De rationibus fidei*, he sees this as a hint that the origin of the Spirit is 'concealed': the source of breath and respiration is concealed from us.[18] This theme of an 'interior and concealed source' will be of particular interest for explaining the way in which the Holy Spirit is the Heart of the Church, for 'the influence exerted by the heart is concealed'.[19] In the *Summa Contra Gentiles*, once he has shown that it belongs to the Holy Spirit to be Love, he brings particularly to the fore that the character of the name 'Holy Spirit' refers us to *impulsive force, inclination, motion,* or *vital momentum*:

[15] *ST* I, q. 27, a. 4, ad 3. Despite its great value, the image of 'breath' ('spiration') must be explained by reference to a more precise notion. It is in aid of this that St Thomas introduces the theme of procession by mode of love. See above, in Chapter 4, 'A Different Procession, Which is That of Love'.

[16] Cf. *ST* I, q. 28, a. 4; q. 32, aa. 2–3. See above, in Chapter 4, '"Notional" Action'; and in Chapter 5, 'Relative Opposition: Paternity, Filiation, Spiration, and Procession'.

[17] I *Sent.* d. 10, q. 1, a. 4.

[18] *De rationibus fidei*, ch. 4. Thomas develops the image of 'wind' at length in his Commentary on John 3.8 (nos. 450–456, with reference to a concealed source and destination, power of motion, impulsion, and so on).

[19] *ST* III, q. 8, a. 1, ad 3.

the beloved in the will exists as inclining the will, as giving it an interior impulsion towards the being which is loved. And this impulse of a living thing from within belongs to his 'spirit'. So it is fitting that God proceeding by way of love be called *Spirit*, in as much as he exists through a kind of spiration.[20]

The *Summa Theologiae* introduces two arguments from congruity. The first touches on the way that the name *Holy Spirit*, which draws two terms together, is a 'community'. It may be that Thomas was drawn to giving primacy to this idea because the three subsequent articles in question 36 treat the theme of the Holy Spirit as proceeding from the Father and the Son. In fact, Augustine had explained that, because he is the Spirit of the Father, who is holy and spirit, and also the Spirit of the Son, who is holy and spirit, the Holy Spirit is given a title common to the two persons whose communion he is.[21] Thomas takes over this explanation.[22] In his Commentary on the *Sentences*, he also alludes to the 'spiritual' nature of the union of two friends: the lover and the beloved are united 'in spirit'.[23] The second reason for its congruity comes from the impulsion which springs from love; this repeats the discussion in the *Summa Contra Gentiles*. Unlike the first, this motif rests on the *proper* meaning of the name Spirit. 'In the physical world, the name *spirit* suggests a sort of impulse or motion: one actually gives the name *spirit* to breath and to wind. And it belongs to love to move and push the lover's will towards that which he loves.'[24] So it is the investigation of the property of the Holy Spirit as *Love*, in question 37, which makes it possible to give a full account of the name *Spirit*.

In relation to *Holiness* (as in *Holy* Spirit), there are two main lines of enquiry. The first one, which is in the Commentary on the *Sentences*, explains the name *Holy* by reference to purity or detachment from things which are unworthy of a spiritual love.[25] The second, in the *Summa contra Gentiles*, the *Summa Theologiae* and the John Commentary gives more prominence to the contiguous idea of consecration to God, and affinity with God.[26]

---

[20] *SCG* IV, ch. 19 (no. 3566). Cf. *In Ioan.* 14.17 (no. 1916): 'the word *Spirit* suggests a certain impulsion, and this is why we call the winds "spirits"'. The theme of the 'instinct of the Holy Spirit' is connected to this way of looking at it: like an amorous impulse, the Holy Spirit produces 'the interior instinct which incites and moves us to believe, and this is why he draws numerous men to the Father and the Son through the instinct of the divine action which moves the human heart from within to believe' (*In Ioan.* 6.44; no. 935); etc.

[21] Augustine, *De Trinitate* XV. XIX. 37; *De Civitate Dei* XI.24.

[22] *ST* I, q. 36, a. 1.

[23] *I Sent.* d. 10, q. 1, a. 4. Such Augustinian explanations were widespread; St Albert also allies himself with the image of the lovers' kiss (Albert, I *Sent.* d. 10, a. 13). See also St Bonaventure, I *Sent.* d. 10, a. 2, q. 3.

[24] *ST* I, q. 36, a. 1. Thomas also adds the aspect of immateriality suggested by the name *Spirit* (ibid., ad 1).

[25] I *Sent.* d. 10, q. 1, a. 4, ad 4; *De rationibus fidei*, ch. 4; cf. *ST* I, q. 36, a. 1, ad 1.

[26] *SCG* IV, ch. 19 (no. 3568); *ST* I, q. 36, a. 1; *In Ioan.* 14.26 (no. 1955): 'He is Holy because he consecrates us to God.' But the *Summa Theologiae* also repeats the purity theme (*ST* I, q. 36, a. 1,

Thus, once its profound 'congruity' has been shown, which does not arise from the meaning of its terms taken strictly in themselves, but from the scriptural way in which the Church has used them, the name *Holy Spirit* indicates a person, that is, a relation, the property of the Holy Spirit in his connection to the Father and the Son. 'Although Holy Spirit is not itself a relational expression, still, as an accommodation, it is posited to designate one person, distinguished from others through a pure relation.'[27] In this way, the name *Holy Spirit* is found to be on a level with the names *Father* and *Son*. So far as one can, it is necessary to pinpoint what the *relative* property of the Holy Spirit is. This is the task Thomas sets himself when he studies the names *Love* and *Gift*.

2. THE HOLY SPIRIT IS LOVE IN PERSON

The indications of where the thesis is going are already given in Thomas' study of the processions, in q. 27: to be able to grasp the procession of the divine persons in a way that avoids the pitfalls of Arianism and Sabellianism, one has to conceive it as an *immanent* procession, and not like an external action. One's understanding of it must also be congruent with God's spiritual nature. These theological exigencies frame the doctrine of the Word.[28] Unless one wants to slip into the stream of semi-Arianism, one also has to disclose how the procession of the Holy Spirit is different from that of the Son. Without that, one could perfectly well make a faith-based assertion that the Holy Spirit is a divine person distinct from the Father and the Son, but one could not disclose this to the minds of believers and one's rationale for the faith would be threadbare.

These theological requirements oblige one to look for an immanent action within God himself. And, in a spiritual being, such an immanent action can only come about through the activity of the mind or the will. Thus, from the *Summa Contra Gentiles* onwards, Thomas developed an original doctrine of the Word and Love which is his own personal extension of the legacy of St Augustine; the ultimate synthesis of this is in the *Summa Theologiae*. He first of all treats the procession of the Word, making him distinct from the

ad 1). The *Compendium of Theology* makes a close connection between the two lines of thought (*CT* I, ch. 47) of purity and consecration.

[27] *ST* I, q. 36, a. 1, ad 2.
[28] *ST* I, q. 27, a. 1; see above, in Chapter 4, 'The Problems of Arianism and of Sabellianism' and 'A Procession which is the Generation of the Word'; on the doctrine of the Word, see above, Chapter 9.

Father, his principle, and yet remaining within God himself. This directs us to discerning the procession of a 'Love' within God, with which God the beloved is present to God who loves, in a way analogous to the procession of the Word, according to which God the known is present in God who knows himself, and immanently.[29] He also shows that this love has a connection of origin (an 'order') in relation to the Word: it belongs to the very notion of *love* to proceed from the word with which a spiritual being links himself to a known reality.

Investigating the processions had already shown that love is not the presence of a 'likeness' of the beloved being in the one who loves; such likenesses belong to the life of the mind, the formation of the word, and enable one to conceive divine generation. Love consists, rather, in a lively momentum, a movement, an impulse towards the beloved being, arising in the will when one loves something: the one whom I love is present in my will, inclining me towards him. Thomas infers that,

Hence, what proceeds in God by way of love does not proceed as begotten, or as Son, but rather as spirit; which name expresses a certain vital movement and impulse, according to which anyone is described as moved or impelled by love to perform an action.[30]

This is how one can conceive of an immanent procession in God which is different from generation. One has to use an analogy. As with the Word, one can pick out an originary relation. With human beings, it is a matter of the relation which a 'love' has to that volition from whose act love dawns. This analogy gives us a grasp of the divine relation which Love enjoys with the Father and with his Word, from whom he eternally issues forth.[31] St Thomas has shown that this divine Love is a subsistent relation whose nature is that of God himself. 'The procession [relation of the Holy Spirit to the Father and Son] is the Holy Spirit himself in person, proceeding.'[32] Before making a critical evaluation of the other ways in which theologians have thought of presenting it, Thomas shows the profound value of this idea: this way is compelling for any theology which wants to conceive the procession of the Holy Spirit as a genuinely immanent process, bypassing the heresies and, so far as theology can do so, transmitting an authentic grasp of the Trinitarian mystery. Remember the conviction which summarizes what his study of the Trinity seeks to achieve:

There cannot be any origination in God, but only what is immaterial and congruent with an intellectual nature. Such is the origin of Word and of Love. This is why, if the

[29] *ST* I, q. 27, a. 3.   [30] *ST* I, q. 27, a. 4.
[31] *ST* I, q. 28, a. 4; q. 37, a. 1.   [32] *ST* I, q. 30, a. 2, ad 1; cf. q. 29, a. 4.

procession of Word and Love is not enough to point towards a personal distinction, there will be no such distinction within God.[33]

Thomas' unravelling of this theory closely binds together the study of human affectivity, the theory of analogy, the authentic demands of Trinitarian doctrine, such as the requirement of immanent processions, the idea of relation, and the notion of what a divine person is. As with the Father and the Son, one sees again to what extent the reflection on the Holy Spirit presupposes the whole of the introductory discussion of the processions, the relations, and the notion of the divine person.

Without going back over the idea of procession 'by mode of love', of which we gave a detailed account earlier on,[34] what is now needed is to say precisely what one means by 'Love', and how understanding him as Love fits the Holy Spirit. What personal property does one express by naming the Holy Spirit as *Love*? St Thomas builds up to this in two stages, both of them carrying his research in one single direction. Just as with the names *Father* and *Word*, so, as he now articulates what the word 'Love' means, he commences by showing that to call the Holy Spirit *Love* is to use a proper name. Having made this clear, he promptly goes on to show that this Love is, as such, the mutual love of Father and Son.

The study turns back once again to the timbre of our language. When we say 'divine Love', does the name Love refer to the person of the Holy Spirit alone?[35] Because it creates real problems, the vocabulary we use has to be at the forefront of our attention here, even more than elsewhere. St Thomas begins by commenting on the 'paucity' of our language for the Holy Spirit, something he had noted several times before. The usage of Scripture and the Church gives us a 'circumlocution' with which to refer to this person; the logic of the precise and given meaning of these words is not what enables us to say *Holy Spirit*.[36] Likewise, we make use of the name *procession* to indicate the origin which belongs to the Holy Spirit, even though, of itself, the term 'procession' fits both the Son and the Spirit.[37] We adapt the name of an action (*spiration*) or of an origin (*procession*) to signify the relation of the Father and the Son in respect of the Holy Spirit, and the corresponding relation of the Spirit to Father and Son.[38] A similar accommodation rebounds on us in the use of the name *Love*. There are not two loves within God, but one single love, to wit, the love with which the three persons love, the love which is God himself: 'God is love' (1 Jn 4.8). But, for want of another word, since our

---

[33] *De potentia*, q. 9, a. 9, ad 7.
[34] See above, in Chapter 4, 'A Different Procession, Which is That of Love'.
[35] *ST* I, q. 37, a. 1.   [36] *ST* I, q. 36, a. 1. See above, 'The Name "*Holy Spirit*"'.
[37] Cf. *ST* I, q. 27, a. 4, ad 3.   [38] *ST* I, q. 28, a. 4.

language is so meagre, we make use of the same name to refer to the person of the Holy Spirit, that is, to indicate the one who proceeds as a 'fruit of love', and thus we give this word a different, personal meaning.

Why do we have this linguistic problem when it comes to the Holy Spirit, when nothing in the study of the Son presents anything like it? For Thomas, the reason is that we have a better understanding of mental procession, whereas that of the will is much more obscure for us. In the study of human beings, just as in that of Trinitarian faith, we have therefore a much more detailed and more accurate vocabulary for designating intellectual things than those connected to volition and love.[39] But Thomas does not give up on achieving the same level of doctrinal vision with the Spirit as with the Word. It is true that there is an outstanding difference between the procession of knowledge and that of love: knowledge is brought about by means of a similitude (the very notion of the Word who proceeds implies such a similitude, and this is why the speaking of the Word is, as such, a generation). But, on the other hand, as we have seen,[40] the procession of love does not come about through a likeness. The amorous procession does in fact presuppose the similitude which one can see in the speaking of the Word, but what it consists in is an impulsion, a vital momentum toward the beloved. Despite this difference, St Thomas maintains that procession by way of intellect (the generation of the Word) and procession by way of the will (the procession of Love) have a comparable structure. Thomas writes that,

All the same, it is necessary to understand both processions in a similar way. Thus: the fact that someone knows something brings about an intellectual conception of the known reality, a conception which we call a *word*; and in like manner, the fact that someone loves a thing brings about in the lover's affectivity what one might call an imprint of the loved reality. It is by means of this imprint that the loved reality is present in the one who loves, just as the known reality is in the knower. In this way, whenever someone knows and loves himself, he is present to himself not simply through actual identity, but also as an object known in one knowing and as an object loved in one loving.[41]

In this key passage, Thomas accents the features of the analogy which he plans to bring into play. On the one hand, we are looking at an immanent procession, where that which proceeds remains within the principle from which it issues. In the same way that the word remains *in* the knowing subject, the imprint of love emerges *within* the lover's own affectivity. Thus it achieves the basic condition set out at the outset of the Trinitarian treatise (q. 27, a. 1).

---

[39] *ST* I, q. 37, a. 1.
[40] See above, in Chapter 4, 'A Different Procession, which is that of Love'.
[41] *ST* I, q. 37. a. 1.

On the other hand, just as he noticed that the knowing mind forms a word, so St Thomas discerns that there is within the loving will an 'imprint' of the beloved thing. For what comes about in the will through the act of love, Thomas uses either the active vocabulary of *principle of impulsion* (vitality, movement towards, inclination, affection for, attraction)[42] or a formal vocabulary relating to an *imprint*.[43] This imprint is precisely a *principle* of impulsion toward the good loved, it pushes the will toward this good. These two registers are complementary expressions of the two faces of love. Love is inclination and attraction toward the loved one, and it is also the presence or grip of the beloved in the heart of the one who loves. In the passage which we have just considered (q. 37, a. 1), Thomas brings the language of *imprint* to the fore, doubtless because it indicates more precisely the immanent fruit which is produced within the will, whereas the inclination language suggests the driving dynamism of the act of love. His analyses of this subject emerge in the context of Trinitarian theology,[44] but they are not an artificial contrivance aimed at making sense out of Trinitarian doctrine. The anthropological texture of the theory is well grounded: the will is seized by the good which it takes as its object, it is attracted by the one which it loves; this follows from that inner inclination which makes the beloved being present to the one who loves, inclining him towards the beloved. It is not the act of love as such, but this *imprint* which flows up through the loving will which gives us an analogical understanding of the procession of the Holy Spirit within the Trinity. Thomas especially underlines the real relation (the relation of origin) which the 'imprint' involves, and not within love itself, but with the principle from which this imprint-impulsion proceeds, that is, within the one who utters the word and within the Word himself, that is, for God, the Father and the Son.[45]

One last nuance puts the finishing touch to the analysis. The one who knows and loves himself is in himself not only by a real identity, but also

[42] *ST* I, q. 36, q. 1: 'a certain imprint and motion'. *ST* I, q. 37, a 1: 'affection for the beloved being'. *SCG* IV, ch. 19: 'inclination' (nos. 3559, 3566), 'movement' (no. 3560), 'impulsion' (no. 3566), 'affection for' (no. 3559). *De potentia*, q. 10, a. 2, ad 11: 'entering upon coalescence'. *CT* I, ch. 46: 'attraction of the lover towards the beloved'.

[43] *ST* I, q. 37, a. 1; *De potentia*, q. 10, a. 2, ad 11. In his Commentary on the *Sentences*, St Thomas conceives love as an 'informing' of the loving will by the loved reality. But the 'imprint' which is at issue in the *Summa Theologiae* must be understood in a more dynamic way, that is, 'like something which pushes and moves' toward the beloved object (*ST* I, q. 27, a. 4). In the *Summa Contra Gentiles* (IV, ch. 19, no. 3560), Thomas had illustrated the dynamic character of love with the example of the movement of *fire*. The *Summa Contra Gentiles* is the turning-point here, as we showed when we spoke of St Thomas' development in relation to this question: see above, in Chapter 4, 'A Different Procession, which is that of Love'.

[44] These analyses of love recur when the *Summa* discusses ethics: see particularly *ST* I–II, q. 28, a. 2, sol.: 'The beloved is said to be in the lover, inasmuch as it is in his affection, by a kind of complacency'; ibid., ad 1: 'The beloved is contained in the lover, by being impressed on his heart (*impressum in affectu eius*) through a kind of complacency.'

[45] Cf. *ST* I, q. 27, a. 3, ad 3; q. 28, a. 4; q. 32, aa. 2–3; q. 36, a. 2.

under the rubric of the way the known is in the knower, and the beloved in the lover. By the Word who arises eternally as the conception of the Father who knows himself (and who, in knowing himself, knows all things), God is 'present' to himself in the mode of knowledge. Through the imprint of the love which from all eternity arises in the love with which God loves himself (and through which he also loves all creatures), God is 'present' to himself in the mode of love. The 'self-presence' of the spiritual being is a fundamental feature of Thomas' Trinitarian theology and of his anthropology. This is how God is in himself through a real identity (God *is* God), but he is also in himself as God known in the God who knows (with the procession of the Word), and as God beloved in the God who loves (with the procession of the affection or imprint of Love).[46] This take on the question makes the complete *immanence* of the procession of Love evident. By a further analogy, this analysis will also enable one to conceive the way the Trinity is present in the saints: when he is known through faith and vision, the Triune God makes himself present in the fruits of charity.[47]

From this vantage point, Thomas goes to work on the linguistic difficulties which we mentioned earlier, directing his attention to the *relations* which are involved in the procession of the 'imprint' of love. Commencing with what he has by now established about the Word, he initially reviews his analysis of the generation of the Word so as to draw up a parallel which indicates the meaning of the language which we use to speak of the Holy Spirit.

In the context of intellectual actions, we have a fitting language at our disposal. We use the verb 'to know' (*intelligere*) to refer to the essential act of each divine person: each person knows himself and knows others. God knows himself through his essence; this knowledge does not entail a real relation or introduce a distinction of persons into the Trinity. We also have to hand an apposite language for referring to the divers aspects of the personal procession and the real relations which it implies. We can actually supply a proper name for the principle, that is, the Father: 'The one who speaks' (*dicens*); the attendant notional action: to speak (*dicere*); and finally for the conception thus formed or begotten: the 'Word' (*Verbum*).[48] But, when it comes to the action of love, we can no longer deploy such linguistic precision. Thomas observes that,

In connection to will, we do indeed have the verb 'to love' (*diligere* and *amare*), which bears on the relation of the one who loves to the beloved being. But there is no proper vocabulary to designate the relation between its principle and that affection or 'imprint' of the loved thing, that 'imprint' which comes about in the one who loves

---

[46] See also *SCG* IV, ch. 19 (no. 3564); *De potentia*, q. 10, a. 2, ad 11; *CT* I, chs. 45–46.
[47] *ST* I, q. 43, a. 3; cf. q. 8, a. 3.
[48] *ST* I, q. 37, a. 1; cf. q. 34, a. 1, ad 3; see above, in Chapter 9, 'The Son, Word of God'.

from the very fact of his loving; and there is no longer a word to suggest the converse relation. Because of this poverty of our vocabulary, we refer to these relationships by using the terms 'love' or 'dilection'; it is as if we were to call the Word 'thought conceived' or 'begotten wisdom'.[49]

We thus have to take on board three revisions to our language. (1) Whereas we refer to the Word through the proper name which exclusively means the person of the Son, we do not have an exact term to refer to the 'imprint' of love. By default, we have to employ the word *Love*. This calls for caution: of itself, love refers to the essential action through which God loves himself and through which each divine person loves himself and the others. It is through an accommodation, and not in the proper meaning of the term, that we use the same word to signify something else, that is, that imprint of love which proceeds and which, despite the identical words, must not be confused with love itself. (2) Whereas we have a proper word to refer to the action of the Father which begets his Word (the word 'to speak' refers to the same action as 'to beget'), we do not have the corresponding word properly to signify the action which makes the imprint of love arise: for want of a more precise term, we have to use the word *to love*. Here again, one has to mind one's language. In its own connotation, the verb 'to love' refers to an action common to the three persons. It is not by the proper meaning of the term, but only after adjusting it, that we make use of the same word also to refer to the 'notional' action of the Father and Son, whose fruit is the imprint of love identical to the Holy Spirit himself. (3) Whereas we have a proper word to refer to the procession of the Word ('to be spoken', 'to be begotten'), we have no parallel term properly to refer to the origin of the imprint or affection of love: we have to make up for the lack by using the verb 'to proceed' or the expression 'to be breathed'.

St Augustine noticed this difficulty when he was thinking about how Love could be the key to the Holy Spirit's personality. He formulated it as follows: on the one hand, the name Love or Charity indicates the Holy Spirit himself, but on the other, since the whole Triune God *is* Charity, one cannot reserve this name exclusively for the Holy Spirit. He explains it like this:

If thus one can properly call one of the three persons *charity*, why should this name be best suited to the Holy Spirit? This is not to say that, in this holy and sovereign nature, substance and charity could be different: the substance itself is charity, the charity itself is substance, either in the Father, or in the Son, or in the Holy Spirit; and yet, nonetheless, it is the Holy Spirit who is given the proper name of Charity.[50]

[49] *ST* I, q. 37, a. 1.
[50] Augustine, *De Trinitate* XV.XVII. 29. Cf. *De Trinitate* XV. XIX. 37: 'We doubtless believe and we understand that charity is not the privilege of the Holy Spirit alone within the Trinity, but also that it is not without foundation that one gives the name of charity to him.' Cf. Thomas, *ST* I, q. 37, a. 1, arg. 1 and ad 1.

Thomas gave his full attention to this problem. His comeback was to point out that the word *Love*, or *Charity*, does not mean the same thing in both cases. (1) In relation to the Love which one must acknowledge in each person, and which St Thomas calls 'essential' love (Augustine identified it with the 'substance'), it relates to God's inclination to his own goodness, and does not introduce any real distinction into God, since the relation which one observes here is that of God loving, where that which is loved is nothing else than God himself. (2) When it comes to referring Love more precisely to the person of the Holy Spirit, one is dealing with what Thomas touched on by means of the terms *affection, attraction, imprint, impulsion*, and which give us an analogical grasp of the person who thus proceeds, as a real relation distinct from his principle. This is how he explains it, as he concludes his exposition:

So thus, where love and dilection simply suggest the relationship of lover to loved, the words *love* and *to love* are spoken of the essence, just as the terms 'knowledge' and 'to know' are. But in as much as we use the words *love* and *to love* to express the relation of the one who proceeds by mode of love in relation to his principle, and, conversely, that is to say, if by *love* we understand: *the love who proceeds*, and by *to love* to breathe the love which proceeds, then Love is the name of a person, and *to love* is a notional verb, like 'to speak' or 'to beget'.[51]

There is therefore no variety of loves within God, and nor is the essential love in God compounded with the personal love. There is, on the one hand, the essential action of love exercised by the whole Trinity. And, on the other hand, there is the action of the Father and the Son who breathe the Holy Spirit, and, which because we are so poor in words, we also designate by the verb *to love*, even though the reality formally intended by this word is not the same as the other. One thus distinguishes the essential love of the three persons and the personal Love which is the Holy Spirit. In calling the Holy Spirit *Love*, we thus do not indicate an essential attribute, but the One who proceeds within the Trinity in a manner analogous to the 'imprint' which one finds in the human will. This has to be accentuated: in designating the personal property of the Holy Spirit with the name Love, Thomas *absolutely does not* understand this as an appropriation (that was the danger in some medieval interpretations of Augustine), and he does not confuse the Holy Spirit with God's nature as love. This is his mature interpretation of the Augustinian doctrine, and it is a very personal and original one.

In this discussion, St Thomas thinks that, by drawing out a cogent analogy to descry the *personal relation* which constitutes the Holy Spirit, he has faithfully observed the requirement of conceiving the procession of the

---

[51] *ST* I, q. 37, a. 1.

Holy Spirit as an *immanent action*. He can thus integrate the fruits of his analysis of the person as a 'subsistent relation' into his meditation on the Holy Spirit. Since one can find a real relation here, and since it touches on an immanent procession, remaining within God himself, the Love which proceeds has the very nature of God, and so we can conceive that this Love is in fact a person: 'like the Word, Love is subsistent'.[52]

Simultaneously with its disclosure of what belongs to the Holy Spirit as a person, this idea of the Love gives an account of his action in creation and in the economy of grace. Here again, the doctrine of the Holy Spirit has a similar focal point to that of the Word. Immediately after having presented love as the property belonging to the Holy Spirit, in the *Summa Contra Gentiles*, Thomas shows that this doctrine proves its worth by enabling one to grasp the multiple aspects of the economy of the Spirit, since it illuminates the economy as well as it does theology.[53] In the *Summa Theologiae*, the economic repercussions of the theme of Love-Spirit will be more fully developed in the other treatises; the Trinitarian treatise itself integrates them into the study of the mutual Love of Father and Son, then of the Gift, and finally into the consideration of the divine missions.

3. THE MUTUAL LOVE OF FATHER AND SON

Using the analogy of love proceeding from the will, Thomas has begun by picking out the personal property of the Holy Spirit. So he had first looked at the love through which God loves himself ('God loves' within loving himself: q. 37, a. 1). The second stage of the discussion is about mutual Love (q. 37, a. 2). The investigation of the Holy Spirit as the 'mutual Love of Father and Son' puts itself forward as the next step from the foregoing analysis. But exegetes are far from unanimous on the best way to interpret the idea of mutual love. Before we tackle the texts, we shall briefly mention the main points of controversy.

For one stream of interpretation, Thomas gave pole position to the theme of the 'mutual love of Father and Son' in his Commentary on the *Sentences*, but drops it in the *Summa Theologiae*. Against Richard of Saint-Victor's stand for 'mutual love', Thomas firmly adopted Anselm of Canterbury's essentialist orientation, directed by the divine nature (the love through which God loves himself), because the image of mutual love is only a minor metaphor, lacking any theological pertinence or acuity. Cut out altogether in the *Summa Contra*

---

[52] *ST* I, q. 37, a. 1, ad 2.   [53] *SCG* IV, chs. 20–22.

Gentiles, it makes a fresh appearance in the *Summa Theologiae*, but is relegated to a subsidiary position, because the theme of mutual love no longer has any real work to do, since the love between Father and Son has become simply their own essence, as love. One must acknowledge Thomas' merit in attempting the reform which will be carried out definitively by Duns Scotus, when he eliminated the idea of the Holy Spirit as mutual love.[54]

At the precise opposite end of the spectrum from this reading of St Thomas, others underline the significance which the theme of the mutual love of Father and Son has in his writing. They have no difficulty in drawing out texts explaining that, because his Love constitutes his personal relation, the Holy Spirit is properly the mutual Love of Father and Son. Instead of seeing the lines of thought coming from Anselm and Richard of Saint Victor as being opposed to each other, one can view Thomas' analyses as an elucidation of the view which Augustine himself passed on. For Augustine himself suggested that the Holy Spirit can be considered in two ways: one way which starts off from the analogy of the mind, the word and love (the 'psychological' analogy), and another way in which the Holy Spirit is manifested as communion, the bond of unity between Father and Son, in which the holiness and unity of the Church is brought about.[55] Augustine's two trains of thought invite us to consider the Holy Spirit on the analogy of the soul's love, but also on that of the reciprocity of persons within mutual love.[56]

So as to attempt to see this topic a little more clearly, one must observe that, widespread prejudice to the contrary notwithstanding, Thomas does not in fact open the investigation of the Holy Spirit with the idea of mutual love. In Thomas' 'Writing on the *Sentences*', the study of the Holy Spirit is introduced through the theme of God's love for creatures, leading one to recognize a procession of Love within God himself. Mutual love actually only enters in the second act of the *Sentences*.[57] In its turn, the silence of the *Summa Contra Gentiles* on the idea of mutual love can be explained by the peculiar genre of

[54] As the outstanding witness to this interpretation, see M. T.-L. Penido, 'Gloses sur la procession d'amour dans la Trinité', *EThL* 14 (1937), 33–68; and M. T.-L. Penido 'A propos de la procession d'amour en Dieu', *EThL* 15 (1938), 338–344.

[55] Cf. especially, Augustine, *De Trinitate* XIV.VIII.11; the *mind* remembers itself, knows itself, and loves itself; *De Trinitate* XV.VII.12: *mens, notitia*, and *dilectio*; or *memoria, intelligentia*, and *dilectio* or *voluntas*; *De Trinitate*, VI.V.7, on mutual love; etc.

[56] As witness of this second school of interpretation, see especially F. Bourassa, 'Sur la propriété de l'Esprit, Questions Disputées', *SE* 28 (1976), 243–264; F. Bourassa, 'Le Saint-Esprit unité d'amour du Père et du Fils', *SE* 14 (1962), 375–415 (reprinted in *Questions de théologie trinitaire*, Rome, 1970, pp. 59–123); F. Bourassa, 'L'Esprit Saint, "Communion du Père et du Fils"', *SE* 29 (1977), 251–281, and *SE* 30 (1978), 5–37; F. Bourassa, 'Dans la communion de l'Esprit Saint', *SE* 34 (1982), 31–56; 135–149; 239–268.

[57] I *Sent.* d. 10, q. 1, a. 1 and aa. 2–3. Cf. our book, *La Trinité créatrice*, pp. 368–383.

the work, by the structure of its Trinitarian treatise, and by the need for concision. Mutual love is not the only topic affected by this. For example, the theme of the Holy Spirit as Gift, to which Thomas constantly attends in his works (he is still giving it a whole question to itself in the *Summa Theologiae*) is only touched upon briefly, without any special prominence, and without even examining the meaning of the word 'Gift'.[58] As the *Summa Theologiae* testifies, this definitely does not imply that St Thomas henceforth denigrated the idea of the Gift, any more than he did this to mutual love, relegating such theologically empty notions to the sidelines.

More importantly, one must consider what the *Summa Theologiae* is aiming at. We have remarked several times upon the fact that Thomas wants to disclose an inward or 'intimate' procession, one which is *immanent*. So he is looking to pin down an analogy through which to grasp the immanent procession of love. And, *in our own world*, interpersonal love does not give us an adequate example of an immanent procession. This is not just because of the clumsy ideas which some theologians have linked to mutual love, such as that the divine love *must* be mutual, because if it were just 'the love of an individual', it would be imperfect.[59] It is, rather, a matter of the nature of mutual love as it comes about in this world: it consists in a double external impulsion, flowing between two different people each of whom is external to the other. If one takes this analogy as one's *starting point*, one will have a very hard time getting to grips with the *unity* of the Holy Spirit's immanent procession, or with his consubstantiality; and this is indicated by the requirements laid down in the first article of the Trinitarian treatise.[60] It is moreover for an analogous reason (for the two cases are not identical) that he did not *commence* from the analogy of human sonship in order to disclose the personality of the Son. He began by using the analogy of the *interior* formation of the word in the human mind to establish that the Son is the Word, and he discloses the meaning of *Son* as a proper name by making the Word theme work towards it.

---

[58] *SCG* IV, ch. 21 (no. 3575).

[59] On this argument, see especially *De potentia*, q. 9, a. 9, sed contra 2. In the twelfth century, Richard of Saint-Victor distinguished the 'gratuitous love' of the Father who communicates himself (the *amor gratuitus* of the Father which 'receives absolutely nothing from any other'), and the 'obligated or owed love' of the Holy Spirit which receives everything from its principle (the *amor debitus* of the Holy Spirit); cf. *De Trinitate*, Book V, chs. 16–18 (*SC* 63, pp. 342–349). In the thirteenth century, William of Auxerre made his own distinction between God's 'natural' love and his 'gratuitous' love, in order to show the difference between the essential and the personal love in God (*Summa Aurea*, Book I, tract 8, ch. 7, ed. J. Ribaillier, vol. 1, p. 150). St Thomas cuts out these anthropomorphisms. The distinction between 'gratuitous love' and 'love which we owe' applies to human beings but not to the divine persons (*De potentia*, q. 10, a. 4, ad 8).

[60] *ST* I, q. 27, a. 1. See above, in Chapter 4, 'The Problems of Arianism and of Sabellianism'.

This does not mean that the idea of 'mutual love', any more than that of the Son, must be seen as incapable of rising above the level of a metaphorical pointer, and set down in an accessory region of theology. But using this theme as the immediate entrance to the study of the person of the Holy Spirit as love cannot be congruent to the purpose of disclosing the *unity* of an *immanent* procession, giving rise to a relation, whose being is substantially the same as that of the principle of the procession.[61] To put it another way, to disclose the manner in which the divine person of the Holy Spirit is the mutual Love of Father and Son, one must begin by showing why grasping Love as an immanent procession enables one to conceive a relation which subsists within God. This is why Thomas takes as his point of departure the case of the procession of the 'imprint' of love which comes about in the will of the lover. When it is transposed into God, the imprint of love which arises from God's love for himself can be understood as a subsistent relation, the very person the Holy Spirit is. Once he has set these bases into position, Thomas can erect the second tier of his analysis, and show that the Father and the Son love one another through the Holy Spirit. This is not a mere accommodation. We are looking at a proper expression of the Trinitarian doctrine which explicates or elaborates a thread which the first stages of the thinking enabled us to disengage.[62]

There is one further way of putting this. In our world, a father and a son are two different beings: the process of generation is carried out 'from the outside'. But, within God, the Father and the Son are distinct by their relations, but nonetheless of the same divine substance, by virtue of an immanent procession: a point which one can convey with the analogy of the word. In the same way, in our world, a mutual love is exercised by two different people, in dual moves, and 'from without'. The shared Love of God has his own singularity, because an immanent procession gives him the same substance as the Father and the Son. The analogy of the imprint of love in the loving will gives us a window on this. So St Thomas shows the property of the

[61] This point has been emphasized by A. Keaty in 'The Holy Spirit Proceeding as Mutual Love: An Interpretation of Aquinas' *Summa Theologiae* I.37', *Angelicum* 77 (2000), 533–557. The idea of the Holy Spirit as Love in the two articles in q. 37 must be read in the light of the objectives fixed in questions 27 and 28 on processions and relations.

[62] Our interpretation is fundamentally in agreement with that of Fr Hyacinthe Dondaine (*La Trinité*, vol. 2, pp. 393–401). Nonetheless, perhaps under the influence of the controversy aroused by Penido (see above, n. 54), Fr Dondaine puts a very strong emphasis on the opposition of Anselm and Richard of Saint-Victor; but, in our opinion, this played a minor role in determining Thomas' aims. In other words, some of Fr Dondaine's formulae tend to undermine the value of the theme of mutual love, not only within the order of the exposition of the doctrine of the Trinity, but in relation to the reality of that which we call the 'mutual love' within God. For a balanced presentation, see J.-P. Torrell, *St Thomas: Spiritual Master*, pp. 183–188.

Holy Spirit as Love by considering the love through which God loves his own goodness,[63] and then by reflecting on the mutual love of Father and Son, the second theme being founded on the first.[64]

Thomas has already introduced the idea of the mutual love of Father and Son when he explains that we designate the very person of the Holy Spirit by using the name *Love*. He did this when pointing out the dual perspective on which our own approach to the mystery of the Trinity hangs: one can consider the persons either purely under their aspect of *reciprocity*, or under the aspect of *origin*, which includes reciprocity. Under the first aspect, the Holy Spirit appears as the bond of love between Father and Son. Thus, to repeat, purely in relation to our own understanding of the mystery, we thus grasp the Holy Spirit as 'between' the Father and the Son, being their mutual love:

the Holy Spirit is called the bond (*nexus*) between Father and Son, in that he is Love, since the Father loves the Son and the Son loves the Father by the one single love; and thus the name of the Holy Spirit as Love implies a relation of the Father to the Son, and vice versa [a relation of the Son to the Father], that is to say a relation of the one who loves to the beloved one.[65]

The Holy Spirit is thus looked upon as the core of the love of Father and Son; being the mutual union of two persons, he comes across in this capacity as a 'mediating' (*medius*) person. But this initial approach only exhibits one partial aspect of the mystery, for it barely gives us a glance at the single procession of the Holy Spirit, who proceeds from one single principle. This is why Thomas *reinterprets* the theme of mutual love in the light of his own idea of love:

But, the fact that Father and Son love one another mutually requires that their mutual love, who is the Holy Spirit, proceeds from both. Therefore, so far as his origin is concerned, the Holy Spirit is not a 'medium' (*medius*), but a third person in the Trinity.[66]

What stands out here is precisely the aspect under which the theme of mutual Love will be exposed: the Holy Spirit is not mutual Love in the way that the middle term of the reciprocal love of Father and Son would be, but rather the *Love who proceeds* from their mutuality (cf. q. 37, a. 1, sol.).

When he treats mutual love on its own merits, Thomas once again tackles the question by relating it to the orientation of our language, taking into account a traditional expression modelled after Augustine: 'The Father and

---

[63] *SCG* IV, chs. 19 and 23; *CT* I, chs. 45–48; *ST* I, q. 37, a. 1.
[64] *ST* I, q. 37, a. 1, ad 3; q. 37, a. 2; cf. q. 36, a. 4, ad 1; *De potentia*, q. 10, a. 4, ad 10.
[65] *ST* I, q. 37, a.1, ad 3. Cf. I *Sent.* d. 10, q. 1, a. 3; a. 5, ad 1.
[66] *ST* I, q. 37, a. 1, ad 3.

the Son love one another *through the Holy Spirit.'* This formula runs parallel to
a contiguous issue, which Augustine had raised on the topic of the Son: is the
Son 'the wisdom through which the Father is wise'?[67] The problem partly
derives from the Latin language in which these questions are formulated, for
this requires the use of the ablative.[68] And the ablative, concealed in an
English translation, 'through the Son' or 'through the Spirit' could suggest
that the Son or the Holy Spirit play a role of principle or cause in relation to
the Father; but the *order* within the Trinity forbids one to affirm this; Son and
Holy Spirit do not function as a principle of the Father, but the Father is the
principle of Son and Holy Spirit.[69] The explanation had already been ham-
mered out in respect of the Son as Wisdom: the Son is the Wisdom of the
Father in that he is *begotten* Wisdom; the Son is not the source of the Father's
wisdom, but is, rather, the conception formed by the Father, that is, the Word
in which the Father *exhibits* the whole of his wisdom.[70] Matters are a little
more complicated in respect of the Holy Spirit as mutual love. St Thomas
finds himself here in the midst of many ways of responding which had been
invented by theologians, and which he presents and discusses at some length,
in good scholastic style, before putting forward his own reply. We shall briefly
review the five opinions which he cites.[71]

When they examined the formula 'the Father and the Son love one another
through the Holy Spirit' (*Spiritu Sancto*), some theologians saw it as a
defective expression—because the Holy Spirit is not a 'principle' in relation
to the Father and the Son[72]—or else they regarded it as an improper use of
words. Closer to Thomas' time, the outstanding example of this is in the
Summa attributed to Alexander of Hales.[73] Bordering on this attitude were
the theologians who considered such a formula to be an 'appropriation' of
love to the Holy Spirit.[74] Thomas was entirely dissatisfied by these initial ways

[67] These two questions had been brought together by Peter Lombard, who also provided a
collection of Augustinian texts on this matter (*Sentences*, Book I, dist. 32).
[68] Cf. Thomas, I *Sent.* d. 32, qq. 1–2; does the Father love the Son 'through the Holy Spirit'
(*Spiritu Sancto*); do the Father and the Son love one another, and love us, 'through the Holy
Spirit' (*Spiritu Sancto*); is the Father wise 'through begotten wisdom' (*sapientia genita*)?
[69] *ST* I, q. 37, a. 2.
[70] *ST* I, q. 34, a. 1, ad 2.
[71] *ST* I, q. 37, a. 2.
[72] This rejection does not date from the period of High Scholasticism. It is already noted by
Peter of Poitiers, for instance, as one of the current opinions amongst the Masters (I *Sent.*, ch. 21;
PL 211. 872).
[73] *Summa fratris Alexandri*, Book I (ed. Quaracchi, vol. 1, p. 657), no. 460, ad 1–4: 'The
expressions "the Father and the Son love one another through the Holy Spirit" or "through the
Holy Spirit" are, properly speaking, false, and one must absolutely never take them on board,
but always give them an explanation instead.'
[74] *Summa fratris Alexandri*, loc. cit., *solutio*.

of solving the problem, because they discount the legitimate claim which the formula expresses. He did not confuse essential and personal love, and he was determined to acknowledge the particular property of the Holy Spirit in the mutual love of Father and Son.

Other theologians had explained the formula by taking the Holy Spirit as the 'sign' of the mutual love of Father and Son. That was how Simon of Tournai had solved the problem.[75] Thomas did not reject this,[76] but he viewed it as inadequate. Others again had seen the formula as presenting the Holy Spirit as being akin to the 'formal cause' by means of which Father and Son love one another. This answer, which had been put forward by William of Auxerre,[77] was barely acceptable in those terms, because it makes the Holy Spirit a sort of principle in relation to Father and Son. An ultimate resolution proposed to conceive the Holy Spirit like a 'formal effect', that is, styled as the Love which formally *unites* the Father and the Son, but only in that he *proceeds* from the Father and the Son: this idea was expressed by Richard of Saint-Victor in an opuscule[78] which thirteenth-century theologians wrongly attributed to Hugh of Saint Victor.[79] Once he has added some important refinements to it, it is this final solution which Thomas chose to extend: 'those who hold this are closer to the truth'.[80]

The theme of the Holy Spirit as mutual Love brings two threads together: the *procession* and the *union of love*. On the one hand, Thomas holds on to the idea of the union of love as a constitutive feature of the Augustinian tradition to which he remains fully attached. His comments on this are quite unambiguous: 'without the Holy Spirit there would be no way of grasping a unity of connection between Father and Son'[81]; 'since the Holy Spirit proceeds as love, it is by way of his mode of procession that he comes to be the union of Father and Son'[82]; 'since the Holy Spirit proceeds by the mode of will as Love, it is

[75] Simon of Tournai, *Disputationes*, disp. 65 (ed. J. Warichez, Louvain, 1932, pp. 180–182).

[76] *ST* I, q. 37, a. 2. Cf. *In Ioan.* 5.20 (no. 753) and 17.24 (no. 2262).

[77] William of Auxerre, *Summa aurea*, lib. I, tract. 8, ch. 7 (ed. J. Ribaillier, vol. 1, Grottaferrata and Paris, 1980, pp. 146–152).

[78] Richard of Saint-Victor, *Quomodo Spiritus sanctus est amor Patris et Filii* (in *Opuscules théologiques*, ed. J. Ribaillier, Paris, 1967, pp. 163–166).

[79] Cf. Bonaventure, I *Sent.* d. 32, a. 1, q. 2; Thomas, I *Sent.* d. 32, q. 1, a. 1.

[80] Thomas, *ST* I, q. 37, a. 2. Bonaventure also backed this solution (I *Sent.* d. 32, q. 1, a. 2) as did St Albert the Great (I *Sent.* d. 32, a. 1), who presents an overview of this which is like Thomas'. In his Commentary on the *Sentences*, Thomas notes that Richard's solution 'contains more truth than the others' and somehow manages to include those of Simon of Tournai and William of Auxerre (Thomas, I *Sent* d. 32, q. 1, a. 1). For a more detailed presentation and the bibliographical material, see our book, *La Trinité créatrice*, pp. 205–206, and pp. 430–434.

[81] *ST* I, q. 39, a. 8; cf. *De potentia*, q. 10, a. 5, ad 11.

[82] I *Sent.* d. 10, q. 1, a. 3, ad 1: 'It is from his mode of procession that the Holy Spirit comes to be the union of the one who loves and the beloved.' See also ad 2 and ad 3, plus the *Responsio de 108 articulis*, q. 25: 'He proceeds as the bond of the two, which could not be said of a creature.'

necessary that he proceeds from two who love one another'[83]; 'the Holy Spirit proceeds from them [the Father and Son] as the Love who unites them both'.[84]

On the other hand, since within the Trinitarian order the Holy Spirit does not play the role of principle in relation to Father or Son, St Thomas highlights the fact that the Holy Spirit is not the principle of the union of Father and Son, but is rather the one who *proceeds* from the Father and Son in their union. In order to show this, he uses the illustration of a bloom coming forth from a blossoming tree: 'one can say, "A fire is a heating agent by its heating", even though the heating is not the warmth that is the fire's form, but the action issuing from the fire; we say, "By its flowers a tree is blossoming", even though the blooms are not the tree's form, but effects coming forth from it.'[85] In this illustration, the action of blooming is named after that which proceeds from its act—the blooms. Now, from a grammatical standpoint, the formula *the Father and Son love by the Holy Spirit* seems to suggest that the Holy Spirit would play the role of a form with respect to the Father and Son. But in fact, as the example of the flowers shows, the Holy Spirit is not the form of the Father and Son's act of loving; rather, the Holy Spirit is the one who proceeds from the Father and Son. So, just as the tree is said to be blossoming *by its flowers*, insofar as the flowers are effects produced by the tree; so the Father and Son are said to love (or: to be lovers) *by the Holy Spirit*, insofar as the Holy Spirit, who is Love in person, proceeds from the Father and Son. Thomas writes that,

If one takes the act of *loving* [as pertaining to Father and Son] in a notional sense, it means exactly to breathe love. It is just in this way that *speaking* is producing a word and *blossoming* is producing a bloom. In the same way that we say that a tree blooms through its blooms, so likewise one says that the *Father speaks himself and creatures by his Word, or his Son*. And again, it is thus that one says that *by the Holy Spirit or Love proceeding, that the Father and the Son love each other and us*.[86]

One can see from these analyses what has been gained by the earlier discussion, inviting us to think of the Holy Spirit as the imprint or affection of the love which proceeds in a will. St Thomas does not consider the Holy Spirit as an action which proceeds (that had been his original idea, in his Commentary on the *Sentences*), but as the imprint of love which blossoms from the unity of Father and Son. In this sense, to love is to breathe Love; and the bloom of Love is the Holy Spirit.[87] It is as proceeding from the Father and Son that the

---

[83] *De potentia*, q. 9, a. 9, ad 3 (second series).

[84] *ST* I, q. 36, a. 4, ad 1; cf. q. 37, a. 1, ad 3. One could multiply such passages.

[85] *ST* I, q. 37, a. 2. When it comes to the Holy Spirit, one cannot keep the word 'effect', just as one cannot really name the Father or the Son as 'cause' in relation to the Holy Spirit. On this exclusion of the terminology of 'cause' and 'effect', see above, in Chapter 8, 'The Father: Principle and Source'.

[86] *ST*, q. 37, a. 2.   [87] Ibid., ad 2.

Holy Spirit is their mutual love, the 'bloom of love' through which we name the act of Father and Son itself, their shared union. Thus, the Holy Spirit is not conceived as the formal principle of the love of Father and Son (that would be to reduce the Holy Spirit to nothing more than the essential core of love through which God loves himself, or to love as appropriation), but is rather understood to be the 'bloom' of the Father and Son's acting as spirators: 'from the fact that Father and Son love one another mutually, their mutual Love, the Holy Spirit, necessarily proceeds from both'.[88] The procession of love accounts for the *union* of Father and Son, not by calling it the principle of their union, but as the 'bloom' or 'fruit' which proceeds thereby.

Because he has attached these nuances to his understanding of mutual love, Thomas is able to explain that the Communion of Father and Son, their mutual Bond or their love-Knot is the Holy Spirit who proceeds as their mutual Love. The *communion* of Father and Son and the *procession* of the Holy Spirit are so wholly caught up with one another that the communion is inconceivable without the procession of the Holy Spirit.[89] And this approach enables Thomas to succeed in doing justice to Augustine's intuition. From one angle, love is common to the whole Trinity: it is essential love, identical to the substance of the Trinity, by means of which Father, Son, and Holy Spirit love one another, and love us. From a different angle, we use the name *Love* to refer to the mark of affection into which this proceeds: it is in this way that the Father and the Son characteristically love one another and ourselves through the Holy Spirit who proceeds from them.

The idea of mutual Love and of a communion Bond will lead one to discern the Holy Spirit at every juncture at which the Father and Son are mentioned in Scripture. St Thomas draws this out with particular reference to the New Testament's 'binary' formulae, that is, the formulae which name Father and Son without explicitly speaking of the Holy Spirit. There is an Augustinian exegetical rule for such passages: 'Sacred Scripture sometimes names three persons, sometimes two [the Father and the Son], and then it is necessary to understand the Holy Spirit since he is the Bond of the two.'[90] The same kind of exegesis is applied to the salutations with which Paul begins his letters. Paul 'mentions the Father and the incarnate Son, by which it is necessary to understand also the Holy Spirit who is their mutual bond';[91] 'he does not explicitly mention the Holy Spirit, since his presence is indicated in the gifts

---

[88] *ST* I, q. 37, a. 1, ad 3.
[89] *De potentia*, q. 10, a. 5, ad 11; see J.-P Torrell, *St Thomas Aquinas: Spiritual Master*, pp. 186–188.
[90] *In Ioan.* 8. 17–18 (no 1156); *In Ioan.* 17.3 (no 2187).
[91] *In Thess.* 1.1 (no. 5).

of grace and peace; and also because the Holy Spirit must be grasped within the Father and Son whose Union and Bond he is';[92] 'since the Holy Spirit is the Bond of Father and Son, wherever mention is made of the person of Father or the person of Son, the person of the Holy Spirit is necessarily also comprehended'.[93]

One can also observe the immediate soteriological dimension of this investigation of mutual Love. In his meditation on mutual Love, St Augustine had seen the bond of Father and Son as that in which unity and sanctity are given to be shared within the Church. Thomas pursues this close association between theology and the economy: it is through the Love which proceeds from them that the Father and the Son love one another and *love us*. Thomas said that,

> In the same way that we say that a tree blooms through its blooms, so likewise one says that the *Father speaks himself and creatures by his Word, or his Son*. And again, it is thus that one says that *by the Holy Spirit or Love proceeding, that the Father and the Son love each other and us*.[94]

The discussion of this soteriological dimension appears with more fine-shadings in the response to an argument where, because of the way the objection is formulated, and also in order to link up his presentation of Love and Word, Thomas considers the Love through which the Father loves himself. But, drawing on the context and the nuancings which he had introduced earlier, what comes across here also concerns the mutual love of Father and Son, since this is a matter of *the same personal Love*:

> The Father utters himself and every creature by the Word which he begets, in as much as the begotten Word represents the Father and all creatures. And in the same way, he loves himself and loves all creatures by the Holy Spirit, in as much as the Holy Spirit proceeds as love for the original goodness, the motive for the Father's loving himself and every creature. Thus it is manifest that, as with the Word, a second aspect of Love proceeding is a reference to creatures.[95]

This discussion connects Love with the Word. The Father knows himself through his divine nature, but he *speaks* himself in his Word. The Word is not 'that through which' the Father knows himself, but is rather the conception which the Father forms or engenders by his fruitful act of knowledge, which is *speaking*. Receiving the whole substance of the Father and perfectly expressing him, the Son is thus the bearer of the creatures which he will express and create: the Father achieves all things through his Son. In a comparable way,

---

[92] *In Rom.* 1.7 (no. 73). St Thomas also notes in the same context that 'the works of the Trinity are inseparable' (*In Gal.* 1.1; no. 7).

[93] *In 2 Cor.* 1.2 (no. 10).   [94] *ST* I, q. 37, a. 2.   [95] *ST* I, q. 37, a. 2, ad 3.

the Father loves himself through his own divine nature, but he *breathes* the Holy Spirit, something which Thomas describes in terms of the 'imprint' or 'affection' of love. The Holy Spirit is not 'that through which' the Father loves, not the 'formal principle', the 'by which' the Father and the Son love one another, but the 'bloom' which proceeds in the notional act of love, which is *breathing*. The Spirit does not have the property of exhibiting creatures (such expression or representation belongs to the Word's personal character), but he proceeds as the *impulsion* of love. And, in the Father as in the Son, this impulsion of love is borne towards a goodness which is none other than the divine Goodness itself.[96] Thomas states that,

A being is loved in so far as it is good. Hence since one and the same goodness belongs to the Father, the Son, and the Holy Spirit, it is with one and the same Love, which is the Holy Spirit, that the Father loves himself, loves the Son, loves the Holy Spirit, and all creatures; just as it is through one and the same Word, which is the Son, that he speaks the Son, that he speaks the Holy Spirit, and all creatures.[97]

It is in the act of loving his own goodness that God loves his creatures. For God, to love creatures is to will their good, which means to create and infuse goodness into creatures.[98] Thomas finds the pattern and the source of the goods which the creating and gracious God assigns to creatures in the love through which God loves himself and through which the Father and the Son love one another. The Father and the Son love one another and love us through *one single Love*, which is the Holy Spirit.

As with the name *Word*, the name of Love thus primarily designates an intra-Trinitarian, person-to-person relation: it is this eternal relation which accounts for the personality of the Holy Spirit. The Holy Spirit is not constituted as a divine person by his relation to creatures, an idea which would take us back to semi-Arianism, but through his relation of origin in regard to the Father and Son, from whom he proceeds. Like the name *Word*, so the name *Love* also has a secondary reference to creatures, in that the immanent acts of God are the pattern of his action in the world.[99] In the passage cited above, Thomas speaks of the causality of the divine goodness. By virtue of its own formality, the procession of the Holy Spirit as love includes the goodness of the divine nature.[100] This affirmation must not be understood in a restricted sense, as if it were just the essential attribute, common to all

[96] By definition, love is the movement of the appetite towards the good: cf. *ST* I, q. 20; see above, in Chapter 4, 'A Different Procession, which is that of Love'.

[97] *De potentia*, q. 9, a. 9, ad 13.

[98] *ST* I, q. 20, a. 2.

[99] See above, in Chapter 3, 'Immanent and Economic Trinity', and in Chapter 9, 'The Word, Creation, and the Economy: the Father Acts through his Son'.

[100] Cf. *ST* I, q. 45, a. 6.

three persons, which is at issue in the relationship that the Holy Spirit has with creatures. It *is* the essential attribute which comes into play in the relationship with creatures,[101] but it is brought into play here because it is formally included in the personal property of the Love which the Holy Spirit is, that is to say, in as much as the Holy Spirit is the personal *origin* and *pattern* of the gifts which the Father and the Son give to creatures.

The Commentary on the *Sentences* explained this in more detail: by affirming that the Father and the Son love us through the Holy Spirit, we say that they 'breathe the personal love' which is the pattern of the gifts made by God for creatures.[102] It is not a question of an appropriation, but properly speaking, the primary thing signified in this affirmation is the intra-Trinitarian relation, the relationship to the created world being secondary. This is because the causality of the divine nature, which is common to all three persons, only exhibits one aspect of God's action in the world. In order fully to understand the creative and saving action of God, it is equally necessary to take the properties of the three persons into account. In other words, one must bring two rules together: 'the procession of the divine persons is one certain origin of the procession of creatures...and the efficacy with respect to creatures is attributed to the common essence'.[103] It is the linking, or rather, the integration of the two rules that comes about when one considers the divine person, which one conveys when one says that the Holy Spirit proceeds as Love in person, the pattern of the goods given to creatures.[104]

Whilst the Eastern tradition followed a separate path,[105] the Augustinian elucidation of the character of the Holy Spirit as Love did not confine itself to illuminating the immanent mystery of God, but also showed how this works out in the Spirit's economy. This idea was brought into play to show the 'necessity' of the revelation of the Trinity: indeed to grasp the creation of things and, above all, human salvation. Thomas states that,

When we affirm that in God there is a procession of love, we show that God produced creatures not because He needed them, nor for any other extrinsic reason, but on account of the love of his own goodness.... In another way, and chiefly, [the knowledge of the divine persons is necessary to us] so that we may think rightly concerning the salvation of the human race, accomplished by the incarnate Son and by the gift of the Holy Spirit.[106]

---

[101] As we have already observed whilst investigating the Word: *ST* I, q. 34, a. 3, ad 1.
[102] I *Sent.* d. 32, q. 1, a. 3.
[103] Ibid. See below, Chapter 14.
[104] See our book, *La Trinité créatrice*, pp. 430–443.
[105] The idea of the Holy Spirit as Love is not absent here, but it is not understood in the same way. See especially J. Lison, 'L'Esprit comme amour selon Grégoire Palamas,' *Connaissance des Pères de l'Eglise* no 69 (1998), 40–45.
[106] *ST* I, q. 32, a. 1, ad 3. See above, Chapter 1, 'Revelation, Creation, and Salvation.'

We will thus trace out the economic repercussions of understanding the Spirit as Love, first as creative Love, operating universally, and turning next to the economy of grace, in which men and women receive the gift of the Holy Spirit.

4. CREATIVE LOVE: THE UNIVERSAL OPERATION OF THE HOLY SPIRIT

Because of the way the topics are ordered in the *Summa Theologiae*, the creative acts of the Holy Spirit and the way he acts providentially on behalf of creatures are treated in different places: in the section dedicated to creation and then in that concerned with divine 'government' (in the *Prima Pars*).[107] Thomas takes the entirety of the creative causality of the Word and of the Holy Spirit into consideration.[108] He makes a more detailed treatment of the actions of Son and Holy Spirit in the *Summa Contra Gentiles*, putting it directly into line with his doctrine of Word and Love. In relation to the Son, we saw earlier that the character of *Word* accounts not only for the distinction and subsistence of the Son within the Trinity, but also for what Scripture describes as his actions within this world: creation, maintaining creatures in existence, their providential guidance, inspiring the prophets, illuminating the minds of angels and men, giving knowledge of God, manifesting the Father, and all of the works carried out in the Incarnation.[109] The property of being *Word* enables one to explain the biblical teaching about the person of Christ.

St Thomas follows the same procedure with the Holy Spirit. After having shown that the property of Love, understood after the *imprint* of love, discloses the existence of the Holy Spirit as a distinct person within the Triune God,[110] he continues: 'In harmony with what has been said, one must put one's mind to the effects which sacred Scripture attributes to the Holy Spirit.'[111] In other words, the idea of the Holy Spirit as Love does not just enable one to present the Holy Spirit as within the immanent Trinity, but also

---

[107] *ST* I, q. 45, aa. 6–7 (the Trinitarian mode of creation); q. 74, a. 3 (the Trinitarian interpretation of Genesis 1); q. 93 (the creation of humanity in the image of the Trinity).

[108] See especially *ST* I, q. 45, aa. 6–7; see below, Chapter 14.

[109] See above, in Chapter 9, 'The Word, Creation, and the Economy: the Father Acts through his Son'; 'The Word Discloses and Reveals the Father'; 'The Son Gives Us a Share in his Sonship'; 'The Image of the Father, First-Born of Creation'.

[110] *SCG* IV, ch. 19.

[111] *SCG* IV, ch. 20 (no. 3569).

gives one a profound and coherent way of understanding the action of the Holy Spirit as it is witnessed to by revelation. The *Summa Contra Gentiles* discusses this activity in three sections: the Holy Spirit acting universally, the gift of the Holy Spirit to human beings, and the Holy Spirit acting to unite human beings to God. The first section begins with an exposition of the creative causality of the Holy Spirit.[112] Thomas affirms that,

As we have already seen above, the goodness of God is his reason for willing that other things be, and it is by his will that he makes things to be. The love, then, by which He loves His own goodness is the cause of the creation of things: this is why some ancient philosophers held that 'the love of the gods' is the cause of all things, as Aristotle says in the first book of the *Metaphysics*; and Dionysius says in the *Divine Names* book four that 'the divine love does not allow itself to be without seed'. But it was held in the foregoing that the Holy Spirit proceeds by way of the love with which God loves himself. Therefore, the Holy Spirit is the principle of the creation of things. And this is signified in the word of the Psalmist: 'Send forth thy Spirit and they shall be created' (Ps. 103.30).[113]

It fits into the outlook of the *Summa Contra Gentiles* for God to be taken to be present to himself by loving himself through the Holy Spirit, understood as the imprint of love. As we have seen, the *Summa Theologiae* follows up this gambit with the notion of mutual love. And love is the direct source of every activity. All beings act in search of the good matched out for them, where 'the good' means their end. With God, there is no action for the sake of obtaining an end which he had hitherto missed out on; he is, rather, his created reality's end: he communicates his goodness to them, and this is what it means for the Creator to love.[114] Here the theologian assimilates the philosophical reflection which, at its own level, can conceive the universal causality of divine love: even some Presocratic philosophers had an obscure sense of this.[115]

---

[112] The same teaching is observable in Thomas' biblical commentaries. Thus, for instance, in his John Commentary, Thomas explicates the work of the Spirit in a like-minded way. Revelation, teaching within us, the remission of sins, the gift of grace, sanctification and filial adoption, indwelling, and so forth, are the works of the Holy Spirit. See *In Ioan.* 14.17 (no. 1916: because he is Love in person, the Holy Spirit reveals the mystery of God); *In Ioan.* 4.10 (no. 577: the Holy Spirit himself is given to us in grace); *In Ioan.* 20.22–23 (nos. 2541–2544: the Holy Spirit gives life and remits sins because he is charity in person); *In Ioan.* 14.26 (no. 1957: the Holy Spirit conforms believers to the Son and confers filial adoption upon them); *In Ioan.* 7.38 (no. 1090: the Holy Spirit who dwells in the hearts of believers is the source of all gifts); and so on.

[113] *SCG* IV, ch. 20 (no. 3570).

[114] *ST* I, q. 20, a. 2; q. 44, a. 4.

[115] Thomas notes in his Commentary on Aristotle's *Metaphysics* (I, lect. 5, no. 101) that some Presocratics had perceived that love is the first principle, 'even though they did not formulate this explicitly or clearly'. In this same ambience, there is a similar reference to the philosophers in I *Sent.* d. 10, q. 1, a. 1; cf. Albert the Great, I *Sent.* d. 10, a. 2 (in the context of speaking about the Holy Spirit as the mutual love of Father and Son); see our book, *La Trinité créatrice*, p. 377.

The procession of the Holy Spirit includes the essence of the love of God, not just because the Holy Spirit is God, but because he proceeds in that very mode of Love.

So it is because he proceeds in this way (because of the 'structure' of his procession) that, when creation is considered as a work of love, that is, when created things are treated as effects of divine love, the Holy Spirit comes to be the principle of creation. In this light, the personal procession of the Holy Spirit is the source and structuring principle of creation. St Thomas is so convinced of this idea that his Commentary on the *Sentences* uses it to introduce the procession of the Holy Spirit.[116] In the passage cited above from the *Summa Contra Gentiles* he shows, with reference to just one of many relevant biblical passages, that the idea of Love enables one to account for the creative action of the Holy Spirit. The mode of such creative activity differs from that of the Son: whereas that of the Son tracks his property as Word, that of the Holy Spirit arises from the property of Love. What creation effects is common to all three persons; creation is not the work of one person 'more' than any other (as will be explained by the idea of appropriations), for the Father accomplishes all things through his Son in the Holy Spirit. But the creative action of each divine person is patterned after his personal property. The Holy Spirit acts as Love, and, according to Thomas, it is this which enables one to make sense of the biblical passages which attribute creation to the Holy Spirit.

The exposition continues by way of the other effects of the Holy Spirit's universal activity. The movement of created beings, their inclinations, the orientations given them under providence are all participations in the personal property of the Holy Spirit:

The Holy Spirit proceeds by way of love, and love has an impelling and moving force. This is why the movement in creatures which comes from God is properly attributed to the Holy Spirit.[117]

We come back here to the idea of the *impulsion* of love, which enabled us to disclose the personal property of the Holy Spirit. Since the Holy Spirit is characterized by an impulsion, the motion of creation (meaning, the movement towards the good which comes from God) is linked to him. Thomas takes this as a base from which to consider various 'movements' in the created world. As the Augustinian exegesis of the Genesis narrative would have it, the first movement is that of the 'formation' of matter. St Thomas sees in the *Spirit of God*, moving on the surface of the waters (Gen 1.2), the Holy Spirit,

---

[116] I *Sent.* d. 10, q. 1, a. 1; cf. G. Emery, *La Trinité créatrice*, pp. 368–383.
[117] *SCG* IV, ch. 20 (no. 3571).

shaping beings into appropriate species. He also discerns the Holy Spirit in the fact that 'good' presides over the creation ceremony, within the first creation narrative, in Genesis.[118] He finds the Holy Spirit once again in the care which God takes for his creatures in guiding them towards their end:

God's government of things comes about through a certain motion, in that God directs and moves all things to their proper ends. If, then, impulsion and motion belong to the Holy Spirit, by reason of Love, it is congruous that Scripture attributes the government and propagation of beings to the Holy Spirit. This is why . . . the Psalm says: *Thy good spirit shall lead me into thy right land* (Ps. 142.10, Vulgate).[119]

By 'government', Thomas means the entire working of divine providence, that is, the concrete realization of the divine plan disposing the whole universe of creatures to its fulfilment.[120] He understands 'propagation' as the multiplication of creatures within the processes of generation,[121] that is the process through which species extend themselves, in space and over time. The impulsion of love characterizing the Holy Spirit leads one to recognize him as the source of this creaturely 'impulsion' toward their goods and their proper ends, carrying out God's plan.

The divine 'government' properly belongs to what we designate as the *Lord*, meaning God as the master and sovereign of the universe, who takes care of his creatures. Thomas sees this as authorizing the Creed's attribution of the name *Lord* to the Holy Spirit: 'I believe in the Holy Spirit who is the Lord.'[122] Continuing in this vein in his reading of the Creed, he also finds the reason why Scripture attributes *vivification* to the Holy Spirit in the fact that he is characterized as the impulse of love. In many other places, when he explains the vivification which the Holy Spirit achieves, Thomas foregrounds the gift of the life of grace, that is, sanctification (this is doubtless the primary sense envisaged by the Creed),[123] but he does not relinquish holding the term to its entire extension: the Holy Spirit is the source of all life. Thomas states that,

The highest way in which life manifests itself is movement. So if beings are self-moving, we call them *living*, and this applies universally to all things which move to act of their own accord. This is why it is fitting that life should be attributed to the

---

[118] *SCG* IV, ch. 20 (no. 3571); cf. *ST* I, q. 74, a. 3: 'The person of the Holy Spirit is indicated by the satisfaction with which God saw that whatever was made was good.'

[119] *SCG* IV, ch. 20 (no. 3572); cf. *CT* I, ch. 147.

[120] Cf. *ST* I, q. 22, a. 1, ad 2; q. 103. See J.-P. Torrell, '"Dieu conduit toutes choses vers leur fin": Providence et gouvernement divin chez Thomas d'Aquin', *Miscellanea Mediaevalia* 29 (2002), 561–594, especially 586–592.

[121] 'Propagation' follows on the first creation: propagation of plants, animals, humans, etc.; cf. especially *ST* I, q. 69, a. 2.

[122] *SCG* IV, ch. 20 (no. 3573).

[123] Cf. *In Ioan.* 6.64 (nos. 992–994); *SCG* IV, ch. 17 (no. 3529).

Holy Spirit, since impulsion and movement belong to him, because of love. This is why John says '*It is the Spirit that quickeneth*' (6.64), and Ezekiel: *I will send Spirit into you and you will live*' (37.5). And, in the Symbol of our Faith, we profess our faith in the Spirit *the giver of life*.[124]

These passages show in an eloquent way that nothing is more alien to St Thomas than a 'static' vision of the universe. The Holy Spirit is the divine impulse of love: the world and its history are formed by this impulsion, in which they participate. One could add other texts, especially from the biblical commentaries, but these are enough to let us see the method and the content of Thomas' doctrine of the Holy Spirit. It is by means of the eternal property of the Spirit as Love, in the style of a 'love-impulse', that one can set forth the deep reason for the acts attributed by Scripture to the Holy Spirit. Its aptitude for elucidating the economy confirms the idea of the Spirit as Love.

Thus far we have only considered creation and the universal activity of the Spirit. St Thomas gives a much more extended elaboration to the acts of the Spirit on behalf of humanity, and particularly to his gifts within the life of grace. But, before we open this window, we have to examine a different face of the Holy Spirit's personality. The Holy Spirit supplies his gifts to the entirety of creation, and he is also given in person to human beings and to angels: he is the *Gift* in person.

5. THE GIFT OF THE FATHER AND THE SON

As with the idea of love, that of the Gift arises as a deepening of the Trinitarian tradition handed on by Augustine. Augustine actually acknowledged *Gift* as a proper name of the Holy Spirit: the Spirit is the only one within the Trinity whom we call *Gift*, the Gift common to Father and Son, the Gift which the resurrection of Christ obtains for men.[125] This is evidently a biblical idea: the Holy Spirit is the highest gift which the Father makes to his children by hearing their prayers (Lk. 11.13); it is by him that spiritual gifts are conveyed to the Church (1 Cor. 12.4–11), he is God's gift, whom Christ extends to us,

---

[124] *SCG* IV, ch. 20 (no. 3574). Thomas finds here a new congruity explaining the name 'Spirit', by analogy with the theme of life: it is effectively through 'spirit' (*spiritus*) that life is communicated to the members in living beings endowed with animal life (ibid.). Cf. *CT* I, ch. 147.

[125] See especially *De Trinitate* V.XV.16–XVI.17; XV.XVII.29; XV.XVIII.32; XV.XIX.33–36; etc. Peter Lombard collected the documentation on the topic of the name 'Gift' (*Sentences*, Book I, dist. 18). All of Thomas' references on this question (in *ST* I, q. 38) are taken from Augustine. See F. Bourassa, '*Don de Dieu*, Nom propre du Saint-Esprit', *SE* 6 (1954), 73–82; id., 'Le don de Dieu', *Gregorianum* 50 (1969), 201–235.

fulfilling every desire (cf. Jn 4.10). According to Thomas, the idea of *Gift* is directly linked to that of grace. Since he is the Gift, it belongs to the Holy Spirit to be uncreated Grace.[126] Under this rubric, 'the Holy Spirit is himself the unfailing source from which all the gifts of grace flow'.[127] The first of these gifts is the charity which the Holy Spirit spreads into the heart.[128]

Following the method it always applies to the names of the divine persons, the *Summa* proceeds in two stages. Thomas first examines what makes the name *Gift* apt for meaning not just the Trinity but one single person in a distinct manner (q. 38, a. 1), then he shows that it concerns the name of the person who is the Holy Spirit (q. 38, a. 2). This way of speaking about it brings one facet of the Holy Spirit into focus.

The peculiarities of the name *Gift* need to be highlighted before we can see how it works as a personal name for the Holy Spirit. One can detect four characteristics which are entirely unique to this name. First, the name 'Gift' always means a certain relationship to creatures. By definition, a gift is connected to a beneficiary, and it is to 'rational creatures', that is, human beings and angels, that the Holy Spirit is given. The relationship which the divine person has with creatures is thus more marked here than in the names *Father*, *Son*, *Word*, or *Image*. Second, the Holy Spirit is given in time, in history: one will need to show how the name *Gift* belongs to the Holy Spirit not only because of how he acts in the economy, but primarily in a way that transcends time, as through an eternal property. Third, in order for a divine person to be recognized as *Gift*, it is necessary not only that a creature can benefit from the divine action, but also that this creature can receive the divine person himself. Does that mean we are capable of receiving not only created effects, but the divine person as such? Finally, Thomas notes that, in begetting him, the Father gives the Son the fullness of divinity. In this sense, the divine essence is *given* by the Father to the Son and the Holy Spirit. Otherwise put, the divine nature is itself a 'gift' which the Father makes eternally to the Son and the Holy Spirit. So one will have to show what enables one properly to apportion the name Gift to one particular person.

Thomas develops the explanations set out by Augustine to take these different angles into account. The latter explained that the Holy Spirit *is* the Gift from eternity, but, in practice he is only *given* in time.[129] Thomas follows

---

[126] II *Sent.* d. 26, q. 1, a. 1: 'There is a gratuitously bestowed Gift who is uncreated: this is the Holy Spirit.'

[127] *In Ioan.* 4.10 (no. 577).

[128] *In Rom.* 5.5 (no. 392). We will see later on Thomas' theological interpretation of this idea: the Holy Spirit spreads charity because he himself is, in his personal character, the Charity of Father and Son (ibid.).

[129] Augustine, *De Trinitate* X.XV.16–XVI.17.

this up with a refinement: 'the name *Gift* involves an aptitude for being given'.[130] He thus distinguishes: (1) the aptitude, congruence or disposition for being given and (2) the donation of the Holy Spirit to those who receive him. The aptitude belongs to the Holy Spirit from all eternity, from before the creation of the world: it is this aptitude or disposition for being given to which we refer by the name *Gift*. But the actual donation only happens in the course of time.[131] This analysis thus distinguishes the Holy Spirit as Gift (*donum*) and as given (*datum*). Under the first heading, Gift refers to the eternal character of the Holy Spirit; under the second, it designates this character in so far as the Holy Spirit is effectively or actually received by any one creature within history.[132] Thomas writes that,

One can speak of a gift prior to the actual donation, because the thing is apt for being given. This is why a divine person is called *Gift* from all eternity, even though he is actually given only in the course of time.[133]

This first refinement is important. In practice, the Holy Spirit is given because he is Gift, but even so, the name *Gift* is not owing to him because of his acts within this world.[134] It is due to him primarily because of an eternal relation at the heart of the Trinity. This enables us to recognize that the name *Gift* has the same prerogatives as the names *Father, Son, Word,* and *Love*. Referring to an eternal property, it can thus signify the divine person as such. Otherwise put, it is not the economy of grace which founds the eternal property of the Holy Spirit, but rather it is this eternal property which founds the economy of the Holy Spirit.

This immediately calls forth two corresponding points. For there to be a 'gift', there must be a donor, since the gift implies a connection to the one who gives. And for there to be a real donation, there must also be a beneficiary, since the gift implies a relationship to a receiver. The first aspect enables one to expose the relation of origin which one must recognize in the divine Gift;

---

[130] *ST* I, q. 38, a. 1.

[131] Latin scholasticism had many terms at its disposal for distinguishing these two aspects: *donum* (the gift, meaning the 'aptitude'), *datio* or *donatio* (the actual donation, implying the factual reception of the gift by its beneficiaries); cf. I *Sent*. d. 18, q. 1, a. 2; d. 15, q. 3, a. 1.

[132] I *Sent*. d. 18, q. 1, a. 2. Distinguishing the dual aspects ('aptitude' for being given and actual donation) is the path taken for explaining the question taken by all theologians contemporary with St Thomas: see especially Bonaventure (I *Sent*. 18, a. 1, q. 2) or Albert the Great (I *Sent*. d. 18, a. 2). On many points, the question of the Gift represents a common doctrine amongst these theologians.

[133] *ST* I, q. 38, a. 1, ad 4.

[134] If the name *Gift* only referred to the action exercised by the Holy Spirit in the course of time, it would be unable to disclose the immanent and eternal procession of the divine person, and likewise for the relation which eternally constitutes this person.

the second implies a linking with creatures. We note first of all the primary aspect:

That which is given has a relation to the one who gives . . . If someone gives something, this is because that thing is 'from someone' who gives. . . . For a divine person, one says that he is 'of another' as to origin; it is thus, for example, that the Son is 'of the Father'. . . . One also says of a thing that it is 'of someone' by reason of its origin alone. It is thus that the Son is 'of the Father' and the Holy Spirit is 'of the Father and the Son'. It is in this sense that one refers the Gift to the Donor, since the Gift is distinguished as a person from the Donor, and the name *Gift* is a personal name.[135]

This is thus the relation of origin: as *Gift*, the Holy Spirit proceeds from Father and Son and this is comprehended within the meaning of the name *Gift* which we attribute to the Holy Spirit as a person. It is this relation of origin which enables us to see this as a personal name. One can of course understand the name 'gift' without reference to such an originary relation: it is thus that the Father gives himself, or the Holy Spirit gives himself; one can equally well say that the divine nature is the 'gift' which the Father makes to the Son in begetting him. In the latter two instances, 'gift' is not properly spoken as a personal name. The name *Gift* is thus a personal name in so far as it entails a relation of origin, that is, a personal distinction, and this occurs when we take it in the sense of 'Gift *of the Donor*', that is, *Gift of the Father and the Son.*[136]

Being Gift involves, not only a relationship to the Donor, but also one to the beneficiaries within a genuine donation. For the Gift fully to deserve that name, one thing which is necessary is that he can be received by his beneficiaries, emerging within the creatures to whom the Holy Spirit is given. The stakes here are high: in the life of grace, we do not just receive the effects of the Holy Spirit, but the Holy Spirit in person. For the donation to be authentic, the recipient must truly be able to walk freely in the Gift, as that which is 'possessed' (*habere*) by him. Such a privilege is handed to rational creatures alone, that is, to angels and human beings, because only they can enjoy the divine person himself, and, they alone can make use of the diverse gifts which the divine person gives. The idea of the image of God meets up with us once more at this juncture. Thomas writes,

A divine person can be possessed only by a rational creature conjoined to God. Other creatures can be mobilized by a divine person, but not in such a way that they enjoy the divine person and put his effects to use. The rational creature herself does sometimes achieve this: when it is given to her to participate in the divine Word and in proceeding Love, in such a way that she can freely know God in truth and love

---

[135] *ST* I, q. 38, a. 1, sol. and ad 1; cf. I *Sent.* d. 18, q. 1, a. 1.
[136] *ST* I, q. 38, a. 1, ad 1 and 2.

him rightly. This is why only the rational creature can 'possess' a divine person. But she cannot come to this by her own resources: so it must be given to her from above; for we say that something is given to us that we have from someone else.[137]

This central analysis takes us to the heart of Trinitarian theology. We will come back later to the ideas of the indwelling of the divine persons and the image of the Trinity in human beings; their significance is already clear. Along with angels, human beings alone can know and love God. The capacity for this knowledge and love is written into human nature at creation, as the divine image: but it cannot achieve union with God himself, that is, true knowledge and right love, without a gift. This gift is the grace through which a human being, made to the image of the Triune God, is lifted right up to objective participation in the procession of the Word and of Love.[138] The elevation in which grace consists can be explained by the gift of the divine person himself, the giving of the Holy Spirit in person. The question of the relationship between 'created grace' and 'uncreated grace' is centred here, at the heart of the investigation of the person of the Holy Spirit.

Thomas actually emphasizes the necessity of a *created* grace. When the Holy Spirit is given to human beings, he does not enter into a synthesis with someone with whom he is 'mixed' or 'fused'. Even in Christ, there is no mixture or conflation between the divine and the human nature. For a human being's own nature to be raised into communion with God, it is necessary to recognize, from the moment of their participation in God onwards, a gift in her which will be the intrinsic principle of her sanctification, a reality which has a human size, and so is a created one, situated on the ontological plane of creatureliness: this is the grace which is called 'created'. This gift comes from God alone, because it is God alone who divinizes, God alone who makes human beings participants in his own divine nature.[139] But, even when he gives himself, God remains distinct from human beings. In the scholastic terminology, it is necessary to see that God is not the 'formal cause' of the life of grace, because he does not enter into formal composition with the human (both God's simplicity and the created condition of human beings make this unthinkable; for we would then be faced with a conflation of the divine and the human nature).[140] In this light, grace is a created disposition which human beings receive from God. It is, so to speak, a gift from God which puts itself onto the ontological level of human nature, proportioning

[137] *ST* I, q. 38, a. 1.
[138] Cf. *ST* I, q. 93: Thomas explains here the different degrees taken by the image of God in human beings.
[139] *ST* I–II, q. 112, a. 1.
[140] 'God gives life to the soul, not as a formal cause but as an efficient cause' (*De veritate*, q. 27, a. 1, ad 1).

itself to the human in order to make it possible for men and women to be united to God from within their own human life.[141] Such created grace *disposes* human beings to receiving the divine person. Thomas states that,

the gift of sanctifying grace disposes the soul to possess the divine person; this is what the formula 'the Holy Spirit is given through the gift of grace' means. But the gift itself is the grace coming from the Holy Spirit; this is what Paul means when he says, *The charity of God is poured forth in our hearts by the Holy Spirit.*[142]

The insistence on the necessity for a created gift (habitual grace with its gifts of wisdom and charity) must not make us forget that its aim is to make human beings capable of receiving the Holy Spirit himself, and, beside the Holy Spirit, the Father and the Son, who come to build their dwelling in the saints ('to possess the divine person'). St Thomas is very clear on this:

through the gift of sanctifying grace, the reasonable creature is not only perfected in such a way as to be able to make use of the created gift, but also in such a way as to enjoy the divine person himself.[143] . . . the grace of the Holy Spirit is given to human beings in such a way that the actual source of the grace is given, to wit, the Holy Spirit himself.[144]

Hence, there are two aspects under which the gift of the Holy Spirit can be considered. The two sides or complementary perspectives are: that of the human being who receives grace, and that of the Holy Spirit who is given to us. In a question which is formulated in such thoroughgoing scholastic-speak that we might underestimate its importance, Thomas asks himself what comes about 'primarily' in the experience of grace: is it the uncreated Gift, that is, the Holy Spirit, or is it the created gift, charity flowing from sanctifying grace? In other words, is it the uncreated Gift who accounts for the presence of created gifts in human beings, or vice-versa, created gifts which explain the gift of the Holy Spirit? Thomas answers that,

A natural ordering between two elements can be looked at in two ways. On the side of the receipient, . . . the disposition takes priority over the disposer: in this sense, the receipt of the gifts of the Holy Spirit has priority over that of the Holy Spirit himself, since it is by receiving these gifts that we are conformed to the Holy Spirit. But on the side of the agent and end, priority belongs to what falls closer to the agent and end: in this sense, the receipt of the Holy Spirit has priority over that of his gifts . . . and this kind of priority is absolute.[145]

[141] *ST* I–II, q. 106; q. 110, aa. 1–2. On this topic, see J.-H. Nicolas, *Les profondeurs de la grâce,* Paris, 1969, pp. 150–160.
[142] *ST* I, q. 43, a. 3, ad 2.
[143] *ST* I, q. 43, a. 3, ad 1. On this topic, one can consult A. N. Williams' illuminating book, *The Ground of Union: Deification in Aquinas and Palamas,* New York and Oxford, 1999.
[144] *In Ioan.* 4.10 (no. 577).   [145] I *Sent.* d. 14, q. 2, a. 1, qla 2.

To our knowledge, this analysis supplies one of Thomas' clearest expositions of the relationship between created and uncreated grace. Like the fine-tunings which we mentioned earlier, it does not appear in the treatise on grace, but rather in the study of the Holy Spirit, in Trinitarian theology. The 'priority' in question is not a matter of temporal order, or 'before' and 'after'. It concerns a metaphysical and structural priority, that is, of the reality whose presence explains that of something else. From the point of view of our assimilation to the Holy Spirit in the condition of our human nature, created gifts are primary, because they represent the priority of a disposition. But from the point of view of the Author or Agent of grace, and the end to which grace disposes us, that is, receiving the Holy Spirit, the gift of the Holy Spirit himself is absolutely primary. And it is this which Thomas has in mind when he discusses the name *Gift*, which refers to the person of the Holy Spirit.

One last shading relates to the personal meaning of the name 'Gift'. As we have seen, this name always involves some sort of link with creatures,[146] since it touches on the real donation of the Holy Spirit in time, or his eternal 'aptitude' for being given. But, it follows on from the innermost rules of Trinitarian theology that a divine person exists in his eternal, personal relation at the heart of the Trinity. The divine person is not 'constituted' as such through his relationship to the world (the trap door into Arianism and Sabellianism), but, rather, through an intra-Trinitarian relation. In other words, the Holy Spirit is not 'more' in relation to creatures than Father and Son are, or, he is no 'more' given to the saints than they: the connection with creatures is common to the three persons, belonging to the way we understand the divine nature, in which the three persons share. Thomas' response to this point is like the ones he gave for the names *Word* and *Love*.[147] *Gift* has an intrinsic involvement with creatures, in that the very notion of Gift 'includes in itself an essential attribute, just as the notion of person includes that of the essence'.[148]

This affirmation must not be taken in the confined sense of the essential attributes common to the three persons, which comes into play in the Holy Spirit's giving himself to the saints. It is in fact the essential attribute which is engaged in the relationship with creatures,[149] but its engagement is based in

---

[146] I *Sent.* d. 27, q. 2, a. 3, ad 2.
[147] *ST* I, q. 34, a. 3, ad 1; q. 37, a. 2, ad 3.   [148] *ST* I, q. 38, a. 1, ad 4.
[149] We have already seen this in the investigation of the names *Word* and *Love*. Yet another locus is I *Sent.* d. 18, q. 1, a. 1, ad 1: 'A name can connote an effect occurring in the creature . . . such that, by denoting a relationship of principle to the creature, it also implies something else. In this case, even though the relationship to the creatures gives an understanding of the essence (for the effect enables one to grasp the cause), because of the other aspect which it signifies, a name can concern a person. . . . I thus say that, over and above the relationship which it implies to that to which it lends itself to being given, the name *Gift* involves a relationship to that from which it proceeds . . . and under this aspect it is personal [notional].'

its formal inclusion in the precise character of the Gift who is the Holy Spirit, that is, in the fact that the person of the Holy Spirit is the Gift of Father and Son. Otherwise put: it is not the relationship with creatures as such which makes *Gift* a properly personal name, just as it is not the relationship with creatures which constitutes the Holy Spirit as a divine person. From all eternity, the Gift is a person, by dint of his originary relation towards the Giver (the Father and Son), or in other words, in that he proceeds from the Father and the Son, distinguishing himself from them precisely through this relation. Yet another way of putting it is that we receive the Holy Spirit in person, because he is the Gift, constituted as such through his relation to Father and Son, who is thus given to us.

This discussion indicates that the name *Gift* is in fact a personal one. It remains to be shown that this name properly belongs to the Holy Spirit, and is not a name for the Father or the Son. The exposition flows limpidly out of the idea of love. St Thomas begins by connecting gift and love, emphasizing the *gratuitous* character of every gift. He states,

according to Aristotle, a gift is a giving that can have no return, that is, which is not given intending that it be repaid. 'Gift' thus implies a gratuitous giving. The basis for such a gratuitous giving is love: we give something gratuitously to someone when we give it willing their good. And so the first thing that we give them is the love with which we will their good. Clearly, then, love is itself the first gift, through which all others are given.[150]

What a gift represents within our own human experience provides an entrance into the topic. Something is an authentic gift not when it is driven by fear, or by the greedy desire for getting an even bigger pay-back (that would be an act of commerce, or compensation, not one of giving), but when it is moved by genuine open-handedness. And, in our own experience, where does such open-handedness come from amongst human beings? It emerges from the fact that we want someone else's good: and this, precisely, is the definition of love.[151] Love is not just the source of the gifts which we give, but it is, rather, the very first gift. This can be interpreted as offering a profound analogy for the pathways of the love of God. God's love is perfect, because he loves without any compulsion, in a purely gratuitous way, and because he loves perfectly, he also gives perfectly, with an absolute open-handedness to which no recompense can be returned. And what he gives first is his own love, communicating the goodness through which he renders us able to love. Love is not all that God gives, but it is by love that he gives, and loving is his first gift to us. Thomas thus

---

[150] *ST* I, q. 38, a. 2.
[151] Cf. *ST* I–II, q. 26, a. 4: 'As Aristotle says, to love is to will good to someone'; cf. I *Sent.* d. 18, q. 1, a. 2.

applies these elements of love to the person of the Holy Spirit, adding this to what he has shown in the reflection on the processions and the property of Love:

Since, then, the Holy Spirit proceeds as Love, as has been shown [cf. q. 27, a. 4; q. 37], he proceeds as being the first Gift. This is what Augustine means when he says that *through the Gift who is the Holy Spirit, a multitude of gifts are distributed to Christ's members.*[152]

The Spirit is personally the Gift because he is the person of Love, in the precise meaning given to *Love* when it designates the personal character of the Holy Spirit, as the fruit of the love of the Father and Son proceeding as an impulse or affection. Otherwise put, even though the names *Gift* and *Love* are not synonyms, they refer to the same personal property of the Holy Spirit, the Gift overtaking our spirits as the immediate result of Love: 'the notion of *Gift* unfolds from that of *Love*'.[153] As the bond of unity which proceeds from Father and Son, the Holy Spirit is Love, eternally inclining toward being given. This same property, which constitutes his personality, leads to his being communicated to men by the Father and Son. As an origination-relation, this character always remains present, for it is because he flows from Father and Son that the Holy Spirit is the Gift in person:[154] he is the Gift of the Father and the Son who give themselves to human beings in him, and it is by way of him that all other gifts are bestowed.[155] The Father also gives himself, and the Son is no less given, but the Holy Spirit holds this as his personal property: to be Gift formally belongs to his distinct character. This is why the Father and the Son are given to us *in the Holy Spirit.*[156] Thomas states that,

Since the Holy Spirit is Love, the mode of procession properly belonging to him entails that he has it in himself *to be given* and to be *the pattern of giving*. He is thus *Gift through his own self*, and this is the primary way of being so. Other things which are given are only gifts to the extent that they participate in this Love, that is to say in so far as they are given in love.[157]

This takes us back to the absolute priority of uncreated grace in relation to created gifts, the latter being participations (dispositions, or help in action and

[152] *ST* I, q. 38, a. 2; cf. Augustine, *De Trinitate* XV.XIX.34.
[153] I *Sent.* d. 18, q. 1, a. 2, ad 4. The Holy Spirit is Love and Gift, just as the Son is Word, Son and Image.
[154] *ST* I, q. 38, a. 2, ad 2.
[155] Ibid., ad 1 and ad 3.
[156] Thomas explains this in relation to the Son, who himself is given: 'That the Son be given to us derives from the Love of the Father: *God so much loved the world that he gave his only Son* [Jn 3.16]', *ST* I, q. 38, a. 2, ad 1.
[157] I *Sent.* d. 18, q. 1, a. 2.

expression) of the uncreated Gift who is the Holy Spirit. It is thus through the Holy Spirit that all other gifts are given: beginning with gifts of the natural order (not forgetting creation itself, for the first gift of all is to be[158]); the charisms which come after it, given for the common good and the building up of the Church; and above all the gifts in which the Holy Spirit is given in person, to wit, the gifts of sanctifying grace, and, at the summit of the life of grace, the gift of charity.[159] In sum: 'the Holy Spirit is the pattern of all gifts'.[160] He is also, in this sense, the divine person 'closest to us', so to speak, the one who is most intimate with us, because he is given to us. It is through him that we receive the Father and the Son, and it is through him that we receive all gifts.[161]

6. THE HOLY SPIRIT'S GIFTS TO HUMAN BEINGS

Having shown that the Holy Spirit is the source of creation and in fact the source of all the gifts which God makes to men, St Thomas draws the whole economy together under the sign of the Holy Spirit: creation, the exercise of providence, human life, human action under the motivation of the Holy Spirit, Christology, the sacraments, and union with God in the beatitude in which the human vocation is fulfilled. This is not the place for a detailed description of the presence of the Holy Spirit in every region of Thomistic theology. There are other books one can consult which have eloquently shown this: 'if one does not find the Holy Spirit here or there in the work of Thomas Aquinas, this is because he is everywhere'.[162] We caught a glimpse of this earlier on, in the discussion of the creative action of the Holy Spirit. Thomas speaks of it at greater length when revelation and the life of grace are in question.

He had supplied a miniature synthesis of this in the *Summa Contra Gentiles*, confirming the power of his idea of Love. He sets off from Scripture so as to use the theory of Love to disclose the Holy Spirit's being as person. Then he returns to Scripture, to collect up the witnesses of the Holy Spirit's action, which he is now able to account for in the light of the idea that the character of the Holy Spirit is Love. Without pretending to set up a complete overview, he notes one

[158] I *Sent.* d. 10, q. 1, a. 1; cf. our study, *La Trinité créatrice*, pp. 372–376.
[159] I *Sent.* d. 18, q. 1, a. 3, ad 4. Charisms (gifts of tongues, of teaching, etc.), given for the edification of the Church, do not inherently imply sanctifying grace, and this is why the Holy Spirit is not formally given *in them*, even though these gifts (just like natural gifts, which do not imply sanctifying grace either), clearly come from the Holy Spirit.
[160] I *Sent.* d. 18, q. 1, a. 3.
[161] III *Sent.* d. 2, q. 2, a. 2, qla 2, ad 3: 'The Holy Spirit is the closest to us, because it is through him that all gifts are given.'
[162] J.-P. Torrell, *St Thomas Aquinas: Spiritual Master*, p. 154; cf. pp. 153–157.

scriptural lesson in particular: the Holy Spirit gives human beings the charity which enables them to love God and to become 'friends of God', he is the source of all divine blessings, he dwells in the heart of the saints with the Father and the Son, he reveals mysteries, he inspires prophets and supplies charisms, he communicates all the gifts of God to men, he leads them to beatitude, he makes human beings children of God in filial adoption, he pardons sins, he renovates and purifies sinners, he gives to us the contemplation and the enjoyment of God, he gives human beings the power to practise God's commandments, he obtains liberty for the children of God.[163]

The diverse aspects of these gifts are multiplied in the biblical commentaries and in the *Summa Theologiae*. The Holy Spirit obtains divinization or 'deification' for the saints, recreating them in the image of the Son, he introduces them into the mystery of Christ, he constructs the Church in holiness and unity,[164] since he himself is the 'heart' of the Church, he is the *'interior master'* and instructs human beings from within, he gives the saints the *instinct* enabling them to act spontaneously under the divine hand, supplies them with the virtues, the gifts, the fruits, and the beatitudes.[165] If it were necessary to lay out a complete list, it would go on forever. Thomas paints the action of the Father and the Son with care, but he dedicates the widest fresco to the Holy Spirit.[166] He also finds it necessary to give a detailed presentation of the presence and action of the Holy Spirit in the life of Christ and in the celebration of the sacraments: it is from the unction of the Holy Spirit, which the Son bears in his humanity, that the flesh of Christ derives its life-giving power.[167] Father Jean-Pierre Torrell has given such a fine

---

[163] *SCG* IV, chs. 21–22. Whereas, in the *Summa Contra Gentiles,* the discussion of these works of the Holy Spirit is drawn together into one piece, the *Summa Theologiae* presents them when the questions at issue call for it, so they are spread across the *Prima, Secunda,* and *Tertia Pars* (including in the life of Christ and the sacraments).

[164] This is a constant theme: 'Christ, the Son of God, consecrated his Church through the Holy Spirit who is his mark and seal' (*CEG* II, ch. 32); cf. *ST* II–II, q. 1, a. 9, ad 5; etc.

[165] The presence of the Holy Spirit at the heart of Thomas' moral theology has been brought out by S. Pinckaers: see especially *The Sources of Christian Morality,* trans. Mary Thomas Noble OP, Edinburgh, 1995, pp. 151–163 and *passim.* It is also worth looking at U. Horst's discussion in *Die Gaben des Heiligen Geistes nach Thomas von Aquin,* Berlin, 2001.

[166] We ourselves have attempted this fastidious exercise in the course of our own research: one can cover many pages just by enumerating the works of the Spirit and the effects appropriated to the Spirit in Thomas' writings. Some themes are constantly recurring, and there are others which one scarcely would have expected: for example, transubstantiation is attributed to the Holy Spirit—for the Son brings about the eucharistic conversion through the Holy Spirit: see IV *Sent.* d. 10, exp. text.

[167] *In Ioan.* 6.64 (no. 993). This also applies to the humanity of Christ in the sacraments, especially the Eucharist; see our article, 'Le fruit ecclésial de l'Eucharistie chez St Thomas d'Aquin', *Nova et Vetera* 72/4 (1997), 25–40.

exposition of Thomas' teaching on the Holy Spirit that we can only invite the reader to take the measure of his outstanding exposition.[168]

What we want to bring to the fore instead, in relation to speculative Trinitarian theology, is that it is *by means of his idea of Love and of Gift* that Thomas constructs his searching examination of the entire work of the Holy Spirit. This speculative doctrine provides the *key for reading* sacred Scripture's teaching about the Holy Spirit. We will just take a few examples from amongst many others, which illustrate this theological reading of Scripture.

The Charity of God has been spread in our hearts by the Holy Spirit who has been given to us (Rom. 5.5). God's charity can be taken in two ways: either as the charity through which God loves us ... or as the charity with which we love God. And both forms of the charity of God have been spread in our hearts by the Holy Spirit who has been given to us. For the Holy Spirit is the Love of the Father and the Son: he is given to us when we are led to participate in the Love who is the Holy Spirit. It is through this participation that we are made friends of God (*Dei amatores*). And if we love him, it is a sign that he loves us: *I love those who love me* (Prov. 8.17); *It is not us who have* first *loved God, but it is him who has first loved us* (1 Jn 4.10).[169]

This exegesis is a good illustration of Thomas' method. Approaching the topic theoretically, so as to disengage the doctrinal meaning of Scripture, he has begun by showing that the Holy Spirit is Love in person. When he comments on Scripture, he makes use of his doctrinal investigation. The personal character of the Holy Spirit enables one to explain why the love with which God loves us and through which we love God is attributed to the Holy Spirit. As one is, so one acts: the Holy Spirit acts in conformity with the property of his person. His action discloses his personal property (as theology learns from the economy), and this property enables one to grasp the depth of the Spirit's action on our behalf. By acting so, the Holy Spirit joins us to him, he communicates a participation of that which he is, that is, the Love of the Father and the Son. The gift of filial adoption is explained in an analogous way,[170] as is vivification. Thomas says that, 'The Spirit unites us to God through love, because he himself is the Love of God, and this is why he gives life.'[171] The Holy Spirit's enunciation of revelation ('he has spoken through the prophets') is likewise illuminated by the character of Love:

[168] J.-P. Torrell, *St Thomas Aquinas: Spiritual Master*, pp. 152–174; one finds numerous bibliographical pointers here.

[169] *In Rom.* 5.5 (no. 392).

[170] *SCG* IV, ch. 21 (nos. 3580–3581). On this topic one can look at the many texts brought together by L.-Th. Somme, *Thomas d'Aquin: La divinisation dans le Christ*, Geneva, 1998, especially pp. 51–63.

[171] *Homilies on the Creed*, art. 8 (no. 961).

It is the proper mark of friendship that one reveal his secrets to his friend. For since friendship unites our volitions and makes of two friends a single heart, it is from this true heart that a friend reveals his secret to his friend. This is why the Lord said to his disciples: *I will not now call you servants, but friends, because all things I have heard from my Father I have shown to you* (Jn 15.15). Since it is by the Holy Spirit that we are established as friends of God, it also fits his inclination that we attribute to him the revealing of the divine mysteries to human beings. This is why the apostle wrote, *It is written that eye hath not seen, nor ear heard, nor hath it entered into the heart of man, what things God hath prepared for them that love Him. But to us God hath revealed them, by his Spirit* (1 Cor. 2.9–10).[172]

The inspiration which the Holy Spirit brings about in his personal capacity as 'breath of Love' is not restricted to the prophets or to the authors of the canonical books of Scripture,[173] but stretches just as much to those who truly interpret the Scripture: 'It is through the same Spirit that the Scriptures are published and also explained...and this applies centrally to that which touches upon faith, because faith is a gift of God.'[174] The Church's inerrancy in matters of faith springs from within the extended line of this inspiration.[175] At an even deeper level, it is the Holy Spirit who ensures the continuity between revelation and ecclesial practice, because it is he who creates practices which fit the teaching of Scripture. Following in Christ's footsteps, the Church's praxis is thus seen to be an integral feature of the tradition by which revelation is interpreted. Thomas tells us that,

As Augustine says, the statements and precepts of sacred Scripture can be interpreted and understood from the actions of the saints, since the same Holy Spirit who inspired the prophets and the other sacred authors is the Spirit who drives the actions of the saints. As we read, *Moved by the Holy Spirit holy men of God spoke* (2 Pet. 1.21); and *For all who are led by the Spirit of God are sons of God* (Rom. 8.14). Thus, sacred Scripture should be understood according to the way Christ and the other saints observed it in their practice.[176]

[172] *SCG* IV, ch. 21 (no. 3578). In keeping with the primary intention of the Symbol of Constantinople, Thomas' sermons on the Creed emphasize the *divinity* of the Holy Spirit: 'If the Holy Spirit were not God, one could not say he had spoken through the prophets.'

[173] This is a repeated affirmation: 'The principal author of holy Scripture is the Holy Spirit'; see especially *Quodlibet* VII, q. 6, a. 1, ad 5; *De potentia*, q. 4, a. 1; etc. Cf. II *Sent.* d. 12, q. 1, a. 2, ad 7: 'The Holy Spirit fertilizes Scripture with the truth.'

[174] *Quodlibet* XII, q. 16, a. un.

[175] *Quodlibet* IX, q. 8, a. un: 'If one considers the divine providence which directs the Church through the Holy Spirit in order that it does not err, according to Christ's promise, *When the Spirit of truth comes, he will lead you into the whole truth* (Jn 16.13), that is, in all that is necessary to salvation, it is then certain that the judgement of the universal Church in matters of faith cannot be in error.'

[176] *In Ioan.* 18.23 (no. 2321).

This explanation brings us back to the 'imprint of love' by which the Holy Spirit as Love is characterized, and which thus also typifies his way of acting. In another domain, the remission of sins provides a good example of Thomas' theological exegesis, all the more so because it solidly teaches that in the Christian virtue of penitence, as in the sacrament in which it partakes, the remission of the fault springs from the charity created by faith, through the gift of the Holy Spirit:[177]

Receive the Holy Spirit: those whose sins you remit, they are forgiven (Jn 20.22–23). The forgiving of sins is a fitting effect of the Holy Spirit. This is because he himself is Charity, and through the Holy Spirit charity is given to us, as it says in Rom. 5.5: *the charity of God has been spread in our hearts through the Holy Spirit who has been given to us.* Now it is only through charity that sins are forgiven, for *charity covers all offences* (Prov. 10.12); *charity covers a multitude of sins* (1 Pet. 4.8).[178]

Because the interpretation is shaped so transparently, there is no need to linger over it. The personality of the Holy Spirit is Love, and this is why he spreads love: from within the heart of the Trinity, he joins human beings to the property personal to him. This doctrine enables one to show *why* Scripture ascribes the remission of sins to the Holy Spirit, by pointing out *that in which* the remission of sins consists—the gift of charity. All of these explanations are set under the aegis of divine friendship.[179]

The study of the works of the Holy Spirit makes use of the speculative idea of Love, but without always calling on all of its diverse features. Often, Thomas just brings to mind what he has established elsewhere: the Holy Spirit is properly and personally Love. This does not mean that the theme of *mutual* Love is being dropped; it is present implicitly in the indication of the personal property of the Spirit who proceeds from Father and Son. And when the context specifically requires that focus, it will be mentioned explicitly. Thus, for example, in respect of the Church's unity:

---

[177] Cf. *ST* III, q. 85, a. 5; q. 86, a. 2; q. 86, a. 6 ad 2. There can be no remission of sins without the charity sown by the Holy Spirit. It is no different in the justification of the sinner which takes place in the first conversion which is baptism: justification is brought about in 'faith formed by charity' which the Holy Spirit brings to bear (*ST* I–II, q. 113, a. 4). See our article, 'Reconciliation with the Church and Interior Penance: The Contribution of Thomas Aquinas on the Question of the *Res et Sacramentum* of Penance', trans. Robert E. Williams, *Nova et Vetera* 1/2 (2003), 283–301.

[178] *In Ioan.* 20.22–23 (no. 2541).

[179] Cf. *SCG* IV, ch. 21 (no. 3582): 'Since it is the Holy Spirit who establishes us as God's friends (*Dei amici*), it is also through the Holy Spirit that God remits our sins.'

the Father and the Son are one by the Love which is not a participated gift, for the Father and the Son love one another through the Holy Spirit; and we are one by participating in this higher love.[180]

The *impulsion* which is typical of love is brought to the fore more often. Since this feature enables one to show how Love constitutes the character of the Holy Spirit, we meet it in many analyses: it comes to disclose the universal action of the Church, and we meet it yet again in the discussions about the life of grace. Thomas says that,

The Spirit is the most excellent gift because he is the spirit of truth. ... He is called the Spirit to indicate his power, because he moves us to act and work well. 'Spirit' indicates a certain impulsion, and that is why the word *spiritus* can also mean the wind: *For all who are impelled by the Spirit of God are sons of God* (Rom. 8.14). *Let thy good spirit lead me on a level path* (Ps. 142. 10, Vulgate).[181]

because the name *Spirit* suggests an impulse, and since every motion produces an effect in harmony with its source (as heating makes a body hot), the Holy Spirit renders those to whom he is sent like the one whose Spirit he is [that is, here, the Son]; this is why, since he is the Spirit of Truth, *he teaches all truth* (cf. Jn 16.13); and Job says, *The inspiration of the Almighty gives understanding* (Job 32.8).[182]

Like a *stimulus*, the charity of Christ stimulates us to achieve what it commands, that is, to bring salvation to our neighbours. Such is the effect of charity. One sees this in Romans: *Those who are driven*, that is to say, who are 'blown' by the Spirit of God [these are sons of God] (Rom. 8.14).[183]

One could also multiply examples here. As Love in person, the Holy Spirit communicates his own impulse, he drives, he gets things going, his force stirs up a momentum.[184] The idea of the mutual presence of friends is connected to this. The doctrines of the Word and of Love have both equally shown us that the begetting of the Son and the procession of the Holy Spirit are divulged through the analogy of a spiritual being's modes of self-presence: a spiritual being is in itself not only identically, but again, 'as the known is in the knower' and 'as the beloved is in the lover'.[185] This approach proved to be

---

[180] *In Ioan.* 17.11 (no. 2214); cf. *In Ioan.* 17.21 (no. 2240); *ST* III, q. 23, a. 3: 'a creature can be likened to the eternal Word as to the oneness of the Word with the Father, and such a likeness is made by grace and charity'.

[181] *In Ioan.* 14.17 (no. 1916).

[182] *In Ioan.* 15.26 (no. 2062).

[183] *In 2 Cor.* 5.14 (no. 181). The play upon words in the interpretation of Romans 8.14 is very suggestive in Latin but not easy to render in the vernacular: '*Qui spiritu Dei aguntur,* id est *agitantur*': both verbs involve the idea of 'putting into action', the second emphasizing the intensity of the motivation given us by the Holy Spirit.

[184] *In 2 Tim.* 1.7 (no. 14).

[185] See especially *SCG* IV, chs. 11, 19 and 26; *CT* I, ch. 50; *ST* I, q. 27, a. 3; q. 37, a. 1.

fruitful for exhibiting the eternal procession of the persons, and it is still more so for their missions to human beings, and, especially, the indwelling of the Holy Spirit in the hearts of the saints. So the Father and the Son come with the Holy Spirit to make their home with those whom grace has chosen:

Since the charity by which we love God is in us by the Holy Spirit, the Holy Spirit himself must dwell in us, in that charity is in us. This is why the apostle says, *Know you not that you are the temple of God, and that the Spirit of God dwells in you* (1 Cor. 3.16). Therefore, it is by the Holy Spirit that we are made friends of God. And, every beloved is in the one who loves as such. And so it is necessary that, by the Holy Spirit, the Father and Son also dwell in us. This is why the Lord said, *We will come to him*, that is, to those who love God, *and will make our abode with him* (Jn 14.23). And it is written that, *In this we know that he abideth in us: he hath given us his Spirit* (1 Jn 3.24).[186]

The immanence of the three divine persons within one another overflows into grace, achieved, so to speak, by the indwelling of the Holy Spirit: 'the beloved is in the lover'. The gift of the Holy Spirit in grace is taken as an applied analogy of the presence of love in the eternal procession of the Holy Spirit. This presence has a dual countenance. It is the presence of the Trinity to the saints, and it is also the presence of the saints to the Triune God. Thomas tells us that,

Every beloved is in a lover. Therefore, by the Holy Spirit, not only is God in us, but we also are in God. Hence we read that, *He that abideth in charity abideth in God, and God in him*, and, *In this we know that we abide in Him and He in us: because He hath given us his Spirit* (1 Jn 4.16, 13).[187]

One could scarcely find a more striking formula for the divinization which the Holy Spirit brings about: presence of the Trinity in human beings and presence of human beings in the Trinity. The treatise on the divine missions pursues this line of thought, explaining that it is by the sending of the Son and the Holy Spirit that the Trinity comes to dwell in the saints. The Triune God makes himself present to the person who adheres to him by knowledge, through living faith and then by vision, and he lives in the man who loves from a love of charity, 'as the known in the knower and as the beloved is in the lover'.[188] One of the first fruits of this is the contemplation of God. Being Love in person, the Holy Spirit nests human beings into friendship with God, making them 'contemplators of God', and giving them through this contemplation a 'dwelling in God'.[189]

---

[186] *SCG* IV, ch. 21 (no. 3576).   [187] *SCG* IV, ch. 21 (no. 3577).

[188] *ST* I, q. 43, a. 3. The treatise on the image will have its own way of reflecting on the grace given to the saints whose actions adhere to the eternal utterance of the Word and the procession of Love (q. 93, aa. 7–8). See below, Chapter 15.

[189] *SCG* IV, ch. 22 (no. 3585).

The aspect which we want to emphasize thus looms into view: all of the elements of the idea of the eternal procession of the Holy Spirit are drawn out into the account of his action in the world. The characteristic features designated by the name 'Holy Spirit' are Love (as the imprint which proceeds and which personally characterizes the Holy Spirit), the spiritual presence of the beloved in the one who loves, the mutual Bond of Father and Son, and the Gift. These themes are not sequestered into the theological study of the distinctness and eternal existence of the Holy Spirit within the immanence of the Trinity, but also weigh heavily on our understanding of the economic action of the Holy Spirit. One finds the same idea on both sides, the two aspects mutually illuminating one another.

In the next chapter, we will present the doctrine of the procession of the Holy Spirit *a Patre* and *a Filio*, but we need to begin to indicate here that this teaching itself also sheds light on the work of the Holy Spirit. It can already be perceived in the theme of the mutual Love or Bond of Father and Son. The soteriological significance of the Holy Spirit's procession *a Patre* and *a Filio* is constantly accentuated. The procession of the Spirit *from the Son* is not only tied into a speculative consideration of the opposition relations within the Trinity, but also puts itself forward as an explanation of the filial and Christological character of the grace given by the Holy Spirit.[190] At an even deeper level, St Thomas observes that, because of his eternal procession, 'the effect of the mission of the Holy Spirit is to lead the faithful to the Son'.[191] The Spirit leads us to the Son because he proceeds from the Son. The Spirit glorifies the Son, he gives it into men's hands to receive the Son through faith, because he proceeds from him, and it is for the same reason that the Son is manifested by him.[192] Thomas says that, 'the reason why the Holy Spirit will glorify Christ ... is because the Son is the principle of the Holy Spirit. For everything which is from another manifests that from which it proceeds: the Son manifests the Father, because he proceeds from him. And so, because the Holy Spirit proceeds from the Son, it typically belongs to him to glorify him.'[193] We will come back to this in greater detail in the next chapter: the mission of the Holy Spirit on behalf of humanity grows out of the fundamental structure of his eternal procession. This is why it is in his consideration of the eternal procession that St Thomas uncovers the doctrinal grounds for understanding the work of the Holy Spirit.

---

[190] See below, in Chapter 11, 'The Doctrinal Weight of the Holy Spirit's Procession *a Patre* and *a Filio*'.

[191] *In Ioan.* 14.26 (no. 1958).

[192] *In Ioan.* 16.15 (nos. 2109–2115).

[193] *In Ioan.* 16.14 (no. 2107). Cf. *De potentia*, q. 10, a. 4.

The Holy Spirit adapts, deploys, and actualizes believers' antennae for the living action of Christ: the entire action of the Holy Spirit comes from Christ, the Son of God, and leads through him to the Father. The work of the Holy Spirit is not *different* from that of Christ, it has the same object and end as that of the Son, giving it root and deepening it, and making Christ's work bear fruit in believers, in the life of faith and charity in the Church. The gifts of the Holy Spirit are the gifts of the Son himself. The action of the Holy Spirit is thus the same as that of the Son (recalling the Trinitarian law of the three persons' unity in action), even though each of them exercises this action in the distinct mode of his personal character: the Son acts in that he receives being and action through his eternal begetting by the Father; the Holy Spirit acts in that he receives being and action from the Father and the Son in his eternal procession from them. 'We have access to the Father through Christ, because Christ works through the Holy Spirit. *If any one has not the Spirit of Christ, he does not belong to him* (Rom. 8.9). And this is why that which is brought about by the Holy Spirit is also brought about by Christ.'[194]

Thomas particularly brings out the unity of action between Son and Spirit in his exegesis of the Fourth Gospel, when he is examining the name *Paraclete*. He explains that the name *Paraclete* refers to the Holy Spirit's own action, the mission which the Spirit receives from Father and Son: to dwell amongst the disciples so as to obtain the presence of Father and Son for them, leading the disciples to the full understanding of Christ's teaching, witnessing to them on behalf of the Son. In his initial steps, Thomas explains briefly the meaning of the name 'Paraclete', and why it is ascribed to the Holy Spirit. The term *Paraclete* means the consoler, the advocate, the intercessor. This clearly comes down to the Holy Spirit, 'since he is the Spirit of Love': it is love which brings spiritual consolation, joy, intercession.[195] He notes nonetheless that the New Testament does not exclusively restrict the name Paraclete to the Holy Spirit. The Fourth Gospel designates the Holy Spirit with the name *Paraclete* (Jn 14.16–17; 14.26; 15.26; 16.7), but also calls him 'another Paraclete' (Jn 14.16), since Christ is himself also called *Paraclete* (1 Jn 2.1). So will the acts of the Spirit-Paraclete differ from those of Christ-as-Paraclete? Or will they be fused into the action of Christ the Paraclete? The answer deserves to be pondered over in depth. Thomas states that,

---

194 *In Eph.* 2.18 (no. 121).

195 *In Ioan.* 14.15 (no. 1911); St Thomas' commentary refers us to Gal. 5.22 and Rom. 8.26. The Greek term *Parakletos* translates into Latin in a more polyvalent way than into English. The Latin Fathers give various translations of it, such as *advocatus* (Tertullian), *consolator* (Hilary), *deprecator* (Rufinus); see *Dictionnaire de la Bible Supplément*, vol. 1 (1991), cols. 364–365. Thomas has a special affinity for translating it as *advocatus* and as *consolator*, but he also often connects the Holy Spirit with the familial terms related to *deprecator*.

The word *Paraclete* suggests an action of the Holy Spirit. But, by saying *another Paraclete* [Jn 14.16] does one designate another nature? For a diversity of action indicates a diversity of nature, and thus the Holy Spirit would be of a different nature to that of Christ. I reply that the Holy Spirit is a consoler and advocate, and so is the Son. One reads that the Son is the Advocate in 1 Jn 2.1, *We have an advocate with the Father, Jesus Christ*, and he is also a consoler, as one can see from *The Spirit of the Lord has sent me to comfort those who mourn* [Isa. 61.1; cf. Lk. 4.18]. Yet the Son and the Holy Spirit are not consolers and advocates in the same way, if we go from what is uniquely congruent to each person. Christ is called Advocate in that, in his humanity, he intercedes for us to the Father [cf. 1 Jn 2.1]; and the Holy Spirit is called Advocate in that he gives it to us to pray [cf. Rom. 8.26]. Again, the Holy Spirit is called Consoler in that he is formally Love; whereas the Son is called Consoler in that he is the Word, and this in two ways: because of his teaching and because the Son gives the Holy Spirit and ignites love in our hearts. Thus the word *another* [as in, *another Paraclete*] does not indicate a different nature in the Son and in the Holy Spirit. Rather, it indicates the different mode (*alius modus*) in which both of them are each an advocate and a consoler.[196]

The effect of the activity of the Son and the action of the Holy Spirit in helping the disciples is identical: it is consolation, joy, forceful witnessing, adhesion to the word of God, assurance in prayer. But if the *action* of the Son is like that of the Spirit (in this capacity, both of them are Consoler), this action takes a distinct mode. The Son acts in the mode of the property personal to him, which is being the Word of the Father. Under this rubric, the Son gives teaching and spreads the Holy Spirit (who belongs to the Word as Word). On the part of the Holy Spirit, action comes from the mode of his personal property as *Love*: he spreads charity, that is, communicates a participation in the property personal to him, obtaining consolation and joy (this formally belongs to the Spirit as Love).

Related passages about the exegesis of the name *Paraclete* explain that the Holy Spirit gives receptivity to Christ's teaching, for 'to disclose the truth converges with the property of the Holy Spirit'. The Holy Spirit is Love proceeding from the Word as Truth. He leads the faithful to the Word for the reason that he proceeds from him, and he makes the Word teach us from within ('it is love which leads to the revelation of secrets'[197]). There is thus a *unity of action* amongst the Holy Spirit and the Son, based in their identity of nature and their mutual relations (this accounts for the close parallelism of the action of the Son and the Holy Spirit, as much in the Fourth Gospel as in the Pauline letters), and a *distinct mode or pattern of action*, founded in the personal properties through which the Holy Spirit and the Son are distinct (this will justify the method of appropriation). The object of the mission of

---

[196] *In Ioan.* 14.16 (no. 1912).   [197] *In Ioan.* 14.17 (no. 1916).

the Holy Spirit as Paraclete is to receive the mystery of the Son at greater depth, to give knowledge of the Son through faith, and to witness to the Son who leads to the Father.

By way of a conclusion, it is worth noting that Thomas accounts for the gifts of the Holy Spirit in the same way that he did for the action of the Son: he uses his provisional constructions of speculative themes which has been made to disclose the distinct personal existence of the Spirit. Two doctrinal themes play a central role here. The first is the property of the Holy Spirit as *Love* and as *Gift*. Being eternally and personally Love, the Gift of the Father and the Son, the Holy Spirit operates as Love and thus he brings about those works whose source is love within the economy. The second principle consists in *his relation to the Father and to the Son*. The Holy Spirit discloses the Father, leads to the Father, because he proceeds from the Father; the Holy Spirit discloses the Son, leads to the Son, and roots the Son's work in the hearts of believers, because he proceeds from the Son. So his personal relation, his distinctive property at the heart of the Trinity, illuminates his work in the economy. Thomas thus has an authentic doctrine of the Trinity in its economic action *because* he has a doctrine of the Trinity in itself, through a speculative return to the Scriptures from which the reflection set out. As we put it, in our contemporary way of speaking:[198] it is the doctrine of the 'immanent' Trinity which enables him to give not just a presentation of the Trinitarian economy, but a speculative understanding of that economy, that is a *doctrine* of the economic Trinity.

[198] Even though he was familiar with the terminology of 'immanence' and 'economy', Thomas prefers to speak of the Triune God 'according as he is in himself' and 'according as he is the principle and end of creatures' (cf. *ST* I, q. 2, prol.).

11

The Holy Spirit Proceeds
from the Father and from the Son

St Thomas has the same respect for the doctrine of the procession of the Holy Spirit from the Father and Son as all the Latin theologians of his time. His perspective on this topic has considerable breadth. We will not restrict ourselves to the well rehearsed theoretical arguments which Anselm had put forward (he made a special point of relative opposition). We wish to show here why this doctrine is important, its patristic and biblical credentials, the theoretical meditation, and some of its consequences. It is also necessary clearly to distinguish: (1) the doctrine itself and (2) the addition of the *Filioque* clause to the Constantinopolitan creed, which constitutes a distinct problem.[1]

1. THE DOCTRINAL WEIGHT OF THE HOLY SPIRIT'S
PROCESSION *A PATRE* AND *A FILIO*

Thomas accepts the procession of the Holy Spirit from Father and Son as a truth of faith which there can be no question of demonstrating, in the proper sense of the term, but whose intelligibility can be disclosed from the focal point of Trinitarian faith. Even when he is establishing that the procession of the Spirit *a Filio* is a required belief for those who accept the Trinitarian faith as a mystery inaccessible to the grasp of pure reason, he intends to show that the confession of the Catholic Church is the truth. On this basis, his reflection on the procession of the Spirit draws out the many elements within it which express what is at stake in this doctrine.

(1) *The defence of the faith against heresies.* It was the defence of the faith in response to heresies which sparked off the development of Trinitarian

---

[1] This chapter condenses some elements in our article, 'La procession du Saint-Esprit *a Filio* chez Thomas d'Aquin', *RT* 96 (1996), 531–574; this is where to look for useful bibliographical references and more fine-shading.

doctrine and the explanation of the procession *a Filio*. Arianism was the initial issue: in professing that the Holy Spirit proceeds from the Father and from the Son, we recognize that the Son is of the same substance as the Father; this shows that the Son and the Holy Spirit are not creatures.[2] The idea that the Holy Spirit proceeds *a Patre* and *a Filio* is intimately bound in with the recognition of the unity in being of Father and Son.[3] The accent placed on the divinity of Christ seems to be closely connected with the history of the Latin doctrine, in which the resurgence of various kinds of adoptionism, particularly in Spain, played an important part.[4] Thomas notes that the confession of the Holy Spirit's procession *a Filio* was also tied in with the Christological question of the unity of the person of Christ, in response to Nestorianism.[5] His theoretical assessment is, ultimately, that the affirmation of the Spirit's procession *a Filio* seems necessary to avoid Sabellianism, because within the structure of Latin Trinitarian doctrine, to reject the *Filioque* is to take away the differentiation of the persons of Son and Holy Spirit. If one cannot accept that the Holy Spirit proceeds from the Son, one will not be able to conceive their personal distinctness, and 'this undermines faith in the Trinity'.[6] The concern to preserve the faith from the errors which rejecting this article creates is constantly present.

(2) *Christ's dignity and prerogatives.* Highlighting the fact that everything we say when we profess our faith has Christological repercussions, this second theme is an extension of the former. The prerogatives of Christ's person are at the heart of this question, to the extent that the rejection of the Spirit's procession *a Filio* seems to diminish Christ's dignity.[7] The reasoning behind this is the unity of the Father and the Son as principle-spirator of the Holy Spirit, a unity in virtue of which that which belongs to the Father is also attributed to the Son, except for the first person's constitutive property of paternity. The theme of the dignity of Christ implies a determined hold on the Nicene *homoousion*. Thomas' affirmation of the dignity of Christ is an outstanding positive feature of his attachment to the Nicene doctrine.

(3) *The concrete Son-shapedness of salvation.* The Spirit's procession *a Filio* does not only engage us in theoretical reflection on the oppositional relations within the Trinity, but also seems to be a prerequisite for explaining the

---

[2] *Homilies on the Creed*, a. 8 (no. 962).

[3] See for instance *In Ioan.* 16.15 (nos. 2114–2115).

[4] See Jaroslav Pelikan, The Christian Tradition: A History of the Development of Doctrine, vol. 2: *The Spirit of Eastern Christendom (600–1700)*, Chicago, 1977, pp. 185–186. It seems to have been the need to respond to Arianism that created a favourable bias or orientation to the *Filioque* amongst Western theologians.

[5] *ST* I, q. 36, a. 2, ad 3; see also *De potentia*, q. 10, a. 4, ad 24.

[6] *ST* I, q. 36, a. 2; *SCG* IV, ch. 24 (no. 3616).

[7] *CEG* II, prol.

fundamentally Son-shaped reality of the grace given by the Holy Spirit. Since his procession from the Son gives him the Son's nature,[8] the Spirit is the Spirit *of Christ*, remaking us in the shape of the Son (Rom. 8.29): 'one is configured to a thing in the mark which belongs to it ... Now the Holy Spirit is from the Son as being his mark'.[9] The Spirit leads us to the knowledge of the Truth who is the Son because he is the 'Spirit of Truth' (Jn 14.17), which is to say, 'because he proceeds from the Truth'.[10] The Spirit *glorifies* the Son and tells us what it is to be the Son (Jn 16.15) because he proceeds from him, and it is for the same reason that he *discloses* the Son.[11] 'Now we see the reason why the Spirit will glorify Christ (Jn 14.17): it is because the Son is the principle of the Holy Spirit. In fact, everything which proceeds from another discloses the one from whom he proceeds: the Son discloses the Father, because he exists as coming from the Father. Thus, since the Holy Spirit's existence is owed to the Son, he owes it to him to glorify him.'[12] In the same way again, when Christ 'breathes' the Holy Spirit 'on' the disciples (Jn 20.22), this happens because he proceeds from the Son: following Augustine, St Thomas takes the Easter 'breathing' to mean that the Holy Spirit, given by the Son, proceeds from the Father *and also* from the Son,[13] 'for if the Holy Spirit did not proceed from him, he would not breathe him upon his disciples after his resurrection'.[14]

One could multiply the illustrations, but these are sufficient for us to see that the Christological and soteriological impact of the Spirit's procession *a Filio* is at the heart of Thomas' reading in Scripture and is the central pillar of his conviction about it. (One can note, on this topic, that, in the twentieth century, in a very different theological and historical milieu, Karl Barth is led by a comparable analysis vigorously to uphold the Latin doctrine of the procession of the Holy Spirit *a Filio*.[15]) This teaching can be summarized in the principle of the economic Trinity which was formulated by Albert the Great: 'the Spirit who is sent leads back (*convertit*) to himself and to the Son, the Son leads back to himself and to the Father... Following the order of nature, the person who proceeds from another carries back to him that which

---

[8] *SCG* IV, ch. 24 (no. 3606); *De potentia*, q. 10, a. 4; cf. *In Ioan.* 14.26 (no. 1957).

[9] *De potentia*, q. 10, a. 4; cf. *CEG* II, chs. 6–7: the Holy Spirit is the mark (*character*) or the seal (*sigillum*) of Christ, the Son of God.

[10] *In Ioan.* 14.17 (no. 1916).

[11] *In Ioan.* 16.15 (nos. 2109–2115).

[12] *In Ioan.* 16.14 (no. 2107). Cf. *De potentia*, q. 10, a. 4.

[13] *In Ioan.* 20.22 (no. 2538); Augustine, *De Trinitate* IV.XX.29; cf. Thomas, *Catena in Ioan.* 20.22 (ed. Guarienti, vol. 2, 1953, p. 582).

[14] *Catena in Ioan.* 15.26 (ed. Guarienti, vol. 2, p. 535); Augustine, *Tractate 99 on John* (CCSL 36, p. 586).

[15] K. Barth, *Church Dogmatics* I/1, trans. G. W. Bromiley, Edinburgh, 1936, 2nd edn. 1975, pp. 473–481; *Church Dogmatics* I/2, trans. G. T. Thomson and H. Knight, Edinburgh, 1956, 1996, pp. 250–251.

he takes from him'.[16] The structure of the Holy Spirit's mission displays or exhibits the fundamental structure of his eternal procession. The Christological and filial nature of the grace of the Holy Spirit, which draws us to Christ and assimilates us to him, is thus intrinsically bound to the Spirit's eternal procession *a Patre* and *a Filio*.

2. BIBLICAL AND PATRISTIC DOCUMENTATION

Rational theological argumentation is not the bedrock of this teaching. As Hyacinthe Dondaine has rightly emphasized, 'only the Word of God as explained by the Church is directly homogeneous with the faith. The conviction of the Latins was also founded on the Word.'[17]

Materially, the centrality given to the scriptural foundations varies in all the different places where Thomas deals with the Spirit's procession *a Filio*. So we find that, in keeping with the methods and aims of that work, the *Contra Gentiles* starts off from Scripture, in the chapters about the procession of the Spirit *a Filio*.[18] The same reasoning explains the predominant position given to the Fathers in the opuscule which was maladroitly labelled the *Contra errores Graecorum*, and also the largely speculative orientation of the Disputed Questions *De potentia* and the *Summa Theologiae*. But despite the differences in the way it is fitted in, one still finds the unchanging triptych: Scripture, Fathers and Councils, theological reason. One single great work is the exception to the rule: the Commentary on the *Sentences*. In this first synthesizing work, where Thomas' thinking about the Spirit's procession *a Filio* is hugely dependent on Albert the Great, one cannot fail to be struck by the exclusively rational climate which drives the question: a meagre position is given to Scripture, and references to the Fathers are also scanty.[19] St Thomas' work in Pneumatology was continually enriched and deepened, not only in its theoretical aspect, but in its patristic and biblical bases.

We have already noted the many New Testament passages which illustrate the soteriological gravity of this question. Three biblical themes are taken as

---

[16] Albert the Great, I *Sent.* d. 31, a. 14, ad quaest. 2; cf. Thomas, *In Ioan.* 14.26 (no. 1958). For a wider view of this topic, see E. Bailleux, 'Le Christ et Son Esprit', *RT* 73 (1973), 373–400.

[17] H.-F. Dondaine, 'La théologie latine de la procession du Saint-Esprit', *Russie et Chrétienté* (1950), 211–218; this citation is on p. 217.

[18] *SCG* IV, ch. 24 (Scripture—Fathers and Councils—reason) and ch. 25 (Scripture—Fathers and Councils—reason).

[19] All the arguments in I *Sent.* d. 11, q. un., a. 1, are taken from Albert, Bonaventure and the *Summa fratris Alexandri*.

primary: (1) the character of the Holy Spirit as the Spirit *of the Son*; (2) the mission or sending of the Holy Spirit by the Son; (3) the verse in John 16.14, *He shall glorify me: because he shall receive of mine and shall show it to you.* These three themes enable us to understand Thomas' exegesis of John 15.26: *The Spirit of truth who proceeds from the Father.*

The first theme reflects on the relationship between Spirit and Son intended by the expression 'Spirit of the Son'.[20] This theme, which is usually given pole position in the discussions, and which is taken to have a 'manifest' scriptural basis,[21] brings together several biblical expressions, such as *Spirit of Jesus* (Acts 16.7), *Spirit of Christ* (Rom. 8.9), *Spirit of Truth* (Jn 15.26), *Spirit of Life* (Rom. 8.2), and *Spirit of the Son of God* (Gal. 4.6). On the one hand, Thomas works at showing that the Spirit of the Father is the Spirit of the Son, and that the relationship indicated by the genitive (*of*) is not restricted to meaning the grace-filled humanity of Jesus (Lk. 4.1), but has a deeper meaning, touching on his divinity. This is the cue for the entrance of the soteriological argument: the Spirit given by the Father really makes us 'sons of God' because, being the Spirit of the Son, he configures us to the 'natural' Son by assimilation to him (Rom. 8.29; the filiation brought about by grace is a participation in Christ's natural, divine Sonship). We become members 'of Christ' because we receive the Spirit *of Christ*, uniting us to the one from whom he proceeds.[22] One can question whether this mutual 'belonging' of the Son and the Holy Spirit really implies, as Thomas holds, the procession of the Holy Spirit *a Filio.* But he maintains—as a decisive point in his biblical exegesis—that every relationship involving a real distinction of divine persons must be understood to flow from a specific origin; and every originary relationship, however it is formulated, necessarily leads one to posit a procession 'from the other (*ab alio*)'. This interpretation of the texts will be put to work in the examination of all the main themes.

The second major biblical theme is the sending of the Holy Spirit by the Son. St Thomas carefully distinguishes the eternal procession and the mission or temporal procession. But the mission of the Spirit *a Filio* entails the eternal procession *a Filio*, because the eternal procession is 'included' in it; what it adds to it is the temporal outworking of grace in which the divine person is 'sent' or 'given'.[23] The mission is the eternal procession encountered in time at the behest of grace. Because of this, even though linking up with temporality belongs only to the mission, the personal relation engaged in the sending is

[20] *CEG* II, ch. 1; *SCG* IV, ch. 24 (no. 3606); *De potentia*, q. 10, a. 4; *In Rom.* 8.9 (no. 627); cf. *ST* I, q. 36, a. 2.
[21] *SCG* IV, ch. 24 (no. 3606).
[22] *In Rom.* 8.9 (no. 627).
[23] I *Sent.* d. 14, q. 1, a. 2; *ST* I, q. 43, a. 2. See below, in Chapter 15, 'The Theory of Mission'.

strictly identical to that of the eternal procession. This is why Thomas, who shows complete agreement with the Eastern theologians in rigorously distinguishing the mission from the eternal procession,[24] nonetheless argues for the Latin doctrine: the person's mission is a temporal unveiling of his eternal procession. The Holy Spirit eternally proceeds from the Son by whom he is sent (*a Filio*). Still more precisely, it is because he eternally proceeds from the Son that the Holy Spirit is given to humanity by the Son. To express it in a different manner of speaking: the 'economy' is rooted in the 'theology' whose intimate structure it displays.[25] This close parallel between theology and the economy is one of the elemental features of Latin and Alexandrian patristic theology.[26] This doubtless makes it different from Orthodox theology in the Byzantine tradition, whose teaching about the eternal Trinity does not give the same value to the economy of salvation.[27]

The analysis of the verse in John 16.14 (*He shall glorify me: because he shall receive of mine and shall show it to you*) holds a place of honour right the way across Thomas' writings. He gives a recapitulation of its importance in the *Summa*: 'We must not say anything about God that we do not find in Scripture either in words or in meaning. Even though we do not find it in so many words (*per verba*) in Sacred Scripture that the Holy Spirit proceeds from the Son, we do find it in meaning (*quantum ad sensum*), and especially where the Son says of the Holy Spirit: *He shall glorify me: because he shall receive of mine.*'[28] The decisive status of this position is confirmed by the absence of similar scriptural passages in this article in the *Summa*. We are thus directed to making a careful examination of how it is being interpreted.

St Thomas explains that the expression *of mine* indicates the consubstantiality of the Son and the Holy Spirit: the Spirit receives the whole substance of Father and Son, that is, the divine nature in its plenitude. In receiving what belongs to the Father and Son, the Spirit is not given paternity or filiation,

---

[24] One can see for instance the passage from Theophylactus cited in the *Catena in Ioan.* 15.26 (ed. Guarienti, vol. 2, p. 535).

[25] *In Ad Gal.* 4.6 (no. 213): 'Ex quo Filius mittit eum, manifestum est quod ab ipso procedit.'

[26] See B. Studer, *Mysterium caritatis: Studien zur Exegese und zur Trinitätslehre in der Alten Kirche*, Rome, 1999, pp. 329–373 (esp. p. 368) and pp. 409–424.

[27] According to the analysis of the Orthodox theologian John Zizioulas: 'With the idea of *Filioque*, the West showed that *mission* is at the foundation of Pneumatology. The fact that Christ sent the Spirit grounds theological speech about God. ... It is the opposite in the East, which insists precisely on the marked distinction between the mission of the Spirit and his eternal procession. The East refuses to develop an ontology of God which begins from history; it prefers to elaborate a theophanic or meta-historical view of God ...' J. Zizioulas, 'Implications ecclésiologiques de deux types de pneumatologie', in *Communio Sanctorum: Mélanges offerts à J.-J. von Allmen*, Geneva, 1982, pp. 141–154 (p. 149).

[28] *ST* I, q. 36, a. 2, ad 1. The translation 'of mine' (*de meo*) nicely suggests the movement of argument from *de meo* to *a Filio*.

since these touch on the incommunicable properties of the divine persons, but he does receive the nature; and the nature is actually identical, in each divine person, to the personal property. This verse in John thus leads us firmly to uphold both the distinctness of the persons as to their properties and their perfect consubstantiality. And the being communicated by the Triune God (that is, the divine nature) is actually identical to that by which this being is communicated, in such a way that the principle of communication is really identical to the communicated being.[29] It is the same nature or divine substance *who* is communicated or handed to the Son and to the Holy Spirit and *by which* the Father hands or communicates. Hence, if the divine nature is communicated to the Holy Spirit, this communicated nature (*of mine*) is actually identical to the principle of communication. And the nature is common to the Father and the Son, with nothing held back (*everything which the Father has is mine*). The conclusion is evident: since the Holy Spirit receives *from the Father*, he likewise receives *from the Son*.

There is an unmistakable emphasis here on the divine essence: this is not a matter of reverting into an implausible 'essentialism', one that makes the essence the agent of the spiration of the Holy Spirit. What Thomas wants to ensure is the assimilation of the person who proceeds to the person-principle, an assimilation in which their consubstantiality is grounded, without preju-dicing their incommunicable character, by virtue of the principle of commu-nication of the divine nature. To put it another way: if the Spirit receives 'that which is of the Son' (*quod est Filii*) without receiving from the Son (*a Filio*), that would mean that the Son would be cut out of the notional act, the content of which is nonetheless 'his own' (*de meo*). But, according to what Christ says in John's Gospel, '*All things whatsoever the Father hath are mine. That is why I said that he shall receive of me and show it to you*' (Jn 16.15).[30] From Thomas' point of view, one must at all costs avoid dividing the divine essence or undercutting the perfect consubstantiality of the Father and Son. This analysis extends to the economy since that which the Holy Spirit will make known to the disciples (*he shall show it to you*) is precisely the 'mine' of the Son, received by him in his eternal procession, and thus making us participants in the divine nature of the Saviour.

The patristic sources of this interpretation are highlighted in the *Catena* on John. They reflect Augustine's *Tractates on John*, and, at an even deeper level, Hilary of Poitiers and Didymus the Blind. Thomas effectively copies a text

---

[29] *In Ioan.* 16.15 (nos. 2114–2115). This identity is also developed in *De potentia*, q. 2, a. 1. See G. Reichberg, 'La communication de la nature divine en Dieu selon Thomas d'Aquin', *RT* 93 (1993), 50–65.

[30] *In Ioan.* 16.15 (nos. 2114–2115).

from Hilary which explains that 'the Lord is not open to doubt if it is required to think that the Paraclete-Spirit is *ex Patre* and *ex Filio*'. Hilary's exegesis, containing the seed which Thomas will cultivate, also shows that for the Holy Spirit to receive *a Patre* likewise implies receiving *a Filio*.[31] Didymus, who is quoted from Jerome's Latin translation, provides this exegesis: the substance of the Holy Spirit is precisely what he is given to be *a Filio*, in such a way that what the Spirit receives from the Father is identical to what the Spirit receives from the Son.[32] These citations from the Fathers are repeated in many works, especially in the John Commentary, which leads one to think that this is what convinced Thomas of the central position of this Johannine passage for understanding the procession of the Spirit.

The absence of reference to the Son in John 15.26 (*The Spirit of truth who proceeds from the Father*) calls for particular attention. As was common amongst medieval theologians, Thomas draws Augustine's explanation of this into his own interpretation. He sees it as indicating not only the Holy Spirit's mission, but his eternal procession as well, as it is in fact held to do within a tradition that was entrenched in both East and West.[33] The problems of the lack of reference to one divine person and that of 'exclusive expressions' (mentioning one divine person to the exclusion of another) were the kinds of question the scholastics often tackled, and Thomas has little hesitation in borrowing from their results.[34] The accepted rule was as follows: the divine persons are always included in the references to one another, and everything that is said of one divine person must be equally ascribed to the other divine persons, excepting what touches on the incommunicable personal property (paternity, filiation, procession). The outstanding illustrations of this tradition are Matthew 11.27 (*No one knows the Father except the Son*) and John 17.3 (*That they may know you, the only true God*). Thus, since breathing the Spirit does not formally derive either from the property of paternity or that of filiation, 'when it is said in the Gospel that the Holy Spirit proceeds from the Father, it is necessary to understand that he proceeds also from the Son, even though the Gospel does not add it'.[35]

In his Gospel commentaries, Thomas specifically construes this as deriving from Christ's 'discretion'; he says that Jesus' 'custom is to refer everything to

---

[31] *Catena in Ioan.* 16.14–15 (ed. Guarienti, p. 541); Hilary, *De Trinitate* VIII, ch. 20 (SC 448, pp. 406–409).

[32] *Catena in Ioan.* 16.14–15 (ed. Guarienti, p. 541). Didymus, *De Spiritu Sancto* (Sancto Hieronymo interprete), ch. 37 (PL 23. 134–135). Cf. *SCG* IV, ch. 24 (no. 3609); *In Ioan.* 16.15 (no. 2114).

[33] See *In Ioan.* 15.26 (nos. 2061–2062).

[34] See especially *ST* I, q. 31, aa. 3–4; cf. I *Sent.* d. 21, qq. 1–2.

[35] *CEG* II, ch. 28; *SCG* IV, ch. 25 (no. 3622); *De potentia* 10, q. 4, ad 12; *ST* I, q. 36, a. 2, ad 1; *In Ioan.* 17.3 (no. 2187); *In Gal.* 4.6 (no. 213); etc.

his Father from whom he has everything whatsoever he possesses'.[36] This commonplace scholastic exegesis[37] does no more than to repeat Augustine's interpretations of these matters.[38] But Thomas does observe in relation to John 15.26 that 'our Lord was not altogether silent about his being the principle of the Holy Spirit. He called Him *the Spirit of Truth* after calling himself *the Truth* (Jn 14.26).'[39] This fine-tuning, given to scholastic thought by Peter Lombard,[40] involves a final confirmation of the interpretation of John 15.26, concerning which Thomas was in no doubt. He is quite robust about this, calling the argument which uses John 15.26 against the Latin doctrine 'entirely frivolous'.[41] In sum, Thomas thinks that the Spirit's procession *a Filio* is not literally stated in so many words in the New Testament, but that expressions having this meaning are in fact present here. As we have seen, the *meaning* of Scripture is thought to present itself when Scripture is read in a solidly doctrinal way, one which draws on speculative principles of Trinitarian theology. This is doubtless where the main difficulty lies for the modern reader, because Thomas' idea of how to make a literal reading of Scripture is to set off from a wholly doctrinal reading.

Thomas' study of the patristic sources reflects a progression parallel to that of the biblical references. Highly restrained in the Commentary on the *Sentences*, which just presents the same texts as his predecessors, the references to the Fathers first become fuller in the *Contra errores Graecorum*, then progressively accumulate in the *Contra Gentiles*, the *Catena Aurea* on John, and the Disputed Questions *De potentia*. The *Summa*'s *Prima Pars* and the lectures on John draw out the fruits of this engagement. This attempt to go back to the sources, whose significance has been rediscovered in our own day, merits a detour, because it shows how Thomas founds his reading on the patristic texts.

From amongst the Latins, Thomas especially calls on Augustine: 'It is clear from Augustine, in numerous passages, and especially in the *De Trinitate* and the [sermons] on John, that the Holy Spirit exists *a Filio*.'[42] The explicit references to Augustine's texts are perhaps less frequent than one might

[36] *SCG* IV, ch. 25 (no. 3622), using the illustration taken from Jn 7.16, *My doctrine is not mine.*

[37] See for instance Bonaventure, I *Sent.* d. 11, a. un., q. 1, ad 5.

[38] See for example the long quotation from Augustine in the *Catena in Ioan.* 15.26 (ed. Guarienti, p. 535). Cf. Augustine, *Tract. in Ioan.* 99.8.

[39] *SCG* IV, ch. 25 (no. 3622); cf. *In Ioan.* 14.17 and 15.26 (nos. 1916, 2062, and 2065).

[40] Peter Lombard, *Sentences*, Book I, dist. 11, chs. 1–2 (vol. I/2, pp. 115–116). Thomas also cites the Venerable Bede on this point, in the *Catena in Ioan.* 14.17 (ed. Guarienti, p. 521).

[41] *SCG* IV, ch. 24 (no. 3622).

[42] *SCG* IV, ch. 24 (no. 3611). These are the two main works of Augustine to which Thomas refers in his investigation of the procession of the Holy Spirit.

expect, doubtless because there is hardly any reason for Thomas to insist on it, and because he can easily integrate Augustine into his own thought. Alongside Augustine, one also finds many references to Hilary of Poitiers, whom Thomas follows in his exegesis of John 16.14–15, and whom he also uses for his analysis of the procession *per Filium*.[43]

But Thomas also tries out what the Greek Fathers had to say, either to draw them into the Latin practice of Trinitarian doctrine, or to probe their divergence from it. In the case of the practical application, the main reference points are Cyril of Alexandria, the so-called 'Athanasian Creed',[44] and the passage from Didymus the Blind which we mentioned earlier.[45] Historically, it is notable that the anthology can already be found in Peter Lombard, who benefited from Abelard's research on the topic. As we sought to show earlier, one probably has to think back to Alcuin's *De processione Spiritus Sancti* to get to the bottom of the Latin transmission.[46] Other patristic texts are called into play, including some from Athanasius, from Epiphanius of Salamis, Denys, the *Passion of the Apostle Andrew*, and so on.[47] Amongst these texts, an extract from Cyril's letter to Nestorius, called *Salvatore nostro*, is especially important. Thomas cites it from the translation of the *Acts* of the Council of Ephesus which was available to him in the *Collectio Casinensis*: 'The Spirit is called *de Veritate* and he is the Spirit of Truth, he comes from the Truth just as he comes from the Father.'[48] He also backs himself up with this passage in the *Summa Contra Gentiles*, specifying that Cyril's Letter *Salvatore nostro* was received by the Council of Chalcedon.[49]

It is worth taking the trouble to follow the progress of Thomas' citations from this part of Cyril, because it provides a good illustration of his

---

[43] See especially *Catena in Ioan.* 16.14–15 (ed. Guarienti, p. 541); *In Ioan.* 16.15 (no. 2114); *ST* I, q. 36, a. 3, contra.

[44] *SCG* IV, ch. 24 (no. 3609): 'Spiritus sanctus . . . a Filio procedens'. Thomas shared the view of all Latin theologians of his time that the *Quicumque* Creed is authentically Athanasian. He draws on this text in the *De potentia*, q. 10, a. 4, contra 1, and in the *ST* I, q. 36, a. 2, contra.

[45] *SCG* IV, ch. 24 (no. 3609); *Catena in Ioan.* 16.13–15 (ed. Guarienti, pp. 540–541); cf. *In Ioan.* 16.15 (no. 2114).

[46] Peter Lombard, *Sentences*, Book I, dist. 11, ch. 2 (vol. I/2, pp. 116–117); Abelard, *Theologia Scholarium* II. 157–159 (CCCM 13, pp. 483–485); Abelard, *Theologia christiana* IV. 127–129 (CCCM 12, pp. 328–329); Alcuin, *De processione Spiritus Sancti* (PL 101, pp. 69–78).

[47] See our study, 'La procession du Saint-Esprit *a Filio* chez Thomas d'Aquin', pp. 550–552.

[48] 'Spiritus Veritatis nominatur et est Spiritus Veritatis et profluit ab eo, sicut denique et ex Deo Patre' (*SCG* IV, ch. 24, no. 3609); cf. *Acta Conciliorum Oecumenicorum*, vol. I/3, ed. E. Schwartz, Berlin and Leipzig, 1929, p. 32. See also *De potentia*, q. 10, a. 4, ad 13 and ad 24. For Thomas, the transition from the verb 'profluere' to the notion of 'procession' is legitimate, because the relationship or order of the procession of the Holy Spirit from the Son implies origin *a Filio* (cf. *CEG* II, ch. 27; *De potentia*, q. 10, a. 4, ad 13, where this passage is cited at greater length; *ST* I, q. 36, a. 2).

[49] *SCG* IV, ch. 24 (no. 3609); *De potentia*, q. 10, a. 4, ad 13. Cf. *ACO* II/3, p. 137.

investigative initiative. In the Disputed Questions *De potentia*, he calls on the extract from Cyril's Letter to Nestorius, to which he then contrasts a letter from Theodoret of Cyrus to Cyril on the procession of the Spirit:[50] in one Letter to John of Antioch, Cyril had retracted a previous acceptance of the procession of the Spirit *ex Filio*. Thomas tracked down the letter concerned and effectively succeeded in finding the offending passage, discovering that in fact Cyril does not reject the procession *a Filio*. By reading it with an Antiochene slant, Theodoret has precisely reversed the meaning of Cyril's text. The difficulties raised by the letters of Cyril and Theodoret (his accusations, Cyril's altering his tone in an effort to achieve reconciliation, and so forth), was discussed in 1979 by André de Halleux, who identified the texts exposing their disagreement.[51] These conclusions show that not only was Thomas right in inferring that Theodoret had qualified Cyril's viewpoint, but also that his identification of the documents was completely on target. Since he cites these passages from the translation in the *Collectio Casinensis*, there can be little doubt that they put us face to face with the historical research which he had put together during his time in Italy.[52]

So he has no hesitation in claiming that, like Didymus, Cyril affirms the eternal procession of the Spirit *a Filio*.[53] He makes himself particularly at home in the Alexandrian theological tradition, in texts which are open to the Spirit's procession *a Filio*.[54] In the Middle Ages, Theodoret of Cyrus' 'Nestorian' affiliations had given him a bad reputation in the West. A Dominican who wrote from Constantinople on the topic in 1252 could also have made Thomas aware that Theodoret was amongst the ancient authors to whom the Easterners laid claim to back up their rejection of the Western doctrine.[55] St Thomas excludes Theodoret's opinion on this with the comment

---

[50] *De potentia*, q. 10, a. 4, ad 24.

[51] A. de Halleux, 'Cyrille, Théodoret et le *Filioque*', *Revue d'Histoire Ecclésiastique* 74 (1979), 597–625; reprinted in *Patrologie et oecuménisme*, Recueil d'études, Leuven, 1990, pp. 367–395.

[52] Given the available resources at the time, Thomas is doing a piece of pioneering research. The texts quoted in the *De potentia*, q. 10, a. 4, ad 24 are: Theodoret of Cyrus, the Letter *Deus qui sapienter* to John of Antioch (*ACO* I/4, pp. 131–132); Cyril of Alexandria, the Letter *Exultent caeli* (or, *Laetentur caeli*) to John of Antioch (*ACO* I/3, p. 191). Thomas connects this with the affair of the condemnation of the Nestorian creed at Ephesus.

[53] A. de Halleux ('Cyrille, Théodoret et le *Filioque*') has shown that Cyril's formula of reconciliation does not imply any underlying change or recasting of his thought. It also appears that Cyril's thinking does not only set its sights on the economy, but also takes in the eternal being of the divine persons; B. de Margerie, 'Vers une relecture du concile de Florence grâce à la reconsidération de l'Écriture et des Pères grecs et latins', *RT* 86 (1986), 31–81, cf. pp. 39–40; M.-O. Boulnois, *Le paradoxe trinitaire chez Cyrille d'Alexandrie*, Paris, 1994, pp. 492–529.

[54] B. de Margerie, 'Vers une relecture'.

[55] *Contra Graecos* (PG 140. 489). For this text, see Antoine Dondaine, '*Contra Graecos*. Premiers écrits polémiques des Dominicains d'Orient', *AFP* 21 (1951), 320–456. We now know that Theodoret of Cyrus cannot simply be put down as a 'Nestorian'.

that it was condemned by the second Council of Constantinople, alongside that of Theodore of Mopsuestia.[56] In sum, although it contains some contrary notes, the voice of the Patristics as a whole consolidates the conviction that the doctrine of the Spirit's procession *a Filio* is not heard of only amongst the Latin Fathers, but is also not alien to the Greek Fathers themselves.[57]

3. THE TERMINOLOGY: THE SPIRIT 'PROCEEDS' FROM THE FATHER AND THE SON

We have alluded several times to the terminological difficulties connected with the Holy Spirit's *procession*.[58] One question remains to be raised now: did Thomas' lack of understanding of the Byzantine tradition derive from the fact that the Latin terminology makes no distinction between *procession* and *ekporeusis*, although the Greek text of John 15.26 creates the possibility? Many people take it that this linguistic problem bears much of the weight of the responsibility for the Latin theologians' incomprehension of their Eastern contemporaries.[59] The Easterners used the word *ekporeusis* to designate the origin of the Holy Spirit from the Father, considered as sole Origin; whereas, as we have seen, the Westerners used the word *procession*, as signifying origin from a principle in a broader sense, making it just as applicable to the Son as to the Holy Spirit. In fact, Thomas did not know why those whom he calls the 'Greeks' sometimes agreed to say that the Spirit *flows out* from the Son (*profluit*), but not that the Holy Spirit proceeds from the Son (*procedit, ekporeuetai*); it was that, for them, *ekporeusis* can only have the Father as principle.

One should begin by noticing that there is a plethora of Latin terms here: the Spirit is 'breathed' (*spirare*), and 'originated' (*deoriginare*) by the Father and Son; he 'emanates' (*emanare*) and 'flows out' (*profluere*) from

---

[56] *De potentia*, q. 10, a. 4, ad 24; *ST* I, q. 36, a. 2, ad 3. These texts also explain why Thomas sidelines a passage in which St John of Damascus argues that the Holy Spirit is the Spirit of the Son but he is not *ex Filio* (*De potentia*, q. 10, a. 4, arg. 24 and ad 24; *ST* I, q. 36, a. 2, ad 3; cf. I *Sent.* d. 11, q. 1, a. 1, arg. 3 and ad 3); Thomas' interpretation of John's text is defective.

[57] *CEG* II, chs. 1, 28, 31; *SCG* IV, ch. 24 (no. 3609). It is also worth consulting A. Patfoort, 'Le *Filioque* dans la conscience de l'Eglise avant le concile d'Ephèse', *RT* 97 (1997), 318–334; B. Pottier, 'La Trinité chez Grégoire de Nysse', *Connaissance des Pères de l'Eglise* 76 (1999), 11–21, especially pp. 19–20.

[58] See above, in Chapter 4, 'The Word "Procession"', and in Chapter 10, 'The Name "Holy Spirit"', and 'The Holy Spirit is Love in Person'.

[59] V. Grumel, 'St Thomas et la doctrine des Grecs sur la procession du Saint-Esprit', *Échos d'Orient* 25 (1926), 257–280, especially pp. 267–272; cf. Yves Congar, *I Believe in the Holy Spirit*, vol 3, pp. 174–179.

the Father and the Son, who are called 'principle' (*principium*), 'author' (*auctor*), and 'source' (*fons*) of the Spirit.[60] Amongst these expressions, the terminology of procession and principle is best tailored to designating the origin of the Holy Spirit.

Despite his evident limitations, Thomas was not as naive or ignorant about the meaning of *ekporeusis* as people often imagine. Even though the distinction between the words *processio* and *ekporeusis* escaped him, he nonetheless grasped the heart of the matter when he observed that the Latin preposition *a* or *ab* translates the Greek *ek* or *ex*, that is to say, 'from' or 'out of' ('the Spirit who proceeds *from* the Father' does not follow the text of John 15.27, which uses a different preposition, but the text of the Constantinopolitan Creed; the word *ek-poreusis* likewise contains this root in its prefix). Thomas makes this observation in his Commentary on the *Sentences*:

It is said that 'the Holy Spirit principally proceeds from the Father', because the *auctoritas* [authorship] of the spiration resides in the Father, and since it is from the Father that the Son receives the power to breathe the Spirit . . . One accurately says that 'the Spirit proceeds from the Father (*a Patre*)', mainly because, for the Greeks, the preposition 'a' designates the relation to the primary point of origin (*prima origo*); this is why one does not say that the lake proceeds from the river, but from the source (*a fonte*); and this is the reason why they will not concede that the Holy Spirit proceeds from the Son (*quod sit a Filio*). Nonetheless, one cannot say that the Spirit does not really proceed from the Son, who together with the Father forms the single principle of the Holy Spirit.[61]

This fine-shading is repeated in the John Commentary: 'some of the Greeks assert that one should not say that the Holy Spirit proceeds from the Son (*procedere a Filio*), because for them the preposition "a" or "ab" indicates a principle which is not from a principle (*principium non de principio*), and this only fits the Father. But this is not compelling, because the Son forms one single principle of the Holy Spirit together with the Father.'[62] So St Thomas does touch on the narrower meaning of the preposition *ek* (which is translated in the Latin here as *a* or *ab*). He accurately reports on the meaning contained in *ekporeusis* for the Greeks, as relation of origin to the Source, principle not from a principle. He notices the different or more precise meaning which the 'Greeks' ascribe to the words. One should take this into account: terminological misunderstanding is not enough to explain the difference between East and West. Thomas does not object to the idea that the terms can refer the relation to the 'first point of origin'. But he does contest the exclusion of the Son, 'because the Son and the Father together form one

---

[60] *CEG* II, chs. 15–27.
[61] I *Sent.* d. 12, q. 1, a. 2, ad 3.   [62] *In Ioan.* 15.26 (no. 2065).

single principle of the Holy Spirit'. The procession of the Holy Spirit has two sides to it: the distinction of the Father and the Son (since the Father is the principle not from a principle, it is the Father who gives the Son his breathing of the Spirit), and the unity of Father and Son, as one single principle.[63] One cannot fail to see that, in Thomas' opinion, the basic problem is not located in the field of terminology, some of whose aspects he saw, but in the metaphysical field of Trinitarian doctrine.

4. THE COUNCILS AND THE PROBLEM OF ADDING TO THE SYMBOL

In order to give evidence for the Roman Church's doctrine and to justify the insertion of the clause 'and from the Son' into the Symbol of Constantinople, Thomas calls on the ancient Councils. There was nothing new about it: the Latin theologians could point out a conciliar tradition going back to Alcuin, at the least; in fact, he refers to this in some detail.[64] The *Filioque*, which is to be held on the basis of the faith professed by the Councils, is in conformity or 'in harmony' with the ancient faith.[65] The hermeneutic of 'explicating the implicit' drives this approach to the problem of making an addition to the Creed, and, in general, the understanding of the development of dogmatic formulae as a whole. The Latin Church had *explicated* what the Symbol of Constantinople contained *implicitly*. This analysis, which comes particularly from Albert the Great, who took it from Anselm of Canterbury, spans his entire work.[66]

This interpretative rule is not presented as a baseless postulate, and, making use of his background research, Thomas makes precise reference to the texts confirming it. He begins by recalling what an ancient tradition, which goes back to before Constantinople I, called the principle of the 'sufficiency' of the

---

[63] See below, in this chapter, 'Balancing Out the Nuances: the Distinction and the Unity of Father and Son'.

[64] Alcuin, *De processione Spiritus Sancti* (PL 101, pp. 69–73), which discusses the first five councils.

[65] *De potentia*, q. 10, a. 4, ad 13.

[66] I *Sent.* d. 11, exp. text.; *SCG* IV, ch. 25 (no. 3624); *De potentia*, q. 10, a. 4, ad 13; *ST* I, q. 36, a. 2, ad 2. Cf. Albert, I *Sent.* d. 11, a. 9. Anselm, *De processione Spiritus Sancti*, ch. 13; *Anselm of Canterbury: The Major Works*, ed. Brian Davies and Gillian Evans, Oxford, 1998, pp. 425–426. One finds the same arguments, particularly this observation: the Symbol of Constantinople did not explicitly formulate everything which is the object of faith; and so, for example, the descent of Christ into Hell, which is affirmed in the Apostles' Creed, goes unmentioned.

Nicene Creed.[67] It is worth noting that Thomas had first-hand knowledge of this principle. The prohibition on adding to the Symbol of the Council of Nicaea, under pains of anathema, appears within his writings in the course of a long quotation from the *Acts* of Ephesus. He remembers also that the Council of Chalcedon proscribes professing any other faith.[68] If the Symbol of Constantinople completes that of Nicaea, this is not because it contains a doctrine which is new or alien to it, 'another faith', but because it carries out an explication required by the needs of the times. It was thus in service to the faith that 'a later Council had the power to interpret the Symbol established by an earlier Council'.[69] Thomas often draws out this thesis, producing a long quotation from the *Acts* of the Council of Chalcedon which explains that, so as to defend it against heresies, the Fathers of Chalcedon did no more than to proclaim and 'corroborate' the faith of Nicaea regarding the Holy Spirit.[70] So the Council of Chalcedon itself testifies to the legitimacy of an explication of the faith: and the Western addition of the *Filioque* sails on this current.

Adding to the Symbol of Constantinople could thus be legitimate, in principle. But what is the competent authority to decide on such an addition? And, historically, what was the authority? Thomas has shown that the Councils themselves practise an explication of the faith. He invokes the authority of the Roman pontiff as the extension of this conciliar practice. He reminds us that councils are recognized as ecumenical by being confirmed as such by the Pope and that it is a Pope who calls a Council: the Pope has the competence and authority to make such an insertion in the Creed.[71] These observations correlate with the place which Thomas gives the Pope in his ecclesiology.[72] But one should note that in all the passages about the *Filioque*, it is only at the very end of the exposition, as a kind of *ultima ratio*, that Thomas brings in the prerogatives of Peter's successor. Perhaps more than later theologians, who could view it as being definitively laid down by the solemn declaration of the second Council of

---

[67] See A. de Halleux, 'Pour une profession commune de la foi selon l'esprit des Pères', in *Patrologie et oecuménisme*, Recueil d'études, Leuven, 1990, pp. 3–24.

[68] *De potentia*, q. 10, a. 4, arg. 13. Cf. *ACO* I/3, p. xviiii; *ACO* II/3, p. 138 (the *Collectio Casinensis* version). Thomas refers back to the principle without citing the texts in *ST* I, q. 36, a. 2, arg. 2.

[69] *De potentia*, q. 10, a. 4, ad 13.

[70] The passage is cited at length in the *De potentia*, q. 10, a. 4, ad 13; more briefly in *SCG* IV, ch. 25 (no. 3624); *ST* I, q. 36, a. 2, ad 2. Cf. *ACO* II/3, pp. 136–137; see also G. Geenen, 'En marge du Concile de Chalcédoine. Les textes du Quatrième Concile dans les oeuvres de S. Thomas', *Angelicum* 29 (1952), 53–56.

[71] *De potentia*, q. 10, a. 4, ad 13; *SCG* IV, ch. 25 (no. 3624); *ST* I, q. 36, a. 2, ad 2.

[72] See in particular S.-Th. Bonino, 'La place du pape dans l'Église selon St Thomas d'Aquin', *RT* 86 (1986), 392–422.

Lyons, in 1274,[73] St Thomas engages in scriptural, patristic, and speculative arguments to account for the doctrine, in conformity with his task as a theologian.

But what did the intervention of the magisterium amount to, historically? For good reasons, Thomas takes pains to respond to this question, bringing various aspects of his answer into play over the course of his writing. It is only in the *Summa Theologiae* that he hits the nail full on the head. On the one hand, he recalls that the ancient councils had no reason to proclaim the Spirit's procession *a Filio*, since the contrary error had not yet been developed. On the other hand, he ascribes the magisterial explication of the *Filioque* and its addition to the Creed to 'a Council which came together in the West' under papal authority.[74] What Council could he be thinking of? Despite the particular interest of this passage, the texts do not permit us to answer this question.

Thomas no longer marks down the 'Greek error' as a sign of the need for a magisterial intervention on this topic (which was Albert's opinion, and Thomas' original take on it[75]), seeing it as merely 'the error of some'. He had probably recognized the role which some forms of adoptionism had played in the explication of the Western doctrine. This reference to a Council 'in the West' (*in occidentalibus partibus*) is effectively identical to the one we find in the *Contra Graecos*, an opuscule composed by a Dominican in Constantinople in 1252. As Père Antoine Dondaine has shown, it is highly probable that Thomas' thinking on this is linked to the latter.[76] According to this text, which is very close to Thomas' own, the proclamation of the *Filioque* is not opposed to the Eastern doctrine, but relates to a heresy emerging *in the West*, and condemned by a Western Council in the absence of the Easterners, since it touched on a purely Western problem. But neither the polemicist in the Dominican priory in Constantinople nor St Thomas tell us any more than that. It was not until the fourteenth century, after the idea of a Council coming together under papal authority to oppose the denial of the procession *a Filio* became an unlikely event that people tried to investigate the Toledo Councils in more detail.[77]

---

[73] In the opinion of P. H. Dondaine, this element was not unimportant for the theories of Henry of Gand and Duns Scotus; coming on the scene after Lyons II, they did not give the same weight to the idea of relative opposition (*La Trinité*, vol. 2, p. 387, n. 1).

[74] *ST* I, q. 36, a. 2, ad 2: 'in quodam concilio in Occidentalibus partibus congregato'.

[75] Albert, I *Sent.* d. 1, a. 9; Thomas, I *Sent.* d. 11, exp. text.

[76] *Contra Graecos*: 'in Occidentalibus partibus ... de licentia et auctoritate summi pontificis'; A. Dondaine, '*Contra Graecos*. Premiers écrits polémiques des Dominicains d'Orient', *AFP* 21 (1951), 320–446, here pp. 390–391. Cf. also PG 140. 502.

[77] See especially the Council of Toledo III, in 589; Toledo IV, in 633; Toledo VI, in 638; Toledo XI in 675 (cf. Denzinger, nos. 470, 485, 490, 527). According to A. Dondaine, who examined the aftermath of the *Contra Graecos* in some detail, we owe the discovery of this genuine means of resolving the historical question to Philip of Pera, writing in 1359 ('*Contra Graecos*', p. 393).

5. THEORETICAL ARGUMENTS

Following on from its biblical foundations and patristic anchorage, the third window on the question is constructed from speculative theological arguments. These are what come to the fore in the *Summa Theologiae*.[78] There are few theological questions in which St Thomas turns his hand to generating such a wealth of argument. Just as he constantly extended the range of his biblical and patristic references, so he also progressively enriched his speculative reflection (at least from the *De potentia* onwards), proposing a dozen 'evident reasons' on behalf of the procession of the Holy Spirit *a Patre* and *a Filio*.[79] We will limit ourselves to presenting the three arguments which survive into the *Summa Theologiae*.

(a) Distinction by Relative Opposition

The first argument, present throughout Thomas' work, refers to the divine persons' being distinguished by relative opposition alone.[80] This is incontestably the main metaphysical point. The reflection behind it runs like this. The divine persons could not be distinguished from each other by something 'absolute' (since that would lead to three gods): only relation or a relational characteristic can account for this distinction whilst leaving the unity of the divine nature intact. And, only a relational opposition can produce an explanation of the distinctness of the persons: this has already been established.[81] This is not just one opinion amongst many others: the 'truth of the faith' compels one to accept relative opposition, because it is the only means of giving a reasonable account of Trinitarian monotheist faith.[82] Thomas is tenacious about a principle which he often legitimated with the following argument: the Father has two relations (one in respect of the Son and the other in respect of the Spirit) and these two relations do not divide the Father

---

[78] *ST* I, q. 36, a. 2.

[79] The expression is taken from the *SCG* IV, ch. 24 (no. 3612: '*evidentibus rationibus*'). For a more complete survey of this theoretical side of Thomas' writing, see our study, 'La procession du Saint-Esprit chez S. Thomas d'Aquin', *RT* 96 (1996), 559–569.

[80] I *Sent*. d. 11, q. un., a. 1; *CEG* II, chs. 29–30; *SCG* IV, ch. 24 (no. 3612); *De potentia*, q. 10, a. 4 and a. 5; *ST* I, q. 36, a. 2. Thomas is not innovative here: see for example Albert the Great's development of Anselm's position in I *Sent*. d. 11, a. 6, contra 1–5.

[81] *ST* I, q. 28, aa. 3–4; cf. q. 40, aa. 2–3. See above, in Chapter 5, 'Relative Opposition: Paternity, Filiation, Spiration, and Procession', and in Chapter 6, 'Relation at the Heart of Trinitarian Theology'.

[82] Cf. *Quodlibet* XII, q. 1, a. 1.

into two persons, precisely because the relations (of paternity and active spiration) are not in mutual opposition.[83] And, for the same reason, if there were no relational opposition between the Son and the Holy Spirit, they would be one and the same person, which comes down to Sabellian monarchianism.[84] And, as the final step in the argument, the relation of opposition can only be founded in *origin*, the sole source of personal distinction in God.[85] If one does not take this step, the affirmation of the personal distinctness of the Son and Holy Spirit becomes, not just problematic but self-contradictory. And *intellectus fidei* as a theological endeavour would come to an end.

On the basis of this analysis, the Spirit's procession *a Filio* asserts itself as the means of safeguarding the Spirit's distinctness from the Son, that is, the Spirit's own personality. Thomas authenticates this by reviewing all of the possible foundations for a real relation, and showing that only an origination of the Holy Spirit *a Filio* can found the distinct relation of the Holy Spirit. But could not one just hold that the Son is *engendered* by the Father, whereas the Holy Spirit *proceeds* from the Father: are not the two modes of generation and procession enough to distinguish them from one another? According to St Thomas, this answer to the problem is superficial: the origin of the Son, as generation, and that of the Spirit, as procession, are not distinct within the divine nature which they communicate, but within the purview of the relations they involve, that is, within relationship to a principle. In other words, the distinction between the Son's generation and the Spirit's procession hinges on their *order*, and this order entails that the Spirit proceeds from Father and Son.[86]

One can see how the exposition works: it is in no way a demonstration of the Trinity, since the argument presupposes Trinitarian faith. It is a matter of doing as much as theological reason can to disclose the real distinction of the persons. Thomas develops a reflection which, because it eliminates every other sufficient hypothesis, entails the necessity (*supposita Trinitate*) of relational opposition and thus of the Spirit's procession *a Patre* and *a Filio*.

(b) Love and the Word

The second argument, which is maintained on through to the *Summa*, takes us back to the theological conception of the properties of the Son and the

---

[83] Cf. *SCG* IV, ch. 24 (no. 3613); *De potentia*, q. 10, a. 5; *ST* I, q. 30, a. 2; q. 36, a. 2.

[84] In other words: if the Holy Spirit did not proceed from the Son, he could not be personally distinct from him. There is a long discussion of this in the *De potentia*, q. 10, a. 5.

[85] See above, in Chapter 4, 'Action, the Source of Relation'.

[86] We have said enough about why Thomas thinks this answer is insufficient: see above, in Chapter 4, 'The Order of the Trinitarian Processions'. Cf. *SCG* IV, ch. 24 (nos. 3615–3616); *De potentia*, q. 10, a. 2; q. 10, a. 4; q. 10, a. 5, sol. and ad 1–6; *ST* I, q. 36, a. 2, sol. and ad 7; q. 40, a. 2.

Holy Spirit: Love proceeds from the Word.[87] The consideration is not just about the activities of love and thought, but, more precisely that relationship which the affection or 'imprint' of love has with the conceived or formed word, which is to say: the relationship enjoyed by the two 'ends' issuing from procession by way of mind and procession by way of love. The explanation in the *Summa* is very concise: 'It is necessary that Love proceeds from the Word; this is why we cannot love something unless we have first conceived of it in our mind. It is thus evident that the Holy Spirit proceeds from the Son.'[88] Otherwise put: the inclination of the spiritual faculty of will carries us toward the object which the intellect presents to it. By observing this relationship of word and love first of all in human beings, one can rediscover an analogy for what the Son and Holy Spirit are actually like, because such a relationship is constitutive of the actual notions of 'word' and 'love'. So the Holy Spirit's proceeding as the 'fruit of love' involves an origination relation with respect to the Word, who is the 'conception' of the Father's mind.

This does not mean that there would be a 'uni-directional' relationship between mind and love, because love itself also exerts an influence on intellectual activity. But, by its very nature, the dynamism of love is rooted in this presence of the known being to the mind: 'we cannot love anything if we have not conceived it as a word in our heart'.[89] One can see this from the perspective of love, but also from that of the word. The Augustinian idea of the 'perfect word', that is to say, the word emerging from accomplished spiritual acts in their fullest blossoming, which is love, is an especially suggestive way of showing this:

As Augustine says in Bk. IX of the *De Trinitate*, 'the Word which we seek to disclose is knowledge with love'. Thus, when an act of knowledge does not give rise to a free act of love, we are not dealing with a likeness to the Word, but only with a simulacrum of something about the Word. There is only a likeness to the Word when the knowing is of such a kind that love proceeds from it.[90]

The idea of the image of the Trinity in human beings touches directly on this Trinitarian exemplarism, and its spiritual repercussions carry a long way:[91]

The Son is the Word, not any sort of word, but one Who breathes Love. As Augustine says in Bk. IX of the *De Trinitate*, 'the Word which we seek to disclose is knowledge

---

[87] *ST* I, q. 36, a. 2; *SCG* IV, ch. 24 (no. 3617); *De potentia*, q. 10, a. 5; *De rationibus fidei*, ch. 4; *Compendium Theologiae* I, ch. 49; *In Ioan.* 14.17 (no. 1916).
[88] *ST* I, q. 36, a. 2.
[89] *SCG* IV, ch. 24 (no. 3617).
[90] I *Sent.* d. 15, q. 4, a. 1, ad 3; cf. d. 10, q. un., a. 1, contra 2; d. 27, q. 2, a. 2, arg. 1; Augustine, *De Trinitate* IX.X.15. On this important notion, see R. Spiazzi, '"Conoscenza con amore" in Sant' Agostino e in San Tommaso', *Doctor Communis* 39 (1986), 315–328.
[91] *ST* I, q. 45, a. 7; q. 93, aa. 4–5.

with love'. This is why the Son is sent [into human souls] not in accordance with any and every kind of intellectual perfection, but only according to the intellectual illumination which breaks out into the affection of love.[92]

In the great synthesizing texts, this argument is never presented as the primary way of exhibiting the Spirit's procession *a Filio*. It is always preceded by the theory of oppositional relations, and sometimes by other arguments as well. It is only in the smaller-scale work, destined for a wider audience, that Thomas puts this idea of the Word and Love in the foreground. Thus, in the *Compendium of Theology*, and in the opuscule, *De rationibus fidei*, the idea of Love as proceeding from the Word is the sole evidence for the procession of the Spirit *a Filio*. The reason for this decision must lie in the method of these works, which calls for simplicity of exposition, as well as in the suggestive power of the analogy of the word and love. This argument rests on a theological elaboration which, along with oppositional relation, lays out the basic structure of Trinitarian doctrine.

(c) The Trinitarian Order

The third approach used by the *Summa Theologiae* is the *order* within the Trinity.[93] One must not regard this as a marginal theme; it touches on a fundamental element of Trinitarian doctrine. There is within the Trinity an 'order of nature' (*ordo naturae*), which does not imply anything like antecedence or posteriority amongst the divine persons, but purely a relation of origin:[94]

if two persons, Son and Spirit, proceed from the one person of the Father, they must have some sort of order between them. And it is not possible to assign any but the order of nature whereby one person is from the other.[95]

To deny any such ordering within the Trinity will lead to the construction of internal conflations which the distinctions in the Trinity should exclude. Doubtless more than it would for us today, the context for Thomas' understanding of such order is the order he can observe in the world, in human affairs, amongst the angels, and in the whole universe which shines with the beauty ordained for it by the divine wisdom. But the argument is not merely 'aesthetic', but actually has a metaphysical value, closely tied to the idea of being: such an order is involved in every kind of distinction and plurality.

---

[92] *ST* I, q. 43, a. 5, ad 2.
[93] *ST* I, q. 36, a. 2; *SCG* IV, ch. 24 (no. 3618); *De potentia*, q. 10, aa. 4 and 5.
[94] *ST* I, q. 42, a. 3.   [95] *ST* I, q. 36, a. 2.

The faith, which rules out any 'conflation' of the persons, leads one to see that there is within God something analogous to this order. The idea of oppositional relation by origin comes in here because for Thomas this order can only inhabit an origination relation. In Thomas' Latin Theology, *unity with no conflation of persons* within the Trinity requires that one acknowledge the Holy Spirit's procession *a Filio*.

One cannot fail to be struck by the fact that the force of 'necessity' is repeatedly and explicitly attributed to this theological reasoning. This shows that the Spirit's procession *a Filio* is engraved in the inner structure of Thomas' Latin Trinitarian doctrine, in such a way that if one starts from these basic principles (oppositional relation as from origin, the ideas of the Word and Love, Trinitarian order), they will impose themselves throughout. Outside all misplaced polemics, and independently of the restrictions on his understanding of Eastern tradition, it is worth considering what is at stake here, as much on the level of history as that of theory. St Thomas is seeking to give an account of Trinitarian faith which works within a structured body of ideas. And, under every angle which he examines, he shows that this basic project cannot be achieved unless one accepts the Spirit's procession *a Filio*.

6. BALANCING OUT THE NUANCES: THE DISTINCTION AND THE UNITY OF FATHER AND SON

Once he has indicated in the *Summa Theologiae* that the Holy Spirit proceeds from the Father and the Son, Thomas makes two crucial points of detail, each the object of a whole article (q. 36, aa. 3–4). On the one hand, acknowledging the Holy Spirit's procession *a Filio* does not imply the conflation of Father and Son. And nor does it imply that the spiration derives from an impersonal principle: the Father and the Son breathe the Holy Spirit as distinct persons. On the other hand, this does not 'divide' the Holy Spirit, because the Spirit does not have a dual origin: Father and Son are 'one single principle of the Holy Spirit'. These two ideas constitute two complementary sides whose juncture needs to be connected with the foregoing analysis. The first expresses the 'condition' of the Father and Son as two distinct persons: the second concerns 'that by which' Father and Son breathe the Holy Spirit; expressing, that is, one single common notion of active spiration. Thomas states that,

Does the Holy Spirit proceed from the Father and the Son *in so far as they are one*? ... I answer that 'in so far as' can designate here either *the condition of the agent* or *the principle of action*. If 'in so far as' designates the condition of the one who acts or operates, the Holy Spirit proceeds from the Father and Son in the plural [that is: two hypostases], and in so far as they are distinct persons, since he proceeds from them as from many [distinct] persons. But if 'in so far as' refers to the condition of the principle of the action, then I answer that the Holy Spirit proceeds from them in so far as they are one. Since the operation comes from one single principle alone, it is necessary that there be in Father and Son something which is singular and which will be the principle of that action which is spiration, an act which is one and simple, and by which the single and simple person of the Holy Spirit proceeds.[96]

Under the first aspect (the 'condition' of the agent), the Father and the Son are taken in relation to their plurality as persons. From this angle, the spiration of the Spirit 'requires distinction of the supposita [the hypostases of the Father and Son] as a precondition, since it comes in a certain way from the two supposits in their distinctness, because it relates to a personal operation'.[97] The shared Love of Father and Son also sheds light on this plurality: 'if we consider the supposita of the spiration, then we may say that the Holy Spirit proceeds from the Father and the Son as distinct; for He proceeds from them as the Love which unites them'.[98] This personal distinction is particularly brought out in the formula: the Holy Spirit proceeds from the Father through the Son (*per Filium*). This is a traditional expression whose value Thomas repeatedly affirms from his Commentary on the *Sentences* onwards.[99] The Son takes from the Father the breath with which to breathe, with him, the Holy Spirit. In other words, this formula puts the spotlight on the *order* amongst Father and Son, that is, the Son's relation of origin coming from the Father:

Since therefore the Son has it from the Father that the Holy Spirit proceeds from him, one can say that 'The Father breathes the Holy Spirit through the Son', or, what amounts to the same thing, 'The Holy Spirit proceeds from the Father through the Son.'[100]

These two formulae present a profile of the utterly *personal* character of the spiration of the Spirit. On the level of personal operations, they express the *authority* belonging to the Father, that is to say the Father's legitimate position within the Trinity as source, principle without principle.[101] The Father and the Son breathe the Spirit, not as a consortium, but out of their distinction. The distinction to which the expression 'through the Son' refers does not touch on that which we grasp as the formal principle of the action of the Father and the Son: this principle is the 'active spiration', a notion common to

---

[96] I *Sent.* d. 11, q. 1, a. 2.   [97] I *Sent.* d. 29, q. un., a. 4, ad 2.

[98] *ST* I, q. 36, a. 4, ad 1; cf. also ad 7; I *Sent.* d. 10, q. un., a. 5, ad 1.

[99] I *Sent.* d. 12, q. un., a. 3 (mainly ad 4); *CEG* II, ch. 8; *De potentia*, q. 10, a. 4; q. 10, a. 5, ad 14; *ST* I, q. 36, a. 3.

[100] *ST* I, q. 36, a. 3.   [101] I *Sent.* d. 12, q. un., a. 3, ad 4; *ST* I, q. 36, a. 3.

and identical in the Father and the Son. Rather, the distinction relates to the persons as such, because the subject of action is always the 'hypostasis', that is, the person.

Following the lead of Augustine (and of Albert, who was particularly fond of this formula), Thomas explains that 'the Holy Spirit proceeds *principally* from the Father'.[102] In this expression, the adverb *principally* means that it is the Father who gives it to the Son to be the principle of the Holy Spirit along with himself: this is precisely what one articulates when one says that the Holy Spirit proceeds from the Father *through* the Son. It is necessary to avoid any priority of one person over another,[103] and likewise any idea of a 'more' or 'less': the Holy Spirit proceeds neither 'more', nor 'more fully', nor 'more directly' from the Father than from the Son.[104] In saying that the Holy Spirit proceeds *principally* from the Father, one accentuates the Son's origin-relation in respect of the Father, an origin in virtue of which the Son receives his breathing of the Holy Spirit from the Father.

The procession of the Spirit 'through the Son' must be understood in a strong sense. To say that the Holy Spirit proceeds from the Father *through the Son* implies that the Holy Spirit also proceeds *from the Son*. For any kind of origination relationship which one recognizes between the Son and the Spirit, and thus the origin-relationship expressed in the formula 'through the Son', entails procession or existing *a Filio*.[105] The idea of procession 'through the Son' expresses a very ancient feature of Latin Trinitarian theology, which goes back as far as Tertullian,[106] and which cannot purely be reduced to simple procession *a Filio*. It brings us to a complementary theme, bringing an important aspect of the Holy Spirit's procession to light, and this is the reason why the *Summa* gives over an entire article to it. The expressions *per Filium* and *a Filio* are not interchangeable. The one looks more toward the distinction of the persons, the other to their unity. The first prevents us from seeing this unity as being founded in a monolithic essence; the second avoids conceiving the *per Filium* like a different or secondary principle. As Venance Grumel has observed, 'one has to join them together to have a full expression of the doctrine of the procession of the Holy Spirit'.[107]

---

[102] *ST* I, q. 36, a. 3, ad 2; I *Sent.* 12, exp. text. Cf. Augustine, *De Trinitate* XV.XVII.29. Augustine's teaching that the Holy Spirit proceeds *principally* from the Father was passed on by Peter Lombard's *Sentences* (Book I, dist. 12, ch. 2). See also, Albert, I *Sent.* d. 12, aa. 4–5.

[103] I *Sent.* d. 9, q. 2, a. 1; d. 12, q. un., a. 1. Like the Father and the Holy Spirit, the Son is '*simpliciter primum*' (I *Sent.* d. 9, q. 2, a. 1, contra).

[104] I *Sent.* d. 12, q. un., a. 2.

[105] *CEG* II, ch. 8; *De potentia*, q. 10, a. 4; *ST* I, q. 36, a. 2.

[106] Tertullian, *Adversus Praxean*, 4.1: 'The Spirit comes in no other way than from the Father through the Son (*a Patre per Filium*)'.

[107] V. Grumel, 'St Thomas et la doctrine des Grecs', p. 275.

After having presented the distinction of the Father and Son as the personal subjects who breathe the Holy Spirit, Thomas glosses their unity. This is the second aspect which we mentioned above: no longer the 'condition of the agent', but the principle of the action. Under this second aspect, Father and Son are one single principle (*unum principium*) of the Holy Spirit.[108] Like the earlier point, this way of fine-tuning things comes from Augustine.[109] It is important because it excludes any kind of duality of principles, and thus any 'division' within the Holy Spirit, and every notion of the Son being subordinate to the Father, conveying a diminution of the equality and simplicity of the divine persons. There is in fact a perfect unity in the principle behind the spiration: not the identity of Father and Son, since they are two distinct persons, but the identity of 'that through which' or 'that in virtue of which' the Father and the Son breathe the Holy Spirit. This principle of action is notional power (power is, by definition, the *principle* of action), communicated to the Son in his begetting by the Father as 'power to breathe the Holy Spirit', and which is numerically one and identical in the Father and in the Son. It is this which justifies the affirmation of the oneness of the principle and which legitimates the proposition that there is one single 'Spirator' (*unus Spirator*, Father and Son).[110]

This analysis tries to maintain the equilibrium between the *plurality* of the persons who breathe the Holy Spirit, and the *unity of the principle* of the Spirit. This balance is ensured by the absolutely fundamental distinction between the person or hypostasis on the one hand, and the notional power on the other. If one bears in mind that 'procession' as the Spirit's personal characteristic actually designates a *relation*, that enables one to grasp the reciprocity of the persons and the mutual implication of generation and spiration. The Father and Son are not 'first of all' constituted in their personal being through paternity and filiation, as if the Holy Spirit came about 'later' or as if the begetting of the Son were in some way 'independent' of the procession of the Holy Spirit. For the purposes of exposition, certainly, Thomas first tackles the generation of the Son, then the procession of the Holy Spirit. But this order should not become a cause of misunderstanding: 'Neither on the part of the nature, nor on the part of the relations, can one person be prior to another, not even in the order of nature and reason.'[111]

[108] I *Sent.* d. 29, q. un., aa. 3–4; *ST* I, q. 36, a. 4.
[109] Augustine, *De Trinitate* V.XV.15: 'The Father and the Son are, in respect of the Holy Spirit, one single principle (*unum principium*) in a relational way.'
[110] *ST* I, q. 36, a. 4, ad 7. In his Commentary on the *Sentences* (I *Sent.* d. 11, q. un., a. 4; d. 29, q. 1, a. 4, ad 2), Thomas maintains the formula 'two spirators'. Yet the evolution is less a matter of doctrinal principle than a deepening of his understanding of how the term 'Spirator' means what it says.
[111] *ST* I, q. 42, a. 3, ad 2.

The Father is constituted in his personal being by his character of paternity, that is, through his relation to the Son. The Son is constituted as a person through his character of filiation, that is to say through his origin-relation to the Father. Breathing the Spirit does not in itself 'constitute' either the person of the Father or that of the Son. The procession of the Holy Spirit does not constitute the Father and the Son; it constitutes the person of the Holy Spirit.[112] This does not mean that the Holy Spirit is either absent from the begetting of the Son or detached from the paternity of the Father and the Son's filiation. The idea of mutual love has thoroughly indicated this, and the study of the principle of spiration discloses it yet more profoundly. In effect, the Father *as Father* gives it to the Son to breathe the Spirit with him, and the Son *as Son* receives the power of co-breathing the Holy Spirit from the Father. Otherwise put: the Son takes his being the principle of the Spirit from the Father, and everything which the Son takes from the Father, he takes through his begetting. Thomas says: 'The Son has this from the Father that of himself he pours forth the Holy Spirit.'[113] The 'virtue' of breathing the Holy Spirit is thus *included* in the generation through which the Son receives his being as principle of the Holy Spirit.[114]

What Thomas explains in terms of the 'power' or 'virtue' of breathing the Holy Spirit, he also puts in terms of relations: 'In line with the relation through which it flows from the Son, the procession of the Holy Spirit also flows from the Father:...for the Son flows from the Father.'[115] The Holy Spirit's relation with the Son *implicates* the Spirit's relation with the Father, for it implies the relation through which the Son himself is referred to the Father. Thomas' explanation of this carries over into love: 'It is the same love whereby the Father loves and whereby the Son loves, yet this love, the Son takes from the Father, but the Father has it from no one else.'[116] Thus, the Father and the Son are constituted as persons through paternity and filiation, and not formally through the breathing of the Holy Spirit. But nonetheless, the spiration of the Spirit is present in paternity and filiation: that the Father is constituted by his relation to the Son carries an implication of his relation to the Holy Spirit; the Son is constituted Son through his relation to the Father inseparably involving his relation to the Holy Spirit. The *intrinsic* bonds of generation and spiration appear in a more evident way in the idea of the 'perfect Word': the generation of the word involves a perfect knowledge

---

[112] *ST* I, q. 30, a. 2, sol. and ad 1.

[113] *De potentia*, q. 10, a. 4, ad 2; cf. arg. 2; I *Sent.* d. 12, q. 1, a. 2; *ST* I, q. 36, a. 3, ad 2: 'The Son takes this power [of breathing the Holy Spirit] from the Father.'

[114] See also *In Ioan.* 16.15 (nos. 2114–2115).

[115] I *Sent.* d. 12, q. 1, a. 2, ad 4. [116] *De potentia*, q. 10, a. 4, ad 8.

from which Love comes forth; the divine Word is thus always the 'Love-breathing Word'.[117]

We have not given an explanation which updates St Thomas' view in order to 'rehabilitate' him in some way, in response to the criticisms which some people have made of Latin theology (such as, being separated into two parts, 'Father–Son' followed by 'Father, Son, Spirit', and obliviousness to the role of the Holy Spirit in the generation of the Son). Rather, we have proposed one which touches on a feature which authentically belongs to Thomas' own original thought. Thomists have been prompt in pointing it out. At the beginning of the fourteenth century, confronted by the Scotist school which tended to disassociate the generation of the Son from the procession of the Holy Spirit (by conceptually separating the two), the Thomists stressed that their Master had taught that the Holy Spirit proceeds from the Son *in so far as the Son is begotten by the Father*: the procession of the Holy Spirit 'is attached in itself' (*per se*) to the generation of the Son. It is from his begetting as *Son of the Father* that the Son derives the 'virtue' of breathing the Spirit and thus of being 'Spirator' of the Holy Spirit along with the Father. In the words of one Durandellus, an ardent defender of St Thomas against Durand de Saint-Pourçain in the first decades of the fourteenth century: 'It is *as engendered* that the Son is a "*breather*" or has the *virtue of breathing* the Holy Spirit: this is why the Spirit who is breathed proceeds through the Begotten as such.'[118] To put it another way, the procession of the Holy Spirit is attached, implied, or included in the relation of the Father and Son precisely as Father and Son.[119] The paternity of the Father and the filiation of the Son can thus not be fully conceived without the procession of the Holy Spirit: the begetting of the Son is irremovably connected to the procession of the Holy Spirit, and each of the three persons is present within the others.

7. THE ATTITUDE TO THE EASTERN ORTHODOX

The student of texts relating to the Holy Spirit's procession encounters a number of pejorative expressions which add a negative note to the atmosphere of the discussion and which often present an obstacle to today's reader,

---

[117] *ST* I, q. 43, a. 5, ad 2; I *Sent.* d. 15, q. 4, a. 1, ad 3.

[118] See our article, 'La théologie trinitaire des *Evidentiae contra Durandum* de Durandellus', *RT* 97 (1997), 173–218, esp. 212–214.

[119] Durandellus refines on this: spiration is 'virtually' included in generation, the term 'virtually' designating the power or 'virtue' of breathing the Holy Spirit which the Father communicates to the Son through generation. One can make a conceptual distinction between the *power* and the *act* of breathing the Holy Spirit, but this does not relate to two different realities within God: the power and the act are really identical (Thomas, *ST* I, q. 41, a. 5, ad 2).

to such an extent that their presence seems to be a stumbling-block, and one is tempted to pass over them in silence. But it is necessary to point them out in an up-front way, and to situate them in their historical context. Effectively, for Thomas, the Greeks who explicitly reject the Spirit's procession *a Filio* are not just mistaken; some of their arguments are called 'ridiculous', others are 'frivolous', and others still 'could easily be refuted by a first year theology student'. The Greeks' formulations of their objections are in general assessed very severely.[120] It is true that the level of argumentation opposed to the Latin doctrine was not always very elevated.[121]

Thomas often frankly suspected that the Byzantine theologians' rejection of the procession of the Holy Spirit *a Filio* was based on ignorance or bad faith. He also signals 'another reason'[122] for the denial, of which, sadly, he says nothing (is he hinting that opinions of a theological order are not the basic point at issue?). In order to assess his expressions of incomprehension, one must put them back into their historical context. One finds them in St Thomas' contemporaries, as for instance, in Bonaventure and Albert.[123] Sadly, the tone to the discussion dates from the era of Photius, and the two parties criticized one another for the same things.

It is in the first place necessary to emphasize that these pejorative notes qualify the discussion of the Western Medievals with their Byzantine contemporaries, and never touch their attitude to the Eastern Fathers, for whom Thomas manifests, in theory as in practice, the greatest respect.[124] It is the divergent ways in which the Byzantines and the Latins interpret their patristic heritage which is at issue. In the second place, one must note the fundamentally positive attitude which Thomas takes to the Greeks of his own time on the level of faith:

if we take careful note of the statements of the Greeks we shall find that they differ from us more in words than in meaning.[125]

This is not an isolated remark within Latin medieval theology. Peter Lombard makes the same assessment.[126] One also finds many such testimonies[127] on the Eastern side, notably in the writings of Saint Maximus the Confessor and

---

[120] See for instance *SCG* IV, chs. 24 and 25 (nos. 3605, 3610, 3621, 3622, 3625).

[121] For instance: the Holy Spirit would be the 'grandson' of the Father or else he would proceed from himself, etc.

[122] *De potentia*, q. 10, a. 5.

[123] Bonaventure, I *Sent.* d. 11, a. un., q. 1; Albert, I *Sent.* d. 11, a. 6.

[124] See our brief article, 'St Thomas d'Aquin et l'Orient chrétien', *Nova et Vetera* 74/4 (1999), 19–36.

[125] *De potentia*, q. 10, a. 5: '*magis differunt in verbis quam in sensu*'. The context shows that this refers to contemporary Greeks and not the Fathers of the Church.

[126] Peter Lombard, *Sentences*, Book I, dist. 11, ch. 2 (vol. I/2, p. 116).

[127] See Yves Congar, 'Quatre siècles de désunion et d'affrontement. Comment Grecs et Latins se sont appréciés réciproquement au point de vue ecclésiologique', *Istina* 13 (1968), 131–152.

Theophylactus. St Thomas doubtless recognized that the 'Greeks' have the same faith as the Catholic Church, but expressed in different words and thus giving rise to controversy. He finds the expression of this convergence in faith in respect of the procession of the Holy Spirit in the fact that the Easterners recognize that the Holy Spirit is the 'Spirit of the Son' and in the fact that they accept the formula 'the Holy Spirit proceeds from the Father through the Son': 'one could not say this if the procession of the Spirit were entirely separate from the Son; this shows that the Greeks themselves understand that the procession of the Holy Spirit has some connection with the Son'.[128]

This basic attitude explains why the Greeks are never described as 'heretics' in the texts which we have encountered. One might think this does not amount to much, but this restraint is less banal that it may appear. Amongst the theologians of the thirteenth century, and even the greatest of them, there is no lack of accusations of heresy against the Greeks. Saint Bonaventure, for instance, does not hesitate to rank the Greeks as *haeretici*.[129] With Thomas, the Greeks certainly appear in the lists of those who err on the side of the heresies which his doctrine avoids,[130] but when he deals specifically with the Holy Spirit's procession, he confines himself to describing their view as 'erroneous'.

One must weigh the meaning of these terms. Looking at the question from the point of view of Thomas' understanding of Catholic doctrine, the main heresy at issue is Sabellianism (the real lack of distinction between Son and Holy Spirit) to which the denial of the procession *a Filio* leads; the second issue is subordinationism, the failure to acknowledge the equality of Father and Son.[131] And he evidently knew that the Byzantine Christians were certainly no Arians, and still less Sabellians, but wholly orthodox. This is the basis of his incomprehension, for, if one took it to its conclusion *within the internal 'logic' of the Latin* doctrine, the denial of the procession leads 'necessarily' to Sabellianism: and it is *this* which is heretical.[132] But the Greeks drew no such conclusion! For the Latin theologian which Thomas Aquinas was, the rejection of the Holy Spirit's procession *a Patre* and *a Filio* by orthodox Christians was incomprehensible. The denigratory tones which we have drawn out above communicate precisely this incomprehension.

---

[128] *De potentia*, q. 10, a. 5; cf. *ST* I, q. 36. a. 2.

[129] Bonaventure, I *Sent.* d. 11, a. un., q. 1: 'they have become heretics, because they deny the truth of the faith'; Albert the Great, I *Sent.* d. 11, a. 6. There is nothing parallel to this in Thomas' writings.

[130] Cf. especially *CEG* I and II, prol.

[131] See above, in this chapter, 'The Doctrinal Weight of the Holy Spirit's Procession *a Patre* and *a Filio*'.

[132] *ST* I, q. 36, a. 2.

In conclusion, one can sum up St Thomas' attitude to the medieval East from a doctrinal and historical perspective by noting on the one hand the deep unintelligibility which the negation of the Spirit's procession *a Filio* had in his eyes, within a lack of comprehension which derived from the fundamental structure of Latin and Greek Trinitarian doctrine, and, on the other hand, his conviction of the unity of faith in the Holy Spirit amongst both parties. The historical and doctrinal understanding which we now have permits us to grasp the internal form of the Orthodox tradition better. Thomas Aquinas' role is to show us the internal form of the Catholic tradition. The path to an authentic ecumenical agreement can hardly lie in a higher synthesis of the two traditions, but, rather in the deepening of the convergence noted by witnesses to both traditions: using different words, and within a doctrine whose theoretical principles differ, how can West and East articulate the same faith?

12

The Reciprocal Interiority
of the Divine Persons

In his presentation of Father, Son, and Holy Spirit, Thomas considered each person for themselves, within their own distinctive properties. The expository order of Trinitarian faith exacts this approach: in order to disclose the Trinity one must pick out what distinct feature characterizes each person as to his own incommunicable property. But a procedure which pictures the divine persons one after another does not constitute the last word in Trinitarian theology, because the divine persons exist and act inseparably, in reciprocated communion. This is why the treatise in the *Summa* comes to rest in a comparison of the divine persons (qq. 42–43). Its teaching about this re-engages the expositions given in the earlier studies of the processions, the relations and the persons, but this time takes them under the aspect of reciprocal communion, which is at the heart both of the eternal Trinity and of the working of grace for human beings, as central to the equality of the persons as it is to the persons' missions.

We have already had many occasions to draw attention to the equality of the persons. One element of this discussion still merits especial attention: the reciprocal presence of the divine persons (q. 42, a. 5). This question gives us a real synthesis of the whole of Trinitarian doctrine, touching on both the eternal immanence of the persons and their activities in the economy. All of the features of Trinitarian theology return to us here, brought together under the sign of the unmixed distinction and unconfused unity of the Trinity.

1. THE PATRISTIC LEGACY

The Father, the Son, and the Holy Spirit are 'within one another', and indivisibly so. This reciprocal immanence is given a high profile in the doctrinal formulations of numerous patristic authors. It finds its most eloquent expression in St John's Gospel: *Do you not believe that I am in the Father and the Father in me? . . . The Father who abides in me, he does the works. Believe me, I am in the*

Father and the Father in me (Jn 14.10–11; cf. also Jn 10.38).[1] The development
of Trinitarian doctrine led to extending what Christ says about himself and
the Father in the Fourth Gospel to the Holy Spirit. Like all his contemporaries,
St Thomas benefited from Peter Lombard having put together a sampler of the
Patristics. Lombard had threaded the diverse testimonies of the Latin Fathers
around the spool of the equality of the divine persons. Thomas' *Summa* and
his Commentary on the *Sentences* draws them out in the same context. The
three most prominent writers are Hilary of Poitiers, the *Ambrosiaster*, and
St Fulgentius. These three, whose first concern is the unambiguous disclosure
of the orthodox faith as against Arianism and Sabellianism, emphasized
the communal presence of the persons in the aspect of their *unity of nature*,
that is to say, of their consubstantiality. Thus, for example, Ambrosiaster
explains:

The Father is in the Son and the Son is in the Father, because their substance is one:
there is unity here where there is no diversity.[2]

As we will see again later on, Thomas refers more often to St Hilary of Poitiers.
He calls on many of Hilary's texts known to him not only because of Peter
Lombard's databank, but also through his own research (the *Catena* on John
is a good resource for this). Here is a particular example of his selection:

The immutable God, so to speak, followed his nature in begetting an immutable God.
It is thus...the subsistent nature of God that we recognize in this....for God is in
God.[3]

The Latin Fathers give evidence of grasping the communal presence of the
divine persons as being founded on their consubstantiality: 'Following the
three doctors invoked in the text of the *Sentences*, that is, Augustine, Hilary
and Ambrose', the Father is in the Son and vice-versa 'because of the unity of
nature, for the nature of the Father is in the Son, and the Father does not leave
go of his own nature: where his nature is, there the Father himself is'.[4] This
line of explanation, typical of fourth-century anti-Arian Trinitarian theology,
is not exclusive to the Westerners: one also finds it in the Greek Fathers.

---

[1] Thomas often finds the occasion to accentuate the mutual presence of the persons in his
Commentary on the Fourth Gospel: John 1.18; 10.38; 14.10–11; 14.20; 16.28; 17.21.

[2] Ambrosiaster, *2 Cor. 5.19*, cited by Peter Lombard, *Sentences*, Book I, dist. 19, ch. 4 (vol. I/2, p. 163).

[3] Hilary of Poitiers, *De Trinitate* V.37. Thomas cites this passage in the *Catena on John* (ed.
Guarienti, p. 518) and in the *Summa Theologiae* (*ST* I, q. 42, a. 5). See also Hilary, *De Trinitate*
III. 1–4 (SC 443, pp. 336–343; *De Trinitate* VII.39 (SC 488, pp. 362–367).

[4] Thomas, I *Sent.* d. 19, q. 3, a. 2. Like Peter Lombard, Thomas conflates St Ambrose with the
Ambrosiaster, and attributes to Augustine a work which really belongs to Fulgentius of Ruspe;
cf. Peter Lombard, *Sentences*, Book I, dist. 19, ch. 4 (vol. I/2, pp. 161–163).

St Thomas can call on the exegesis of St John Chrysostom which, in this context, equally accentuates the consubstantiality of Father and Son.[5]

In its extension of this first line of enquiry which draws on the substantial unity of the divine persons to account for their communal presence, the theological tradition developed the more capacious notion of *perichoresis* which could also integrate other aspects of the Trinitarian mystery. The word *perichoresis*, which can be translated as interpenetration, makes its first appearance in Christology, becoming clearly observable in the seventh-century writings of Maximus the Confessor (following St Gregory Nazianzus, who had earlier employed the verb *perichorein* in a Christological sense), where it is used to mean that, in Christ, the human nature is united and bonded to the divine nature within a reciprocal communication: there is a 'perichoresis' of the two natures in Christ.[6] Such perichoresis represents a reciprocation of activities, the interaction of the divine and human natures in Christ: the two natures are united, without confusion, in a reciprocal exchange. Within Christology, it is a consequence of the Council of Chalcedon's affirmation of the hypostatic union: the two natures of Christ are neither separated nor detached from one another, but united in a reciprocity.

In its second innings, this Christological terminology will be extended to Trinitarian theory by St John Damascene.[7] The Trinitarian notion of perichoresis makes its appearance within the history of theology after the doctrine of the Trinity has come to full maturity. When it functions within Trinitarian theology, perichoresis means the communal immanence, or the reciprocated interiority of the three persons. Through a kind of reciprocal compenetration, each person is contained in the other. As John Damascene puts it,

> We do not say that there are three gods, the Father, the Son and the Holy Spirit, but one God . . . They are united but not confused, and they are in one another, and this perichorĕsis (*perichôrêsis*), each in the others, is without fusion or mixture.[8]

Perichoresis is an expression of the unconfused unity of the three persons: it excludes Arianism or tritheism, since each person is contained in the others, and it excludes Sabellianism, since the three persons remain distinct within

---

[5] See *Catena in Ioan.* 14.9 (ed. Guarienti, p. 518). This explanation of the reciprocal immanence of the persons through their identical divine substance will be repeated at the Council of Florence in 1442 (*Bull of Union with the Copts*, cf. Denzinger, nos. 1330–1331).

[6] See Maximus the Confessor, *Opuscula theologica* XVI and *Ambigua* 112 b.

[7] For a sketch of the history of this, see P. Stemmer, 'Perichorese. Zur Geschichte eines Begriffs', *Archiv für Begriffsgeschichte* 27 (1983) [1985], 9–55.

[8] John Damascene, *The Orthodox Faith* I. 8. Cf. *The Orthodox Faith* I. 14: 'The hypostases remain and are each in the others, for they are inseparably and indivisibly one in the others by their perichoresis (*perichôrêsis*), one in the others without confusion, nor in fusion or mixture but by the fact of one being conveyed into the others.'

their reciprocal immanence. When, in the twelfth century, St John Damascene was translated into Latin by Burgundio of Pisa, the latter translated the Greek word *perichoresis* by the Latin terms *circumincessio* and *circuitio* ('circulation').[9] In his Commentary on the *Sentences*, written before Thomas', St Bonaventure is already fluent in this use of the word *circumincessio*: 'There is in God a sovereign and perfect circumincession. One speaks of "circumincession" to say that one is in the other, and vice-versa.'[10] Other writers will select the Latin term *circuminsessio* ('circuminsession'). St Thomas himself uses neither of these Latin words, but he draws on the biblical expression 'being in' (cf. Jn 14.10–11): each person 'is in' the other (*esse in*).

From John Damascene, Thomas especially appropriates the theme of *relation*: the divine persons are each 'in one another' not only because of their common nature, but also *by reason of their communal relations*.[11] It was very probably Albert the Great who drew his attention to this perspective.[12] There is more to it than meets the eye. In dealing with the 'circumincession' of the divine persons, Bonaventure had explained it without direct reference to the role of relations. But St Bonaventure very clearly emphasizes the personal distinction which the idea of perichoresis implies: 'Since sovereign unity and distinction lie in God alone, in such a way that the distinction is unconfused and the unity without distinction, it is therefore in God alone that there is a perfect circumincession. The notion of circumincession effectively means a perfect unity of essence within the distinction of persons.'[13] St Thomas benefits from the contributions of his forerunners: he follows Albert very closely in his observations on the relations, and he keeps close to Bonaventure in finding the expression of their unity and plurality in the reciprocated presence of the persons; he synthesizes these two elements into a Trinitarian doctrine.

---

[9] *De Fide orthodoxa*, Versions of Burgundio and Cerbanus, ed. E. M. Buytaert, New York and Louvain, 1955, pp. 45 and 64.

[10] Bonaventure, I *Sent.* d. 19, p. 1, a. un., q. 4. But in his Commentary on John 14, Bonaventure does not employ the term 'circumincession': he observes the unity of substance or essence of the persons, and thus their unity of operation (cf. *Opera omnia*, vol. 6, pp. 438–439).

[11] Thomas, I *Sent.* d. 19, q. 3, a. 2: 'According to Damascene, in the third book of *The Orthodox Faith*, [the mutual presence of the Father in the Son] is to be understood through the notion of relation, in so far as a correlate is grasped in the other.'

[12] Albert, I *Sent.* d. 19, a. 8, arg. 4 and ad 4.

[13] Bonaventure, I *Sent.* d. 19, p. 1, a. un., q. 4. As with Albert and Thomas, the context is the equality of the persons.

2. A SYNTHESIS OF TRINITARIAN DOCTRINE

The communal 'in-being' of the persons creates the opportunity to gather the diverse aspects of the Trinitarian mystery into a single portrait: the substantial unity of the persons, the relations, the processions of Son and Holy Spirit, their unity of action and their shared presence within the grace given to human beings. As we have seen, St Thomas employs neither the word 'perichoresis', nor the word 'circumincession', nor the term 'circuminsession'. In presenting the 'in being' of the persons, he uses, rather, the expressions *union* or *intrinsic conjunction, interiority,*[14] *intimacy,*[15] *existing in,*[16] *being in that which is the most intimate and most secret* (this is how the Son is in the Father),[17] *reciprocal communality of 'in being',*[18] *communal union,*[19] etc. In every case, the communal presence of the persons excludes their confusion, because it is based in their real distinction.[20] It rules out the 'isolation' of one person, since it implies a communal relationship of persons.[21] The divine persons are not 'solitaries':[22] they are 'inseparables'.[23]

In making this exposition, Thomas' Commentary on the *Sentences* suggests a two-way explanation: unity of essence and of relations.[24] Taking the reflection further in the *Summa Theologiae*, he no longer sees just two, but three aspects in which each of the persons is within the others: unity of essence, relation and origin (procession). He first of all considers the Father and the Son, on the basis of the text of the Fourth Gospel (Jn 14.10),[25] so as to give them an immediate link to the Holy Spirit:

In the Father and in the Son, there are three perspectives to consider: that is, essence, and relation and origin. These three angles are the reason that the Father and the Son reciprocate their being. . . . And the same applies to the Holy Spirit.[26]

---

[14] *In Ioan.* 1.1 (no. 45): 'conjunctio intrinseca', 'intrinsecum'.

[15] Cf. *SCG* IV, ch. 11 (no. 3461): 'intimum'.

[16] *In Ioan.* 1.1 (no. 32): 'existentia Filii in Patre'.

[17] *In Ioan.* 1.18 (no. 218).

[18] *Super Dion. de div. nom.* II, lect. 2 (no. 155): 'Mutuo enim Pater est in Filio et Filius in Patre.'

[19] *Super Dion. de div. nom.* II, lect. 2 (no. 148): 'unitio ad invicem'.

[20] Cf. *In Ioan.* 14.10 (no. 1895).

[21] Cf. *Catena in Ioan.* 14.9–11 (ed. Guarienti, pp. 518 and 519). St Thomas goes with Hilary of Poitiers in emphasizing this aspect in particular: see above, in Chapter 7, 'The Theological Terminology of Plurality'.

[22] *ST* I, q. 31, a. 2; cf. a. 4.

[23] *In Ioan.* 8.29 (no. 1192).

[24] I *Sent.* d. 19, q. 3, a. 2; cf. I *Sent.* d. 21, q. 1, a. 2, ad 4.

[25] *ST* I, q. 42, a. 5, sed contra: 'It is said in Jn 14.10: *I am in the Father and the Father is in me.*'

[26] *ST* I, q. 42, a. 5.

(a) The Essential Unity of the Three Persons: Consubstantiality

Like nearly all of the scholastic writers, St Thomas foregrounds God's unity of
nature. As we mentioned a moment ago, this is how the Fathers contextualize
the issue. His explanation is particularly close to that of Hilary of Poitiers:

> As to essence, the Father is in the Son because the Father is his essence and he shares it
> with the Son without any change taking place in himself; therefore because the
> Father's essence is in the Son, it follows that the Father is in the Son. Equally, the
> Son being his own essence, it follows that he is in the Father, in whom the same
> essence is present. This is Hilary's teaching . . . [27]

This discussion accentuates the real identity of a divine person with the
divine nature: it is not enough to say that a divine person 'has the divine
nature'; one must say rather that the 'divine person is his nature'. God is in
reality exempt from the composition of subject and essence which is of the
character of creaturehood (for instance, a human individual is not humanity,
but the Father is the divine nature, just as the Son and the Holy Spirit are the
divine nature). God is perfectly simple.[28] And so, wherever the Father's nature
is, the Father's person is, and the same goes for the Son and the Holy Spirit.
This is the basis for Thomas' treatment of the divine processions: the Father
does not communicate in his begetting part of his divine nature to the Son,
but the fullness of the divine nature; thus, 'the nature of the Father is in the
Son, and conversely, the Father is in the Son and reciprocally'.[29] It works in the
same way for the spiration of the Holy Spirit: here too, the Father and the Son
communicate the divine nature in its fullness. The communal presence of the
divine persons is thus a presence in complete *equality*. Because of their
consubstantiality, the persons are '*intrinsically at one*'.[30] Hilary received such
careful attention from Thomas because of his having focused this real identity
of person and nature: 'Hilary explains it well.'[31]

The communal presence of the persons thus rests on their *consubstantiality*.
For what is implicated in this is that the three divine persons do not just have
a similar nature, but the very same nature, identically one, that is to say
numerically one.[32] The reason why the persons are each mutually within the
others is that 'the fullness of divinity' dwells in each one.[33] Insisting on this

---

[27] *ST* I, q. 42, a. 5. The text from Hilary is the same one we quoted above (*De Trinitate* V.37).
[28] *ST* I, q. 39, a. 1; cf. q. 3, a. 3; see above, in Chapter 7, 'The Consubstantiality of the Persons'.
[29] *In Ioan.* 10.38 (no. 1466); 14.10 (no. 1891); *SCG* IV, ch. 9 (no. 3445).
[30] *In Ioan.* 1.1 (no. 45).
[31] *In Ioan.* 10.38 (no. 1466); cf. *ST* I, q. 42, a. 5.
[32] *In Ioan.* 14.9 (no. 1887).
[33] I *Sent.* d. 19, exp. text.

was not idiosyncratic to St Hilary and St Thomas: one can easily find it in connection not only with the great scholastic writers (especially Albert and Bonaventure), but also in many of the Fathers, as much in the West (as with Augustine) as in the East (the outstanding examples are Athanasius, Cyril of Alexandria, and John Damascene). What this shows us is that, the genuine idea of perichoresis is no substitute for that of the unity in nature. Perichoresis is a richer concept than unity of nature, but one cannot replace the idea of consubstantiality with that of perichoresis, because unity of nature is included within the concept of perichoresis.

(b) Relations

But the communal presence of the three persons has more to it than their essential unity. St Thomas also conducts an investigation into the role played here by the *relations*. This is an original feature, which was probably suggested to him by Albert's exegesis of John Damascene: 'Likewise as to the relations, it is clear that each of the relative opposites is in the notion of the other.'[34] We come back to the notion of relation itself: in its own formal notion, relation consists in a relationship to another. Relatives (words or things which are relative) are defined like this: 'in their own proper meaning' they 'signify only what refers to another (*ad aliud*)', that whose being consists in 'relating to another thing.'[35] As a correlative term, this 'other' enters into the very definition of a relative being, since it is implied by the very nature of a relative reality as such, because 'one of the relatives is included in the other.'[36] This is why 'one person is in the notion of another; as the Father is in the notion of the Son, and reciprocally.'[37] It is not just that a relative reality cannot be *thought* without its correlative. It cannot *exist* as such without it: 'a relative cannot be without its correlate.'[38] For this reason, correlatives are essentially simultaneous:[39] the Father has no other existence than in his relation to the Son.

The persons are not just *characterized* by means of a relative property, they *are* a relation which subsists, a 'subsistent relation'.[40] For this reason, reciprocal interiority is really only carried off by *divine* persons. Each person is

---

[34] *ST* I, q. 42, a. 5.
[35] *ST* I, q. 28, a. 1; a. 2, arg. 3.   [36] I *Sent.* d. 19, q. 3, a. 2, sed contra 2.
[37] *ST* I, q. 31, a. 4, arg. 3.   [38] *De potentia*, q. 8, a. 1, arg. 10.
[39] *ST* I, q. 40, a. 2, ad 4. The simultaneity of the correlates is not just logical but 'factually' real. It is a simultaneity of nature (cf. I *Sent.* d. 9, q. 2, a. 1). St Thomas pinpoints it like this: 'In God, it is from the same reality that the Father has it to be someone and to be the Father: this is why he exists with the Son in a simultaneity of nature, not only insofar as he is Father, but absolutely' (ibid., ad 3).
[40] See above, in Chapter 6, 'Subsistent Relations'.

within the others in virtue of the relation constituting him as a person. So this presence within the other is not a secondary feature of the person, but belongs to the very nature of Trinitarian 'personality':

In God, the Son is also properly in the Father from the perspective of *relation*—and that in a more fitting way than amongst human fathers and sons—because it is by his relation that the Son is a subsisting person: his relation is his personality.[41]

The communal interiority of the persons is also *reciprocal*. It is not inter-changeable or identical in the three persons. This is the important edge which the idea of relation brings to that of perichoresis. The Father's relation is actually not that of the Son or of the Holy Spirit. Saint Bonaventure had hit on this problem: if the Father is in the Son, and the Son is in the Father, is the personal relationship intended by this 'in being' identical for each of the three persons or is it different in each of them? It is identical, replied the Franciscan Master: it is not a matter of distinct relationships, but of the same relation-ship, 'since it concerns a relation of identity or consubstantiality'.[42] But with his idea of relation to hand, Saint Albert came back with a different response: 'On the side of relationship as relation, the Father is not in the Son in the same way that the Son is in the Father, and this works just the same for the Holy Spirit.'[43] Thomas goes with his own Master, Albert: the Son is in the Father precisely in that he relates himself to the Father as his Son, whereas the Father is in the Son in that he is his Father. Paternity and filiation thus entail two distinct modes of reciprocal presence:

From the perspective of relation, the mode [of the presence of the Father in the Son and of the Son in the Father] is crosswise, consequent on the different relationships of the Father to the Son, and the Son to the Father.[44]

This observation is particularly evocative for the way one understands Trinitarian *reciprocity*. From the perspective of unity of nature, the Father is in the Son and the Son in the Father in the same way; that is to say, through an identity of nature. But nonetheless, from the perspective of the relations, the communal presence of the persons divulges the *proper mode* of the relation. These modes are not interchangeable, but distinct within their reciprocity. When Thomas envisages the persons' interiority under the third perspective,

---

[41] I *Sent.* d. 19, q. 3, a. 2, ad 1.

[42] Bonaventure, I *Sent.* d. 19, p. 1, a. un., q. 4, ad 5; this explanation keeps to the level of unity of nature.

[43] Albert, I *Sent.* d. 19, a. 8; cf. also Albert, *In Ioan.* d. 14 (ed. Borgnet, vol. 24, pp. 534–535). The nature of the Father and the Son is one and the same, but each has it in a *distinct mode*; the Son has the divine nature as received from the Father, whereas the Father has it as communi-cating it. These distinct modalities are precisely the relations which characterize each person.

[44] Thomas, I *Sent.* d. 19, q. 3, a. 2, ad 3; cf. ad 1.

of origin, he will follow the same track: the Father is in the Son as the Son's principle, the Son is in the Father in that he is begotten by the Father. The idea of the Holy Spirit as communal Love or Bond of communion between Father and Son has already brought this out: 'As Love, the Holy Spirit implies a relationship of the Father to the Son, that of the lover to the beloved, and that this is reciprocated.'[45] So the relations are not tethered to 'distinguishing' the persons through the 'oppositions' which they entail, but are also, by their very nature, the reason for the *unity* of the persons they distinguish.[46] Relation is the foundation of Trinitarian communion.

(c) Procession

Finally, perichoresis draws its light from origin, that is, from the way it orients us to the interiority of the spiritual processions. From the first question in the treatise onwards, the idea of origin laid the foundations for its theoretical Trinitarian doctrine. It also illuminates the persons' communal interiority. Thomas writes that,

As to origin it is evident that the procession of the intelligible Word is not something 'outside', but dwells within the One who utters the Word. And that which is expressed in the Word is contained in it. And the same reasoning goes for the Holy Spirit.[47]

The processions of the persons are 'immanent' (they *dwell* in God himself) or 'interior' (*ad intra*).[48] It was because of this immanence that, at the outset of his treatise, Thomas held onto the analogies of the processions of word and love as the means by which a spiritual being is present to itself, 'as the known is in the knower' and 'as the beloved is in the lover'. This immanence, which is accentuated from the study of the processions on, implies that the person who proceeds is *interior to* the principle from which he issues. In an analogous way to that in which our mental word dwells in our conceiving mind, so the divine Word dwells in the begetting Father, he is intimate and interior to the Father. The Word 'comes out' of the Father by remaining entirely 'within him'.[49] And analogously to the way that the impression of love rises at the centre of the loving will, so the Holy Spirit is interior to Father and Son.[50] The Holy Spirit

---

[45] *ST* I, q. 37, a. 1, ad 3. See especially F. Bourassa, 'L'Esprit Saint "Communion" du Père et du Fils (II)', *SE* 30 (1978), 5–37.

[46] *ST* I, q. 42, a. 5, ad 3; cf. I *Sent.* d. 21, q. 1, a. 2, ad 4. Thomas notes here the dual function of relation: the distinction and the communal interiority of the persons.

[47] *ST* I, q. 42, a. 5.

[48] Cf. *ST* I, q. 27, a. 1, ad 2.

[49] Cf. *ST* I, q. 42, a. 5, ad 2.

[50] *ST* I, q. 27, a. 1 and a. 3. See above, Chapter 4.

does not proceed 'outside' of the Father and Son, but dwells within the Father and the Son from whom he proceeds.[51]

As with relation itself, the communal interiority as from origin involves each person being present to the others in a distinct mode. Applying this to the Father and Son, Thomas explains that, 'The Son is in the Father as the one who comes forth is in the originating principle, and the Father is in the Son as the originating principle is in the one who takes his origin from him.'[52] Thus, the very nature of the Trinitarian processions can show the reciprocal interiority of the persons. The processions do not just give us the basis for understanding the real relations making the persons distinct, but also ground the communion of the persons.

The Commentary on John 16.26 (*I came forth from the Father and am come into the world: again I leave the world and I go to the Father*) gives an outstanding exposition of this. In the course of showing that the Son who 'comes forth' from the Father still dwells in the Father, Thomas explains that the Father and Son do not make their common immanence in autonomy from this 'coming out', or in despite of it, but make the space for it within the 'coming out' of generation itself. Thomas states that,

> In material things, what comes forth from another is no longer in it, since it comes from it by a separation from it in essence or in space. But in God, coming forth does not arise in this way. The Son came forth eternally from the Father in such a way that the Son is still in the Father from all eternity. And so, when he is in the Father, he comes forth. And when he comes forth, he is in him, in such a way that he is always coming forth, and always in him.[53]

Thus, the explanation of the communal presence of the divine persons rests on the central pillars of Trinitarian doctrine: procession, relation (especially the idea of subsistent relation), and the persons' unity of nature. We find here as before the characteristic features of his Trinitarian doctrine, bringing into view the weight which the patristic sources carry (very much present on the subject of the unity of nature, as the John Commentary makes very clear), and, in particular, the attention devoted to heresies. The study of the aim of speculative Trinitarian theology alerted us to the role of heresies, and how this links up with the patristic sources, and we see it again in the investigations of

[51] Cf. *ST* I, q. 37, a. 1, ad 2.

[52] I *Sent.* d. 19, q. 3, a. 2, ad 1. Thomas is focusing on relation here, but the language he uses indicates clearly that this reciprocity applies to *origin* (i.e. procession) as such.

[53] *In Ioan.* 16.28 (no. 2161). For Thomas, the first part of this verse from John (*I came forth from the Father*) relates to the eternal generation of the Son, and the second part (*and am come into the world*) relates to his 'temporal procession': that is to say his 'mission' which includes his eternal generation (see below, in Chapter 15, 'The Theory of Mission').

the processions, the relations, the persons, and so on. The theory of the communal presence of the persons is no exception to the rule.

The confrontation with Sabellianism and Arianism leads us to the nub of the exegetical problem of the divine persons' communal 'in-being'. Through their reading of Hilary and Augustine, the medievals knew that the verse in John 14.10 had been used on behalf not only of Sabellianism but also of Arianism. Modalist exegesis invoked the common presence of Father and Son (*I am in the Father and the Father in me*) in order solely to acknowledge one single person as real, whereas the Arians found it to be an expression of the inferiority of the Son (*The words that I speak to you, I speak not of myself*). Sabellianism and Arianism turned to John 14.10 to shore up their opinions; or, more than that, the verse was one of the occasions for their errors.[54]

Thomas' own exegesis explains how the teaching of Christ in John's Gospel is far from Sabellianism or subordinationism. One index of this is that, if one puts the two heresies alongside each other, then, given their contradictory aims, they can be seen to rule each other out.[55] As against Arianism, the presence of the Father in the Son displays the *unity* of Father and Son. As against Sabellianism, it also shows the *distinction* of Father from Son.[56] The communal presence of the persons 'exhibits the Trinitarian faith',[57] since this theme indicates the unity of the persons (their 'in-being') as well as their distinction (it is from within their real distinctness from each other that the persons are in one another). And in this way, the reciprocal interiority of the persons contains and recapitulates the orthodox Trinitarian faith.

3. THEOLOGY AND ECONOMY

Perichoresis does not just shed light on the being and the relations of the Trinity in itself, but also on the Trinity's action within this world. Thomas makes an effectual bond between the communal 'in-being' of the divine persons and the common action of the Trinity, and thus shows that the persons are inseparably present in the gift which they make of themselves.

---

[54] *In Ioan.* 14.10 (no. 1895); cf. 14.9 (nos. 1887–1888); *SCG* IV, ch. 5 (no. 3376) and ch. 9 (no. 3445).

[55] *In Ioan.* 14.10 (no. 1895). St Thomas takes over this principle from the Fathers, particularly Hilary (*De Trinitate* I.26 and VII.7; SC 443, pp. 248–251, and SC 448, pp. 290–291). The heresies themselves contain an index of the truth out of the fact that they do not just oppose truth but one another (*SCG* IV, ch. 7, no. 3426). This is why knowledge of the heresies comes into the exploration of truth.

[56] *In Ioan.* 14.9–10 (nos. 1887–1888, 1895); cf. *In Ioan.* 8.16 (no. 1154).

[57] *In Ioan.* 14.11 (no. 1896).

For, in the first place, the communal 'in-being' of the persons implies that they act in common. In the same way that the persons *exist* indivisibly, so they *act* undividedly. We have seen St Thomas saying this from the outset of our presentation of the Trinitarian mystery: the works manifest the nature of the one who acts. By carrying out the Father's own works, Christ shows himself to be of the same nature as the Father, since 'the clearest indication of the nature of a thing is taken from its works'. Thus, the divine activities of the Son induce one to recognize that unity of nature through which he is in the Father, and conversely.[58] The Son's action is not 'diverse' or different from the Father's, but rather the persons act within one single operation.[59] The Father who acts is in the Son and Holy Spirit, the acting Son is in the Father and the Holy Spirit, the Spirit who acts is in the Father and in the Son. The undivided operation of the three persons thus constitutes one aspect of their communal 'in-being'. St Thomas found this teaching through his reading of the Patristics,[60] and, closer to home, Bonaventure had also underlined it.[61]

The idea of perichoresis extends to the economy of grace. The gift of the Holy Spirit creates the living presence of the Son in believers.[62] Because of the internal communality of the persons, believers are united to the Father, by the gift of the Holy Spirit and through the presence of the Son. Thomas writes that,

Just as the Son acts because the Father dwells in him by a unity of nature, so also believers act through Christ dwelling in them by faith, as it says in Ephesians, *that Christ may dwell in your hearts through faith* (Eph. 3.17).[63]

Looking at things from the perspective of action takes us to what is known as 'divinization'. This is the idea of the 'marvellous exchange' between the Trinity and human beings in the person of the Word incarnate. The Father's action is no different from that of the Son: each indwells the actions of the other. In an analogous way, the action of believers is propelled by the power of Christ living in them. The communal presence of Father and Son rests on the divine *nature* which the Son eternally receives from the Father in his begetting, whereas, the presence of the incarnate Son in believers comes from the *faith* which enables believers to participate in Christ's divine sonship, by becoming children of God. Thus it is Christ's own power which achieves the works of the faithful. The communal presence of the divine persons is in some sense

[58] *In Ioan.* 10.38 (nos. 1465–1466).
[59] *In Ioan.* 5.19 (no. 752); cf. 14.10 (no. 1893).
[60] See the extracts from Hilary and Augustine in the *Catena* on John 14.10–11 (ed. Marietti, p. 519). The 'inseparable' action of the persons is directly connected here with their communal 'in-being'.
[61] Bonaventure, *In Ioan.* 14.10, no. 11 (*Opera Omnia*, vol. 6, p. 438).
[62] Cf. *SCG* IV, ch. 21 (no. 3576); through the Holy Spirit, Father and Son come 'to dwell' in us.
[63] *In Ioan.* 14.12 (no. 1898).

extended into their communal action on our behalf. St Thomas has a parallel explanation for this which refers to the action of the Son and the Holy Spirit: 'We have access to the Father through Christ, because Christ works through the Holy Spirit. . . . And this is why everything which the Holy Spirit brings to pass is also brought about by Christ.'[64] We have access to the Son in the Holy Spirit, and, we have access to the Father through faith in the Son. The inseparable action of the divine persons is one of the foundations of this doctrine.

Whilst working inseparably in the economy, the three divine persons are also thus inseparably *present*. At its most basic, this presence touches on the mysteries of the Son of God in his flesh: because of the divine consubstantiality and the Trinitarian relations, the whole Trinity makes itself present to human beings in Christ, the Son incarnate. This presence comes about likewise in grace, when the Son and the Holy Spirit are sent to the spirit of the saints (the 'missions' of the divine persons). The Father is not 'sent', since he cannot be from a principle: he is the sender. But, the Father comes to dwell in the hearts of the saints, along with the Son and the Spirit whom he sends. Thomas explains this in connection with the 'invisible mission' of the Son, that is, the sending of the Son in grace, his coming to build his home in the hearts of those who receive him. St Thomas writes,

The Father is in the Son, the Son is in the Father, and both are in the Holy Spirit. For this reason, when the Son is sent, the Father and the Holy Spirit come simultaneously. This takes place in the Son's advent in the flesh, as he says himself in John 8.16: *I am not alone, but I and the Father that sent me.* This is also so for his spiritual coming [to the saints], as he also says himself in John 14.23: *We will come to him and we will make our home in him.* This is why the advent and the indwelling are configured to the whole Trinity.[65]

Perichoresis makes it that the coming of the Son in the economy of salvation is not only a presence of the Son, but of the whole Trinity. This is also why the Incarnation and the mysteries of the life of Christ are a *revelation of the Trinity*. And, in the gift of grace, the perichoresis of the divine persons is extended even to us. When the Holy Spirit is given with the charity which he spreads,[66] when the Son comes to live in human beings as living faith, it is the whole Trinity which makes itself indivisibly present, as much in virtue of the common essence of the persons as of their relations. Thomas observed this in the course of presenting the foundations of ecclesial unity. The unity of believers in the Church is a participation in the unity of Father and Son: by

---

[64] *In Eph.* 2.18 (no. 121).   [65] I *Sent.* d. 15, q. 2, ad 4.

[66] Cf. *SCG* IV, ch. 21 (no. 3576). This is why the Father and Son also come to live in the human beings to whom the Holy Spirit is given.

their unity of nature, but also by the unity of Love which the Holy Spirit is, their mutual Bond.[67] Thus, the internal reciprocity of the divine persons constitutes an axis of the Trinitarian mystery. Their communal immanence, explained by the pillars of Trinitarian doctrine—the theories of the processions, relations, and nature—illuminates the inseparable unity of their action and their presence in the economy.

[67] *In Ioan.* 17.11 (no. 2214); cf. 17.21 (no. 2240).

13

Appropriation

Once having set out the essential attributes and discussed the properties of the persons, St Thomas investigates appropriation. Appropriation is the name for the theological procedure in which a feature belonging to the nature of God, common to all three persons, is specially ascribed to one of the divine persons. This process aligns the persons' properties with their essential attributes.

We have to start by keeping in mind that the enquiry into the person as 'subsistent relation' has already reconnected the persons in their distinctness with their unitary nature. That allowed us to present a Trinitarian monotheism which respects both the persons' plurality and their consubstantiality: since each person is the divine essence, the three distinct persons are one single God. This identity of person and nature is frequently emphasized in the investigation of the notion of person (q. 29). The treatise in the *Summa* takes this over in its comparison between what it means for Father, Son, and Holy Spirit to be the divine *persons* they are, and what it means for each of them to be *divine* (q. 39). We have already pointed out many aspects of this: the identity of nature and person, the consubstantiality of the three persons who are 'of one single essence', the name 'God' being applied to the Trinity and to each person, and so forth.[1] Appropriation is assigned to the same framework and it is by means of this idea that the Trinitarian treatise rounds off its investigation of the 'persons in relation to the essence'.[2]

The significance of this context is twofold. In the first place, the reservations which are often expressed today about the doctrine of appropriations are narrowly focused on the context of God's relationships with this world. But scholastic theology—and St Thomas is no exception to this rule—does not restrict appropriation to the Trinitarian works of creation and salvation. The setting for appropriation is much wider. Most of the appropriations it discusses do not belong to the divine action within this world but to the Trinity in itself. Secondly, theologians often suspect the idea of appropriation of harbouring a confusion between personal properties and essential attributes;

---

[1] On these different aspects of question 39 in the *Prima Pars*, see above, Chapter 7.
[2] *ST* I, q. 39, prol.

the smokescreen of appropriation would then conceal an 'objectless verbal trick'.[3] But, its very definition entails that appropriation is based in a very clear distinction between personal properties and essential attributes. This is the reason why, using the earlier discussion of the distinction of the two orders as a springboard, appropriation comes in once the Trinitarian treatise has reached an advanced stage, during the reflection which looks into the relationships of the persons with the nature. Its definition also gives it an orientation toward language. The mature doctrine of appropriations aims at taking account of a certain way of speaking which is found in Scripture and Tradition, in order to show what function or value to ascribe to it in connection with how we think about the divine persons. The appropriations figure within that very careful attention to the *words* of Scripture, the *words* of tradition, which characterizes scholastic method.[4]

In order to assess the value of the idea of appropriation and to see its self-imposed limitations, one has to situate it within the movement in which it slowly came to maturity, and in its context in theological doctrines. As against a widespread prejudice, one will then perceive that the idea of appropriation is neither facile nor superficial. It calls for a serious and deep reflection on the theology of the Trinity.

1. THE ORIGINS OF THE IDEA OF APPROPRIATION

Patristic tradition was aware of a number of triads of attributes linked to the three divine persons. We will come back to the way St Augustine often worked from such triplicate attributions. But the origin of the theory of appropriations is more directly bound to one specific triad: *power, wisdom,* and *goodness* (or benevolence). In and of itself, this does not spontaneously convey the central meaning of appropriation, but it was what made theologians pursue the enquiry further. It was Abelard who made this triad famous, but it appears to have been Hugh of Saint Victor's *De tribus diebus* to which we owe the linking of the triadic formula *power, wisdom,* and *goodness* to the

---

[3] See for instance B. Sesboüé, 'Appropriations', in *Dictionnaire critique de théologie*, ed. J.-Y. Lacoste, Paris, 1998, p. 80.
[4] One can see this in a very indicative way in the *Summa* ascribed to Alexander of Hales: the investigation of the essential attributes and the divine persons (which can deal with 'absolute' personal terms: *hypostasis, persons,* or with terms which distinctly designate each person: *Father, Son, Image, Word, Holy Spirit, Gift*) constitutes a chapter within the study of the 'divine names'. Appropriation is no exception to this: 'the appropriated personal names' (Book I, ed. Quaracchi, vol. 1, nos. 448–461, pp. 640–647).

Father, Son, and Holy Spirit. Hugh of Saint Victor knew this triad of divine attributes from his patristic sources, and he applied it to his own Trinitarian reflections with finesse and nuance. Hugh made a light and sparing use of it. When Peter Abelard took this triadic formula over from Hugh, it took on a primary role, and this primary function was something out of the ordinary.[5]

Reacting against what he perceived as Roscelin's leaning to tritheism, Abelard wanted to make a defence of traditional Trinitarian teaching against the way the new 'dialecticians' were talking. This is what Abelard's *Theology of the Sovereign Good* sets out to do, as do its revised editions (the *Theologia Christiana* and *Theologia Scholarium*). One of the main features of Abelard's thesis consisted in disclosing the three divine persons on the basis of power, wisdom, and benevolence (*potentia, sapientia, benignitas*). The Father 'is called Father because of the unique power of his majesty'; the Son is called Son 'because one can see authentic wisdom in him'; and the Holy Spirit is so called 'according to the grace of his goodness'. Thus, 'power is designated by the name Father; Wisdom by the name Son; a favourable feeling for creatures by the name Holy Spirit'. In sum, 'That God would thus be three persons— Father, Son, and Holy Spirit—comes down to saying that the divine substance is power, wisdom, goodness.' Abelard's reasoning about the Trinity leads him to envisage it *on the basis of* the 'sovereign good' which consists in the three notes of 'power, wisdom and goodness'.[6]

Abelard had as definite a conception of the unity of God, as a single and singular substance, as he did of the properties by which the persons are distinguished.[7] He had a good grasp of the Trinity in the light of the relative properties and processions (generation and procession), but he nonetheless tried to explain these properties by means of the triadic formula mentioned above. The properties of Father, Son, and Holy Spirit are distinct 'because the Father is said to be Father purely because he is powerful, the Son from the fact that he can know, and the Holy Spirit on account of his being good'.[8] Abelard could see perfectly well for himself that the problem raised by this analysis is how to use these attributes to distinguish the persons, given that one

---

[5] See D. Poirel, *Livre de la nature et débat trinitaire au XIIe siècle: Le De tribus diebus de Hugues de Saint-Victor*, Turnhout, 2002, pp. 381–383.

[6] Abelard, *Theologia Summi Boni*, Bk I, ch. II (CCCM 13, pp. 86–88).

[7] Ibid., Bk II, ch. I (CCCM 13, pp. 124–125).

[8] Ibid., Bk II, ch. IV (CCCM 13, pp. 150–151). The same thesis is repeated at the conclusion of the chapter: 'because the Father, who is a Person by the very meaning of the word, must be defined precisely as divine Power, that is to say, God-as-Power; God the Son, as divine Wisdom; the Holy Spirit as divine Goodness. Thus the Father is different from the Son by his property or definition; that is to say, he is another than him; likewise, both are different from the Holy Spirit.' (p. 152; cf. pp. 87–88).

acknowledges that they also designate that which is divine as such, or that power, wisdom, and goodness are common to the three persons.

Abelard's response to this drew on the linguistic and grammatical structure of our statements: 'Words maintain the same value or bear an equivalent meaning when they are taken in themselves, but do not retain this value when put together into a sentence or phrase.'[9] So, within the statements we make about the Triune God, one must distinguish those which touch on the common identity (the power shared by the three persons), and those which deal with the distinct property of a person (where we are attributing wisdom and benevolence personally to Father, Son, and Holy Spirit). The words 'power, wisdom, goodness' can thus contain two different meanings, depending on the context: the one personal, the other substantial, that is, shared by all three persons. This conceptual paradigm enabled Abelard to illuminate the Trinitarian dimension of creation and salvation history: that which deals in power (such as creation *ex nihilo*, sending the Son) is attributed to the Father; what touches on wisdom (such as judging and discerning) is ascribed to the Son; and we attribute that which belongs to the action of divine grace to the Holy Spirit.[10]

Abelard clearly would not dream of attributing to the Father a powerfulness of essence which is higher than the Son's, and he also avoids any suspicion of Sabellianism. He may have figured out how to apply the attribute of power in a way which connects essential power to what would later be called 'notional' power (power to beget and power to breathe).[11] The Master of Pallet did not minimize the real distinctness between the divine persons, and he recognizes that the reasons he puts forward are approximations, drawn from what creatures can teach us about God, and which could never enable us to 'comprehend' the Trinity on any level.[12] But the fact remains that Abelard's theory was discernibly controlled by his anti-'tritheist' polemics, aimed at Roscelin, that his employment of the triad-formula 'power—wisdom—goodness' is ambiguous, and that its emphasis is therefore on the unity of the divine substance. Abelard rapidly drew a two-pronged objection: that of rationalism and that of modalism (that is, distilling the Trinity into the divine unity).[13] Being less up to date with what was original in Abelard's work, Bernard of Clairvaux also threw in accusations of Arianism and

---

[9] Ibid., Bk III, ch. I [XI] (CCCM 13, p. 173).

[10] Ibid., Bk III, ch. I (CCCM 13, pp. 177–179).

[11] S. P. Bonanni, *Parlare della Trinità: Lettura della Theologia Scholarium di Abelardo*, Rome, 1996, pp. 86–102, 184.

[12] Abelard, *Theologia Summi Boni*, Bk II, ch. III (CCCM 13, pp. 138–139).

[13] See the Letter from Roscelin, which accuses Abelard of a kind of Sabellianism (PL 178. 357–372).

subordinationism.[14] Abelard underwent an initial censure at the Council of Soissons in 1121, with the condemnation of his *Theologia*, and then another at Sens in 1141. In the lists of 'heretical theses' which would be imputed to him, the number one error was the use of the triad wisdom—power—goodness in relation to the Trinity.[15] Abelard had thus stimulated a vast field of reflection which would absorb scholastic theology for a long time to come: what are the relationships between the divine persons and the essential attributes?

Within his own counter-offensive against Abelard, Hugh of Saint Victor interpreted the application of this triad of attributes to the three divine persons in a way that limited their scope. Since they are part of the substance of divinity, power, wisdom, and goodness belong equally to Father, Son, and Holy Spirit: they have no bearing on the properties of the divine persons. Rather, as Hugh explains them, these attributions have a corrective or negative implication. We use words forged within our world to signify the divine persons. The triad-formula of power—wisdom—goodness balances this out. In connection with actual human life, the name 'father' can evoke a grandfather's impotence, whilst the name 'son' can conjure up inexperienced youth. The attribution of power to the Father and wisdom to the Son avoids both such anthropomorphisms. Likewise, the name 'spirit' can connote either rigour or acerbity: attributing benevolence, that is, goodness, to the Holy Spirit introduces a 'qualifier' on the comparisons which our language puts our way. Hugh used this analysis to set clear blue water between his own view and Abelard's. The value of the attributions of power, wisdom, and goodness is reduced to a minimum. It functions as a corrective within human discourse about the divine persons, rather than being based directly on what is really given by the personal properties.[16]

In addition to this 'negative' or corrective view of the 'power—wisdom—goodness' triad, and whilst freely conceding the problematic character of the enterprise, Hugh also outlined a 'positive' analysis. He drew this from Richard of Saint Victor. The 'positive' proposal looks to the order of the attributes and the divine persons; just as power does not proceed from another faculty, so the Father is without origin; in an analogous way to how wisdom presupposes power, the Son takes his origin from the Father; and like love presupposing power and wisdom, so too the Holy Spirit proceeds from Father and from

---

[14] For the accusations of heresy levelled at Abelard, see J. Hofmeier, *Die Trinitätslehre des Hugo von St. Viktor*, Munich, 1963, pp. 26–56.

[15] 'Quod Pater sit plena potentia, Filius quaedam potentia, Spiritus Sanctus nulla potentia': *Capitula haeresum* XIX, n. 1; ed. C. J. Mews, 'The Lists of Heresies Imputed to Peter Abelard', *Revue Bénédictine* 95 (1985), 73–110, here 108.

[16] Hugh of Saint Victor, *De Sacramentis* I.II.8. See D. Poirel, *Livre de la nature*, pp. 330–332. But Hugh's *De tribus diebus* seems to give a more positive interpretation of the triad formula: see CCCM 177, pp. 62–64.

Son.[17] At the same time, Hugh brings out the fact that whereas these three aspects are distinct in the mind of the creature-image, they are one same single reality in God, and thus do not distinguish the three persons.

The analyses of later theologians would bear the traces of both Hugh and Abelard, but Hugh of Saint Victor had the upper hand. Peter Lombard used his *Sentences* vigorously to reanimate the Victorine's 'negative' explanation.[18] It would flow from the Lombard into all of the *Sentences'* commentators. But some theologians, like Robert of Melun for example, did try to do justice to the element of truth enshrined in Abelard's intuition.

Richard of Saint Victor made an important breach. Along with Alan of Lille and the author of the *Sententiae divinitatis*, Richard is one of the first theologians to use the word 'appropriation' (*appropriatio*) to designate a special attribution to one specific divine person[19] (the terminology was still very varied, and it would long remains so, even in St Thomas, who often speaks of 'attribution'). Richard also builds on Hugh of Saint Victor's 'positive' analysis. He does not just give a negative reason for appropriations, but recognizes in them a positive value deriving from the *order* taken up amongst the essential attributes: power does not in itself presuppose wisdom or goodness; wisdom presupposes power; and goodness can only exist where there is power and wisdom. Thus, for Richard, the three attributes disclose the order of the personal properties: the Father comes from no one (and this is why one especially attributes power to him), the Son is engendered by the Father (wisdom is thus a way of expressing the Son's character), and the Holy Spirit proceeds from the Father and the Son (and goodness is thus especially ascribed to the Holy Spirit).[20] Appropriation thus rests on the correlation between the two sets of relationships, those within essential attributes and those amongst personal properties.

This Ricardian theory of the bases of appropriation will exert a serious influence, one that is still evident in the writings of Thomas' contemporaries. One example of a work in Thomas' neighbourhood is the *Summa* ascribed to Alexander of Hales: this explains that the appropriation of the triad power—wisdom—goodness primarily fits the objective of avoiding error, as Hugh had said; showing something true is given second place, and explained by reference to Richard of Saint-Victor.[21]

[17] Hugh of Saint Victor, *De Sacramentis* I.III.27.
[18] Peter Lombard, *Sentences*, Bk I, dist. 34, chs. 3–4 (vol. I/2, pp. 251–253). Since he tiptoes around it, the Lombard steers clear of showing any kinship between the Abelardian triad and the triplicate formulae of Augustine and Hilary.
[19] See the texts in D. Poirel, *Livre de la nature*, pp. 395–398.
[20] Richard of Saint-Victor, *De tribus appropriatis*, ch. 2 (*Opuscules théologiques*, ed. J. Ribaillier, Paris, 1967, pp. 186–187).
[21] *Summa fratris Alexandri*, Book I (ed. Quaracchi, vol. 1), no. 450.

When St Thomas began to compose theology, the doctrine of appropriation was already mature. Its relatively slow fermentation, and the prudence which Abelard's excesses encouraged, had contributed to its ripening, and its widespread adoption. Writers had the shared recognition that appropriation was not just made up by theologians. If the *theory* was articulated by theologians, the *practice* of appropriation was already a given in sacred Scripture: Scripture especially ascribes to one divine person traits which, taken absolutely, belong to all the persons.[22] Typical examples are, for instance, the attribution of wisdom to the Son (1 Cor. 1.24) or the closing salutation of the second epistle to the Corinthians which links grace to the Lord Jesus Christ (the Son), love to God (the Father) and communion to the Holy Spirit (cf. 2 Cor. 13.13).

When the theologians come to considering actual *triads* of appropriated attributes in their systematic writings, most of them originate with the Patristics. Peter Lombard held onto four of these: (1) *aeternitas—species—usus* (Augustine on Hilary of Poitiers);[23] (2) *Unity—equality—connection* (Augustine);[24] (3) *power—wisdom—goodness* (Abelard and Hugh of Saint Victor; when later writers commonly credit this triad to Augustine, they erred on the side of generosity);[25] (4) the School of Chartres was especially fond of *through him—with him—in him* (cf. Rom. 11.36), pursuing a medieval reading of, and embroidery on, Augustine.[26]

This ranking of the triads is the one which most authors followed.[27] Thomas was no exception. When he examines these appropriations in the *Summa Theologiae* he introduces them by explaining that it is a matter of authenticating the congruence 'of the essential attributes ascribed to the persons by the *sacri doctores*'.[28] These 'sacred doctors' are mainly Augustine

---

[22] Cf. Peter Lombard, *Sentences*, Book I, dist. 34, ch. 3 (vol. I/2, p. 252).

[23] Peter Lombard, *Sentences*, Book I, dist. 31, ch. 2 (vol. I/2, pp. 225–227); Hilary, *De Trinitate* II.1 (SC 443, pp. 276–277); Augustine, *De Trinitate* VI.X.11.

[24] Augustine, *De doctrina christiana* I.V.5. Cf. Peter Lombard, *Sentences*, Book I, dist. 31, chs. 2–3 (vol. I/2, pp. 228–229).

[25] Peter Lombard, *Sentences*, Book I, dist. 34, chs. 3–4 (vol. I/2, pp. 251–253).

[26] Peter Lombard, *Sentences*, Book I, dist. 36, chs. 3–5 (vol. I/2, pp. 261–263). On the Augustinian sources and the place of Rom. 11.36 in the medieval theory of appropriations, see J. Châtillon, '*Unitas, aequalitas, concordia vel connexio*. Recherches sur les origines de la théorie thomiste des appropriations (*Sum. theol.*, I, q. 39, art 7–8)', in *St. Thomas Aquinas 1274–1974: Commemorative Studies*, vol. 1, ed. A. Maurer, Toronto, 1974, pp. 337–379, cf. pp. 340–343.

[27] Peter Lombard, *Sentences*, Book I, dist. 31, 34 and 36. See the typical presentation in the *Summa fratris Alexandri*, which examines each of the triads taking them in that order (Book I, ed. Quaracchi, vol. 1, nos. 448–461).

[28] Thomas, *ST* I, q. 39, a. 8. One can clearly observe that in this article Thomas does not use the specific terminology of 'appropriation', but the more general one of 'attribution'. This way of speaking is second nature to him.

and Hilary. One can also see that Abelard's triad is not situated first and that the appropiations range much further than God's action in the world.

2. THE BASES FOR APPROPRIATION

Like his peers, Thomas held that the attributions in Scripture and the Fathers of the Church are not confined to being a purely linguistic fact which only connects to the way we ourselves understand the divine mysteries (as Hugh of Saint Victor would have preferred). Their meaning is also safeguarded with a foundation in the object. We will begin by noting how Albert and Bonaventure brought this off; they enable us to get a better understanding of Thomas' background, but also of his originality.

(a) The Analyses of Saint Bonaventure and Saint Albert

Saint Bonaventure explains that one can consider appropriated personal attributes in two ways: either as to what they *mean* (what eternity or unity really means), or as to the *order which they connote.*[29] (1) Under the first aspect of what is meant by the name of any one attribute, the appropriations are not founded in God but in our minds, that is, in our own conception of God's mystery, and ultimately they are a way of side-stepping erroneous ideas. Here Bonaventure assimilates Hugh of Saint Victor's analysis: If one takes *power* in the strict sense of the word, when one attributes it to the Father the appropriation will serve as a corrective to anthropomorphisms, and thus of their unfortunate consequences. (2) But, under the second aspect, when one considers the order which the attributes connote, the appropriations are really founded in God ('from the side of the reality'). Bonaventure also takes over another of Richard's analyses which we mentioned earlier: in the same way that, taken in itself, power does not presuppose either wisdom or goodness, so the Father proceeds from no other person—and so on. For the Franciscan Master, the foundation of the appropriation thus consists in the affinity ('congruity') of the two orders, that is, of the appropriated attributes in their mutual comparison and that of the personal properties themselves.

Bonaventurian appropriation consists therefore in a kind of analogy between relationships, a parallelism between a pair of serried relationships: those of the appropriated essential attributes and those of the personal

---

[29] Bonaventure, I *Sent.* d. 34, a. un., q. 3; cf. ad 2.

properties. So Bonaventure strictly limits appropriations to attributes which connote an order or an origin: the other attributes cannot be appropriated.[30] This analysis does not just cover *power, wisdom, and goodness* as a triad, but is applied first and foremost to the Augustinian triads of *aeternitas—species— usus* and *unity—equality—harmony*.[31] In and of themselves, the appropriated names remain shared by the whole Trinity, but considered *as from within their relationships*, they induce us to grasp the personal properties.[32]

Although the roots of the two theories are evidently the same, Albert's explanation is different from Bonaventure's. An appropriation is built on an essential attribute being akin to a personal property. For this to be possible, the appropriation must be based on an attribute's 'rationale', which means on the intrinsic signification of the attribute, expressed in its definition.[33] Albert still mentions Richard of Saint-Victor's analysis, but only marginally.[34] He sharpens the issue in two important respects. The first touches on the foundation for appropriation, the second on the relationship between essential attributes and properties.

Albert explains that appropriation is not just based in our own peculiar way of knowing God, nor in the artistry of theological language, but has an objective foundation in God. (1) This foundation is the proximity or likeness which the very notion of an attribute has toward one divine person. Such a likeness makes the essential attribute 'appropriable', that is, 'fitted' for being appropriated. Albert clearly emphasizes the objective value of a foundation of this kind: it does not rest on one of our mental conceptions, but is solidly founded 'on the side of the reality itself'.[35] For this reason, the appropriation hangs on the formal meaning of a divine attribute, that is, on the perfection which each distinct attribute signifies. (2) In the second place, making appropriations is a given within our way of speaking, one which is not brought about in an arbitrary way but by 'men who were experts on Sacred Scripture' (one cannot improvise around appropriations!). In this capacity, the attribute is not just 'appropriable' (objective foundation) but is existentially appropriated in a linguistic act, and that for various purposes: to exclude error (as in Hugh of Saint Victor's analysis), to express the truth

---

[30] Bonaventure, I *Sent.* d. 34, a. un., q. 3; cf. *Summa fratris Alexandri*, Book I (ed. Quaracchi, vol. 1, no. 450).

[31] Bonaventure, I *Sent.* d. 31, p. 2, a. 1, q. 3 and a. 2, q. 3: the first Augustinian triad rests on *origin*, the second more specifically on *order* (first, second, third person).

[32] Cf. Bonaventure, *Breviloquium* I, ch. 6 (*Opera omnia*, vol. 5, p. 215).

[33] Cf. Albert, I *Sent.* d. 31, a. 5.

[34] Albert, I *Sent.* d. 34, a. 5, ad 3. This feature is all the more striking because Albert's *Sentence* Commentary pre-dates Bonaventure's. This is clear evidence that the differences do not just reflect historical developments, but derive from theological choices.

[35] Albert, I *Sent.* d. 34, a. 5; cf. ad quaest.; d. 31, a. 1 and a. 2.

about the Trinity and 'further to bring out the distinction between the properties'. The former aims always presuppose the latter, of showing the difference between the properties. And so, from our own point of view, the foundation of appropriation is pragmatic.[36] Its function is to highlight each of the distinct personal properties: appropriation thus makes it possible to avoid mix-ups and to show the truth.

Saint Albert also pinpoints the nature of the relationships between the appropriated essential attributes and the properties. Making an appropriation assumes a given knowledge of the personal properties. It could never be used to establish the personal properties, since it is not the essential attributes which distinguish the persons, but their incommunicable characters. 'If one has no initial property, one will have no appropriated attribute.' This view involves a very tight conception of how an understanding of the divine nature and of the distinct persons is open to us. (1) Considered 'materially,' that is, as to its intrinsic meaning, one can get a perfectly good grip on an essential attribute without the personal property. A non-Christian believer who does not profess the Trinity can recognize that God is eternal, powerful, or wise; taken in itself, the attribute of eternity or that of power is not conditional on the personal property. (2) Considered 'formally', that is, as *actually appropriated*, the appropriated essential attribute presupposes and includes the property of the person. Taking Albert's own example, the appropriated attribute of eternity is not the notion of divine eternity alone but eternity *in as much as* it 'aligns with the person of the Father', that is, eternity as joined to Fatherhood. Seen as appropriated, the notion of 'appropriated attribute' thus includes the notion of essential attribute *and* the personal property kindred to it. The concept of an 'appropriated attribute' is a complex notion which joins both aspects in itself.[37] Despite what many people think, appropriation takes real understanding of Trinitarian doctrine; it is not a 'walkover'.

This analysis takes into account what Bonaventure had meant by the terms 'meaning' and 'connotation'. But there is no space for 'connotation' in Albert's view. One could say that, for Albert, it is not a matter of using one aspect to 'extend' the other, but of 'uniting' two distinct aspects. In other words, Albert does not base his interpretation frontally on the mutual order amongst the attributes, but on the notion or special 'rationale' of any particular essential attribute, that is, on the meaning of the name of that attribute, which presents a 'congruence' with the notion of this personal property. Albert formulates this doctrine in relation to the Trinitarian triads worked out by the Church Fathers which we mentioned above. Their analysis undergirds both the general theory and the terms of its application.

[36] Albert, I *Sent*. d. 34, a. 5.   [37] Albert, I *Sent*. d. 31, a. 2.

(b) Thomas' View

There are two main theoretical explorations of the process of appropriation in Thomas' writing: one in the Commentary on the *Sentences*, the other in the *Summa Theologiae*. The *Sentences* exposition has strong affinities to Albert's thinking, in the care it takes to show the value and objective grounding for appropriations, and it also assimilates some important features which Bonaventure emphasized. St Thomas remains very close to his precursors. He takes over Albert's analysis in his observation that appropriation can be considered in two ways: either from the side of the divine reality, or from the side of our knowledge.

(1) From the standpoint of the reality of the Triune God, appropriation is based in the likeness that its notion or 'rationale' makes an essential attribute have for one person rather than another. This kinship or likeness 'is the first and main reason for the appropriation'.[38] Thus, for instance, power is akin to the character of the Father, because power means a principle (a principle of action), and, within the Trinity the Father is the principle without principle. Wisdom has a kinship with the character of the Son who is the Word; and likewise goodness is akin to the property of the Holy Spirit as love. In each of these cases, it is the particular notion of the essential attribute which is linked to the notion of the property. Like St Albert, Thomas is very clear on the objective value of the appropriation, which he presents in terms of 'congruence' (the word 'congruence' must be taken in a strong sense, as the context shows: it concerns the basis for appropriation, that is to say, what accounts for its real and objective value). 'From the standpoint of the reality, the likeness of the appropriated attribute to the person's character creates the congruity of the appropriation, *a congruence which would be there even if we did not exist*.'[39] If there is any need to do so, this should remove any doubt about the realism with which Thomas treats appropriation and the value which he accords it. It is certainly not just a linguistic ploy.

(2) From our own standpoint, appropriation is driven by the 'function which it achieves'. This function is 'the disclosure of the faith' (Albert's third reason). Once the properties of the persons have been laid down, appropriation enables us to supplement our presentation by way of their essential attributes. But such a disclosure is imperfect. Like St Albert, Thomas observes that the prefix 'ad' in the phrase 'appropriation' (*ad-propriatio*) indicates both proximity and distance.[40] To show this, he reverts to Bonaventure's analysis: like the personal properties, the appropriated attributes are *distinct* and have a

---

[38] Thomas, I *Sent.* d. 31, q. 2, a. 1, ad 1.   [39] Thomas, I *Sent.* d. 31, q. 1, a. 2.
[40] Ibid., ad 1; cf. Albert, I *Sent.* d. 31, a. 2, ad 2.

certain *order* amongst themselves. But whereas, in the case of the properties, distinction and order are real, they are purely conceptual ('according to reason') in the case of the essential attributes. Thomas thus says that,

The [appropriated] essential attributes do not open the way to a sufficient knowledge of the persons. Nonetheless, we observe in the appropriated [attributes] some kind of likeness to the persons, and this is how an appropriation has the quality of a disclosure of the faith, however imperfect.[41]

What kind of 'likeness' to the divine persons do the essential attributes need to have if they are to 'disclose the faith'? Thomas' analysis develops those of his predecessors: the very notion of the appropriable attribute must present a kinship with the character of one person; in addition, the appropriated essential attributes must be distinct, as Albert indicated, and they must have an internal order and indicate origin, as Bonaventure specified.

On the one hand, tracking St Albert's meditation, Thomas pinpoints the fact that, even though they belong to the reality of the God who is simple, the essential attributes are different in their 'notion' or 'rationale'.[42] As Thomas explains it in an addendum which he slipped into his Commentary after first writing it, this difference of 'rationale' does not just exist reflexively in the theologian's mind, but 'flows from the character of the reality itself'. The plurality of distinct essential attributes is tied to the incomprehensibility of the God who surpasses our understanding, but what we recognize in these divine attributes is authentically divine, for they really exist in God (God is eternal, powerful, one, wise, good, in the mode of unity). Thomas affirms that,

The plurality of these 'rationales' [of divine attributes] does not only exist from the perspective of our human minds, but also from within God himself, in so far as his perfection transcends every conception we can think of. This is why there is indeed something which corresponds within the reality of God to the plurality of these 'rationales': not a real plurality, but a plenitude of perfection, from which it follows that all these 'rationales' of attributes are authentically attributed to him.[43]

The plurality of divine attributes is thus also founded 'from the standpoint of the divine reality itself'.[44] We are certainly not in the order of personal properties, where the plurality is real, but this point is very important, because it is the ground of the value of the appropriation of the essential attributes that, since they also authenticate some kind of distinction and plurality 'from the standpoint of the reality', they are fitted to 'disclosing' a distinction and a plurality.

---

[41] Thomas, I *Sent.* d. 31, q. 1, a. 2.   [42] Ibid., ad 2.
[43] I *Sent.* d. 2, q. 1, a. 3.   [44] I *Sent.* d. 2, q. 1, a. 3.

Following St Bonaventure, on the other hand, Thomas observes that the appropriated essential attributes put forward a mutual *order* and an *origin*. 'There is an actual distinction and an order amongst the divine attributes and amongst the persons, but in different ways: for the distinction and order are real in the persons, whereas they are conceptual ('as to reason') in the [essential] attributes.'[45] Thomas had learned these ideas from others; but he puts more emphasis on the 'rationale' or notion belonging to each attribute. The illustration he gives comes from Hugh and Abelard's triad. Power is appropriated to the Father because it has a likeness to the Father's character as principle of the Son and Holy Spirit: it is *origin* which is being underlined here, since we can see origin both in the notion of power and in the property of the Father. Wisdom and goodness are appropriated respectively to the Son and to the Holy Spirit, since the Son proceeds as Word (Wisdom as begotten) and the Holy Spirit as Love (love travels toward the good): it is thus the *mode of origin* which is brought into play.[46] St Thomas does not do much to highlight the structural parallelism which Bonaventure had taken over from Richard of Saint-Victor—linking two orders of analogous relationships. Rather, he puts the stress on the kinship which each distinct essential attribute has with the origin or origin-mode of each one of the divine persons.[47]

One can test whether this theory works in practice by applying it to the Augustinian triads.[48] Thus, for instance, *unity* is appropriated to the Father because 'one' is the basic numerical principle, and thus possesses a certain kinship with the beginningless Father who is the principle of Son and Holy Spirit. The foundation of the appropriation is origin, as linked here to the distinct notion of 'unity'. *Equality* is appropriated to the Son, because equality is inscribed within the Son's own mode of procession; by definition, a son proceeds within a nature like that of his father, and thus within an equality of nature: this belongs to the very notion of generation, as much in our world as in God. *Connection* (or the 'bond', *nexus*) is appropriated to the Holy Spirit, because it is by dint of his precise mode of procession as Love that the Spirit binds the Father and the Son, and it is by virtue of his procession as Gift that the Holy Spirit binds us to God (this bond is inscribed within the mode of procession belonging to the Holy Spirit as Love and Gift). We can say that, with the Son and the Holy Spirit, it is the close investigation of the *modes of*

---

[45] I *Sent.* d. 31, q. 1, a. 2.   [46] I *Sent.* d. 31, q. 1, a. 2, ad 2.

[47] But in some instances, Thomas turns directly to the *order* in which the attributes belong to the three persons: see for instance *ST* I, q. 45, a. 6, ad 2.

[48] The four 'traditional' triads indicated above are considered one at a time, following Peter Lombard's text: I *Sent.* d. 31, q. 2, a. 1; d. 31, q. 3, aa. 1–2; d. 34, q. 2; d. 36, q. 1, a. 3, ad 5.

procession, linked to the distinction of attributes, which makes it possible for appropriation to disclose the persons in a valuable and grounded way.[49]

In these analyses, Hugh of Saint Victor's negative interpretation, which still has an important position in Bonaventure's presentation, and which Albert also notes, has disappeared. In his *Sentence* Commentary, St Thomas does not rely on this when he presents the general doctrine of appropriations: it only comes in much later, in the exposition of the triad wisdom—power—goodness.[50] It is doubtless that, for Thomas, the difference between the general doctrine of appropriations and the specific case of the triad of power—wisdom—goodness stands out more than it did for his predecessors. Even though, historically speaking, the question about the triad which issued from Abelard and Hugh had been the occasion for the development of the idea of appropriation, it could hardly be called the focal point of Thomas' theoretical position. His theoretical idea rests much more on the positive disclosure of the faith, founded on a precise analysis of the personal properties and Trinitarian processions, and on a no less precise reflection on the distinction of 'rationales' of essential attributes.

Thomas continues Albert's practice of fine-tuning the nature of the relationship between the appropriated essential attribute and the personal property.[51] (1) Considered in its proper notion ('materially'), our minds grasp an essential attribute minus the personal properties. A philosopher, or a non-Christian believer, can recognize that God is wise without having embraced the Trinitarian faith. This distinction is also binding on the Christian theologian: what one expresses when we attribute wisdom to God does not include that divine person *in and of itself*. In other words, if one takes account of the route which our knowledge travels, one must recognize that, in our thinking, the notion of divine wisdom comes about before we grasp the divine person:[52] one cannot grasp a person without having grasped the divine substance (the notion of person includes that of divine substance, for one could not otherwise grasp the person as a reality existing in God), and thus, in our thinking, the understanding of the essential attribute as such 'comes before' understanding the person who has this attribute. (2) But, *in so far as it is appropriated*, or 'formally', the attribute includes the person's character, since its appropriation rests on the kinship which it has with the personal property.

---

[49] I *Sent.* d. 31, q. 3, a. 1.

[50] I *Sent.* d. 34, q. 2. But the *Summa Theologiae* does reproduce this argument at the end of the presentation of the general doctrine of appropriations (*ST* I, q. 39. a. 7).

[51] I *Sent.* d. 31, q. 1, a. 2, ad 3.

[52] This anteriority is not temporal but conceptual: it is a matter of the ordering of concepts, that is, of the process of our thought.

Thus, the notion of an appropriated attribute as such embraces the notion of this attribute, and also includes the personal character.[53] From this angle, the person's character must be seized upon before the appropriated attribute: it is the personal property which controls the appropriation of an essential attribute. This analysis is reproduced in the *Summa*.[54]

So one must avoid confusing an 'essential attribute' with an 'appropriated essential attribute'; the later is a much thicker complex notion. Combining the attribute of power and the person of the Father, 'power as appropriated to the Father' says more than 'divine power'. The appropriated attribute is envisaged in the person: one finds unity 'in the Father', equality 'in the Son', and bonding 'in the Holy Spirit'.[55] Otherwise put, the appropriated attribute is the attribute considered *within the person to whom it is appropriated*.[56]

3. DISCLOSING THE PERSONS

Having just run through it, it is perhaps worth mentioning that, in his Commentary on the *Sentences*, Thomas is not especially concerned about giving a definition of appropriation. He prefers to show what the foundations of appropriation are, and then to present the triads which the scholastic tradition accepted for use. One could perhaps consider this observation from the Disputed Questions *De Veritate* as a definition: 'To appropriate is nothing other than to draw what is shared towards what is proper.'[57] That explanation has absorbed this one from Albert the Great: '[to be] appropriated is nothing other than for a real and linguistic congruity to enable something to be aligned with the property of one person rather than another'.[58] What is going on here is description rather than definition. In his early works, Thomas is concerned above all with carefully presenting the bases

---

[53] I *Sent.* d. 31, q. 1, a. 2, ad 3. Cf. also I *Sent.* d. 9, exp. text.: 'the notion of what is "proper" is included in the "appropriated" as such'.

[54] *ST* I, q. 39, a. 7, ad 3; cf. q. 33, a. 4, ad 1. Bonaventure (I *Sent.* d. 34, a. un., q. 3, ad 3) likewise observes that the appropriated attribute as such presupposes the notion of the property.

[55] I *Sent.* d. 31, q. 3, a. 2.

[56] St Thomas also explains this by reference to Hilary's triad: *aeternitas—species—usus* (I *Sent.* d. 31, q. 2, a. 1). Eternity is the eternity 'which is in the Father as having been appropriated to him'; splendour or beauty (*species*) is considered 'in the Image, that is to say, in the Son who is genuinely Image'; and the fruition and use of gifts (*usus*) is 'in the Gift, that is, in the Holy Spirit'. One sees here that Thomas interprets the terms *species* and *usus* in the meaning given them by Augustine (for beauty and fruition, see Augustine's *De Trinitate* VI.X.11) rather than in Hilary's original sense (Hilary, *De Trinitate* II.1; see the notes in SC 443, pp. 276–277).

[57] *De veritate*, q. 7, a. 3 (in relation to the appropriation of 'book of life' to the person of the Son).

[58] Albert, I *Sent.* d. 31, a. 2.

for appropriation and organizing the internal features of the procedure. Coming after the 'Writing on the *Sentences*', and considering appropriation from a new angle, the *Summa* puts forward a definition of it.

In the first place, the context has changed. In his first systematic work, tracking the Lombard's text, St Thomas connected the general idea of appropriations to the equality of persons, and then dealt with the diverse triads in their order of appearance within the text upon which he was commenting.[59] In the *Summa*, the context is the comparison of the persons with the divine nature, in the middle of a block of text which delves into how the persons own the features faith ascribes (nature, properties, acts, and equality, in qq. 39–42). This block of fine-shadings comes immediately after the presentation of each person in his distinctive character, in qq. 33–38. As thus pursued under diverse aspects, the study of the persons enables one to unify the whole doctrine of God around the persons themselves. This is an illuminating context. Thomas has shown the features proper to each person; then, in the comparison of the persons, he reassembles and integrates all of the elements of the Christian doctrine of God. Put together through discreet complementary touches, this is the authentic synthesis of the doctrine of the persons which these questions aim to offer, and appropriation is positioned here.

The more immediate context is also highly indicative: the comparison of the distinct persons with their common nature, in q. 39. Grasping the Father, Son, and Holy Spirit is not just knowing their distinctive characters, but also being able to recognize how the three persons relate to their shared nature, and being capable of *formulating* this relationship between the Trinity and the Unity, and thus ultimately of entering upon a deeper understanding of the persons. This investigation progresses from its inception in the divine unity to the disclosure of the distinctness of the persons. Thomas begins by studying the expressions of the strict *unity* of the three persons (the nature is identical to the person, the three persons are 'of one single nature') and he ends his journey amongst the expressions of the *distinction* of the persons: such are appropriations. The context indicates that what appropriation aims to do is to make a thorough disclosure of the personal plurality within God. This plurality has been established within faith through the properties of the persons, which—so far as theology can do so—give adequate ('sufficient') evidence of the personal alterity amongst Father, Son, and Holy Spirit. Moving on further ahead, and no longer offering sufficient evidence, but merely an imperfect showing, Thomas indicates that *the investigation of the divine nature can benefit from the light given by the properties*, and in this way it can be integrated into *the single overall purpose of disclosing the Trinity*.

---

[59] See above, n. 48.

This discussion is set out in two stalls: (1) the general doctrine of appropriations (q. 39, a. 7); (2) the explanation of why scholastic tradition generally set a value on the appropriations it garnered from its exegesis of the Bible and the Church Fathers (a. 8). The presentation of common doctrine is rather surprising. On the one hand, one finds nothing of the analysis of appropriation 'from the standpoint of reality' which we encountered in the *Sentence* commentary. On the other hand, much more attention is paid to the route by which we know the Trinity. From the first sentence, the whole doctrine of appropriations is placed under the ensign of its function of giving us a deeper perception of the divine persons:

In order to disclose the faith, it is fitting to appropriate essential attributes to the persons.[60]

As we saw earlier, this is the third theme which Albert drew on in order to show the value of appropriations 'from our perspective',[61] and it is Thomas' own end-point in his *Sentence* commentary.[62] In the *Summa*, this becomes the *point of departure* driving the entire meditation. Thomas has not given up either his conviction that there is an objective basis for appropriations or his conception of the internal features of appropriation (they will reappear in the examination of particular triads), but nonetheless, everything is directed towards one single value and goal: to give human contemplation a better window on the persons themselves.[63] This is the precise purpose of Trinitarian theology,[64] and appropriations have no other function than to serve this aim. What is suggested by the context, is shown with complete clarity by the text itself. The basis foregrounded here is the path which our knowledge of the Trinitarian mystery takes:

as we have shown [q. 32, a. 1], the Trinity of persons cannot be demonstratively proven. But it is still congruous to place it in the light of some things which are more manifest to us. And the essential attributes stand out more to our reason than the properties of the persons do, for, beginning from the creatures from which we derive our knowledge we are able to arrive at certain knowledge of essential attributes, but not at the knowledge of the personal properties, as we have said [q. 32, a. 1]. Thus, just as to disclose the persons we make use of vestigial or imaged likenesses of the Trinity

---

[60] *ST* I, q. 39, a. 7.

[61] Albert, I *Sent.* d. 34, a. 5.

[62] Thomas, I *Sent.* d. 31, q. 1, a. 2. Bonaventure also takes note of this final aim: 'The appropriated attributes put the properties on record' (I *Sent.* d. 31, dubium 1; cf. *Breviloquium* I, ch. 6).

[63] This characteristic feature of the *Summa Theologiae* was emphasized in a study by Fr Dominique-Marie Cabaret, which made me aware of it: 'Les appropriations trinitaires chez S. Thomas d'Aquin', Mémoire de licence, University of Fribourg, 2001.

[64] *ST* I, q. 32, a. 1, ad 2.

in creatures, so too we use their essential attributes. And what we call *appropriation* is the disclosure of the persons through the essential attributes.[65]

Appropriation is defined by its utility or final aim of disclosing the persons, and likewise by its means, the essential attributes. The backward glances at question 32 are good indicators that St Thomas connects appropriation with the pathways of our knowledge of God. He begins by reminding us of the prerogatives of faith, our only means of access to knowledge of the divine persons. In accordance with his strong conviction, he rules out any attempt to establish Trinitarian faith with necessary proofs.[66] He also clearly distinguishes between the two orders within our knowledge: that of the relational personal properties and that of the essential attributes. One cannot deduce the former from the latter. The personal properties do not flow from the divine nature, but rather our understanding of the Trinitarian mystery is brought about by the linking or integration of the 'common' and the 'proper', following a procedure which, as we have seen, can call the best patristic sources to witness.[67] Theology does not attempt to demonstrate the Trinitarian faith, but to disclose it to our minds more clearly, within a contemplative exercise which is addressed to believers. This exercise obeys the basic laws of the human mind, which the understanding of the faith cannot avoid: we illuminate that which is less known, or more obscure, by that which is more accessible, that is, through realities which are better proportioned to what our own thinking is suited to know. Unless one does this, one can *affirm* the Trinitarian faith, but one cannot *make it more evident* to the mind of believers, which is the very task of theology.

And the essential attributes are precisely that within God which is 'more evident' to our minds than the personal properties. One can see this from the fact that our human reason can achieve some knowledge of the essential attributes under its own steam. The essential attributes are certainly not 'pigeon-holed', since they remain beyond our human grasp,[68] but we know enough to say that it is necessary to recognize their presence in God. Why? Because, starting from what is creaturely, we are led to find that which necessarily belongs to God in so far as he is the source of creatures.[69] This metaphysical notion is proportioned to our natural mental resources and to the structure of human cognition whose starting-place is knowledge of the sensible. In this capacity, it is 'more evident' or 'more on our level' than the

[65] *ST* I, q. 39, a. 7.

[66] See above, in Chapter 2, 'The Aim of Speculative Trinitarian Theology'.

[67] See above, in Chapter 3, 'The Essence and the Distinction of Persons: the Common and the "Proper"'.

[68] See above, in Chapter 6, 'Person and Analogy'.

[69] *ST* I, q. 12, a. 12.

knowledge of the personal properties, which rests purely on the reception of revelation through a gift from God surpassing our reason. Thus, for example, the divine goodness is 'more evident' to our mind than *ekporeusis*, the hypostatic property of the Holy Spirit.

This is why, when he wanted to disclose the persons' properties, Thomas went to work on the analogies of word and love (the analogy of the image), scrupulously purifying them until he could discern in them the means of grasping the properties of Son and Holy Spirit. Even if we can understand these 'likenesses' as offering a route into knowledge of the personal properties, nonetheless, the parallel with the idea of image[70] calls on us to notice an important nuance. The investigation of the personal properties has shown in practice how the distinction between the word and its principle, in the human mind, gives us an analogy of faith through which to grasp the eternal procession of the divine Word, as other from the Father. But in the case of appropriations, the resemblance which we are drawing on is of a different order: it is the resemblance between a divine essential attribute and a divine personal property. The goal of the appropriation is to throw more light on a property which the theologian has already fine-tuned in a more adequate or 'sufficient' way, and without conflating the essential attribute and the property: 'the essential attributes are not appropriated to the persons as though one were calling them properties'.[71]

The outlook of this first article about appropriation differs from the way appropriation is usually tackled by contemporary theologians. Thomas is not showing that we need appropriation in order to respect the unity of nature of the three persons, but the reverse: his explanation of its worth is that we need it to disclose the distinct persons. The service it can perform can take two shapes: (1) 'by way of likeness' and (2) 'by way of dissimilitude'.[72] The second form, the way of dissimilitude, is that which thirteenth-century authors had taken over from Hugh of Saint Victor, which was mistakenly ascribed to Augustine. We have discussed it above. It hardly applies to anything other than the triad wisdom—power—goodness, and its place in Thomas' thought is very marginal. It was perhaps the erroneous ascription, lending it the prestigious authority of Augustine, which made him mention it at all.

The first form, the way of likeness, is positive appropriation, and Thomas uses it in nearly every instance. Working from the order or mode of origin, one attributes to the person that which has a kinship with his personal property. One example he gives is this: 'That which touches on intellect is appropriated to the Son, because he proceeds by an intellectual mode, in so

---

[70] Thomas mentioned this already in the same context in I *Sent.* d. 31, q. 1, a. 2.
[71] *ST* I, q. 39, a. 7, ad 1; cf. ad 2.   [72] *ST* I, q. 39, a. 7.

far as he is the Word.'[73] The essential attributes which are connected with mental life (like divine wisdom, divine truth, eternal law, splendour and beauty, providence, God's disposition of creatures) are appropriated to the Son, by dint of the kinship they have with the Word's property, that is to say, to what belongs to the precise notion of 'Word' on the basis of his own mode of procession. Likewise, that which touches on the divine volition can be appropriated to the Holy Spirit by virtue of his personal property, that is, by dint of that which belongs to the specific notion of his mode of procession as personal Love (impulsion, amorous impression, or affection).[74] And that which concerns the source or origin of a reality or principle (eternity, unity, power, creation) will be attributed to the Father because of his property within the Trinity as principle without principle.

In each of these cases, appropriation is a disclosure of the person. The personal property has already created an initial capacity to conceive the divine person in his distinctness. The essential attributes which one connects to this property—or which one observes *in* that person—are now adduced to enrich our contemplation of the person, making the persons more evident to our vision, like an auxiliary cluster of lights which one could not conflate with the light of the properties.

4. THE REGIONS IN WHICH APPROPRIATION APPLIES

Once it has established the function and value of appropriation, the *Summa* shows the 'congruity' of the traditional appropriations (q. 39. a. 8). First theory, then practice. The attributes he examines are those which the scholastics received from the 'sacred doctors', that is, the scriptural thinking of the Fathers of the Church.[75] Thomas presents no inclination either to multiply appropriations or to invent novel ones. He deals dryly with the received appropriations. The peculiar structure of this article brings this out very well: no *sed contra* argument, nor any responses to objections after the master's response. Thomas is content to give a list of the received appropriations, stressing which of their features can cause problems, articulating a principle on which to organize them, and finally interpreting them in a way

---

[73] Ibid.

[74] The terminology makes this formulation more complex, because, as Thomas explains it, we use the same word 'love' in two different senses, the one personal and the other essential: see above, in Chapter 10, 'The Holy Spirit is Love in Person'.

[75] *ST* I, q. 39, a. 8. Thomas calls on the 'sacred doctors' where Albert spoke of 'men who were experts on sacred Scripture'.

that shows the value of each appropriation. This is a question of the four famous triads maintained by Peter Lombard, and of some singular attributes which did not make up a triad. These latter also belong to the common pool of scholastic tradition. One can easily show that many authors have access to this: one appropriates *virtus*, *truth*, the *book of life*, the expression *He Who Is* (Exod. 3.14) to the Son, and so on.

Thus, appropriation is not only practised in relation to the triads. Even when unattached to a triad, an essential attribute's kinship with a personal property is enough to give rise to an appropriation. One can see that, taken outside any triad, these singular attributes frequently appear within Thomas' customary practice. He often appropriates a single attribute to a person, and sometimes two attributes to two persons, and sometimes uses triads, ascribing three attributes to three persons. The position of triads is uncontrovertibly larger in this article in the *Summa* than in Thomas' ordinary usage, especially when he comments on Scripture. In addition, one can observe in his exegetical and theological works that he also sometimes considers a single attribute which could be fitted into a triad.[76]

The particular interest of this discussion of 'traditional' appropriations lies in the way Thomas suggests it should be organized. The principle of this organization bears the characteristic stamp of his theological thought:

> Since our mind is led from creatures to knowledge of God, its way of thinking about him has to follow a mode deriving from them. And, our knowledge of creatures has four stages, in the following order. First we examine it in itself, in so far as it is a *being*. The second consideration is the thing in so far as it is *one*. The third is the thing as possessing the *power to act and to cause*. And the fourth consideration is that of its *relationship to its effects*. The same quadrant presents itself for consideration when we think about God.[77]

These comments take us back to the principle which legitimated the process of making appropriations: our knowledge of God sets off from an object proportioned to our minds, the knowledge of creatures. The *mode* of our knowledge of God (not the reality towards which we orient ourselves, but our own way of reaching it) thus continues to be linked in with the mode of our knowledge of creatures. Our earlier discussion of analogy called upon this fundamental law of human thought. The mode by which we know things intellectually and the mode by which our words convey meaning are both

---

[76] For example, Thomas appropriates *eternity* to the Father without mentioning the appropriation of *beauty* to the Son or *usus* to the Holy Spirit (*ST* III, q. 59, a. 1, ad 2). And he appropriates *wisdom* to the Son without mentioning the appropriation of *power* to the Father and *goodness* to the Holy Spirit (*ST* III, q. 3, a. 8, sed contra), and so on.

[77] *ST* I, q. 39, a. 8.

connected to the mode of existence which is perfected within creaturehood. Our 'consideration' of God and our words for naming God remain bound to the mode of being of our sensible world, from which we take our knowledge.[78]

On this basis, Thomas reaffirms that we initially grasp an object as a thing which is an entity: 'what first enters our mental conception is the being (*ens*)'.[79] This is a fundamental principle of the idea of knowledge: that which our intellect first conceives, as the best known to itself, and from which it draws all its other conceptions, is the being, that is, the thing in so far as it exists in act. The other conceptions which our mind forms about the thing we know are, so to speak, adjuncts to this first seizure of its being as such. The next step which St Thomas mentions as a second element in the process of knowing is the *unity* of the being. Our minds grasp the known thing as a reality which is internally undivided, that is, one.[80] We can see the doctrine of the transcendentals in this.[81] He adds to these first moments the no less basic principle of the 'first act' and the 'second act', that is, of being and of *action*. Knowledge of its action entirely belongs to knowledge of a being: 'one does not know a reality perfectly unless one knows its operation'.[82] A thing acts and exercises its influence on other realities because of what it is. What is first stressed here is the precise capability, the intrinsic power of action, that is, the principles of action, that through which a being acts. Then, as a last step, and without specifying the kind of causality in question, Thomas envisages the relations which a being's action makes it have with the realities which it 'causes', that is to say, the relationships given to an entity by the influence it exercises on behalf of others.

Thus, this approach pictures four regions in which appropriation can be applied, to wit, appropriations of attributes touching on: (1) God in his absolute being (as in *aeternitas—species—usus*, the triad important to Augustine and Hilary); (2) God considered as One (as in the Augustinian triad unity—equality—connection); (3) God under the aspect of his power of causation (power—wisdom—goodness, the triad of Hugh of Saint Victor and Abelard; *virtus* appropriated to the Son); (4) God in the relationships which he enjoys with creatures (as in the triad deriving from Rom. 11.36: 'through him, with him, in him'; different aspects of divine causality: efficient, formal, and final).[83]

---

[78] See above, in Chapter 6, 'Person and Analogy'.　　[79] *ST* I, q. 5, a. 2.
[80] *ST* I, q. 11, a. 1.　　[81] Cf. *De veritate*, q. 1, a. 1.　　[82] *SCG* II, ch. 1 (no. 852).
[83] *ST* I, q. 39, a. 8; cf. q. 46, a. 3. In his Commentary on the final salutation in 2 Corinthians (*In 2 Cor.* 13.13, no. 544), Thomas introduces a further distinction: appropriation 'by essence' and appropriation 'through cause'. Appropriation 'through cause' aims at taking this particular biblical passage into account.

St Thomas has held onto these four aspects in relation to his doctrine of God. We can appreciate that they correspond precisely to the structure of the treatise on God and especially to the structure of the investigation of the divine nature. In the *Summa*, the first question shows that the subject of theology is either God himself, or creatures in their relationship to God as their principle and end.[84] This second aspect (the relation to creatures) runs parallel to the fourth consideration within the making of appropriations, whereas the first aspect (God himself) corresponds to the first three considerations. In other words, in his investigation of what concerns the divine nature, Thomas first investigates 'what God is, or rather what he is not' (qq. 3–11):[85] this deals with the divine attributes which belong to God's being (simplicity, perfection, goodness, infinity, eternity, and so forth); this enquiry culminates in the examination of God's unity (q. 11). The first and second consideration for appropriations (being and unity) correspond to this treatise. Finally, he studied 'that which relates to God's operation' (qq. 14–26)[86]: this block examines knowledge and will with their connected attributes (life, love, mercy, justice, providence, and predestination), and concludes, before the study of divine beatitude, with 'the power of God, the principle of the divine operation as proceeding to the exterior effect'.[87] These operative attributes correspond to the third consideration for appropriations. Beyond that, Thomas examines the 'processing of creatures *from God*' (qq. 44 ff.), which, as we said, runs parallel to the fourth consideration for appropriations, that is, the relations between God and the world.

One can thus see the following mirrorings between the treatise on God and the regions in which appropriations can be applied:

1. God as to his being (cf. qq. 2–10): first region for appropriations
2. God in his unity (cf. q. 11): second region for appropriations
3. God in his operation (cf. qq. 14–26): third region for appropriations
4. God in his relations to creatures (cf. qq. 44 ff.): fourth region for appropriations.

Since Thomas' main aim is to organize the appropriations he has received from others, one should take these correlations as being flexible rather than rigid. Moreover, it is not as if every single divine attribute gave rise to an appropriation; for instance, since they have no kinship with any one personal property, essence and operation are not appropriated. But one can see that the appropriations are a *Trinitarian re-enactment* of what comes before them, and presage what is to follow, in the treatise on 'that which concerns the

---

[84] *ST* I, q. 1, a. 7.   [85] *ST* I, q. 2, prol.
[86] *ST* I, q. 2, prol.; q. 14, prol.   [87] *ST* I, q. 14, prol.

distinction of the persons' (qq. 27–43, which we call the Trinitarian treatise). In this way, thanks first to the properties themselves, and second to the ensuing appropriations, Trinitarian doctrine has the whole of theology within its sights. Thomas evidently wants to show that Trinitarian theology is not an isolated arena within theology: *it contains the entire Christian mystery.*

This is not the place to make a detailed examination of every region of appropriation. But we can note in passing that Thomas applies the rules which he formulated in his Commentary on the *Sentences* in the explanations he gives here. In each case, and within each of the four regions, he establishes the kinship or 'likeness' of an essential attribute with a personal property. The explanations generally work from the property itself rather than from the Trinitarian order or mode of procession, but, as we have seen, the personal properties imply an order and a mode of procession. So, for instance, anything dealing with the life of the mind is appropriated to the Son because of its kinship with his property as *Word*, and what deals with the affective life is attributed to the Holy Spirit as being kindred to his character as *Love*. Even when St Thomas makes no explicit reference to the processional modes of mind and will, his analyses implicitly presuppose them. Likewise, he frequently calls on the property of the Father as 'principle without principle' (this justifies the appropriation of eternity, unity, power, and so on), which implies the order theme. The results of the investigation of the personal properties are rigorously applied. These properties are precisely those which the treatise on the persons had brought to light: the paternity of the Father who, being without principle, is the principle of the Son and the Holy Spirit; the property of the Son as Word, Son and Image; the property of the Holy Spirit as Love, mutual Love of Father and Son, and Gift. All the characteristics worked out in the prior investigation are drawn in.

In the fourth region, that of 'God's relations to his effects', the kinds of appropriation diversify. It could be a matter of a divine action: so, for instance, creation is appropriated to the Father. Thomas also appropriates clusters of actions. He attributes the stages of the divine economy to distinct persons: creation is appropriated to the Father, re-creation to the Son, and glorification or 'consummation' to the Holy Spirit.[88] He also appropriates general aspects of the divine operations: efficient causality is appropriated to the Father, formal causality to the Son, and final causality to the Holy Spirit. The words expressing these aspects are likewise appropriated: '*from* him, *through* him, *in* him'.[89] He also appropriates to the three persons a selfsame action considered under different aspects; it is thus that, for instance, our filial

[88] III *Sent.* d. 1, q. 2, a. 2, ad 3.
[89] *ST* I, q. 39, a. 8; cf. I *Sent.* d. 36, q. 1, a. 3, ad 5; *ST* I, q. 46, a. 3; *In Ad Eph.* 4.6 (no. 203).

adoption is appropriated to the Father who is its author, or to the Son who is its model, or to the Holy Spirit, who engraves it in our hearts.[90] Appropriation can be applied to a created effect (a gift is appropriated to the Holy Spirit),[91] but also to aspects or internal elements of an effect (this is the case with the vestige of the Trinity in all creatures and with the image of the Trinity in human beings[92]). This requires making a careful, case by case study of the realities under question. The appropriation of created effects rests on the bedrock appropriation of the immanent essential attributes, for it is by dint of these essential attributes that the Triune God is the source of the effects which he brings about within the world.

Finally, we should mention that certain analyses, in question 39 of the *Prima Pars*, are an important way into appreciating some of St Thomas' themes. Thus, for instance, research into Thomist aesthetics cannot fail to observe the appropriation of *beauty* to the Son, or that beauty is said to have three features: integrity, proportion, and clarity. At this point, Thomas is extending the Augustinian interpretation of *species* which Hilary found in the property of the Son.[93]

5. THE ADVANTAGES AND LIMITATIONS OF APPROPRIATION

The value of appropriation must be understood in relation to its foundation, and, in particular, to its final aim: the disclosure of the persons by way of the essential attributes. As we have already observed, the foundation is solid: 'The likeness of an appropriated attribute to the property of a person is the basis of the congruity of the appropriation from the standpoint of the reality, which would be there even if we did not exist.'[94] Its final aim has also been tried and tested: appropriation renders the divine persons more evident to our minds. We cannot *directly* attain the property of the person from the essential attributes, but, starting from a knowledge of the persons' properties, we can *indirectly* shed light on the person's character through the mediation of an

---

[90] *ST* III, q. 23, a. 2, ad 3.
[91] *ST* I, q. 43, a. 5, ad 1. All the gifts, qua gifts, are appropriated to the Holy Spirit. But if one considers the gifts in their distinct nature, then the gifts which perfect the understanding (faith and wisdom) are appropriated to the Son, and those which perfect the will, like charity, are appropriated to the Holy Spirit.
[92] *ST* I, q. 45, a. 7.
[93] *ST* I, q. 39, a. 8. See above, n. 56.
[94] I *Sent.* d. 31, q. 1, a. 2.

essential attribute. This indirect illumination enables us to give a better disclosure of each person in his distinctness, even though the means are still imperfect. When we appropriate omnipotence to the Father, for example, this profiles the property of the Father as Source, principle without principle. Appropriation nourishes our capacity to contemplate all things in the light of the Trinity.

Appropriation is a process of understanding and of language. It derives from an *analogical judgement* based in faith, and it is in this capacity that it introduces us to a deeper understanding of the mystery of the divine persons. In order to be illuminative, appropriation draws on specific theological rules, as we can see in Thomas, as well as in St Albert and St Bonaventure. These writers invite us to maintain a very precise usage of appropriation, not to descend into arbitrariness. This requires an exact notion of the persons' properties, of the Trinitarian order, and of the modes of procession. Appropriation is ineliminably bound to an organic view of Trinitarian theology.

The process of making appropriations also involves limitations. More precisely, it is necessary to evaluate appropriation in terms of what it can give us, not in relation to tasks which do not belong to it. By definition, the appropriated attributes are no substitute for the personal properties, and are not to be conflated with them. It does not belong to appropriations to give us a proper notion that could really distinguish each divine person; this is the task of the properties or Trinitarian 'notions', knowledge of which is assumed within the process of appropriation. Appropriation can never in any way replace theological study of the persons' properties, for it presupposes it. Appropriation is concerned *exclusively* with the region of that which is absolutely common to the three persons, that is to say, with that which is 'attributed to the nature'. It is here, and here alone, that it applies, and can show its worth. For this reason, appropriation was not called for in the exposition of the processions, the relations, or the personal properties. But reflection on the action of the Trinity is not exhausted by appropriation. The study of creative and salvific action will enable us better to perceive the Trinitarian grounds of the divine action, and, in return, will help us to grasp the value of appropriation more deeply.

14

Trinitarian Creation and Action

The idea of appropriations would be intellectually dissatisfying if it became the only route to the persons, and one had to imagine divine activity in its *entirety* as bearing on the divine essence. In other words, one is misusing appropriation if it lends itself to a 'monistic' conception of the divine activity. And this misapplication is what puts one on the slippery slope to making it a verbal game. Grasping Thomas' thought in the round requires us to reckon with the fact that his teaching on the creative activity of the Trinity is rather more extensive than this.

In fact, St Thomas developed a profoundly Trinitarian idea of creation. Weaving a coherent synthesis which closely binds together faith in the Triune God, creation, and the economy of grace, Thomas systematically presented the Trinitarian principles acting within creation, and their repercussions for our understanding of the created world. Without saying everything that could be said, it makes sense to sketch what follows on from the earlier chapters on Trinitarian action: from the facts that the Father creates and achieves all things through his Son and Spirit and that the procession of the divine persons is the cause of creation. We can thus attempt to discern the way in which the property of each person comes into play within the divine action (this will serve to consolidate the bases of appropriation), and ultimately to observe the Trinitarian structure of the economy of creation and grace as envisaged thus.

1. THE FATHER CREATES AND ACHIEVES ALL THINGS THROUGH HIS SON AND BY HIS SPIRIT

The study of the Father, Son, and Holy Spirit has made it clear that the personal properties do not only throw a spotlight on how the persons subsist in distinctness within the immanence of the Trinity, but also illuminate their activity within this world. St Thomas bound 'theology' and 'economy' tightly together at every step. In his study of the Father, he showed that Paternity primarily designates the intra-Trinitarian relation of Father to Son; divine paternity goes on to refer in a secondary way to the relation which God the Father has with the world, and that in many different ways (divine paternity as to nature and as to grace, paternity towards 'irrational' creatures and toward creatures made in the image of God): all creatures have God as their Father by participating in the relation which the Son has to his Father.[1]

In his study of the Son, he has shown that the property of the Word's personality relates him to creatures. For the Father achieves everything through his Word: in its very notion, *Word* signifies the Son as exemplar and effective cause, and enables one to grasp the grounds of the revelation of the Father which the Son brings about. Like its companion thread of *Image*, the enquiry into the name Son sheds light on both how the Son acts to create and how he acts to save. The entire thematic enables one to illuminate the incarnation of the Son.[2] We cannot attempt to condense this immense teaching into one of its features. But we can simply bring to mind the governing idea which steers these analyses:

God makes nothing except through the conception of his intellect, that is, the Word of God and the Son of God. So it is impossible that God make anything other than through his Son. And so Augustine says in *The Trinity* that the Word is the art full of the living patterns of all things. Thus it is clear that everything which the Father makes, he makes through him.[3]

The Father's acting 'through his Word' touches on creation (the Word is the expressive and productive source of creation), providence, the disclosure and revelation of the Father, salvation and the gift of enfiliation; in short, the whole of divine creative and salvific activity. In each case, Thomas presents the Son's action by means of his property as *Word, Son,* and *Image,* that is, by way of that which gives him his distinctive character within the Trinity. In an analogous way, he shows that the property personal to the Holy Spirit does not only enable us to grasp his eternal distinction and his existing, but also allows us to exposit his action in creation and the economy of grace. He uses the property of *Love* to display the Holy Spirit's activity of creating, exercising providence, moving creatures, vivifying, sanctifying, and building our life in grace. Being the Gift-personality, the Holy Spirit is given to the saints and dwells in them, he communicates the Father's presence, and that of the Son,

---

[1] *ST* I, q. 33, a. 3. See above, in Chapter 8, 'The Paternity of the Father: Father of the Son and Father of his Creatures'.

[2] *ST* I, q. 34, a. 3. See above, in Chapter 9, 'The Word, Creation, and the Economy: the Father Acts through his Son'; 'The Word Discloses and Reveals the Father'; 'The Son Gives Us a Share in his Sonship'; 'Image of the Father, First-Born of Creation'.

[3] *In Ioan.* 1.3 (no. 77).

replenishing the Church with his gifts.[4] We can recall again here the governing idea behind this teaching:

> The Father utters himself and every creature by the Word which he begets, in as much as the begotten Word represents the Father and all creatures. And in the same way, he loves himself and loves all creatures by the Holy Spirit, in that the Holy Spirit proceeds as love for the original goodness, the motive for the Father's loving himself and all creatures. Thus it is manifest that, as with the Word, a second aspect of Love proceeding is a reference to creatures.[5]

As we have indicated earlier, this argumentation means that the Love through which both Father and Son are together one is also the Love through which they net us into their communion: 'The Father and the Son love one another and they love us through the Holy Spirit, through "the Love" who proceeds.'[6] The theological exposition of divine activity rests on the study of the persons in their common essence and particular properties. St Thomas' analysis of the names *Word, Love,* and *Gift* showed that these names involve a relationship to creatures.[7] His exact point is that the divine person (Father, Son, Holy Spirit) is not directly related to creatures through the originary relation he enjoys within the eternal Trinity, but through the aspect in which the relationship includes the divine essence:

> The name of a divine person does not involve relationship to creatures as to personal relation, but as to that [within it] which touches on the nature. This does not obstruct a divine person's name from involving a relationship to creatures, in so far as this name includes the essence within its meaning. Thus, in the same way that it is proper to the Son to be *Son*, so it is proper to him to be *begotten God* and *Creator as begotten*.[8]

These nuances are at the heart of the matter. Once applied to the Trinitarian economy, they bring us back to the elemental features of the notion of *person* and of the structure of *relation*. Running over it quickly once more: relation has two sides to it, (1) it is a pure relating to another, and (2) it has existence within a subject. The first aspect (the relationship to another) constitutes the notion or 'rationale' proper to the relation and the second aspect renders the being (*esse*) of the real relation. Both aspects are required for any real relation. Within God, the first aspect consists in the pure person-to-person relating in terms of origin (paternity, filiation, spiration, procession). Under the second aspect, the divine relation is identical to the very being of the divine essence; it

---

[4] See above, in Chapter 10, 'Creative Love: The Universal Operation of the Holy Spirit'; 'The Gift of the Father and the Son'; 'The Holy Spirit's Gifts to Human Beings'.

[5] *ST* I, q. 37, a. 2, ad 3.

[6] *ST* I, q. 37, a. 2.

[7] For the *Word, ST* I, q. 34, a. 3, ad 1; for *Love,* q. 37, a. 2, ad 3; for *Gift,* q. 38, a. 1, ad 4.

[8] *ST* I, q. 34, a. 3, ad 1.

is the divine essence: it *is* God.[9] It is by plugging these two sides into each other that we can conceive the divine person as a relation who subsists: the person is distinct within the first side of the relation, the aspect of relating to another as to origin, and, within the second side of the relation, he subsists in virtue of the divine being he has.[10] Thomas applies this analysis to the relationship which the divine persons have to creatures. We can view the two sides of relation from closer to hand.

(1) The relationship to creatures does not enter into the first aspect of divine relations, that is, into the side consisting in pure relating to another; this contains the intrinsic rationale of the relation. Under this first aspect, intra-Trinitarian relations are purely person-to-person relatings, through origin. Each divine person is distinguished and constituted through the relation he has with the other divine persons; it is not the relationship to creatures which distinguishes and constitutes the divine person. If one brings the relationship to creatures into this region, it will lead one back into thinking that the Trinity's very existence as three distinct persons, depends on how God acts in the world, as if the world could fashion a divine person's being. This way of envisaging the matter implies a pantheistic conception of the Trinity or leads into Arianism or Sabellianism, which conceived the processions of the persons as God acting within creation. One will thus no longer be able to give an account of the divinity of the persons or of their perfect equality.[11]

(2) A relationship to creatures enters into the second side of the divine relation, that is, into the relation as 'including' the divine essence and having the being of the divine essence. The divine nature contains all creatures as pre-existing within it, and the divine nature is likewise the cause and the source of created things. Thomas exposed the main lines of this in his study of the essential attributes, where he speaks about the divine operations (God's knowledge, his will, his love and power). God creates through his essence, that is, through his wisdom, his will, and his power. And, this creating gives creatures a participation in the attributes which God has in their fullness ('essentially'), in an eminent mode.[12] In other words, God creates because he is God *and in so far as he is God*. This is why the relationship to creatures does not enter into the first aspect of personal relation, as pure 'relating to another',

[9] *ST* I, q. 28, a. 2; see above, in Chapter 5, 'The Being of Divine Relations'.

[10] See above, in Chapter 6, 'Subsistent Relations' and 'Relation the Heart of Trinitarian Theology'.

[11] Cf. *ST* I, q. 27, a. 1; see above, in Chapter 4, 'The Problems of Arianism and of Sabellianism'.

[12] With this nuance: the relationship to creatures is gratuitous, imposing no necessity on God. God does not create the world through a natural necessity. Rather, creation is God acting freely, through his wisdom and will (*ST* I, q. 19, a. 3).

but into the second aspect of relation, as the divine being. And what one says about *relation* can also be put in terms of *person*. The divine person is not implicated in a relationship to creatures in its aspect as a pure relation to another person, but it is involved in such a relation in the aspect in which it is divine. The Holy Spirit saves and the Son creates, because the Son and Holy Spirit are *divine* persons, that is, because they are God.

This is what St Thomas explains in reference to the Word, Love, and Gift: the relationship to creatures does not enter into the 'person relation', as a pure relating to another, but into the divine essence which the person 'includes', since the person is the divine essence. It is in this capacity that the Son is 'engendered Creator': the word *engendered* signifies the Son in his relationship to the Father, and the word *Creator* means the Son in his divine being. These two aspects of relating to another and divine subsisting are enfolded in the notion of 'divine person'. One has to take hold of the fundamental elements of the synthetic theory of relation and person in order to understand the relationship which the divine persons have to the world.

Do we not camouflage the personal facets of the Trinitarian economy if we affirm that God's relationship to creatures derives not from the pure person-to-person relation, but from the divine nature, common to the three persons? Do we not then mean that only the nature, and not the persons as such, enter into creation and the economy of grace? Absolutely not, because the person is not only constituted by the pure relating to another, but also through the nature in virtue of which it is a person. This is why Thomas explains that a relationship to creatures can indeed be 'included' in the notion of the divine person, where it comes into play within the divine person 'as a second step' after the eternal personal relation. When we profess that the Son is the Word of God, or when we recognize that the Holy Spirit is the Love and Gift of God, a relationship to creatures is 'included' in that 'just as the essence is included in the notion of the divine person'.[13] Thomas' explanation of God's relationship to the created world as flowing from the divine essence maintains that the relationship belongs to the divine persons, since the person is a person by owning the nature.

We need to take one additional step if we want to attempt to discern the personal dimension of creative and salvific action. What 'role' does that which is proper to each particular person play in the relationship to creatures? How do the properties of each of the persons enter into the Trinity's action in the world? Before we can answer this, we need to extend this preliminary discussion with a reminder of the idea of the 'causality of the Trinitarian processions'.

[13] *ST* I, q. 38, a. 1, ad 4.

2. THE 'EFFICACY' OF THE TRINITARIAN PROCESSIONS

In his first theological synthesis, the Commentary or Writing on the *Sentences*, Thomas formulated this central idea: 'the eternal processions are the cause and the rationale (*causa* et *ratio*) of the making of creatures'.[14] The words *cause* and *rationale* are rounded out with other terms in order to pin down the Trinitarian ground of creation. The procession of the persons is the *origin*,[15] the *principle*,[16] and the *exemplar*[17] of the procession of creatures. This affirmation is put forward as a theological exegesis of the biblical texts concerning the action of the Son and the Holy Spirit. The idea is not peripheral. One comes upon it nearly twenty times in Thomas' works, either in the same words[18] or in formulae contiguous to them: 'the temporal procession of creatures derives from the eternal procession of the persons';[19] 'the coming out of the persons in their unity of nature is the cause of the coming out of creatures in their diverse nature'.[20]

Thomas could have learned this thesis from his teacher, Albert the Great, who formulated it in his commentary on the *Sentences*.[21] It is also obviously inspired by Bonaventure who, without using precisely these words, also taught that the processions of the Son and Holy Spirit have a causality and exemplarity in relation to creation: the reason for the 'extrinsic diffusion' of created goodness is the 'intrinsic diffusion' of the sovereign Good within the divine persons, in the way that the *primary* reality is the cause of all the secondary things which derive from it. But the creative causality of the Trinitarian processions held far more meaning for Thomas than it had for Albert or Bonaventure: it is as if the character of his theology were shaped by its systematic mining of this thesis.[22]

When it is addressed to the divine creative act, Thomas calls the causal function of the Trinitarian processions the 'order of creation'.[23] An *order* is made up of a particular way in which things are related to a principle. It involves three elements.[24] In relation to the created order, these are: first, an

---

[14] I *Sent.* d. 14, q. 1, a. 1.   [15] I *Sent.* d. 32, q. 1, a. 3.   [16] I *Sent.* d. 35, div. text.

[17] I *Sent.* d. 29, q. 1, a. 2, qla 2; *De potentia*, q. 10, a. 2, sed contra 2.

[18] I *Sent.* d. 10, q. 1, a. 1; I *Sent.* d. 14, q. 2, a. 2; I *Sent.* d. 26, q. 2, a. 2, ad 2; I *Sent.* d. 27, q. 2, a. 3, ad 6; *De potentia*, q. 10, a. 2, arg. 19 and ad 19; *ST* I, q. 45, a. 6, sol. and ad 1; q. 45, a. 7, ad 3.

[19] *Sent.*, prol.; *Super Boetium de Trinitate*, prol.

[20] I *Sent.* d. 2, div. text.

[21] Albert, I *Sent.* d. 20, a. 3, sed contra; I *Sent.* d. 29, a. 2, sed contra 2.

[22] We examine this at length in *La Trinité créatrice*, and more briefly in 'Trinité et création. Le principe trinitaire de la création dans les commentaires d'Albert le Grand, de Bonaventure et de Thomas d'Aquin sur les *Sentences*', *RSPT* 79 (1995), 405–430.

[23] Thomas Aquinas, General Prologue to the Commentary on the *Sentences*.

[24] I *Sent.* d. 20, q. 1, a. 3, qla 1; cf. *ST* I, q. 42, a. 3.

essential distinction between God and the world, which excludes pantheism; second, the absolute primacy of God, as against the secondariness of the created world, which exists through participation in the divine perfection (the doctrines of participation and analogy);[25] and third, the threefold causality which is God's character as principle in relation to the world—efficient, exemplary, and final.[26] All the elements of the 'order of creation' are present in the affirmation that the Trinitarian processions are the cause and rationale for the procession of creatures. Exemplary causality has a privileged position here. St Thomas sets the Trinitarian processions under the following rule: that which is first and has the highest degree of perfection is the cause and rationale of what comes later and has the perfection to a limited extent.[27] The use of this principle, one which animates the *Summa's* fourth proof of the existence of God,[28] indicates that we are at the nerve-centre of the Thomist metaphysics of participation. As applied to the Trinity, this principle entails that the Trinitarian processions are the exemplary, efficient, and final cause of the procession of creatures; the Trinitarian processions are the 'rationale' of God's creative action, the creature's principle both in the ontological order and in the order of intelligibility. Thus, one has to know about the procession of the divine persons in order fully to understand creation.

This analysis does not pick out any one particular divine person and exclusively or properly ascribe creation to him. God is creator in virtue of the divine nature common to the three persons: the three persons are 'one single Creator'.[29] Creative causation cannot precisely be ascribed to one single divine person; it should be wholly attributed to the Trinitarian processions. The word *procession* stands for an origin or entry into existence, a reality's coming into being from its principle.[30] In considering the Trinity and creation under their analogous aspect of *procession* (Son and Spirit eternally *proceed* from God, and creatures also *proceed* from God, in a different order), one makes use of a concept which leads one into the analogous modes of the communication of existence. Creation and the economy of grace are not

[25] I *Sent. Prol.*, q. un., a. 2, ad 3; cf II *Sent.* d. 3, q. 3, a. 3, ad 2.

[26] Cf. *ST* I, q. 44. The notion of 'cause' is a spacious one, including all of the complex and differentiated influences which one reality can exert on another. Causal interrelationships are not simply univocal: whether it is material, formal, efficient, or final, causality comes about in analogous ways. This analogous character comes to the foreground when one is conceiving God's activity in 'causal' terms. It reckons with the diverse aspects of the action of the God who freely gives a participation in his perfection to creatures: this causation is efficient, exemplary, and final.

[27] *Sent.*, prol.; I *Sent.* d. 18, q. 1, a. 3, contra 2; I *Sent.* d. 32, q. 1, a. 3; etc. I investigate this further in *La Trinité créatrice*, pp. 276–285. For other ways of applying it, see J. Tonneau, 'L'accessoire suit le principal', in Thomas Aquinas, *Somme théologique, La Loi nouvelle, 1a2ae, Questions 106–108*, Paris, 1999, pp. 215–233.

[28] *ST* I, q. 2, a. 3.   [29] *ST* I, q. 45, a. 6.   [30] I *Sent.* d. 13, q. 1, a. 1.

connected to any one divine person but to the Trinity: the entire 'Triune processus' comes into play here.

With God, procession represents the personal communication of divinity in its fullness: the Father eternally communicates the plenal deity to the Son; he and the Son together communicate it to the Holy Spirit. One is addressing the dynamic quality of the persons, as eternally communicating their divinity, when one speaks of 'procession' in God. In its own, different order, creation consists in the creature's participation in the being and perfections of God. Trinitarian causation is located in the frame of the *communication of a participation in the divine perfections*; this meshes with the theory of analogy. The intercommunication of the entire divine nature amongst the persons of the Trinity is the cause and rationale of the communication to creatures of a participation in the divine nature. The order of creation is radically different, and yet, 'the coming out of the persons in their unity of nature is the cause of the coming out of creatures in their diversity of nature'.[31] We can see that this comes down to the distinction and connection between the action *immanent* to the Trinity and the way that God acts *transitively* in the world:[32] the first is the 'rationale' of the second.[33]

St Thomas presented two interpretations of the 'efficacy' of the Trinitarian processions: chronologically, the first comes in his *Sentence* commentary and the second in the *Summa Theologiae*. There is an observable deepening in his perceptions. In his earlier work, Thomas explains that a viable take on the divine persons' action will take two complementary rules into account: (1) the efficacity common to the divine nature and (2) the eternal procession of the divine persons. He wrote that,

The procession of the divine persons is in a certain way what originates the procession of creatures, since what is first in any genus is the cause of what comes after it; but efficacity with respect to creatures ought to be ascribed to the common nature.[34]

Thomas draws on this dual principle to explain the way in which 'the Father and the Son love us through the Holy Spirit'. It also enables one to show how 'the Father speaks all things *through his Word*'. The divine action is not wholly explained by reference to the divine nature, that is, by the creative knowledge and will of the Trinity. It also has its roots in the Trinitarian processions which are the exemplar-model and rationale of the works God brings about in the world. When he refers to the 'causation of that which is first', Thomas means that speaking the Word is the model of the way that God

---

[31] I *Sent.* d. 2, div. text.
[32] See above, in Chapter 3, 'The Plan of the Trinitarian Treatise in the *Summa Theologiae*'.
[33] *SCG* II, ch. 1 (no. 854).
[34] I *Sent.* d. 32, q. 1, a. 3.

communicates himself to creation. In the same way, the Holy Spirit is the rationale of all that God communicates in the generosity of his love. Within God, the only person who proceeds 'by the mode of mind' is the Son: he is in this capacity the uncreated model and rationale of the procession of creatures from God as works of wisdom. The only person in God who proceeds by the mode of love is the Holy Spirit: he is the rationale of the procession of creatures as coming from God in the form of a divine gift. On this analysis, creative causation—as 'efficiency'—belongs to the divine nature, whereas the 'rationale of this causation'—'rationale for efficiency'—retraces the format of the procession of the divine persons.[35] In their common work of creation, the three persons act through their common nature, each person bringing his own property into play.

Because he now has to hand his developed theory of relation, St Thomas is able to bring more precision to bear on the exemplarity and causality of the Trinitarian processions by the time he writes the *Summa*. His analysis is marked by the progress in his Trinitarian theology. Whereas Thomas' first writing founded his Trinitarian doctrine on the notion of *procession*, the *Summa* structures it more clearly around the notion of *relation*. Drawing on the two facets we mentioned above, relationship to another and divine nature, Thomas writes that,

the divine persons have causality with respect to the creation of things in the rationale [*rationem*] of their procession. For, as was shown in the discussion of God's knowledge and volition, as the craftsman is to the works of his art, so God is the cause of things through his mind and his will. And the craftsman works through an idea conceived in his mind and through love in his will bent on his work. Likewise, God the Father wrought the creature through his Word the Son, and through his Love, which is the Holy Spirit. And thus, carrying in them the essential attributes of knowing and willing, the comings forth of the divine Persons are patterns [*rationes*] of the coming forth of creatures.[36]

Thomas explains this by drawing on the analogy of intellect and will. The relations which the 'immanent' acts have with the acts oriented to a reality external to them is once again made explicit. We should not be misled by the simplicity of the craftsman example: this analogy is wedded to a freighted metaphysical reflection on the principles of divine action. What should engage our attention here is the conclusion: so far as they 'carry' the essential attributes, the processions of the persons are the 'rationale' or 'cause of

---

[35] Ibid. This relates to the rationale for efficiency from the standpoint of the effects (*ex parte effectorum*). On this important article, see my book, *La Trinité créatrice*, pp. 430–443.

[36] *ST* I, q. 45, a. 6. On the continuity and development within Thomas' thought on this point see G. Marengo, *Trinità e Creazione: Indagine sulla teologia di Tommaso d'Aquino*, Rome, 1990.

creation'.³⁷ Thomas no longer relies on *two* complementary rules, as in his *Sentence* Commentary. One is now enough: personal procession includes the divine nature. The upshots of the analysis yielded by his ideas of person and relation are now vigorously applied to the divine action. God does not act in two separate ways, through his nature and through his personal processions. The 'linchpin' of the divine activity is the relations which flow from the processions, and the persons who combine distinction and commonality. Beginning from the fact that the divine nature is drawn out into the processions, since these processions and relations are *divine*, one can say that it is through such processions that the persons achieve creation. This is precisely the same analytic route through which Thomas led us earlier on, when he studied the properties of Word, Love, and Gift.

3. THE QUESTION OF THE 'ROLE PROPER' TO EACH OF THE PERSONS

The discussion of the 'causation' exercised through the personal processions takes us back to a question which was raised earlier in relation to the personal properties: what 'role' do the things which properly belong to each of the persons play in the divine action? On Thomas' view, we have to avoid two possible answers. We can quickly glance in their direction.

One unsatisfactory way out is to say that, since the persons act purely through what is entirely common to them, no one divine person brings anything 'proper' to himself into his mode of action: the principle of action is the divine nature. This solution can draw on the Orthodox axiom of the three persons' unity of 'energy', or on the Augustinian principle of the indivisibility of the Trinitarian works *ad extra*. The personal distinctions come into their mutual relationships, but the actions they exercise on our behalf are void of them. This response is common in early modern scholasticism, and one can find it in the neo-scholastic manuals of the nineteenth and twentieth centuries. It can lead one to graft creation into the investigation of the 'One God' (*De Deo uno*), since the Trinitarian plurality plays no role in the divine action. By the same token, it weakens the value of the idea of appropriations, by making the appropriations the *sole means* of displaying the Trinitarian dimension of divine action.

Our own reading of the issue does not shrink from accentuating the significance of the axiom of the unity of action in the Trinity: it is fundamental,

---

³⁷ *ST* I, q. 45, a. 6, ad 1.

and lies at the centre of the treatise on the Trinity.[38] Creation and grace are not the proper or exclusive work of any single divine person. The three persons are at the source of all things together, by dint of their common divine nature. Failure to perceive this leads to the denial of the consubstantiality of the persons of the Trinity. Appropriation is likewise an invaluable process, as Thomas showed in some detail. The drawback in this way of tackling the question is not that the principles it draws on are false, but that the principles are applied in an *exclusive* way, as if the axiom of the unity of operations constitutes the single lever which relays the action of the Trinity. In other words, the axiom of the indivisibility of the Trinity when it acts *ad extra* is accurate and fundamental, but one takes it too far if one presumes one can reduce the entirety of the activity of the divine persons to this point.

In powerful reaction against this way of responding to the question, the second answer maintains that each divine person exercises his own particular action on our behalf. This way of conceiving the activity of the divine persons is attractive to many contemporary theological writers. Some people then go on to pin down the 'personal causality' and the 'proper function' of each divine person. For instance, bestowing grace will be seen as a characteristic activity of the Holy Spirit, as if the Holy Spirit himself brought about this grace independently of the other divine persons. Or again, in reference to the gift of adoptive sonship, people will emphasize that enfiliation makes us children of the Father, to the exclusion of the other persons. The idea that one divine person exercises a 'quasi-formal causality' is especially popular in relation to the graces given by the Holy Spirit.[39] Personally present to the saints, the Holy Spirit himself exercises the role of the immanent principle of the human acts of faith and charity. That explains the distinct and proper work of one divine person on our behalf.

Even apart from the problem that a theory of 'formal causality' creates a confusion between God and the world—since a form is by definition inherent in a creature, one of its ontological constitutive features, it is really part of the creature's make-up[40]—there is an insurmountable problem in the idea of an

---

[38] See for example *ST* I, q. 32, a. 1; q. 45, a. 6.

[39] Talking about 'quasi-formal' causality amongst the divine persons was not unknown to the scholastics. For instance, Albert used it to refer to the Holy Spirit as the one through whom we love God and neighbour. But he immediately specifies that neither the *habitus* nor the act of charity are the Holy Spirit 'in essence'; they are, rather, the effects of the Holy Spirit (Albert, *Summa theologiae* I, tract. 8, q. 36, ch. 3; ed. Colon. vol. 34/1, p. 282). And we then come back to the affirmation of the inseparable causality of the Trinity, using the idea of appropriations (ibid., tract. 7, q. 32, ch. 2, p. 254).

[40] Thomas clearly shows the *exemplarity* belonging to the Holy Spirit, but without making the Holy Spirit a formal and inherent cause, and without excluding the Father and Son: 'charity has the whole Trinity as its efficient cause, and the Love which is the Holy Spirit as its exemplary cause' (I *Sent.* d. 17, q. 1, a. 1); cf. *ST* II-II, q. 23, a. 2; *ST* I-II, q. 110, a. 1.

'action proper' to one divine person. Setting aside one action or one divine gift for one person rather than another casts suspicion on the oneness of the Trinity, raising doubts as much about its unity in nature as about its relations.[41] Creation is the most obvious example,[42] but looking into any number of the divine actions could show us the basic principle that, from their single nature, the three persons act in one single operation or *action*,[43] and that the source of the *effects* of the divine action is therefore always the entire Trinity.[44] Theological reflection on the Trinitarian economy can never run counter to this rule, which is a foundational presence throughout this topic.

What we learn from this about how to elaborate the Trinitarian dimension of the divine action can be summed up as follows: whilst the rule of the essential unity of the three persons gives us one of the basic criteria which guides our meditation on the action of the Triune persons, it nonethless cannot be the sole feature of divine action.

4. THE PERSONS' DISTINCT MODES OF ACTION AND THEIR UNITY IN ACTION

The three divine persons act inseparably, in virtue of their common divine nature, and the whole Trinity is the source of all their works. But each person acts within the distinct mode of his relationship to the other persons within this common action. Before explaining the theoretical foundations of this, we can look at how the creative acts of the Word illustrate it. In his exegesis of John 1.3 (*through him all things were made*), St Thomas explains that the Word is the one *through whom* the Father brings all things into being, and he then moves on to a more focused reflection on the activity of the Word. What does it mean to be the one '*through whom*' the Father brings all things to be? One can consider it from two angles.[45]

(1) If the intention of the phrase *through whom* is the 'formal principle' of the action, that is the Father's principle of action, that 'in virtue of which' the Father acts, then we must see this as meaning the divine nature. Like the Son

---

[41] We have already seen this in relation to the economic dimension of Trinitarian perichoresis. See above, in Chapter 12, 'Theology and Economy'.

[42] *ST* I, q. 45, a. 6.

[43] See for instance *SCG* IV, ch. 25 (no. 3625), '*una actione*'.

[44] See for example *ST* III, q. 23, a. 2. The incarnation of the Son is no exception. The Son alone assumes humanity into the unity of his person; this is why the Son alone is the '*term* of this assumption' but 'what belongs to the act of assuming belongs to the three persons'; for 'the three persons caused the human nature to be united to the one person of the Son' (ST III, q. 3, a. 4).

[45] *In Ioan.* 1.3 (no. 76).

and the Holy Spirit, the Father acts through his own nature: every being acts by its nature. Thomas speaks here of the 'formal' principle in order to avoid bringing in any idea of an 'efficient' principle, since nothing and nobody can stimulate or move the Father to act. Neither the Son nor the Spirit is a 'principle' of the Father's action, because the Son and Spirit are not related as principles in respect of the Father: the Trinitarian order prevents us from seeing the Son or the Holy Spirit either as principles of the Father's being or as principles of the Father's acting. Thus, when one takes it as indicating a 'formal' principle, the expression *'through whom'* is appropriated to the Son, because God the Father acts through his essential wisdom which is appropriated to the Son. In this sense, formulae like *of whom, through whom,* and *in whom* (Rom. 11.36), are appropriated rather than being proper to any one person.[46]

This analysis may seem to have taken us a long way from the obvious meaning of John 1.3, but it was necessary to specify that when the Father acts *through his Word* this does not make the Word principle to the Father. We do not say that the Father acts 'through the Son' in the way that one would say of a human being that he acts 'on what he has learned' or 'through his own freedom'. In this sense, the Father acts through himself or through his nature. This had already been observed by Augustine: when one maintains that 'the Father is wise through his begotten wisdom', one does not mean to say that the Son could cause the Father's wisdom, since that would lead us into the *reductio ad absurdum* that the Father is not wise in himself but only through the Son, and that the Father therefore derives his nature from the Son. The Son is not the wisdom through which the Father is wise, but 'begotten wisdom', flowing from the Father.[47] The same theory will go for the Father's action.

(2) But if one takes *through him* in John 1.3 to mean the causation the Word effects in relation to creatures,[48] then this must be fully understood to mean a *property of the Son.* This is doubtless the most obvious meaning of John 1.3. Taken in this sense, the expression *through him* does not denote the Father's principle of action, but the principle or cause of creatures, and this must be acknowledged to go beyond appropriation to being a trait proper to the personality of the Word. Thomas writes that,

if the preposition 'through' denotes causality from the standpoint of the thing produced, then when we say *The Father does all things through the Son,* it is not simply appropriated to the Word, but is proper to him (*proprium*). For the fact that he is the

---

[46] *ST* I, q. 39, a. 8.
[47] Augustine, *De Trinitate* VII.I.1–2; XV.VII.12. Cf. Thomas, I *Sent.* d. 32, q. 2, a. 1; *ST* I, q. 34, a. 1, ad 2.
[48] See also II *Sent.* d. 13, q. 1, a. 5.

cause of creatures is had from someone else, namely the Father, from whom he has being.[49]

The Son is the one 'through whom' the Father acts, because he is the Father's begotten Son and Word. In relation to the Father and Son's action, the preposition 'through' means the Father's *authority*, the property as principle to the Son which belongs to the Father. The Son exists in the eternal reception of his being from the Father, and the way he acts conforms to this, that is, he eternally receives his action from the Father. Father and Son perform one single *action*, and the *principle of this action* is also single, the divine nature or essence; the *effects* of this action are common to Father and Son. But the subjects of this action, the *actors* themselves, are distinct, and what one can call their *mode of action* is also distinct.[50] Although this observation has escaped most commentators, perhaps because it is set in the question on appropriations, Thomas says as much in the *Summa Theologiae*: 'in some contexts the [preposition] *through* does not mean an appropriation, but a property of the Son, as with John 1.3, *through him all things were made*'.[51]

This is the route that Thomas takes to show us the importance of distinctions within the three persons' action. Here the personal distinction is not a matter of the three persons' action, which is one and single, or their power and principles of action, which come from their common nature and so are common to the three persons. Nor is it related to the effects of the divine action: these effects issue from the three as persons executing one single action. The doctrine of perichoresis shows this quite well: the Father is in the Son, the Son is in the Father, the Holy Spirit is in the Father and in the Son, as they are present in him. This makes the actions of the three persons inseparable. So, for instance, Thomas explains this by saying that 'The Son acts because of the Father who indwells him, in their unity of nature';[52] 'Christ works through the Holy Spirit... and this is why everything brought about by the Holy Spirit is also brought about by Christ.'[53] The depth of the perichoresis is such that the Father himself acts in the Son's actions, and the Holy Spirit acts inseparably with them both. The action of Son and Holy Spirit is thus no different from the Father's, since, because they are immanent

---

[49] *In Ioan.* 1.3 (no. 76). One can see that, for Thomas, John 1.3 is not tied down to meaning creation in the strict sense, but encompasses every inner-worldly divine action.

[50] Cf. II *Sent.* d. 13, q. 1, a. 5; ad 4: 'It is because of the Father's *authority* with respect to the Son, the fact that the Son takes his being and action from the Father, that the Father acts "through the Son".'

[51] *ST* I, q. 39, a. 8: '*proprium Filii*'.

[52] *In Ioan.* 14.12 (no. 1898).

[53] *In Eph.* 2.18 (no. 121).

to one another, the persons indwell one another's actions; they have one single operation.[54]

But the acting persons are distinct, and their acting modes reflect their relative personal property. The mode of action exhibits nothing more or less than the personal character itself. The Father's acting through the Word makes a good case-study on this. The Son's distinct mode of action (the Son is the one *through whom* the Father acts) does not consist in his way of being related towards creatures; it is rather the relationship to the Father which is proper to the Son within the heart of the Trinity. Another way of putting it is to say that this proper modality entirely resides in the person-to-person relations within the Trinity, and not in a relation to creatures which is other to this.

This is precisely what Thomas explains, from another perspective, in connection with the names *Word, Love,* and *Gift*: personal distinctness within the Triune actions does not emerge from the ways of being related to creatures, but from the intra-Trinitarian relations. It properly belongs to the Father to be the one who acts through his Son in the Spirit: he is the only one in the Trinity who acts in this way, in virtue of the property personal to him. It properly belongs to the Son to be the one through whom the Father creates and achieves all things: the Son is the only one in the Trinity who acts in this way, because it is his property to be Son, Word, and Image. And it properly belongs to the Holy Spirit to be the one in whom or through whom the Father and the Son act, because of his property as Love and Gift. Thomas explained this when he showed that 'the Father speaks all things through his Son' and that 'the Father and the Son love us through the Holy Spirit', or when he explained that 'the processions of the persons are the cause of the procession of creatures'.[55] Expressions like this are used properly; they are not just appropriations. Appropriation is not the only way we have for grasping the Trinitarian dimension of God's activity.

These observations can be authenticated within many areas of Thomas' teaching, for instance the relationship between the persons' mode of being and their mode of action. How a being acts follows from what he is: as one is, so one acts. The mode of action is bound to the mode of being which it reflects.[56] But if the *being* of the three persons is in fact identical, their *mode of*

---

[54] See above, in Chapter 12, 'Theology and Economy'.

[55] Cf. *ST* I, q. 34, a. 3; q. 37, a. 2, ad 3; I *Sent.* d. 32, q. 1, a. 3; etc.

[56] See for instance *ST* I, q. 89, a. 1: 'As nothing acts except in so far as it is actual, the mode of action (*modus operandi*) in every agent follows from its mode of existence (*modus essendi*)'; see also *ST* I, q. 50, a. 5: 'Since everything acts according as it is actual, the operation of a thing indicates its mode of being'; *ST* I, q. 75, a. 2: 'Only what actually exists acts, and its manner of acting follows from its manner of being.'

being is distinct. This mode of being consists in the way in which each person's relative property functions in his possession of the divine nature: 'Even though the same nature exists in Father and Son, one can see here another mode of existing (*alius modus existendi*), that is to say, a different relation.'[57] The essence of the three persons is one and the same, but each person has, or more precisely, *is*, this divine essence after a distinct relation. Thus, the nature is given in each person within a distinct 'mode of existence'.[58] Thomas lays this out with the utmost clarity:

Although the nature of the Father, Son and Holy Spirit is the same, nonetheless [the nature] is not had in the same mode of existence in the three, and I speak of the mode of existing as to relation. For in the Father it is not received from another, in the Son it is received from the Father.[59] Although the Godhead is wholly and perfectly in each of the three Persons according to its proper mode of existence, yet it belongs to the perfection of the Godhead that there be several modes of existence in God, namely that there be one from whom another proceeds yet proceeds from no other, and one proceeding from another. For there would not be full perfection in God unless there were in him procession of the Word and of Love.[60]

It is clear that this teaching on the 'modes of existence' is a reappropriation of Cappadocian Trinitarian doctrine: their *tropoi tês hyparxeôs* are literally *modes of existence*.[61] The relation each person has gives him to exist in his own distinct way. The personal property fashions the mode of relational being proper to each person. The Father exists in the mode of the unengendered source; receiving his existence from the Father's begetting, the Son exists in the mode of filiation; the Holy Spirit exists in the mode of the love which proceeds from Father and Son. Each person is thus characterized by a relational mode of existing. This distinct mode does not vanish into thin air in the persons' action. It remains present. In the same way that one can perceive distinct modes of being in the three persons, one can see distinct modes of action. A very precise picture of the matter imposes itself on us: the distinction amongst the persons touches neither on the divine being or nature of the persons, nor on their power of action, nor on their action itself. But the persons are distinct under the perspective of the *mode* of existing of the divine nature in them, and thus, under the perspective of the mode of action corresponding to this mode of being. In every field, the distinction of these modes thus concerns the

---

[57] *De potentia*, q. 2, a. 1, ad 13.   [58] *De potentia*, q. 2, a. 5, ad 5.

[59] *De potentia*, q. 3, a. 15, ad 17: 'quod licet eadem natura sit patris et filii et spiritus sancti, non tamen eumdem modum existendi habet in tribus, et dico modum existendi secundum relationem. In patre enim est ut non accepta ab alio, in filio vero ut a patre accepta.'

[60] *De potentia*, q. 9, a. 5, ad 23.

[61] See for instance Basil of Caesarea, *On the Holy Spirit* 18.46 (SC 17 2nd edn., pp. 408–409).

relation proper to the person, that is the intra-Trinitarian person-to-person origination relation. Each person exists and acts or 'operates' after his personal relation. It is this which Thomas is unravelling when he says that it properly belongs to the Son to be the one *through whom* the Father acts.

So no occultation of the persons is in hand when he attributes creation, or the divine action *ad extra* to the divine nature. It really is the divine nature which is the source of creation in each person; and a nature which each person has after the mode of his relative property. The first way one can justify this is from our ordinary use of language. We speak of the three persons as 'one single Creator', but we say there are 'three who create', or three 'Creatings'. The name *Creator* signifies the principle of creation; and we have said that this principle is the common essence of the three persons: 'creation is the work of three persons, not as distinct, but in as much as they are united in the essence'.[62] To put it another way, the three persons do not create the world in function of what distinguishes them, but by force of what unites them—their divinity. The three persons create because they are God. And if we could really say 'three creators' in the full meaning of the words, that would mean three different natures, three Gods. One must recognize that the truth lies elsewhere: the persons are three who create, three *Creatings*. In this place also, Thomas looks very carefully at our way of speaking. Unlike the substantive noun *Creator*, the verbal participle *Creating* does not immediately signify the principle of action, which is single, but the *subjects* of the creative action, who are distinct.[63]

So to outline the Trinitarian dimension of creation, one has to look at the acting persons, that is, the subjects of the action, the 'operators', keeping focused at the same time on the divine persons' mutual *relations*. Thomas says that, 'It is from the Father that the Son takes his being and action, and this is why the Father acts through the Son'; 'The acting Son exists from the Father'; 'The Father acts through the Son, because the Son is the cause of that which is achieved from one and the same indivisible power, a power which the Son has in common with the Father but which he nonetheless receives from the Father's begetting.'[64] The property signified by the name *Word* puts this in the spotlight: in calling the Son by the name *Word*, we say that he is the 'operative' cause of the works which the Father achieves through him.[65]

---

[62] I *Sent.* d. 11, q. un., a. 4, ad 2; d. 29, q. un., a. 4, ad 2: 'creation is the work of the divine nature'; *ST* I, q. 36, a. 4, ad 7, 'creatures do not proceed from the three persons as they are distinct but as they are one in essence'.

[63] I *Sent.* d. 11, q. un., a. 4, ad 2; d. 29, q. un., a. 4, ad 2.

[64] II *Sent.* d. 13, q. 1, a. 5, sol., ad 4; d. 13, exp. text.

[65] See above, in Chapter 9, 'The Word, Creation, and the Economy: the Father Acts through his Son'.

The interpretation of John 1.3 refines on this: in creating, the Son is the subject of an action (an operation) distinct from that of the Father.[66] The Father acts 'through the Son' because the Father's eternal begetting gives the Son the divine essence through which the Son acts.

The discussion of the Holy Spirit accents his personal distinction in a similar way. In breathing the Holy Spirit, Father and Son give the Holy Spirit the divine nature, and with it his operative power. This is why Father and Son act 'in the Holy Spirit' or 'through the Holy Spirit'.[67] In this respect, in as much as they communicate the divine power of action to him, the Father and Son are the principle of the action which the Spirit performs.[68] Thomas specially brings this out in reference to the property intended by the personal names *Love* and *Gift*. In recognizing the Spirit as Love and Gift we signify him as the source of the effects which Father and Son bring about through him, that is as the Love through which Father and Son love us and from which they give us their gifts.[69]

In sum, 'whatever the Son does, he has from the Father'.[70] And likewise, the Holy Spirit acts as receiver of his own action from Father and Son, because he receives the divine nature from them: the Holy Spirit receives his being and action from the Father and Son, and it is in this reception that he exercises his activity.[71] The three persons act in the same action, but each of them performs this act in the distinct mode of his personal relation, that is after the 'mode of existence' which fits the Trinitarian order. The Father acts as source of Son and Spirit, the Son acts as Word of the Father, the Holy Spirit acts as Love and Gift of Father and Son. We are not in the milieu of appropriations, but solidly within that of the persons' *properties*, as Thomas says explicitly with reference to the Word.[72] To repeat, what we have called the 'distinct mode' of the persons' actions is not purely a relationship of the person to creatures but strictly concerns the eternal relations of one divine person to another.

In conclusion, while clearly emphasizing the divine persons' unity of *action*, the unity of their *principle of action*, and the unity of the three persons in their relationship to *created effects*, this doctrine invites us to spot a relational *mode of action* which belongs to each person in a distinct way; this mode of action consists in the intra-Trinitarian personal relation.

---

[66] *In Ioan.* 1.3 (nos. 76 and 85).   [67] *De potentia*, q. 10, a. 4; *CEG* II, ch. 4.

[68] *CEG* II, ch. 4: 'the Son is the principle of the Holy Spirit's acting (*principium operandi Spiritui Sancto*), because he gives him his acting force'.

[69] See above, in Chapter 10, 'Creative Love: The Universal Operation of the Holy Spirit'; 'The Gift of the Father and the Son'; 'The Holy Spirit's Gifts to Human Beings'.

[70] *In Ioan.* 15.26 (no. 2061).

[71] *In Ioan.* 16.13 (no. 2103).

[72] This strengthens the significance of the appropriations which flow from the personal properties.

5. TRINITY AND CREATION: THE MEANING
OF THE PLURAL

When he discusses the plurality characteristic of our world, Thomas stresses the goodness of the plurality and diversity which God wills for it. The multiplicity of creatures is not the result of the fall, but is created by God: it expresses the goodness of God. The most common theme to which Thomas turns to show this is that of the representation of the divine perfection. In short, he looks at it like this: God created the world through love, giving creatures a participation in his goodness; and, any one single creature, in its finitude, does not suffice to represent the divine good; God has therefore created a universe (*universum*); that is to say a plurality of creatures within an ordered multiplicity, apt to represent his goodness.[73] This thesis, the product of Christian Neoplatonism, is not his only explanation for the goodness of creaturely multiplicity. Trinitarian faith also illuminates the plurality of things within our world:

as to the order of dignity and causality, this distinction [of the divine persons] excels all distinctions; and likewise the relation which is the principle of the distinction, excels in dignity every distinguishing amongst creatures: not because it is a relation, but because it is a divine relation. It excels them in causality, since all creaturely procession and multiplicity proceeds out of the procession of the divine persons.[74]

This analysis emerges within the study of relation. Thomas has shown that, within the Trinity, personal *distinction* does not divide the three persons' unity of being. As we have seen, this personal distinction rests on *relation*. Following Aristotle and Averroes, he notes that relation has the weakest kind of being had by worldly things, since, unlike the other categories of being, relation does not intrinsically determine or modify the subject. Taken in itself, relation purely consists in a relating to another. Distinction through relation is thus 'the most minuscule' of all real distinctions. This is why Thomas deployed the notion of relation to exhibit the distinction of the persons in God: relation can make sense of genuine plurality within unity.[75]

Relation to another is not however the only aspect of a real relation: in our world, a relation exists in a subject from which it takes its existence. In God, relation has the being of the divine nature: its being is identical to the divine nature.[76] This is why, considered in their 'dignity' and 'causality', distinction

---

[73] *ST* I, q. 47, a. 1.

[74] I *Sent.* d. 26, q. 2, a. 2, ad 2. There is a detailed exposition of this passage in *La Trinité créatrice*, pp. 445–454.

[75] Cf. *ST* I, q. 40, a. 2, ad 3. See above, in Chapter 5, 'The Being of Divine Relations'.

[76] *ST* I, q. 28, a. 2; q. 29, a. 4; q. 39, a. 1; q. 40, a. 1.

and relation within the Trinity excel all other distinctions and relations. The personal relations do not achieve this prerogative simply through what a relation notionally consists of, being a relationship to another, but because the relation in question is *divine*: within God, personal relation has the same existential flavour as the divine nature, and this properly belongs to the divine relations as such. This is why the divine relations exercise the universal causality which belongs to the divine nature. Thomas does not only treat the divine relations in their efficient causality, but also as exemplar causes. The divine relations, and thus the distinctions which flow from these relations, are the cause of the procession and the diversification of creatures.

Thus, the Trinitarian *distinctions* and *relations* throw light on creation. The first distinction, that of the divine persons, is the cause of that other distinction which is the creation; for creation is the production of a world really distinct from God, so creation creates a distinction. In the same way, the plurality of persons, the principle of which is relation, is the cause of the 'multiplication' of creatures: the plurality of genus and species amongst creatures, and the multiplicity of individuals within species, the multiplicity of events produced within history, have the Trinitarian relations as their source. It is difficult to emphasize strongly enough what a positive value the multiplicity within the created world has. Plurality is not a falling away from unity, but rather a participation in the fullness of Trinitarian life. As the principle of distinction at the heart of the Trinity, personal distinction comes to be seen as the ultimate source of creation and of every kind of multiplicity in our world.[77] Thomas' teaching on this throws an immense light on the meaning of the manyness and difference within our world.

6. THE TRINITARIAN STRUCTURE OF THE ECONOMY

In the preceding analyses, creation was in the foreground. But the Trinitarian dimension of the divine action is not limited to creation. As the first step of the economy, creation is located in the complete divine plan as understood in the light of Trinitarian faith. The influence of the begetting of the Son and the procession of the Holy Spirit extends to the economy. The thematic of the 'causality' of the procession of the divine persons enables one to articulate that the economy has a Trinitarian structure. According to St Thomas,

---

[77] Writers often invoke the fact that Thomas' 'metaphysics of being' enables us to grasp the relationships between God and our world. Although this aspect of his thought is fundamental, we also need to complete or extend this into a 'metaphysics of relation', which, from within his doctrine of being, constitutes one of the essential features of Thomas' theological thought.

Trinitarian Creation and Action

in the same way that the procession of the persons is the rationale for the production of creatures by the first principle, so likewise the procession of the persons is the rationale of this return to the end; since, in the same way that we have been created through the Son and the Holy Spirit, so likewise it is through them that we are united to the ultimate end.[78]

The economy pivots on the begetting of the Son and the breathing of the Holy Spirit. Thomas is conceiving creation and grace here in terms of the coming out (*exitus*) and return to God (*reditus*). All creatures come from the Father who creates them through his Son and by the Holy Spirit (*exitus*). This is the primary domain of God's gift of existence to creatures, that is the goods of nature in the widest sense. As we have seen, it is the act of the Son to deal out these goods: begotten by the Father, the Son is the model and source of this communication in which God confers a participation in the goods of nature upon creatures. Because he proceeds by a mode of intellect as the Word of the Father, the Word is the Art by which the Father achieves his works of wisdom in the world: the Father creates through his Word.[79] And likewise the Holy Spirit is the pattern and source of this communication in as much as it flows from God's love. Proceeding as the Love with which Father and Son love one another, the Holy Spirit is also the Love by which Father and Son communicate a participation in the divine goodness to creatures as an act of love.[80] In this initial domain, the Trinitarian processions shed light on the benefits which creatures receive from the wisdom and goodness of God, 'the natural gifts in which we subsist'.[81]

In his *Sentence* commentary, Thomas makes an observation about the parallelism between the divine works. If we receive the grace to return to God by participating in his beatitude (*reditus*), this also happens under the influence of the Trinitarian processions: they are as much the cause and rationale of the *reditus* as of the *exitus*. The image of 'circulation' is brought forward to signal the unity of the economy of creation and of grace, and to emphasize the unity of the Trinitarian mode of action: creation and union with God are achieved through the same Trinitarian processions, plying their influence in diverse ways. The *Summa* speaks of God in more Aristotelian terms, as 'principle and end', but the same 'exitus–reditus' structure can be seen in both. In the second domain of *reditus*, God no longer appears simply as the source from which all good things come, but as the 'end', that is, as the goal and fulfilment of human life. All creatures exist and act with a view to the end of assimilation to God, that is, participation in the divine goodness. But

---

[78] I *Sent.* d. 14, q. 2, a. 2; cf. I *Sent.* d. 14, q. 1, a. 1. We discussed this passage earlier, in Chapter 8, at 'From Father to Father'.

[79] I *Sent.* d. 10, q. 1, a. 1, sol and ad 3: 'The Son proceeds as the Art of everything made by the divine mind.' This comes back to the mode of his procession (*ST* I, q. 34, a. 3).

[80] I *Sent.* d. 10, q. 1, a. 1; cf. *ST* I, q. 37, a. 2, ad 3.

[81] I *Sent.* d. 14, q. 2, a. 2.

when it comes to spiritual creatures, this participation is no longer just an assimilation to the divine goodness. It is a participation in the very *happiness* of God. Thomas states that,

> since everything proceeds from God insofar as he is good, as Augustine and Dionysius say, therefore, all creatures receive from their Creator an imprint inclining them to seek the good, each after its own modality; and thus a certain 'circulation' is found in things; now, issuing from the good, they incline to the good. This circulation is perfected in some creatures, whilst remaining imperfect in some others. For there are creatures which are not ordained to touch upon the first good from which they proceed, but only to obtain some sort of likeness of him; these do not have a perfect 'circulation'; . . . this only belongs to the rational creature, who can attain God through knowledge and love: and in this attainment their beatitude consists.[82]

One can see here one of the basic issues at stake in the exitus–reditus structure: the end of human beings is not to enjoy God's created goods, but is God himself.[83] As God is the source, so God is the end. Human beings obtain through grace the vocation of attaining, 'obtaining' or 'possessing' God, of 'being with God', of 'attaining God in person'.[84] This comes about through the Trinitarian processions, but is new-fashioned, different from what came before. The goods of creation surely give participation in the divine goodness, but they do not unite us to God. This union is achieved through the spiritual activity of knowing and loving God, through a new divine gift, that of grace, and later that of 'glory'. In the return (*reditus*), the influence of the divine processions is brought to bear in these gifts 'through which we adhere to the end'.[85] Such are the 'missions', the 'temporal processions' of Son and Holy Spirit into the hearts of the saints: the persons *themselves* are given, and 'possessed in a new way, as leading to or uniting with the end'.[86] The treatise in the *Summa* reaches its climax in its teaching on the 'missions' of the Son and Spirit. It deserves special attention because it offers a genuine synthesis of Trinitarian doctrine. This will be the subject of our concluding chapter.

---

[82] IV *Sent.* d. 49, q. 1, a. 3, qla 1. St Thomas explains elsewhere: 'The goodness of God is the end of all things, but these things are related to God's goodness in diverse ways. God himself has this goodness perfectly in his own being: this is why he is sovereignly good; and he also has it in the operation through which he knows and loves his goodness in a perfect way: this is why he is happy, because beatitude is perfect operation, according to the Philosopher . . . For its part, the intellectual creature does not achieve the goodness of God to the point of identifying its own being with the sovereign good, but it does achieve it through its operation, by knowing and loving: and this is why the intellectual creature participates in the beatitude of God and not just in the divine goodness. Whereas creatures who lack reason can be assimilated in a way to the divine goodness, they don't actually touch on it either in their operation or in their own being: this is why they participate in goodness, but not beatitude.' (II *Sent.* d. 1, q. 2, a. 2, ad 4); see also II *Sent.* d. 1, q. 2, a. 2, sol.; IV *Sent.* d. 49, q. 1, a. 2, qla 2.

[83] Cf. *ST* I-II, q. 2, a. 8.   [84] I *Sent.* d. 37, exp. prim. part. text.

[85] I *Sent.* d. 14, q. 2, a. 2.   [86] I *Sent.* d. 15, q. 4, a. 1.

15

Missions

We have come to see that the processions of the divine persons underpin both the coming out of creatures from God and their return to him. Our returning will go beyond being endowed with a distant resemblance to God; it will mean being gathered into God himself. This is God's gift to rational creatures, by which one means angels and human beings:

Even though they are given a likeness to God from God's own hand, the other creatures do not attain to God himself; and this is why, although God is in them, they are not with God. But, as one who knows and loves, a rational creature receives the grace to be regathered to God himself, and this is why we can say that she is with God. One can for the same reason say that her perfecting consists in the capacity objectively to intend God. And again, one can say on these grounds that she is the temple of God and that God dwells in her.[1]

These cursory observations reflect the main features aligned to the divine persons' missions: the human capacity to attain to God himself (*capax Dei*), which also brings out the theme of the divine image; the fulfilment or 'perfection' of the human being in God himself;[2] union with God himself through the theological act of knowledge and love which takes God as its object; inhabitation by the Triune God. This is a union in which the Triune God enters into intimacy with the human person, and the human being comes into the personal reality of God. So the idea of a 'return' to God does not mean returning to a pre-existent state, but being lifted up toward the God who gives human beings the grace to come to meet him in his own personal mystery: this is the fruit of the missions of the Son and the Holy Spirit.

The mission of the divine persons has raised more problems and outstanding disagreements within Trinitarian theology than any other topic; rivers of ink have flowed into it.[3] One can easily see why it has exercised a deep

---

[1] I *Sent.* d. 37, exp. prim. part. text.

[2] 'The perfection [of the rational creature] does not only consist in that with which it is naturally endowed, but also in that which is given to it through a sort of participation in the divine goodness' (*ST* II–II, q. 2, a. 3).

[3] The best place to look for a bibliography is J. Prades, '*Deus specialiter est in sanctis per gratiam*': *El misterio de la inhabitación de la Trinidad en los escritos de Santo Tomás*, Rome, 1993.

magnetism and caused tremendous controversy: the heart of St Thomas' spiritual teaching is in this question. That makes it clear why the compass of our exposition cannot extend to all of the nooks and crannies of this doctrine. We have to confine ourselves to presenting the context and format of this question, and then explaining the idea of mission, the sending of the Son and the Holy Spirit into the spirits of the saints, the divine persons' indwelling and the experiences to which it gives rise, the growth of the divine image within human beings, and then the 'visible' missions of Son and Spirit.

1. CONTEXT AND FORMAT OF THE QUESTION ABOUT DIVINE MISSIONS

Thomas' commentary on the *Sentences* runs in tandem with Peter Lombard's text, and so the persons' missions feature in the discussion of the Holy Spirit, in a huge section of more than twenty questions considering the 'temporal procession of the Holy Spirit'.[4] The study of the Spirit's mission thus integrates that of the mission of the Son. The reasoning behind situating the treatise on the missions in the context of Pneumatology is the idea of 'temporal processions', which arises within a treatment of the procession of the Holy Spirit. The Holy Spirit proceeds as Love, and this makes it 'tend' or 'proceed' toward a beloved, whether an eternal person, to whom he proceeds eternally, or a created person, to whom his temporal procession is directed. On the other hand, the idea of the 'begetting of the Son' does not inherently imply the idea of being related to a term. The only meaning generation has is relation to a principle, that is, the relation to the Father who begets the Son.[5] The discussion of the name *Gift* brought out the fact that this is a character trait of the Holy Spirit: it is because of the property personal to him that the Holy Spirit is eternally primed or 'cut out' for being given.[6]

Without dismissing the notion of 'temporal procession' from consideration, St Thomas' discussion in the *Summa Theologiae* (*Prima Pars*, q. 43), foregrounds the idea of *mission*. He no longer puts mission in the study of the

---

[4] I *Sent.* d. 14–16. This section is followed by one on the charity given by the Holy Spirit (d. 17), and then by a consideration of the name 'Gift' (d. 18); cf. d. 14, div. text.

[5] I *Sent.* d. 14, q. 1, a. 1, sol. and ad 1; cf. d. 15, q. 5, a. 1, qla 1, ad 3. This is a feature common to much scholastic thought. For instance, Albert observes that 'temporal procession' is congruent to both Son and Spirit, but is particularly well fitted to the Holy Spirit because of the nature of his procession (Albert, I *Sent.* d. 13, a. 1).

[6] I *Sent.* d. 18, q. 1, a. 2; cf. *ST* I, q. 38, aa. 1–2; see above, in Chapter 10, 'The Gift of the Father and the Son'.

Holy Spirit: it is now set after the question of the equality of the persons, within his investigation of 'the comparison of the persons to each other'.[7] A panorama comes in view at this point. The enquiry into the missions brings the study of the persons' mutual relations to a head: to think about the missions is still to consider the persons in their relationships, their divine being, and their own properties. In fact, by pinning down which of the persons are sent and which of them 'send', this question will examine the personal interrelationships implied by one person's sending. So when theologians turn to the Trinity's work of sanctification, they do not shift their attention away from the mystery of the Trinity in itself; and conversely, our investigation of the Trinity in its mysterious intimacy comes to completion when we reflect upon the Trinitarian economy.

This structure is a good indication that the consideration of the persons in their immanent divine life is not separated from the Trinitarian economy: the question of the missions closes the investigation of 'the distinction of persons in God' or 'the Trinity of persons in God':[8] it creates the bridge between the field which studies God's mystery as it is in itself, and the field of God's design in creation. The missions of the divine persons are what ultimately make sense of the gift of existence, human work and vocation, the mysteries of the humanity of Christ (the 'mission of the Son'), the sacraments and eschatology.

Question 43, on the divine missions, has a peculiarly complex internal structure. One can describe it like this: (1) the preliminary features of the notion of 'mission' (aa. 1–2: the fact of divine missions, the notion of mission, and how it is related to the person's eternal procession); (2) the 'invisible' missions of the divine persons, that is, how the giving of grace to the saints is a sending of the Son and Spirit (aa. 3–6: the gifts which are the evidence for a person's mission, which person is sent, to whom is he sent); (3) the 'visible' missions of Son and Holy Spirit (a. 7); (4) the author of the sending: which person brings the sending about? (a. 8). This structure shows what Thomas is setting out to do: after having pinpointed what one means by 'mission', we examine the sending and gift of the Son and Holy Spirit in grace, followed by the embodied sending of the Son in the incarnation, and then the Holy Spirit being sent to Christ and to the Church. The last article, discussing by whom the person is sent, brings one last fine-tuning to bear on the personal relationships that are involved in the notion of mission, and largely aims at bringing St Augustine's way of speaking about this on side.

We should note at the outset that question 43 is not restricted to the mission of the persons into the hearts of the saints, but also involves the Incarnation as the 'sending of the Son' and likewise the manifestation of

---

[7] *ST* I, q. 42, prol.; cf. q. 39, prol.   [8] *ST* I, q. 2, prol.; q. 27, prol.

the Holy Spirit in Christ and in the primitive Church. The treatment of the general notion of mission in the first two articles makes this very clear. Both of the *sed contra* arguments are drawn from the incarnation as the 'mission' of the Son.[9] In this way, the treatment of the missions lays down the Trinitarian ground-plans both for the mysteries of Christ's life and for the giving of the Holy Spirit. When the *Summa* reaches its *Tertia Pars* and turns to 'Christ who, as man, is our way to God',[10] it is springing off from this discussion of the missions. On its own level, when it examines 'the rational creature's movement toward God',[11] the *Secunda Pars* is likewise drawn out of how the missions are treated, since it is the sending of the divine persons which brings our human act of returning to God round to completion. When they come up in the *Prima Pars*, it works in the same way for the angels' return to God, and for the growth of the divine image in human beings.[12] Thus, the theory of the economy of grace, to be elaborated later in the *Prima*, in the *Secunda*, and in the *Tertia Pars*, is given its groundwork when Thomas expounds what he technically calls the 'invisible mission' and the 'visible mission'.

Question 43 is a crossroads within the progression of the *Summa Theologiae*. In what comes after, the *Summa* will consider the economy of grace from the window of the creatures receiving the gifts of God, and from the portal of the Incarnation. In question 43, we look down on this same economy 'from above', from the perspective of the mutual relations of the divine persons. The question about the missions exhibits the ground-plan of the economy of grace within the Trinity itself.

There can be no debate about the fact that the question Thomas gives to the missions is one of the most difficult in the whole Trinitarian treatise. It would be a mistake to imagine that, since its spiritual repercussions matter so much, the topic itself should be easier to get at. One has to realize that the opposite is the case: the theological explication is that much more demanding precisely because it relates to the heart of the Christian experience of the Trinity.

2. THE THEORY OF MISSION

Thomas' exposition in the *Summa* begins by pinning down some basic features of mission (q. 43, aa. 1 and 2), and then goes on to think through the tangible effects of the missions of Son and Holy Spirit. When he comes to dividing their

---

[9] Jn 8.16 (*ST* I, q. 43, a. 1, sed contra) and Gal. 4.4 (a. 2, sed contra).

[10] *ST* I, q. 2, prol.; the sacraments and eschatology are drawn out of the mystery of Christ (*ST* III, prol.).

[11] *ST* I, q. 2, prol.   [12] *ST* I, q. 62, and q. 93.

visible and invisible missions, this build-up enables him to focus his presentations on the elements idiosyncratic to each of them. And, as his treatise comes to its close, he can round it off with a discussion of the person who sends (a. 8). These different insights give us all the basic features of the theory of mission. We have to examine it very carefully, and perhaps even repetitively, because this analysis is decisive for the outcome of the study of the Trinity.

(a) Mission

The idea of the missions of Son and Spirit is thoroughly biblical. The *Summa Theologiae* does not give detailed expositions of the Johannine and Pauline passages which he had expounded at length in his commentaries, but Thomas indicates that he is working from Scripture: 'In the fullness of time, God *sent* his Son' (Gal. 4.4); 'it is not I alone who judge, but I and he who sent me' (Jn 8.16); 'through the Holy Spirit he has given us' (Rom. 5.5).[13] The *Summa* does not do word-by-word analyses of specific scriptural passages, but rather gives us a theological synthesis of Thomas' reading of the New Testament; the back-up for what he does here can be found in his biblical commentaries.[14]

This particular synthesis puts itself forward as a personal take on the common acceptation of Augustine.[15] A divine person's mission will have two constitutive features: (1) this person's eternal procession; and (2) the divine person's relation to the creature to whom this person is made present in a new way. One could formulate the two sides of it either in terms of *procession* or of *relation*. In terms of procession: mission consists in the person's procession toward a creature; including the eternal procession in itself, it adds to it a created effect, whose force is to make this person present in a new way (one thus speaks of the 'temporal procession' of the divine person).[16] Thomas also sets out the theory of mission in terms of relations or relationships:

The meaning of 'being sent' [or mission] implies two things: one is the orientation of the one who is sent to the sender; the other is the orientation of the one sent to the goal to which he is sent.[17]

[13] *ST* I, q. 43, a. 1, sed contra; a. 2, sed contra; a. 3, arg. 2.
[14] See for instance *In Ioan.* 15.26 (no. 2061) and 16.28 (nos. 2161–2162); *In 1 Cor.* 3.16 (nos. 172–173).
[15] For the Augustinian bases, see especially *De Trinitate* II.IV.6–V.10; IV.XIX.25–XXI.32.
[16] *ST* I, q. 43, a. 2, ad 3; cf. I *Sent.* d. 14. aa. 1–2. There is a common basis for this teaching: see Albert, I *Sent.* d. 14, aa. 5, 7, 9–10; or Bonaventure, I *Sent.* d. 14, aa. 1–2; d. 15, p. 1, a. un., q. 2.
[17] *ST* I, q. 43, a. 1; cf. I *Sent.* d. 15, q. 1, a. 1. The idea of tackling the topic via relations is not unique to St Thomas; see for instance the *Summa fratris Alexandri*, Book I (ed. Quaracchi, vol. 1), no. 497 and no. 511 (ad contra *a*). Thomas is drawing here on received assumptions.

This generic definition is formulated in terms that could be applied to any mission whatsoever, whether that of a creature or of a divine person. As is his wont, Thomas uses analogy as a way into the topic, because it is by an analogous usage that we can say that a divine mission genuinely takes place, and in the proper sense of the word 'mission'. One can go on from these premises to show more exactly what is peculiar to the mission of a *divine person*.

(1) The first aspect of this consists in the divine person's relation of origin or 'procession of origin'.[18] This eliminates any possibility of anthropomorphism: when one says a divine person is 'sent', this sending is not that of a minion carrying out his boss's orders, nor is it about receiving instructions from a higher intelligence, and nor is the sending a displacement, spatially separating the sender from the one sent. A sending that happens in God is purely a matter of the origination relation: a relation of unseparated equality. The notion of missions is part of the integrated theory of immanent processions and Trinitarian relations of origin: a divine mission 'includes' an eternal procession in itself.[19] So the premier feature of mission is an origination relation as between one divine person and another. This relation is eternal and uncreated, like the divine persons themselves.

Since only the Son and Holy Spirit proceed from a principle, taking their origin from another person, only they are 'sent'. The Father does not proceed from anyone: he is principle without principle. This is why he is not sent. 'As we have shown,' Thomas says, 'mission implies by definition a procession from another, and a divine mission a procession as from origin. Since the Father does not proceed from another, it is not fit for him to be sent, but only the Son and the Spirit, into whom being from another is fitted.'[20] This is why 'the Father alone is nowhere said to have been sent';[21] Trinitarian theology has to work from the fact that Scripture refers only to a sending of the Son and the Holy Spirit. Thomas remarks elsewhere that this is why the Creed sets out several articles of faith about the Son and Holy Spirit, but expresses what we believe about the Father in one single article. We need not make any professions about missions here, because the Father was not sent.[22]

---

[18] *ST* I, q. 43, a. 1, sol. and ad 2.

[19] Cf. *ST* I, q. 43, a. 2, ad 3; a. 4, ad 3; cf. I *Sent.* d. 14, q. 1, a. 2; d. 15, q. 1, a. 1.

[20] *ST* I, q. 43, a. 4.

[21] Augustine, *De Trinitate* II.V.8. Cf. Thomas, *ST* I, q. 43, a. 4, sed contra. For the sending of the Son, Thomas refers to Jn 8.16, Jn 10.36 and Gal. 4.4 (a. 1, sed contra and sol.; a. 2, sed contra). Rom. 5.5 is one of his bases for the mission of the Holy Spirit, but he also takes note of the sending of the Spirit to Christ at his baptism (Mt. 3.16), the manifestation of the Spirit at Christ's transfiguration (Mt. 17.5) and at Pentecost (Acts 2), and the gift of the Spirit by the Resurrected One in John (20.22–23), and so on (*ST* I, q. 43, a. 3, arg. 2 and ad 2; a. 7).

[22] *ST* II–II, q. 1, a. 8, ad 4.

(2) The second aspect of mission is the 'orientation of the one sent to the goal to which he is sent'. Here one comes up against a constitutive feature which ranges across missions of every type, from the human to the divine: when someone is sent on a mission, the mission is accomplished when the envoy reaches his destination, that is, where we find 'a new way of being present somewhere'. As with the first aspect of mission, Thomas notes that here too there is a difference between what mission is for human beings and what it is for God. A human being takes himself off to where he previously was not, or even to where he has never been before, whereas a divine person is not sent into a world from which he was previously absent, for God is never absent from his creatures: the divine person is already there, either in the way a cause is present in its effect, that is, as the common presence of the Triune Creator in all his creatures, or simply as grace. When a divine person is sent, he 'does not begin to be present where before he was not', but rather, he has 'a new way of being present somewhere', being here 'in a way in which he was not present before'.[23] And, in the same context, the divine person is not separated from the one who sends him. Thomas writes that, 'even as the divine person sent does not begin to be present where he before was not, so he does not cease to be present where he was. Consequently, this kind of mission involves no separation but only distinctness by origin'.[24]

By investigating the two constitutive sides of mission and authenticating the applicability of both of them to a divine person, Thomas has shown that we can really speak of *mission* here, in the proper senses of the term and of the reality.[25] And this in turn will impact on how he understands the formal meaning of the word; he can now bring out what typifies a divine mission by comparing it to a human one. He thus puts forward a common notion of mission, applying analogously to creatures and to God: as such, any mission involves an orientation of the envoy to the one who sends (such as procession or origin), and likewise an orientation to the goal (such as a new mode of being for the one sent). The notion of mission peculiar to creatures will imply, on the one side, distance, and, on the other, movement or change in the one sent, whereas, the notion of mission which is peculiar to the divine person is characterized by, on the one side, the person's having an eternal origin, and, on the other, a new mode of being for the person who is sent.

---

[23] *ST* I, q. 43, a. 1, sol. and ad 2; a. 2, ad 2.

[24] *ST* I, q. 43, a. 1, ad 2.

[25] When applied to the Son and to the Holy Spirit, the word 'mission' has a proper sense if its meaning is determined by features which fit the divine persons (that is, the eternal origin and the new mode of being present for the person sent). But if we retain the properties which can only belong to creatures (movement, separation, and so on), this proper sense disappears. See Bonaventure, *De mysterio Trinitatis*, q. 6, a. 1, ad 7.

In this analysis, the characteristic features of a divine mission are the absence of separation amongst the divine persons, the absence of change from the divine person (the change or movement happens in the creature receiving the divine person), and thus an eternal procession. The absence of separation in the divine persons is a point of particular significance to Christology: the Son is not separated from the Father who sends him.[26] It is no less crucial in Pneumatology: the Spirit is never present without the Son or without the Father. Moreover, the mission of a divine person is based on the presence which that person already has through his creative and providential action. The person who is sent does not begin to be where hitherto he was not, but begins to be in a new way, and one which presupposes the presence which is already given. The doctrine of mission assumes the Trinitarian doctrine of creation.

A divine mission thus consists in a *new mode of presence* in the person sent, his rendering himself present *in an innovative way*.[27] Where English has 'being present' or 'rendering himself present', Thomas writes, 'being in'. The kind of language used in speaking about mission is very like that for perichoresis. The incarnation of the Son gives us the best illustration of this: 'One says that the Son has been sent into the world by the Father (cf. Jn 10.36) meaning that he has begun to be visible through the flesh he has assumed, even though he was already in the world before that, as it says in Jn 1.10.'[28] And just as the divine emissary's being is invested in the recipient in a new way, so that person's being is also 'possessed' (*haberi*) in a new way.[29]

At this juncture, Thomas does not elaborate on what the divine person's 'new presence' or 'new being' in the world consists in. He will explicate it further on, when he describes the divine persons' visible and invisible missions. The only specification he gives of what it means is that the Son 'proceeds temporally so as to be man by reason of his visible mission and so as to be in man by reason of his invisible mission'.[30] This is the goal of it all: in the visible mission, the uniting of man to God in the very person of the incarnate Son, or, in the invisible mission, the presence of the Son in the human reception of a living faith. In neither instance does this new presence or existence entail any alteration or novelty in what is divine in the person, because the person's divine nature is immutable. Everything that changes

---

[26] This was particularly well illustrated by the theory of perichoresis, as above, Chapter 12.

[27] This teaching is another one which Thomas could have found amongst his forerunners: see for instance the *Summa fratris Alexandri*, Book I (ed. Quaracchi, vol. 1), no. 511, contra *c* and response; Albert, I *Sent.* d. 14, a. 7; d. 15, a. 5.

[28] *ST* I, q. 43, a. 1. The case in point is the Son's 'visible mission'.

[29] *ST* I, q. 43, a. 2, sol. and ad 2.

[30] *ST* I, q. 43. a. 2.

comes about in the creature to whom the divine person makes himself present.[31] Thomas turns to his idea of 'mixed' relations to explain the relationship of the divine person to those gifted with a mission. The relation is 'real' in the creature, in whom the mission brings about something new, but it has a being of 'reason' in the divine person. There is no internal alteration within the divine person. Rather, the divine person is the source or cause of the creature's changing, his being united to God in a fresh way.[32]

In sum, the notion of relation is once again brought into play in making sense of faith in the Triune God. The divine person's mission actually 'includes two relations in its meaning': an eternal relation to the person from whom the envoy proceeds, and a temporal relation to the creature in whom the sent person exists in a new way, by the force of a new relation.[33]

(b) Mission, Temporal Procession, and Donation

Thomas can also use this construct to clarify the terms in which one commonly speaks of the sending of the divine persons: procession, missions, and donation.[34] He analyses each of these terms and differentiates precisely amongst the relationships each one implies.

The person's origin is designated by the word *procession*. In and of itself, the word procession refers only to the one principle from which the person comes forth, that is, the origin-relation in which the real distinction of the divine persons is given. This is the eternal procession. One can also use the phrase *temporal procession* to mean the same thing as mission: when one speaks thus, qualifying the procession as *temporal* refers to the created effect in which the divine person is in this world in an innovative way. The temporal procession is an embassy of the eternal, bringing a part of its home country into our history. There are not two different processions, one eternal and one temporal. The phrase *temporal procession* means the eternal procession *joining itself to* the effect through which the divine person makes himself newly present in the world. In other words, a procession is called eternal or temporal by virtue of its 'end-point': the divine person proceeding within the unity of the divine being is an eternal 'end-point'; and the created effect in which the

---

[31] *ST* I, q. 43, a. 2, ad 2.

[32] I *Sent.* d. 14, q. 1, a. 1, ad 2. This idea is applied to all the relationships between God and the world. It does not only touch on the invisible mission; Thomas also applies it to the 'visible' mission; he uses this double relationship to present the hypostatic union in Christ (*ST* III, q. 2, a. 7). See above, in Chapter 5, 'Real Relations in God', for this 'mixed relation'.

[33] I *Sent.* d. 15, q. 1, a. 1.

[34] *ST* I, q. 43, a. 1; I *Sent.* d. 15, q. 1, a. 1. The way he clarifies the meaning of these words is contiguous with the way Albert uses them (I *Sent.* d. 14, a. 5).

earthly presence of the divine person is given is a temporal 'end-point'. One and the same procession somehow reaches as far as ourselves, in a new form of the divine person's presence.

As we have seen, mission is also two-sided, involving both a relationship to a person-principle, and a relationship to creatures. So *mission* indicates the same territory as *temporal procession* does, but the two phrases are not synonyms. Thomas explains this nuance in his *Sentence* commentary: in the proper meaning of the words, an intention to refer to the relationship of origin has the upper hand in the phrase 'temporal procession', because procession means a relationship to a principle, whereas the primary meaning of 'mission' intends a relationship to a created effect, that is, the relationship to the destination *to which* the divine person is sent. For the same reason, an intention to designate the differentials of the divine persons is in the foreground of *temporal procession*, with the divine nature as a background meaning, whereas the two sides come the other way round in *mission*.[35] In the *Summa Theologiae*, Thomas' stress is more on the fact that procession can be qualified as either eternal or temporal, whereas mission, like donation, is always something temporal.[36]

The very notion of divine mission implies the person's donation (*datio*). The person is sent in order to be *given* to the creature to whom he is sent. The person does not just hand over created gifts, but is actually given himself: we saw this particularly clearly in our examination of the name *Donum*,[37] and we will come back to it again later. Since he is really *given*, the person is also 'possessed' by the one who receives him. But there is still a difference between the relationships involved in *donation* and those in *mission*. As we have said, mission entails relationships to a recipient and to the sent person's eternal principle. On the other hand, the notion of *donation* does not necessarily imply that the person who is 'given' proceeds from another person: it only entails the divine person's being related to the one who receives it.[38] For this reason, although the Father is not 'sent', since he does not proceed from anyone, he nonetheless 'gives himself'; he 'is given' along with the Son and the Holy Spirit,[39] and he 'indwells' the saints together with them.[40]

---

[35] I *Sent.* d. 15, q. 1, a. 2.   [36] *ST* I, q. 43, a. 2, sol. and ad 3.

[37] See above, in Chapter 10, 'The Gift of the Father and the Son'; cf. I *Sent.* d. 14, q. 2, a. 1.

[38] I *Sent.* d. 15, q. 1, a. 1; cf. a. 2.

[39] I *Sent.* d. 15, q. 3, a. 1; *ST* I, q. 43, a. 4, ad 1. If one brings out the particular modes of donation which belong to the Son and the Holy Spirit, then the kinds of donation implied by the origin-relation of the given persons are that the Son is 'given' by the Father, the Holy Spirit is 'given' by the Father and the Son from whom he proceeds.

[40] *ST* I, q. 43, a. 4, sol. and ad 2.

The *donation* of the divine person corresponds to the *possession* of the divine person on the part of its creaturely recipient. Like those of the Franciscan theologians,[41] Thomas' ways of putting this are highly realistic and concrete: 'something is given in order that it may be possessed'.[42] The divine person is freely handed over to be 'possessed' (*haberi, habere*) by the recipient of this donation, that is, so that the recipient can enjoy the divine person and his gifts.[43]

(c) The Person who Sends

One final clarification is required concerning the 'personnel' of a divine mission. Only the Son and the Holy Spirit are actually 'sent'. But *by whom* are they sent? The *Summa* dedicates an entire article to this problem, the last in the Trinitarian treatise. This initially looks like an odd question to ask. The obvious reply which the general idea of mission seems to imply is that the Son is sent by the Father who engenders him, and the Holy Spirit is sent by the Father and Son from whom he proceeds. Nonetheless, like all the scholastics, Thomas has to build on the way Ambrose and Augustine spoke of this. The Bishop of Hippo had explained that, 'The invisible Father and the invisible Son sent the Son to become visible.'[44] The context for this is that Augustine must show that the Son and Holy Spirit are not inferior to the Father, but his equals in their being and operation. The whole Trinity brings about the incarnational mission of the Son through one single and undivided action.[45] Peter Lombard's *Sentences* describe and sum up this Augustinian teaching: the Son is sent by the Father, by himself and by the Holy Spirit; on the same rationale, the Holy Spirit is sent by Father and Son, and also sent by himself.[46] It is easy to imagine that expressions like this brought the theologians out in a sweat. 'On this question,' as Bonaventure observed, 'the wise contradict the wise.'[47]

Thomas acknowledges that this language poses a genuine 'difficulty'.[48] His earlier analysis tended rather to the conclusion that a divine person is only

---

[41] See the *Summa fratris Alexandri*, Book I (ed. Quaracchi, vol. 1), no. 511, ad contra *a*; Bonaventure, I *Sent.* d. 14, a. 2, q. 1.

[42] *ST* I, q. 43, a. 2.

[43] *ST* I, q. 43, a. 3; cf. I *Sent.* 14, q. 2, a. 1.

[44] Augustine, *De Trinitate* II.5.9: 'Even the Son is sent by the Father and the Son.'

[45] Augustine, ibid.; cf. also Thomas, *ST* III, q. 3, a. 4: 'The three persons bring it about that the human nature is united to the person of the Son.'

[46] Peter Lombard, *Sentences*, Book I, dist. 15, chs. 1–4 (vol. I/2, pp. 130–134). The patristic texts here are all taken from Ambrose and Augustine.

[47] Bonaventure, I *Sent.* d. 15, p. 1, a. un., q. 4.

[48] I *Sent.* d. 15, q. 3, a. 1. The precise issue does not concern the person who is sent (Thomas has already explained that only the Son and the Holy Spirit are sent; the Father is not sent, because he has no origin). The question touches on the origin of the sending, that is, the sender.

sent by the one(s) from whom he eternally proceeds. He also observed that the Eastern Fathers, with whose explanations he concurs, reserve the sending of the Son to the Father alone: for the Greek Patristics, only the Father sends the Son. But, according to Augustine, one can *also* say that the whole Trinity sends one of the persons.[49] The authority of Augustine, relayed and ramified by Peter Lombard, could not just be ignored.[50] Like his peers, Thomas suggests a solution which genuinely contains both teachings, by showing that, for all their limitations, it is not improper to use the Augustinian expressions.[51] He does this by coming back to the structure of mission, as initially construed. As we have seen, there are two features in a mission: the divine emissary's relation to the *sending person* and the relation to the *created effect* for whom the mission is carried out. A consideration of both of these elements brings out the legitimacy of the dual perspective. Thomas writes that,

If the one who sends is taken to mean a principle of the person sent, then not each of the persons is the one who sends, but only a person to whom it belongs to be a principle of the person sent. Accordingly the Son is sent by the Father alone; the Holy Spirit by Father and Son together. If, however, the person sending is taken to mean the principle of the effect in which the mission becomes observable, then it is the entire Trinity that sends the person sent.[52]

The distinction of the persons and the effects of the mission are not put into separate compartments. These two features are grasped together, in their conjunction, but the duality is nonetheless necessary to the integral notion of mission. One can see from this that, like Augustine, Thomas strictly holds that only the Son and the Holy Spirit are sent. But here we have to specify what it means *to send* a person. One can see it from two different points of view. On the one hand, aligning oneself with the intra-Trinitarian relation of origin, one can conceive of mission in terms of one person sending another: the Father and the Son send the Holy Spirit to the Church. On the other hand, one can look for the effects of mission, seeing the sending person as their source, and in that case, the Father, Son, and Holy Spirit together make the Spirit indwell the Church to which he is sent.[53] This dual-perspective could be considered as a way of interpreting what Augustine himself is saying, since

---

[49] *CEG* I, ch. 14.

[50] I *Sent.* d. 15, q. 3, a. 1: 'Since the Holy Fathers commonly use these expressions, and above all since Augustine and the Master of the Sentences [Peter Lombard] do concede it.' On Augustine's authority in this question, see also Bonaventure, I *Sent.* d. 15, p. 1, a. un., q. 4.

[51] See Albert, I *Sent.* d. 15, a. 5 and a. 11; Bonaventure, I *Sent.* d. 15, p. 1, a. un., q. 4.

[52] *ST* I, q. 43, a. 8; cf. I *Sent.* d. 15, q. 3, aa. 1 and 2; *CEG* I, ch. 14.

[53] Cf. I *Sent.* d. 15, q. 3, a. 1. From the perspective of the relationship to the created effects, the three persons act inseparably.

he does emphasize the persons' relations of origin, and reckons with both sides of mission.

One can find analyses contiguous to those in this initial presentation of mission in many other theologians of Thomas' time. But we ought to note that most other authors define mission as a *manifestation* of the divine person. For instance, for Bonaventure, the *key* feature of mission is the manifestation of the divine person: 'In itself, mission involves two things: the emanation [of the divine person] and his manifestation; and the idea of mission principally designates the manifestation.'[54] Down to this point, Thomas has not gone into manifestation as an aspect of mission: what he puts in the foreground is rather the divine person's new mode of existence. But we will come upon this theme later, when Thomas discusses the invisible missions, and yet again in the context of the visible missions of Son and Spirit.

3. THE 'INVISIBLE' MISSION: THE GIFT OF THE SPIRIT AND THE SON TO THE SAINTS

The first type of mission which Thomas discusses is the one which, together with the whole scholastic tradition, he calls the 'invisible mission', in distinction from 'visible' mission.[55] Basing himself on Augustine, Peter Lombard had organized his presentation of mission around these two types.[56] 'Visible mission' means the manifestation of the Son in the Incarnation and the manifestation of the Spirit in physical signs. 'Invisible mission', conversely, means the sending of the Son and Holy Spirit into the hearts of the faithful.[57] In question 43, aa. 3–6 of the *Summa*, Thomas begins by showing that what the persons' invisible mission builds upon is a gift in the order of sanctifying grace. He then lays it down that only the Son and Spirit are sent; even though the Father is given and inhabits the souls of the saints, he is not sent. Thomas works especially hard to show how it comes about that not the Holy Spirit alone but the Son also is sent 'invisibly' into each sainted soul. A final article polishes it off by showing that everyone who lives from grace is a beneficiary of this mission.

---

[54] Bonaventure, I *Sent.* d. 15, p. 1, a. un., qq. 4; cf. d. 15, p. 2, a. un., qq. 1 and 2; dist. 16 a. un., q. 1.

[55] One finds different but comparable expressions in other authors. For instance, Albert also speaks of 'manifested' mission (meaning the visible type), and 'hidden', that is, invisible, mission.

[56] See Peter Lombard, *Sentences*, Book I, dist. 15, chs. 7–8; dist. 16, ch. 1; dist. 17, ch. 1 (pp. 135–143).

[57] Ibid.

(a) Initial Clarifications

These analyses are the bedrock of the doctrine to which we now turn. Within the dynamic of the gifts by which the saints are conformed or 'assimilated' to the Word and Love in sanctifying grace, the Son and Spirit are sent into human hearts, they and the Father dwell there, these persons are really given and they are 'possessed' by the hearts which receive them. This teaching rests on the notion of *mission*: mission consists in the person's new way of being present. So invisible mission engages a *newness* and a real *presence* of the divine person who is sent. Thomas writes that,

a divine person is *sent* in that he exists in someone in a new way; and he is *given* in that he is possessed by someone. Neither of these occurs outside of sanctifying grace.[58]

One might be surprised to learn that this reply bases itself in a created effect (sanctifying grace) when it has to reckon with the gift of the uncreated persons themselves. We can get hold of Thomas' angle on this by considering the divine persons' action. The persons' donation is an idiosyncratic divine action, quite different from other divine actions like creating the world and maintaining creatures in existence. How is one to distinguish amongst these different creature-related actions within God himself? The action or operation of the Triune God is as singular as God's being. When we acknowledge many divine actions on behalf of the creature, we are not introducing a real differentiation into God himself: within the divine persons, such diverse actions only present a distinction 'of reason', not a real distinction.[59] But on the part of the creaturely beneficiaries of God's action, that is, within the divine action's 'effects', the distinction is thoroughly real. The gifts of grace with which human beings are sanctified are a different kind of reality from nature, and from the other goods which we receive through creation. Thomas had already said as much when he put forward the general notion of 'mission': the new presence of the divine persons does not consist in a change in the persons themselves, but in a change within the creature who is enlarged by a new gift of the divine person.[60] This is why Thomas exhibits mission by way of considering the effects of the divine persons within creatures, or the new presence of the persons who are given.

---

[58] *ST* I, q. 43, a. 3. This is another doctrinal commonplace; see for instance the *Summa fratris Alexandri*, Book I, no. 512; Albert, I *Sent.* d. 15, a. 16; Bonaventure, I *Sent.* d. 15, pars 2, q. un., a. 1.

[59] Cf. I *Sent.* d. 17, q. 1, a. 1, sed contra 3; I *Sent.* d. 37, q. 1, a. 2. The only real distinction in God is that amongst the divine persons. God's action upon the world does not bring a real distinction into God himself. The three persons act through their unitary essence, in an action that is unitary.

[60] Cf. *ST* I, q. 43, a. 2, ad 2.

The analysis will engage several elements: (1) the efficient action of the Trinity and the unique influences of the sent persons (exemplarity, assimilation and conformation to the Son and Spirit); (2) the effect which is received in a human being; (3) the theological or Godward action which the effect enables a person to perform; (4) the gift of the divine person himself. The account of the sending of the divine persons in the *Sentence* commentary bases its presentation on the efficacity of the Trinitarian processions. The *Summa* itself focuses on the gift of sanctifying grace and the Godward action which grace makes possible, but without isolating this one thread alone (article 3 does not give the final word on what missions are): the analysis will be worked out through the discussion of the gifts which conform the just to the Son and the Spirit, their opening us to receive the divine persons and to enjoying their substantial presence.

In our explanation of this, we will speak of 'ontological presence' and 'operative presence'. This distinction necessitates an opening word which should help us avoid over-simplification. It is not unusual for works about this matter to set the two approaches to the subject in opposition, as if there were two kinds of analysis, one in the 'Writing on the *Sentences*' and the other in the *Summa Theologiae*.[61] But this fails to take account of what St Thomas says. The *Summa* doubtless breaks new ground,[62] and gives the master synthesis; but one would still err if one opposed what he writes here to his *Sentence* commentary. Despite the differences in the order and emphases within the two expositions, Thomas threads the same features into both. The *Summa* sets off from God's presence in grace, 'in the way that the known is in the knower and the loved in the lover' (the operative way), so as to specify, at a later stage, by reference to the way of assimilation, the proper mode of presence of the Son and Holy Spirit in the just. In both instances, it is a matter of showing the action of the Trinity, the exemplary influence of the Son and Spirit, the gifts which conform the just to the Son and Spirit, the experience of the sent persons and the indwelling of the whole Trinity. We can get a more accurate view of Thomas' analysis by beginning from his commentary on the *Sentences*.

---

[61] See for instance, J. Prades, *Deus specialiter est in sanctis per gratiam*, pp. 376–389.

[62] The great Spanish Dominican, Domingo Bañez could already spot this. Commenting on *ST* I, q. 8, a. 3, he writes, 'Going from I *Sent.* d. 37, the scholastics explain the special mode by which God is in the just by the fact that God "operates" grace and the virtues in them, elevating the just to participation in the divine nature. But here St Thomas appears to explain this mode of existence by the fact that the just tend to God through the knowledge and desire of God himself, that which is an effect of grace' (in I^{am}, q. 8, a. 3, in F. Domingo Bañez, *Scholastica Commentaria in Primam Partem Summae Theologiae sancti Thomae Aquinatis*, ed. L. Urbano, Madrid and Valencia, 1934, p. 212).

(b) The Seal of Son and Holy Spirit

The 'Writing on the *Sentences*' puts the divine missions in the light of the Trinitarian processions as causes: in the same way that the person's procession is the cause and rationale of creation, it causes and explains the creature's return to God.[63] But one and the same procession of persons is the cause of creation and the cause of the return to God in different capacities. In the first case, when we take it as the rationale of creation, the personal procession is the source of the natural goods in which we subsist. In the second, considered as causing the return to God, the processional causality can be seen in the gifts which unite us to God, and that means not only the gifts in which God presents himself as the principle of our existence, but also the gifts which make us attach ourselves to God as our end. To be precise, these are the gifts of sanctifying grace.

Thomas' presentation begins with the mission of the Holy Spirit. When the Holy Spirit is sent, within a sanctifying gift, he is really given to the person who 'possesses' him. The person who receives the Holy Spirit's mission 'enjoys' the divine person himself. A mission takes place where his recipient can 'enjoy' not just created gifts, but the divine person himself.[64] The words which we are translating as 'enjoyment' or 'fruition' are the technical theological words—*frui, fruitio*. 'Enjoyment' or 'fruition' touches on the highest human act, in which we achieve our good, uniting ourselves with God. This union is achieved through that knowledge of God which blossoms in love, enabling us to enter upon God's communion. 'Fruition' is the possession of the one in whom human persons have their end, their fulfilment and genuine happiness.[65] Fruition is the purpose of the donation and indwelling of the divine persons, of their mission. The divine persons can be given either within a 'perfect fruition', which means the blessedness of the saints in heaven, or in an 'imperfection fruition', which is how the saints possess the divine gift of sanctifying grace on earth. To put it more precisely, the Son and Spirit are given to us,

---

[63] I *Sent.* d. 14, q. 2, a. 2; see above, in Chapter 14, 'The "Efficacy" of the Trinitarian Processions'.

[64] Such enjoyment or 'fruition' is central to the interpretation of mission given by the *Summa fratris Alexandri* (Book I, no. 511), and by Bonaventure (I *Sent.* d. 14, a. 2, q. 1; d. 15, p. 2, a. un., q. 1; d. 18, dubium 5; II *Sent.* d. 26, a. un., q. 2, ad 1). On this issue, Thomas' teaching is an extension of the Franciscans'.

[65] Formally speaking, fruition is an act of the will and of love: the will's adhesion to its final end, resting upon an act of the mind. Cf. I *Sent.* d. 1; *ST* I–II, q. 11.

As the power through which we are united to the reality which we enjoy, in as much as the divine persons mark us with their seal (*sui sigillatione*) by leaving the gifts through which we formally enjoy, that is, love and wisdom.[66]

Thomas sees the gift of the divine persons in their mission from a dynamic perspective, as the uniting of the human to the divine. The Son and Holy Spirit are given us on our journey to our last end so that we can attain fruition in the Triune God, within the divinizing acts of wisdom and love. Every recipient of a mission receives not only the divine person's gifts, but the divine person himself. We looked at this earlier on, in relation to the name *Donum*: the created gifts are 'dispositions', which make their bearers open to receiving the divine person himself.[67] As far as the recipient is concerned, the created gifts have to arrive before the divine person does, because they dispose us to receive him. But in so far as it is a matter of God acting to bring about the goal at which the mission aims, the gift of the divine person himself is absolutely primary.[68]

Thomas gives a more explicit version of this analysis when he shows us the format of the Son's invisible mission to the saints. Once having reminded us that creatures receive a 'likeness' to the communicated divine goodness in *creation*, he turns to the causality of the divine persons' processions within the *return* to God which grace effects. Thomas argues that,

the restoration of the rational creature to God is comprehended in the procession of the divine persons, and this is also said of their missions, in that the proper relation belonging to the divine person is re-presented in the soul through a sort of received likeness, whose exemplar and origin is the property of this same eternal relation. Just as the mode through which the Holy Spirit is referred to the Father is love, so the proper mode of reference of the Son to the Father is to be the Word who manifests him. And this is why, just as the Holy Spirit proceeds invisibly in the spirit through the gift of love, so likewise the Son [proceeds in the spirit] through the gift of wisdom, and this manifests the Father himself, the ultimate end to which we return. And since the likeness to the properties is effected in us through the reception of these two, the [person] is after a new mode of existence in us, in that a thing is in its likeness, and the divine persons are said to be in us in that our assimilation to them takes on a new modality. And it is on this basis that both processions are called mission.[69]

In this context, Thomas is looking at mission from the perspective of how the Son and Holy Spirit influence us. He does not explicitly talk about 'sealing', but this is what he is touching on. The divine person is sent to transmit a

---

[66] I *Sent.* d. 14, q. 2, a. 2, ad 2.   [67] I *Sent.* d. 14, q. 2, a. 1, qla 1.
[68] I *Sent.* d. 14, q. 2, a. 1, qla 2; see above, in Chapter 10, 'The Gift of the Father and the Son'.
[69] I *Sent.* d. 15, q. 4, a. 1; we discuss this passage in *La Trinité créatrice*, pp. 402–413.

participation in his eternal property: the Son conveys a likeness or resemblance to the modality through which he is referred to the Father; the Holy Spirit communicates a resemblance to the mode through which he proceeds. This resemblance is the imprint with which the Son and Holy Spirit mark the saints, for their union to God will come about through being integrated into the personal relations which Son and Holy Spirit have with the Father. Reflecting the way in which the Holy Spirit proceeds as Love, the Spirit impels our return to the Father through the love which he makes over to us when he makes himself our own. And just as the Son proceeds as the person who is the Word of the Father, so he gives us to return to the Father through the wisdom which he gives us in coming to be in us. The Father himself is not sent, but the missions of Son and Holy Spirit culminate in him. And thus the missions of Son and Holy Spirit present and disclose the Father.[70]

The importance of the personal properties within this discussion must now be obvious. Union with God is brought about by wisdom and charity as reflections of the properties with which the Son and Holy Spirit are related to the Father. Thomas focuses on the exemplarity of the divine persons in respect of the gifts of wisdom and love. It is this exemplarity which differentiates amongst the effects of the missions of the Son and the Holy Spirit, a point to which we will return. The created gift is appropriated to a divine person rather than being the exclusive effect of any one person.[71] Although the efficient cause of such gifts is the undivided Trinity, the divine persons do have special affinities to the properties which they exemplify, and Thomas picks these out.[72] He highlights the fact that this exemplarity has to be brought out to perfection when we are speaking about God as the *goal* of the human–divine relationship. At the giving of the Holy Spirit, 'the influx of charity culminates in a likeness to the personal procession of the Holy Spirit'.[73] The properties of the Son and Holy Spirit stand at the base of our unification to the divine persons through the gifts which assimilate us to their exemplars. The modality of our union is set in motion by the gifts assimilating us to the divine persons. 'The gift which conforms us to the person achieves our union to God within the proper mode of a particular divine person.'[74] The gifts derive their power to unite us with God from the divine persons. If the gifts unite us to our 'end', they do so 'in the power of the divine persons, since the impression contains the power of the agent who impressed the form

---

[70] See above, in Chapter 8, 'From Father to Father'.
[71] I *Sent.* d. 14, q. 2, a. 2, ad 3; d. 15, q. 2, a. 1, ad 2.
[72] Thus, for instance, 'The efficient cause of charity is the whole Trinity, but its exemplar-cause is the Love which is the Holy Spirit' (I *Sent.* d. 17, q. 1, a. 1).
[73] I *Sent.* d. 30, q. un., a. 2. See our *La Trinité créatrice*, pp. 314–316.
[74] I *Sent.* d. 14, q. 2, a. 2, ad 3.

on it'.[75] The divine efficacity and the exemplarity of Son and Spirit are thus the twin foci of this explanation.

St Thomas thinks this analysis sufficient to set out the sending and donation of the divine persons. When we receive the gifts of wisdom and love, the divine persons are present in a way they had not been before, 'in the way that the divine goodness is re-presented in the creature through its likeness', that is, 'our assimilation to the divine persons takes on a new mode'. We should understand the presence of the divine person 'in his similitude' as a dynamic 'assimilation'. 'One who receives these gifts possesses the divine persons in a new way, like conductors or conjointers to our end.'[76] The 'similitude' does not merely consist in a static likeness, but in the theological or God-inclining behaviour which someone achieves under the influence of these gifts, our bearing fruit in the acts of knowing and loving God. Thomas' detailed discussion of this comes when he is showing that it is the Holy Spirit who sanctifies us: the Holy Spirit acts in us by giving us the *habitus* of charity and he repeats the performance when he makes us to *act in charity*.[77] The divine persons' bearing fruit in us is thus bound to the efficacity and exemplary influence of each of the sent persons, that is, to the given effects for humans beings and likewise to the theological actions which these effects enable us to perform.

This exposition by means of the assimilation to the divine persons can be qualified as 'ontological' because it directly accentuates divine efficient and exemplary causality (the 'seal' of the Son and Holy Spirit). Thomas does not leave this behind when he comes back to the question in the *Summa Theologiae*: but when it reappears here, it is within the context of showing the new bearing within the divine persons' presence. The backdrop is now the gift of sanctifying grace, as enabling us to know and to love God. To an extent, the *Sentence* commentary also uses this idea: 'grace enables the reasonable creature to return to God himself, through the knowledge and love of God'.[78] A human being reaches God 'through his own operation', that is, 'when someone adheres to the first truth through faith and to this sovereign good through charity: and this gives rise to another mode, that in which God is specially present in the saints through grace'.[79] Because it makes its exposition

---

[75] I *Sent.* d. 15, q. 4, a. 1.

[76] Ibid.: '*quasi ductrices in finem vel coniungentes*'.

[77] I *Sent.* d. 17, q. 1, a. 1, ad 1. But this indwelling does not require an actual knowledge of the divine persons; an habitual knowledge is enough: 'that is, as the property of the divine person is represented as it were in the form of its likeness in the given gift, which is an *habitus*' (I *Sent.* d. 15, q. 4, ad 1). We will come back to this later: the act is a virtual reality within the habitus.

[78] I *Sent.* d. 37, exp. prim. part. text.

[79] I *Sent.* d. 37, q. 1, a. 2.

commence with it, the *Summa* highlights its use of this aspect more clearly than the *Sentence* commentary does. This way can be qualified as 'operative' (it stresses the theological operation) or as 'intentional' (the terms *intentional* or *spiritual* designate, by contrast with *natural,* the mode of being which a reality has in the subjects which know and will it).[80] The *Summa* develops this side of the story.

(c) God's Presence as Known and Loved

In order to show that the *mission* and *donation* of Son and Holy Spirit are only attested within the gift of sanctifying grace, the *Summa* considers them from within the framework of a general doctrine of the modes in which God 'is in' his creatures.[81] What one has to put one's finger on is precisely what new event occurs when the divine persons are 'sent' and 'given'. Thomas' exposition begins with mission, and then goes on to donation. Since mission has been defined through the presence of the divine person, 'existing in a new way in someone', one must consider how the divine persons are present in the world. Thomas here discusses two of God's modes of presence in the world. He mentions elsewhere a third one, the Son's incarnation, which is actually unique, for in this mode the Son is personally united to the humanity which he assumes, in a hypostatic union.[82] So we need to look at these two modes of God's presence.

Thomas affirms that, 'as the cause present in those that share his goodness, God is in everything by his essence, power and presence'.[83] Because it can be seen throughout creation, the first mode is described as 'common'. God is in everything he creates, not as a feature of creation, but 'as the agent is present in that which he makes'. God gives creatures existence, and preserves them in existence. To exist (*esse*) is God's first created effect. God thus communicates to creatures a participation in what he himself is, that is, in the One whose essence is his very existing. Thomas notes that, 'no matter how long a thing exists, it is necessary that God be in it, after the manner in which the thing has existence'.[84] This first mode is not just on the surface of things. God 'is in' his creatures at the depth at which these creatures participate in existence:

[80] The philosophical terminology used here is originally Islamic, coming from Averroes: see R. A. Gauthier's note on this in the Leonine edition of the *Sentencia libri de anima,* vol. 45/1, p. 169.

[81] *ST* I, q. 43, a. 3. As we have seen, Thomas is already looking at it in this way in his *Sentence* commentary: cf. I *Sent.* d. 37, q. 1, a. 2.

[82] I *Sent.* d. 37, q. 1, a. 2.

[83] *ST* I, q. 43, a. 3.

[84] *ST* I, q. 8, a. 1.

'The *esse* is that which is most intimate in each thing, and that which is deepest in all things.... So God must be in all things, and innermostly.'[85] In order to convey this common mode of God's presence, St Thomas takes over a formula from the *Ordinary Gloss* on the Song of Songs (5.17), which, like everyone else at the time, he ascribes to Gregory the Great: 'Through his presence, his power and his substance, God is in all things in common.'[86] He is in them through his *power* because all things are subjected to the exercise of his power; through his *presence* because all things are naked before the God who knows them; through his *essence* because God is in all things as the cause of their being.[87]

Father, Son, and Holy Spirit are present in the way that an agent is present within his effects, that is, because the divine persons act upon all created things. In his *Sentence* commentary, Thomas explains there is already a kind of union (*coniunctio*) with the Triune God within the first mode. By dint of God's acting in them, creatures have a communicated participation in or 'likeness' of the divine goodness.[88] It is thus just as much in their being as their doing that creatures are assimilated to God, or receive the divine 'resemblance', and all because God operates upon them. But this first mode does not enable creatures to attain to God in himself. It is more a matter of achieving a likeness to God, through his act of creation and his constant operation within the creatures he has made and makes still.[89]

Thomas writes that,

Over and above this, there is a special presence congruent with the nature of an intelligent being, in whom God is said to be present as the known is in the knower and the beloved in the one who loves.[90]

Within the second, 'special' mode, the creaturely recipient of God's action does not just achieve a 'likeness' to God, but 'touches the very substance of God';[91] reaching up to 'God in person', he or she is 'with God'.[92] Within this special mode, God is not solely present as a cause is in its effects, but present 'as the object under operation is present in the operator'.[93] The word 'object' has a peculiar meaning in this context. It does not suggest any sort of anonymization or depersonalization of God (as it would today, when we distinguish relating to someone else 'as a subject' from relating to them 'as

---

[85] *ST* I, q. 8, a. 1.   [86] See for instance *ST* I, q. 8, a. 3, sed contra.
[87] *ST* I, q. 8, a. 3.   [88] I *Sent.* d. 37, q. 1, a. 2.
[89] IV *Sent.* d. 49, q. 1, a. 3, qla 1. We discussed this passage in the 'Writing on the *Sentences*' in Chapter 14, at 'The Trinitarian Structure of the Economy'.
[90] *ST* I, q. 43, a. 3.
[91] I *Sent.* d. 37, q. 1, a. 2.
[92] I *Sent.* d. 37, exp. prim. part. text.; cf. *ST* I, q. 8, a. 3.
[93] *ST* I, q. 8, a. 3; cf. I *Sent.* d. 37, q. 1, a. 2; d. 37, exp. prim. part. text.: 'in an object mode'.

an object'). Rather, *object* is taken in its formal meaning, designating that which an action immediately attains or reverts to, in this instance, the God to whom creatures are carried by their action or 'operation'.

In that case, what is the action or operation in which God is thus present? It can only be a spiritual activity, an action of the mind or of volition. Creatures who do not have intelligence or free will can achieve a specific good, by participating through their own existing in the divine goodness or through their material sensibility, but they cannot attain to the universal good. Thomas claims, on the other hand, the 'created rational nature, in as much as it apprehends the universal notion of good and being, is immediately related to the universal principle of being':[94] alone among creatures, it can reach all the way up to God. This analysis echoes what we have said earlier about the Trinitarian processions. Through the procession of the word in the knowing mind, 'the known reality is in the knower'. And likewise, the 'operation of the will within ourselves involves also another procession, that of love, whereby the object loved is in the lover'.[95] In the spiritual order, our union with another comes about in the form of the other's being present within ourselves. Since the two modes are distinct, the other is present to us in different ways depending on whether it is realized in the mind or in the will. When we have an intellectual presence, the known reality is present through its likeness; whereas, in the will, the beloved entity is present through a dynamic momentum, as attracting us toward itself.[96]

Thomas originally used this thought to give an analogical explanation of how we can grasp the *immanent* processions in God: 'that which knows itself and loves itself is in itself not only by a real identity, but also in the capacity of the known in the knower, and the beloved in the lover'.[97] This is why, from the *Summa Contra Gentiles* onwards,[98] the idea of Word and Love is treated as the best way of disclosing how the divine persons are distinct within the unity of the divine essence: immanence and distinction (through originary relations) belong to the very notions of *Word* and *Love*. One can also show in this way

[94] *ST* II–II, q. 2, a. 3.
[95] *ST* I, q. 27, a. 3.
[96] *SCG* IV, ch. 19 (no. 3560); cf. *ST* I, q. 27, a. 4. We presented this teaching, about the presence of the known and the beloved in the one who knows and loves, way back in Chapter 4, at 'A Different Procession, which is that of Love'.
[97] *ST* I, q. 37, a. 1.
[98] *SCG* IV, ch. 11 (no. 3469): 'God must be in himself as the thing understood is in the one who understands. But, the thing understood is in him who understands the intention understood and the word. There is, therefore, in God understanding Himself the Word of God, as it were, God understood'; ch. 19 (nos. 3563–3564): 'God Himself is in his will as the beloved is in the lover'; God is 'in his will by way of love'; 'the love by which God is in the divine will as a beloved in a lover proceed[s] both from the Word of God and from the God whose Word He is'.

that, whilst the two are distinct from their principles, Word and Love proceed from and remain in God himself. The enquiry into the divine missions also gains from the earlier discussion of the processions and persons. In the application of this analysis to the question of mission, an important role is carried by an elaboration upon the idea of Word and Love. Using analogous bases to disclose both the eternal processions and the divine persons' missions enables Thomas to present a unified theory.

Thus, a consideration of the intrinsic nature of intellect and love allows Thomas to show the conditions under which God is present in a new mode, one distinct from the divine omnipresence in the whole of creation. This novel mode only comes about in 'intelligent creatures',[99] since they alone are capable of knowing and loving God. Thomas states that,

because, by these acts of knowing and loving the intelligent creature touches God himself, by reason of this special way of being present we have the teaching that God is not merely in the intelligent creature, but dwells there as in his temple. No effect other than sanctifying grace, then, could explain a divine person's being present to the intelligent creature in this new way. The conclusion is that there is no mission or temporal procession of a divine person except in the shape of sanctifying grace.[100]

This is not a matter of natural knowledge of God, nor of some sort of natural bond to God. Natural knowledge of God, which in other contexts must be accorded a genuine value, only grasps what necessarily belongs to him as the first cause of all things;[101] it does not enable us to know the missions of the divine persons.[102] This is a field for the knowledge and love which unite us to God as the end in which all human beings, and angels, discover their final beatitude. The knowledge and love at stake here enable us to reach 'right up to God himself' (*ad ipsum Deum*). Such expressions enable us to see the typifying feature of the theological virtues: gratuitously given by God alone, they have God himself as their 'object', an ultimate end which surpasses the creatures' intrinsic resources.[103] In the knowledge given by faith and in the love given by charity, and finally in the vision and enjoyment of God in the blessed, God is not just attained as the cause reflected by his effects, but touched upon in his own being, as the ultimate end, pure and simple. Faith achieves a knowledge of God 'after the mode of the divine reality itself', a knowledge of God 'in and for himself', through assimilation to God's self-knowledge.[104] And likewise, rooted in faith, charity is love of God in and for himself, enabling us to reach his own precise mystery.[105] Thomas affirms that,

---

[99] One could just as well say: to creatures which are *persons*. See above, Chapter 6, 'What is a Person?'
[100] *ST* I, q. 43, a. 3.   [101] Cf. *ST* I, q. 12, a. 12.   [102] Cf. *In 1 Cor.* 3.16 (no. 172).
[103] *ST* I–II, q. 62, aa. 1–2.   [104] *Super Boetium de Trinitate*, q. 2, a. 2.
[105] *ST* II–II, q. 23, a. 5, ad 2; a. 6.

Now, 'to possess' means to have something at our disposal to use or enjoy as we wish. A divine person can be possessed in this sense only by an intelligent creature conjoined to God. Other creatures can be acted upon by a divine person, but not in such a way that they have it in their power to enjoy the divine person or to have the use of his effect. But in some cases the intelligent creature does reach that state, wherein he becomes a sharer in the divine Word and in the Love proceeding, so that he has at his disposal a power to know God and to love him rightly. He cannot, however, come to this by his own resources; it must be given to him from above.[106]

Just as he did in his *Sentence* commentary, so here too Thomas emphasizes that, within this new mode, God is attained 'through the operation' of the intelligent creature. The implication of this stress on operation is obvious. It is through the *activity* of knowing and loving that the known and beloved reality is present in the one who knows and loves. Thomas' discussion of the new mode of God's presence foregrounds *activity* just as his study of the divine image will do. It is in their activity of knowing and loving God that human beings express the Trinity to which each of them will be united.[107] The presence of God in the saints is not restricted to the acts which they perform: 'for, otherwise, when the just are asleep, God would only be in them in the way that he is in other creatures'.[108] This new mode of the divine presence is thus attested also in habitual knowledge and love of God, that is in the supernatural virtues (which are dispositions to act) from which actions issue, and 'in which the acts exist in a virtual way'.[109] This enables us to account, for instance, for the presence of God in little children, who live from grace but who are not yet able to exercise personal acts of intelligence: 'God dwells spiritually in the saints as if in his own home . . . even when they do not carry out acts of knowing or loving him, because grace gives them the *habitus* of faith and charity, as in the case of baptized babies.'[110]

These analyses have shown that God 'dwells' in the intelligent creature through the missions of the Son and Holy Spirit. Even though he does not refer to them in so many words in this article of the *Summa Theologiae*, this teaching echoes the Pauline and Johannine language to which it responds;[111] 'Do you not know that you are the temple of God and that the Spirit of God dwells in you' (1 Cor. 3.16); 'Your body is a temple of the Holy Spirit' (1 Cor. 6.19); 'we will come to him and make our dwelling with him' (Jn 14.23); 'Those who keep his commandments, live in God and God in him' (1 Jn 3.24),

---

[106] *ST* I, q. 38, a. 1.   [107] *ST* I, q. 93, a. 7.

[108] I *Sent.* d. 17, q. 1, a. 1, sed contra 3.

[109] *ST* I, q. 93, a. 7; I *Sent.* d. 15, q. 4, a. 1, ad 1: 'the mission of a divine person does not require an actual act of knowing that person, just an habitual one'. Cf. Albert, I *Sent.* d. 15, a. 17.

[110] *In 1 Cor.* 3.16 (no. 173). This contains a striking miniature exposition of the modes of the divine presence.

[111] Cf. *SCG* IV, ch. 21 (nos. 3576–3577).

and so forth. It is by living in human beings that God makes each of them his dwelling place and temple. In his commentary on the first letter to the Corinthians, St Thomas sums up his teaching on this in a single, terse formula: 'God dwells in human beings through the faith which operates by charity.'[112] This is the conclusion the theologian was after. Only sanctifying grace, as the source of faith and charity, affects and explains the *mission* or *temporal procession* of the divine persons. In human beings, grace is the root or the condition of the possibility of receiving the divine persons. Commenting on John 14.23, Thomas remarks that,

> God is said to come to someone because he is there in a new way, in a way he had not been before, that is, by the effect of his grace. It is by this effect of grace that he makes us approach him.[113]

In his reflections on the general notion of 'mission', Thomas had underlined that fact that the divine person is not only sent, but *given*, and given in order to be *possessed*. Here again, only gifts of sanctifying grace make sense of the donation of the divine person:

> In the same way, one says that we 'possess' that which we can freely enjoy. And one can only enjoy a divine person by reason of sanctifying grace.[114]

This brings us back to the explanation given in the *Sentence* commentary, and which had already been formulated in Bonaventure's own commentary and in the *Summa* of Alexander of Hales.[115] The recipient of the missions of Son and Spirit 'enjoys' the divine persons themselves. And this 'fruition' is Everyman's blessedness: union with God. The theme of fruition showcases the focal place of charity and of union with God as our beatifying end, for 'fruition touches on the love or delectation which one experiences at the ultimate term of his journey, which is his end'.[116] Fruition will achieve its perfection when the final end has been achieved in its fullness. In their pilgrim condition on earth, human beings only receive this fruition imperfectly, 'because of the imperfect way in which the end is possessed'. But one can properly speak of 'fruition', since the ultimate end is really possessed, in an inchoate way.[117] St Thomas clearly conceives this enjoyment in the light of the divinizing acts of the knowledge and love of God.

---

[112] *In 1 Cor.* 3.16 (no. 172).
[113] *In Ioan.* 14.32 (no. 1944).   [114] *ST* I, q. 43, a. 3.
[115] *Summa fratris Alexandri*, Book I (ed. Quaracchi, vol. 1), nos. 511–512. Bonaventure, I *Sent.* d. 14, a. 2, q. 1; d. 15, p. 2, a. un., q. 1.
[116] *ST* II-II, q. 11, a. 1.
[117] *ST* II-II, q. 11, a. 4; cf. ad 2.

As in his 'Writing on the *Sentences*', Thomas insists that it is the divine persons themselves who are given. The gift is not restricted to sanctifying grace, but extends to the uncreated persons. In a sense, the pathway for the presentation of this has been turned around the other way. In his *Sentence* commentary, Thomas had taken off from the divine person who 'proceeds' in creatures, that is, from the temporal procession, and gone on to show that the divine person is given in the gift of sanctifying grace. In the *Summa*, the elucidation begins from the divinizing acts and from grace, in order finally to show that the divine person is really given. This analysis is, in some ways less complex that that of the 'Writing on the *Sentences*'. It is also more readily integrated into the Trinitarian theology of the *Summa* (with its doctrine of the presence of the known and the loved in the knower and lover). But we find the same thesis in both texts. Thomas argues that,

Still as, when sanctifying grace is given, it is the Holy Spirit himself who is possessed and dwells in a person, so it is he himself who is given and sent. The gift of grace perfects the intelligent creature not only by putting him in a state in which he has this created gift at his free disposal, but also to enjoy the divine person himself. The invisible mission is cut out for the gift of sanctifying grace, but the divine person is altogether given in it.[118]

The connection between the created gift of grace and the uncreated gift of the divine person is explained in a way that is like the one we find in the *Sentence* commentary: the gifts of grace, that is, of wisdom and charity, are a *disposition* to receiving the divine person, and it is because of this that the weight is on the human side of the event. Created gifts of grace are necessary in order to 'proportion' a human being to the divine persons, that is, in order to raise the human soul so as to make it capable of attaining God, or of being divinized.[119] They achieve the purpose for which they are given, by paving the way for the enjoyment of the divine persons. And it is the divine person who gives this grace: just as the divine person is the end or aim of grace (grace is given with a view to the enjoyment of the divine person), so he is its cause. Thomas brings this out in the course of elucidating a verse from Paul which is located at the heart of this discussion: 'The charity of God has been spread in our hearts through the Holy Spirit who has been given to us' (Rom. 5.5). Thomas comments that,

---

[118] *ST* I, q. 43, a. 3, sol. and ad 1. Cf. *In Ioan.* 4.10 (no. 577), in relation to the 'living water': 'The grace of the Holy Spirit is given to human beings in such a way that the very source of grace is given, that is, the Holy Spirit himself.'

[119] *ST* I-II, q. 112, a. 1; cf. q. 110, a. 1.

Grace prepares the soul to receive the divine person and this is what the statement that the Holy Spirit is given by reason of the gift of grace means. Nonetheless, the Holy Spirit is the source of the gift of grace and this is what the text, 'The charity of God is spread in our hearts by the Holy Spirit' means.[120] The principle of habitual grace, which is given with charity, is the Holy Spirit; who is said to be sent inasmuch as he dwells in the mind by charity.[121]

Thomas has put the theological activity of the knowledge and love of God, rooted in grace, at the front of the picture in order to make sense of the gift of the divine persons themselves. Of course God's action and efficacy has a decisive part to play in the exposition, but it does not make its entrance until the final act. We could sum up the main features of the mission and donation of the divine persons as consisting in: the theological or Godward actions of knowledge and love of God (or God's 'operative' or 'objective' presence), the effect of grace as the elevation of nature toward God, the gift of the divine persons themselves (or the 'fruition' brought about by the persons), and, along with the action of the whole Trinity, the Holy Spirit and Son operating like exemplars in the way they influence those to whom they are sent.

The 'fruition' which the divine persons effect is not reserved for the occasional ecstasies attained by some mystics at the height of their ascetic lives. Thomas sees it as being there in every single sending of the divine persons. It stamps the character of union with God for everyone who lives in grace by receiving the divine persons.[122] The divine persons' missions are thus coextensive with the whole life of grace, whether it be the just living out the fruits of the mission they have been given,[123] or when they are graced with a new mission. In an even more marked way than in his *Sentence* commentary, the *Summa* acknowledges the presence of new missions not only in exceptional spiritual experiences, but also in a progress in the virtues or in the growth in grace, and whenever the indwelling of the divine persons seems to have brought some 'new thing' to bear,[124] that is, when progress toward union with God encounters a new state of grace or inspires new acts, which could be voluntary poverty or the acceptance of martyrdom, but also the reception of the sacraments, or charity enabling one to conquer temptation or carry a

---

[120] *ST* I, q. 43, a. 3, ad 2.

[121] *ST* III, q. 7, a. 13; Thomas is speaking of the sending of the Holy Spirit to Christ at the moment of his conception.

[122] *ST* I, q. 43, a. 6; cf. I *Sent.* d. 15, q. 5, a. 1, qla 2.

[123] *In Ioan.* 14.16 (no. 1914): 'The Spirit is truly given because it is given forever. Thus [Christ] says, *the Spirit of truth will remain with you forever.* When something is given to a person only for a time, this is not a true giving; but there is a true giving when something is given to be kept forever. And so the Holy Spirit is truly given, because he is to remain with them forever.'

[124] *ST* I, q. 43, a. 6: 'in the recipient of a mission we should take into account both the indwelling by grace and a quality of newness brought about by grace'.

demanding task to completion.[125] And so the missions envelop the graced life in its entirety, both through its ongoing, permanent fruition and in the springtimes of the new sendings of the divine persons. They are also coextensive with the whole of history, from the creation of the first human beings until God brings his design to its ultimate fulfilment.[126]

We must add one finishing touch to this discussion of grace and the gifts of grace. Sanctifying grace ('habitual grace') is at the root of it, the principle which germinates in us the disposition to receive the divine persons: grace is required for the uplifting of the creature's *nature*, rendering it capable of receiving the divine person. Nonetheless, the *formal* achievement of the mission of the divine person comes about in the gifts of wisdom and love, that is, it comes about when the supernatural habit is *operative* as the knowledge and love of God; habitual grace lies at the root of this fulfilment. These operational habits are needed to enable the creature whose nature has been upraised by sanctifying grace to return to God through the supernaturally charged habits and acts of knowledge and love. Through the gift of these operational habits, the mission's beneficiaries are *assimilated* and *conformed* to Son and Holy Spirit. The Son is sent to confer the gift of knowing God and this gift is a participation in the character of the Word. The Holy Spirit is sent so that the enamoured saints can reach up to God in a way that participates in the personal character of the Holy Spirit—love. In a formal perspective, sanctifying grace is a participation in the divine nature and does not relate to the divine persons in their Trinitarian distinction: the personal relation to Son and Spirit comes about in the operative gifts of wisdom and love (in the 'gifts of sanctifying grace') which are the formal effects of sanctifying grace (the 'effects of grace'), and which are *given with this grace*. Thus, properly speaking, the divine missions hit their target in a formal sense with the sanctifying gifts of wisdom and charity, which are the effects of habitual grace.

(d) The Gifts of the Son and Holy Spirit: Two Inseparable and Distinct Missions

One cannot compartmentalize the Triune presence; the divine persons are present inseparably.[127] Thomas notes that 'we will come to him and make our dwelling with him' (Jn 14.23) means that 'sanctifying grace makes the whole

---

[125] *ST* I, q. 43, a. 6, ad 2 and ad 4; I *Sent.* d. 15, q. 5, a. 1, qla 2. Thomas acknowledges that there are new missions even amongst those who contemplate God in beatitude, as when God gives them new revelations on the mysteries, right down to the last judgement (*ST* I, q. 43, a. 6, ad 3; I *Sent.* d. 15, q. 5, a. 1, qla 3).

[126] Cf. *ST* I, q. 43, a. 6, ad 3.

[127] I *Sent.* d. 15, q. 2, ad 4. See above, in Chapter 12, 'Theology and Economy'.

Trinity to abide in the soul'.[128] But, the meaning of 'mission' entails that, although the whole Trinity is given, only the Son and Spirit are *sent*. Once having pinned down the 'new modality' in which the persons are present as an inhabitation in grace, the theologian can explain that,

A divine person's being to someone invisibly through grace means a new manner of presence as well as origin from another divine person. Because, then, being present through grace and being from another person fit the Son and the Holy Spirit, as does being sent invisibly.[129]

The missions of Son and Holy Spirit should not be conflated; they are distinct from each other. Thomas shows this by drawing out the implications of the two elements of mission, with the diverse things they entail: the person's origin and the effect of grace. (1) In relation to the origin of the person, Thomas states that, 'the Son's mission is distinct from the Holy Spirit's, just as being begotten is from proceeding'.[130] As we have seen, each person's eternal procession is a factor of his mission. It is the person *as proceeding*, the person taken in his procession, or the person within his personal relation, who is sent and given. On this point, the doctrine of missions ties together the highest flights of Trinitarian theology. The person is sent and given after the mode which is proper to him and characterizes him within the heart of the Trinity, that is, within the modality of his personal property. (2) The missions of Son and Holy Spirit are also distinct in reference to their effects. 'By grace,' St Thomas says, 'the soul is con-formed to God,' and therefore

that a person is sent to someone requires an assimilation to the person sent through some particular gift of grace.[131]

The idea of 'assimilation' carries reverberations of the 'sealing' mentioned in the 'Writing on the *Sentences*'. The recipient of a mission gains a likeness or resemblance to the divine person, in the character personal to him. When the saints receive the Son and the Holy Spirit in their knowledge and love of God they are 'conformed' to them; they are made 'con-formable' with the God in whom Word and Love proceed. One can thus witness a 'conformity of union in the saints who know and love the same reality which God knows and loves'.[132] And here again, Thomas makes use of his speculative theory of the divine persons, claiming that,

Since the Holy Spirit is Love, the likening of the soul to the Holy Spirit occurs through the gift of charity, and it is thus the gift of charity which attests a mission of the Holy

---

[128] *ST* I, q. 43, a. 5; cf. a. 4, arg. 2.   [129] *ST* I, q. 43, a. 5.
[130] *ST* I, q. 43, a. 5, ad 3; cf. I *Sent.* d. 15, q. 4, a. 2.   [131] *ST* I, q. 43, a. 5, ad 2.
[132] *De potentia*, q. 9, a. 9. The idea of the graced image of God articulates just this conformity.

Spirit. The Son in turn is the Word; and not just any word, but the Word breathing Love; this is why Augustine says in the *De Trinitate* Book IX, 'The Word which I seek to disclose is knowledge with love.' Consequently not just any mental advancement indicates the Son's being sent, but only that sort of enlightenment which bursts forth into the affect of love.[133]

Those who benefit from a mission are conformed to the divine persons within the habits and acts through which they attain to God: through the charity reflecting the Holy Spirit's personal relation, and through that knowledge which inspires love which 'renders us like' the Son. The two missions are thus at one in bringing about an effect of grace, but distinguished in the effects of this grace, to wit, 'the illumination of the mind and the enkindling of the affections'.[134] One has to go back to the language of appropriation in relation to the effects, because the effects are not the proper or exclusive work of any particular divine person. Wisdom is appropriated to the Son, and charity is appropriated to the Holy Spirit.[135] The truth is that Thomas lays little stress on appropriation within the question on the missions, but it has to come into its own when he explains how the *effects* are related to the divine persons.[136] We need to be clear how appropriation figures in this discussion. It touches on the connection between the created gifts of wisdom and love and the personal properties of the Son and the Holy Spirit. Any created effect as such has the whole Trinity as its efficient cause.[137] The mission itself is certainly not an appropriation, but proper to a given divine person. Thomas remarks that 'The proper mode in which the Son is said to be in the creature is not the proper mode in which the Holy Spirit is present there: one is present in wisdom, the other in love.'[138] By bringing about an assimilation to a divine person, the created gift opens the way to a real recognition of which divine person has been sent. The function of Son and Holy Spirit as exemplars takes centre-stage in the analysis of this. Thomas adduces that,

Looking to the effects which God properly produces in the rational creature, we must give consideration to this fact: When we are somehow assimilated to a divine perfection, this perfection is said to be given us by God; so wisdom is said to be a

---

[133] *ST* I, q. 43, a. 5, ad 2. Cf. Augustine, *De Trinitate* IX.X.15.

[134] *ST* I, q. 43, a. 5, ad 3.

[135] *ST* II-II, q. 1, a. 8, ad 5.

[136] There is only one reference to appropriation in the discussion of missions in q. 43, where St Thomas says that, 'certain gifts taken in their individual meaning are in a certain way appropriated to the Son, that is, the gifts which grace the intellect' (*ST* I, q. 43, a. 5, ad 1). He is more explicit in his *Sentence* commentary (I *Sent.* d. 14, q. 2, a. 2, ad 3; d. 15, q. 2, arg. 3, arg. 5, ad 2, ad 3, ad 5; d. 15., q. 4, a. 1, arg. 3). The appropriation of the created gifts belongs to what all the scholastic theologians have to say on this topic.

[137] See for instance *SCG* IV, ch. 21 (no. 3576).

[138] I *Sent.* d. 15, q. 4, a. 2.

gift from God to us when we are somehow assimilated to the divine wisdom. Since, then, as we have seen, the Holy Spirit proceeds through the mode of the Love by which God loves himself, . . . when we are assimilated to this Love in becoming friends of God, we are given the Holy Spirit . . . The 'word of wisdom' (Dan. 1.20) by which we know God, and which God pours into us, is properly representative of the Son. And likewise the love by which we love God is properly representative of the Holy Spirit.[139]

The fruition which issues in the enjoyment of the divine persons in their personal reality works on the same lines. Thomas constantly comes back to the point that the person *himself* is given for the possession of the one in whom he abides. 'We enjoy', he says, 'what is proper to each person.'[140]

Although they are distinct, the missions of Son and Holy Spirit are nonetheless inseparable.[141] Like their distinction, their inseparability appears on every level of the discussion. Within the eternal processions, which are included in the person's mission, the Son and Holy Spirit are inseparable. Thomas uses the idea of the 'perfect Word' to show this, that is, drawing from Augustine, the idea of the 'Word breathing Love': the Word cannot be dissociated from Love, and vice versa. As we have seen, the idea of subsistent relations enables us to display the bedrock foundation of this inseparability. One should also notice that this analysis is framed by an intrinsic relatedness of the generation of the Son and the procession of the Holy Spirit. One cannot fully grasp the begetting if one thinks only in terms of the relation of Father and Son, for the begetting of the Son cannot be detached from the procession of the Holy Spirit.[142] In the same way that the Holy Spirit is the Love who proceeds from Father and Son so, in the immanence of the Trinity as in his mission, the Son is always the 'Word breathing Love'.[143]

The persons give themselves inseparably in our 'fruition'. As we have seen, such fruition is the heart of the theological elucidation of the indwelling of the divine persons. And those who receive Son and Holy Spirit do not enjoy the persons through different fruits, as if there were one fruition for the Holy Spirit and another fruition for the Son, and yet another for the Father. 'We enjoy the three persons', Thomas notes, 'by dint of one and the same fruition.'[144] St Thomas gives two reasons for this. One is that the object of fruition and of charity is the sovereign goodness of the Triune God. And

---

[139] *SCG* IV, ch. 21 (nos. 3575–3576).

[140] I *Sent.* d. 1, q. 2, a. 2, ad 2.

[141] Here Thomas differs from the *Summa* attributed to Alexander of Hales, which claims that one divine person could be sent without another (Book I, no. 506, ad 1).

[142] See above, in Chapter 11, 'Balancing Out the Nuances: The Distinction and the Unity of Father and Son'.

[143] *ST* I, q. 43, a. 5, ad 2; I *Sent.* d. 15, q. 4, a. 1, ad 3 (with the same reference to Augustine's *De Trinitate*).

[144] I *Sent.* d. 1, q. 2, a. 2.

there are not different degrees of goodness amongst the divine persons; all of them have the same divine goodness, within three hypostases. So it is through one and the same love and fruition that we are conveyed toward each of the three persons, and to all of them taken together. The oneness of the fruition is not buried in the property of each person. When we are united to the Son, we relate the Son's fruition to the Father, within the unity and equality which is such that only the order of origin distinguishes Father from Son.[145] In the second place, St Thomas reminds us that the divine persons must be grasped in their relations. These persons distinguish themselves from one another through their relations, and they are these subsisting relations. And, by dint of the very nature of a relation, each of the relations is included in the other.[146] Thus, 'anyone who knows one of the relationships knows the others' and 'one who enjoys one of the relationships in itself, also enjoys the others'. As a result, 'the fruition of one divine person is engaged in the fruition of another'.[147] This brings us back to one of the central features of the doctrine of perichoresis. In the same way that each person 'is in the other', so union to one person includes union to the other persons.

The missions are also inseparable from the perspective of the effect, and that in two capacities: because grace, the root of this effect, is attested in both missions, and because the knowledge and love in which the mission is evident are inseparable. Charity proceeds from faith, and that faith is dead which does not flower in charity. And here the exemplar function of the divine persons becomes very clear: in the same way that the divine Word is the 'Word breathing love', so the kind of knowledge which the mission gives us is a knowledge fulfilled in love. Without charity, knowledge would not even reflect the property of the Word, and would not allow us to recognize that the Son is its emissary. From the same standpoint of the donation of the divine persons, one can even pick out a certain priority of the gift of the Holy Spirit. This is not a temporal priority, but a priority deriving from the nature of love: 'since the original dynamic which moves and is inclined toward being given is love, the donation of the Holy Spirit comes before the donation of the Son'.[148] In every respect, there is an absolute solidarity and simultaneity

---

[145] Ibid., arg. 3 and ad 3.
[146] Cf. *ST* I, q. 42, a. 5; I *Sent.* d. 19, q. 3, a. 2.   [147] I *Sent.* d. 1, q. 2, a. 2.
[148] I *Sent.* d. 15, q. 4, a. 2, ad 2. This observation relates to donation rather than to mission. From the standpoint of the divine persons themselves, the Trinitarian order leads us to recognize that, without there being priority or posteriority amongst them, the Son is the Holy Spirit's principle. And likewise from the standpoint of the sending, it is the Son who, together with the Father, sends the Holy Spirit. And again, from the standpoint of the effects, supernatural knowledge (or the mission of the Son) is the source of charity (or the mission of the Holy Spirit). The priority of the gift of the Holy Spirit which Thomas spots here is attested 'from the standpoint of the donating' (*ex parte dantis*) alone.

between the missions of Son and Holy Spirit, the one entailing the other. Thomas states that,

The one mission never takes place without the other: for love results from knowledge; and perfect knowledge, which follows from a mission of the Son, always implicates love. This is why both [gifts] are infused at one and the same time, and they increase at one and the same time.[149]

Underneath their formal dress, these observations contain a rich teaching whose consequences are important for every theological discipline: Christology, the sacraments, ecclesiology, and moral theology. In creation as in the economy of grace, God never acts other than through his Word and by his Spirit. The economy of Son and Spirit are never 'autonomous' or detached from each other, but always at one.[150] It is thus that the presence of the Son can be weighed by that of the Holy Spirit, and conversely.

(e) Experiencing the divine persons of Son and Holy Spirit

Within the life of grace, the mission of the Holy Spirit is attested in the gift of charity, and that of the Son in the gift of a kind of knowledge that is bound in with love. This teaching comes straight out of Augustine, as passed on by Peter Lombard. Augustine had explained that the mission of the Son is realized within his coming into the world and through his presence in human souls. The mission of the Son does not only consist in his being born from the Father, but in his *manifestation*, either in the flesh he assumed or in the hearts of those who receive him by faith. This theology of mission is evidently inspired by the Johannine writings. The Son is sent into the world and he remains with his disciples afterward, whenever faith recognizes him as the Envoy and Son of God. Augustine used contiguous language to grasp the mission of the Holy Spirit:

The Son is sent to someone when he knows and understands him . . . For the Son to be born is for him to be from the Father, and for the Son being sent is being known to have his origin in the Father. And likewise, for the Holy Spirit, just as to be the Gift of God is to proceed from the Father, so being sent is being known as proceeding from the Father; and moreover, we cannot deny that the Holy Spirit also proceeds from the Son.[151]

---

[149] I *Sent.* d. 15, q. 4, a. 2.

[150] On the many biblical and theological aspects of this idea, see Yves Congar's beautiful book, *The Word and the Spirit*, trans. David Smith, London, 1986.

[151] Augustine, *De Trinitate* IV.XX.28–29. This teaching is repeated in Peter Lombard's *Sentences*, Book I, dist. 15, chs. 7–9 (vol. I/2, pp. 135–137).

Along with his peers, St Thomas broadly echoes this teaching and constantly cites Augustine's analyses.[152] The divine person is disclosed in his mission; it makes him known through the gifts which represent him, and which are appropriated to him.[153] And when the person is thus disclosed, he is given in the relation personal to him. The Son makes himself known as his relation to the Father: faith receives him as the Envoy and Son of the Father. And correlatively, the Holy Spirit makes himself known as his relation to Father and Son: he is received as the Spirit of Father and Son.[154] This knowledge of the divine person via his originary relation is part of the meaning of 'mission'.[155] But what is the nature of this 'disclosure' and 'knowledge' of the divine person? Thomas explains it in particular detail when he presents the 'knowledge with love' which characterizes the Son's mission, stating that,

not just any mental advancement indicates the Son's being sent, but only that sort of enlightenment which bursts forth into the affect of love, the kind namely described in John: 'Everyone that hath heard from the Father and hath learned, cometh to me' (John 6.45); and in the Psalm which says, 'In my meditation a fire shall come forth.' So Augustine says in a very indicative way that 'the Son is being sent *whenever someone has knowledge or perception of him*,' for 'perception' points to a kind of experiential knowledge, and this is precisely what wisdom is, that is, a knowing that is as it were tasted; thus the phrase in Ecclesiasticus, 'The wisdom of doctrine is according to her name' (6. 23 in the Vulgate).[156]

For this reason, knowledge of the divine person is a graced knowledge, or a sanctifying gift's enabling us to recognize a divine person. This is why the Son is only sent when he is received in grace, with charity. If one knows the Son through a mere external knowledge or within a dead faith, then the Son does not dwell in one's heart and he is not possessed.[157] It works the same way for the Holy Spirit. The Spirit is not given if he is only known symbolically, without the reception of the grace that sanctifies.[158] Thomas says that,

Knowledge is not enough for there to have been a mission. Rather, it is necessary that there be knowledge deriving from a gift appropriated to a person, and by which we are united to God after the mode proper to this person, that is, when the Holy Spirit is sent, through love. And such a knowledge is of the experiential order.[159]

---

[152] *ST* I, q. 43, a. 3, arg. 3 and ad 3; a. 4, ad 2; a. 5, ad 1 and ad 2; a. 6, ad 2. Cf. I *Sent.* d. 14, q. 2, a. 2, arg. 3 and ad 3; d. 15, q. 2, a. 1, arg. 2 and ad 2; arg. 5 and ad 5; d. 15, q. 3, a. 1, sed contra 1; d. 15, q. 4, a. 1, sed contra 2; etc.

[153] I *Sent.* d. 15, q. 4, a. 1, ad 1.

[154] Cf. I *Sent.* d. 15, q. 2, a. 1, ad 2; d. 15, q. 3, a. 1.

[155] I *Sent.* d. 15, q. 2, a. 1, ad 2; d. 15, q. 4, a. 1, ad 1; cf. *ST* I, q. 43, a. 4, ad 2.

[156] *ST* I, q. 43, a. 5, ad 2; cf. Augustine, *De Trinitate* IV.XX.28.

[157] *ST* I, q. 43, a. 3, ad 3.

[158] *ST* I, q. 43, a. 3, ad 4.

[159] I *Sent.* d. 14, q. 2, a. 2, ad 3; cf. Albert, I *Sent.* d. 15, a. 17.

The experiential knowledge in question in this passage refers to the grasp of the Son and Holy Spirit within their sending. And such a knowledge is bound to the conformation within which the just are assimilated to the Son and to the Holy Spirit. Only a graced knowledge, in charity, opens the door to the divine persons. This is one reason why the missions of Son and Holy Spirit are inseparable: genuine wisdom is inseparable from love, which is what makes it bring about the 'union with God'. In articulating this knowledge of the persons, Thomas speaks of an *'experiential* knowledge'. Coming from his pen, this expression is not infrequent in this context: one often encounters it, as much in the *Sentence* commentary as in the *Summa,* and elsewhere, and always in reference to the love which perfects our knowing.[160]

What does this experience-shaped knowledge consist in? It does not come down to some sort of affective colouring of our knowledge of God. It is much rather the grasp of the divine person in his presence and action, for the gifts of wisdom and love assimilate us to the divine persons and allow for an authentic 'enjoyment' of the persons. It is precisely this fruition that the idea of 'experiential knowledge' articulates: it is not just a 'speculative' or conceptual kind of knowledge,[161] but the fact of experiencing the divine person, and testing out an objective oneness with him. This experience is given to those who receive the missions of the divine persons, for 'experiential knowledge is requisite to a mission'.[162] The love bound to this knowledge must thus occupy a key position, for it is this which unites us most deeply to God. This does not mean that we can have an absolute certainty either of the supernatural authenticity of the acts we perform, or of the dispositions in which we live (that is, certitude of being in a state of grace), because experiential knowledge of the sent persons is not of the same order as reflexive consciousness of our acts and habits.[163]

Along with the idea of 'sealing', the theology of missions, the 'possession' and 'fruition' of the persons is set forth as an invitation to experience it. How can one fail to imagine that it was this which St Thomas experienced in December 1273, when he ceased to write, leaving the *Summa* unfinished?

[160] I *Sent.* d. 14, q. 2, a. 2, ad 3; d. 15, q. 2, a. 1, ad 5; d. 15, exp. text.; d. 16, q. 1, a. 2; *ST* I, q. 43, a. 5, ad 2. On this notion, see in particular, A. Patfoort, '*Cognitio ista est quasi experimentalis* (I Sent. d. 14, q. 2, a. 2, ad 3m)', *Angelicum* 63 (1986), 3–13; id., 'Missions divines et expérience des Personnes divines selon St Thomas', *Angelicum* 63 (1986), 545–559; J.-P. Torrell, *Thomas Aquinas: Spiritual Master,* pp. 94–98.

[161] Cf. I *Sent.* d. 15, exp. text: 'The divine person is sent to someone when he is known by him. This cannot be comprised of speculative knowledge alone, but must contain a knowledge which is, in a certain way, experiential.'

[162] I *Sent.* d. 15, q. 2, a. 1, ad 5. Cf. Albert, I *Sent.* d. 15, a. 17.

[163] Cf. I *Sent.* d. 15, q. 4, a. 1, ad 1 (knowledge 'through certain hypothetical signs'); cf. *ST* I-II, q. 112, a. 5.

When his secretary and friend Reginald of Piperno expressed astonishment that Thomas was to abandon work before completing his masterpiece, Thomas responded by saying, 'I can no more.' When he went on insisting, Reginald received the same answer: 'I can no more, for everything I have written seems to me as straw by comparison with what I have seen.'[164] Historians have been reserved about the cause of this event. It should probably be ascribed to an extreme nervous and physical fatigue; but the last year of Thomas' life is marked by deep spiritual experiences. However that may be, this piece of evidence suggests that Thomas had come to the same reality of which he had spoken, and that theological speech was no longer sufficient to contain it. He himself had observed this in his reading of John, commenting on Jesus' response to the two disciples who asked him where he lived (Jn 1.38–39):

'Rabbi, which means master, where do you dwell?' Jesus said to them, 'Come and see.' In the mystical sense, [Jesus' response, 'come and see'] means that the dwelling of God, whether of glory or of grace, cannot be known except by experience: for it cannot be explained in words. Revelation 2.17: 'To him who conquers I will give a white stone upon which is written a new name, which no one knows but he who receives it.' And so Jesus says, 'Come,' by believing and working, and 'see' by having the experience and the grasp.[165]

Christ's indwelling in human hearts can only be recognized in experience (*agnosci non potest nisi per experientiam*): words fall short of adequately explaining it. The theologian can make sense of the indwelling in a speculative meditation thereupon, which has a value on its own level. One explanation can be truer or more complete than another. But the reality of the divine indwelling is tested neither by precision concepts nor in their orderly formation, but in an experience of faith acting through charity, opening the way to the grasp of the very being of the divine persons.

4. THE IMAGE OF THE TRINITY

Thomas' view of the *imago Dei* is extraordinarily close to his teaching on the divine presence and on the missions of the divine persons. Both of them deal with the same reality. But, whereas, in question 43 of the Trinitarian treatise, the doctrine of mission and indwelling considers this reality from the standpoint of the divine persons, his profile of the image in q. 93 of the treatise on

---

[164] See J.-P. Torrell, *St Thomas Aquinas: the Person and his Work*, p. 289.
[165] *In Ioan.* 1.39 (no. 292).

the creation of human beings is drawn from the standpoint of creatures. Moreover, his image-theory reflects on one particular feature of our union with God, that of the 'resemblance' or 'likeness' of the Triune God in each human being. As we have learned, this specification is also at the heart of the teaching on mission: those to whom the divine persons are sent receive a likeness of the divine persons or are 'sealed' by them, and it is through this conformation that a human person is given the ability to touch on God himself, in fruition. So the image-theory does not only establish the anthropological bases for the indwelling of the divine persons. It also pins down what 'assimilation' to the divine persons means, from the perspective of the human recipient of the persons' mission. This is the aspect which we wish to highlight here, even though we cannot go into the features of the image doctrine which escape the purview of this study.[166]

The presence of the divine persons is linked to the image-theory in Thomas' *Sentence* commentary. Through the graced habits and their concomitant acts, the human soul which lives in grace is to the image of God, 'imitating God' and 'grasping God': the soul is united to God as the 'object' of his acts of knowledge and love; such is the human being's 'perfection'.[167] Thomas' idea of the image is proximate to this. He connects the indwelling of the divine persons to the idea of the human being as 'capable of God' (*capax Dei*). To be 'capable of God' means to have the inbuilt aptitude for being raised to God in such a way as to know and to receive him. Thomas says that, 'God dwells spiritually in the saints whose knowing and loving soul is capable of God.'[168] In this connection, Thomas explains that the given end of human beings is to know and love God. Such a union with God surpasses the intrinsic resources of human nature; it must be raised through God's own gratuitous action. But this capacity is nonetheless inscribed in the nature of humankind, because human beings are cut to the image of God: 'The soul is naturally capable of grace; as Augustine says, 'simply from the fact that it is to the image of God, it is capable of God through grace.'[169]

---

[166] For a more complete consideration, and for bibliographical references, see J.-P. Torrell, *St Thomas Aquinas: Spiritual Master*, pp. 84–85; A. Patfoort and A. Gardeil, 'Notes explicatives' and 'renseignements techniques' in the recent French edition of Thomas' *Summa, Les origines de l'homme, 1a, Questions 90–102*, Paris, 1998, pp. 302–319 and 380–421.

[167] I *Sent.* d. 3, exp. text.

[168] *In 1 Cor.* 3.16 (no. 172); cf. I *Sent.* d. 37, exp. prim. part. text.: 'Through grace, the intelligent creature returns to God himself, in that he or she knows and loves him. This is why one says that he is with God. For the same reason, one says that someone is capable of God, because having God as an object is his perfection. And for the same reason again, one says that she is the temple of God and that God dwells in her.'

[169] *ST* I-II, q. 113, a. 10; cf. Augustine, *De Trinitate* XIV.VIII.11. See J.-P. Torrell, *St Thomas Aquinas: Spiritual Master*, p. 347.

The notion of the image had been refined in the study of the person of the Son. The image involves a 'specific resemblance' and an originary relation, which is to say that it is the expression of an exemplar.[170] What makes a human being an image of God is thus that he has a likeness to the character- istics proper to the Triune God, and that he receives this likeness from God himself.[171] When he presses deeper into what this resemblance consists in, Thomas promptly goes for what is really characteristic of God: not just existence, but life and intellectuality or spirituality, that is, wisdom and love.[172] This makes for the fact that God's expression or resemblance in human beings cannot be contained in the 'static' way that an impression or a trace-mark would be. Rather, it consists in moving into participation in God's spiritual action, that is, the knowledge and the love in God. Thomas states that,

the image of God is in human beings on three levels. Primarily, inasmuch as the human being has a natural aptitude for understanding and loving God; and this aptitude rests in the very nature of the mind, which is common to all human beings. Secondly, in as much as human beings know and love God, though imperfectly; and this image consists in the conformity of grace. Thirdly, inasmuch as a human being knows and loves God perfectly; and this image consists in the likeness of glory.[173]

These analyses have many points of interest. Firstly, using a theological framework which we have often encountered before, the image of God is pictured as a rising vector: first of all the created nature which is common to all human beings, then grace and finally its fulfilment, in glory. The image is an analogical thing, whose development follows the rhythm of the economy of creation and grace. The progress which the image makes traces out the levels of assimilation to the person of the Son, and also the same levels as belong to our relation to God the Father: creation means that every human being has God as their Father; this Fatherhood points toward something even higher, which is that the grace of the Holy Spirit can make human beings 'adopted children' (the enfiliation of grace), and so receive the patrimony of eternal life (the enfiliation to glory).[174] The image thus puts assimilation to God in the frame of an increasing conformation to the Son in an ever-closer relation to the Father.

---

[170] *ST* I, q. 35. See above, in Chapter 9, 'The Word, Image of the Father'.
[171] *ST* I, q. 93, a. 1: 'some likeness to God derived from God as from an exemplar'.
[172] *ST* I, q. 93, a. 2.
[173] *ST* I, q. 93, a. 4.
[174] Cf. *ST* I, q. 33, a. 3; and see above, in Chapter 8, 'The Paternity of the Father: Father of the Son and Father of his Creatures'.

Secondly, on each of the levels that the image occurs, the resemblance to God is a matter of *knowing and loving God*. It is by knowing God and loving him that one 'resembles' or is 'assimilated' to him, whether this falls under the heading of a natural aptitude, or under that of an activity or habit acquired in grace or in glory. One can see two very typical things in this exposition. One is that the image does not consist in any sort of intellectual engagement or just any sort of love, but *in the knowledge and love of God*. A second is that Thomas puts the weight on the *action* of knowing and loving God. Thirdly, when he scrutinizes these two constitutive features of the image, Thomas shows that the issue is entirely one of the *image of the Trinity*. This is a precise replay of what he said in his doctrine of the indwelling: the divine persons are present as the 'object' of our *action*, when in faith or vision we know in the love which is charity. We shall take on these aspects in brief.

Human beings are to the image of the Trinity in their mind or soul. More precisely, the image resides in the *mens*.[175] This word is not easy to translate into modern languages: it means the highest faculties of the intellectual soul. The *mens* is 'the highest part of the soul's power'. *Mens* indicates either the soul as it unfolds into intellectual power, or the superior faculties or 'powers' of the soul (the intelligence and will).[176] The image is tied to what distinguishes a human being from other embodied creatures, which means those authentically spiritual faculties which make him a *person*. And the image consists in a representation of the Triune God, an expression of the 'specifics' or characteristics which belong to God. Thomas notes that,

As a result, if the image of the Divine Trinity is to be found in the soul, we must look for it where the soul comes the nearest to a representation of the species of the Divine Persons. Now the divine persons are distinct from each other by reason of the procession of the Word from the One who is his Speaker, and the procession of Love connecting both. But in our soul word 'cannot exist without actual thought,' as Augustine says (*De Trinitate* XIV.7). So, primarily and chiefly, the image of the Trinity is to be found in the acts of the soul, that is, inasmuch as from the knowledge which we possess, we form an internal word in an actual thought; and thence break forth into love. But, since the principles of acts are the habits and powers, and everything exists virtually in its principle, therefore, secondarily and derivatively, the image of the Trinity may be considered as existing in the powers, and still more in the habits, forasmuch as the acts exist virtually in them.[177]

---

[175] *ST* I, q. 93, a. 6.
[176] *De veritate*, q. 10, a. 1; see Ambroise Gardeil, *La Structure de l'Ame et l'expérience mystique,* Paris, 1927, pp. 21–45 and 349. Cf. *ST* I, q. 79, a. 1.
[177] *ST* I, q. 93, a. 7.

Human beings are not only cut to the image of the divine nature, but to the image of the three divine persons.[178] Other creatures have a certain resemblance or 'vestige', which the Trinity sprinkles throughout the entire creation. But since these creatures lack intellect and volition, their nature cannot articulate the characteristic lines of the Speaker of the Word, of the Word himself, or of Love.[179] Such an expression of the Trinity can only belong to creatures endowed with intelligence and will, that is, those capable of spiritual knowledge and of love. Here Thomas fuses two features of his Trinitarian doctrine with his notion of the image. By definition, an image consists in a specific resemblance, that is, a base characteristic which makes something what it is. And, within the Trinity, this base-line feature is personal distinction via the processions of Word and Love, that is, the distinction through a relation grounded in an *act*: the action of the Father who 'speaks the Word' and the actions of Father and Son in 'breathing the Holy Spirit'.[180] So, a human soul expresses the Trinity to the degree that it represents the Trinitarian actions in which it participates by conceiving a word and by rising to an impulse of love.

Hence, it is through its actions of knowing and loving, or, to be more precise, through the acts of conceiving a word and by the procession of an impress of love, that the human soul represents or expresses the Trinity. And if the image also lives in our habits, or dispositions to know and to love, it is in the degree that these actions themselves are virtually present in the habits from which they flow. This is a matter of the natural faculties and the habits of knowledge and love, and, more particularly (as in the doctrine of indwelling, with the image of grace), the supernatural habits of faith and charity, which are gratuitously poured into the saints by God.

What is primary and key to the image of God in human beings is the action that takes place immanently within them, one which is spiritual and fertile, the speaking of a word, and the procession of an impress of love. Under the new guise of the representation or expression of the Trinity, this takes us back to one of the central features of the doctrine of indwelling: the divine persons inhabit the soul of the saints when they are known and loved, present 'as the known is in the knower and as the beloved is in the lover', by dint of theological acts or 'operations', or at least because of habits which have been infused in order to bring such acts about.[181]

---

[178] Ibid., a. 5.   [179] Ibid., aa. 2 and 6.   [180] See above, Chapter 4.
[181] We have already mentioned this point: see *In 1 Cor.* 3.16 (no. 173); I *Sent.* d. 17, q. 1, a. 1, sed contra 3; I *Sent.* d. 15, q. 4, a. 1, ad 1: 'the mission of a divine person does not require an actual act of knowing that person, just an habitual one'.

The finishing touch on the doctrine of the image will be to pinpoint the object of the acts of knowledge and love: knowledge and love *of what*, or rather, *of whom*? Thomas' answer to this question draws on what Augustine had to say about it in *De Trinitate*. Augustine had begun from the image of the Trinity which one can see when one catches the soul in the act of knowing and loving itself,[182] and he showed that the image which has been defaced by sin is remade by grace:

> If the soul's trinity is the image of God, this is not because it remembers itself, knows itself, and loves itself; but because it can recall, know, and love the One through whom it has been created.[183]

Here again, Thomas binds his ideas of the Trinity and of the image tightly around each other. (1) From the standpoint of Trinitarian doctrine, he has shown that the human soul is cut to the image of God in that it represents the divine actions of speaking the Word and breathing Love. And, in the Triune God, the eternal begetting of the Word does not issue from a knowledge derived from creatures; rather, it is by knowing *himself* that God engenders his Word; and likewise, the Holy Spirit does not flow from the love which God bears for creatures, but proceeds as the Love God has for *himself*, the Love of the Father and Son for their own goodness.[184] Knowledge and love of creatures is not absent from the begetting of the Word and the procession of the Holy Spirit; they belong to the Trinitarian processions in that these processions are the cause and rationale of creation. (2) From the standpoint of human beings, we can observe that our interior word and the love we experience are conditioned by the object which specifies them: the word expressing a vegetable or mineral is not the same as one which articulates something spiritual, and the love which is linked to this word follows suit.[185] By combining these two points, Thomas is able to show that the image of God in human beings takes off from knowledge *of God* and from love *of God* because this is what makes for the most expressive articulation of the Trinitarian processions:

> Hence we refer the divine image in human beings to the verbal concept born of the knowledge of God, and to the love which comes from it. Thus the image of God is found in the soul according as the soul turns to God, or has a nature capable of turning so.[186]

[182] See for instance *De Trinitate* IX.II.2–IX.V.8.
[183] Augustine, *De Trinitate* XIV.XII.15 (BA 16, p. 387, with footnote 48 on pp. 635–637). See Thomas, *ST* I, a. 93, a. 8, sed contra.
[184] See above, in Chapter 3, 'Immanent and Economic Trinity'.
[185] *ST* I, q. 93, a. 8: 'in the human mind the concept of a stone is specifically different from that of a horse, while also the love regarding each of them is specifically different'.
[186] *ST* I, q. 93, a. 8; cf. *De veritate*, q. 10, a. 7. Thomas makes a decisive move here, whereas his response in the *Sentence* commentary had been more ambivalent (I *Sent.* d. 3, q. 4, a. 4).

But Thomas does not eliminate the Augustinian theme of the soul's self-knowledge and the soul's self-love. Thomas appreciates its importance, but draws it on into the deeper or higher panorama of the knowledge and love of God. An image of the Triune God is actually there in the soul when it knows and loves itself: 'not because the mind reflects on itself absolutely, so as to come to a halt in itself, but so that it can ultimately go on to turn toward God'.[187] It follows that, whether in an unmediated way or with some indirection, the soul which knows and loves itself is transported toward God. Thomas explained this at greater length in his *De veritate*:

Within the knowledge through which the soul knows itself, there is an *analogous* representation of the uncreated Trinity, in that, as the soul knows itself it engenders of itself a word, and love proceeds from both. Thus the Father, in speaking himself, begets his Word from all eternity, and the Holy Spirit proceeds from both. Whereas, in the knowledge through which the soul knows God, the soul itself is *conformed to God*, in the way that any knowing thing is, in some way, assimilated to the known object.[188]

The most perfect resemblance, that of the image of grace and of glory, is that realized by an objective assimilation of our spiritual faculties to the Triune God. It is faith in God, and charity toward God, paving the way for the vision of God and its fruition in our heavenly homeland, which fulfils the image of God in humankind. The believer who loves God finds that he has been assimilated or 'transformed' into that which he knows and loves: this is what divinization is. Commenting on 2 Cor. 3.18, 'We all with unveiled faces reflect as in a mirror the glory of the Lord; thus we are transformed into his likeness, from glory to glory, as by the Lord who is Spirit', Thomas writes that we know

the glorious God by the mirror of reason, in which there is an image of God. We behold him when we rise from a consideration of ourselves to some knowledge of God, and we are transformed. For since all knowledge involves the knower's being assimilated to the thing known, it is necessary that those who see be in some way transformed into God. If they see perfectly, they are perfectly transformed, as the blessed in heaven by the union of fruition: 'When he appears we shall be like him' (1 Jn 3.2); but if we see imperfectly, then we are transformed imperfectly, as here by faith: 'Now we see in a mirror dimly' (1 Cor. 13.12).[189]

This teaching corresponds closely to Thomas' analyses of mission and of the indwelling of the divine persons. The divine persons dwell in the saints

---

[187] *ST* I, q. 93, a. 8.

[188] *De veritate*, q. 10, a. 7.

[189] *In 2 Cor.* 3.18 (no. 114); this exegesis is inspired by Augustine, *De Trinitate* XV.VIII.14. The knowledge consists in an *assimilation*: see above, in Chapter 4, 'A procession which is the generation of the Word'.

when they are carried toward God as the 'object' of the divinizing acts of knowledge and love. The saints are assimilated to the divine persons, united and made like unto the persons, 'transformed' by the known and beloved God. The image theory shows from a human standpoint precisely what the theory of the missions showed from a divine one. One can see that both belong to an identical set of ideas. And, at this height, the theologian and the spiritual master are made as one.

5. OUR RELATION TO EACH DIVINE PERSON IN GRACE: OBJECTIVE UNION

We explained in the previous chapter that, since the three divine persons are together the efficient and exemplifying source of the gifts of nature and grace, creation and grace train us 'ontologically' toward the whole Trinity.[190] This way of looking at it is Thomas' way of inviting us to acknowledge the unity of the Trinity: since the three persons exercise a single causal action in unison, an 'ontological' or 'entitative' perspective on created effects will refer us to the three persons in their undivided efficacy.[191]

But does the experience of faith not give us a relation to each particular divine person? And would not the acknowledgement that the gift of grace opens the way to a relation not only with the unified Trinity but to each person grasped in his distinct personality follow from this? As we have seen, Thomas clearly says yes: when the Son and Holy Spirit are sent to the saints in grace, the saints enjoy each person in his own personal property. But the context of this relation to each distinct person of Father, Son, and Holy Spirit is no longer exclusively concerned with the ontological and entitative framework of the Trinity's causality. We are now dealing with a human being's *intentional* or *objective* hold on the divine persons, who are really 'given' and 'possessed' by the recipients of grace. The importance of this issue makes it worthwhile to pause and recall Thomas' analysis.

In the gifts of grace, the Trinity dwells in a human being 'as the known is in the knower and as the beloved is in the lover'.[192] The Trinity with its distinct persons gives itself to human beings to become the 'object' of acts of

---

[190] See above, Chapter 14, and also, in Chapter 8, 'The name "Father": The Person of the Father and the Trinity'.

[191] Without forgetting that the divine action or the created effect can be appropriated to one specific person, we still have to say that such appropriations occur within the common causality of the whole Trinity; see above, Chapter 13.

[192] *ST* I, q. 43, a. 3.

supernatural knowledge, such as faith-knowledge and the beatific vision, and the object of acts of charity, like fruition. The persons are not simply given as causing the effects which we receive, but are present and given, 'in the same way as the object of an activity exists in the acting subject'.[193] When it is applied to God in the context of grace, the word 'object' means that the human habits or acts of wisdom and charity enable them to grasp or 'possess' the divine persons so as to be united to these persons in knowledge and love. This is why the Thomist tradition speaks of the 'objective' presence of the Trinity, or the 'intentional' presence of the divine persons, which comes about in the conformation or assimilation to the Son and Spirit.

One can sum up what Thomas has to say about this as follows. The Trinity as a whole and with one single action is the source or cause of sanctifying grace (grace is appropriated to the Holy Sprit because of the kinship it has with the Holy Spirit's property as Love and Gift of Father and Son). Whilst adoption is appropriated to the Father as its author, and to the Son as its model, and to the Holy Spirit as the one who imprints it in our hearts, the entire Trinity is the source or cause of our filial adoption.[194] And whilst the gifts illuminating the intellect are appropriated to the Son and those which enkindle charity to the Holy Spirit, the cause of the gifts of wisdom and love is the whole Trinity.[195] But deification consists in the reception of *the divine persons themselves*: the presence of the Son and the Holy Spirit who are sent to us, and the presence of the Father who abides in the hearts of his children along with the Son and Spirit whom he sends.[196] The created gifts which the Trinity cause to be in us, such as sanctifying grace, wisdom, and charity, are dispositions given to human beings to make them capable of receiving divine persons who are really given as themselves, and present in their very substance.[197] Thomas calls this relationship to the divine persons 'fruition' (*frui, fruitio*):[198] 'We enjoy (*fruimur*) the property of each person.'[199] To enjoy or 'possess' (*habere*) the divine persons[200] is to be united to the divine persons through their being the 'object' of our knowledge and love, that is to encounter the divine persons as known and loved in faith (and then in vision), and in charity (fruition).

---

[193] *ST* I, q. 8, a. 3: 'sicut objectum operationis est in operante'; cf. I *Sent.* d. 37, q. 1, a. 2; dist. 37, exp. prim. part. text.: 'per modum objecti'.

[194] *ST* III, q. 23, a. 2, ad 3.

[195] *ST* I, q. 43, a. 5, ad 2 and ad 3.

[196] Cf. *ST* I, q. 43, a. 4.

[197] I *Sent.* d. 14, q. 2, a. 1, qla 1; dist. 14, q. 2, a. 2, ad 2; dist. 15, q. 4, a. 1; cf. *ST* I, q. 43, a. 3, sol., ad 1 and ad 2.

[198] *ST* I, q. 43, a. 3; cf. *ST* I, q. 38, a. 1.

[199] I *Sent.* dist. 1, q. 2, a. 2, ad 2: 'proprietate uniuscujusque personae fruimur'.

[200] *ST* I, q. 43, a. 3.

We have found that the doctrine of the Triune image in human beings worked from the same basis. We are conformed to the divine persons by knowing and loving them, and that is how the image of the Trinity in us achieved its greatest heights, in the image of grace and glory. A human being arrives at perfectly imaging God when he is *conformed* to the Trinity through his *acts* of knowledge and love (this is the 'objective union'), that is, when, by being configured to the emissaries of Son and Spirit, a human person is united to the known and beloved Trinity.[201] The fruition of the divine persons occurs within this 'objective' ordering; it is thus that the divine persons abide in the human heart. The divine persons are not ontologically conflated with the creature, but the creature is united to the objectively real presence of the divine persons after the mode of a known and beloved 'object'.

Thomas' analyses make it necessary to distinguish the 'ontological' and the 'intentional' aspects of grace.[202] (1) In its 'objective' or 'entitative' side, or considered in itself within the subject to whom it is given, grace is the effect of the action of the whole Trinity and so the gifts of grace refer us to the Trinity taken in the unity of the three persons.[203] Within this frame, we can, for instance, recognize the whole Trinity as 'our Father'. (2) But on its 'intentional' side, considered in relation to that to which it is heading, that is, from the perspective of the *object* or term which we orient ourselves towards, when the known and beloved persons manifest themselves as 'objects', the gifts of grace refer us to the three divine persons as distinct from each other, and grasped in their proper peculiarity, one as Father, the other as Son, and the third as the Holy Spirit issuing from Father and Son. Within this second frame, it is not a matter of appropriation, but of a relation to three divine persons, each grasped in the distinct personality proper to him. Such is the Trinitarian personalism of the Christian spiritual life.

6. THE 'VISIBLE' MISSIONS OF THE SON AND HOLY SPIRIT

Who hath saved us, and called us with a holy calling ... according to his own purpose and grace, which was given us in Jesus Christ before the world began, but is now made manifest by the appearing of our Saviour Jesus Christ. (2 Tim. 1.9–10)

---

[201] *ST* I, q. 93, aa. 7–8: the image of God comes about in human beings within the *acts* which take God as their object.

[202] For a lengthier discussion of this, see Charles Journet, *L'Eglise du Verbe Incarné, Essai de théologie spéculative*, vol. 2: *Sa structure interne et son unité catholique*, Saint-Maurice, 1999, pp. 454–468.

[203] This is the place for appropriation.

After discussing the invisible missions of Son and Holy Spirit within the souls of those who live in grace, St Thomas turns to the 'visible missions'. He uses this expression to mean the historical manifestation of the incarnate Son, and the gift of the Holy Spirit in the visible signs which the New Testament attests. He is drawing on a way of speaking which the scholastic theologians had extracted from their understanding of Augustine. Why does he wait until after the invisible missions to take on the visible missions? The reason is contained in the notion of a 'visible mission': a visible mission makes an invisible mission manifest. And so Thomas firstly presents invisible mission, the donation and indwelling of the Triune God in the life of grace, and then he tackles the visible mission which is a sensible disclosure of the sending of the Son and Holy Spirit.

It is necessary to take the terms 'visible' and 'invisible' in the sense in which they are intended, and that is, not too rigidly. The missions of Son and Holy Spirit are called 'invisible' because they occur within the graced soul; but it is not the case that every indwelling is invisible down to its last details. It also expresses itself externally, in a sensible or visible way, through the actions of those who live in grace. And the 'visible mission' by which the Church was implanted on earth implicates the sensible manifestation of the Holy Spirit just as much as it does that of the incarnate Son. And yet these two manifestations look very different. The incarnation of the person of the Son is not of the same order as the manifestation of the Holy Spirit at Pentecost. So one has to take the notion of 'visible mission' as being analogous, with all the differences that creates. And, because 'visible' is used here as an analogous term, these two manifestations have a common feature which makes sense of using one combined word for both. They constitute the summit of the historical revelation of the Triune God within the manifest events which give rise to the New Covenant.

True to form, Thomas puts across what visible mission is by looking at the specific way in which human beings know realities: sensible experience is the basis of all human knowing. This is definitive not only for our natural knowledge, but also for the revelation of the Triune God. God providentially proportions himself to the human beings he addresses. The revelation of the Triune God is ordered to the mode in which those for whom it is destined can receive it. St Thomas observes that,

God's provision for all things matches the mode of their being. And the mode connatural to human beings is to be guided by the seen toward the unseen; this is why the invisible mystery of God had to be made known to them through visible things. And thus, God has in some sense shown himself and the eternal processions of the persons by making the visible creatures present certain revelatory indicators (*indicia*); similarly, it was congruent for the invisible missions of the divine persons to be manifest through visible creatures.[204]

Although this looks like an easy move, the initial steps of this response call for our attention. Divine providence follows a rule which entails important consequences: 'God's provision for all things matches the mode of their being.' Thomas sees this as a perfection of providence and he dwells on it with particular force when he discusses divine justice, human liberty, the action of grace, the communication of virtue, and even when he reflects on the mystery of evil.[205] Providence uses the mode which it has inscribed within human nature to guide human beings to the divine realities: it takes off from sensible experience. Thus, sensible experience is our entrance to the natural knowledge of God,[206] and, in his revelation too, God signals his own mystery to us with bodily realities.[207]

And so God has shown the mystery of the eternal procession of the persons by way of certain 'indications' (*indicia*). Thomas may be thinking as much of the coming of the incarnate Son as of the signs of the sending of the Holy Spirit: as he explains in his John commentary, 'the mission shows the origin'.[208] But he also finds that such 'indications' are present to the light of faith in all the actions and effects of God (the vestige of the Trinity and the divine image tie in with this), and in the whole of Scripture, from the first chapter of Genesis onwards.[209] And if God has providentially shown the eternal processions of the persons through 'visible creatures', he has also shown that the persons are sent *to dwell in the hearts of the saints*. The visible missions of the Son and Spirit thus involve a dual disclosure: they manifest the procession of the person,[210] and they manifest the donation of this person in grace, in the 'invisible mission'.[211] And so the 'visible mission' contains three threads: (1) the divine person's eternal procession; (2) the divine person's new presence;

---

[204] *ST* I, q. 43, a. 7.

[205] Cf. *SCG* III, ch. 71 (no. 2470); ch. 73 (no. 2489); ch. 79 (no. 2544); ch. 148 (nos. 3211–3212); ch. 150 (no. 3231), and so on.

[206] *ST* I, q. 12, aa. 12–13; cf. q. 2, aa. 2–3; q. 32, a. 1.

[207] *ST* I, q. 12, a. 13 (this is where Thomas mentions the Holy Spirit's invisible mission at Christ's baptism).

[208] *In Ioan.* 5.23 (no. 769); see above, in Chapter 1, 'The Revelation of the Trinity through its Works'.

[209] Cf. *ST* I, q. 74, a. 3, ad 3.

[210] See for instance *In Ioan.* 20.22–23: Jesus' 'breathing' on the disciples is a sign of the Holy Spirit, showing that the Holy Spirit proceeds from Father and Son. Cf. Augustine, *De Trinitate* IV.XX.29.

[211] 'The visible mission of the Holy Spirit does not differ in essence from his invisible mission: it simply adds a visible sign to it' (I *Sent.* d. 16, q. 1, a. 1). This teaching is a refinement on a doctrine which Thomas could have found in his precursors (see for instance the *Summa fratris Alexandri*, Book I, no. 514).

and (3) the disclosure of the eternal origin and new presence through a visible sign.[212] The 'invisible mystery' of the processions and of grace is manifested to witnesses by these visible signs. The expression which we translate as 'the invisible mystery of God' is a remarkable one: literally, it is 'that which is invisible of God', the *invisibilia Dei*. This is the expression which the Vulgate uses to indicate that which God has disclosed of himself.[213]

Thomas is well aware that, since the Son's incarnation is of a different order of manifestation to the Holy Spirit's visible indicators or signs, the Son's donation is not disclosed in the same way as the Holy Spirit. Thomas states that,

> It makes a difference whether it is the Son or the Holy Spirit. The Holy Spirit proceeds as Love and he is cut out to be the Gift of sanctification. As the Holy Spirit's principle, it belongs to the Son to be the Author of this sanctification. This is why the Son gives this sanctification to us visibly, as its Author, whereas the Holy Spirit's sending takes the shape of a sign of sanctification.[214]

Thomas' analysis aims at distinguishing how the gift of grace is disclosed in the missions of Son and Holy Spirit, without setting them apart from each other. The Son's 'visible mission' has pole position and nothing can be done to diminish it because the Incarnation is the heart of Christian faith. The 'visible mission' of the Holy Spirit is more problematic. What does it mean to talk about the Holy Spirit's being visibly disclosed, and how is this disclosure connected to the manifestation of the Son? By making a comparison of the two missions, Thomas tries to show that, not just the Son, but the Holy Spirit too, has a visible mission of his own.[215] This requires him to make sense of the commonality within the contrast.

The two visible missions of Son and Spirit are drawn together in their being oriented to the sanctification which an invisible mission brings about. What makes them differ is something rooted in the relative properties of the persons. The character of the Holy Spirit is to proceed as Love, because, since he is Love, the Holy Spirit is the Gift in person:[216] Love is the first Gift in whom all gifts are given.[217] It is thus the Holy Spirit who brings off our interior sanctification. Thomas often articulates this by speaking of the 'grace

---

[212] I *Sent.* d. 16, q. 1, a. 1.

[213] Cf. *In Rom.* 1.20 (no. 117); in this context, this relates to the divine attributes which human beings can know by means of the effects of divine action. In the question on the missions, Thomas returns to this way of speaking, but applies it to the revelation of mysteries which faith alone can know.

[214] *ST* I, q. 43, a. 7.

[215] Most of the objections in question 43 article 7 deal with the precise problem of the 'visible mission of the Holy Spirit'. The lie of the land can be seen from the first argument, introducing the article: 'It would seem that it is incongruous for the Holy Spirit to be sent in a visible manner.'

[216] *ST* I, qq. 37–38. See above, Chapter 10.   [217] *ST* I, q. 38, a. 2.

of the Holy Spirit'. On the other hand, it is the character of the Son to be the Son of the Father, the Image and Word who breathes forth the Spirit side by side with the Father. In this capacity, he joins with the Father in being the 'principle' of the Gift, the 'author' and giver of the Holy Spirit.[218] It therefore accrues to him to be the author of sanctification: together with the Father, the Son sends the Gift which proceeds from them to human beings, the Holy Spirit who sanctifies. The persons' missions come from the eternal procession, which shapes it. This gives us one of the basic features of mission. It enables us to explain what unites and divides the different missions:

We have said that it fits for the Son to be manifested as the author of sanctification. This makes it necessary for the visible mission of the Son to come about in an intelligent nature, one which is capable of action, and which could be used as an instrument of sanctification. But other creaturely things could suffice for the sign of sanctification: this does not have as its prerequisite that a purpose-built, visible creature be assumed by the Holy Spirit into the unity of his person, because it was not assumed or used for the purpose of action, but only in order to be a sign.[219]

St Thomas sees a close correlation between the person's eternal procession, his action of sanctification, and how the person is manifested in our world. The Son acts as he is; that is, he works our salvation in a way that correlates with his personal property. And so he sanctifies in his capacity as giver of the Spirit and author of sanctification. This is one of the means by which the Incarnation fits the way things are: the Son becomes man to save human beings with the active co-operation of the humanity he assumes. He assumes a humanity to sanctify humanity in and through it.

On the one hand, the Son co-opts the humanity he takes into the work of human salvation, because 'divine wisdom requires that God takes care of each thing in a style that is congruent to it' (this is the providential rule we mentioned above). God saves humanity with the co-operation of a free humanity.[220] When Thomas explains that the visible mission of the Son is brought about 'in an intelligent nature, one which is capable of action, and which could be used as an instrument of sanctification', he does not mean that a creature could be intrinsically capable of sanctifying or giving the Holy Spirit: only God can sanctify.[221] Instead, it should be understood as the action

[218] *ST* I, q. 36. Thomas sometimes restricts the name 'author' to the Father, to the exclusion of the Son (I *Sent.* d. 29, q. 1, a. 1). Other times, the term indicates the same reality as the name 'principle' (cf. *CEG* II, ch. 23). For more details, see above, in Chapter 8, 'The Father: Principle and Source'.

[219] *ST* I, q. 43, a. 7, ad 4.

[220] *SCG* IV, ch. 55 (no. 3935); cf. *ST* III, qq. 18–19.

[221] I *Sent.* d. 14, q. 3: no creature could give the Holy Spirit, unless as a minister or an instrument of the divine action. Cf. *ST* I–II, q. 112, a. 1.

of a creature who is endowed with his own free action, and thus has an instrumental part to play in the divine operation: the humanity of Christ. Thus, right in the middle of his treatment of missions, Thomas takes on the action of the humanity assumed by the Son. The discussion in the *Summa Contra Gentiles* is very good on this:

The only creature capable of acting through itself is the one with reason. Since the other creatures lack reason, it is less a matter of them acting through themselves than one of their being guided by a natural impulse; these creatures are used as instrumental causes rather than being engaged as principal agents. And the creature assumed by God must be such that it can act through himself, engaging himself as principle agent. The things which act purely like instruments act in that they are driven to do so: but the principle agent acts through himself. And thus it would not fit the way things are for God to assume an irrational nature: it had to be an intelligent nature.[222]

On the other hand, as Thomas explains when he speaks about Christ, the unique dignity of Christ's humanity is manifested in his operation. This dignity is the affinity of the human nature to the person of the Word.[223] And what we rediscover here are the ideas of imaging and indwelling. Thomas says that, 'the likeness of the image comes down to the fact that it is capable of God, that is, capable of attaining God through its own operations of knowledge and love. This is the reason why it was congruent for the Word to unite itself to a human being.'[224]

This is not the place for a discussion of Thomas' Christology, but we should at least note that this touches on Christ's fullness of grace, the complete outpouring of the Holy Spirit in the soul of Christ. This renders the humanity of Christ capable of 'attaining God himself through knowledge and love' and of 'making this grace flow out onto others'.[225] The divine Son is the principle and giver of the Holy Spirit. And in his visible mission, his incarnation, the Son puts himself across as the Author of sanctification in the way that, through the collaboration of his human operations, in an 'instrumental efficient causality',[226] he communicates the grace of the Holy Spirit to men (as, knowledge and love of God, inhabitation, fruition), which he himself

---

[222] *SCG* IV, ch. 55 (no. 3936). Free action 'through oneself' suggests a constitutive feature of the persons: see above, in Chapter 6, 'What is a Person?'.

[223] *ST* III, q. 3, a. 8; see above, in Chapter 9, 'The Word Discloses and Reveals the Father'.

[224] *ST* III, q. 4, a. 1, ad 2; cf. sol.: 'In so far as it is endowed with reason and intelligence, the human nature is capable of somehow attaining to the Word through its own operation of knowledge and love.'

[225] *ST* III, q. 7, a. 1. See J.-P. Torrell, 'La grâce du Christ', in Thomas Aquinas, *Somme théologique, Le Verbe incarné*, vol. 2: *3a, Questions 7–15*, Paris, 2002, pp. 395–415.

[226] On this theme, a key to Thomas' Christology, see J.-P. Torrell, *St Thomas Aquinas: Spiritual Master*, pp. 126–137.

possesses in its fullness. As God and man, Christ is the Author of sanctification, the 'principle of all grace'.[227]

The Holy Spirit is the One who, in keeping with his personal property as
Love and Gift, brings the sanctification to achievement within us. When
Thomas speaks of 'indicators' or signs in relation to the Holy Spirit, he
does not mean to say that the Holy Spirit or his sanctifying acts are the
signs in question. The indicator (*indicium*) is the fire or dove which shows
that the Spirit acts, right here, the Holy Spirit sanctifying. The visible mission
of the Holy Spirit is thus ordered to the sanctification of human beings, but it
is realized in a different way to the Son's sanctifying mission. The Holy Spirit
internalizes the life of grace in us, bringing about sanctification and the divine
indwelling. He himself is what the Son communicates to human beings in
the mysteries of his flesh. In other words, the Holy Spirit is not the Giver
but the *Gift himself*, spread in human hearts. And so the visible indicators of
the Holy Spirit do not display him as the Giver but as the sanctifying Gift: the
Holy Spirit is present as the 'indicated is in the indicating'.[228]

St Thomas adds a few concrete touches to this teaching by looking at the
various 'visible missions' of the Spirit. These visible missions are simply
the making manifest of the Spirit's invisible mission, his sanctifying gift,
and they are all bound to *the establishment of the Church*. A very beautiful
passage in the *Sentence* commentary gives a brief synthesis of the doctrine of
missions which explains this:

In the invisible mission of the Holy Spirit, the fullness of the divine love is poured out
in the soul through grace and, as an effect of this grace, the recipient of the mission is
given an experiential knowledge of the divine person. And likewise, in the visible
mission, his 'overflow' rises to a new level: because of its plenitude the interior grace
overflows into a visible disclosure which reveals the indwelling of the divine persons
beyond the one who receives it to others. So two things are requisite to a visible
mission: it is necessary that there be a plenitude of grace in the recipients of the
mission, and that this plenitude be ordered to others, so that this abounding grace
overflows in some way onto others. So the interior grace is not only manifest to the
one who possesses it, but also to others. And this is why the visible mission came first
to Christ and then to the Apostles, because it is through them that grace has been
spread to many other human beings; it was through them that the Church was
planted.[229]

A visible mission consists in two kinds of outpouring. (1) The pouring out of
the eternal procession of the person (his personal property) in the gifts
of grace which bring about the indwelling of the person and the experience

[227] *De veritate*, q. 29, a. 5.   [228] *ST* I, q. 43, a. 7, ad 5.
[229] I *Sent.* d. 16, q. 1, a. 2; cf. *ST* I, q. 43, a. 7, ad 6.

of this person. (2) The rebounding of this plenitude of grace into a disclosure to *witnesses* in order to found the Church in faith ('so that the faith be confirmed and spread'[230]). The reason Thomas gives for only accepting the occurrence of visible missions in 'Christ, the Apostles and some of the earliest saints' is that 'it is by them that the Church has been in some way founded'.[231] The outpouring of grace is realized in two ways: through the sanctifying action of Christ that is conveyed through the sacraments (*per operationem*), and through the teaching of Christ that is passed on through the Apostles (*per instructionem*).[232]

The visible missions made to Christ during his earthly life thus displayed his plenitude of grace to others. They do not give Christ a plenitude of grace which he hitherto lacked, since Christ is fully blessed from the moment of his conception.[233] So Christ does not receive any 'new grace' but he does go forward into new acts which he cumulatively achieves by dint of the grace with which he is filled:[234] 'the visible mission [of the Holy Spirit] to Christ shows the invisible mission which has been made to him not at this precise moment, but at the first instant of his conception'.[235] According to the Gospels, a particular sign attaches to each of the visible missions made to Christ. At his baptism, the Holy Spirit appears and descends on Christ 'like a dove' (Mt. 3.16–17). Here at the beginning of Christ's public ministry, the Holy Spirit is sent 'to disclose in Christ the power (*auctoritas*) to regenerate people's spirit by giving them grace'. At the transfiguration, the Spirit is sent to Christ 'to disclose the fecundity of his teaching, and this is why he said: 'Listen to him!' (Mt. 17.5)'. The Holy Spirit is given to the Apostles in the form of the Lord's 'breath' (Jn 20.22–23) 'to show the power of their ministry of the dispensation of sacraments'; and the Spirit poured upon the Apostles at Pentecost (Acts 2.1–4) is manifested in the form of 'tongues of flame' 'to disclose their teaching ministry'.[236]

A thorough exposition of the visible manifestations of the Spirit would detain us too long. Thomas' exegesis draws in numerous patristic sources which he arranges within his own theological synthesis.[237] One should note that the main orientations of this exegesis are: the manifestation of interior

---

[230] *ST* I, q. 43, a. 7, ad 6.   [231] Ibid.
[232] I *Sent.*, dist. 16, q. 1, a. 3; cf. *In Ioan.* 20.22 (no. 2539).
[233] *ST* III, q. 7, a. 12.   [234] Ibid., ad 3.
[235] *ST* I, q. 43, a. 7, ad 6; cf. III, q. 7, a. 13.
[236] *ST* I, q. 43, a. 7, ad 6.
[237] For the manifestation of the Holy Spirit at the baptism and transfiguration of Christ, which Thomas presents in the Christological portion of the *Summa Theologiae* (III, q. 39 and q. 45), see J.-P. Torrell, *Le Christ en ses mystères: La vie et l'oeuvre de Jésus selon St Thomas d'Aquin*, vol. 2, Paris, 1999, pp. 199–205 and 293–297; see also pp. 127–129, on Christ's plenitude of grace from the instant of his conception.

grace (the invisible mission, the indwelling of the Holy Spirit), the over-flowing onto another to stimulate his faith (the hearing of the Word, the teaching of Christ and the preaching of the Apostles), and the affirmation of charity (the gift of grace through Christ and the sacramental ministry of the Apostles).

When it reaches this juncture, Trinitarian theology can speak directly to the mystery of Christ. This is what Thomas did in the *Summa Contra Gentiles*.[238] The *Summa Theologiae* presents the breadth of the economy: the creation of human beings within the universe, the human faculties, the wound of sin and the restoration of human nature by grace, an act through which humankind returns to God, the mystery of Christ, and the consummation of grace in the beatific vision of the Triune God. The rest of the *Summa* is 'suspended' from the treatment of the missions. By presenting them, the theologian has shown the heart of the economy which God uses on behalf of his children. This is the perspective with which the treatise on the Triune God concludes: a mystery which communicates itself.

---

[238] After the Trinitarian doctrine, in *SCG* IV, chs. 2–26, Thomas moves on to the mystery of the Incarnation (chs. 27–78).

Conclusion

The *Summa's* Trinitarian treatise is not closed in on itself. At the end of his study of the persons' missions, Thomas affirms that, 'after the consideration of the divine persons, it remains to treat the procession of creatures from God' (q. 44. prol.). One could almost say that the rest of the *Summa* is the conclusion to the Trinitarian treatise—that is, that it comes to a close by studying the economy of creation and grace, God's action in the world. As we have seen, the economy begins from within the treatment of the Triune God; this is its third segment, after the reflection on the essential attributes and the immanent properties of the divine persons. However surprising it may sound, one has to say that the best way of rounding off our interpretation would be to discuss the questions that follow it. So our concluding remarks can only be a piece of provisional bridge-building. We will not attempt to run back over everything we have said in the fifteen chapters of this book. What we want to do instead is to foreground some of the features which our reading of the treatise has covered: the connection between economy and theology, the focus on the divine persons, especially the Holy Spirit, the key place given to relation, and lastly, the contemplative dimension of Trinitarian theology.

The *Summa's* exposition of Trinitarian faith makes a close fit between immanent mystery and the workings of the economy. It comes up in every question, and our examination of the structure of the treatise showed why. The strategy of Trinitarian doctrine is to make this intimate alliance plain. As against the reductionist thesis that the economy is just the extension of the *De Deo Uno*, Thomas Aquinas taught that the Father creating the world through the Son and in the Spirit runs so deep that the Trinitarian processions are the cause, rationale, and exemplar of the world and its creatures, and of their return to God. He has a genuinely Trinitarian doctrine of action.

Moreover, his concern for the Trinitarian economy is already apparent in the study of the immanent mystery of God. As against another widespread prejudice, the idea of the Word and Love cannot be boiled down to the extension of a 'psychological analogy', one which leaves the Trinity shut in on itself. To contrast this psychological analogy with the biblical economy is to forget one of its major strengths. The analogy of word and love enables one to disclose the eternal distinctions of the persons, but it also allows us to put the profound personalism of the divine action in the world in the picture. The Father acts through his Word and his Love. The divine persons act in virtue of who they are, to the power of their characteristic properties. Created to the image of God, human beings are inspired by grace to return to the Triune God through faith and charity: through the gift of Son and Holy Spirit, they are conformed to the inmost properties of Word and Love, that is, to the relations which the Word and Love have with the Father. As this theologian makes clear, the Word and Love are at the foundation of the economy, with its Trinitarian modality. The fact that soteriology comes into the heart of his Trinitarian doctrine requires a radical revision of the unconsidered judgements which we still find today in writings about the relations between the immanent and economic Trinity in St Thomas' thought. The charge that it misses out on soteriology should just be abandoned.

The Trinitarian treatise makes it evident that theology and economy are intimately connected, to such a point that one would make a blunt error if one devolved the economy to a secondary rank. It is true that the overall exposition begins by considering the immanent processions of Word and Love. The structure of Trinitarian theology calls for this layout. But the full power of the idea of Word and Love comes to light when it is reflected toward the economy and can illuminate the action of the divine persons there. On the other hand, it is when one knows it as rooted in the immanent life of the Trinity that the true nature of the economy comes to light. The expository order distinguishes these two faces, but each is present within the study of the other: one cannot get a panoramic view of God's action without reflecting on the 'immanent Trinity'; and without a deep study of the 'economic Trinity' theology would have no bite. The singular merit of the doctrine of Word and Love is that it brings these two faces together within a coherent synthesis.

It would take another book to give detailed evidence for the interweaving of speculative theology and Trinitarian economy. Research into this topic has as yet scarcely begun. All that our reading of the *Summa* did was to draw attention to this soteriological dimension whenever the texts explicitly called for it. For us to rediscover the Trinitarian faith within the entirety of St Thomas' theology, we would have to make a much closer study of the biblical commentaries, which play a decisive role here. It would also be necessary to examine the presence of the Trinity in the other parts of the *Summa*, perhaps making a fresh start on tackling certain questions. For example, the study of what Thomas says about the image of God cannot rest when it has looked into his anthropology: it demands a deep awareness of his Trinitarian theology. The image is directly linked to God's fatherhood over human beings, to the progressive assimilation to the Son-Image, and thus to the reception of the Holy Spirit. One has to approach it through Trinitarian theology rather than through anthropology. In the same way, one cannot comprehend the treatise on grace without the question about missions: what the treatise on grace examines from a human standpoint is delivered in the doctrine of missions from the perspective of the divine persons who are the source and end of grace. For its part, the question on missions hangs on the earlier conversation in the Trinitarian treatise, which it sums up. This invites us to redesign our reading of the questions on moral theology in the light of the Trinitarian treatise. It works the same way for Christology, soteriology, the sacraments, and eschatology. One could only make such an exploration if one began from the lines marked out for the disclosure of Trinitarian faith.

Notwithstanding its limitations, our reading opens the view to the deep structural connection between theology and economy. When he presents the divine persons' action in the world, Thomas does not list the works of Father, Son, and Spirit, and leave it at that. He presents these works within a real doctrine of the Trinitarian economy, using the properties and order of the persons, and making use of metaphysical reflection on action, participation, and the like. Our reading lends itself to criticism of the common opinion that the biblical history can be viewed as providing a 'doctrine of the economic Trinity', whilst the 'doctrine of the immanent Trinity' can be produced by a subsequent, posterior analysis. For St Thomas, teaching on the economic Trinity is just as speculative as reflection on the immanent Trinity. The doctrine of the economic Trinity is seen as the fruit of a meditation which, with the helping hand of the study of the Trinity in itself behind it, elucidates the Trinitarian economy by the eternal being of God. In the theological exposition, the *doctrine* of the economic Trinity is not given the upper hand: it is, rather, the final fruit of the exploration, the result for which the meditation on the nature and properties of the divine persons paves the way.

The elaboration of a theology works in three stages, which one can formulate as follows. The first comes from the acknowledgement of the revelation of the Trinity through its action in the world, listening to and following the witness of Scripture. The economic and soteriological current runs through the heart of this unfolding of the Trinitarian mystery. We signposted some of its features in our first chapter. The reading of Scripture and Christian experience are its main resources. A good example is the soteriological point which Thomas liked so much: the Son and Spirit show us their divinity by making us participate in the divine life; they show us their distinction by taking us into the Father's communion, rhymed with their personal relations. In the second stage, beginning from their economic revelation, this theologian puts forward a speculative reflection on the persons, in their distinction and their unity. This is the doctrine of the 'immanent Trinity', or in Thomas' own language, the doctrine of the Trinity 'in itself'. A third and final phase uses the two initial moments as a guide into a speculative reflection on the action of the persons within this world. This is where a genuine *doctrine* of the 'economic Trinity', the Trinity as 'principle and end of creatures', is conveyed. In the same way that it sets off from Scripture in order to lead us back to Scripture afresh, Trinitarian reflection begins from the action of the persons in the world in order to come round to that action anew.

This structure is especially transparent in the serial study of each of the divine persons. The chapters about the Holy Spirit are perhaps the best example of it. When Thomas presents the work of the Holy Spirit, he applies his reading of Scripture to show the Spirit's divinity (with the soteriological argument), his hypostatic subsistence (the Holy Spirit acts as a person), and his personal distinction: the Holy Spirit is not conflated with the Father and Son from whom he proceeds and to whom he guides us. This is precisely what the *Summa* wants to put before our eyes. And, as we have seen, its most extended teaching is dedicated to the Holy Spirit: far from being obviated, the Holy Spirit receives the most attention. The first move the theologian makes is to concentrate his mind on the intra-Trinitarian property, because this is what enables him to disclose the eternal subsistence and personal distinction of the Holy Spirit. What we clumsily call the 'psychological analogy' is found at this initial step. But he goes on without a pause to take up the idea of the *mutual Love* of Father and Son, widening his approach out to the Trinitarian communion. The economic current now makes itself evident: the Spirit is the Love through which the Father and the Son love one another and love us. He then follows up on this teaching by showing that the Holy Spirit is the person of the Gift, the source of all participation in the Trinitarian communion. Sanctity and communion are given to share from within the Holy Spirit; it is in him that the Church is created. These threads are not just laid alongside one another. Thomas interrelates them by bringing them cumulatively to light. The conclusions can then be applied to the economy, through a return to Scripture which legitimates the power of Love and enables the presentation of a synthetic doctrine of the Holy Spirit. The Spirit's economy is communicated by means of his property as Love and Gift, that is, his relation to Father and Son. The exposition of the action of the Holy Spirit thus rests on the speculative principles which the theologian had positioned at the core of his synthesis, to wit, relation and the doctrine of Word and Love. The study of the economy of grace is not an appendix more or less loosely hooked on to Trinitarian theology, but is riveted right into it.

The obstacle to our seeing this is doubtless the way the *Summa* is organized, and the extent of the materials with which it deals. When one moves on to the *Secunda* and *Tertia Pars*, one runs into the danger of losing sight of their connection with the treatise on God. Some hurried readers can even forget that one is still speaking of the Triune God when one speaks of grace! If one does not keep the structure of the *Summa* constantly in one's thoughts, if one neglects the doctrine of Love (and the themes which spring from it), if one forgets the doctrine of missions or fails to grasp the importance of appropriations, one will be blind to where the Spirit stands in all this. As the door to reading the rest of the *Summa* properly, the treatise on the Triune God deserves our renewed attention. If, as we hope, Thomistic theology is due to move forward, Trinitarian thought will play a decisive role in this development.

Turning to speculative matters, the reader cannot fail to notice that relation has an axial position amongst them. From the first question onward, the theologian's meditation is guided by relation: it takes him to the basis of the processions, and enables him to grasp the divine person and to explain how Trinitarianism is monotheistic. The doctrine of Word and Love, whose directive role we have tried to show, takes its power from the relations it makes it possible to disclose. The treatise on God comes together as a unity in the divine person grasped as a 'subsistent relation'. When he puts forward a relational conception of the divine person, Thomas commits himself to disengaging everything that flows from his discovery, right down to the amazing notion of a 'transcendental multiplicity'. Every doctrinal move calls on relation: the Trinitarian order, the personal plurality, perichoresis, and so forth. There is not a single question which does not engage the analysis of relation. It entails the most typical features of Thomistic theology by contrast to other schools. The unwavering option of the Dominican master for a relational conception of the divine persons is reflected on every page. It is worth noting that the importance of relation does not disappear when the theologian deals with the Trinitarian economy. Relation appears at the centre of the Trinitarian missions, and the next step is to find that the sending of the persons consists in a dual relation: a relation to the person who sends and a relation to the recipient of the mission. The effect of Trinitarian relation runs all the way to our world. Thomas considers divine relation as the source of the multiplicity of creatures, throwing a particularly effective cast on the meaning of created plurality.

If it is true that the theology and philosophy of Thomas Aquinas is characterized by his theory of being, it is no less true that his thought takes its character from the extraordinary centrality it accords to relation within its doctrine of being. We have pointed it out every time it appeared, but without developing it as much as it deserves. The theory of relation is something he inherits from the philosophers and theologians of the past, but at the same time it brings a new treasure into Christian theology. The innovation lies in the systematic application of this feature: our grasp of all the varied aspects of the mystery is integrated by relation. A vast field for research offers itself to other, more directed studies. The reading of the treatise on God shows that its author provided a rare breadth to the disclosure of the implications of Trinitarian monotheism.

When the analyses scale the heights of complexity, as in the disputed questions, and the works of synthesis, it is important not to lose sight of what Trinitarian theology is for. It constitutes a spiritual exercise in the authentic meaning of the term: a contemplative and speculative exercise on the part of the theologian who seeks to grasp 'something of the truth' in order to disclose the faith 'for the consolation of believers'. A rationalist approach defaces St Thomas' thought. It takes a serious misreading to imagine one can find that he gives a demonstration of the Trinity or that he detaches theology from the experience of faith. Opposing or contrasting his explorations to the spiritual aims of the Fathers is the other side of the same false coin. His thought certainly marks a watershed: the spiritual aim is achieved within an academic and, in the sense which he gave the term, 'scientific' theology. The resources of culture are harnessed to the understanding of faith. But it is always faith that guides the exploration.

What the modern reader may find most puzzling is that this spiritual aim can include such great attention to heresies. We have seen that the care taken to avoid heresy colours the whole treatise: it overshadows the elaboration of the doctrine of processions, relations, persons, plurality and unity, and so forth. Trinitarian doctrine seeks to disclose the intelligibility of the faith of the Church by distinguishing it from error: these are the two faces of a single theological enterprise. Thomas puts the progression of faith face to face with the revealed writings to show their deep convergence. But he also knows that, within the history of Christianity, speculative theology only emerges when Christians meet the challenges which human reason addresses to faith. Can Trinitarian theology face up to being questioned by reason? Can the Christian square up to a debate over his faith against the objections raised by other doctrines? Thomas is convinced that the theologian can and must respond to questions. Looking for a response gives him a better grasp of what he believes. It is faith which seeks understanding. Such is the ulterior aim of Trinitarian theology, which is ordered to the beatific vision. Did Augustine, Gregory Nazianzus, or Gregory of Nyssa pursue any other end? In his teaching and his preaching, the theologian wants to help believers to contemplate an object beyond the power of human reason, but which does not nullify that reason. He shows that, without imposing itself as a necessity of reason, Trinitarian faith is not an obstacle to the God-given light of our minds. Christians can speak of their faith in debate, enter into dialogue with other believers, both religious and secular, and progress in human knowledge without weakening their adherence to the mystery or imposing what they see on others. This aim has yet to lose its relevance.

The purpose of this book has been to create a better understanding of the Trinitarian theology of the *Summa*. If it comes anywhere near showing which paths are taken by saint Thomas, and why they matter, it has achieved its goal. But, to repeat, we have only covered part of the journey. It remains to read the rest of the *Summa* in the light of the analyses offered by the treatise on the Triune God. Trinitarian theology will prove how fruitful it can be when other fields of theological enquiry draw from it. The Christology and soteriology of the *Summa* are in particular need of revisiting in the light of Trinitarian doctrine.

The knowledge of the divine persons was principally necessary to us in order properly to grasp the human salvation which is achieved by the incarnate Son and the gift of the Holy Spirit. (*ST* I, q. 32, a. 1, ad 3)

Easter Sunday
20 April 2003

Bibliography

1. Sources plus Ancient and Medieval Authors

This is a list of the books and articles used in this book. The classical and medieval authors in the Latin or Greek Patrologia (PL, PG), the Corpus scriptorum ecclesiasticorum latinorum (CSEL), and in the Corpus christianorum (CCSL, CCCM) are not listed here.

Acta Conciliorum Œcumenicorum, vol. I/3, ed. E. Schwartz, Berlin and Leipzig, 1929; vol. II/3, ed. E. Schwartz, Berlin and Leipzig, 1936.

Albert the Great, Saint, *Opera omnia*, ed. A. Borgnet, 38 vols., Paris, 1890–1899.

—— *Opera omnia*, ed. Coloniensis, Münster, 26 vols. since 1952.

Alexander of Hales, *Summa theologiae* (*Summa fratris Alexandri*), 4 vols., ed. PP. Collegii S. Bonaventurae, Quaracchi, 1924–1948.

—— *Glossa in quatuor Libros Sententiarum Petri Lombardi*, 4 vols., ed. PP. Collegii S. Bonaventurae, Quaracchi, 1951–1957.

Anselm of Canterbury, Saint, *Opera omnia*, ed. F. S. Schmitt, 6 vols., Seckau and Edinburgh, 1938–1961; (reprinted in 2 vols., Stuttgart and Bad Cannstatt, 1968.

—— *L'Œuvre*, ed. M. Corbin, Paris, 7 vols. since 1986.

Aristotle, *Metaphysics*.

—— *Nichomachean Ethics*.

—— *Organon*: I. *Categories*; II. *On Interpretation*.

—— *Physics*.

Athanasius of Alexandria, Saint, *Lettres à Sérapion sur la divinité du Saint-Esprit*, introduction and translation by J. Lebon, SC 15, Paris, 1947.

—— *Sur l'incarnation du Verbe*, critical text, translation and notes by Ch. Kannengiesser, SC 199, Paris, 1973.

—— *Werke*, vol. III/1, ed. H.-G. Opitz, Berlin and Leipzig, 1935.

Augustine, Saint, *Œuvres*, Bibliothèque Augustinienne, Paris, 1936–.

Bañez, Dominicus, *Scholastica Commentaria in Primam Partem Summae Theologiae S. Thomae Aquinatis*, ed. L. Urbano, Madrid and Valencia, 1934.

Basil of Caesarea, Saint, *Contre Eunome*, and Eunomius, *Apologie*, introduction, text translation, and notes by B. Sesboüe, with the collaboration of G.-M. de Durand and L. Doutreleau, 2 vols., SC 299, 305, Paris, 1982 and 1983.

—— *Lettres*, ed. Y. Courtonne, 2 vols., Paris, 1957 and 1961.

—— *Sur le Saint-Esprit*, introduction, text, translation, and notes by B. Pruche, 2nd edn., SC 17 bis, Paris, 1968.

Boethius, *Traités théologiques*, presented and translated by A. Tisserand, Paris, 2000.

Bonaventure, Saint, *Opera omnia,* ed. PP. Collegii S. Bonaventurae, 10 vols., Quaracchi, 1882–1902.

—— *Collationes in Hexaëmeron et Bonaventuriana quaedam selecta,* ed. F. Delorme, Quaracchi, 1934.

Cajetan, *Commentarii in Summam theologiae,* in Sancti Thomae Aquinatis..., *Opera omnia iussu Leonis XIII. P.M. edita,* vols. 4–12, Rome, 1898–1906.

Denys (Pseudo-Denys the Areopagite, Saint), *Dionysiaca,* in the collection of Latin translations of writings ascribed to Dionysius the Areopagite, ed. Ph. Chevallier, 2 vols., Paris and Solesmes, 1937 and 1950.

Denzinger, H., *Symboles et définitions de la foi catholique,* ed P. Hünermann for the original edition (Freiburg, 1991) and J. Hoffmann for the French edition (Paris, 1996).

Duns Scotus, *Opera Omnia,* vol. 17: *Lectura in Librum primum Sententiarum a distinctione octava ad quadragesimam quintam,* Vatican City, 1966.

Ephèse et Chalcédoine: Actes des Conciles, trans. A.-J. Festugière, Paris, 1982.

Eunomius of Cyzicus: *see* Basil of Caesarea, *Contre Eunome.*

Gilbert of Poitiers (Gilbert de la Porrée), *Expositio in Boecii de Trinitate,* in *The Commentaries on Boethius by Gilbert of Poitiers,* ed. N. M. Häring, Toronto, 1966, pp. 51–180.

Gregory of Nazianzus, Saint, *Discours 20–23,* introduction, critical text, translation, and notes by J. Mossay, SC 270, Paris, 1978.

—— *Discours 27–31,* introduction, critical text, translation, and notes by P. Gallay, SC 250, Paris, 1978.

—— *Discours 38–41,* introduction, critical text, and notes by Cl. Moreschini, translation by P. Gallay, SC 358, Paris, 1990.

—— *Discours 42–43,* introduction, critical text, translation, and notes by J. Bernardi, SC 384, Paris, 1992.

Henry of Ghent, *Opera omnia,* vol. 10: *Quodlibet VI,* ed. G. A. Wilson, Leuven, 1987.

Hilary of Poitiers, Saint, *La Trinité,* introduction by M. Figura and J. Doignon, critical text, and translation by G. M. de Durand, Ch. Morel, and G. Pelland, notes by G. Pelland, SC 443, 448 and 462, Paris, 1999–2001.

Hugh of Saint Victor, *Didascalicon,* ed. Ch. H. Buttimer, Washington DC, 1939.

Irenaeus of Lyons, Saint, *Contre les hérésies: Dénonciation et réfutation de la gnose au nom menteur,* trans. A. Rousseau, 3rd edn., Paris, 1991.

John of Damascus, Saint, *De fide orthodoxa: Versions of Burgundio and Cerbanus,* ed. E. M. Buytaert, New York, 1955.

Justin, Saint, *Apologie pour les chrétiens,* ed. and trans. Ch. Munier, Fribourg, 1995.

—— *Œuvres complètes,* trans. G. Archambault, L. Pautigny, and E. Gaché, Paris, 1994.

Les Conciles Œcuméniques: Les décrets, ed. G. Alberigo *et al.,* vol. II/1: *Nicée I à Latran V,* Paris, 1994.

Maximus the Confessor, Saint, *Ambigua,* introduction by J.-C. Larchet, translation by E. Ponsoye, Paris and Suresnes, 1994.

—— *Opuscules théologiques et polémiques,* trans. E. Ponsoye, Paris, 1998.

Peter Abelard, *De l'Unité et de la Trinité divines (Theologia Summi Boni)*, introduction, translation, and notes by J. Jolivet, Paris, 2001.

Peter Lombard, *Sententiae in IV Libris distinctae*, 2 vols., Spicilegium Bonaventurianum 4 and 5, Grottaferrata, 1971 and 1981.

Prevostin of Cremona, *Summa 'Qui producit ventos', Liber primus: De divinis nominibus*, ed. G. Angelini, in *L'ortodossia e la grammatica: Analisi di struttura e deduzione storica della Teologia Trinitaria di Prepositino*, Rome, 1972, pp. 191–303.

Richard of Saint-Victor, *La Trinité*, Latin text, introduction, and notes by G. Salet, reprint of the first edition, revised and corrected, SC 63, Paris, 1999.

—— *Opuscules théologiques*, critical text with introduction, notes, and tables by J. Ribaillier, Paris, 1967.

Simon of Tournai, *Disputationes*, ed. J. Warichez, Spicilegium sacrum lovaniense, études et documents 12, Louvain, 1932.

Thomas Aquinas, Saint, *Opera omnia*, Leonine edition, Cura et studio fratrum praedicatorum, Rome and Paris, 1882–; 37 vols. to 2002.

—— *Catena aurea: Commentary on the Four Gospels Collected Out of the Works of the Early Church Fathers*, 4 vols., intro. J. H. Newman, trans. M. Pattison, J. D. Dalgairns, and T. D. Ryder, 3rd edn., London, 1997.

—— *Catena aurea in quatuor Evangelia*, ed. A. Guarienti, 2 vols., Turin and Rome, 1953.

—— *Commentaire sur l'Evangile de saint Jean*, vol. 1: *Le Prologue, La vie apostolique du Christ*, translation and notes edited by M.-D. Philippe, Paris, 1998.

—— *Commentary on the Gospel of John*, pt. I, trans. James A. Weisheipl and Fabian R. Larcher, Albany, NY, 1980; also on CD-Rom, www.nlx.com; pt. II, trans. Fabian R. Larcher, Albany, NY, 1998.

—— *Commentary on Saint Paul's Epistle to the Ephesians*, trans. M. L. Lamb, Albany, NY, 1966.

—— *Commentary on Saint Paul's Epistle to the Galatians*, trans. F. R. Larcher, Albany, NY, 1966.

—— *Commentary on Saint Paul's First Letter to the Thessalonians and the Letter to the Philippians*, trans. F. R. Larcher and M. Duffy, Albany, NY, 1969.

—— *Compendium of Theology*, trans. C. O. Vollert, St Louis, 1947.

—— *Faith, Reason, and Theology: Questions I–IV of his Commentary on the De Trinitate of Boethius*, trans. A. Maurer, Toronto, 1987.

—— *In librum beati Dionysii de divinis nominibus expositio*, ed. C. Pera, Turin and Rome, 1950.

—— *Le Credo*, introduction, translation, and notes by a monk of Fontgombault, Paris, 1982.

—— *Le Pater et l'Ave*, introduction, translation, and notes by a monk of Fontgombault, Paris, 1982.

—— *Liber de veritate catholicae fidei contra errores infidelium seu Summa contra Gentiles*, ed. C. Pera, P. Marc, P. Caramello, 3 vols., Turin and Rome, 1961–1967.

—— *On the Power of God*, Third Book: *Questions VII–X*, literally translated by the English Dominican Fathers, London, 1934.

—— *On Truth*, 3 vols., trans. R. W. Mulligan, J. V. McGlynn, and R. W. Schmidt, Chicago, 1953.

—— *Opuscula theologica*, vol. 1, ed. R. A. Verardo ; vol. 2, ed. R. M. Spiazzi and M. Calcaterra, Turin and Rome, 1954.

—— *Quaestiones disputatae*, ed. P. Bazzi *et al.*, Turin and Rome, 1965.

—— *Question disputée: L'union du Verbe incarné (De unione Verbi incarnati)*, introduction, translation, and notes by M.-H. Deloffre, Paris, 2000.

—— *Questions disputées sur la vérité, Question IV, le Verbe*, introduction, translation, and notes by B. Jolles, Paris, 1992.

—— *Questions disputées sur la vérité, Question X, L'esprit (De mente)*, introduction, translation, and notes by K. S. Ong-Van-Cung, Paris, 1998.

—— 'Reasons for the Faith Against Muslim Objections (and one objection of the Greeks and Armenians) to the Cantor of Antioch', trans. Joseph Kenny, *Islamochristiana* 22 (1996), 31–52.

—— *Scriptum super libros Sententiarum* (Books I–II), ed. P. Mandonnet, 2 vols., Paris, 1929; (Books III–IV down to dist. 22), ed. M. F. Moos, 2 vols., Paris, 1933 and 1947; (Book IV, dist. 23–50), ed. Parme, vol. 7, 1857, pp. 872–1355.

—— *Sententia super Metaphysicam*, ed. M.-R. Cathala and R. M. Spiazzi, Turin and Rome, 1950.

—— *Sententia super Physicam*, ed. P. M. Maggiolo, Turin and Rome, 1965.

—— *Somme contre les Gentils: Livre sur la vérité de la foi catholique contre les erreurs des infidèles*, trans. V. Aubin, C. Michon, and D. Moreau, 4 vols., Paris, 1999.

—— *Somme théologique*, French translation, 4 vols., Paris, 1984–1986.

—— *Somme théologique, La Trinité*, translation and explanatory notes by H.-F. Dondaine, vol. 1: *1ᵃ, Questions 27–32*, Paris, Tournai, and Rome, 1943, 1950, 1997; vol. 2: *1ᵃ, Questions 33–43*, Paris, Tournai, and Rome, 1946, 1950, 1997.

—— *Somme théologique, Le Verbe incarné, 3ᵃ, Questions 1–26*, translation, notes, and appendices by J.-P. Torrell, 3 vols., Paris, 2002.

—— *Summa Contra Gentiles*, trans. Anton C. Pegis, James F. Anderson, Vernon J. Bourke, and Charles J. O'Neil, 5 vols., Notre Dame, 1975.

—— *Summa Theologiae*, Blackfriars English Translation, 60 vols, London and New York, 1964–1976.

—— *Summa theologiae*, ed. Instituti Studiorum Medievalium Ottaviensis, 5 vols., Ottawa, 1941–5.

—— *Super Epistolas S. Pauli lectura*, ed. R. Cai, 2 vols., Turin and Rome, 1953.

—— *Super Evangelium S. Ioannis lectura*, ed. R. Cai, Turin and Rome, 1952.

—— *Super Evangelium S. Matthaei lectura*, ed. R. Cai, Turin and Rome, 1951.

—— *The Sermon-Conferences of St. Thomas Aquinas on the Apostles' Creed*, trans. N. Ayo, Notre Dame, 1988.

—— *Traités: Les raisons de la foi, Les articles de la foi et les sacrements de l'Église*, introduction, translation, and notes by G. Emery, Paris, 1999.

William of Auxerre, *Summa aurea*, ed. J. Ribaillier, 4 vols., Spicilegium Bonaventurianum 16–19, Grottaferrata and Paris, 1980–1985.

2. Modern Works

Angelini, G., *L'ortodossia e la grammatica: Analisi di struttura e deduzione storica della Teologia Trinitaria di Prepositino*, Rome, 1972.

Aranda Lomeña, A., 'Santo Tomás frente a Sabelio: un modelo de refutación teológica', *Studi tomistici* 13 (1981), 145–152.

Ayres, Lewis, *Nicaea and its Legacy: An Approach to Fourth-Century Trinitarian Theology*, Oxford and New York, 2004.

Bailleux, E., 'Le Christ et son Esprit', *RT* 73 (1973), 373–400.

—— 'Le personnalisme de St Thomas en théologie trinitaire', *RT* 61 (1961), 25–42.

Barnes, M. R., *The Power of God: Dunamis in Gregory of Nyssa's Trinitarian Theology*, Washington DC, 2001.

—— 'De Régnon Reconsidered', *Augustinian Studies* 26 (1995), 51–79.

Barth, K., *Church Dogmatics*, vol. I/1, 2nd edn., 1975; vol. I/2, 1958, 1994; vol. II/2, 1957, 1992.

Bauckham, Richard, *God Crucified: Monotheism and Christology in the New Testament*, Carlisle, 1998.

Beretta, B., *Ad aliquid: La relation chez Guillaume d'Occam*, Fribourg, 1999.

Bergeron, M., 'La structure du concept latin de personne', *Études d'histoire littéraire et doctrinale du XIIIe siècle*, Second series, Paris and Ottawa, 1932, pp. 121–161.

Boespflug, F., *Dieu dans l'art: Sollicitudini nostrae de Benoît XV (1745) et l'affaire Crescence de Kaufbeuren*, Paris, 1984.

Boismard, M.-E., *Moïse ou Jésus: Essai de christologie johannique*, Leuven, 1988.

Boland, Vivian, *Ideas in God According to St Thomas Aquinas: Sources and Synthesis*, Leiden, New York and Cologne, 1996.

Bonanni, S. P., *Parlare della Trinità: Lettura della Theologia Scholarium di Abelardo*, Rome, 1996.

Bonino, S.-Th., *Thomas d'Aquin, De la vérité, Question 2 (La science en Dieu)*, Fribourg and Paris, 1996.

—— 'La place du pape dans l'Église selon St Thomas d'Aquin', *RT* 86 (1986), 392–422.

Bougerol, J. G., 'Saint Bonaventure et la Hiérarchie dionysienne', *AHDLMA* 36 (1969), 131–167.

Boulnois, M.-O., *Le paradoxe trinitaire chez Cyrille d'Alexandrie*, Paris, 1994.

Bourassa, F., 'Dans la communion de l'Esprit Saint', *SE* 34 (1982), 31–56, 135–149, 239–268.

—— '*Don de Dieu*, Nom propre du Saint-Esprit', *SE* 6 (1954), 73–82.

—— 'L'Esprit Saint, "Communion du Père et du Fils"', *SE* 29 (1977), 251–281; 30 (1978), 5–37.

—— 'Le don de Dieu', *Gregorianum* 50 (1969), 201–235.

—— 'Le Saint-Esprit unité d'amour du Père et du Fils', *SE* 14 (1962), 375–415.

—— 'Sur la propriété de l'Esprit Saint, Questions Disputées', *SE* 28 (1976), 243–264; 29 (1977), 23–43.

—— *Questions de théologie trinitaire*, Rome, 1970.

Bouthillier, D., '*Splendor gloriae Patris*: Deux collations du *Super Isaiam* de S. Thomas d'Aquin', in *Christ among the Medieval Dominicans*, ed. K. Emery and J. Wawrykow, Notre Dame, 1998, pp. 139–156.

Brown, R. E., *Jésus dans les quatre évangiles*, Paris, 1996.

Burrell, David B., *Aquinas: God and Action*, Notre Dame, 1979.

—— *Faith and Freedom: An Interfaith Perspective*, Malden, MA, and Oxford, 2004.

Butterworth, Edward J., 'The Doctrine of the Trinity in St Thomas Aquinas and Saint Bonaventure', diss. Fordham University, New York, 1985.

Cabaret, D.-M., 'Les appropriations trinitaires chez S. Thomas d'Aquin', Mémoire de licence, University of Fribourg, 2001.

Chatillon, J., '*Unitas, aequalitas, concordia vel connexio*: Recherches sur les origines de la théorie thomiste des appropriations (*Sum. theol.*, I, q. 39, art. 7–8)', in *St. Thomas Aquinas 1274–1974 Commemorative Studies*, vol. 1, ed. A. Maurer, Toronto, 1974, pp. 337–379.

Chenu, M.-D., *Introduction à l'étude de St Thomas d'Aquin*, reprint, Montreal and Paris, 1984.

Chevalier, I., *La théorie augustinienne des relations trinitaires*, Fribourg, 1940.

—— *Saint Augustin et la pensée grecque. Les relations trinitaires*, Fribourg, 1940.

Cirillo, A., *Cristo Rivelatore del Padre nel Vangelo di S. Giovanni secondo il commento di S. Tommaso d'Aquino*, Rome, 1988.

Congar, Y., *I Believe in the Holy Spirit*, 3 vols., trans. David Smith, London and New York, 1983, 1997.

—— *The Word and the Spirit*, trans. David Smith, London, 1986.

—— 'Quatre siècles de désunion et d'affrontement. Comment Grecs et Latins se sont appréciés réciproquement au point de vue ecclésiologique', *Istina* 13 (1968), 131–152.

—— 'Valeur et portée œcuméniques de quelques principes herméneutiques de St Thomas d'Aquin', *RSPT* 57 (1973), 611–626.

Conrad, Richard, *The Catholic Faith: A Dominican's Vision*, London and New York, 1994.

Dahan, G., *L'exégèse chrétienne de la Bible en Occident médiéval, XIIe–XIVe siècle*, Paris, 1999.

Dauphinais, Michael, and Levering, Matthew (eds.), *Reading John with St. Thomas Aquinas, Theological Exegesis and Speculative Theology*, Washington DC, 2005.

David, Brian (ed.), *Thomas Aquinas: Contemporary Philosophical Perspectives*, Oxford and New York, 2002.

Davis, Stephen T., Kendall, Daniel, and O'Collins, Gerald (eds.), *The Trinity: An Interdisciplinary Symposium on the Trinity*, Oxford and New York, 2000.

De Ghellinck, J., *Le mouvement théologique du XIIe siècle*, Brussels and Paris, 1948.

Den Bok, N., *Communicating the Most High: A Systematic Study of Person and Trinity in the Theology of Richard of St. Victor (+1173)*, Paris and Turnhout, 1996.

Dewan, L., 'The Individual as a Mode of Being according to Thomas Aquinas', *The Thomist* 63 (1999), 403–424.

Dobler, E., *Zwei syrische Quellen der theologischen Summa des Thomas von Aquin, Nemesios von Emesa und Johannes von Damaskus*, Fribourg, 2000.

Dodds, Michael J., *The Unchanging God of Love: A Study of the Teaching of St. Thomas Aquinas on Divine Immutability in View of Certain Contemporary Criticism of this Doctrine*, Fribourg, 1986.

Dondaine, A., '*Contra Graecos*. Premiers écrits polémiques des Dominicains d'Orient', *AFP* 21 (1951), 320–456.

Dondaine, H.-F., 'La théologie latine de la procession du Saint-Esprit', *Russie et Chrétienté* (1950), 211–218.

—— 'Notes explicatives' and 'Renseignements techniques', in St Thomas Aquinas, *Somme théologique, La Trinité*, vol. 1: *1ᵃ, Questions 27–32*, Paris, Tournai, and Rome, 1943, 1950, 1997; vol. 2: *1ᵃ, Questions 33–43*, Paris, Tournai, and Rome, 1946, 1950, 1997.

Dubois, M.-J., *Aristote, Livre des acceptions multiples: Commentaire philosophique*, Saint-Maur, 1998.

Emery, G., *La Trinité créatrice: Trinité et création dans les commentaires aux Sentences de Thomas d'Aquin et de ses précurseurs Albert le Grand et Bonaventure*, Paris, 1995.

—— 'Biblical Exegesis and the Speculative Doctrine of the Trinity in St. Thomas Aquinas' Commentary on St. John', in id., *Trinity in Aquinas*, Ypsilanti, MI, 2003.

—— 'Dieu, la foi et la théologie chez Durand de Saint-Pourçain', *RT* 99 (1999), 679–687.

—— 'Essentialisme ou personnalisme dans le traité de Dieu chez St Thomas d'Aquin?', *RT* 98 (1998), 5–38.

—— 'La procession du Saint-Esprit *a Filio* chez S. Thomas d'Aquin', *RT* 96 (1996), 531–574.

—— 'La réconciliation avec l'Église et la pénitence intérieure: l'apport de Thomas d'Aquin sur la question du *res et sacramentum* de la pénitence', in *Praedicando et docendo: Mélanges offerts à Liam Walsh O.P.*, ed. B. Hallensleben and G. Vergauwen, Fribourg, 1998, pp. 31–47.

—— 'La relation dans la théologie de saint Albert le Grand', in *Albertus Magnus: zum Gedenken nach 800 Jahren: Neue Zugänge, Aspekte und Perspektiven*, ed. W. Senner, Berlin, 2001, pp. 455–465.

—— 'La théologie trinitaire des *Evidentiae contra Durandum* de Durandellus', *RT* 97 (1997), 173–218.

—— 'Le fruit ecclésial de l'Eucharistie chez St Thomas d'Aquin', *Nova et Vetera* 72/4 (1997), 25–40.

—— 'Le mode personnel de l'agir trinitaire suivant Thomas d'Aquin', *Freiburger Zeitschrift für Philosophie und Theologie* 50 (2003), 334–353.

—— 'Le Père et l'œuvre trinitaire de création selon le Commentaire des *Sentences* de St. Thomas d'Aquin', in *Ordo sapientiae et amoris: Image et message de St Thomas d'Aquin: Hommage au Prof. J.-P. Torrell OP*, ed. C.-J. Pinto de Oliveira, Fribourg, 1993, pp. 85–117.

—— 'Le photinisme et ses précurseurs chez St Thomas', *RT* 95 (1995), 371–398.

—— 'Le traité de St Thomas sur la Trinité dans la *Somme contre les Gentils*', *RT* 96 (1996), 5–40.

—— 'St Thomas d'Aquin et l'Orient chrétien', *Nova et Vetera* 74/4 (1999), 19–36.

—— 'Trinité et création. Le principe trinitaire de la création dans les commentaires d'Albert le Grand, de Bonaventure et de Thomas d'Aquin sur les *Sentences*', *RSPT* 79 (1995), 405–430.

—— 'Trinité et Unité de Dieu dans la scolastique, XIIᵉ–XIVᵉ siècles', in *Le christianisme est-il un monothéisme?*, ed. P. Gisel and G. Emery, Geneva, 2001, pp. 196–201.

—— *Trinity in Aquinas*, Ypsilanti, MI, 2003.

Feuillet, A., 'Les *ego eimi* christologiques du quatrième évangile', *Recherches de Science Religieuse* 54 (1966), 5–22, 213–240.

Floucat, Y., *L'intime fécondité de l'intelligence: Le verbe mental selon St Thomas d'Aquin*, Paris, 2001.

Fortman, Edmund J., *The Triune God: A Historical Study of the Doctrine of the Trinity*, Grand Rapids, 1982.

Gauthier, R.-A., *St Thomas d'Aquin, Somme contre les Gentils, Introduction*, Paris, 1993.

Geenen, G., 'En marge du Concile de Chalcédoine. Les textes du Quatrième Concile dans les œuvres de St Thomas', *Angelicum* 29 (1952), 43–59.

Geiger, L.-B., 'Les rédactions successives de *Contra Gentiles* I, 53 d'après l'autographe', in *St Thomas d'Aquin aujourd'hui*, Recherches de philosophie 6, Paris, 1963, pp. 221–240.

Grelot, P., 'La traduction et l'interprétation de Ph 2, 6–7. Quelques éléments d'enquête patristique', *NRT* 93 (1971), 897–922, 1009–1026.

Grumel, V., 'St Thomas et la doctrine des Grecs sur la procession du Saint-Esprit', *Échos d'Orient* 25 (1926), 257–280.

Gunten, F. von, '*In principio erat Verbum*. Une évolution de St Thomas en théologie trinitaire', in *Ordo sapientiae et amoris: Image et message de St Thomas d'Aquin: Hommage au Prof. J.-P. Torrell OP*, ed. C.-J. Pinto de Oliveira, Fribourg, 1993, pp. 119–141.

Hall, Douglas C., *The Trinity: An Analysis of St. Thomas Aquinas' Expositio of the* De Trinitate *of Boethius*, Leiden, New York, and Cologne, 1992.

Halleux, A. de, *Patrologie et œcuménisme: Recueil d'études*, Leuven, 1990.

—— 'Cyrille, Théodoret et le *Filioque*', *Revue d'Histoire Ecclésiastique* 74 (1979), 597–625.

Harris, M. J., *Jesus as God: The New Testament Use of Theos in Reference to Jesus*, Grand Rapids, 1992.

Healy, Nicholas M., *Thomas Aquinas: Theologian of the Christian Life*, Aldershot, 2003.

Hill, William J., *The Three-Personed God: The Trinity as a Mystery of Salvation*, Washington DC, 1982.

Hipp, Stephen A., *'Person' in Christian Tradition and the Conception of Saint Albert the Great: A Systematic Study of its Concept as Illuminated by the Mysteries of the Trinity and the Incarnation*, Münster, 2001.

Hofmeier, J., *Die Trinitätslehre des Hugo von St. Viktor*, Munich, 1963.

Horst, U., *Die Gaben des Heiligen Geistes nach Thomas von Aquin*, Berlin, 2001.

Hülsewiesche, R., 'Monotheismus', in *Historiches Wörterbuch der Philosophie*, vol. 6, ed. J. Ritter and K. Gründer, Basel and Stuttgart, 1984, cols. 142–146.

Imbach, R., and Putallaz, F.-X., 'Notes sur l'usage du terme *imago* chez Thomas d'Aquin', *Micrologus* 5 (1997), 69–88.

Jenkins, John I., *Knowledge and Faith in Thomas Aquinas*, Cambridge, 1997.

Kasper, Walter, *The God of Jesus Christ*, trans. Matthew J. O'Connell, London, 1983.

Keaty, A., 'The Holy Spirit Proceeding as Mutual Love: An Interpretation of Aquinas' *Summa Theologiae* I.37', *Angelicum* 77 (2000), 533–557.

Krempel, A., *La doctrine de la relation chez St Thomas d'Aquin*, Paris, 1952.

Ladaria, L. F., 'Dios Padre en Hilario de Poitiers', in *Dios es Padre, Semanas de estudios trinitarios*, Salamanca, 1991, pp. 141–177.

Lafont, G., *Peut-on connaître Dieu en Jésus-Christ?*, Paris, 1969.

Le Guillou, M.-J., *Christ and Church: A Theology of the Mystery*, preface by M. D. Chenu, trans. Charles E. Schaldenbrand, New York, 1966.

Levering, Matthew, 'Wisdom and the Viability of Thomistic Trinitarian Theology', *The Thomist* 64 (2000), 593–618.

—— *Scripture and Metaphysics: Aquinas and the Renewal of Trinitarian Theology*, Malden, MA, and Oxford, 2004.

Levering, Matthew, and Dauphinais, Michael, *Knowing the Love of Christ: An Introduction to the Theology of St. Thomas Aquinas*, Notre Dame, 2002.

Libera, A. de, *La querelle des universaux de Platon à la fin du Moyen Age*, Paris, 1996.

—— 'Suppositio', in *Dictionnaire du Moyen Âge*, ed. C. Gauvard, A. de Libera, and M. Zink, Paris, 2002, pp. 1358–1360.

Lison, J., 'L'Esprit comme amour selon Grégoire Palamas', *Connaissance des Pères de l'Eglise* 69 (1998), 40–45.

Malet, A., *Personne et amour dans la théologie trinitaire de St Thomas d'Aquin*, Paris, 1956.

Marengo, G., *Trinità e Creazione, Indagine sulla teologia di Tommaso d'Aquino*, Rome, 1990.

Margerie, B. de, 'Vers une relecture du concile de Florence grâce à la reconsidération de l'Écriture et des Pères grecs et latins', *RT* 86 (1986), 31–81.

Merriell, D. Juvenal, *To the Image of the Trinity: A Study in the Development of Aquinas' Teaching*, Toronto, 1990.

Mews, C. J., 'Introduction', in *Petri Abaelardi Theologia 'Summi Boni', Theologia 'scholarium'*, ed. E. M. Buytaert and C. J. Mews, CCCM 13, Turnhout, 1987, pp. 39–81.

—— 'The Lists of Heresies Imputed to Peter Abelard', *Revue Bénédictine* 95 (1985), 73–110.

Milano, A., *Persona in teologia, Alle origini del significato di persona nel cristianesimo antico*, 2nd edn., Rome, 1996.

Morard, M., 'Une source de St Thomas d'Aquin: le deuxième concile de Constantinople (553)', *RSPT* 81 (1997), 21–56.

Morerod, Ch., 'Trinité et unité de l'Eglise', *Nova et Vetera* 77/3 (2002), 5–17; ET 'The Trinity and Unity of the Church', *Nova et Vetera English Edition* 2/1 (2004), 115–127.

Nedoncelle, M., '*Prosopon* et *persona* dans l'Antiquité classique', *Revue des Sciences Religieuses* 22 (1948), 277–299.

Nicolas, J.-H., *Les profondeurs de la grâce*, Paris, 1969.

O'Collins, Gerald, *The Tripersonal God: Understanding and Interpreting the Trinity*, London, 1999.

Olson, Roger E., and Hall, Christopher A., *The Trinity*, Grand Rapids, 2002.

Pagnotta, S., 'La figura di San Tommaso d'Aquino nell'arte, Tentativo di analisi storico-teologica dell'iconografia tommasiana', Mémoire de licence, University of Fribourg, 1995.

Paissac, H., *Théologie du Verbe, Saint Augustin et St Thomas*, Paris, 1951.

Patfoort, A., *La Somme de St Thomas et la logique du dessein de Dieu*, Saint-Maur, 1998.

—— '*Cognitio ista est quasi experimentalis* (I *Sent*, d. 14, q. 2, a. 2, ad 3m)', *Angelicum* 63 (1986), 3–13.

—— 'Le *Filioque* dans la conscience de l'Eglise avant le concile d'Ephèse', *RT* 97 (1997), 318–334.

—— 'Missions divines et expérience des Personnes divines selon S. Thomas', *Angelicum* 63 (1986), 545–559.

Patfoort, A., and Gardeil, A., 'Notes explicatives' and 'Renseignements techniques', in St Thomas d'Aquin, *Somme théologique, Les origines de l'homme, 1ᵃ, Questions 90–102*, Paris, 1998, pp. 302–319, 380–421.

Pedrini, A., *Bibliografia Tomista sulla Pneumatologia*, Studi Tomistici 54, Vatican City, 1994.

Pelikan, J., *The Christian Tradition: A History of the Development of Doctrine*, vol. 2: *The Spirit of Eastern Christendom (600–1700)*, Chicago, 1974.

Penido, M. T.-L., 'A propos de la procession d'amour en Dieu', *EThL* 15 (1938), 338–344.

—— 'Gloses sur la procession d'amour dans la Trinité', *EThL* 14 (1937), 33–68.

Pinckaers, S., *The Sources of Christian Ethics*, translated from the 3rd edn. by Sr Mary Thomas Noble, Edinburgh, 1995.

—— 'Recherche de la signification véritable du terme "spéculatif"', *NRT* 81 (1959), 673–695.

Poirel, D., *Livre de la nature et débat trinitaire au XIIᵉ siècle: Le De tribus diebus de Hugues de Saint-Victor*, Turnhout, 2002.

Prades, J., '*Deus specialiter est in sanctis per gratiam*', El misterio de la inhabitación de la Trinidad en los escritos de Santo Tomás, Rome, 1993.

Quasten, J., *Initiation aux Pères de l'Eglise*, vol. 3, Paris, 1963.

Rahner, K., *The Trinity*, trans. Joseph Donceel, London, 1970.

—— 'Dieu dans le Nouveau Testament', in id., *Ecrits théologiques*, vol. 1, Paris, 1959, pp. 11–111.

Reichberg, G., 'La communication de la nature divine en Dieu selon Thomas d'Aquin', *RT* 93 (1993), 50–65.

Rey, B., *A la découverte de Dieu, Les origines de la foi trinitaire*, Paris, 1982.

Richard, R. L., *The Problem of an Apologetical Perspective in the Trinitarian Theology of St. Thomas Aquinas*, Rome, 1963.

Riestra, J. A., 'El error de Macedonio y la doctrina de Santo Tomás', in *Credo in Spiritum Sanctum*, ed. J. Saraiva Martins, vol. 1, Vatican City, 1983, pp. 461–471.

Robb, Fiona, 'The Fourth Lateran Council's Definition of Trinitarian Orthodoxy', *Journal of Ecclesiastical History* 48 (1997), 22–41.

Rocca, Gregory P., *Speaking the Incomprehensible God: Thomas Aquinas on the Interplay of Positive and Negative Theology*, Washington DC, 2004.

Ruello, F., 'Le commentaire inédit de saint Albert le Grand sur les *Noms divins*. Présentation et aperçus de théologie trinitaire', *Traditio* 12 (1956), 231–314.

—— 'Une source probable de la théologie trinitaire de St Thomas', *Recherches de Science Religieuse* 43 (1955), 104–128.

Ruggiero, G., 'Il monastero di Sant'Anna di Nocera. Dalla fondazione al Concilio di Trento', *Memorie Domenicane* NS 20 (1989), 5–166.

Schlapkohl, C., *Persona est naturae rationabilis individua substantia: Boethius und die Debatte über den Personbegriff*, Marburg, 1999.

Schmaus, M., 'Die Texte der Trinitätslehre in den Sententiae des Simon von Tournai', *RTAM* 4 (1932), 59–72.

Schmidbaur, H. C., *Personarum Trinitas, Die trinitarische Gotteslehre des heiligen Thomas von Aquin*, St Ottilien, 1995.

Schneider, J., *Die Lehre vom dreieinigen Gott in der Schule des Petrus Lombardus*, Munich, 1961.

Schönberger, R., *Relation als Vergleich, Die Relationstheorie des Johannes Buridan im Kontext seines Denkens und der Scholastik*, Leiden, 1994.

Sesboüé, B., *Saint Basile et la Trinité, Un acte théologique au IVe siècle*, Paris, 1998.

Sesboüé, B., and Meunier, B., *Dieu peut-il avoir un Fils? Le débat trinitaire au IVe siècle*, Paris, 1993.

Simonin, H.-D., 'Autour de la solution thomiste du problème de l'amour', *AHDLMA* 6 (1931), 174–276.

Smith, Timothy, *Thomas Aquinas' Trinitarian Theology: A Study in Theological Method*, Washington DC, 2003.

Somme, L., *Fils adoptifs de Dieu par Jésus Christ*, Paris, 1997.

—— *Thomas d'Aquin, La divinisation dans le Christ*, Geneva, 1998.

Spiazzi, R., '"Conoscenza con amore" in Sant'Agostino e in San Tommaso', *Doctor Communis* 39 (1986), 315–328.

Stemmer, P., 'Perichorese. Zur Geschichte eines Begriffs', *Archiv für Begriffsgeschichte* 27 (1983), [1985] 9–55.

Studer, B., *Mysterium caritatis, Studien zur Exegese und zur Trinitätslehre in der Alten Kirche*, Rome, 1999.

—— 'Credo in unum Deum Patrem omnipotentem', *Connaissance des Pères de l'Eglise* 73 (1999), 2–17.

—— *Trinity and Incarnation: The Faith of the Early Church*, trans. Matthias Wester-hoff, Edinburgh, 1993.

Sweeney, E., 'Supposition, Signification, and Universals: Metaphysical and Linguistic Complexity in Aquinas', *FZPT* 42 (1995), 267–290.

Tonneau, J., 'L'accessoire suit le principal', in St Thomas d'Aquin, *Somme théologique, La Loi nouvelle, 1ᵃ2ᵃᵉ, Questions 106–108*, Paris, 1999, pp. 215–233.

Torrell, J.-P., *St Thomas Aquinas*, vol. 1: *The Person and his Work*, trans. Robert Royal, Washington DC, 1996.

—— *St Thomas Aquinas*, vol. 2: *Spiritual Master*, trans. Robert Royal, Washington DC, 2003.

—— 'Autorités théologiques et liberté du théologien. L'exemple de St Thomas d'Aquin', *Les Échos de Saint-Maurice* NS 18 (1988), 7–24.

—— '"Dieu conduit toutes choses vers leur fin". Providence et gouvernement divin chez Thomas d'Aquin', *MM* 29 (2002), 561–594.

—— 'La grâce du Christ', in St Thomas d'Aquin, *Somme théologique, Le Verbe incarné*, vol. 2: *3ᵃ, Questions 7–15*, Paris, 2002, pp. 395–415.

—— *Le Christ en ses mystères: La vie et l'œuvre de Jésus selon St Thomas d'Aquin*, vol. 2, Paris, 1999.

—— 'Le savoir théologique chez St Thomas', *RT* 96 (1996), 355–396.

—— 'Philosophie et théologie d'après le Prologue de Thomas d'Aquin au *Super Boetium de Trinitate*. Essai d'une lecture théologique', *Documenti e Studi sulla tradizione filosofica medievale* 10 (1999), 299–353.

Valkenberg, W. G. B. M., *Words of the Living God: Place and Function of the Scripture in the Theology of Thomas Aquinas*, Leuven, 2000.

Van Nieuwenhove, Rik, and Wawrykow, Joseph (eds.), *The Theology of Thomas Aquinas*, Notre Dame, 2005.

Vanier, P., *Théologie trinitaire chez St Thomas d'Aquin*, Montreal and Paris, 1953.

—— 'La relation trinitaire dans la Somme théologique de St Thomas d'Aquin', *SE* 1 (1948), 143–159.

Ventimiglia, G., *Differenza e contraddizione*, Milan, 1997.

Wainwright, A. W., *The Trinity in the New Testament*, London, 1962.

Weinandy, Thomas G., *Does God Suffer?* Notre Dame, 2000.

Weinandy, Thomas G., Keating, Daniel, and Yocum, John (eds.), *Aquinas on Doctrine: A Critical Introduction*, London and New York, 2004.

Weisheipl, J. A., *Friar Thomas D'Aquino: His Life, Thought and Work*, New York, 1974.

Wetter, F., *Die Trinitätslehre des Johannes Duns Scotus*, Münster, 1967.

Williams, A. N., *The Ground of Union: Deification in Aquinas and Palamas*, New York and Oxford, 1999.

Williams, Michael E., *The Teaching of Gilbert Porreta on the Trinity as Found in His Commentaries on Boethius*, Rome, 1951.

Witherington, Ben, and Ice, Laura M., *The Shadow of the Almighty: Father, Son, and Spirit in Biblical Perspective*, Grand Rapids, 2002.

Wolinski, J., 'Le monothéisme chrétien classique', in *Le christianisme est-il un mono-théisme?*, ed. P. Gisel and G. Emery, Geneva, 2001, pp. 141–183.

Worrall, P., 'St. Thomas and Arianism', *RTAM* 23 (1956), 208–259; 24 (1957), 45–100.

Zizioulas, J., 'Implications ecclésiologiques de deux types de pneumatologie', in *Communio Sanctorum, Mélanges offerts à J.-J. von Allmen*, Geneva, 1982, pp. 141–154.

Name Index

Abelard 22, 137–138, 141, 278, 313–319, 324–325, 333
Alan of Lille 317
Albert the Great 1, 23, 78, 85–86, 88, 90–91, 93, 95, 107, 110, 112, 114–117, 125–129, 131–132, 139, 162, 166, 171–172, 181, 213, 224, 239, 246, 251, 271–272, 282, 284, 291, 295, 301, 304–305, 320–321, 322–323, 325–326, 328, 337, 343, 348, 361, 364, 368, 371–373, 383, 393, 394
Alcuin 278, 282
Alexander of Alexandria 79–80
Alexander of Hales 23, 85, 129, 132, 139, 148, 213, 238, 313, 217, 384, 390
Saint Ambrose 134, 204, 299, 370
Angelini, G. 32
Anselm of Canterbury 23–24, 97–98, 137–138, 186, 233–234, 236, 269, 282, 285
Aristotle 41, 53–55, 58–59, 80, 83–85, 87, 91, 105–106, 109, 132, 183, 192, 206, 246, 256, 356
Arius 56–57, 60, 76–77, 79, 98, 133–134, 153
Athanasius of Alexandria 12, 14, 62, 76, 80, 143, 147, 153, 158–159, 199, 209, 217, 278, 304
Augustine 1, 3, 11–12, 21, 29–30, 54–55, 58–59, 63, 76, 79, 82–83, 85, 92, 100, 114–115, 143, 155, 163, 168, 170, 172–174, 177, 179, 183, 197, 199, 202, 206, 210, 213, 316, 221, 224–225, 231–232, 234, 237–238, 241–242, 249–250, 257, 261, 271, 275, 277–278, 287, 291–292, 299, 308–309, 313,

317–318, 326, 330, 333, 339, 347, 350, 359, 362, 364–365, 370–372, 389–390, 392–393, 396, 398, 400–401, 405–506
Averroes 91, 356, 379
Avicenna 54, 87

Bailleux, E. 103, 272
Banez, D. 374
Barnes, M. R. 11, 47
Barth, K. 108, 271
Basil of Caesaria 10, 14, 16, 45–46, 71, 80–82, 98, 135, 147, 153, 158, 170, 209, 222, 353
Venerable Bede 278
Bellarmine 2
Beretta, B. 86
Bergeron, M. 115
Bernard of Claivaux 90, 315
Boethius 19, 79, 83–85, 90, 92, 104–107, 109–112, 114, 116, 118–119, 132, 142
Boespflug, F. 2
Boismard, M.-E. 11
Bonanni, S. P. 315
Saint Bonaventure 24–26, 78, 100, 107, 110–112, 115–117, 122, 124–125, 129–130, 135–137, 160, 166, 171–172, 181, 213, 224, 239, 251, 272, 319–326, 328, 337, 343, 364, 366, 370–373, 375, 384
Bonino, S.-Th 38, 195, 283
Borgnet, A. 23, 305
Bougerol, J.-G. 160
Boulnois, M.-O. 80, 279
Bourassa, F. 234, 249, 306
Bouthillier, D. 193
Brown, R. E. 13

Subject Index

Printed in Great Britain
by Amazon